W9-BKB-893

Human Communication

Motivation, Knowledge, & Skills

Sherwyn P. Morreale
National Communication Association

Brian H. Spitzberg
San Diego State University

J. Kevin Barge
Baylor University

WADSWORTH
THOMSON LEARNING™

Australia • Canada • Mexico • Singapore • South Africa • Spain
United Kingdom • United States

WADSWORTH
THOMSON LEARNING™

Executive Editor: Deirdre Cavanaugh
Publisher: Clark Baxter
Development Editor: Mimi Melek
Executive Marketing Manager: Stacey Purviance
Signing Representative: Cindy Yates
Project Editor: Cathy Linberg
Print Buyer: Barbara Britton
Permissions Editor: Bob Kauser
Technology Project Manager: Jeanette Wiseman

Production Service: Thompson Steele, Inc.
Text Designer: Marilyn Perry
Photo Researcher, Copy Editor, and Compositor: Thompson Steele, Inc.
Illustrators: Marilyn Perry and Thompson Steele, Inc.
Cover Image: © Peter Horjus, 2001
Cover Printer: Phoenix Color Corporation
Printer: Quebecor/World, Versailles, Kentucky

COPYRIGHT © 2001 Wadsworth, a division of Thomson Learning, Inc., Thomson Learning™ is a trademark used herein under license.

ALL RIGHTS RESERVED. No part of this work covered by the copyright hereon may be reproduced or used in any form or by any means—graphic, electronic, or mechanical, including photocopying, recording, taping, Web distribution, or information storage and retrieval systems—without the written permission of the publisher.

Printed in the United States of America
2 3 4 5 6 7 04 03 02

For permission to use material from this text, contact us: **Web:** http://www.thomsonrights.com
Fax: 1-800-730-2215 **Phone:** 1-800-730-2214

ExamView® and *ExamView Pro®* are trademarks of FSCreations, Inc. Windows is a registered trademark of the Microsoft Corporation used herein under license. Macintosh and Power Macintosh are registered trademarks of Apple Computer, Inc. Used herein under license.

COPYRIGHT © 2001 Thomson Learning, Inc. All Rights Reserved. Thomson Learning *Web Tutor*™ is a trademark of Thomson Learning, Inc.

Wadsworth/Thomson Learning
10 Davis Drive
Belmont, CA 94002-3098
USA

For more information about our products, contact us:
Thomson Learning Academic Resource Center
1-800-423-0563
http://www.wadsworth.com

International Headquarters
Thomson Learning
International Division
290 Harbor Drive
Stamford, CT 06902-7477
USA

UK/Europe/Middle East/South Africa
Thomson Learning
Berkshire House
168-173 High Holborn
London WC1V 7AA
United Kingdom

Asia
Thomson Learning
60 Albert Street, #15-01
Albert Complex
Singapore 189969

Canada
Nelson Thomson Learning
1120 Birchmount Road
Toronto, Ontario M1K 5G4
Canada

Library of Congress Cataloging-in-Publication Data

Morreale, Sherwyn P.
Human communication : motivation, knowledge, & skills / Sherwyn P. Morreale, Brian H. Spitzberg, J. Kevin Barge.
p. cm.
Includes bibliographical references.
ISBN 0-534-56619-7
Annotated Instructor's Edition ISBN 0-534-56620-0
1. Communication. I. Spitzberg, Brian H. II. Barge, J. Kevin. III. Title.

P90 .M637 2001
302.2--dc21

Brief Contents

Detailed Contents

PART TWO INTERPERSONAL COMMUNICATION

PART FOUR **PUBLIC SPEAKING**

ONLINE EPILOGUE

Communication & Community

Online at http://communication.wadsworth.com/humancomm.html

Preface

Shortly before the 1996 National Communication Association Convention, our annual professional academic conference, we discussed the possibility of collaborating on an introductory textbook based on the work we had done on communication competence. The objectives of the textbook were simple. Most existing books do not take an integrated approach to organizing the content of this course and do not provide adequate assessment of learning outcomes to determine the value of the course of study. Given our respective expertise in the three communication contexts most often included in an introductory course—Brian Spitzberg in interpersonal, Kevin Barge in small groups, and Sherry Morreale in public speaking—we thought it worthwhile to apply ourselves collectively to filling this gap.

We had all developed or co-developed assessment tools specific to our areas of expertise. These instruments have been recognized by the national professional association and used extensively in research and instruction. Furthermore, we had a model of communication competence—motivation, knowledge, and skills—that could provide a conceptually coherent framework for organizing the book's coverage of the communication process and the varied topics relevant to everyday life. The assessment instruments we had developed for the National Communication Association had even been created specifically to be consistent with the model of competence—the Conversational Skills Rating Scale, the Competent Group Communicator, and the Competent Speaker. Given those resources, we set about the task of creating the book you now hold in your hands.

Part One of this new book welcomes you to the study of human communication, defines communication, including communication as community building, and describes the model of communication competence that guides learning in the remainder of the book. Part One also explains the basic processes essential to communicating competently: perception, language, nonverbal communication, listening, and a special feature of this book—mediated communication competence. Part Two introduces you to interpersonal communication from a competence perspective—understanding and managing interpersonal relationships. Part Three investigates small group communication, then focuses on decision making and participating in and leading groups. Part Four first introduces public speaking competence, then applies that model to speech preparation and presentation, and finally to informative and persuasive speaking. An appendix on interviewing provides an overview of this valuable skill and explains how you can apply what you've learned about communication competence to gathering information and getting a job. Our Online Epilogue, located at **http://communication.wadsworth.com/humancomm.html** brings us full circle from Part One by focusing more closely on communication as community building. We invite you to share your thoughts on this issue—and any others presented in the book—with us through a mediated online discussion.

The communication model that serves as the framework for this book, the ways we have embedded assessment of learning, and the unique pedagogical features woven into the text itself, along with the instructional resources that accompany it, result in our integrated approach.

Communication Competence as Motivation, Knowledge, & Skills

Our model for competence is straightforward, so we hope you'll find it valuable for learning about communication. In order to be viewed as competent not only by oneself but also—most importantly—by others, a communicator needs to be motivated, knowledgeable, and skilled in a given context. Competence is an evaluation of the appropriateness and effectiveness of a communicator or a communicator's performance. Because a given behavior may be appropriate and effective in one context but not another, competence exists in the judgments people make of your communication behavior, not in the behavior itself. This makes motivation, knowledge, and skills factors that increase the likelihood that your communication performance will be viewed as competent in any given context. The particular features of motivation, knowledge, and skills will vary according to the context. The three contexts we focus on are interpersonal, small group, and public speaking.

Our Approach to Assessing Student Learning

We encourage you to participate in assessing your own learning processes. To that end and to help faculty evaluate student communication skills, we include the following resources.

- Communication Assumption Tests are integrated in Chapters 1, 8, 11, and 14 to help you identify, at the start of major sections, the preconceived notions you correctly and incorrectly bring to the communication process.
- Building Motivation Assessment Tests are located at the end of Chapters 2, 3, 5, 6, 7, 8, 11, and 14 to provide you with a self-diagnostic to help identify areas in which you can develop your communication competence as you progress through the course.
- Assessing Skills self-diagnostic grids are located at the end of Chapters 6, 10, 12, 13, and 16 to provide a way to categorize behaviors and protocols that will be perceived as more or less competent given a context you specify. A completed grid, based on the communication situation described in the chapter's opening vignette, is provided as a model.
- For faculty, a complete set of essential assessment resources is provided in the instructor's manual. The three skills assessment instruments (the Conversational Skills Rating Scale, the Competent Group Communicator, and the Competent Speaker) are available through NCA or Wadsworth. Guidelines for using each instrument have been prepared specifically for adopting faculty and are included in the *Instructor's Resource Manual.* Faculty are invited to participate in online electronic discussions with the authors—about the three instruments, computerized evaluation tools, and, guidelines for engaging in oral communication assessment.

Pedagogical Features

The following pedagogical features are included throughout the book to encourage both teachers and students to engage actively in teaching and learning about communication competence together:

- Challenges to Competence and Overcoming Challenges to Competence sections close a majority of chapters and help students think critically about the topic at hand and their own communication development.
- Comprehensive coverage of ethics and communication is integrated throughout the book, and most particularly in chapters 2, 6, 7, 8, 13, and the public speaking chapters.
- Coverage of diversity, culture, gender, ethics, and conflict is integrated throughout the book in CloseUps that elaborate concepts in the text as they apply to these important topics.

- Opening vignettes in each chapter describe students having real-world experiences related to the respective chapter content to engage readers and reinforce the application of concepts.
- A two-part pedagogy structure of chapter-opening Learning Objectives and marginal Knowledge Links help develop students' critical thinking skills. Learning Objectives identify goals for content mastery. Knowledge Links connect content across chapters.
- Building Knowledge and Building Skills questions at the end of each chapter offer opportunities for individuals and small groups to discuss and review chapter content. Icons designate World Wide Web and *InfoTrac College Edition* questions that encourage you to take your review online.

Instructional Resources

An unparalleled support package for faculty and students is available from Wadsworth/Thomson Learning. This package is described in detail in the Annotated Instructor's Edition and online at **http://communication.wadsworth.com**.

Acknowledgments

The path from idea to textbook was long, involved, and demanding. From that meeting in 1996 to the present, there have been those who informed, guided, instructed, regulated, cajoled, and most importantly, inspired us. To these people, many of whom are listed on the inside front cover of this book, we extend our sincere thanks and appreciation. In particular, we would like to thank two people, without whose efforts this project would likely have faded away early on. Mimi Melek, developmental editor extraordinare, deserves billing as the "unbilled" ghostwriter of this project. Mimi faced twin responsibilities of assisting us in finding a common writing style and maintaining it at a consistent level throughout. These twin responsibilities have now been replaced by two new real twins who will find Mimi a wonderful mother. Congratulations, and thank you. May you be pleased with what you have given birth to in so many ways.

Second, we owe a great debt of gratitude to Deirdre Cavanaugh, our executive editor at Wadsworth. She was the reason we decided to publish with Wadsworth, and after two and a half years of writing, planning, rewriting, adjusting, revising, and rewriting, we still love Deirdre. Editors are not supposed to be loved so much as be the taskmasters who get the job done on schedule, under budget, and in a position to be competitive. With Deirdre's support, we have fulfilled these editorial objectives, while the joy in our relationship with her has remained constant, and a true source of inspiration.

Cathy Linberg, working with Andrea Fincke and the incredibly talented team at Thompson Steele, has worked miracles in physically bringing this book to life. Stacey Purviance continues to amaze us with her creativity and marketing wisdom. We are grateful for the support of everyone at Wadsworth/Thomson Learning.

Along the way, it is important not to lose sight of our most important source of guidance—our students. We may do the research and writing, but it is our students who tell us the "truth" of our ideas in the everyday crucible of our classes. They are our touchstones, and ultimately, our mission and our charge. As this textbook finds acceptance in the coming years, we will look more and more to our own and our colleagues' experiences with students, and to the students themselves, to tell us not only where the value is in our project, but where the value yet needs to be.

Finally, to all those friends, family members, and peers, who have faithfully tended to our questions, complaints, and ongoing progress reports regarding this project, we thank you for your patience and loving support. The fact that you have remained our supporters throughout is evidence of the wisdom of our choices and luck of our birthrights.

About the Authors

Sherwyn P. Morreale is the Associate Director of the National Communication Association (NCA), following a 15-year career of teaching and research at the University of Colorado at Colorado Springs. She earned an undergraduate degree in communication at the University of Colorado and her Ph.D. at the University of Denver. In her position as NCA Associate Director, she provides consulting services to communication departments and college campuses in her areas, which include public speaking, interpersonal and gender communication, diversity issues, and the assessment of communication competence. She is the National Director of the undergraduate communication honor society Lambda Pi Eta and represents the communication field as the disciplinary liaison to interdisciplinary organizations such as the American Association for Higher Education, the American Association of Colleges and Universities, the Carnegie Foundation, and the Council of Graduate Schools. Sherry lives in Washington, DC. In her spare time, she can be found on a hiking trail, in an aerobics class, or taking advantage of the rich cultural aspects of the nation's capital.

Brian H. Spitzberg is Professor and Director of Graduate Studies in the School of Communication at San Diego State University. A native of Dallas, Texas, Brian engaged actively in forensics in high school and college, majoring in communication. He received his B. A. at the University of Texas at Arlington and his M.A. and Ph.D. at the University of Southern California. He taught for a year as a visiting professor at the University of Wisconsin, Madison, and for six years at the University of North Texas and has been at San Diego State University since 1989. His main research interests are in communication competence, assessment, and areas deemed the "dark side" of interpersonal communication and relationships, including conflict, coercion, violence, and stalking. He has authored, coauthored, and/or co-edited over 50 scholarly works, including two books on communication competence and two edited books on the dark side, and presented over 100 papers at professional conferences. Brian lives in San Diego and enjoys dining out, wine, collecting art, jogging, and trying to write while his two Siamese cats, Ethos and Avatar, sit on his lap (or laptop).

J. Kevin Barge is an Associate Professor of Communication Studies at Baylor University. He has published more than two dozen articles and book chapters, as well as two books: *Leadership: Communication Skills for Groups and Organizations* and *Managing Group Life: Communicating in Decision-Making Groups.* He is an active organizational consultant and facilitator, who works with team members in the United States and Europe to enhance their ability to collaborate, learn, and innovate. He is a member of the Public Dialogue Consortium, a group of academics and communication practitioners who are interested in developing innovative communication forums that allow community members to talk about polarized and polarizing issues in constructive ways. He is currently working with the U.S. Department of Education on increasing parental involvement in the lives of middle school students. Kevin received his B.A. at Millikin University in Decatur, Illinois, and his M.A. and Ph.D. at the University of Kansas. Kevin lives in Waco, Texas, with his wife, Courtney, and enjoys traveling, cooking, theater, and golf.

CHAPTER 1

Learning Objectives

After studying this chapter, you should be able to:

1. Define communication and explain how messages, management, and meaning relate to communication.
2. Compare and contrast viewing communication as information transfer, sharing meaning, persuasion, and community.
3. Distinguish between the interaction and transactional models of communication.
4. Outline the seven assumptions underlying communication.
5. Explain why communication is crucial to constructing healthy relationships, groups, and communities.
6. Distinguish between communication and communication competence.

Introducing Communication

Monday, 8 P.M.—Kathryn returned to her apartment after attending a team-building workshop hosted by her university's Student Life Department. It had been a great workshop and she had picked up a lot of useful information about running committee meetings. Even though she had extensive experience as a committee chair, Kathryn had been looking forward to this workshop because her new position as chair for her service club's fund-raising committee held many challenges, in part because of the committee's diversity. The workshop gave her the tools she needed to plan her Tuesday committee meeting.

As she walked into her apartment, she noticed she had received 10 phone messages; two were from a good friend confirming their lunch date on Tuesday. When she turned on her computer, she downloaded 7 email messages from her classmates. Kathryn immediately called her friend Kwan, and made a note to return the other phone calls and respond to the emails when she had some spare time on Tuesday. Tonight, her task was to finish her presentation for her 9 A.M. marketing class. She had done all her research; it was now time to outline her presentation of the marketing plan. She knew it was going to be a long night because she always had a tough time organizing her material; she had researched so much information she wasn't quite sure which points needed to be highlighted in her presentation. Moreover, speaking to large groups wasn't her strength. Kathryn always felt nervous in front of an audience and as a result, she typically fumbled awkwardly for the right words and phrasings. She began typing an outline for her presentation.

Tuesday, 10:30 A.M.—The speech had gone poorly. Kathryn felt she knew her material, and even her marketing professor told her that her outline highlighted the most important points about the marketing plan. Even though she had prepared thoroughly and knew the information, she still could not overcome her nervousness. She lost her place on more than one occasion and introduced awkward silences into the presentation. Her nervousness did not escape her classmates; their evaluations showed that they felt it distracted from her speech.

Tuesday, 1 P.M.—Kathryn's lunch with her friend Kwan went much more smoothly than her presentation. Kwan was conflicted about whether to transfer to another college. Kathryn didn't have a hard time listening to him but felt awkward giving advice. She knew in her heart that she wanted her friend to stay, but felt that saying so would put more pressure on Kwan. Kathryn wanted to tell Kwan how she really felt but couldn't find a way of putting her feelings into words.

Tuesday, 5 P.M. —The fund-raising committee meeting had gone very well. Kathryn received several compliments from committee members about how well she had organized the meeting and how effective she was in keeping the discussion on track. The workshop she had attended the day before helped her feel well prepared and confident in her ability to lead the group.

Tuesday, 8 P.M.—Kathryn returned to her apartment, exhausted after a long day. She looked at her answering machine and saw that she had 7 new messages. As she accessed her email, 13 new messages posted. She glanced at her date book and noted she had two classes on Wednesday and two other meetings. What would tomorrow be like?

Most of our waking hours are spent communicating with other people. Whether we are talking to someone over the phone, making a presentation to a group, responding to email, working in a committee, or chatting with a friend, we are communicating and relating to people. Sometimes the vast number of people we have to talk to and the wide range of topics we must discuss become staggering and leave us overwhelmed and unconfident about our ability to communicate. Although we may want to cut off communication with others and withdraw as a means of coping with communication overload, a reality of contemporary life is that we must continually engage with others to do work, build relationships, and sustain healthy lives.

The key to all this lies in the quality of our communication with others. High-quality communication is competent—both appropriate and effective for a particular situation. Appropriate communication means that you act in ways that are suitable given the norms and expectations of the groups, organizations, or cultures to which you belong. Effective communication mans that you are able to achieve the most desirable objectives or outcomes in the situation. When you are able to communicate appropriately and effectively, you are perceived by others as competent. Your communication competence can vary from situation to situation. For example, Kathryn was perceived as very competent by her fellow committee members but as less competent by her professor and classmates during her marketing presentation.

What factors influence our ability to communicate appropriately and effectively? Kathryn's story highlights some of the factors that influence others' perceptions of us as competent communicators. One possible explanation for Kathryn's poor performance in her marketing class is that she suffered from stage fright. She had written a solid outline of the most important points, but was held back by her fear of public speaking. In her conversation with her friend Kwan, however, she was not at all nervous or anxious.

Rather, she was highly motivated to help Kwan make a difficult decision and knew what she wanted to say—but couldn't find a way to say it without pressuring him to stay. We could probably attribute Kathryn's ability to communicate successfully in the committee meeting to her motivation to lead the group and her extensive experience and training in leading committees.

As you can see from Kathryn's experience on Tuesday, many factors influence whether we are perceived as competent by other people. What influences whether you are perceived as a competent communicator by others? In what kinds of situations do you feel that you communicate competently? In what kinds of situations do you feel less assured about your communication ability and act less competently? Consider someone who wants to become better at playing chess or bridge—this person would, at the very least, need to know the general rules of the game. Likewise, if you want to become a more competent communicator, you need to know how to play the communication game, which means you need to know how the communication process works.

What Is Communication?

A wide variety of terms have been used to define communication such as *symbols, speech, understanding, process, transmission, channel, intention, meaning,* and *situation* (Littlejohn, 1999). A broad definition of communication that applies to different situations and to a diversity of people is most useful. **Communication** is the process of managing messages for the purpose of creating meaning (Frey, Botan, and Kreps, 2000). Three key terms make up this definition: *messages, managing,* and *meaning.*

MESSAGES

Messages are the words, sounds, actions, and gestures that people express to one another when they interact. Messages may be expressed verbally in words or nonverbally in sounds, actions, and gestures. Messages may be symbolic. A **symbol** is a word, sound, action, or gesture that arbitrarily refers to an object. For example, in the English language, the words *tiger, elephant, zebra,* and *monkey* are symbols that refer to animals. The relationship between the word *zebra* and the animal itself is arbitrary. The animal zebra could just as easily be called anything—the word zebra has been assigned to represent the animal in the English language. Similarly, when we use both our hands to form a "T," we interpret this nonverbal gesture as a symbol for a time-out. The nonverbal gesture to take a time-out could be anything—the "T" gesture has been assigned to represent it. Symbols serve a referential function as they refer or point to intangible objects such as feelings, emotions, thoughts, moods, attitudes, and beliefs, as well as more tangible objects such as people, actions, events, and physical objects.

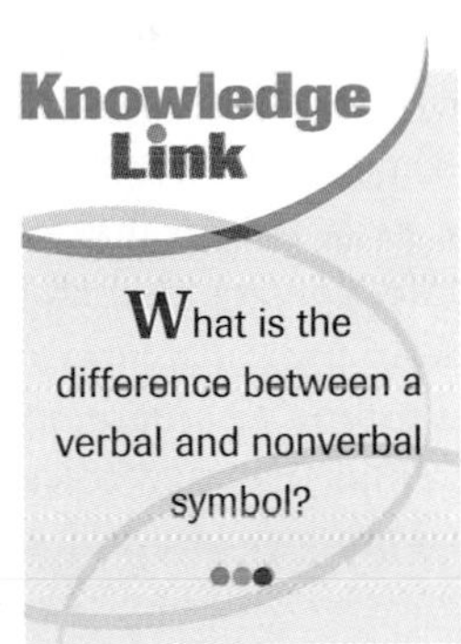

The most common set of verbal symbols we use is language, which we need in order to talk about our physical, social, and psychological worlds. Language is a verbal symbol system that allows us to take messages and utterances, in the form of words, and translate them into meaning. For example, in the English language, we use words such as *house* and *car* to refer to physical objects in our world, and words like *love* and *anger* to refer to our inner feelings. Verbal symbols may take either spoken or written form.

Symbolic behavior is not limited to verbal messages; it can be nonverbal as well. Nonverbal symbols are those sounds, actions, or gestures that people agree have a common meaning. Nonverbal symbols may be communicated by behaviors such as eye contact, posture, gestures, and how we use space and time. An example of a nonverbal symbol in

North America is the joining of the forefinger and thumb to signal to others that we are "OK." However, in some cultures, the same symbol sends an obscene message! Nonverbal symbols can also be used to communicate emotion. When people use email they may include the nonverbal symbol called an *emoticon*, :-), to show they feel good or happy. What distinguishes these symbolic nonverbal gestures from other nonverbal behaviors is that people have arbitrarily agreed on the meaning of the gesture.

Nonverbal symbols represent one way for people to communicate with one another.

MANAGING

Managing refers to the handling or supervising of people or some process or material. In communication, we manage the process of creating, receiving, and responding to verbal and nonverbal messages. Managing and handling messages involves making choices among possible messages. Consider the various choices you make when performing a simple ritual such as greeting a friend in a hallway. You choose between greeting the person verbally or non-verbally. Do you simply say "Hello," wave your hand as you pass your friend, or do both? You make choices among several possible verbal or nonverbal behaviors. When choosing among nonverbal messages, do you wave your hand as you pass by your friend, do you extend a handshake, or do you hug your friend as you greet? When choosing among verbal messages, do you say "Hello!," "Hey, it's good to see you!," or "What's happening?"

Managing messages not only involves making choices about how to initiate communication, but it also encompasses how to respond to another's communication. When someone says "Hello" to you, how do you respond? Do you acknowledge the greeting or ignore it? Do you respond by saying "Hello" back or giving a wave of your hand? Managing communication is challenging not only because it involves choosing among many possible messages but also because the kinds of messages you select influence the meaning you create.

MEANING

Meaning refers to the interpretation people assign to a message—how it is recognized or understood. Meaning for words and events may be personal and unique or it may be shared with others. As people are socialized into a group or culture, they may develop meanings for certain words and events shared with others. As you saw earlier, language can be considered a system of shared meanings in which people have come to agree on what certain words mean. Take for example the words *spam, virus,* and *firewall.* If you are a cook, *spam* refers to spiced ham in a can. If you are a doctor, the term virus refers to an infectious agent that invades and takes over human cells. If you are a forest firefighter, the word *firewall* refers to a line of defense where you will attempt to stop a fire. But if you are a computer programmer, these words take on different meanings. The word *spam* refers to junk mail that you receive on email; *virus* refers to a computer virus that corrupts your computer files; and *firewall* refers to restricting who has access to data on a computer network. Although the words are the same, whether you are socialized as a cook, doctor, firefighter, or computer programmer influences the meaning you assign to those words.

People may agree at some level on the meaning of particular words or events, but meaning can also be personal and unique and depends on your own personal history, your culture, your political and religious beliefs, the volunteer organizations you belong to, and so on. It is not enough to ask, "What does that mean?" Instead, the question needs to be rephrased as "What does that mean to you?" For you, what does it mean to arrive 30

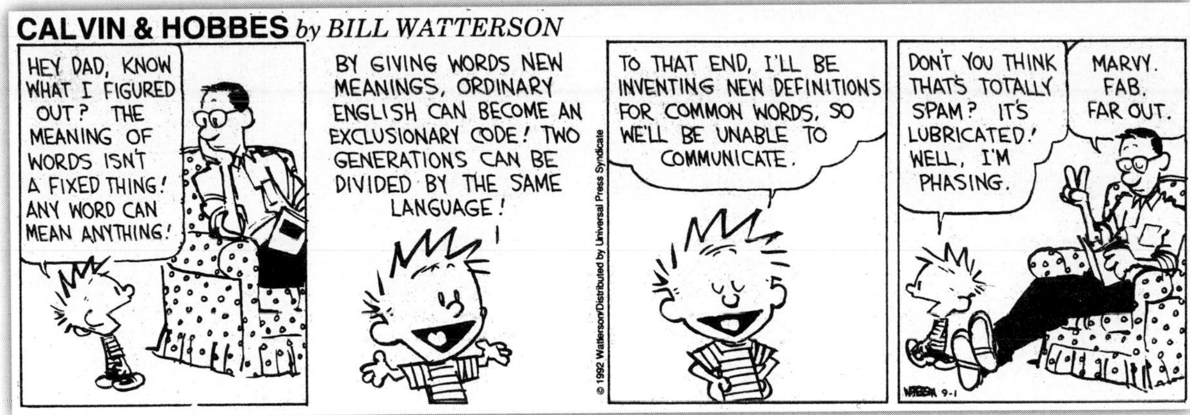

The meaning of words is both shared among people as well as unique to individuals.

CALVIN AND HOBBES © Watterson. Reprinted with permission of UNIVERSAL PRESS SYNDICATE. All rights reserved.

minutes after a meeting is scheduled to begin? If you are from a Western time-sensitive culture, this nonverbal message means you are late, and depending on how you account for your lateness, you might be perceived as inconsiderate. If you were raised in an Eastern culture where time is more fluid, you might interpret this nonverbal message as normal—it is appropriate to arrive 30 minutes beyond the scheduled time. In fact, arriving at the exact time your appointment is scheduled would be inappropriate. One way to sort out meaning is to examine the models that people have created to describe the communication process.

Models of Communication

Communication models highlight certain features of communication and downplay others. Four different models that depict the communication process have evolved over the last century: (1) communication as information transfer, (2) communication as shared meaning, (3) communication as persuasion, and (4) communication as community.

Communication as Information Transfer

An early model of communication still used today is the **information transfer model**. Sometimes called an action or linear model of communication, this perspective adopts a one-way view of communication in which a message is sent by a source through a channel to a receiver. A **source** or sender is the original producer of the message and in human communication is a person. The **channel** is the medium through which a message is sent. Channels may be written, as letters and memos; oral, as in face-to-face verbal communication and telephone conversations; nonverbal, as in shared looks or raised eyebrows; or mediated, as email or videoconferencing. The **receiver** of the message is the person or group of people who is the ultimate audience for the message. As Figure 1.1 illustrates, the source **encodes** a message, or puts a thought into words and transmits it through a channel or a medium through which the message travels to a receiver. The receiver then **decodes** or assigns meaning to the message. These messages may be interrupted, intercepted, or altered by **noise**, which is some type of interference coming from the environment that distracts from the communication. Noise can be competing sounds that make it difficult for the receiver to hear or other distractions in the environment such

What kinds of noise may interfere with a source clearly conveying a message to a receiver?

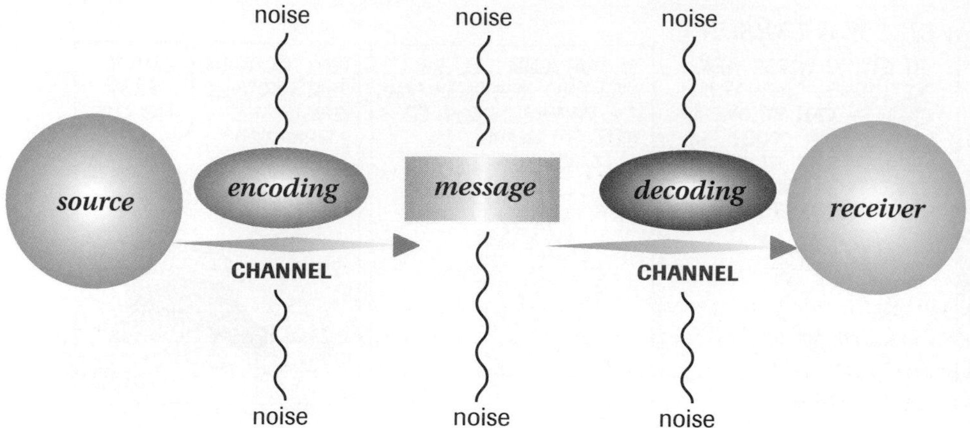

FIGURE 1.1
The Information Transfer Model of Communication

One of the earliest models of communication was the action or linear model of communication developed by Shannon and Weaver (1949). This model views communication as a one-way process in which a source encodes a message through a channel to a receiver who decodes the message. Noise potentially influences whether the message sent by the source is accurately received by the receiver.

as heat or a seat in the back of a crowded room. Noise can also come from within the communication in the form of daydreaming, illness, or nervous tics.

The information transfer model depicts human communication as a satellite television transmission in which a television station broadcasts a signal to its listening audience. The audience's reception of the signal may be interfered with by noise from atmospheric interference or faulty equipment. This model of communication suggests that understanding a communication situation can be accomplished by answering five simple questions (Lasswell, 1948/1964): Who? Says what? To whom? Through what channel? With what effect?

Viewing communication as information transfer emphasizes the role of the message source. Using this model, message sources make intentional choices about the kinds of verbal and nonverbal messages they transmit to make their point. Message sources must find ways to express clearly what they are thinking and wanting. The key question in the information transfer model is "Did the source successfully convey his or her meaning to the receiver of the message? Did the receiver understand precisely what the speaker intended?" (Eisenberg & Goodall, 1997).

Imagine you are a vice president for Student Life at a college and you are trying to evaluate whether students understand the new policies and procedures your office has developed for student organization events, dances, and parties. If you were to use the communication as information transfer model, you would probably ask the following kinds of questions:

- What does the Student Life office want students to understand about the new policies and procedures?
- What is the content of the message that the Student Life office is distributing to students?
- What channels does the Student Life office use to distribute the message? Presentations at club meetings? Posters? Email? Posting on a Web site?
- What might interfere with students' clear reception of the message?
- What message might students perceive that they received?
- Does the message sent by the Student Life office match the message received by students?

As a vice president for Student Life, you would be concerned with clearly identifying your organization's intent and anticipating and observing what obstacles, if any, might have interfered with the reception of the message.

What kinds of noise may interfere with a source clearly conveying a message to the receiver?

COMMUNICATION AS SHARING MEANING

One difficulty with the information transfer model is that it assumes communication travels in only one direction, that it is unidirectional. No way exists for the sender of a message to check and confirm whether the receiver understood the message. Moreover, receivers are viewed as passive absorbers of information sent by sources with no way of responding to the message and communicating their viewpoint.

An alternative to the information transfer model views communication as sharing meaning and assumes that communication flows both ways—from source to receiver and receiver to source. The most important outcome of communication is that each person understand the other and together agree on the meaning of the message. Two distinct models have been developed that view communication as sharing meaning: (1) the interactive model, and (2) the transactional model.

The **interactive model** views communication as sharing meaning and adds a feedback loop that links the receiver to the source. This model shifts the perspective away from viewing communication as a simple linear process and instead views communication as a circular process in which both communicators are senders and receivers of messages. As Figure 1.2 illustrates, the interactive model views people as alternating between acting as senders and receivers of messages. A distinguishing aspect of this model is that people can only perform the role of sender or receiver during interaction; they cannot perform both functions simultaneously.

Unlike the interactive model in which people alternate between acting as message sources and receivers, the **transactional model** maintains that people are senders and receivers of messages simultaneously. According to this model, even when you are listening carefully to another person and receiving his or her message, you are sending nonverbal messages through your level of eye contact, vocal "uh-huh's," hand gestures, and head nods. The transactional model also differs from the interactive model because it accounts for fields of meaning—the values, attitudes, beliefs, and ideas that a person has developed over a lifetime. As Figure 1.3 illustrates, all communicators bring their own personal fields of meaning to all communication situations. The overlap between the receiver and the sender's personal fields of meaning represents their shared field of meaning.

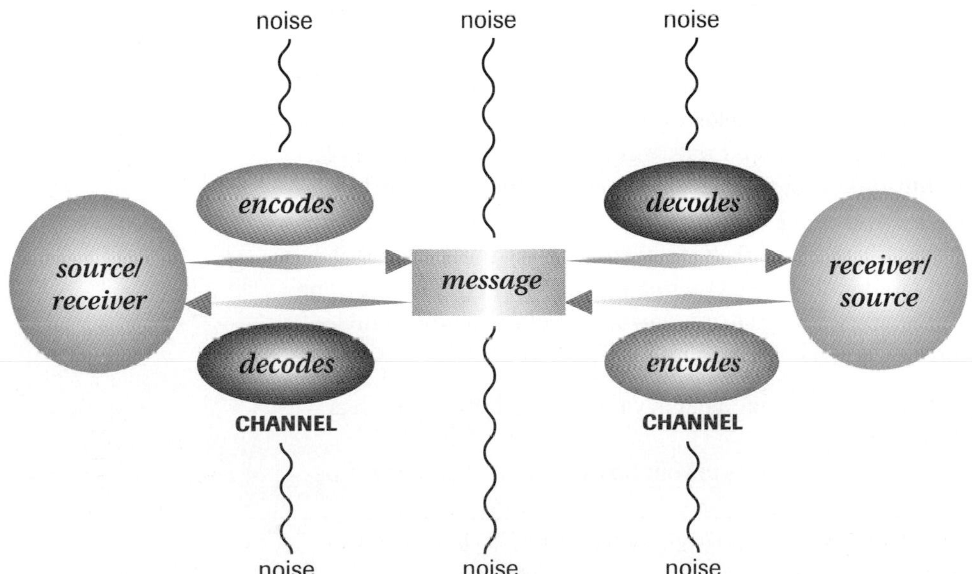

FIGURE 1.2
The Interactive Model of Communication

An interactive model of communication emphasizes two-way communication between communicators. Notice that although both parties perform all the functions of the sender and receiver in the information transfer model (encoding and decoding), they take turns acting as sender and receiver.

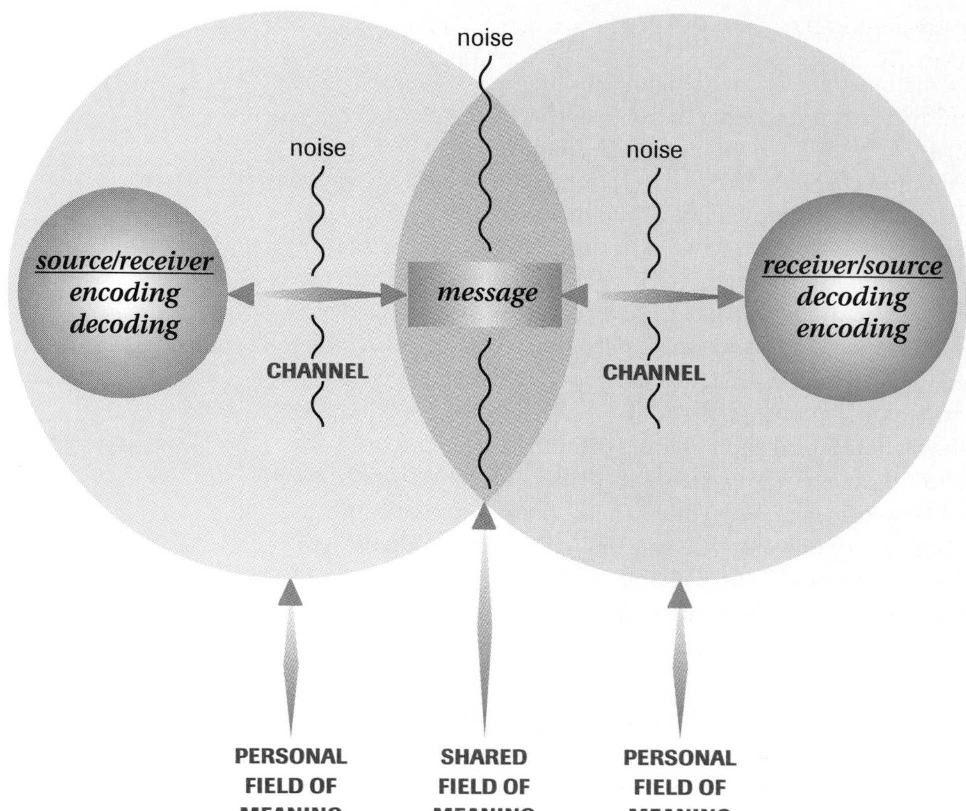

FIGURE 1.3
The Transactional Model of Communication

The transactional model of communication differs from the interactive model because it views the source and receiver as engaging in encoding and decoding simultaneously. Furthermore, it accounts for personal fields of meaning. The personal fields of meaning of the two communicators can overlap, creating a shared field of meaning.

Viewing communication as shared meaning emphasizes the importance of people constructing shared fields of meaning to coordinate our actions and accomplish desirable goals. Communication is viewed as a kind of social glue that can hold relationships, culture, communities, and society together by helping people forge shared understandings of events. In situations where no shared meaning exists among people, communication can help create new shared meanings and, with them, understandings.

The model of communication as sharing meaning focuses on identifying areas where shared meaning exists, areas where people disagree about meaning, and the communication processes people can use to create shared meaning. This model recognizes that individuals come to situations with different fields of personal meaning which may or may not overlap. For example, imagine a friend tells you he has just had a misunderstanding with his boss. The misunderstanding occurred because his boss told him to complete a project "as soon as possible." But when he completed the project, his boss was annoyed with him for being "late" with his work. If you were to apply the model of communication as shared meaning to this situation, you might ask your friend the following kinds of questions to help him understand his boss's personal field of meaning and look for commonalities with his own personal field of meaning:

- What does "as soon as possible" mean to you? What in your personal experience has led you to believe this?
- What do you think "as soon as possible" means to your boss? What in your boss's experience has led her to believe this?
- Where do the two of you agree on what "as soon as possible means"? Where do you disagree?

- For those areas where you disagree, what could you say or do to carve out an agreement on what "as soon as possible" means? What could your boss say or do?

Asking these types of questions can apply the transactional model by identifying areas of agreement and disagreement over meaning and highlighting possible ways of communicating to establish shared meaning where none exists. The first three questions inquire into the personal fields of meaning of your friend and his boss and highlight points of agreement and disagreement. The last question explores what could have been said during the conversation to begin constructing a shared field of meaning over the phrase "as soon as possible."

How can communication be used to create shared meaning? One way is to simply see where shared meaning might exist by asking questions about the other person's field of meaning. Inquiry into fields of experience allows people to discover where meaning is shared and where it is not, and to ask what can be done to create shared meaning. In some cases, asking such questions is enough to create shared meaning; the act of asking questions allows people to clear up misunderstandings and forge new understandings. In other situations, people create shared meaning more actively by using persuasion. When people use persuasion to create shared meaning, one person persuades the other that his or her meaning for people and events should be adopted by the other.

COMMUNICATION AS PERSUASION

Viewing communication as persuasion is a very old model of communication. Dating as far back as when Aristotle offered his first course in rhetoric in the 4th century B.C., the communication discipline has long been concerned with how speakers use the tools of persuasion to convince audiences. **Persuasion** is the use of communication to reinforce, change, or modify an audience's attitudes, values, beliefs, or actions. Persuasion is commonly viewed as a form of influence and occurs in many different contexts, for example when we talk ourselves into performing a certain action or thinking in a certain way or when salespeople try to persuade us to buy their service or product in person, through the mail, email, and over the phone. When faced with decision making in small groups, group members make arguments to sway our thinking. In many arenas of life, politicians and advertisers bombard us with persuasive messages. Especially in election years, politicians use a diverse set of persuasive tools to change our opinions or move us to support their political message. Advertisers specifically design television and radio commercials, billboards, and ads in the print and electronic media to catch our attention and entice us to purchase products and services.

Communication as persuasion involves influencing others in order to achieve your own goals. When trying to persuade others, you might typically ask yourself questions such as these:

- Who am I attempting to persuade? Who is the target of my persuasive attempt? What are the target person's key attitudes, values, and beliefs?
- What kinds of arguments can I use to persuade the target person? How do these arguments fit the target person's key attitudes, values, and beliefs?
- What kinds of appeals or arguments would most successfully persuade my target?
- How will the target of my persuasion need to act in order for me to know I have succeeded?

From this viewpoint, communication is successful to the degree to which you are able to get other people to do what you want. Successful communication is measured by your ability to persuade others and move them in the direction you choose.

Viewing communication as persuasion points to a way that we can work with others to achieve consensus on what a certain action means, as well as what kinds of actions need to be performed. Persuasion can be useful in creating shared fields of meaning. The assumption behind viewing communication as persuasion is that if people hold the same set of values and beliefs they will be better able to work together productively. Organizations such as Coca-Cola, Microsoft, Dell, Ford Motor Company, and Nike use a variety of persuasive techniques such as incentive systems, employee orientation programs, performance appraisals, and in-house newsletters to create shared meaning between the employees and the organization. If employees share an organization's values and views, they will pursue goals beneficial to the organization as well as to themselves. This idea points to a contemporary way of viewing communication: communication as a way of building community within interpersonal, group, and public situations.

COMMUNICATION AS COMMUNITY

Many people have come to view communication as so powerful that it creates our social worlds (Pearce, 1994). A **community** is a group of people who come together in the same physical, mental, or virtual space to interact and/or pursue a common goal. Public institutions such as governments and schools, organizations such as Microsoft, Saturn, or Paine Webber, groups like families, work teams, email lists (listservs), sports teams, and romantic or friendship relationships represent the vast variety of communities to which we belong. How do these various kinds of communities get created? As Figure 1.4 illustrates, communication permeates our environment and creates the various communities we belong to. Moreover, different forms of communication create different forms of community. For example, the kind of community created when people in a relationship express concern and demonstrate support for each other is very different than one created by a couple who are constantly fighting. Similarly, when people in a group show little interest in completing an assigned task, the kind of community these members create is significantly different from the community created by a group where the members feel passionate about the task and are willing to devote the time and energy necessary to complete the task.

This relationship between *communication* and *community* is not surprising. Both terms include the roots "co" and "union." "Co" means with and "union" means to join with another. When you co-sign a loan, you sign it with someone else and become jointly liable for the loan. When Kathryn in the opening vignette met with her fund-raising committee, one of the tasks was to make sure that her mission for the committee converged with the other members' missions for the group. In attending the workshop the day before, Kathryn made sure that her mission and that of the other committee members were joined.

Taking the "co" and "union" in communication and community seriously suggests that we must look at what it is people do with one another to create community. Remember, a community is about people who join together so we must examine their collective behavior. **Collective behavior** focuses on the joint action that links people together. We need to know what a person says, how others respond to that person, and how the first person adjusts to the response given by a second person. To understand this joint action, you might ask yourself the following questions:

- What do people say to each other?
- When?
- Where?
- What gets made by their joint action?

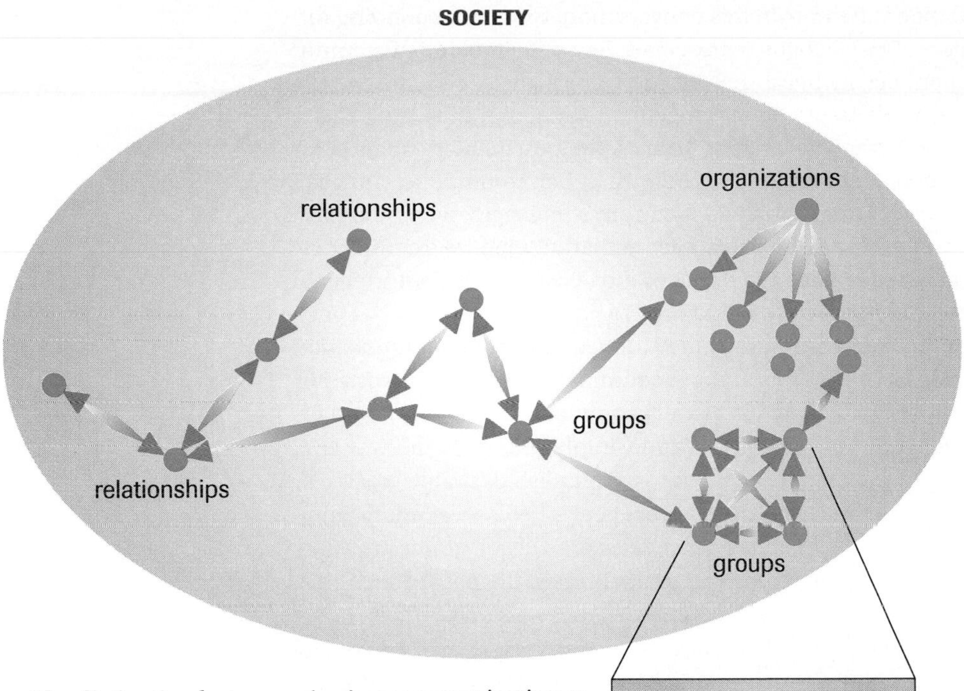

SOCIETY

relationships

organizations

groups

relationships

groups

FIGURE 1.4
The Community and Communication Model

Community permeates our existence as members of society, organizations, groups, and relationships. Understanding the idea of community is challenging because people may belong to multiple communities simultaneously, and the way we communicate can create different types of community. To understand how community is created, examine the form of communication occurring between people as indicated by the lines connecting individuals in their relationships, groups, organizations, and society.

The distinction between viewing communication as community and the transactional model of communication is revealed by the last question, "What gets made by their joint action?" As you recall, the transactional model suggests that what needs to get made as we communicate is shared meaning. However, when viewing communication as community, creating shared meaning is only one possible outcome of communication. This model of communication opens up a wide variety of possible outcomes. Take for example, the following snippet of conversation:

SALLY: I think you really need to get your act together.
CHRIS: [Silence.]
SALLY: Chris, don't you care about what I'm saying?
CHRIS: [Silence.]

What is getting made in this conversation? One possible outcome is a relational community where Sally is the dominant partner in a relationship. Another possible outcome is a relational community where Chris withdraws from the relationship. Other possibilities include an oppressive community where Sally is the oppressor, or even a passive-aggressive community where Chris is the aggressor. Although shared meaning may or may not be one outcome, the outcomes of Sally becoming dominant and Chris withdrawing from the relationship are certainly possible outcomes.

Contrast the first episode with the following conversation:

SALLY: I think you really need to get your act together.
CHRIS: Since when did you become my mother?
SALLY: Chris, don't you care about what I'm saying?
CHRIS: No Sally, I really don't. I wish in the future you'd just keep your mouth shut and let me live my life.

Knowledge Link

What is the key difference between viewing communication as community and the transactional model of communication?

How is this second conversation different? In this conversation, Chris is responding differently; she is no longer silent. This dialogue represents a very different kind of community, one in which an argument occurs because Sally and Chris actively disagree over an issue—whether or not Chris needs to get her act together. The community they create and the way they create it—together—is different from all the possibilities explored for the previous exchange. To understand a relational, group, or public community, you need to focus on what people do together. If we only viewed Sally's messages, we would have interpreted what is getting made in both conversations similarly. When we examine how Chris responds to Sally, we begin to understand that the kind of community being created in their relationship is different in the two conversations.

Given that communication creates community, how do we evaluate communication effectiveness? Communication as community is about coordinating our actions with others to bring about desirable goals. In fact, in this model coordination is the primary standard for evaluating communication effectiveness. More simply put, does the way that people come together in communication allow them to accomplish desirable goals? For example, in the context of a job interview, the interviewer's goal is to discover information about a job applicant that will facilitate making a good decision. The job applicant wants to present information that will promote a positive evaluation on the part of the interviewer. Sometimes these two interests come into conflict: Interviewers may request information less flattering to an applicant and job applicants do their best to avoid divulging that information. In interviews where the communication is coordinated, skillful interviewers and job applicants coordinate their questions and answers seamlessly to achieve their own personal goals. As you might expect, a job interview in which such coordination is achieved is considered effective by both the interviewer and the applicant.

All four models of communication are useful when deciding how to communicate in different situations. The information transfer model is effective when giving instructions to a large group of people. When motivating a work team to partake in an organization's vision, viewing communication as shared meaning may facilitate this process. If a salesperson needs to fulfill a quota to keep his or her job, viewing communication as persuasion may best enable the accomplishment of this task. However, each model only provides partial insight into the communication process because it allows us to only focus on what it highlights as important. If we believe in communication as information transfer, we neglect understanding how shared meaning is created and the persuasive elements of communication. If we believe in communication as shared meaning, we do not focus on how information is transferred or how people persuade one another. If we believe in communication as persuasion, we do not focus on how people create shared meaning.

Consider an example of this dilemma. Many public health campaigns aimed at reducing teen pregnancy adopt an information transfer model of communication. They provide detailed information about pregnancy and contraception. So why do so many of these campaigns fail? One explanation may be that by focusing on disseminating detailed information clearly, the proponents of such campaigns may have overlooked the importance of shared meaning. They may not be providing words and images in a way that taps into a teenager's field of experience. As a result, the message is not heard. The information transfer model focuses on getting the information across; how-

Viewing communication as shared meaning is sometimes useful.

ever, it does not necessarily connect to the audience's field of experience and create shared meaning.

Viewing communication as community is the most useful model because its comprehensiveness allows us to place the other models under its umbrella. However, when analyzing communication situations, keep in mind that people draw on a wide variety of skills and knowledge associated with each communication model. We can examine whether the clarity of communication allows people to coordinate their actions, whether shared meaning facilitates coordination, or whether the fact that one person created consensus through persuasion enhances coordination. Viewing communication as community allows us to examine what elements of information transfer, shared meaning, or persuasion allow people to coordinate their actions as well as other skills and knowledge.

Assumptions About Communication

If we view communication as community and as the process of managing messages to create meaning, what assumptions do we make about communication? Test your assumptions about communication using the test in the accompanying box. To check your answers, read the following detailed descriptions of these common assumptions about communication:

1. Communication is a process.
2. Communication creates our social worlds.
3. Communication is functional.
4. Communication is limiting and liberating.
5. Communication is adaptive.
6. Communication is holistic.
7. Communication involves coordination.

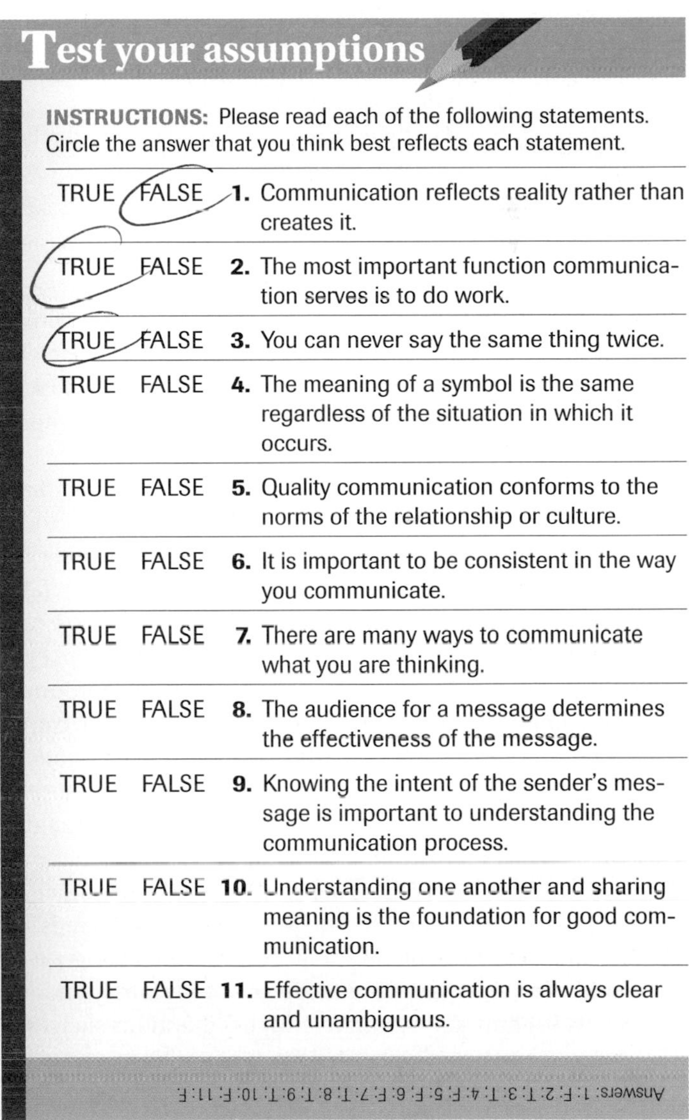

Test your assumptions

INSTRUCTIONS: Please read each of the following statements. Circle the answer that you think best reflects each statement.

TRUE FALSE **1.** Communication reflects reality rather than creates it.

TRUE FALSE **2.** The most important function communication serves is to do work.

TRUE FALSE **3.** You can never say the same thing twice.

TRUE FALSE **4.** The meaning of a symbol is the same regardless of the situation in which it occurs.

TRUE FALSE **5.** Quality communication conforms to the norms of the relationship or culture.

TRUE FALSE **6.** It is important to be consistent in the way you communicate.

TRUE FALSE **7.** There are many ways to communicate what you are thinking.

TRUE FALSE **8.** The audience for a message determines the effectiveness of the message.

TRUE FALSE **9.** Knowing the intent of the sender's message is important to understanding the communication process.

TRUE FALSE **10.** Understanding one another and sharing meaning is the foundation for good communication.

TRUE FALSE **11.** Effective communication is always clear and unambiguous.

Answers: 1: F; 2: T; 3: T; 4: F; 5: F; 6: F; 7: T; 8: T; 9: T; 10: F; 11: F

Communication Is a Process

One of the turning points in any relationship with romantic potential is when two people look each other in the eye and say, "I love you." With these three simple words the relationship moves from a friendship to romantic involvement and love. Look six months into the future of this relationship. After an argument, both people look at each other and utter those same three words, "I love you." Does this phrase mean what it did six months earlier? Although the words may be the same, the meaning is probably quite different. The first time the couple said "I love you," it meant their relationship was moving to a new level of intimacy. The second "I love you" came after the couple had shared many more experiences—both positive and negative. The meaning of "I love you" changes from being a significant milestone to words intended to smooth over a conflict. Although you may be able to say the same words twice, the words never mean the same thing. The answer to Statement 3 in Test Your Assumptions then is true.

As with the relationship just described, communication is an ongoing process where people send messages to one another over time. To understand the communication process, you have to understand what each message means, where it occurs in the unfolding sequence of messages, and the context in which the message takes place. For example, what does the message, "I don't know how" mean? Consider the following two conversations.

Conversation 1

ANGELINA: Could you facilitate this group discussion?
JUAN: I don't know how.
ANGELINA: Oh, that's right. I haven't had time to train you. Let me give you a few tips on how to do it.

Conversation 2

ANGELINA: Could you facilitate this group discussion?
JUAN: I don't know how.
ANGELINA: That's not true. I've trained you before how to do it. I know that you're nervous about trying this, but you've got to jump in and give it a go.

In the first conversation, "I don't know how" means that Juan doesn't have the information necessary to perform the task. Angelina acknowledges that she hasn't trained him when she offers to coach Juan. In the second conversation, "I don't know" means that Juan is not confident in his ability to perform the task; Angelina acknowledges that he has the needed skills but lacks the confidence to perform the task. Although people may utter the same words, the meaning of those words change according to where they fall in the overall communication process.

Describing communication as a process does not mean that communication must follow a specific series of steps in order to be effective. People can communicate effectively in given situations in any number of ways. When talking about communication as a process, the meaning of an utterance depends on where it falls in the process—what has happened before the words are spoken and what happens afterward. Have you ever said something in a conversation and the person you were talking to asked, "What does that mean?" If you view communication as a process, an appropriate answer to the question is "I'm not completely sure yet; we have not finished our conversation" (John Shotter, in Pearce, 1994, p. 123). This is because the meaning of an individual message is not solely determined by the intentions of the message source; rather the meaning of a message is completed only when the receiver responds to it. For example, the words "I love you" mean different things depending on how the recipient responds to the message. The meaning of these words differs depending on whether the recipient says "I love you too", "You've got be kidding", or "I thought we were just friends." Context can influence the meaning of a message. The meaning of "I love you" changes when you utter that phrase to a potential romantic partner, a member of your family, or a close friend. To understand the process of communication we must ask questions such as what was said, to whom, in what context, and how did they respond? Thus the answer to Statement 4 is false.

Communication Creates Our Social Worlds

Return to Test Your Assumptions. Statement 1 claims that communication reflects reality rather than creating it. In popular culture, we see this question debated over the effect of media messages on society. Some argue that violence on television, in the movies, and in video games creates a society desensitized to violence and causes people to act out their violent impulses. Others argue that the violent content of television, movies, and video games simply reflects what is going on in society at large. This debate is typically triggered when people are exposed to media violence and subsequently commit crimes that mimic the violence portrayed in the media. The debate centers on whether life imitates art, art imitates life, or if art and life are totally separate.

Our social worlds are comprised of people, their relationships with others, and the events and objects they create. Communication does so much more than simply transmit our internal states such as thoughts and feelings to others and refer to external events and people. Rather, it creates and reforms our understanding of those states, events, and people. Through communication we create myths, stories, rituals, ceremonies, rules, and other aspects of our social reality. It is communication that provides us with meaning and expectations about people and situations. Because the way we communicate is responsible to a large extent for creating our social worlds, Statement 1 is false.

Knowledge Link

How does communication create our social worlds?

Communication Is Functional

Why do you communicate? Revisiting Test Your Assumptions, note that Statement 2 suggests the central reason for communicating is to accomplish something. This is indeed a primary function of communication. If you are a member of a work team and need to make a decision, communication with other team members helps make that decision. When you are negotiating the purchase of a car, your ability to persuade can help you accomplish your goal by getting a good deal. For a manager conducting a performance evaluation of an employee, communicating constructive feedback and effective goal setting is critical to accomplishing this task. Communication functions by helping us explain, brainstorm, negotiate, direct, and make decisions in many situations. It allows us to complete the task at hand.

Communication performs a variety of functions. It can help us accomplish work as well as build relationships.

Communication is functional—that is, communication serves a particular purpose in any interaction. In addition to getting things done, communication also helps build relationships and maintain a healthy supportive climate. Communication can offer people social support in times of personal crisis. Self-esteem can be built and strengthened through communication. Communication can help build cohesion and enhance commitment and loyalty in small groups and organizations. When communication builds relationships and creates supportive climates, it serves a relational function by focusing on the emotional aspects of a relationship between two people, a group, or an organization.

Communication can serve task and relational functions simultaneously. What does it mean when a parent asks a child for his or her opinion? Such communication serves an important task function—it helps the parent make a decision regarding some issue. At the same time, it serves an important relational function—it conveys the parent's respect for the child's opinion and makes him or her feel valued as a member of the family. To understand the functional nature of communication, ask yourself the following questions:

- What has led the speaker to utter this message?
- What is the effect of this message on listeners?

By understanding the purpose of the message and the effect it has on others, you can begin to determine what functions the message is serving. So Statement 2 is true.

COMMUNICATION IS LIMITING & LIBERATING

When you meet a person for the first time, what do you talk about? Typically, you talk about nonthreatening topics such as your major or occupation, where you are from, common friends or acquaintances, and your hobbies. Growing up you learn that this pattern of communication for initial meetings between people is typical in North America. You quickly learn that in the context of initial interactions with people you don't know, you should limit your communication to superficial topics. But what would happen if you met someone for the first time and said something like, "You know, usually people talk about hobbies and make superficial small talk when they first meet. Instead, I was wondering what has been the high point of living in this town for you?" Such a question may open up new topics to discuss such as that person's feelings about the community he or she lives in, what it is about the community that brings him or her enjoyment, the person's values, and so on. These kinds of topics are not typically covered in initial interactions among strangers, and yet the act of asking this kind of question may liberate you and your new acquaintance from covering the same old topics.

So Statement 5, "Quality communication conforms to the rules and norms of the relationship or culture," is false. Meeting the expectations of the relationship or culture is crucial to competent communication. However, that is only half of the communication puzzle. When people communicate, they base their communication on the preexisting norms, values, and beliefs that characterize groups, organizations, institutions, and societies (Giddens, 1979, 1984). These norms, values, and beliefs set expectations and boundaries for how people are to communicate and they try to conform to them. For example, gangs have created a strong set of norms, values, and beliefs that guide how gang members dress and talk to one another (Conquergood, 1994). Gang members who want to maintain their membership in the gang and avoid punishment or retribution must conform to these expectations.

However, the expectations and boundaries created by preexisting norms, values, and beliefs do not form a limited type of communication where those who violate these boundaries must be punished (Giddens, 1979, 1984). People often communicate in ways that intentionally or unintentionally violate preexisting expectations and boundaries. When people communicate in ways that are creative and liberating, they reshape the norms, values, and beliefs. Moreover, they may do it in such a way that others view as appropriate. For example, in the 1960s, Martin Luther King, Jr. set out to reshape the U.S. views on the civil rights of African Americans. He intentionally led a movement that was determined to change the laws governing African Americans' participation in local and federal government. Moreover, his emphasis on nonviolence as a way of expressing dissent was viewed as appropriate by others.

Said a different way, human beings act *from* and *into* context. When we act from context, that context may impose constraints on our communication. For example, in the context of a college classroom, students know they should take notes during class; they also know playing loud music and dancing is prohibited. When we act into context, we create new ways of communicating that are viewed by others as appropriate and effective. By creating new meanings and understandings, we open up new and creative ways of acting for people and liberate them from their constraints. Therapists, for example, have long recognized communication's power for changing and liberating people's self-images and conceptions of how they must act. Consider someone who is depressed and describes himself to his therapist as "an outsider" and feels isolated, marginal, and alone (Cronen & Lang, 1994). This person has created a self-image that constrains what he can do or say and sustains his depression. A therapist who recognizes that communication can be liberating may focus on the fact that some people who are isolated, at the margin, and alone are viewed as heroes. Heroes are often described as rebels, trailblazers, and revolutionaries and viewed as creative, brave, and energetic—all positive traits. If the person begins to describe his feelings as "heroic," his self-image changes from negative to positive. The power of this new description can transcend previous constraints, opening up new possibilities for action, thus empowering the patient.

Communication Is Adaptive

Imagine you strongly believe it is important to speak openly and honestly about your opinions regarding people and events. Even at the risk of hurting someone's feelings, you feel it's important "to tell it like it is." You recently were hired by a company at the top of your list of desirable places to begin your career. Your first week on the job, your immediate supervisor gives a presentation to the newly hired employees that is truly awful. You feel it was disorganized and didn't make the important points clear. Your supervisor approaches you following the presentation and asks you what you think. How do you respond? Do you tell your boss that it was a dreadful presentation and risk harming this new and potentially significant relationship? Do you tell your boss it was "fine" and betray your strong commitment to speaking openly and honestly?

As this example illustrates, we need to change our communication according to our environment if we are to communicate competently. Adapting your communication to your environment can be difficult because it may involve trade-offs between your beliefs and values and the necessity to maintain quality working relationships with others. Rather than being consistent in our communication and always saying the same thing in the same way, as competent communicators we need to adapt our messages to the time and place in which we are communicating, and the audience we are trying to reach. This is not to say you should change what you say or do to match what other people want you to say or do, however. This type of behavior would compromise your ethical code. People who are rhetorically sensitive recognize the unique characteristics of their environment and create messages that allow them to be heard by others while retaining their own viewpoints.

A good example of rhetorical sensitivity can be found in former First Lady Barbara Bush's speech to the graduating class at Wellesley College. As a homemaker, mother, and wife, she faced an audience comprised mainly of graduating senior women who would soon be pursuing professional careers. What would you say in this situation? In her speech, Bush told her audience that perhaps one of them would be in the White House as a spouse. She then followed up with the line, "and I wish him the very best." What Bush did in this speech was to adapt to her audience. Knowing that the audience was comprised of prospective professionals, she captured their attention by stating that anything is possible—including being the president of the United States. By crafting her message with an emphasis on a belief she shared with her audience—the ability for women to accomplish great things—she created a climate in which the audience was willing to listen to her. By adapting to her audience and establishing common ground, her message was heard. Statement 6 then is false.

The notion of adapting to situations is not limited to public speaking events. We adapt our messages every day whenever we communicate. For example, imagine you are an employee for a nonprofit community theater group. You have a great idea for boosting ticket sales. Yet you know your boss believes that only he can have good ideas. How do you present your idea to your boss? Consider the following choices:

- You can directly tell the boss your idea.
- You ask the boss whether he has heard of any idea that resembles your own.
- You can hint that you heard about another theater group using the ticket strategy, and ask what the boss thinks about it.

These are three possible strategies to introduce your idea to the boss. Given your boss's tendency to believe he has all the answers, you might lean toward the second or third choices rather than directly revealing your idea. In this way, you will have adapted your message to the situation, and considered possible messages once you are in that situation. This is key to competent communication. Returning to Test Your Assumptions, Statement 7 is true.

COMMUNICATION IS HOLISTIC

People commonly believe you must break down complex entities such as countries, organizations, or processes into their component parts in order to learn more about them. For example, imagine you are an economic development officer for a city charged with attracting new business and industry. You have found a strong correlation between the interest a business shows in relocating to your town and the rate of local taxes. Lower taxes increase the likelihood that a company will relocate to your town. Therefore, one of the strategies you pursue to encourage development is to offer tax breaks for incoming business and industry. What problems may be associated with this strategy of economic development? If you focus on the whole, you may see how giving tax breaks to business decreases the amount of money that can be generated, which in turn limits the amount of money earmarked for public education, which may lessen the quality of education and limit the school system's ability to train skilled workers. This would make future relocations to your city less desirable for business and industry because of a poorly skilled labor force. When you think holistically, you begin to see how different parts are related to one another, and how changing one part in a whole system can lead to unintended consequences for other parts within the whole.

Understanding communication holistically means you must examine the speaker (Statement 9), the audience (Statement 8), and most importantly what they do together. To understand communication holistically, focus on:

- what people do together,
- at a specific time,
- in a specific place,
- what has led up to this interaction,
- and what their hopes are for the future.

A holistic approach to examining communication is important because focusing only on the speaker's intent or on the audience's perceptions of a message limits our understanding of the entire communication process. Can we understand the complete communica-

People sometimes adapt their communication to fit into situations. Adapting your communication to the situation may help you achieve your goals.

CATHY © Cathy Guisewite. Reprinted with permission of UNIVERSAL PRESS SYNDICATE. All rights reserved..

tion process if we focus only on the speaker's intention apart from the audience to whom he or she is speaking? Can we say a message is effective if the audience for that message views it as such, but the sender of the message does not? The simple answer is no. Understanding the entire communication requires examining the past, looking to the future, and focusing on the situation itself. Statements 8 and 9, then, are both true.

Communication Involves Coordination

In the late 1970s, Douglas Adams wrote a science fiction book called *The Hitchhiker's Guide to the Galaxy.* In this book, he identifies one problem facing space travelers: the inability to communicate clearly with one another because of the wide variety of languages spoken. As a result, the Babel Fish was invented, a device placed in the ear that would automatically and clearly translate what a person was saying into the listener's own language. However, rather than helping relationships among different races by promoting clear understanding, the end results of using the Babel Fish were some of the bloodiest wars known to the universe. Once people clearly understood one another and assigned similar meanings to words, this clarity sharply defined their differences and led to war.

Most of us assume that for people to communicate well, they must share meanings for events and words (Statement 10) and that people always need to be clear and unambiguous to achieve good communication (Statement 11). Of course, there are times when people need to share meaning and clarity in communication. During crisis situations, medical personnel need to agree on what certain procedures mean and doctors must give clear instructions on the procedures that must be performed. Yet there are times where we may need or want to be less than clear in our communication. Being ambiguous in how you communicate can have two main benefits (Eisenberg & Goodall, 1997). First, ambiguity can help people with diverse sets of opinions collaborate with each other. If there is ambiguity about what beliefs or values are important, people may assume they share the same beliefs and values and be willing to work together. When communication is clear, the differences between people become more distinct and may lead to conflict. Second, ambiguous communication can promote creativity. For example, sometimes teachers may be ambiguous in their instructions about how to complete a particular assignment to encourage students to be creative in the way they accomplish the task. So Statements 10 and 11 are both false.

Why Is Communication Important?

Human beings communicate almost constantly given how much time we devote to speaking, listening, writing, informing, persuading, and talking. The old adage "One cannot *not* communicate" is especially true today (Berlo, 1960). The rise of communication technologies such as the fax, email, teleconferencing, and audio-conferencing bring people closer together to communicate despite long distances. Like Kathryn in the opening chapter vignette, we communicate with a large number of people daily through a wide variety of channels. We literally live in a communication world.

Communication is functional and creates our social worlds. The way we communicate has direct consequences on the kinds of lives we lead, the kinds of relationships we create, and the kinds of communities we build. Do you want to improve your relationships with other people? Do you want to participate in groups that not only produce good work but work well together? Do you want to participate in organizations and communities that are growing and developing? Interpersonal relationships, groups, organizations, and communities are not simply found; they are made by you and others through communication. The choice you have is whether you wish to communicate in ways that create positive relationships among people.

The ability to build strong interpersonal relationships rests on changing the form of communication. For example, when married couples engage in forms of communication that are negative, they are highly likely to get divorced. When couples allow their conversations to be influenced by the Four Horsemen of the Apocalypse—criticism, contempt, defensiveness, and stonewalling—they create relationships that are unstable and prone to divorce (Gottman & Silver, 1999). Rather than choosing to be negative, couples can choose more positive forms of communication that encourage them to describe their conflict, maintain fondness and admiration for each other, craft solutions that allow both people to meet their needs, and offer mutual support. Relationships are constantly being made and remade by communication—changing the form of communication can result in more positive, fulfilling, and long-lasting interpersonal relationships.

The ability to create strong groups and teams also depends on communication. The last decade has seen an explosion in the use of groups in social and work settings. Over 40 million people in the United States currently participate in support groups such as Alcoholics Anonymous, cancer survivor groups, and consciousness-raising groups (Wuthnow, 1994). Moreover, in an era of increased domestic and international competition and corporate downsizing, organizations increasingly rely on work teams to maintain a competitive edge. In both our social and work lives, groups are becoming a more powerful presence. When group members choose forms of communicating that allow the creation of collective goals, the blending of individual members' knowledge, and the promotion of learning, they are more likely to be successful (Katzenbach & Smith, 1994; Senge, 1991).

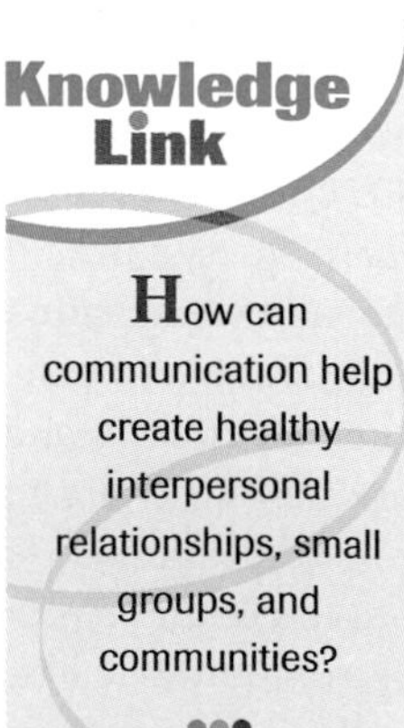

Finally, the way we communicate influences our ability to build strong and healthy communities. Traditional ways of building communities have emphasized debate and argument. For example, the United States has a strong tradition of using town hall meetings to deliberate over important issues within communities. In these settings, advocates for each side of the issue present arguments for their positions. Public issues such as health care, abortion, economic development, and environmental protection have been discussed in such public forums. Yet for debate and argument to work well, people need to come to such forums with similar assumptions and values. The shared assumptions and values serve as a backdrop for the discussion. However, as society becomes more diverse, the likelihood that people share assumptions and values diminishes. As a result, forms of communication such as argument and debate become polarized because people do not share the same foundation for understanding. In this situation, debate and argument may drive communities apart as opposed to bringing them together.

Many people interested in community building contend that we need to shift our forms of communication to include more dialogue (Chasin, Herzig, Roth, Chasin, Becker, and Stains, 1995; Pearce & Littlejohn, 1997). **Dialogue** is a way of communicating that allows people to stand their own ground while being open to other perspectives. A number of groups such as the Public Conversations Project, Study Circles, the Public Dialogue Consortium, and National Issues Forum have been formed to help citizens in a community enter into rich conversations about potentially explosive issues such as race, education, homosexuality, abortion, health reform, cultural diversity, and welfare reform. As people begin to participate in more community dialogues about significant issues, the community pulls together and unifies.

As you've seen, communication creates our social worlds and builds community. However, the choice to make a commitment to communicate in ways that make your relationships, groups, organizations, and communities healthy and functional is yours. The idea that you have a choice in creating the kinds of communities in which you want to participate is not new. Over 2,000 years ago, in the ancient Greek city of Athens, citizens took an oath to leave their city better than how they found it. Like the Athenians, your commitment to such an ideal is just the first step. You must also be able to make wise choices about your communication to select those messages that help you create healthy communities. The second step is to develop your ability to choose among the forms of communication that will allow you to build healthy communities in relationships, groups, organizations, and society.

Communication Competence

As you can see by now, communication is much more complex than it first appears. Like Kathryn at the beginning of this chapter, you probably communicate with a large and diverse number of people, over a number of topics and issues, and in a wide variety of settings. Given this diversity, it is impossible to construct rules for communication that specifically detail what messages are obligated, permitted, or prohibited given a specific situation. Thus building a comprehensive model of communication that can prescribe what people must do or say in all situations is impossible. For example, is it always effective and appropriate to be clear in your communication according to the information transfer model? Is creating shared meaning as suggested by the interactional and transactional models always desirable? Does all communication involve advocating and making arguments for your position as outlined by the persuasion model? The simple answer to each of these questions is "no." There are times when it is effective to be ambiguous in your communication, when shared meaning is not important, and when the goal of the communication is not persuasion. However, if we can't make general rules for communicating, what kind of model of communication can we create? It is possible to construct a model of communication for making informed choices about messages that will help you act in competent ways—ways in which your communication is perceived as appropriate and effective by others.

As you've just seen, communication is the process of making community. This means that the choices we make about how to communicate influence what we create and the

CloseUp on Community

Integrating Community Concerns With Your Experience

OUR COMMUNITIES ARE BECOMING increasingly diverse. How can you begin to understand those who are different from you? How can you begin to grasp how communication can make a difference in building strong, healthy communities? During your college experience, one way to connect with people who may be different from you is to make a commitment to work for social justice, to be willing to engage with and advocate for people in a community who are "economically, socially, politically, and/or culturally under-resourced" (Frey, Pearce, Pollock, Artz, & Murphy, 1996, p. 110). The goal of working for social justice is not only to learn about people who may be different from you, but to take action to help those who are disadvantaged in your community because of a lack of resources.

One way to integrate a commitment to social justice with your education is to engage in service learning, a collaboration between students and communities in which students apply their classroom learning to help communities manage significant issues or problems, and in turn, the community experience broadens the students' classroom learning. Service learning may take several different forms:

- *Courses with service-learning components*: These courses are not designed to be service-learning intensive, but they allow or require you to use a service experience, often something you may be doing already such as tutoring high-risk children, visiting the elderly, working in domestic abuse shelters, supporting the chronically ill, as the basis for one assignment.
- *Courses with service-learning motifs*: These are courses that may or may not have been designed with service learning in mind, but allow or require you to use service as the basis for all or a major part of your course assignments. An example of this would be a class developing and producing radio programs that respond to local community needs and interests.
- *Internship/Fieldwork:* An internship provides an opportunity to spend several hours each week working with a community organization in a position that builds professional skills. Habitat for Humanity, for example, has developed a public relations internship position that offers valuable public relations experience while participating in an effort to provide affordable housing to people who might otherwise live in deplorable conditions. The intern produces press packets, coordinates interviews, writes press releases and public service announcements, and assists in the editing and publishing of a newsletter.
- *Capstone course*: This is a department/program-based, senior-level course that involves significant community service, as well as guided discussion and written analysis of previous service experience based on intellectual frameworks designed by the instructor or team of instructors. (Adapted from Frey et al., 1996, pp. 120–121)

Service learning is one way in which you can learn about people who may be different from you. However, your school may not offer opportunities in service learning. In that case, how could you learn about others who may be different from you and still maintain a social justice commitment? Consider the following ideas:

- Mentor someone who is under resourced.
- Volunteer at a soup kitchen or a homeless shelter.
- Encourage campus groups to make a commitment to service.
- Facilitate the planning and execution of service projects on campus.
- Present a speech about people who are under resourced or about an issue that relates to social justice as an assignment for one of your classes.
- Research the under resourced in your community and submit an article based on this research to your school newspaper.

Even if formal classes that emphasize service and social justice are not offered, you can undertake any number of interpersonal, small group, or public speaking opportunities to facilitate your learning about people who may be different from you and to help those that have fewer resources.

SOURCE: Frey, et at. (1996).

kinds of personal lives, relationships, and communities we build. How do we know what kinds of communication are most helpful for creating the kinds of communities that we desire? Communication competence provides a framework for making these important choices. As you will see in Chapter 2, communication competence involves acting in ways that are perceived as appropriate and effective by yourself and by others. Competent communication can be clear or ambiguous; it can create shared meaning or not; and it can function to persuade others or not. All forms of communication have the potential to be viewed as competent depending on the situation. This idea requires that you develop a framework for choosing among communication messages that will allow you to act competently within a situation.

There are three requirements to constructing messages that are perceived as competent by others. First, you must be motivated to communicate competently. Second, you must be knowledgeable about the situation you are communicating in and the kinds of messages that are obligated, permitted, or prohibited. Third, you must be skilled at actually transmitting the kinds of messages you know you should perform in the situation. Simply knowing what to do is not enough to act competently; you must be able to deliver a skilled performance if you are to be perceived as a competent communicator. Motivation, knowledge, and skills are the foundations to being perceived as competent by others.

Chapter Summary

Communication is a pervasive force in our everyday life as we relate and connect to a wide variety of people through face-to-face and mediated channels in a large number of social and work contexts. The contemporary reality of our lives is that we simply cannot *not* communicate. We must understand that communication is a process of managing messages for the purpose of creating meaning. What do human beings attempt to accomplish by managing messages? The answer to this question depends on the model of communication you adopt. If you accept the model of communication as information transfer, people communicate to get their point across to an audience clearly. The model of communication as sharing meaning suggests that we communicate in order to create a common understanding of people, events, and situations. Viewing communication as persuasion highlights that the purpose of communication is to influence others to accept our points of view or to perform certain actions that we specify. The model of communication as community suggests that we try to communicate to facilitate coordination among people in communities.

The idea that communication is community carries with it several assumptions about the nature of communication. Communication is a process that unfolds over time and creates our social worlds. It does more than simply transfer information, create shared understanding, or control people; it shapes our perceptions of what we think our social worlds are like—how we interpret what they mean and what kinds of actions we think are possible. Communication is functional in that it helps us perform important tasks and build strong relationships. When we communicate, we try to adapt to the situations in which we find ourselves; but at the same time we are not limited to what the situation demands. We can also communicate in ways that open up new ways of thinking and being. Our ability to create new ways of thinking and being requires being sensitive to the holistic nature of communication and taking actions that allow us to coordinate our collective behavior.

Communication is important because it has the power to mold our social worlds. However, there are few clear-cut rules for how to communicate competently in ways that are both appropriate and effective within situations. As a result, to develop your communication competence you need to develop your abilities in three areas: (1) motivation, (2) knowledge, and (3) skills. Developing your abilities in these three areas will help you in a variety of communication situations.

Key Terms

communication
messages
symbol
meaning
information transfer model
source
channel
receiver
encoding
decoding
noise
interactive model
transactional model
persuasion
community
collective behavior
dialogue

Building Knowledge

1. How are relatively new communication technologies such as email, chat rooms, instant messaging, and video conferencing influencing the communication process?
2. Identify situations where it would make sense to use communication as information transfer, communication as sharing meaning, and communication as persuasion.
3. How else can you define communication besides information transfer, sharing meaning, persuasion, and community?
4. In what kinds of situations could a person be able to coordinate his or her actions with those of another person but not share meaning?
5. If all communication is functional—the speaker has a purpose in communicating a message and it has an effect on an audience—can communication ever be dysfunctional? What standards would you propose for classifying communication as functional or dysfunctional?
6. Think of a time when you felt a person was flexible in his or her communication, yet was not perceived as being wishy-washy or adapting just to meet someone else's needs. How did that person make his or her communication flexible?
7. Why is understanding communication important to our daily lives? Are there ever situations where communication doesn't make a difference? Explain.

Building Skills

Individual Exercises

1. Ask four or five friends how they define communication. Do their definitions of communication reflect it as information transfer, sharing meaning, persuasion, or community? Why do you think each person defined communication in the way he or she did?
2. Think of a time when you were able to coordinate your communication with another person to achieve some desirable goal. Write down the dialogue of who said what to whom. Now answer the question, "What in this conversation made it possible for me to achieve my goal?" What kinds of factors influence how we coordinate our actions?
3. Think of a recent conversation that you would characterize as poor communication. On a piece of paper, draw a vertical line dividing the paper in two. In the left-hand column, write down the conversation. Note each speaker's turn on a separate line. In the right-hand column, next to each message write down what you think is the underlying reason for that message. Think about the key assumptions each conversational partner is making and the reasons that guided their interaction. How could you change the conversation to make it better? How would the key assumptions need to change to make the conversation better?
4. Find an opinion piece or an editorial in a magazine or a newspaper. Read the editorial and highlight the key words and phrases that the author uses. Focusing on these key words and phrases, how would you describe how the author perceives his or her community?
5. Consider the following list of labels we use to describe some of the roles that people can play in society and organizations: When a person is labeled in a certain way (e.g., as a AIDS activist), what kinds of communication are permitted? What does it allow him or her to do? Given how a person is labeled, what kinds of communication are prohibited? What does that label prohibit him or her from doing?

professor	CEO
student	construction worker
AIDS activist	lawyer
mother	doctor
politician	

6. Using *InfoTrac College Edition* type in the keywords *communication and community*. Examine the articles that have been written about communication and community during the last two years. Given these articles, generate a list of questions that you think communication scholars are trying to answer.

Group Exercises

1. Form small groups of 4–5 students. Take a blank piece of poster board and draw a picture of a model that captures your view of the communication process. As a group, discuss what features need to be included in the communication model and why. Compare your communication model with those created by other groups in the class.
2. As an individual, complete the following statement: "I dream of a community where . . ." In groups of 4–5 other students, share your dreams for your community. As a group, construct a vision for what an ideal community would look like. Then discuss the kinds of communication that need to happen to make that vision a reality. Who needs to talk to whom? About what? How?
3. Form small groups of 5–6 students. The communication discipline has several national organizations including the National Communication Association (http://www.natcom.org/) and the International Communication Association (http://www.icahdq.org/). Split up and visit each site and write a one-page summary of how that site portrays the communication discipline. Then compare each subgroup's finding on the sites. What is the purpose of communication according to each site? What kinds of issues are studied in communication?

References

Berlo, D. K. (1960). *The process of communication: An introduction to theory and practice.* New York: Holt, Rinehart & Winston.

Chasin, R., Herzig, M., Roth, S., Chasin, L., Becker, C., & Stains, R. R. (1996). From diatribe to dialogue on divisive public issues: Approaches drawn from family therapy. *Mediation Quarterly, 13* (4), 323–344.

Conquergood, D. (1994). Homeboys and hoods: Gang communication and cultural space. In L. R. Frey (Ed.), *Group communication in context: Studies of natural groups* (pp. 23–55). Hillsdale, NJ: Erlbaum.

Cronen, V., & Lang, P. (1994). Language and action: Wittgenstein and Dewey in the practice of therapy and consultation. *Human Systems, 5* (1–2), 5–44.

Eisenberg, E. M., & Goodall, H. L., Jr. (1997). *Organizational communication: Balancing creativity and constraint* (2nd ed.). New York: St. Martin's.

Frey, L. R., Botan, C. H., & Kreps, G. L. (2000). *Investigating communication: An introduction to research methods.* (2nd ed.). Boston: Allyn & Bacon.

Frey, L. R., Pearce, W. B., Pollock, M. A., Artz, L., & Murphy, B. A. O. (1996). Looking for justice in all the wrong places: On a communication approach to social justice. *Communication Studies, 47* (1/2),110–127.

Giddens, A. (1979). *Central problems in social theory.* Berkeley: University of California Press.

Giddens, A. (1984). *The constitution of society.* Berkeley: University of California Press.

Gottman, J. M., & Silver, N. (1999). *The seven principles for making marriage work.* New York: Crown.

Katzenbach, J. R., & Smith, D. K. (1994). *The wisdom of teams.* New York: HarperBusiness.

Lasswell, H. (1964). The structure and function of communication in society. In L. Bryson (Ed.), *The communication of ideas* (pp. 37–51). New York: Cooper Square. (Original work published 1948)

Littlejohn, S. W. (1999). *Theories of human communication* (6th ed.). Belmont, CA: Wadsworth.

Pearce, W. B. (1994). *Interpersonal communication: Making social worlds.* New York: HarperCollins.

Pearce, W. B., & Littlejohn, S. (1997). *Moral conflict: When social worlds collide.* Thousand Oaks, CA: Sage.

Senge, P. M. (1991). *The fifth discipline.* New York: Doubleday.

Shannon, C. E., & Weaver, W. (1949). *The mathematical theory of communication.* Urbana: University of Illinois Press.

Wuthnow, R. (1994). *Sharing the journey: Support groups and America's new quest for community.* New York: Free Press.

CHAPTER 2

Learning Objectives

After studying this chapter, you should be able to:

1. Describe how competence viewed as an impression is different from competence viewed as an ability.
2. Illustrate how clarity, appropriateness, and effectiveness differ.
3. Identify and distinguish the different types of competence and incompetence.
4. Describe how the standards of appropriateness and effectiveness can provide an ethics of communication.
5. Identify and describe the major components of the communication competence model.
6. Distinguish among the types of contexts and identify communication events in terms of contexts.
7. Identify the features that distinguish among the levels of context.
8. Illustrate how perception influences a communicator's competence.

A Model of Communication Competence

Cambria was a transfer student at a prestigious small fine arts university. Shortly after leaving her home-town community college and moving into a small apartment, she was invited to a social for communication majors. She had spent the day hiking in some hills near campus and found that she was more exhausted than she had thought she would be. She got back to her apartment just in time to quickly clean up and get dressed. Upon arriving at a large classical-styled brick and granite building on campus, she saw that she was dressed less formally than most of the other students and faculty attending the social. The gathering was in a large carpeted room with marble columns and fine art on the walls. About 40 people were there, faculty and students from freshmen to seniors.

Cambria joined a small group of students conversing about the program, the courses, the professors, and the major. She repeatedly felt like she couldn't keep up with the conversation. She was not accustomed to conversing with people from cultures so different from her own, and with such strong dialects. She didn't know the names of many of the faculty, nor did she know much about the specifics of the program, but she didn't want to appear ignorant in her first conversations with her peers. She would occasionally make a general comment, but avoided saying much. She really wanted to let her peers and professors know how excited she was to be attending the college, but wasn't quite sure how to do this in the context of these discussions.

About an hour into the social, the department chair asked everyone to form a large circle. After some introductory remarks, he asked everyone to take turns introducing themselves, giving their name, where they were from, and offering something interesting about themselves. As chance would have it, Cambria found herself next to the chair, and she was asked to start. Cambria mumbled in a soft voice her name, that she was from California, and said the first thing that came to her mind: She felt "out of place" that evening.

Cambria, tired from her day's hike, self-conscious about how she was dressed and how uninformed she was compared to her peers, was suddenly cast into the spotlight, and she found herself unable to think of much to say, or to say impressively. As the evening wore on, she felt nervous, unclear about what she was doing there, or simply unable to communicate well. •••

Your success or failure when communicating depends on many factors. As the vignette suggests, three factors influence your communication excellence: motivation, knowledge, and skills. Combined in a variety of ways, in a variety of contexts these factors improve or impair communication. Sometimes only one of these is important. Other times the difference between success or failure depends on motivation, knowledge, and skills together. In this example, Cambria was tired, nervous, and at times unclear about why she was at the social, so her motivation was less than ideal. She wasn't familiar with many of the topics being discussed, and thus could not contribute much to the conversations, so she wasn't very knowledgeable. Finally, she introduced herself in an overly quiet voice and didn't have anything interesting to say when the opportunity came. She did not have the skills to overcome her tiredness and communicate in the way she would have liked. This chapter examines these three factors of communication—motivation, knowledge, and skills—and their implications for improving communication in everyday situations.

No two cultures, races, societies, groups, families, relationships, or individuals are exactly alike. This fact may frustrate those who seek simple answers to questions such as "How should I communicate to make a good impression in this situation?" In fact, there are countless communication situations, given the endless possible combinations of culture, race, individuals, and so on. Although these differences lead you to experience the world in new and interesting ways, they also often make communication more difficult.

Many such differences make communication difficult. However, the desire to be and appear to others as competent is fairly universal across people and situations. Even though at rare times it may be advantageous to appear incompetent (Spitzberg, 1993, 1994), most of the time, people prefer to be perceived as competent, coherent, attractive, effective, and appropriate.

In this chapter we discuss a general model for communication competence to help you understand any communication situation. The model identifies those factors that increase the likelihood of communicating competently in most situations. We then examine these factors in more detail in subsequent chapters. As a departure, first let's understand the types of judgments people make about communication.

What Is Communication Competence?

Communication competence concerns the extent to which something desired is accomplished through communication in a manner that fits a situation (Spitzberg & Cupach, 1984). In other words, competence is how effective and appropriate a person is in a given context. We provide more formal definition later, but for our current purposes, this definition leads us to examine certain issues, such as "How do we know if something has been accomplished?" and "How do we know if a communication behavior fits a situation?" To better answer such questions, we need to examine what impressions people form about communication.

COMPETENCE AS AN IMPRESSION

People reach an infinite number of impressions about communication. For example, when a friend asks to see your notes the night before an exam, you may evaluate your friend's request in a variety of ways, such as "How inconsiderate!" "How nice that she thought of me first." "What nerve!" "I'm flattered that she thinks that highly of my academic abilities." "Her timing is awful!" We can't begin to predict all the possible impressions people make of our communication. In the Luann cartoon Diane's date is making a wide variety of assumptions about what kind of impression his behavior is making, or might make, on Diane. Diane, it turns out, has a different impression altogether. It's not always easy to know what impression we're creating.

Even if the impressions about communication are almost infinite, certain impressions are more important than others. In the cartoon, as in most situations, what seems to matter is whether others understand you, whether your behavior seems appropriate, and whether you achieved what you were trying to accomplish. These situations represent the most important and common impressions and goals of communication: clarity, appropriateness, and effectiveness. You will soon see that clarity is only important to the extent that it is appropriate and effective, so really only two impressions are essential to viewing a communicator as competent.

How are these objectives of clarity, appropriateness, and effectiveness achieved? Most people think a person is competent because of certain skills or abilities. An **ability** is the potential to perform some set of behaviors consistently. We commonly think people are clear, appropriate, and effective because of their abilities, such as listening actively, acting empathic, or behaving assertively.

However, viewing competence strictly as an ability creates problems. The competence of a given skill varies from situation to situation. For example, a loud laugh may be highly competent in response to a joke at a party, but entirely incompetent in response to viewing an open casket at a funeral. So it is not the ability, behavior, or skill that's competent or incompetent. Instead, competence exists in the impressions people form of communication in a given context. Three potential impressions are commonly used to evaluate a person's competence: clarity, appropriateness, and effectiveness. These three impressions are explained next.

What we think we're communicating and what we're actually communicating are often entirely different.

Reprinted by permission of United Media.

Clarity

If you were asked to describe competent communication, you might say it is when what someone says is clear, which generally means understandable. As you saw in Chapter 1, this view of communication competence is most relevant when we view communication solely as information transfer. Many businesspeople and telephone advertisements imply that clarity is the most important feature of communication. This view of communication can be problematic, however. Clarity is important, but for several reasons it is not the most useful standard of competent communication.

First, it is difficult to *know* whether or not you are actually understood. Just because people nod their heads does not necessarily mean they understand the message. Just because two people say "I love you," it doesn't mean they share the same concept of what love means and implies.

A second caution on equating understanding and clarity with competent communication is that it involves grouping together very different concepts. **Clarity** is the precision of the message. Does the message represent the speaker's intentions accurately? If you have ever tried to give directions to someone who doesn't speak your language, you've realized that communicating clearly is quite different from achieving understanding. In such a situation, you can give very clear directions, but the person understands nothing of what you say. **Understanding** is the extent to which someone comprehends the intended meaning of a message. In the opening vignette, Cambria wanted to communicate a sense of excitement about beginning a new life in college. This sense may be an image, or experience, or idea. Understanding occurs to the extent that those with whom she spoke ended up with a similar idea of Cambria's sense of excitement.

Some people also assume that clarity and understanding imply agreement. **Agreement** exists when two people have similar values or beliefs about something. If other new students also felt out of place like Cambria, then they agreed with her. They not only understood her intended meaning, but agreed with her meaning. A politician may express a position on abortion clearly, which you may understand very well, but you may not agree with the position expressed.

A third problem with viewing competence as clarity is that clarity is usually a means to some other, more important goal. Why do people try to be clear? Because they believe clear communication will help them accomplish their goals better than unclear communication. People generally do not seek understanding for its own sake. When engaging in small talk, a large portion of your daily communication, understanding is generally less important than relating. Even in organizations, not all encounters require clear communication. Employees communicate to express emotion, make impressions, begin relationships, and manage conflict. Such encounters are only occasionally about something specific that requires clarity. Therefore, clarity and understanding are often less important than other objectives you may have.

A final problem with clarity may surprise you. Frequently, the most competent form of communication is not to be clear, but rather the opposite. Consider the need to be polite. A friend asks you what you think of her tattoo and you really dislike it. A very direct and honest response may be insulting. Finding something positive to say about it includes some honesty as well as allowing your friend to save face. People tend to use ambiguous messages when they are presented with similar dilemmas (Chovil, 1994).

Leaders often find themselves in the position of building teams out of diverse groups of people who have different and sometimes incompatible interests. In such situations, clear messages may upset some members of the team (Eisenberg, 1984). A CEO who explains to employees that the company is "striving to compete with global competition and still maintain a strong work force" could mean there may be layoffs, or simply that the company is seeking to improve its position in global markets. It is **equivocal communication;** that is, it speaks with many (equi) voices (vocal) or messages. It potentially implies both positive and negative opinions. It sounds good and may often be the best response even if it's not the clearest. If clarity and understanding are not the basis of competence, then what is? The two remaining criteria for competent communication are appropriateness and effectiveness.

Appropriateness

Appropriateness is communication that fits a given context. Appropriate interactions avoid breaking valued rules of behavior developed in all cultures, societies, groups, and enduring relationships. **Rules** are followable prescriptions for what should or should not be done in a given type of situation (Shimanoff, 1980). Rules are sometimes explicit: "Don't call someone names when arguing." Some rules are more implicit: "You should arrive at parties 30 minutes to an hour after the stated beginning time."

Rules are related to **norms,** which are patterns of behavior that recur over time. As a behavior, you may normally say "Fine, how are you?" in response to someone's greeting of "Hi. How's it going?" It also would be acceptable to say, "I'm late and have to run, but I'll call you later." However, if you were to respond, "Why do you ask?" or "Relative to what?" such a response might be perceived as unfriendly or merely odd. Such a norm violation would also reflect a rule violation.

Unlike norms, rules do not necessarily apply to frequently occurring patterns of behavior. Rules can apply to very specific behaviors in very specific situations, which may or may not commonly occur. For example, imagine you approached a member of the opposite sex on campus and asked one of the following three questions: "Would you go out with me tonight?" "Would you come over to my apartment tonight?" or "Would you spend the night with me?" Which of these questions violates the rules for initial meetings with someone to whom you are attracted? The first question probably would not be considered a rule violation, whereas the latter two probably would. In fact, a study of just these scenarios found this to be true, at least for women. Fifty percent of both women and men accepted the date request, but no women accepted the apartment or bed request, whereas almost 70% of men accepted such requests (Clark & Hatfield, 1989)!

Although subtle, people generally communicate their displeasure with inappropriate actions through verbal and nonverbal sanctions, or symbolic punishments.

In general, you know a rule exists when it has been violated. Rule violation typically evokes a behavior called **sanction,** a negative evaluation ranging from a raised eyebrow, to a scowl, to a slap on the face in response to someone's behavior. The sanction is feedback that lets you know you did something inappropriate. In general, appropriate communication tends to be somewhat invisible to the interactants. Only when communication is inappropriate do you elicit sanctions, which tell you that a rule has been violated.

Effectiveness

Effectiveness describes the extent to which communication accomplishes valued outcomes. We all pursue goals, objectives, intentions, and outcomes in our interactions with others. You may call someone to see if you can borrow their notes, ask someone for a date, interview for a job, or speak to a group to persuade them to support a proposal. In this way, communication is functional (see Chapter 1)—it serves to get things done. Culture, society, politics, religion, business, conflict, and relationships are accomplished through interaction, through the behavior of communication. Clearly, to be competent requires that a person be able to accomplish the basic communicative tasks of everyday life. In this sense, competence is the extent to which people are effective in accomplishing what they want through communication.

Getting communication to function effectively is closely related to the concept of goals (Argyle, Furnham, & Graham, 1981). **Goals** are the outcomes, objectives, or purposes sought by communication. Goals and functions are related but not the same. Goals are preferred outcomes that communication may or may not achieve successfully. Communication can function in ways that you never intended. For example, if you ask someone to go see a movie, you may simply intend to get to know the other person and see a movie. However, this request may lead the other person to assume you are interested in a romantic relationship.

Although you pursue your goals through communication, you may not be aware of all your goals. For example, you may not realize you want to negotiate a raise until you find yourself in the context of discussing your performance appraisal with your boss. Thus, if one of your goals is to negotiate a raise, talking about the difficulties you are experiencing with your co-workers is not likely to be very functional.

Effectiveness is defined in terms of "valued" outcomes. However, this does not mean that effective communication is always satisfying. Sometimes we have to choose the lesser of two evils. For example, arguing with someone else can create favorable or unfavorable results. An argument with your boss at work may help you get a raise. An argument with your partner may help you redefine and improve your relationship. Even though arguments bring about positive outcomes, most people view such conflicts as negative or dissatisfying. How can you be dissatisfied yet effective? The answer is fairly simple.

People may dislike having an argument with someone over an important issue. Yet clearly there are better and worse ways of having an argument. Would you rather a person scream at you and criticize you or calmly identify the problems with your position? Even though you may feel uncomfortable with either, most of the time in North American culture, a calm discussion is likely to be viewed as less dissatisfying than screaming and yelling. Thus effectiveness sometimes means choosing the least problematic course of action, even if all available courses of action are viewed as negative.

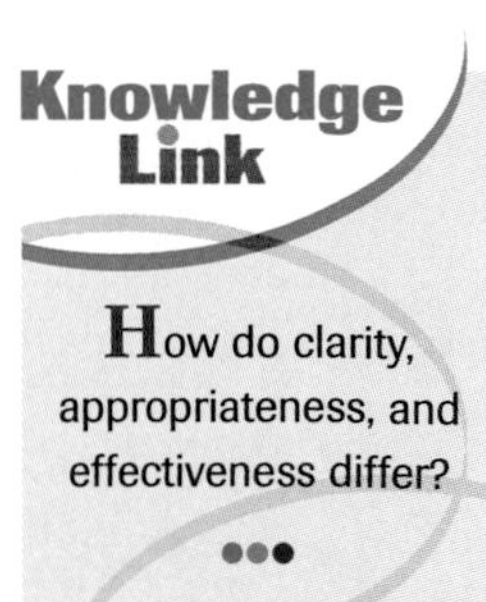

How do you know when you have been effective? In general, your effectiveness is something only you can determine. Usually you consider yourself effective when you obtain (1) something you value, (2) something you set as a goal to accomplish (regardless of how conscious that goal was), and (3) something you expend some effort to obtain (Seibold & Spitzberg, 1982). Unlike appropriateness, which is judged by others, effectiveness is something that generally only you determine for yourself. Only you know when you have obtained a preferred outcome.

THE COMPETENCE GRID

Now you've considered three possible standards of competence: clarity, appropriateness, and effectiveness. As you saw, each standard depends on the other. Clarity is only competent if it is appropriate and effective so there are really only two standards of communication competence. If we consider the possibility that someone can be perceived as inappropriate or appropriate, and ineffective or effective, there are four possible combinations for communication: A person can be inappropriate and ineffective, inappropriate and effective, appropriate and ineffective, or appropriate and effective. Each of these communication possibilities is examined next.

The first possible way to communicate is both inappropriate and ineffective. This represents a **minimizing** type of interaction, in which a person not only fails to achieve any personally desired outcomes in interaction, but also alienates other people through his or her behavior. As an example of someone who is neither effective nor appropriate, consider someone frustrated by waiting in line yelling at the person working behind the counter only to be told that nothing can be done. Indeed, by creating a scene this person may even be escorted out of the room by a security guard, forfeiting his or her goal. This person gets minimum results out of the interaction.

The appropriate but ineffective person interacts in a **sufficing** manner, which enables him or her merely to get by. Although this person's behavior is not inappropriate, it doesn't accomplish much of anything either. For example, Cambria spent most of the early part of the social merely standing in groups while other people talked. Her behavior did not break any rules or norms, but she probably did not get much out of the social, such as making new friends, finding out about upcoming activities, or getting to know faculty members.

The inappropriate and effective type of communicator engages in a **maximizing** form of communication. A person maximizes when he or she is assertive or aggressive without concern for other people's sense of appropriateness. This orientation suggests that winning is all that matters. From a maximizing perspective, lying, cheating, stealing, coercing, exploiting, hurting, and abusing are all fair game if they help you win. But in the context of interactions, the inappropriateness of such activities is destructive to the communicator's relationship.

The communicator who achieves preferred outcomes in a way that preserves the relationship and respects the rules of the situation has chosen **optimizing** communication. This person achieves success through means that others consider acceptable. The optimizing communicator recognizes the importance of self-satisfaction in communication situations and he or she also understands that such satisfaction should not come at the expense of others' satisfaction.

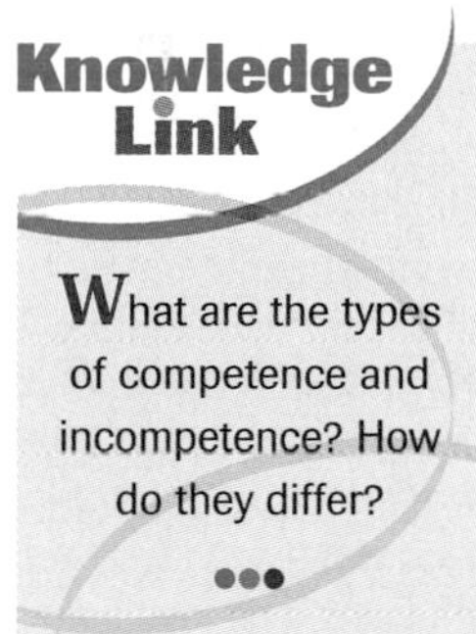

These four types of competence are reflected in the competence grid (see Figure 2.1). The grid displays the four styles of communication just described: entirely incompetent (minimizing), partially competent (sufficing and maximizing), and very competent (optimizing). In some situations you may value your personal effectiveness more than your

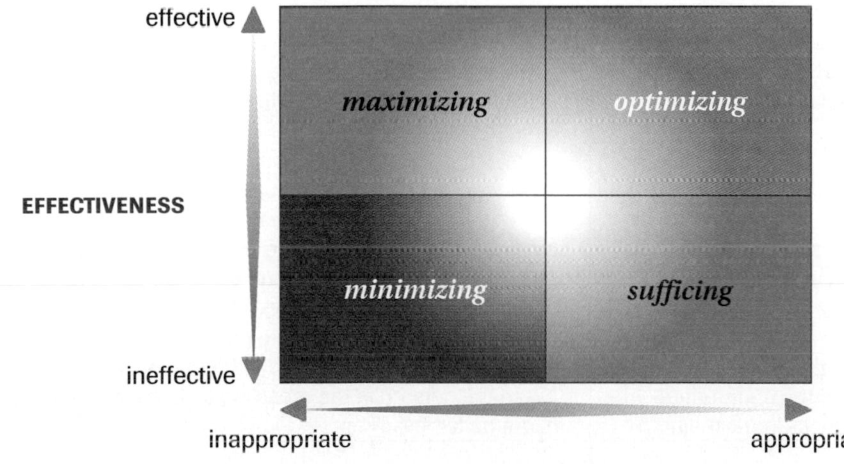

FIGURE 2.1
The Communication Competence Grid

The competence grid allows you to map your communication behavior and to analyze your most important communication goals in any given situation.

CloseUp ON ETHICS

The Ethics of Interpersonal Communication

THE COMPETENCE GRID is a partial attempt to provide an ethical framework for understanding communication. Appropriateness and effectiveness are not just impressions—they can be ethical judgments as well. If effectiveness is viewed primarily as an orientation of self-interest, appropriateness can be viewed primarily as an orientation of interest in the other person(s). Optimizing competence, therefore, involves locating the best course of interaction for the relationship and the people with whom you are interacting while pursuing your own interests.

Let's look at three examples of interpersonal communication. In the first, a friend of yours has a terminal disease and you know she doesn't have much time left to live. But at her bedside, you tell her you believe she will find a way to beat the disease. In the second example, your best friend tells you she is cheating on her boyfriend, but asks you to keep it secret from her boyfriend. In a third example, on a second date a student begins unbuttoning his date's blouse without warning and she slaps him hard. These examples illustrate deception, secrecy, coercion, and violence. Each instance, also opens small windows into the world of communication ethics.

In the first example, lying to a dying person is generally viewed as appropriate because it is motivated out of a sincere desire to help the other person. If this communication were more selfish in nature, such as lying to avoid dealing with the discomfort of facing reality, then it would tend to be viewed as less appropriate. In short, deception is competent to the extent that it is intended to benefit others rather than the self.

In the second example, being asked to cover for a friend's unethical behavior creates a number of ethical problems. You may view your friend's request as unethical because it is selfish and both the infidelity and the request to keep it secret would likely be viewed as inappropriate by her boyfriend. However, if you think the affair is short term and the couple has a strong long-term relationship potential, you may conclude that secrecy will avoid damaging the long-term relationship. Furthermore, your relationship with the girlfriend may involve certain relational understandings. For example, perhaps she has kept secrets of your own indiscretions, and her request provides you with a chance to return the favor. In other words, the ethics are likely to be determined by your assessment of the importance of various goals in relationship to the appropriateness of your behavior. If your effectiveness in maintaining your relationship with the girlfriend outweighs the importance of being appropriate in the boyfriend's eyes, then you would be likely to keep the secret. If, however, your standards of appropriateness are independent of the relationship, for example, if you believe infidelity is simply wrong regardless of context, then you would be less likely to keep the secret. In this case, the result might well be that you and the girlfriend would view each other's response as incompetent.

In the third example, even though we generally view violence as inappropriate even when it is effective, in this instance, most people would view the slap as one of self-defense. As such, the slap is appropriate because it is guarding against an inappropriate and coercive behavior. In other words, the coercion is inappropriate in the context because the woman did not provide a clear indication that such assertive behavior would be appropriate. In turn, the slap would tend to be viewed as appropriate because it negates another person's inappropriate behavior.

These three examples illustrate that the ethics of communication conduct is a constant balancing of the self's goals and effectiveness with others' sense of what is appropriate and legitimate in a situation. In addition, ethical communication sometimes involves balancing one's own sense of appropriateness with what would be effective. Lying, cheating, and coercing may be effective, but they tend to be appropriate only when they are negating others' unethical conduct or when they are intended to benefit the other persons. Even under these circumstances, however, there are times when you will find the benefit of others or protection of the self still do not justify such behavior.

Ethics concern morals, values, and standards of conduct or potential conduct. If asked, most people would probably claim that deception and violence are unethical no matter what the circumstances. Yet, when their everyday life is examined in detail, most people would discover frequent instances of a host of questionable practices. The "white lie," the use of physical force in self-defense, the use of an ambiguous response to avoid an awkward issue, and other such "dark" forms of communication are common practices (Cupach & Spitzberg, 1994). Their commonality raises the question of their ethics. To the person engaging in such behaviors, the actions can be rationalized as ethical, but to the person on the receiving side, such a judgment might be far less likely.

appropriateness (maximizing). In another situation, you might value fitting in more than achieving other personal communicative goals (sufficing). However, there is always the possibility that you can try to achieve all your personal goals in an appropriate way. To the extent you achieve this, you have optimized your communication.

Life is very complex and presents us with many situations in which it is difficult to be a competent communicator: irreconcilable differences, conflicts of interest, and instances in which another person's unreasonableness can only be met with indifference, avoidance, antagonism, and perhaps even violence. You may occasionally need to compromise the standards of appropriateness and effectiveness. The competence grid provides the most important standards by which your communication will be judged, both by you and by others. Awareness of these basic standards helps you make better judgments about what is important in any given communication encounter.

Communication and communicators are judged on many characteristics, such as satisfaction, attractiveness, efficiency, or emotional warmth. However, such characteristics only matter to the extent that they contribute to the appropriateness and effectiveness of the encounter. The key challenge of competent communication in most situations is the delicate balance between the need for appropriateness and the desire for effectiveness (Spitzberg, Canary & Cupach, 1994). Failures to attain that balance are likely to call your competence into question. One of the issues that results from failures of appropriateness or effectiveness is the ethics of one's behavior. We examine this question next.

ETHICS & COMMUNICATION COMPETENCE

Communication ethics, debated for centuries, were first documented by the ancient Greeks. Plato was concerned that any instruction in rhetoric could be misused by unethical people to exploit others. According to Plato, one of the most influential early philosophers, if communication is not used to serve the truth, it can be used to lead people away from the truth. His student Aristotle cleverly countered this argument, claiming that the best defense against such exploitation is to be informed about the ways in which communication can be misused. In a sense, the more competent you are as a communicator, the less likely you are to be exploited because you understand the techniques of exploitation.

Many people since Plato and Aristotle have argued for ethical standards with which to evaluate communication. Such standards would provide a basis for holding communication and communicators alike responsible. For example, the National Communication Association developed a "credo" or statement of belief in ethical communication shown on the next page. This credo illustrates a set of beliefs in the value of freedom of expression, openness of access, accuracy of content, diversity of representation, and respect of persons and opinions. Ethical codes are sets of principles for guiding behavior in ways considered good or moral in nature. Most ethical codes emphasize the nature of the conduct itself, the purposes the conduct serves, or the particular considerations of the context in which the conduct occurs. These three types of codes represent means oriented, ends-oriented, or context-oriented codes.

Means-oriented ethical codes define what behaviors are considered moral or immoral, regardless of their outcomes. For example, if lying is considered immoral regardless of the liar's motive, then it is a means-oriented code. In contrast, if it is not the behavior itself, but the purpose or outcome of the behavior that is considered moral or immoral, then it is an *ends-oriented code*. Using an ends-oriented code, for example lying to help others, might be viewed as ethical, but lying for selfish reasons would be considered unethical. Finally,

NCA CREDO FOR ETHICAL COMMUNICATION

- We advocate truthfulness, accuracy, honesty, and reason as essential to the integrity of communication.
- We endorse freedom of expression, diversity of perspective, and tolerance of dissent to achieve the informed and responsible decision making fundamental to a civil society.
- We strive to understand and respect other communicators before evaluating and responding to their messages.
- We promote access to communication resources and opportunities as necessary to fulfill human potential and contribute to the well-being of families, communities, and society.
- We promote communication climates of caring and mutual understanding that respect the unique needs and characteristics of individual communicators.
- We condemn communication that degrades individuals and humanity through distortion, intimidation, coercion, and violence, and through the expression of intolerance and hatred.
- We are committed to the courageous expression of personal convictions in pursuit of fairness and justice.
- We advocate sharing information, opinions, and feelings when facing significant choices while also respecting privacy and confidentiality.
- We accept responsibility for the short- and long-term consequences of our own communication and expect the same of others.

SOURCE: http://www. natcom.org

context-oriented codes claim that the morality of communication behavior depends on the specific circumstances of the situation. For example, when some Jews lied to Nazis about their religious beliefs during World War II to escape internment and later death, it was to help themselves, but given the extreme nature of the consequences and the immorality of the opposing forces, lying under those circumstances is viewed as ethical.

The concepts of appropriateness and effectiveness provide a hybrid ethical code of communication conduct. The appropriateness standard is often a means standard because within most groups and cultures, certain behaviors tend to be considered ethical and other behaviors are considered unethical. The effectiveness standard is more of an ends-oriented code because it specifies behavior that accomplishes valued outcomes as ethical. In the context of an actual communication event, the participants determine how to balance and evaluate the importance of the two dimensions. Applying the competence grid as a code of ethical communication conduct is not simple. For example, most people consider violent behavior unethical. Yet most people also have little difficulty defining self-defense and disciplinary physical punishment as ethical (Spitzberg, 1997b). But if you ask the child who has just been spanked by a parent after the child almost walked out into a busy street, the child would probably consider the punishment inappropriate. Thus in any given situation, determining whether a communication behavior is ethical will depend on taking into account the means, the ends, and the context. Nevertheless, in general, to the extent that you can optimize a communication situation by achieving desired personal goals while at the same time preserving the sense of appropriateness others apply to the context, your communication is more likely to meet ethical standards of conduct and be considered ethical.

Basic Components of the Communication Competence Model

The competence grid shows that competence in communication is a delicate balance and pursuit of both appropriateness and effectiveness. The grid illustrates what we need to accomplish, but it doesn't show us how. The answer to this question requires consideration of factors that allow us to be more appropriate and effective. These factors are motivation, knowledge, and skills, and form the basic model of communication competence applied to contexts covered throughout this book. The basic communication competence model is displayed in Figure 2.2.

Shakespeare tells us that all the world is a stage and we are merely actors on this stage. This seems truer today than ever. We live in a media-rich, entertainment-oriented culture. Drama, broadly speaking, is everywhere. Movies, television, plays, performances, and concerts abound. We view talk shows that look like soap operas, and sports programs that are talk shows. We read magazines and watch shows devoted entirely to movie stars, musicians, and the entertainment industry. Many theorists and researchers have suggested that the stage is a useful metaphor for our social worlds (Combs & Mansfield, 1976). In essence, we are constantly playing to audiences around us, and we are painfully aware of the spotlight of their evaluations. We behave differently on the public stage than we do when acting in the privacy of the backstage areas of our lives. We sometimes even behave as if we are in front of an audience when we are not. Who has not tripped over the

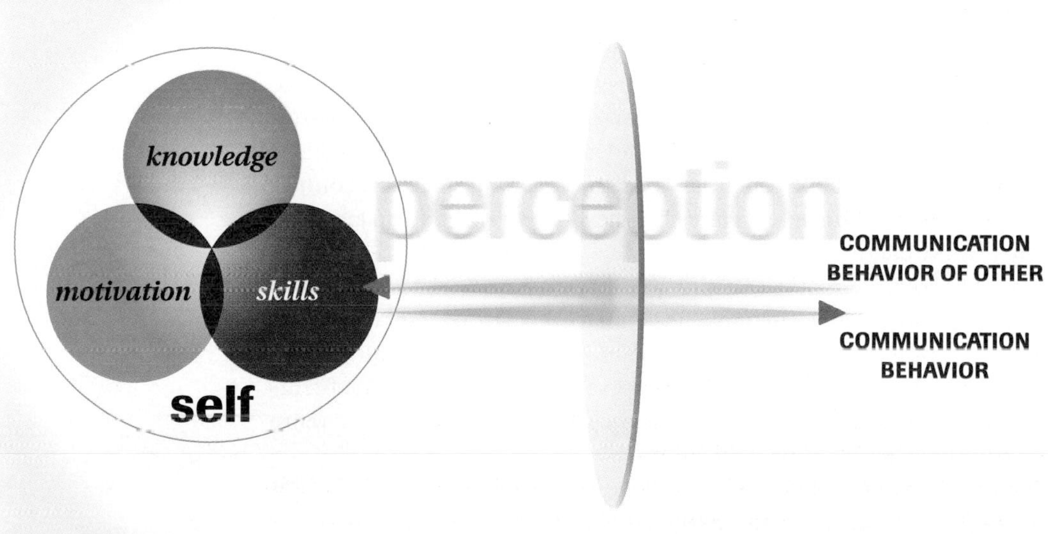

FIGURE 2.2 The Basic Communication Competence Model

Communication competence depends on your motivation, knowledge, skills, the communication context, and the perception process that people apply to your communication.

sidewalk, only to engage in various displays of embarrassment and doing a double take at the crack, even when no one is around?

Thinking about life as drama is very useful in understanding communication (Goffman, 1974). For the purposes of understanding competence, we can ask, "What makes for a competent acting performance?" We've already seen that competence is an impression based on a person's appropriateness and effectiveness. Certain factors are likely to enhance a person's ability to communicate appropriately and effectively. So the question becomes one of determining which factors increase the chances that an actor will be viewed as competent by his or her audience. The model of communication competence identifies these factors as motivation, knowledge, and skills.

MOTIVATION

For an actor to communicate competently, it is important first to *want* to give a competent performance. That is, competence is more likely to the extent a communicator is *motivated* to be so. **Motivation** is the extent to which a communicator is drawn toward or pushed away from communicating competently in a given context. Many communicators never fulfill their potential because of their shyness or fear of communicating. Even if confident and self-assured, some people simply do not have the drive it takes to be excellent communicators. They do what comes easily, rather than exerting great effort to get the most out of their performances.

For now, let's consider two types of motivation: negative and positive. **Negative motivation** refers to the factors that result in fear, anxiety, or avoidance. At the interpersonal level, for example, many people have the basic understanding of how to develop satisfying romantic relationships, but are afraid to initiate conversations, such as actually asking another person for a date. You may have participated in a small group meeting and had ideas to contribute, yet you were afraid to put forth your ideas in front of the group, so you didn't say anything. Some people even choose majors and careers that require very little communication with others because they are terrified of the prospect of public speaking or highly social activities. Problems of shyness adversely influence millions of people's communication every day (Carducci & Zimbardo, 1995).

Positive motivation is the result of efforts and desires that drive your performance toward excellence. People find the motivation to act competently from such sources as the situation and their own goals in the situation. Some situations simply offer greater rewards. For example, you will probably be much more motivated to perform competently on a job interview or a first date than when sitting next to a stranger on an airplane. The stakes for the first two situations are much higher.

Situations vary in their reward potential. People also vary in the degree to which they seek rewards in situations. Some people are more likely than others to set their own communication goals and to pursue these goals. The booming business of motivational speaking is generally based on the simple notion that those who actively motivate themselves and search for goals to pursue in the situations they encounter will achieve more than those who merely follow their natural motivations.

Perhaps like Cambria in the opening vignette, you have found yourself at a social event in which you looked at people talking comfortably among themselves and thought, "I want to join in the conversation, but I don't know how to break the ice and capture the interest of people I don't know." You have the motivation to communicate, but you don't know what to say or do. Motivation alone is not enough—you also need knowledge to communicate competently.

Knowledge

William Shakespeare's "life is but a stage" metaphor also applies to knowledge. As you saw, motivation alone is generally not enough to make you a competent actor. To be competent, an actor also needs to know the script, something about the type of audience, the stage or set, the lines of the other actors, the playwright's intentions, and his or her own acting strengths and weaknesses. Returning to everyday communication, the audience is the person or persons to whom you are speaking, the stage and set make up the communication situation, the lines are others' responses, and the playwright's intentions correspond to the goals of the situation. A competent communicator needs to be knowledgeable about all of these elements in communication situations. **Knowledge** in communication consists of the content of what to say and do, and the procedures by which this content can be performed.

In the Chickweed Lane cartoon below, the woman experiences the precise problem of communicative knowledge that is the topic of discussion. Most of us encounter situations in which we only realize some time later "what we *wish* we had said." We generally can think of what to say and do, but not always when and in the way that would be most competent. Such situations illustrate how difficult it can be to know what to say and do in a communication situation.

Obtaining knowledge of communication is not easy. We learn about communication in informal ways, usually through years of trial and error. We spend a relatively small amount of time in life writing. Most of our waking hours are spent communicating in interpersonal, group, and public settings. Yet, although most of us receive over a decade of formal instruction in writing skills, few people ever receive formal instruction on oral communication. Your parents may teach you general social conventions of politeness like saying "please" and "thank you," but how often do parents take their children aside to explain how to stay on the topic or take turns in conversation? For example, did anyone ever teach you that when you want a turn to speak in a conversation, you should wait for the other speaker to complete a sentence, look for eye contact indicating a readiness to give up a turn, and slightly rigid posture, audible breath, and hand gestures? You probably know about all these cues, but it is probably knowledge you gained informally.

Knowledge can be roughly broken down into the "what" and the "how" of communication, known as content and procedural knowledge, respectively. **Content knowledge** involves knowing what topics, words, meanings, and so forth, are required in a situation. **Procedural knowledge** is knowing how to assemble, plan, and perform content knowledge

We all experience situations in which we are at a loss for what to say or do.

Copyright, Los Angeles Times Syndicate. Reprinted with permission. 1999 in a particular situation. When you get a driver's license, you take a written test on traffic laws and practices (content knowledge), and a driving test of your actual ability to apply that content knowledge in a car while driving (procedural knowledge).

For most of us, the bottom line of a person's driving ability is his or her actual driving performance. The same is true of communication. Performance depends on motivation and knowledge, but ultimately, it is a person's actual behavior, his or her actual skill, that is judged as competent or incompetent.

SKILLS

You may have witnessed both terrible and terrific acting performances. Even the worst actors are motivated to perform well, and they probably know their scripts inside and out. So what makes their performances so bad? The simple answer is that they lack the acting skills to *apply* their motivation and knowledge.

Skills are repeatable, goal-directed behaviors. They must be repeatable, because anyone could accomplish something by accident, but if it can't be accomplished again, it is not a skill the person possesses. You might give a very funny introduction to a speech, but if you can't ever get a laugh again, you can't say you have the skill of creating humorous introductions. Skills are goal directed because they must be designed to accomplish something. If they don't, they are just behaviors, rather than behaviors *skilled* at something. To say a person is a skilled comedian is to say the person's behaviors are effective in accomplishing laughter and audience appreciation.

Communication skills have both general and specific levels. At the general level, for example, regardless of culture people need to be able to ask questions, display certain facial expressions such as anger, sadness, happiness, and perform greeting rituals (such as handshaking, bowing, waving "hi"). All people in all cultures develop routines they use in certain situations. Yet, at the specific level, within each situation every communication event represents a unique interaction. Small talk probably always seems like small talk. Yet every episode of small talk is also different from what you have experienced before. Thus some skills are used across almost all situations, and others are reserved for very particular situations.

We constantly use communication skills that have worked well in the past. Although every first date is different, there is enough similarity that people have some idea, or model, of what is supposed to happen and when, and they can use this knowledge as a working model (Berger, 1987). A communicator, therefore, learns a variety of skills throughout life. Different roles and situations require different combinations of these skills: Skills acquired for one role end up being used for another one. Ultimately, the actor carries this repertoire of skills into each performance, selecting and using those that will yield the most competent performance.

Thus to communicate competently, we must be motivated, knowledgeable, and skilled. These three key components can be used to analyze why a communicator was or was not competent in any situation. When communicating, we apply these components in an actual situation, toward some kind of audience, which brings us to context, the fourth component of our model.

Knowledge Link

What are the components of the communication competence model and how do they differ?

CONTEXT

The communication context is the frame within which action occurs. At a museum, you look at a painting and often don't notice the frame. But it provides a set of boundaries to define what is in the frame and what is not. It defines what you should consider as the art itself. In communication, the **context** consists of the boundaries we perceive that help us know what the communication is, and what it is supposed to be.

So far, we've been using the terms *context* and *situation* almost interchangeably. But context can be viewed in a number of different ways. For some people, context is the climate or feel of a situation; for others, context is the physical location in which communication occurs. For still others, context involves everything in the surroundings, physical and psychological.

Context consists of both types and levels. **Contextual types** are routine ways in which you think about and respond to the communication episode. The most common context types include culture, time, relationship, situation, and function (Spitzberg & Brunner, 1991). **Context levels** refer to the number of communicators in the episode and the extent to which the direction of communication among these communicators is determined by the nature of the episode. The most common context levels are interpersonal, small group, and public communication contexts.

Context Types

Culture consists of the enduring patterns of thought, value, and behavior that define a group of people (Samovar & Porter, 1995). Culture encompasses people's beliefs and attitudes about the world, their spirituality, their sense of status and hierarchy, their use of time and physical space, and their relationships to one another. A culture represents a collection of these mental and behavioral patterns that give people a sense of belonging to a group or community viewed by its members as distinct from other groups. Culture is always present as a backdrop to whatever we do and however we see ourselves and others.

Although culture is commonly thought of as the same as ethnicity, race, and nationality, it is not. Ethnicity refers "to a wide variety of groups who might share a language, historical origins, religion, identification with a common nation-state, or cultural system" (Lustig & Koester, 1993, p. 47). Similarly, nationality simply refers to people born, raised, or with citizenship in a given nation-state. In contrast, race implies a group of people with common genetic or physical characteristics. Many people have expanded the notion of culture to include organizations, chat rooms, and even eras, gender, and sexual preference. Thus we can speak of Microsoft or Barnes & Noble as having different corporate cultures than Apple or Amazon.com, respectively. Culture is also described as the mood of a time, such as the "culture of narcissism" or "culture of complaint." So culture may include ethnicity, race, and nationality, but it usually implies more, including belief systems and ways of thinking and behaving.

In recent years, the Pacific Rim has become the focus of much social, political, and social scientific interest as the economies of North and South America become increasingly interdependent with those of Japan, China, Korea, and other Asian and Pacific nations. In the process, people in both cultures have come to consider the many differences between them and their communication behaviors. As one illustration of this, consider the differences between the Japanese and North American communication styles, displayed in Table 2.1. Although these descriptions are generalized, and may not apply to a particular individual or interaction, the fact that many of these differences appear intuitive illustrates the extent of culture's influence.

People communicating interculturally may experience difficulties as they attempt to bridge their differences in addition to the other tasks they seek to achieve. For example, whereas Japanese business decisions are more group based, business decisions in North America are delegated to individual representatives. Japanese and North American businesspeople may seem to be working at cross purposes as the North American

TABLE 2.1

••• Comparison of Japanese–North American Cultural Contexts •••

NORTH AMERICAN CULTURAL CONTEXT		JAPANESE CULTURAL CONTEXT
Values		
Individualistic	vs.	Collectivistic
Sacrifice for self-gain	vs.	Sacrifice for group gain
Competitive within group	vs.	Cooperative within group
Knowledge		
Knowledge based on rationality	vs.	Knowledge based on intuition
Clear conclusions	vs.	Flexible conclusions
Linear and clock-based time	vs.	Cyclical and nature-based time
Social Structure		
Equal status among all	vs.	Hierarchical status
Status is achievement based	vs.	Status is based on age/gender/family
Flexible group boundaries	vs.	Strict group boundaries
Informality (e.g., first names)	vs.	Formality (e.g., official titles)
Stylistic Patterns		
Priority on verbal communication	vs.	Priority on nonverbal communication
Hostile to silence/silencing	vs.	Prefers silence
Fast-paced interaction	vs.	Slow-paced interaction

SOURCE: Cathcart and Cathcart (1994), Ishii and Bruneau (1994), Javidi and Javidi (1994), and Kim (1994).

negotiator pushes proposals forward while the Japanese organization takes time to achieve consensus among its employees. This is only one among dozens of cultural differences of context listed in Table 2.1 that could affect the competence of communication.

The tendency for Japanese businesses, compared to North American businesses, to want to spend more time developing trust before "doing business" illustrates another type of context: time. If "time is money" in North America, then every minute that ticks by on the clock while a contract is not signed is money lost. But if time is viewed as more natural and cyclical, then there is less rush to push the natural order of things. **Time** is the collective and individual perception of the sequence and progression of events. Some cultures, such as Germanic cultures, are known for their strict punctuality and precise organization of time. Others, such as Mediterranean and Pacific Islander cultures, are much more relaxed when defining time and punctuality. In North America, New York is a fast-paced city, whereas San Diego is considered slower paced. Individually, some people believe rapid development of physical intimacy is appropriate in romantic relationships, whereas other people believe physical intimacy should progress very slowly. Time is a context that weaves its way into everything we experience, and it is a primary dimension along which we make sense of both our own and others' communicative behavior.

Another type of context is relationship. At the most general level, **relationship** is the implication your behavior has for your continued connection with another person or a group of people. To have a relationship with someone is to be interdependent, which means that each person depends on the other to achieve desired outcomes. In collectivistic, or group-oriented cultures, for example, family relationships are viewed as more important than personal goals. Divorce in Japan, for example, tends to be viewed as selfish if pursued merely because the relationship is loveless. Preserving the family is more important than pursuing individual goals. In North America, however, personal happiness and individual pursuit of love are considered reasonable bases for breaking off a relationship.

Relationship can be understood according to two dimensions: power and affiliation. **Power** refers to the status relationship of the people involved—who has the ability to influence whom? Most relationships involve some form of power. For example, relationships between boss–employee, parent–child, professor–student, older sibling–younger sibling, therapist–client, doctor–patient, all imply some hierarchy among the participants, with one person higher in status than the other. In any one of these pairs, however, interaction over time may redistribute the power to make it quite different. Power is always shifting, but shifting it in your favor is always relevant to your competence. Your effectiveness, and for that matter, appropriateness, depend significantly on how much power you command in a relationship. Your manager may have more formal power, but you may be able to use your intelligence and persuasive influence to change your boss's mind on any given decision, thereby shifting the power dimensions of the relationship.

Affiliation refers to the emotional and evaluative dimension of relating; that is, the degree to which you like and are drawn toward someone, or dislike and want to avoid this person. Determining whether you like or dislike someone, and deciding in what *way* you like or dislike this person, is one of the most fundamental evaluations you can make about someone. When you consider all the ways in which people can form connections, several relationship types come to mind.

You can look at affiliation in terms of several continua, including intimacy, kinship, and enmity. On a continuum of intimacy, relationship types vary from strangers to acquaintances, friends, close friends, best friends, boy- and girlfriends, lovers, fiancé(e)s, spouses, and everything in between. Culture affects where people place relationships on a continuum of intimacy. For example, Japanese students tend to view acquaintance (Chijin), roommate (Doshukusha), and best friend (Ichiban no shinyu) relationships as more intimate than U.S. students do, whereas U.S. students tend to view boyfriend/girlfriend (Otoko/onna tomodachi), lover (koibito), and fiancé (Konyakusha) relationships as more intimate than Japanese students do (Gudykunst & Nishida, 1986). Another continuum would be kinship, ranging from parents, siblings, grandparents, aunts, uncles, cousins, nieces and nephews, and so forth. Again, culture affects how people experience these affiliations. Japanese students view uncles (Oji) more intimately than U.S. students, but the reverse is true of son (Musuko) and daughter (Musume) relationships (Gudykunst & Nishida, 1986). Still another continuum, enmity, ranges from friends to enemies, including social, romantic, and even political enemies. Someone who deceives you, exploits you, threatens you, or takes something (or someone) you value is affiliated with you in terms of an "enemyship" rather than friendship.

Your affiliation for someone influences the competence of your communication. Most people perceive communication as becoming more competent as intimacy increases in relationships (Knapp, Ellis, & Williams, 1980). More competent people are more likely to achieve intimacy, and we tend to expect the people we are intimate with to know us better and to want and know how to interact with us more competently.

The fourth type of context is **place,** what most people think of as the environment or physical surroundings. Place includes all the physical characteristics that are present—temperature, lighting, amount of space permitted for movement, objects in the space, and the media through which we communicate. Some public speakers discover the difficulty of keeping an audience's attention if there is background noise in the environment or if the temperature is uncomfortable. Group leaders often find themselves challenged when projectors or teleconference links fail to work. A relationship or business meeting is likely to progress differently through computers than when conducted face-to-face. Surroundings can also help communication, as in the early stages of a romantic relationship in which a participant tries to get the lighting, privacy, and music to match the couple's feelings.

People limit, and are limited by, the places in which communication occurs. When mediators or facilitators select an office at a neutral site with a peaceful view of a wooded area, and a round table and seating arrangements that downplay power differences among parties, they are attempting to create an environment of cooperation. Some aspects of the place are out of our control, however. Politicians often have to compete with crying babies and hecklers. Many peaceful demonstrations turn violent when the heat of the day and closeness of the crowd encourages individuals to express their anger. These expressions of anger then feed into others' rising tempers, and violence erupts.

The final type of context is function. The **function** of communication is what the communication behavior attempts to or actually accomplishes. Many contexts are understood in terms of the function that people pursue through their communication. A funeral is functionally different from an inauguration. A labor negotiation's function is different from that of a team-building meeting. The function of communication on a date is different from that in a class lecture. Contexts in each of these situations are different, independent of the culture, time, relationship, and place in which they occur. They differ because the communicators are attempting to accomplish something different in each context. As you saw earlier, different functions often imply different communication goals, and goals help define the function of the context, and thereby influence the types of behavior considered appropriate and effective.

In the opening vignette, Cambria's competence was challenged by each of these context types. The mix of cultures was alien to her. She felt rushed and therefore somewhat anxious when she arrived. She didn't know anyone well enough to have established a comfortable relationship. The situation was more formal than she anticipated and she didn't realize that one of the functions of the gathering would be to introduce oneself to the entire group. In other words, had she been better able to analyze and anticipate the context types, she could have communicated much more competently.

Context Levels

The levels approach to context understands it in terms of the number of people involved. The three levels of context are interpersonal, group, and public speaking and differ according to whether a person is communicating on a one-to-one, one-to-several, or one-to-many basis. If you are chatting with your significant other or a friend, you are communicating in an interpersonal context. If you are working on a project with five or six other students or briefing your colleagues at work, you are in a small group context. If you are delivering a wedding toast or speaking at a meeting of stockholders, you are in a public speaking context.

The levels are not entirely distinct, however. A communication event may fit more than one level of context. Is a family discussion an interpersonal or a group context? Is a weekly presentation by a department head to middle management a group or public speaking context? The answer in each case is "both." Although context levels frequently overlap, the levels do suggest that the number of people in a context makes a difference in your communication. As the number of people increases, the potential number of meanings attributed to a message increases, and the number of "audience" characteristics to be considered increases. You don't need a podium or microphone in a small group context, and you don't cast votes on a proposed decision in an interpersonal situation. In other words, the level of context affects your communication choices, and thus your communication competence.

In this book, we concentrate on the most common levels of contexts (Powers, 1995). We present **interpersonal contexts** as informal interactions among people involved in social and/or personal relationships. Social relationships are most often defined based on informal, social-emotional roles (e.g., family, friends, lovers, etc.). However, other communications, such as when you speak to a salesperson about a product or service, or another student about an assignment, are also considered interpersonal, even though they are more formal and task based.

The complexity of connections differentiates interpersonal and group encounters. When dealing with only one or two other people, far fewer potential communication exchanges are involved. Messages are targeted to one particular person, rather than to a general group. **Group contexts** involve a larger number of people, typically three to twelve, and usually take place in a more formal, task-oriented context. Although messages may sometimes be directed to specific individuals in the group, there is an understanding that the entire group is the appropriate audience, and other members of the group may respond to the messages. Also, the group usually meets to accomplish some predetermined purpose through its interaction.

Public speaking contexts typically involve one or a small group of people whose task is to speak to a larger number of people. Unlike the group context, the general assumption is that the audience will have little or no "speaking" role. This does not mean they don't communicate, however. Even if audience members do not address the speaker or the rest of the audience with a particular message, they may ask questions and provide feedback at the end of the speech.

People communicate in these three contexts throughout their lives. As you can imagine, almost everyone communicates interpersonally every day of their life. The success of educational systems, civic and religious organizations, private and public organizations, athletic institutions, special interest clubs and organized hobbies, and social events (e.g., concerts, chat rooms, etc.), is based in large measure on group interactions. Finally, many people involved in business, politics, or even community events speak publicly with surprising frequency.

Process Aspects of the Communication Competence Model

The model of communication competence discussed thus far consists of motivation, knowledge, skills, and context. The more motivated, knowledgeable, and skilled we are, in ways that are appropriate and effective to each type and level of context, the more likely we will be perceived as competent communicators.

So far we have discussed these components with only limited reference to people's actual behavior because what constitutes competent behavior, in other words skills, differs from one context to the next. Each part of this text examines the skills relevant to its context level: interpersonal, small group, and public speaking. But first, let's look at those processes common to all contexts: verbal communication, nonverbal communication, perceptions, expectancies, and impressions.

VERBAL & NONVERBAL COMMUNICATION

Communication, in any context, occurs in two basic forms: verbal and nonverbal. Verbal communication is linguistic and can be written, spoken, or otherwise behaviorally or visually transmitted, as in the case of American Sign Language (ASL). All verbal communication uses language, a symbol system consisting of letters and words. The words in turn are understood both in terms of semantics and syntax. Semantics refers to culturally or socially agreed upon meanings, similar to what would be found in a dictionary. Syntax refers to the rules for combining words or symbols into sentences and expressions.

Nonverbal communication involves all forms and aspects of communication that are not based on language. It consists of physical behavior commonly referred to as body language, gestures, use of space, and use of voice. We discuss verbal and nonverbal communication in more detail in Chapters 4 and 5.

PERCEPTION, EXPECTANCIES, & IMPRESSIONS

Any behavior, whether verbal or nonverbal, must make an impression if it is to communicate a message. The behavior must be observed, interpreted, understood, and evaluated through a process called *perception,* the way we make sense of the infinite amount of information provided by the world around us. You may or may not be aware of the lighting, background noise, colors, temperature, and pressures of sitting or lying down while reading this sentence. However, now that it has been mentioned, you will find that you can focus on any one of these stimuli. In the process of focusing on any one stimulus, you selectively place the other types of sensation in the background. If you tried to take in everything at once, you probably would not accomplish much because you would be receiving too much information.

Over time, people experience more and more situations. Eventually, they learn to categorize certain types of situations and people as similar to better understand them. If you had to treat every greeting, every first date, every study group meeting, and every presentation as an entirely new context each time, you would have to find a way of establishing what you were expected to do. In such a world, you might never get anything accomplished. To sidestep this dilemma, people develop expectancies or mental pictures of what ought to be, about the types of situations and individuals that call for certain behaviors. Thus the competence of a person's communication performance is strongly influenced by the way it fulfills others' expectancies in a given situation.

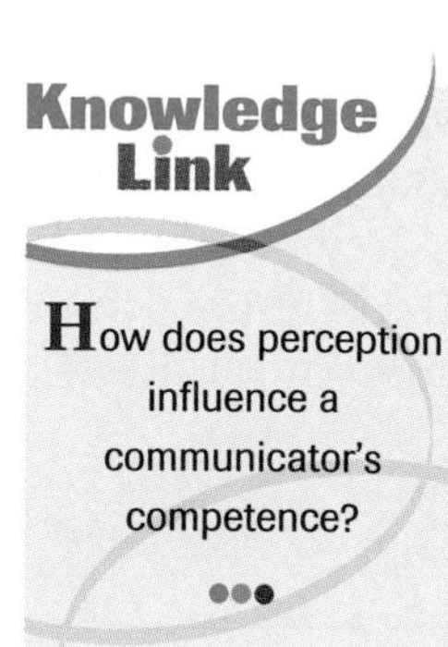

Competent communication requires the use of verbal and nonverbal behavior. However, these behaviors are not competent in and of themselves. Rather, competence is an impression we form about the behavior. This impression is based on how well the behaviors fulfill our expectancies of competence in a given situation (Spitzberg, Canary & Cupach, 1994). Returning to the opening vignette, Cambria was concerned that she was not able to fulfill the expectancies as competently as those around her. If the faculty and the other communication students had expectations that communication majors are articulate and outgoing, especially at a social, their impressions of Cambria's communication behaviors would probably be less than competent.

We examine the entire perception process, closely linked to communication, in greater detail in Chapter 3. However, expectancies and the impressions based on them are particularly important to the way in which we perceive others as more, or less, competent.

THE COMPETENCE MODEL IN ACTION

Communication competence is *the use of verbal and/or nonverbal behavior to accomplish preferred outcomes in a way that is appropriate to the context.* Behavior that accomplishes preferred outcomes is effective. Behavior that is both effective and appropriate optimizes the potential of creating desired impressions of competence in the context.

Figure 2.3 displays the components of communication competence. It shows that motivation and knowledge are internal to individuals, but both influence the individual's skills. These skills, or behaviors, are displayed in communication events with others. Each communicator forms an impression of these behaviors based on the context and the process of perception. The other's judgments of these behaviors, in terms of their appropriateness and effectiveness, then influence the self's motivation and knowledge, which in turn influence his or her skills, and the process continues.

This general model of communication competence touches on all the pieces of the process a person goes through to communicate competently (Spitzberg, 1997a). However, as you saw in this chapter, context plays a substantial role in competent communication. Most of the remainder of this text is concerned with specific contexts, and we discuss the model described in this chapter as it applies to each type of context. Although motivation, knowledge, and skills are important in all contexts, each context may differ concerning what constitutes motivation, or what knowledge is needed, or which skills are ideal.

FIGURE 2.3
The Complete Model of Communication Competence

Achieving competent communication involves the complex interplay of two or more communicators using their motivation, knowledge, and skills in a given context to create impressions of their appropriateness and effectiveness.

Adapted from Spitzberg 1997a.

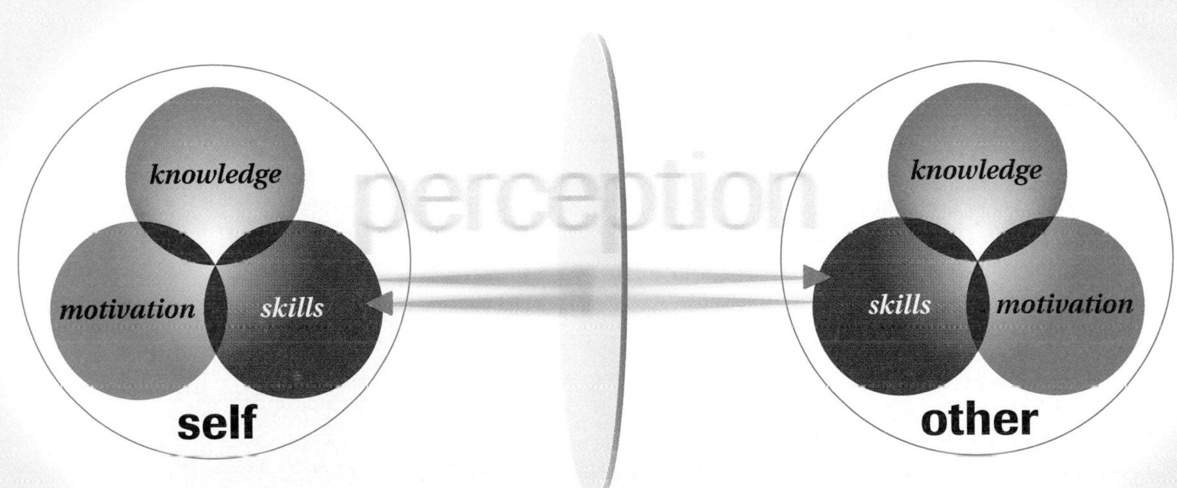

Chapter Summary

Competent communication depends on both the self and others' perception of its appropriateness and effectiveness. Communication low in both appropriateness and effectiveness is a minimizing style of communication. Communication high in appropriateness but low in effectiveness is sufficing, but accomplishes nothing for the communicator. In contrast, communication low in appropriateness but high in effectiveness is maximizing. The maximizing communicator does anything to win, even to the point of engaging in unethical and exploitative behavior. Optimizing communication is most competent; preferred outcomes are achieved in a manner that is viewed as appropriate to the context.

Achieving competence in communication is more likely if a person is motivated, knowledgeable and skilled in a given context. Motivation can be negative, as in anxiety and shyness, or positive, as in recognizing the goals that a context potentially provides. Knowledge can be content based, as in knowing what to say and do, or it can be procedurally based, as in knowing how to say and do something. The more motivated and knowledgeable a person is, the more likely he or she will be able to enact the specific appropriate verbal and nonverbal behaviors, or skills, in the pursuit of preferred outcomes. Finally, motivation, knowledge, and skills occur in a context. What is competent in one context is not necessarily competent in another.

Context types include culture, time, relationship, place, and function. The competence of a person's communication depends on what culture the behavior is enacted in, the timing of the behavior, the relationship and physical space in which the behavior occurs, and the purpose the communication is intended to serve. Context levels refer to the three most commonly recognized communication contexts: interpersonal, small group, and public speaking. These levels differ in the number of communicators involved, and therefore the formality and complexity of the communication process.

Whether or not communication is perceived as competent in a given context depends on the communicator's motivation, knowledge, and skills, but also on the receiver's perceptual process. To be viewed as competent, a communicator needs to fulfill people's expectancies in a given situation.

Key Terms

communication competence
ability
clarity
understanding
agreement
equivocal communication
appropriateness
rule
norm
sanction
effectiveness
goal
minimizing communication
sufficing communication
maximizing communication
optimizing communication
motivation
negative motivation
positive motivation
knowledge
content knowledge
procedural knowledge
skill
context
contextual types
context levels
culture
time
relationship
power
affiliation
place
function
interpersonal context
group context
public speaking context

Building Motivation

See Self-Assessment on page 52.

Building Knowledge

1. Why isn't clarity the best way of defining competent communication?
2. Why shouldn't communication competence be defined as an ability? How is it defined?
3. Are there situations in which either appropriateness or effectiveness (but not both) should be considered more important in determining a person's communication competence? If so, under what circumstances? Why?
4. How do the standards of appropriateness and effectiveness provide an ethical system for communication?
5. Provide an example of each type of competence and incompetence (that is, minimizing, sufficing, maximizing, optimizing).
6. Think back on your own communication experiences. Identify a difficult communication situation you have encountered. Describe how motivation, knowledge, skills, or all three helped your competence in the context.
7. Describe a communication situation in which the culture, time, relationship, place, and/or function influenced your competence.
8. How do people's expectations of you influence their impression of your competence? Describe an example in which your expectations have influenced your view of someone else.

Building Skills

Individual Exercises

1. Identify some recent communication encounters that you feel did not go as well as they could have. Describe these situations in terms of who was involved, what you were hoping to get out of the encounter, what you might have said or done differently, and why you thought the encounter did not go well. Then analyze each encounter in terms of the communication competence model. Were you simply not motivated to make a good impression? Did you lack specific knowledge or say the wrong thing (skills)? Does the model provide a useful basis for understanding what happened? Why or why not?
2. Describe some recent communication encounters that went better than you expected, and then analyze them in terms of the communication competence model. Does the model provide a useful basis for understanding what happened? Why or why not?
3. Locate an example of a communication event that exists in both a video-recorded and written text format, such as Martin Luther King, Jr.'s "I Have a Dream" speech, Shakespeare's *Macbeth*, the president's State of the Union speech, a Woody Allen movie and its script, or Thomas Harris's *Silence of the Lambs*. Obtain both versions. First read a segment of the written form. Evaluate the communicator's competence. Now view and/or listen to the recorded version. What does the nonverbal dimension add to the verbal communication? What, if anything, does it take away from the verbal format? Is one better than the other? Why or why not?
4. Go to the Web sites for automakers Volkswagen (**http://www.vw.com**) and Cadillac (**http://www.cadillac.com**). Assume you are applying for a job in the auto industry. Based on these Web sites, how would you characterize their differences and similarities in corporate culture? Knowing these differences in their contexts, how might this affect your communication behavior if you were to get a job interview?
5. Strike up a conversation with someone from a culture significantly different from your own. Afterward, identify the difficulties in communicating competently, such as any anxiety about approaching the person, maintaining the conversation, knowing what to talk about, and so forth.
6. Using *InfoTrac College Edition*, conduct a search for "communication competence." Locate an article by Robert Duran and Brian Spitzberg on "cognitive communication competence." After reading the article, find the self-report questionnaire assessing your tendency to plan, think about, and analyze your communication situations, that is, your tendency to develop and use communicative knowledge. Answer the questionnaire items, and then reflect on your level of communicative knowledge. How competent are you at developing and using your communicative knowledge? In which of the areas of knowledge covered by the questionnaire are you best, and in which areas do you need the most improvement?

Group Exercises

1. Form groups of 3–5 students. Each group should identify a public speaking current event that is making news, such as a politician engaging in a press conference, a sports figure answering charges of cheating or drug use, a person who engaged in some heroic action. Analyze the event in terms of the person's motivation, knowledge, and skills in the context. How applicable is the model?
2.  Go to the National Communication Association's ethics credo Web site (**http://www.natcom.org/conferences/ethicsconferencedo99.htm**), scroll halfway down the page, and read their ethical guidelines. Individually, come up with an exception to each ethical principle. Then form groups of 3–5 students, and share your exceptions. How do your exceptions differ from the other group members? What kinds of ethical principles do the exceptions suggest? What do the exceptions tell you about the relationship between appropriateness, effectiveness, and ethics?
3. Form groups of 3–5 students. As a group, brainstorm about the contexts in which you have the most difficulty communicating competently in terms of motivation. Repeat the process for knowledge, then for skills. As a group, rank the contexts from most to least difficult. To what extent did you find that others perceive the same or different types of contexts as most challenging? Speculate as a group why these similarities or differences exist, and how they might best be overcome from the perspective of the communication competence model.

References

Argyle, M., Furnham, A., & Graham, J. A. (1981). *Social situations.* Cambridge: Cambridge University Press.

Berger, C. R. (1987). Planning and scheming: Strategies for initiating relationships. In R. Burnett, P. McGhee, & D. Clarke (Eds.), *Accounting for relationships: Explanation, representation, and knowledge* (pp. 158–174). London: Methuen.

Carducci, B. J., & Zimbardo, P. G. (1995). Are you shy? *Psychology Today, 28* (6), 34–48.

Cathcart, D., & Cathcart, R. (1994). The group: A Japanese context. In L. Samovar & R. E. Porter (Eds.), *Intercultural communication: A reader* (pp. 293–304). Belmont, CA: Wadsworth.

Chovil, N. (1994). Equivocation as an interactional event. *The dark side of interpersonal communication* (pp. 105–124). Hillsdale, NJ: Erlbaum.

Combs, J. E., & Mansfield, M. W. (Eds.). (1976). *Drama in life: The uses of communication in society.* New York: Hastings House.

Cupach, W. R., & Spitzberg, B. H. (Eds.). (1994). *The dark side of interpersonal communication.* Hillsdale, NJ: Erlbaum.

Eisenberg, E. M. (1984). Ambiguity as strategy in organizational communication. *Communication Monographs, 51,* 224–242.

Goffman, E. (1974). *Frame analysis: An essay on the organization of experience.* Cambridge: Harvard University Press.

Gudykunst, W. B., & Nishida, T. (1986). The influence of cultural variability on perceptions of communication behavior associated with relationship terms. *Human Communication Research, 13,* 147–166.

Ishii, S., & Bruneau, T. (1994). Silence and silences in cross-cultural perspective: Japan and the United States. In L. Samovar & R. E. Porter (Eds.), *Intercultural communication: A reader* (pp. 246–251). Belmont, CA: Wadsworth.

Javidi, A., & Javidi, M. (1994). Cross-cultural analysis of interpersonal bonding: A look at East and West. In L. Samovar & R. E. Porter (Eds.), *Intercultural communication: A reader* (pp. 87–94). Belmont, CA: Wadsworth.

Kim, Y. Y. (1994). Intercultural personhood: An integration of Eastern and Western perspectives. In L. Samovar & R. E. Porter (Eds.), *Intercultural communication: A reader* (pp. 415–424). Belmont, CA: Wadsworth.

Knapp, M. L., Ellis, D. G., & Williams, B. A. (1980). Perceptions of communication behavior associated with relationship terms. *Communication Monographs, 47,* 262–278.

Lustig, M. W., & Koester, J. (1993). *Intercultural competence: Interpersonal communication across cultures.* New York: HarperCollins.

Powers, J. H. (1995). On the intellectual structure of the human communication discipline. *Communication Education, 44,* 191–222.

Samovar, L. A., & Porter, R. E. (1995). *Communication between cultures* (2nd ed.). Belmont, CA: Wadsworth.

Seibold, D. R., & Spitzberg, B. H. (1982). Attribution theory and research: Review and implications for communication. In B. Dervin & M. J. Voight (Eds.), *Progress in communication sciences* (Vol. 3, pp. 85–126). Norwood, NJ: Ablex.

Shimanoff, S. B. (1980). *Communication rules: Theory and research.* Beverly Hills, CA: Sage.

Spitzberg, B. H. (1993). The dialectics of (in)competence. *Journal of Social and Personal Relationships, 10,* 137–158.

Spitzberg, B. H. (1994). The dark side of (in)competence. In W. R. Cupach & B. H. Spitzberg (Eds.), *The dark side of interpersonal communication* (pp. 25–50). Hillsdale, NJ: Erlbaum.

Spitzberg, B. H. (1997a). A model of intercultural communication competence. In L. A. Samovar and R. E. Porter (Eds.), *Intercultural communication: A reader* (8th ed., pp. 379–391). Belmont, CA: Wadsworth.

Spitzberg, B. H. (1997b). Intimate violence. In W. R. Cupach & D. J. Canary (Eds.), *Competence in interpersonal conflict* (pp. 174–201). New York: McGraw-Hill.

Spitzberg, B. H., & Brunner, C. C. (1991). Toward a theoretical integration of context and competence inference research. *Western Journal of Speech Communication, 56,* 28–46.

Spitzberg, B. H., Canary, D. J., & Cupach, W. R. (1994). A competence-based approach to the study of interpersonal conflict. In D. D. Cahn (Ed.), *Conflict in personal relationships* (pp. 183–202). Hillsdale, NJ: Erlbaum.

Spitzberg, B. H., & Cupach, W. R. (1984). *Interpersonal communication competence.* Beverly Hills, CA: Sage.

Building Motivation

Self-Assessment: Rate each of the following communication situations, indicating the typical level of competence you feel you can or do achieve. Use the scale of 1–4 provided, with 1 minimal competence and 4 high competence. Rate one component (motivation) through all the situations, and then rate the next component (knowledge), and then the third (skills).

Motivation	Knowledge	Skills
1 = Anxious, nervous, or no motivation to be competent	**1** = Completely inexperienced and ignorant about how to behave	**1** = Completely incapable of behaving competently in the situation
2 = Somewhat nervous, but some motivation to be competent	**2** = Minimal experience and knowledge about how to behave	**2** = Barely capable of behaving minimally competently
3 = Somewhat confident and motivated to be competent	**3** = Somewhat experienced and knowledgeable about how to behave	**3** = Fairly capable of behaving competently
4 = Highly confident and motivated to be competent	**4** = Highly knowledgeable about all aspects of how to behave	**4** = Highly capable of behaving competently

INTERPERSONAL CONTEXT

Communication Situations:	Motivation	Knowledge	Skills
1. Interacting socially with people from very different cultures.			
2. Asking someone for a date.			
3. Refusing a date with someone.			
4. Asking/telling some people they can't cut in a line in front of you.			
5. Discussing safe sex with someone you are considering sexual relations with.			
6. Telling a subordinate that she or he has done something wrong.			
7. Telling a boss she or he has done something wrong.			

GROUP CONTEXT

Communication Situations:	Motivation	Knowledge	Skills
1. Reintroducing a topic you think is important after a group has moved on.			
2. Making a spontaneous joke or quip in the middle of a serious group discussion.			
3. Correcting a group leader's minor error in summarizing the group's discussion.			

	Motivation	Knowledge	Skills
4. Making an argument for what you believe in even though you know everyone in the group is against your position.			
5. Telling a group member that he or she interrupted you and should wait.			
6. Explaining to a group that you haven't prepared adequately for this meeting.			
7. Becoming the leader of a group.			

PUBLIC SPEAKING CONTEXT

Communication Situations:	Motivation	Knowledge	Skills
1. Giving a simple, prepared, informative speech in front of a classroom.			
2. Presenting a prepared technical report to a group of employees.			
3. Making an elaborate toast to a large, formal wedding party.			
4. Introducing a political candidate you support to a large crowd.			
5. Giving a persuasive speech at a city council meeting on a proposal the members oppose.			
6. Giving an impromptu speech at a political rally.			
7. Giving an interview on stage after being picked from a live television audience.			

TOTAL SCORES

Interpreting Your Scores: For each context level, total your ratings for each column (motivation, knowledge, skills). You should end up with three scores. The possible range of scores per column is 7–28. Scores 7–14 indicate you are minimizing your competence and have significant room for improvement in this area of competence. Scores 15–21 indicate you think you are average in your competence. You may be sufficing or maximizing your competence, and still have room for improvement. Scores 22–28 indicate you think you are nearing optimizing competence. Although you may still improve, you have a good grasp of the competence process.

CHAPTER 3

LEARNING OBJECTIVES

After studying this chapter, you should be able to:

1. Define perception and explain how the activities of noticing, organizing, and interpreting comprise perception.
2. Discuss how mindfulness, expectations and the self-fulfilling prophecy, and language use influence the ability to notice data about people, situations, and events.
3. State how prototypes, stereotypes, and scripts help people organize information into impressions.
4. Demonstrate how implicit personality theory and attribution theory can be used to characterize individuals' personalities as well as their motives for behavior.
5. Defend the importance of perception by articulating how perception influences responses and behavior.
6. Describe how the self is constructed through communication with others.
7. Distinguish between significant others and generalized others.
8. Compare and contrast the modern and postmodern self.
9. Predict how self-disclosure is influenced by the issues of breadth, depth, valence, reciprocity, and relevance.
10. Discuss the major challenges to perception and the strategies for overcoming those challenges.

Perception

Ann-Chinn and Loern are both enrolled in an 8 A.M. introductory political science class. As Ann-Chinn sees more and more of Loern, she becomes impressed with him as a person. One of the things that first caught her attention was how he always came to class well dressed. This was so completely unlike all the other guys in the class who looked like they had just rolled out of bed and thrown on a ball cap to cover their dirty hair. She also noticed that Loern came to class very well prepared. She saw that he always highlighted sections of his text and prepared two or three questions about the assigned reading that he asked in class. Ann-Chinn was surprised because she did the same thing and thought that no one else did. When the instructor asked Loern questions, Ann-Chinn was impressed with how thoughtful and detailed his answers were. He always referred to the assigned reading and added examples from his personal experience to illustrate the answer further. Although Ann-Chinn also talked about the book when answering the instructor's questions, she felt she could learn from Loern by connecting her personal experiences with the class material. Although others in the class perceived Loern as trying to get on the professor's good side, Ann-Chinn thought of him as a very serious, thoughtful, and dedicated student.

One day Ann-Chinn walked out of class with Loern and began talking. As they walked out into the parking lot, Ann-Chinn noticed several bumper stickers on Loern's truck. Two that stood out were "Earth first, we'll log the other planets later" and "A little nukie never hurt anyone." Ann-Chinn was startled by these messages and asked Loern what those bumper stickers were doing on his truck.

Loern's eyes flashed with passion. "Well, honestly, I'm just sick of these fanatical environmentalists who are trying to halt our economic development. As for nukes, sure, nuclear energy has some problems, but it is a very important energy source for the future."

"But what about a responsibility to our environment?" Ann-Chinn asked in shock. "If we log the old forests, people in the future will never have an opportunity to see a towering redwood tree or hike in a rain forest."

Loern responded, "But what about a responsibility to the economic well-being of future citizens? Sure, seeing old trees would be nice, but we need the lumber. Besides, trees are a renewable resource. If we just have a solid reforesting plan, we can keep the environment going."

Ann-Chinn was bewildered, "I feel I don't know who you are. You're not the same person I take political science with!" ●●●

Many times we form an initial impression of a person only to have that impression disconfirmed later. Ann-Chinn formed an impression of Loern in her political science class only to find her impression was incomplete. She noticed his attention to detail and level of class preparation and given that she focused on her studies in the same way, she assumed he was similar to her in other ways—including attitudes about the environment. When her expectations were violated, she felt she didn't really know the true Loern.

The ability to notice certain characteristics of other people, events, and situations and sort out what these characteristics mean is a complex process. Like Ann-Chinn, our sense of identity influences what we notice and how we interpret phenomena. This chapter first examines how we process the wide variety of information cues we notice and how we interpret those cues. We then discuss how personal identity is created, its influence on perceptions, and the way we express ourselves. The chapter concludes with some practical tips on how to manage challenges arising from perception.

What Is Perception?

Perception involves noticing, organizing, and interpreting data about people, events, activities, and situations. Data refers to any objects of our attention that we are attempting to make sense of. Perception is an active process in which we use the senses of touch, taste, sight, hearing, and smell to gather data about both our external environment and our internal experiences and subsequently try to make sense of these sensations. Understanding perception requires examining the activities of noticing, organizing, and interpreting.

PERCEPTION INVOLVES NOTICING

In the chapter-opening vignette, Ann-Chinn noticed Loern's behavior. What moved her to notice his behavior in class? What caused her to notice and subsequently be surprised about his beliefs regarding the environment? Three major factors influence our ability to notice data within a situation: (1) mindfulness, (2) expectations and the self-fulfilling prophecy, and (3) language use.

MINDFULNESS

Imagine that you have just shown up for class the first day. What do you notice? Most likely, your senses are fully engaged and you probably observe every small detail in the classroom. You may hear who talks to whom. You may note what people wear, and so on.

We become mindful of our surroundings when they are relatively novel. In a new job, we may hang on to every word that's uttered in a weekly staff meeting, but lose such mindfulness when we experience the meetings as routine. When they become regular, we tend to gloss over the details of situations and events.

Mindfulness is paying close attention to the task at hand, absorbing each bit of detail that you possibly can (Langer, 1978). Typically, people become mindful of their own behavior and the situation in which they find themselves when the situation is somewhat novel. But the more others behave in routine ways and the more situations unfold predictably, the more people gloss over the details of the person or the situation and become mindless.

Expectations & the Self-Fulfilling Prophecy

As you saw in Chapter 2, expectations refer to the standards and guides that we develop over time regarding what we anticipate people will do in situations. Expectations function in two different ways. On the one hand, expectations focus our attention on certain phenomena within a situation and create a type of self-fulfilling prophecy. A **self-fulfilling prophecy** occurs when you make assumptions about yourself or another person and then behave or interact with the person as if these assumptions were true. When you have a self-fulfilling prophecy about yourself, you tend to act in ways that confirm your own self-fulfilling prophecy. Not only do your expectations of how you will perform in a given situation affect your actual behavior, but the way you interact with other people makes them act in ways that confirm your assumptions. Our expectations guide our inquiry into a situation as we seek out information and details that confirm these expectations. In employment interviews, as in many social situations, the interviewer forms an impression about the interviewee and then seeks out information that confirms the impression, rather than disconfirming information (Snyder & Gangestad, 1981). Similarly, if you believe you are unqualified for a job or you will botch the interview, often the interview will not go well, confirming your expectations. The idea of the self-fulfilling prophecy takes the old adage "Seeing is believing" and turns it around: "Believing is seeing" (Weick, 1978). We notice what we expect to see.

On the other hand, when our expectations are violated, we engage in a more extensive information search within the situation (Burgoon, Stern, & Dillman, 1995). In this situation, we may ask questions such as these:

- How is the situation different than what I expected?
- What makes the situation different?
- What has caused this change in the situation?

- In what ways is the person behaving differently than I expected?
- What is motivating this person to behave differently?

When our expectations are violated, we feel a need to understand a situation in more detail and seek out what is causing the change and what is motivating people to act in unexpected ways.

Language Use

Language influences our ability to notice data in situations. Words are pointers; they direct our attention toward certain aspects of people and situations. Take for example the debate of whether to refer to a person as "Indian" or as "Native American." What do you notice when you call someone "Indian"? Your attention is directed to this person's general ethnicity. Despite the fact that many tribes in the United States such as the Lakota, the Sioux, the Cherokee, the Navajo, and the Hopi represent different nations, the term Indian glosses over these differences. The term Indian was first used by Columbus to describe the native inhabitants of the land because he mistakenly thought he had arrived in India. What do you notice if you refer to someone as Native American? This language focuses on the person's historical heritage. In the United States the term *Native American* highlights the fact that Europeans are not native to North America and their arrival was preceded by populations of other peoples. In Canada, the term *First People* is used to stress that several tribal peoples were the first inhabitants of the country.

Words are so important in influencing our impressions that we need to be careful not to engage in **linguistic tyranny**, which occurs when people use one set of words that have a certain value or connotation to describe and control the outcome of a situation instead of playing with different words to describe the situation (Pearce, 1994). Politicians typically engage in linguistic tyranny to influence citizens' interpretations of particular events. Consider the words that have been used to describe the war in Kosovo against ethnic Albanians. Politicians have described the situation as "ethnic cleansing" and have also vividly described the mass graves and other atrocities committed against the Albanians. The words they choose closely parallel the description of Nazi atrocities during World War II. When politicians urged U.S. participation in the NATO intervention, these words were particularly potent in influencing the American public to see the war as just, necessary, and urgent. By implicitly making the link to Nazi atrocities, the American public would be more predisposed to enter the conflict. Had this link not been made, Milosevic would have been merely another dictator of another aggressive country far from American shores. Our choice of words to describe people and situations directs attention to different things.

Perception Involves Organizing

Cognitive psychology suggests that people use schemas to make sense of and organize incoming information. A **schema** organizes information and places it into a coherent and meaningful pattern. Imagine that you walked into an art museum and saw a painting by Picasso. Unless you had a schema that included information about cubism and surrealism, you would have difficulty recognizing the various elements in the painting or even finding it beautiful. A schema containing ideas about cubism would help you recognize and appreciate Picasso's work. A variety of schemas help organize our impressions around people, events, situations, and activities: (1) prototypes, (2) stereotypes, and (3) scripts.

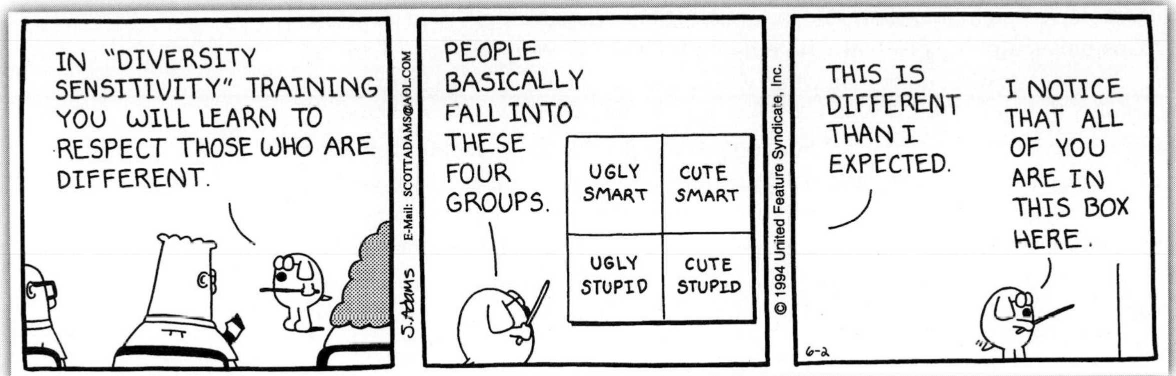

We often categorize people based on our concept of the best possible example, or prototype, of a type of person.

DILBERT reprinted by permission of United Feature Syndicate, Inc.

Prototypes

In the Dilbert cartoon, Dogbert has grouped all people into one of four basic types, making fun of our general tendency to view people as types. These types, in turn, provide us with mental pictures of abstract examples that help us place people, events, activities, and situations into categories called **prototypes**. A prototype can be thought of as a best example of some concept. For example, your prototype of a luxury car might be a Lexus, or any car with the following characteristics: roomy inside, large, powerful, constructed of superior materials, and very expensive. Prototypes help us answer questions such as "Who are you?" "What is it?" and "What's going on?" For example, how do we know whether a person is a competent communicator or not? We may develop a competent communicator prototype to help us make a determination (Pavitt & Haight, 1985). In fact, research shows that people have developed a prototype for the competent communicator as someone who is intelligent, articulate, confident, outgoing, well dressed, and a good listener (Pavitt & Haight, 1985). Similarly, we have prototypes for events and activities. If we walk into a room and see people dancing and hear music blaring in the background, we type the situation as a dance party. Prototypes are useful in that they help us determine the kinds of people, situations, or activities we are experiencing.

Stereotypes

Stereotypes link our perceptions of people, events, activities, and situations to predictions and anticipations. Prototypes provide a general example of a category, whereas stereotypes connect a variety of characteristics we believe to be true of a category to a given person or situation we see as a member or example of that category. For example, we may develop stereotypes about how tourists dress and behave. If you think of tourists, you may think of people running around in tennis shoes, plaid shorts, an uneven sunburn, with cameras hung around their necks. Based on classifying people as tourists, you might predict they will buy cheap and gaudy trinkets from the place they are visiting to give as gifts to friends and family back home. Similarly, we may develop stereotypes about how people look or act on the basis of their ethnicity, sexual orientation, gender, age, religion, and level of education.

Stereotypes can impair communication by relying on the belief that people have a single self or identity. This belief is reflected in the assumption of **allness**, the tendency to conclude that what is believed to be true of one part is true of the whole. If we encounter a rude traffic cop, we may conclude that all traffic cops are rude. In addition, if this traffic cop is also female, we might then start making assumptions about all females in positions of power. This belief allows us to make statements such as "All women are . . ." or "All Asians do . . ."; however, what do you do when you encounter a female Asian Democratic environmentalist like Ann-Chinn? Which stereotypes do you pay attention to? Gender? Race? Political? Environmental activist? Stereotypes are part of the perceptual process because they simplify complex situations. We cannot notice everything, so we seek to group as many things as possible into categories that make them understandable and familiar. In this sense, stereotypes help us cope with new and complex situations. At a minimum, however, we need to recognize that stereotypes can't capture the whole person or situation, and any one person or event can be characterized according to an unlimited number of stereotypes.

Scripts

A **script** is an expected sequence of events that is coherent to the individual (Abelson, 1976). Scripts have an identifiable sequence of actions. Take the following random list of questions you might be asked by a server in a restaurant. Reorder the questions as you would anticipate them to be asked.

- Would you like dessert?
- Would you like a little more time to make your selections?
- What would you like to order as your appetizer?
- Good evening.
- What entrée would you prefer?

More than likely, you reordered the questions as follows:

- Good evening.
- Would you like a little time to make your selections?
- What would you like to order as your appetizer?
- What entrée would you prefer?
- Would you like dessert?

The typical script for ordering food at a restaurant follows chronologically: After the greeting, we begin with ordering our appetizer, then our entrée, and if we have room, our dessert. The script for ordering food follows the order in which we eat the food.

Scripts provide us with guides for interpreting events and organizing our communication. In a restaurant, we know that the question "Would you like a little more time to make your selections?" is a query by the wait staff to determine if the diners are ready to order. Following the script, we know that we are to answer either "Yes" or "No." But, if a member of the wait staff came up to us and said, "I've had a lousy day—I don't even know why I came to work," we would be confused and not know how to act. Such statements don't follow the typical script we have created for ordering food at a restaurant. We usually don't become aware that we are using scripts to guide our interpretations and actions until someone violates the plotline.

PERCEPTION INVOLVES INTERPRETATION

Once we have noticed something and organized it according to some cognitive framework using prototypes, stereotypes, or scripts, we interpret what we have noticed. That is, once we have organized the "data" we have perceived and stored, we have to make sense of this information. We draw conclusions from the data about the kind of person with whom we are interacting or the type of situation in which we find ourselves. There are two ways to look at how we draw such conclusions: implicit personality theory and attribution theory.

Implicit Personality Theory

Implicit personality theory suggests that we use one or a few personality traits to draw inferences about what people are like (Wegner & Vallacher, 1977). **Constructs** represent a continuum of dimensions or traits that make up people's personalities. Constructs can include a variety of personality traits such as happy–sad, strong–weak, close–distant, and so on. Implicit personality theory suggests that certain constructs are central to determining what a person is like. You might make some generalizations about what the person is like on the basis of one construct. For example, you may focus on a single construct such as gender (male–female), economic status (rich–poor), or educational status (grade school–college) and draw inferences about the person based on that construct. Implicit personality theory examines how traits are clustered together and how certain central traits trigger associations with other traits. For example, you may associate the construct of being college educated with being artistic and elitist. However, other people may associate the construct of a college education with prosperity and friendliness. In the opening vignette, Ann-Chinn associates the construct of "good student" with appearance and class participation. Other students may associate the construct of "good student" with class attendance.

Knowledge Link

How does implicit personality theory help explain the role perceptions play in the development of communication competence discussed in Chapter 2?

Implicit personality theory helps explain why first impressions of others are so powerful. The **first impression bias** means that our first impression sets the mold by which later information we gather about this person is processed, remembered, and viewed as relevant. For example, based on observing Ann-Chinn in class, Loern may have viewed her as a stereotypical Asian woman and assumed she is quiet, hard working, and unassertive. Having reached these conclusions, right or wrong, he now has a set of prototypes and constructs for understanding and interpreting Ann-Chinn's behavior. Over time, he fits the behavior consistent with his prototypes and constructs into the impression he has already formed of her. When he noticed her expressing disbelief over his selection of bumper stickers, he may simply dismiss or view it as an odd exception to her real nature because it doesn't fit his existing prototype.

Attribution Theory

Attribution theory provides people with a framework for determining the motives underlying others' behavior (Spitzberg, in press). What reasons or motives do we attribute for why people act and communicate in the way they do? Several key dimensions of the attribution process help us answer this question. Specifically, we tend to make attributions about people based on the principles of consistency and distinctiveness, and we draw conclusions about the importance of these attributions based on the principles of locus and controllability (Seibold & Spitzberg, 1982).

The **principle of consistency** suggests that we make attributions about people based on the similarity of their characteristics or actions across time and space. If a student has a history in both high school and college of getting teachers to accept late assignments, you are likely to attribute persuasiveness to this student. In this circumstance, you might also attribute irresponsibility or laziness to this student. This particular behavior is said to be high in consistency. But, if you saw that this student persuaded one professor to permit a late assignment, but had no success in convincing two other professors, you have no consistent pattern to use in attributing persuasiveness to this student, even if you may still perceive enough consistency in the student's behavior to attribute irresponsibility or laziness. In this case, the student's behavior is low in consistency.

The **principle of distinctiveness** suggests that we make attributions about people based on whether particular characteristics and actions are associated with specific outcomes unique to the situation. Distinctiveness is the extent to which things occur *only* with each other, and not with other things. For example, if the student with the late assignments seems well liked by peers and professors, but is clearly treated harshly by one of the professors, then the student seems to evoke a distinctive reaction from this professor. The action of asking for permission to turn in a paper late is associated with the outcome of harsh treatment for that specific professor. The attribution you make in this situation depends on both the consistency and distinctiveness of both persons. If the professor in question is consistently harsh with many other students, then the behavior is not distinctive to the late student; rather it is low in distinctiveness, and you will tend to consider the professor a harsh person. If, instead, you see this professor being friendly with all students *except* the student with the late assignments, then the student seems to be unique or distinctive in eliciting this response from the professor. In this case, the professor's behavior is high in distinctiveness and you are more likely to attribute that the late student has done something to upset this professor.

Consistency and distinctiveness are related, but separate. For example, if the first time Loern sees Ann-Chinn in a class she is smiling and laughing, he might conclude she is cheerful and fun. If the next time he sees her she is outside having lunch with some friends and is laughing again, the consistency begins to give him more confidence in his attribution. However, if the next time he sees her she seems serious, and he notices that one of the friends he had seen her with the previous times was not there, then Loern might conclude that she tends to be cheerful around this person, but not with others. So it was high consistency that led to the first attribution, and high distinctiveness that led to the second attribution.

People tend to arrive at attributions about others based on the principles of consistency and distinctiveness. The importance of these attributions for how you feel and act toward others depends in turn on the principles of locus and controllability. The **principle of locus** states that we attempt to determine the extent to which a cause of some outcome is internal or external to a person. Is the student who asks permission to turn in assignments late working two jobs, a single parent, and taking 10 courses? If so, many would assume the student is late with assignments not so much out of laziness, an internal condition, but out of the external demands of that student's life. In contrast, if you frequently see this student on campus throwing Frisbees and chatting with friends at the student union, you are more likely to attribute the student's behavior to laziness, a quality inherent in that particular student.

The **principle of controllability** means we try to determine not only whether the cause of a particular action is internal or external, but the extent to which a person is able to alter or change the outcome. Whether you feel sympathy for or dislike the student depends in large part whether your attribution is one of laziness or excessive external demands. But notice that even with the attribution of excessive demands, you could still blame the student for "taking too much on" or failing to prioritize properly. To the extent that you perceive an outcome, such as lateness, as controllable, you are much more likely to hold that person responsible for his or her outcomes, whether positive or negative.

How do these principles become important in communication? Table 3.1 shows how attribution principles might work in the courtroom. How you feel and act toward people

TABLE 3.1

••• Attribution Theory in the Courtroom •••

A student accuses a fellow student she had been dating of engaging in date rape. How might the attorneys attempt to use attribution theory to make their respective cases for their clients?

ATTORNEY	CONSISTENCY	DISTINCTIVENESS	LOCUS	CONTROLLABILITY	SPECIFIC ATTRIBUTION
Definition	How often does one event occur when the other event occurs?	To what extent does one event occur *only* when the other event occurs?	Is the cause of the event "inside" the person or "outside" the person?	To what extent is the person able to change or control what happens?	What caused this person to do what he or she did?
Defense	Low: My client never tried this before with this person.	Low: My client never tried this with any of his other dating partners.	External: The plaintiff teased and led my client on. She didn't say "please don't" until they were undressed, and then only feebly.	Uncontrollable: Both my client and the defendant had had a lot to drink that night.	My client is not a coercive person; he simply got carried away by the context due to mixed signals from plaintiff (e.g., he should not be held responsible).
Prosecution	High: My client claims that the defendant consistently persisted in pressuring her for sexual relations.	Low: Previous dating partners testify that the defendant was sexually aggressive with them.	Internal: The defendant talked and talked about how much he wanted to have sex with my client.	Controllable: The defendant said to her: "I know what you need and I'm going to give it to you whether you want it or not."	The defendant clearly *intended* to have sex with my client, forcing himself on her against her will (e.g, he should be held responsible).
	High: The defendant has a reputation for being very sexually persistent and aggressive.	High: The defendant was clearly uniquely obsessed with my client; he was more aggressive with her than with previous partners.	Internal: The defendant bragged to friends about how he was going to score with my client.	Controllable: Actions on the date—going to a party, to his place drinking, threatening to leave her stranded if she didn't have sex—reveal the defendant's intentions.	The defendant clearly had *planned* to have sex with my client, regardless of her consent and he did things to assure this outcome (e.g., he should be held responsible).

NOTE: Attribution theory explains how we determine what caused some event, but it also guides how we make explanations in everyday arguments. What other types of arguments could be made about either the defendant's or the plaintiff's actions, motives, or background that are based on consistency, distinctiveness, locus, or controllability?

depends on how you attribute outcomes to their actions, particularly in a courtroom where decisions of guilt and innocence are being decided. Consider the communication predicament attorneys might face in dealing with a student accused of date rape. Both the defense and the prosecution must craft stories about the case to convince a judge or jury of the defendant's guilt or innocence. In order to influence the judge or jury the attorneys base their stories on attribution principles to construct a coherent argument regarding the defendant's guilt.

As you can see, the principles of consistency, distinctiveness, locus, and controllability describe the way attributions are likely to be made if people are rational. However, research shows that people tend to be biased in applying these attribution principles (Nisbett & Ross, 1980). The most consistent biases are the fundamental attribution error and the self-serving bias. The **fundamental attribution error** occurs when we assume other people's behavior is due more to internal characteristics such as their personality, whereas we view our own behavior more as a result of factors in the context or situation (Jones & Nisbett, 1971). The **self-serving bias** states that we tend to attribute positive outcomes to our self, which is an internal attribution, and negative outcomes to others or to the situation, which are external attributions (Nisbett & Ross, 1980). Consider students discussing the grades they received on a recent exam. You will find that most people seem to *earn* A's, but are *given* D's. That is, an A is achieved through the internal characteristics of effort and ability on the part of the student, but a D is a product of the external situation such as not having enough time to study, or an overly difficult or demanding professor.

Why Is Understanding Perception Important?

We continually process information about people, events, situations, and activities and create interpretations about those events. Because perception is such a part of our daily lives, it is tempting to dismiss it as relatively unimportant—after all, it happens so often we barely even notice it. However, even though it may be invisible, perception is critical to human communication. Perception is critical to communication because of three of its qualities: It is responsive, relative, and regulative.

PERCEPTION INFLUENCES OUR RESPONSES

How do we know how to act in situations when we interact with people? The simple answer is that the cognitive schemas we have learned help guide our responses. If we classify situations or people in certain ways, using prototypes, stereotypes, and scripts, we draw certain interpretations about the situation or person. Those interpretations guide our subsequent actions.

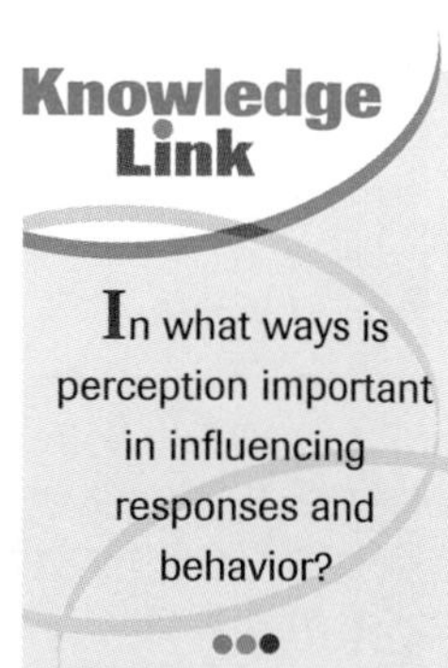

One of the key factors that influences how we know how to respond within a situation is whether we view that situation as following a fixed script or whether the script is flexible and can be changed (Cronen & Lang, 1994). When a script is fixed, a situation has a highly prescribed set of actions for behavior. For example, ordering a meal at a fast-food restaurant is a fixed script; you know that someone will first ask for the order, next take the order, and (eventually) bring you what you ordered. If you perceive the communication situation as following a fixed script, you follow the fixed script for the situation (Pearce, 1994). However, you may perceive a communication situation as involving a flexible script where you can not only change the way you talk but also what you talk about.

For example, sometimes groups need to brainstorm for ideas to solve a particular problem. If you perceive a situation as a group brainstorming session, you know that by definition the script will be flexible because almost anything goes in a brainstorming situation. Moreover, you have the opportunity to take the situation in different directions and, in this case, transform the group meeting. Although you may initially perceive the situation as a brainstorming session, you may be able to guide the discussion toward talking about group members' responsibilities and goals.

PERCEPTIONS ARE RELATIVE

Perceptions are relative. There is no way to view any person, situation, event, or object objectively. Perception depends on who is making the observation, where it occurs, and when it occurs. Consider the question "What is a cow?" At first glance, this seems to be a very simple question to answer. A cow is a four-legged animal raised by farmers. However, the interpretation of a "cow" depends on our relationship to that cow (Morgan, 1995). For a farmer, a cow is a source of income. For a veterinarian, a cow is a patient. For Hindus, a cow is a holy animal that cannot be killed for food or leather. For others, cows are pets. The answer to the question "What is a cow?" depends on your relationship to the cow.

Why should the competent communicator recognize that perceptions are relative? Simply, many difficulties or disagreements between people arise from different perceptions of people, events, and situations. For example, in recent years debates in several southern states have centered on whether the Confederate flag should be flown over state capitols or be incorporated into the state flag. This difficult issue demonstrates the importance of perception. For some people, such as African Americans and northerners, the Confederate flag may be perceived as a symbol of racism and oppression. Yet others, such as southern Anglos whose ancestors fought and died for the Confederacy during the Civil War, may perceive it as a symbol for freedom and states' rights. The assumption that others' perceptions of the world are different from yours allows you to explore the root causes for these differences and determine the best way to manage them through communication.

PERCEPTIONS REGULATE BEHAVIOR

Understanding perception can also help us understand power and influence. **Power** is the ability to influence and control another person's thoughts, feelings, or actions. One way to control a person's actions is to guide and shape the frames of reference they use to perceive a situation. Just as a photographer frames a picture to highlight certain aspects of a subject and background, power can be gained by controlling people's frames of reference so they see certain aspects of the situation.

Consider a parent and a rebellious teenager. Many teenagers are very concerned with their independence and, as a result, challenge everything their parents say and go against their parents' wishes. Figure 3.1 shows the logic that a teenager may use when managing a relationship with his or her parent. Because he or she perceives any act by a parent as a potential limit to independence, the teenager takes actions directly opposite to the parent's desires. A parent experienced in teenage logic can use this knowledge to frame a communication situation to control the behavior of the teenager. Thus a savvy parent may form a request that is the direct opposite of what he or she actually desires. By working with their teenager's perceptions, parents can guide their child toward behaviors in the direction they prefer.

FIGURE 3.1
Regulation of Behavior

How we perceive a situation or person influences how we behave and respond in a situation. In this instance, the parent depends on the teenager's perceptions of the situation to prohibit him from using the car. Notice the parent never says the teenager can't use the car.

Developing Self-Concept

What influences your perceptions? How did you learn what is important to notice about people and situations? Do you see situations from only your perspective or are you able to see them from others' perspectives as well? These questions touch on different issues regarding perception; however, they share two elements. First, they assume there is a self. In order to ask about a "you" or "yours," whoever is asking these questions assumes you can respond by using words like "I," "my," "myself," and "mine." These words illustrate how people tend to view themselves as distinct from others. The idea of having a "self" suggests that people are different from one another, and that to understand a person's self, you need to understand the uniqueness of that particular person.

Second, these questions highlight the importance of the other in understanding the self. We learn about what to notice regarding people and situations through our interaction with others. Moreover, in order to have a "self," we must have a concept of "not self," those individuals, attitudes, behaviors, beliefs, and values distinct from our own. To know your "self" implies you know what is "not your self." Perceiving events through your own senses implies you have a clear sense of the attitudes, behaviors, beliefs, and values central to who you are, and being able to perceive events through other people's eyes suggests you have a clear sense of "others'" attitudes, behaviors, beliefs, and values. The key to understanding ourselves, therefore, centers around how others influence our self, and the way they influence the self is through communication.

THE IMPLIED OTHER IN CONSTRUCTING THE SELF

Theorists have explored the idea of how the self is created using a wide variety of explanations. Most explanations have two ideas in common. First, when you can respond to yourself as an object, then you have created the self. The moment you say "I should do this" or "I should not do this" you have created the self because you have reflected on the actions of an object—"your self." Second, you are aware of yourself as an object in the world only because other people are aware of and perceive you (Wegner & Vallacher, 1980). This second point is crucial for understanding the role of others in the construction of self. Say you view yourself as intelligent. How did you create this self-view? One possible answer is that you thought about it on your own and came to this conclusion. Yet this answer still begs the question of where you initially learned that the idea of intelligence is an important criterion in determining your self-view. Over time, you interacted with others, beginning with your parents, who evaluated you in terms of your intelligence, and you internalized these criteria and used them as criteria for viewing your self. By adopting the perspective of others, you were able to create a self-view that you could then reflect on.

We develop a "self" by reflecting on ourselves as an object as well as through taking in others' reflections of ourselves.

The importance of the other in constructing the self was noted by Cooley (1922), who explicitly argued that the self is a **social self**. According to the social self, the self comes into being through interaction with others and can only be determined through relationships with other people. Cooley (1922) coined the term *the looking-glass self* to demonstrate how our relationships with other people form the self. The **looking-glass self** assumes people imagine the perception that others hold of them, and it is this act of perceiving the self as an object through the eyes of others that creates the self. The looking-glass self consists of three principal elements: (1) the imagination of one's appearance to another person, (2) the imagination of the other person's judgment of that appearance, and (3) a resulting feeling such as pride or shame. For example, consider a positive adjective you would use to describe yourself. How did you come to view this adjective as positive? Why do you view yourself in this way? According to Cooley's looking-glass self, as you interacted with people you imagined how they viewed and judged your behaviors. The adjective you selected emerged from taking the perspective of others and determining whether they thought this quality was worthy of pride or shame.

The role of the other in constructing the self is crucial. Who, then, are the others with whom you interact? Whose perspectives do you use to identify yourself? Two types of "others" influence the construction of the self: significant others and generalized others.

SIGNIFICANT OTHERS

Significant others are those important people who shape your life. For example, in early childhood your mother and father played significant roles in your life. In grade school and middle school, your peers and teachers became important parts of your life. When you began your work life, your supervisor and co-workers may have occupied a central role in your life. Throughout life we encounter people who take an interest in our well-being and for whom we develop tremendous respect and appreciation. When we construct our self, we take into account how these significant others see us.

Generalized Others

The idea of the significant other implies that people develop a self by taking into account the attitudes important individuals direct toward them as they interact in play or work. George Herbert Mead (1934) states that to develop the fullest sense of self you need to consider the attitudes of the **generalized other**—the entire social group or community to which you belong. Significant others are specific people who influence your life such as parents, partners, friends, and teachers, whereas the generalized other is the general class, category, or group of people that you use to assess your actions. The term generalized other includes the communal rules and guidelines that determine how people who belong to a particular social group or community should view situations and act. As an example, assume you are a volunteer for a women's shelter that provides assistance and support to abused women. A new woman comes to the shelter and presents you with a problem you have never encountered before. You ask yourself the following question, "What should a volunteer at this shelter do?" This question evokes the generalized other. Rather than asking what a specific person such as another volunteer or volunteer coordinator should do, you have asked what the general community of volunteers would do. When we ask questions that evoke the generalized other, we can begin to coordinate our actions more successfully because we are drawing on a common base of shared assumptions and beliefs.

COMMUNICATION & PERSONAL IDENTITY

As you've read thus far, the development of the self-concept is a social process that involves significant and generalized others. The meanings and interpretations that we create for ourselves and others result from our interactions with other people. Mead

CloseUp ON COMMUNITY

Managing Multiple "Me's" in a Diverse Society

GEORGE HERBERT MEAD VIEWED the "Me" and the generalized other as the glue that holds society together. By having a common set of values, beliefs, and assumptions, people are able to communicate clearly with one another because they have a shared understanding of what various symbols mean. Moreover, a clear set of rules and norms guide behavior within society. At the time of his writing in the 1930s, the notion of a single "Me" and a generalized other made sense as many people within the United States viewed the country as having a homogeneous set of values and beliefs.

In light of this shared value and belief system, how did society in the 1930s talk about significant issues? The dominant way of talking about significant public issues was debate. In debate, one side advocates a particular position, and the other side argues for the opposing position. One of the reasons that debate historically worked well in communities was that the shared values, beliefs, and assumptions held by community members served as a backdrop for the debate. This shared sense of identity held by members of a community allowed them to argue over significant public issues in a coherent manner. For example, when people argued over whether certain forms of speech—for example, speech that denigrates people on the basis of their gender, race, or ethnicity—should be limited, both proponents and opponents of regulations regarding certain forms of speech have valued free speech. The result was that a common shared standard, the importance of free speech, became the primary criterion used to determine which regulations should be enacted and which should not.

The idea that debate was the best form of communication to talk about significant public issues worked well as long as there was a shared identity among community members. However, today, there is great diversity existing within society, and people have differing values, beliefs, and assumptions about which kinds of behaviors are acceptable and moral and which are not. In such a pluralistic society, the traditional form of debate may actually divide and polarize communities instead of uniting and integrating them.

Consider, for example, the proposal to extend health benefits to the partners of gays and lesbians. For some people, the thought of extending such benefits is horrifying as it legitimizes same sex preference relations and goes against their religious beliefs. For others, such a policy signals that all people within the United States are created as equals and should not be discriminated against—a right that extends to gay and lesbian couples as well. The first group may view the issue of extending health benefits to the partners of gays and lesbians as an issue rooted in morality, while the second may view the issue as one of equal rights. Since these two different groups are using different standards to judge the acceptability of the proposal, it is not surprising that they have difficulty reaching agreement. There is no common standard with which to judge the validity of the proposal.

One of the ways that community members can begin to manage the multiple "Me's" and generalized others of a community is to engage in forms of communication that promote understanding of the values, beliefs, and assumptions that guide people. One form of communication that encourages mutual understanding among people is dialogue. Dialogue is a process of standing one's own ground while being profoundly open to other perspectives (Pearce & Littlejohn, 1998). The characteristics of dialogue include the following:

- We try to understand one another's perspectives.
- Listening is as important as speaking.
- We speak mostly for ourselves.
- We speak from personal experience.
- The atmosphere is one of safety.
- We discover differences even among those with whom we agree.
- We discover shared concerns among those with whom we disagree.
- We discover our uncertainties as well as our deeply held beliefs.
- Questions are asked out of true curiosity and the desire to know more.
- We discover new things.
- We explore the complexity of the issues being discussed.
- We try to work collaboratively.

The notion of dialogue in public life has taken on added importance. A number of groups such as the National Issues Forum, Study Circles, the Public Conversations Project, and the Public Dialogue Consortium are devoted to developing ways of communicating that promote dialogue among people. In a world of diversity comprised of multiple Me's and generalized others, understanding one another's unique perspective is an important first step in managing the identity of a community.

SOURCE: Pearce & Littlejohn (1998).

(1934) argued that the self is comprised of both an "I" and a "Me." The "I" represents the impulsive and unpredictable part of the self. The "Me" represents the generalized other and the patterns of behavior that you share with others. The "I" serves as the driving force for performing an act, but is quickly controlled and guided by the "Me." For example, a mischievous aspect of the "I" may encourage you to shout "Fire!" impulsively in a crowded movie theater; the "Me" controls this impulse because it knows that shouting such words in a crowded movie theater could not only injure people as they stampede for the exits but also lead to your arrest. For Mead, the "Me" serves an important function in regulating behavior in society.

The generalized other is formed through the use of significant symbols. **Significant symbols** are verbal or nonverbal messages that have shared meaning. How does your use of significant symbols lead to you develop the generalized other? Take the example of the significant symbol "Fire!" from the preceding paragraph. When you use a significant symbol, you can imagine how others will hear you and how they will interpret your messages. You can assume the listener's role and empathize with the perception of your message. This process is called **role taking**. By imagining the meaning that others attribute to your behavior, you can take the standpoints of others who view you and your behavior. As you've seen so far, Mead suggests that people experience themselves through the perceptions of others. He further suggests that the way we begin to understand others is through using significant symbols.

The development of self depends on who we talk to and the kinds of significant symbols used in these conversations. As we talk to significant others throughout our lives we develop specific significant symbols that influence how we see ourselves. For example, what do the significant symbols "male" and "female" mean to you? Historically, men and women have been socialized in different ways. Men have been taught to be aggressive, task oriented, and competitive, and women have been conditioned to be deferential, relationship oriented, and cooperative, although behavior of men and women is rarely so starkly different (Canary & Hause, 1993). Through interaction with significant others such as parents, classmates, teachers, and co-workers, we take on the meanings that they have developed for each of these significant symbols.

We also have conversations with ourselves, or self-talk. These internal conversations are important to the development of the self. Through these conversations we reflect on what we are doing well or what we are doing poorly; we reflect on how we have done in the past and what we anticipate doing in the future. The power of self-talk has been demonstrated to help people accomplish their goals (Barrett, 1994). For example, when you are preparing for a speech you may visualize a successful performance. When a speaker thinks positive thoughts such as "I can see what I need to do" as opposed to negative thoughts such as "I hope I don't freeze up" he or she is more likely to perform the desired behavior.

THE POSTMODERN SELF

The notion that the self is comprised of an "I" and a "Me" is the basis for the idea of the **modern self** (Giddens, 1991), the classic, Western tradition of viewing people as having essential natures to their character and personality. Western conceptions of self tend to assume there is a single self that is stable over time. This thinking leads us to believe there is an essential core self. The common expression "just be yourself" reflects this philosophy, implying there is a "true" self that others can perceive accurately or inaccurately.

The concept of a **postmodern self**, in contrast, rejects the notion of a single "true" self and states that the self is actually made up of many different selves, not just one stable self. For example, on any given day, you might face interactions that include the following: You wake up to local, regional, national, and international news stories on a radio alarm clock. You pet your dog and cat, and make sure they are fed. You log on to your computer and download a dozen email messages, some from friends, some from colleagues or fellow students, a few advertisements, and a few jokes that have now made the rounds to tens of thousands. You reply to people and then enter a couple of chat rooms to see who's on. You chat for a while with one person about your hobby and with another about romance. You log on to an online auction site and inquire about a couple of items on which you may want to bid. You call your parents to let them know about your plans to visit. Then you go to a nearby track to meet a friend to go jogging, go back home, clean up, get dressed, and meet with another friend at a local coffeehouse to talk about your social plans this weekend. You go to campus and attend a couple of afternoon classes, and afterward, meet with a couple of students in your study group. Before you leave campus, you talk to a librarian about an overdue fee. You go home, but not before doing some grocery shopping. You call your romantic partner to see about getting together that night with some mutual friends at a club.

During the course of this day, you have communicated with dozens, perhaps even hundreds or thousands of people. You have been an acquaintance, a friend, a counselor, a romantic partner, an instructor, a hobbyist, an athlete, a student, a client, a patron, a potential customer, a provider, and a son or daughter. You have communicated through technology and face-to-face, one on one and in larger groups, through writing and through speech, from close and from afar. In the study group you may be primarily sharing information, however you are managing conflict when interacting with the librarian. In the chat room you offer support, and at the coffeehouse you seek entertainment. In some encounters you are doing all of these activities. In a given day, you end up being many different people, and yet, in the end, you remain yourself. As the world offers more and more opportunities and avenues for communication, the ways in which we present ourselves to the world, and to ourselves, have become more complex. The postmodern self is a product of this increasing complexity.

The postmodern self is multiple, adaptable, and socially constructed (Gergen, 1991). The first of these characteristics, the **multiple self**, means that we create many different versions of "self" across contexts. Examine the selves of two students displayed in Figure 3.2. The figures show the roles that each person plays and the behaviors expected for competent role performance for each role. Furthermore, the arrows show how behaviors from one role connect with other roles. For example, in trying to fulfill the role of a good family member and please parents, Blair needs to be a good student, learn good career skills, sustain her religious practice, maintain relations with her siblings, and uphold ethnic traditions. Both students have personal and academic lives, but Chris's life revolves around a wide variety of activities, all of which are equally important to Chris's self-concept. Success in school is just as central to Chris's self-concept as finding love. In contrast, Blair views all of the self's roles as deriving from relationships with others. Success at school is important for Blair in terms of the impact it has on fulfilling her parents' expectations. However, it is also important to Blair's self as a romantic partner and as a friend, as Blair's networks of relationships and activities overlap.

Knowledge Link

What are the similarities and differences between the modern and postmodern self?

Some of your friends know you primarily as an athlete, through your shared hobbies, as a fraternity or sorority member, or as a work colleague. But in knowing you through these shared activities, they may know little about your hopes and dreams, your sense of humor, your family history, your romantic life, and so forth. In other words, our self has multiple faces, and we give certain faces more prominence in some relationships and in some contexts than in others (Rosenberg & Gara, 1985). All of these faces are true, and yet

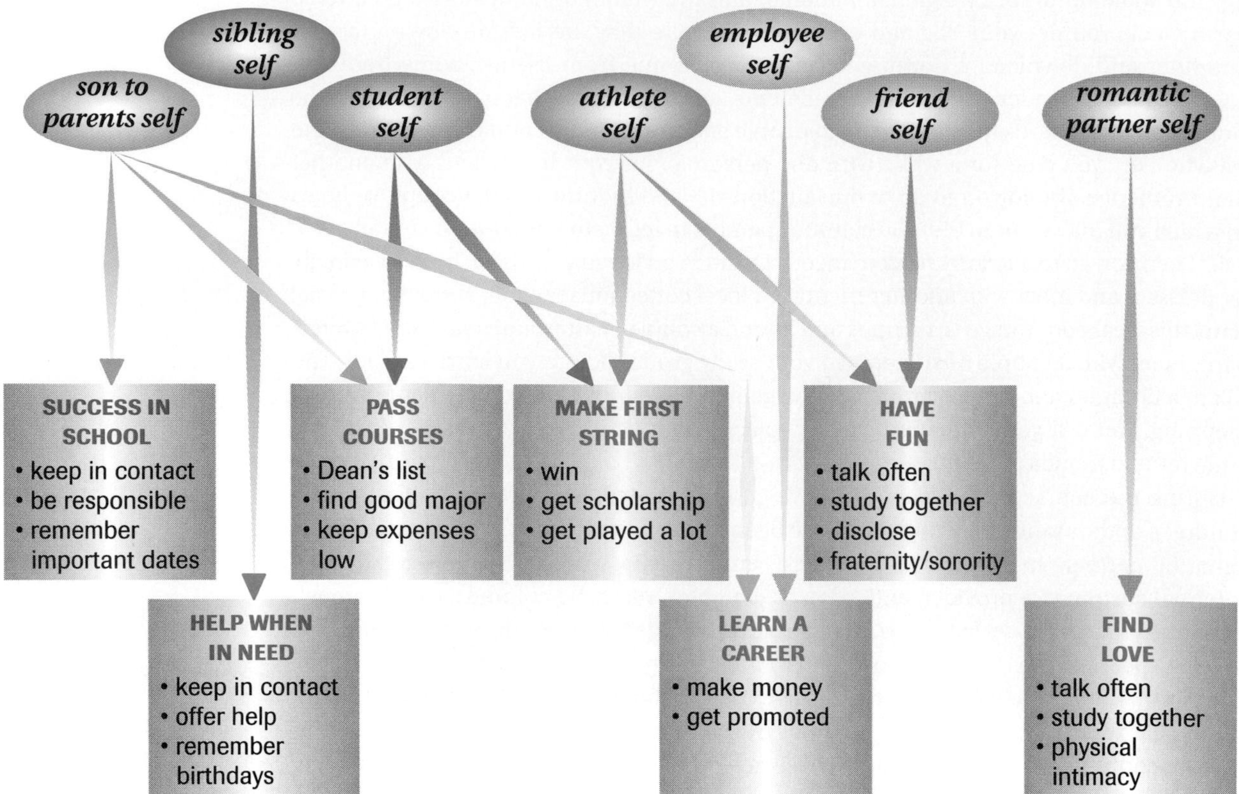

FIGURE 3.2
Different Selves

Chris and Blair both define themselves in terms of the same basic constructs, but they organize these selves very differently. For Chris (above), all the selves are equally important and are somewhat separate from one another. But for Blair (facing page), all these aspects of self are important only to the extent that they fulfill the relationship selves.

different people get very different views of you. These faces also reveal the very complex nature of your own self. You may easily see these multiple selves as parts of a whole, but the fact that you can be polite in one context, aggressive in another, passive in one context and powerful in another, suggests just how many different selves you are capable of revealing.

The second characteristic of the postmodern self is that it is adaptable. Not only do we reveal different selves across contexts, but we show different faces of ourselves within contexts and across time (Zurcher, 1977). That is, we adapt. Think about the last complicated and serious conflict you had with someone close to you. You may have had to play the role of confidant, advocate, friend, counselor, competitor, and victor or loser, all within a single communication episode. Over time, you may discover that you have become more competitive or less forgiving, more expressive or less confident. These adaptations result from life experiences such as marriage, children, divorce, loss of a parent or close friend, or changing jobs. Such adaptations occur not only in a person's behavior, but in the conception of self. Losing a loved one may make one person more

BLAIR 'S "IMPORTANT SELVES"

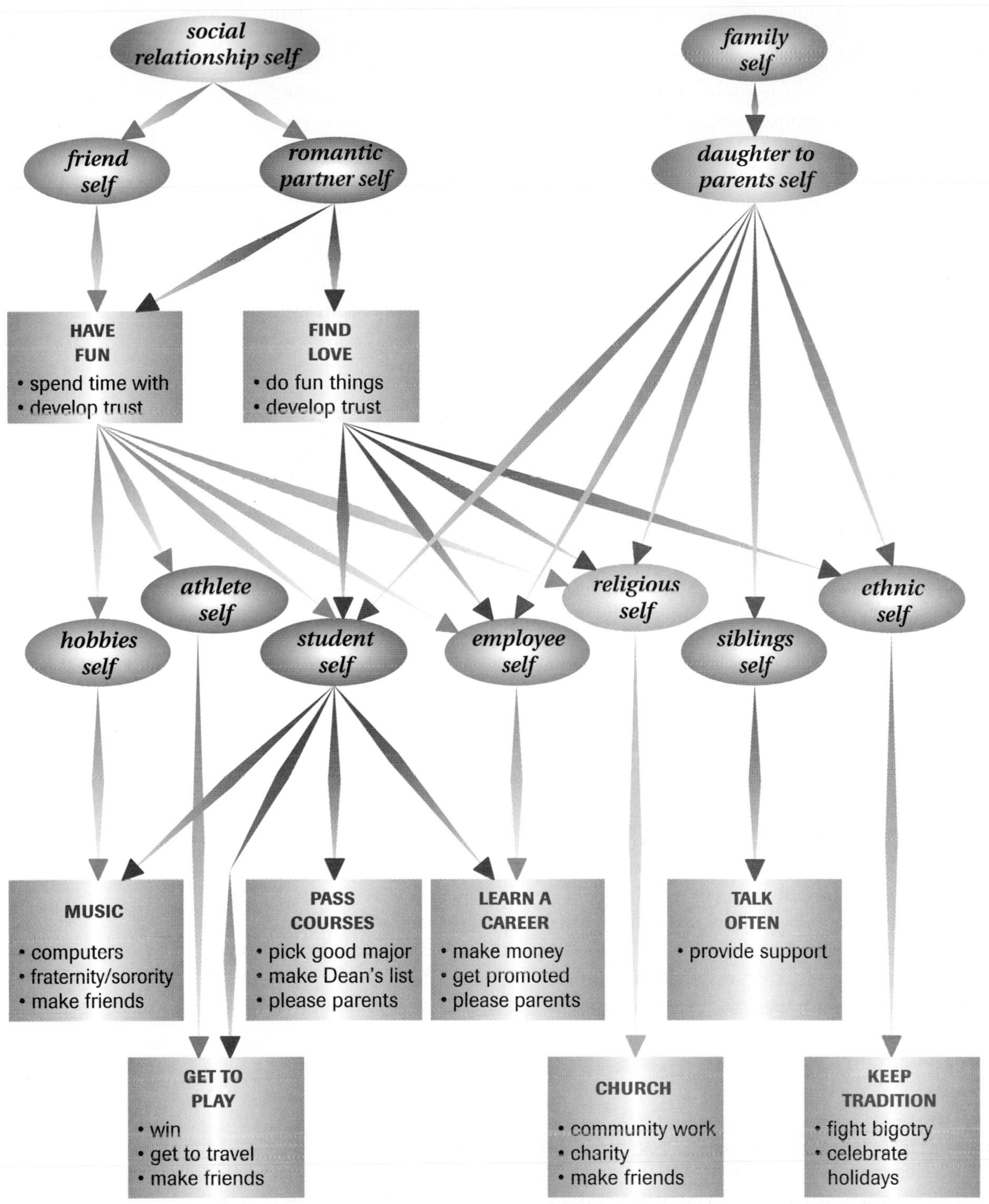

faithful and another less faithful. Getting a good job may make one person more greedy and aggressive and another person more gracious and compassionate. These adaptations can even be specific to particular contexts. Look back at yourself in high school—are you the "same person" you were then? Chances are, you're not. One study found that even victims of childhood sexual abuse sometimes find silver linings from such dark experiences, including a more cautious view of others, greater determination not to repeat the experience with their own children, and a toughened personality (McMillen, Zuravin, & Rideout, 1995). The self often finds ways of adapting to the most severe and varied experiences.

Finally, the postmodern self is socially constructed, which means that how you see and create yourself depends in large part on how others perceive you. Consider the very simple question of how physically attractive you are. Most of us have some idea of our level of physical attractiveness. But where does this idea come from? Is there some objective, universal set of characteristics that defines attractiveness according to a continuum? No. Some characteristics are universally considered more attractive than others (such as a good complexion or facial symmetry); however, how we determine our own attractiveness is based on the communications we receive from our social and cultural worlds. Media depictions of beauty, cultural values as depicted in art and music, and comments and reactions from significant others lead us to develop a sense of our own attractiveness. There is no self-concept of physical attractiveness without others to help define what is and what is not attractive.

The postmodern self is multiple, adaptable, and socially constructed. Through our interactions with many different people and institutions, we find ourselves adapting our "self" to these experiences and to the experiences that others have of us. These interactions provide many opportunities for us to define ourselves as we most want to be seen, but how we want to be seen often varies across time, context, and relationship. Communication, therefore, is not just a situation in which you reveal yourself, but a process in which you co-create yourself with others.

Expressing the Self to Others

Every communication event gives us an opportunity to express ourselves. In doing so, we reveal something about who we are, and who we view ourselves as being. We are generally very selective in what we express about our beliefs, attitudes, and feelings. If we reveal too much, we risk offending others or making ourselves vulnerable. If we reveal too little, others may not know who we are or how to interact with us. Competent interaction involves finding an appropriate and effective balance in how we reveal our many selves to others. The process by which we reveal ourselves to others is self-disclosure.

SELF-DISCLOSURE

Self-Disclosure is the process of intentionally and voluntarily providing others with information about yourself that you believe is honest and accurate and is unlikely to be discovered elsewhere. To be considered self-disclosure, a message must be intentional rather than accidental or unconscious. If Loern is staring at Ann-Chinn while she is talking about her vacations, and responds "What great lips, uh, I mean trips," Ann-Chinn may think he has disclosed something about his thoughts. But if he had no intention, and his comment was purely accidental, then it is not self-disclosure. To be considered self-disclosure, a message must be voluntary. It can hardly be considered self-disclosure if someone is brainwashed, tortured, or coerced to provide information. We come to know someone not only by *what* she or he chooses to tell us, but by the fact that she or he *chooses* to tell us at all. The choice to reveal information is as informative as the information itself. Returning to the opening vignette, the fact that Loern chose to use such blatant bumper stickers is itself a message, not only about these particular environmental attitudes, but about Loern's beliefs regarding freedom of self-expression and perhaps even about the extremity of his opinions in general.

Self-disclosure provides information about the self. If a student sitting next to you tells you she thinks the class is boring, you might consider this information *relevant* to who she is. But is it *about* her? Certainly it reveals information about her attitudes, and this gives you information about her. She may not consider it self-disclosure, but instead may view it as merely expressing an attitude. But attitudes, beliefs, and values make up a significant part of our self-concepts, and disclosing them, in effect, is disclosing who we think we are.

Finally, self-disclosure reveals information that is unlikely to be discovered through other means. If your professor states on the first day of class, "I'm your professor," it is not self-disclosure. Not only did you already know this fact, but your professor knew you knew it. This is similar to when someone tells you a secret you already know—it is no longer a secret. For self-disclosure to occur you must be the sole source of the information being disclosed. You are not "revealing" anything about yourself if you tell someone something he or she already knows. In contrast, if you tell someone something that can only be known because you say it, you have truly opened yourself up to that person.

TYPES OF OPENNESS

The ways in which we open ourselves to others can be understood through a concept known as the **Johari window**. Pronounced as "Joe" plus "Harry," after the first names of the scholars who first developed the ideas, Harry Ingham and Joseph Luft (Luft, 1969), the window is defined by two dimensions: the self-dimension and the other dimension (see Figure 3.3). The self-dimension of openness concerns what is or is not revealed or known to one's own self. The other dimension of openness identifies information about the self that is or is not revealed or known to others. When these dimensions are crossed, they form a window with four areas, called the open, blind, hidden, and unknown self. The **open self** is what is known to the self and to others, the part of you that you are aware of and show to people around you. Your hobbies, your major, your career objectives, whether or not you are married, and the like, are often very open. The **blind self** consists of those aspects of yourself that others know but you don't know yourself. You may not be aware that you come across as overly aggressive or critical, but others know this. The **hidden self** is known to the self but not to others. This area represents those aspects of yourself that you intentionally keep to yourself. Perhaps you did something cruel to a person or animal when you were young that you choose not to reveal to others. Finally, the **unknown self** is the part of you that neither you nor those around you know. You might be terrified of being deep underwater in scuba equipment, but if you have not had the experience, you might not be aware of this reaction. You may want children, but may not realize it at this point in your life because the idea may simply not be very relevant. However, once you experience something in the unknown self, it moves to the hidden self or the open self.

	KNOWN TO SELF	UNKNOWN TO SELF
KNOWN TO OTHERS	*the open self*	*the blind self*
UNKNOWN TO OTHERS	*the hidden self*	*the unknown self*

FIGURE 3.3
The Johari Window

The Johari window illustrates that by revealing different degrees of who we are to ourselves and to others, we constantly create different versions of ourselves.

People vary considerably in their self-disclosure. Some people disclose very little, regardless of the person with whom they are communicating. Others seem to disclose almost everything. In the Test Your Self-Disclosure, you can assess your level of self-disclosure. Take a moment and complete the self-test before continuing.

An important part of any communication situation is to determine the appropriate type of disclosure for the situation. Not only does this depend on how open or private you are as a person, but it also depends on the characteristics of the disclosure itself.

DIMENSIONS OF SELF-DISCLOSURE

Information about the self is not simply "there" or "not there" in a message. The process of self-disclosure is more like a faucet than a light switch. With the typical light switch, the light is either on or off. But with a faucet, we can vary temperature, pressure, direction, amount, and so forth. So it is with self-disclosure. There are several dimensions along which information about the self varies. In particular, we alter our messages about the self in terms of breadth, depth, valence, reciprocity, and relevance.

The vast number of topics we may choose to disclose about ourselves is referred to as the **breadth** of disclosure. People may disclose about their hobbies, family background, religious beliefs, political beliefs, romantic history, fears, hopes, and so on. Some people like to disclose a lot about some relatively specific aspect of their life, such as their exercise regimen or their current romantic relationship, but choose not to talk about their family or their religion. Others may disclose less about more areas of their lives.

Depth of self-disclosure is the importance and relevance of information to our core sense of self. There is a wide range of information about ourselves, from information that has little or no importance to our self-concept to information that is very central to how we view ourselves. *Whether* or not you want to get married may be a fairly superficial piece of information. Disclosing the *type* of person you want to marry may be more personal and central to your conception of self. At the deepest levels might be types of information such as the *meaning* of marriage in your life, including your image of your parents' marriage, your fears about marriage, and your dreams of happiness in a marital relationship. The deeper the disclosure, the closer the information to your most intimate sense of who you are.

Test your self-disclosure

INSTRUCTIONS: Some of us are very open people. Some of us are very private. Several situations in which you might find yourself communicating are described. The five columns list people with whom you might be communicating in each situation. Using a scale from 0 to 2 where 0 = "I would never disclose something of a private or personal nature," 1 = "I would occasionally disclose something of a private or personal nature," and 2 = "I would usually disclose something of a private or personal nature," rate how you would self-disclose according to each situation and audience.

	AUDIENCE				
SITUATION	BEST FRIEND	RECENT ACQUAINTANCE	ROMANTIC PARTNER	FAMILY MEMBERS	COMPLETE STRANGERS
1. In your dorm or apartment					
2. Over lunch in a restaurant					
3. In a classroom before lecture					
4. In a study group					
5. In a speech to a volunteer group					
6. In a job interview					
7. On a long airplane trip					

Generally, a person who discloses everything to anyone (one who answered almost all 2's here) is viewed with caution and distrust. If this person has no sense of privacy, perhaps he or she also has no sense of secrecy and would tell others anything you reveal of yourself. Additionally we often have a negative image of the person who is always talking about himself or herself. We may not trust such a person because his or her motives seem self-serving.

Although you generally don't disclose everything to anyone (if you scored all 1's here), consider a phenomenon known as the "stranger on the plane." On a plane, train, or bus, you don't expect to see the person sitting next to you again, and so you may feel little risk in disclosing personal information. However, in most situations, if you think you may encounter a person again, you are concerned with what he or she might think of you or do with the information you disclose.

In contrast, people who never disclose (a person who scored almost all 0's here) are often viewed with distrust, but for another reason. Trust implies that we know what a person will do. If a person doesn't disclose anything to us, we may find it difficult to know this person, and thus, difficult to trust.

One way of thinking of the breadth and depth dimensions is to think of your self as a planet (see Figure 3.4). A planet is made up of many different substances, such as water, rock, and plants, and yet large areas are made up mostly of one type of substance. In addition, there are many layers, or strata, by which these substances are distributed. You can dig a narrow but deep mine for some of those substances, or you can sow seeds on a vast area of the surface. Similarly, you can dig deeply into your core selves and reveal this information to others, or instead you may choose to disclose only the topics lying close to the surface.

When choosing to disclose information on a first date, most people are very selective in the depth of their disclosure. As you saw in the Test Your Self-Disclosure box, disclosing too much information can make others suspicious, and even more so when they know little else about you.

But controlling the depth of disclosure is only one way in which we are selective about disclosing information on a first date. Another way is by controlling the positive or negative

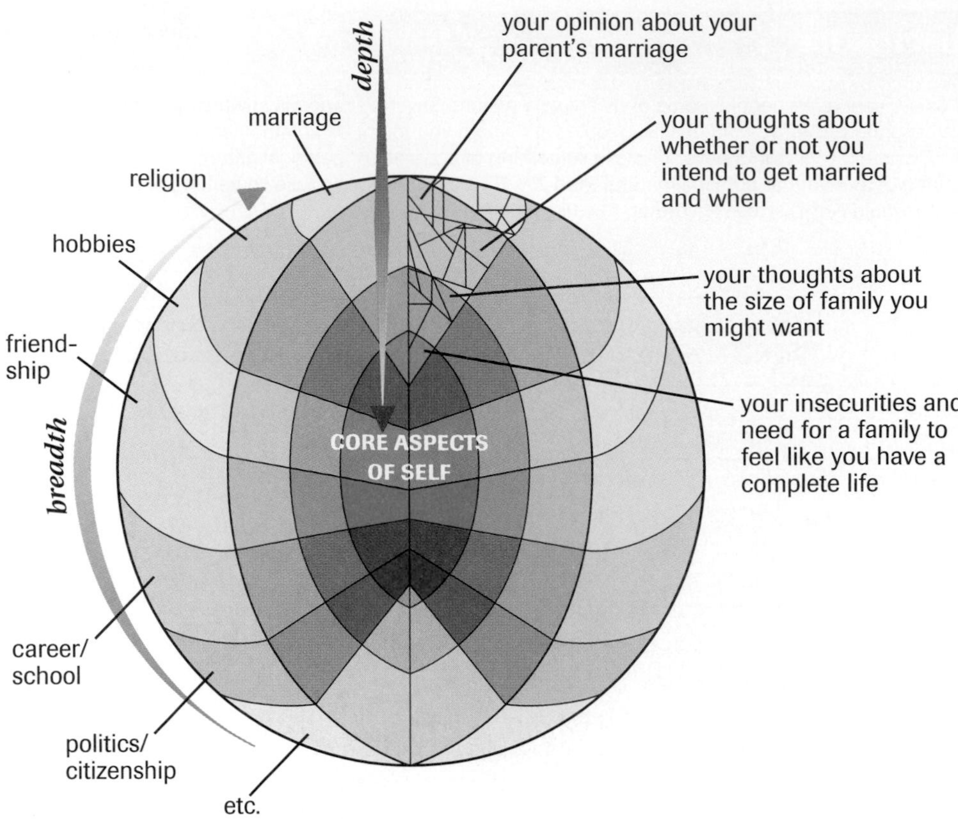

FIGURE 3.4
The Planetary Self

Like a planet, there are many different substances and layers to the self. The vast number of topics shown on the surface represent the breadth of disclosure possible. Moving from the surface toward the core aspects of the self in any one topic represents the depth of disclosure.

implications of the information disclosed. **Valence** is the extent to which a message has good or bad implications for the sender, in this case, the person disclosing the information. Valence is derived from the same root as the word *value,* and thus represents whether a disclosure casts the disclosing person in a positive or negative light. Disclosing that you were class valedictorian has a positive valence, and disclosing that you were once arrested for driving under the influence of alcohol has a negative valence. People tend to view negatively valenced disclosures as significant clues to who a person is, partly because they don't expect people to disclose negative information. Because people generally want to be viewed as attractive, they tend to disclose much more positively valenced information than negatively valenced information. Thus when negative information is disclosed, it tends to carry more weight in our impressions of others.

Returning to this first date, another selective aspect of the disclosure is **reciprocity**, the degree to which the communicators match each other's levels of disclosure. In early stages of relationships, whether among friends, romantic partners, or colleagues, disclosure tends to be highly reciprocal. People tend to disclose at similar rates and similar levels of breadth and depth as others disclose to them. This helps regulate the appropriate unfolding of interpersonal knowledge and understanding. Indeed, research shows that we use the norm of reciprocity when we meet people. If we want to get to know someone better, we can ask this person direct questions, or we can disclose something about ourselves. If this person follows the norm of reciprocity, she or he will soon disclose similar types of information. In contrast, if we experienced the stranger on the plane phenomenon all the time, we would feel constantly out of balance with others. If you disclose your life's story to your first date, but your date discloses virtually nothing to you, you are likely to feel the relationship is lopsided. You may feel you didn't get a good deal because you took risks and engaged in trusting behavior while your date didn't.

Finally, self-disclosure varies in how closely related the information disclosed is to the topic being discussed, or its **relevance**. If during your first date you have just finished talking about your hobbies and your date starts disclosing his or her most embarrassing moment in high school, it would probably seem like an overly abrupt shift of topics. Likewise, in the midst of your study group discussing their attitudes toward the professor, it would seem out of place if you disclose a significant family problem. As you can see from both these examples, relevance is an important feature of disclosure competence. Not only do irrelevant disclosures knock the conversation off track, but you may appear as though you aren't listening or simply aren't sensitive to the other person's concerns.

The dimensions of self-disclosure reveal that letting others get to know us is very complex. Without any self-disclosure, other people are likely to know us primarily through their prototypes of "people like us." Even so, self-disclosure represents a relatively small proportion of our total daily communication with others (Duck, 1994). However, its significance is not in the frequency with which we disclose, but in the depth, breadth, valence, reciprocity, and relevance of our disclosures when we actually *do* choose to self-disclose. One primary way others come to know us and develop relationships with us is through the process of self-disclosure. The more competently we disclose, the more comfortable people will be opening up to us, and the more satisfying the progress of the ongoing interaction is likely to be. In short, the better we are at letting others understand us, the better we become at understanding others and ourselves.

Challenges to Perception & Self

In an old *Peanuts* cartoon, Lucy asks Linus what he wants to be when he grows up. Linus simply replies, "Outrageously happy." Ultimately, people want to live lives that are meaningful and bring them joy. The challenge to creating meaningful lives depends, in part, on how we perceive others and express the the self to others. In the impressions other people and events make on us and the ways in which we disclose information about ourselves, we are confronted with numerous choices about how we can perceive and respond to people and situations. Three choices can be particularly challenging: (1) how to manage the multiplicity of perceptions and disclosures, (2) how to develop complete and more accurate perceptions, and (3) how to change the self for the positive.

Because perceptions are relative, one of the key challenges for people is determining which perception is most important at a particular moment. For example, when meeting a person for the first time, is it most useful to perceive the person as a potential date, business partner, or friend? Similarly, what information is useful to disclose to this person? You could potentially disclose a great variety of information ranging from the more superficial such as your occupation or level of education to more personal such as political and religious beliefs. Determining the breadth and depth of information to disclose is a significant challenge because it will depend on the person you are talking to and the situation. As you saw, what and how much you disclose will affect your competence.

The second challenge revolves around developing rich and detailed perceptions. People have a tendency to form judgments that are not only based on limited information, but also reflect certain biases. A number of potential biasing factors can influence your ability to form perceptions. For example, the fundamental attribution error suggests that we tend to attribute our success to external factors and we attribute others' success or failure to internal factors. One of the key challenges is to guard against such biases in order to form rich, detailed, and accurate perceptions.

Third, how do we manage to develop our self? As the theory of the postmodern self suggests, the self is adaptable—it can change and grow. In what direction do we wish to grow and develop? Given our opportunity to choose how to develop, the challenge becomes determining the best strategy for developing the self. As mentioned earlier, significant others play an important role in the development of the self. Yet it is important also to be proactive in developing the self and not let others dictate who we are to become. One of the challenges is to develop a strategy that allows us to make choices about how we would like to develop and structuring ways to achieve these goals.

Three possible strategies can help you manage these challenges: (1) using multiple perspectives to create descriptions, (2) anticipating the consequences of perceptions and disclosures, and (3) envisioning the future.

Knowledge Link

What are the main challenges to perception?

USING MULTIPLE PERSPECTIVES TO CREATE DESCRIPTIONS

Given our unique life experiences, each one of us may look at people and situations and notice different things. As a result, when we form impressions, we tend to have certain prejudices that shape how we perceive people and events. One way to develop a richly detailed perception of a person or situation is to challenge preexisting prejudices and view a person or an event from a variety of different perspectives.

There are many strategies for seeing a person or an event from multiple perspectives. First, slow down the perception process, suspend your judgment, and explore other ways to interpret the person's actions or the event. This may mean delaying or suspending a judgment until later. This also means that you suspend the assumptions, biases, and prejudices you typically use to make judgments and explore whether they are valid.

One way to explore the process you use to form an impression is by asking a variation of the simple question "Why?" (Senge, Kleiner, Roberts, Ross, & Smith, 1994). If you ask this question five times prior to forming an impression, you can begin to unpack the reasoning and assumptions you used to make this inference. Consider the following example:

I perceive this person as lazy.	Why?
Because he or she didn't turn in his or her assignment on time.	Why?
Because he or she doesn't know how to manage his or her time well.	Why?
No one probably has told him or her how to manage his or her time well.	Why?
Because the high school he or she attended probably didn't assign homework.	Why?

As you can see, asking the question "Why?" helps develop an understanding of the assumptions used to make inferences. In this instance, the professor associates turning in an assignment late with a lack of time management skills, and infers that these skills have not been developed because the student was not assigned homework in previous educational experiences. Having explored this chain of reasoning, the professor might approach the student differently by asking, "What led you to turn in the assignment late?"

Another way to slow down the perception process is to use multiple perspectives for viewing people and events that involve stepping outside your frame of reference and exploring your perceptions of people and events from different vantage points. This strategy can help you gain insights that you otherwise might not have been able to access. For example, the professor might explore how the tardy assignment situation feels from the student's standpoint. The professor might imagine how other colleagues as well as other students might view this situation. As you saw in earlier this chapter, this ability to take other people's perspectives and see the situation through their eyes is called role taking.

One way to create useful impressions of a person is to challenge any preexisting prejudices we may hold. What are some prejudices the professor may hold concerning late assignments? How might the professor try to put himself in the student's place to challenge existing assumptions?

ANTICIPATE CONSEQUENCES

The potential short- and long-term consequences of your perceptions and self-disclosures are important to assess. Consider a person in a romantic relationship. Suppose he or she has a history of infidelity and feels that in order for the present relationship to work, he or she "must come clean and be honest" with his or her new partner. Should this person disclose information about his or her relational history? To answer this question, the person would need to consider the short-term consequences of this disclosure. He or she might attempt to answer the following questions: "Is my relational partner ready for this type of disclosure? What will my relational partner do with this information? Will my partner break off the relationship or let it continue?" The person should also consider the long-term consequences of this disclosure: "Will this disclosure strengthen our relationship over time? By being open and honest, can we build a trusting relationship, or will the disclosure make me untrustworthy in the eyes of my partner?" Many times there are no clear-cut answers to these types of questions. However, by thinking through the consequences of the disclosure, you can gain a better sense of whether it will help or hurt the development of positive relationships.

ENVISION THE FUTURE

Achieving personal growth involves making choices about the kind of person you want to become. As you assess your behaviors, attitudes, and values, you may realize that you are acting in ways that aren't as effective or appropriate as possible. How can you best change your behaviors, attitudes, and values? Two strategies are useful for changing the self.

First, focus on what you have done well in the past as well as on what you are currently doing well. By appreciating what you do well, you can draw on your capacity to appreciate positive possibilities by selectively focusing on your past and current strengths and assets (Barrett, 1994, p. 40). By focusing on your successes instead of your problems, you can more quickly accomplish the results you desire. For example, baseball players like Mark McGuire or Sammy Sosa are able to ignore hostile crowds, the heat of summer, and the difficulty of hitting at night. By doing so, they are able to focus their energy on accomplishing the task—hitting the baseball. Similarly, when people are depressed or anxious about their communication ability, they can lessen these feelings by focusing on situations where they have succeeded in not being depressed and anxious..

A second strategy for changing the self is to set reasonable goals for change. If you make small changes in your behavior, these changes accumulate over time and yield bigger results (Wheatley, 1994). For example, say that you want to become friendlier and perceived as more sociable by others. To accomplish this you might set a goal of greeting everyone with a smile. Over time, these seemingly insignificant changes in your behavior may result in a positive story about your friendliness among your friends and acquaintances.

To set reasonable goals to help you change the self, consider the following guidelines:

1. Identify small changes that can lead to big results if carried through over time.
2. Specify concrete behaviors that are within your control to perform.
3. Know the contexts in which these behaviors need to be performed.
4. Determine the standards you will use to measure whether you have performed the behaviors well.

The multiple ways to perceive people, events, and situations and numerous choices you can make about how to act in situations present significant challenges to the competent communicator. By exploring the multiple perspectives of people, events, and situations and anticipating the consequences of your actions, you can begin to develop ways of acting that allow you to achieve desirable goals. At the same time, you may feel that you typically act in ways that are counterproductive to your goals. In such instances, envisioning the future may allow you to develop new, more productive lines of action that will facilitate achieving your goals.

Chapter Summary

Perception is a process that involves noticing, organizing, and interpreting data about people, events, activities, and situations. Our ability to notice bits of data is directly influenced by how mindful we are within situations, the kinds of expectations and self-fulfilling prophecies we create for situations, and how we use language. How we organize the data depends on the kinds of cognitive schemas such as prototypes, stereotypes, and scripts we use. When we interpret data and form impressions, we must be aware of the role that our first impressions play in creating perceptions and how we go about making attributions of whether particular behaviors are internally or externally motivated.

Why is understanding perception important? Our interpretations of people, events, activities, and situations influence how we choose to respond in situations and regulate our behavior. Perception is also important to understand because of its relativity—people interpret events differently. Understanding the root causes of perceptual differences can facilitate our understanding of potential miscommunication and conflicts.

One of the major reasons why we have different perceptions of people and events is because our perception is influenced by self-concept and each person's self-concept is unique. As we interact with people and groups that influence our lives—significant and generalized others—we begin to form our personal identity. Traditionally, we have thought of ourselves as having a single or modern self that has a central core identity. However, contemporary thought highlights the notion of a postmodern self—an idea that we have multiple selves and who we become, our identity, changes according to whom we are talking in particular situations.

Our self concept not only influences how we perceive situations but also what information we disclose to others. As the Johari window illustrates, in any situation parts of our self are open to others such as the open and blind self, and parts of our self are not open to others, such as the hidden and unknown self. The degree to which we choose to self-disclose depends on the dimensions of breadth, depth, valence, reciprocity, and relevance.

The primary challenge to perception is that we have different perceptions of situations and that we need to find ways to manage our perceptions to grow and develop personally. Three strategies can foster an ability to grow and develop (1) using multiple perspectives to create descriptions, (2) anticipating consequences, and (3) envisioning the future.

Key Terms

perception
mindfulness
self-fulfilling prophecy
schema
linguistic tyranny
prototypes
stereotypes
allness
script
implicit personality theory
constructs
first impression bias
attribution theory
principle of consistency
principle of distinctiveness
principle of locus
principle of controllability
fundamental attribution error
self-serving bias
power
social self
looking-glass self
significant others
generalized others
significant symbols
role taking
modern self
postmodern self
multiple self
self-disclosure
Johari window
open self
blind self
hidden self
unknown self
breadth
depth
valence
reciprocity
relevance

Building Motivation

See Self-Assessment on page 86.

Building Knowledge

1. What is the role of perception in understanding people and situations? How do you see the relationships among noticing, organizing, and interpreting data about people and events? Does noticing influence how we organize data or vice versa? Do the interpretations we draw about people and events at one time influence what we notice at a later time?
2. What is the role of the other in developing the self? What kind of self, if any, develops when people have limited contact with others?
3. In what kinds of situations are people more likely to become mindful of their surroundings?
4. What is first impression bias? How might a competent communicator guard against first impression bias?
5. Think of a recent argument you had with someone. How might the attribution theory principles of consistency, distinctiveness, locus, and controllability help explain the positions that were taken?
6. Consider the last time your romantic relationship with someone broke up. In what ways did the fundamental attribution error play a role in how you interpreted why the relationship ended?
7. Do you think there is a single self or multiple selves? Why? What influences how you create and present yourself?

Building Skills

Individual Activities

1. How well do you know yourself? Review the following scenarios. Put yourself in each situation described and then answer the following questions.

    Situation A: Your best friend tells you that he or she is having an affair and then asks you not to tell his or her spouse about it, even though you consider yourself a close friend to the spouse as well. What do you do?

Situation B: A friend and classmate asks if you want to study the answers he purchased from someone who stole them for the upcoming examination. How do you answer?

Situation C: Someone you are really attracted to has just asked you out to a social event, but you had already agreed to do something with a friend of the opposite sex that evening. How do you answer?

Situation D: You are purchasing an item that costs $5, for which you gave the cashier a $10 bill. The cashier apparently thought you presented a $20 bill, and you get $10 more back than you should have. Do you call the mistake to the cashier's attention? Why or why not?

Situation E: You have been waiting in line for 35 minutes to get tickets to a hot concert and three people cut in front of you when they see someone they know in line two people ahead of you. What do you do?

Reflect on how easy or difficult it was to respond to the situations. What role did your self-concept play in your responses? What role did others' possible impressions of your behavior play in your responses?

2. Return to the situations in question 1, and predict what a good friend of yours would do. Is it easier to predict your behavior or your friend's? Why? Who looks better in their responses to the situations, yourself or your friend? Review the implicit personality theory and fundamental attribution error principle covered in this chapter. How might they account for your responses to this question?

3. On a blank sheet of paper, describe your best friend. Next, review what you have written to see if there is anything you would add or change. Go through your description very carefully, looking for any "constructs" you have used to describe your friend. Remember, a construct is any dimension along which you understand the concept of "friend." Thus if you described your friend as thin, tall, dark-haired, and attractive, these all represent a single construct of "physical characteristics." Count the number of constructs you use to understand the concept of your best friend. How well do these constructs describe friendship? What constructs might you include if you wanted to describe friendship more completely? How might a simpler or smaller set of constructs result in different behavior with your friend than a more complex or larger set of constructs?

4. Using *InfoTrac College Edition*, look up articles that have appeared within the last five years with the word *personal identity* in the title. Using the titles and abstracts as guides, make a list of those factors that influence people's personal identity.

5. Briefly describe your most prominent impressions of yourself using each of the following areas:

   Personality
   Physical characteristics
   Morality
   Activities/hobbies
   Career (or career objectives)
   Intelligence

   Select a parent (or parent figure), best friend, (present or former) romantic partner, professor, and the student sitting next to you in some class. Ask these people to answer the same question about yourself (e.g., "How would you describe my key or most prominent characteristic in terms of the following concepts?"). To what extent did these people mention the same things? To what do you attribute their similarities or differences to each other's and to your own answers?

Group Activities

1. Pair off with another person. Each person in your dyad should write down a common emotion or adjective on each of five separate note cards, such as happy, sad, boring, angry, intelligent, and so on. Collect the ten cards and shuffle them. Each person should select a card without revealing the card to the other person. Have a conversation with each person acting in ways that are consistent with the emotion or adjective provided on the card. After the conversation, each person should guess the emotion or adjective the other person is acting out. After guessing, reveal the emotions that were being performed. Discuss what cues were used to make judgments about the emotions performed. How accurate were the guesses? Discuss what principles of perception may have influenced your abilities to assess each other's emotion.

2. Form a group of 4–5 people. Each group member should write a brief personal advertisement describing themselves to prospective dates and then share the personal advertisement with the group. Each person should answer the following questions: "Why did you decide to feature certain aspects of yourself and not others?" "How did the 'other' in the form of the prospective date influence how you wrote the advertisement?" Compare each group member's answers.

3. Form a group of 4–5 people and locate the Web site for Kids in Crisis (**http://www.geocities.com/Heartland/Bluffs/5400/**) that focuses on challenges children and teenagers face in daily living. As you examine the Web site, list all the challenges that youth face as they are developing their personal identity. What challenges do you perceive as significant that are not included on the Web site? Why are these challenges significant? What suggestions does the Web site offer for developing a healthy self-concept?

References

Abelson, R. (1976). Script processing in attitude formation and decision-making. In J. S. Carroll & J. N. Payne (Eds.), *Cognition and social behavior* (pp. 33–45). Hillsdale, NJ: Erlbaum.

Barrett, F. J. (1994). Creating appreciative learning cultures. *Organizational Dynamics, 23,* 36–39.

Burgoon, J. K., Stern, L. A., & Dillman, L. (1995). *Interpersonal adaptation: Dyadic interaction patterns.* Cambridge: Cambridge University Press.

Canary, D. J., & Hause, K. S. (1993). Is there any reason to research sex differences in communication? *Communication Quarterly, 41,* 129–144.

Cooley, C. H. (1922). *Human nature and the social order* (rev. ed.). New York: Charles Scribner's Sons.

Cronen, V., & Lang, P. (1994). Language and action: Wittgenstein and Dewey in the practice of therapy and consultation. *Human Systems, 5,* 5–43.

Duck, S. (1994). *Meaningful relationships: Talking, sense, and relating.* Thousand Oaks, CA: Sage.

Gergen, K. K. (1991). *The saturated self: Dilemmas of identity in contemporary life.* New York: Basic Books.

Jones, E. E., & Nisbett, R. E. (1971). The actor and the observer: Divergent perceptions of the causes of behavior. In E. E. Jones & R. E. Nisbett (Eds.), *Attribution: Perceiving the causes of behavior* (pp. 70–94). Morristown, NJ: General Learning Press.

Langer, E. J. (1978). Rethinking the role of thought in social interaction. In J. H. Harvey, W. J. Ickes, & R. F. Kidd (Eds.), *New directions in attribution research* (Vol. 2, pp. 35–58). New York: Wiley.

Luft, J. (1969). *Of human interaction.* Palo Alto, CA: National Press Books.

McMillen, C., Zuravin, S., & Rideout, G. (1995). Perceived benefit from child sexual abuse. *Journal of Consulting and Clinical Psychology, 63,* 1037–1043.

Mead, G. H. (1934). *Mind, self, and society.* Chicago: University of Chicago Press.

Morgan, G. (1995). *Imaginization.* Thousand Oaks, CA: Sage.

Nisbett, R., & Ross, L. (1980). *Human inference: Strategies and shortcomings of social judgment.* Englewood Cliffs, NJ: Prentice-Hall.

Pavitt, C., & Haight, L. (1985). The "competent communicator" as a cognitive prototype. *Human Communication Research, 12,* 225–241.

Pearce, W. B. (1994). *Interpersonal communication: Making social worlds.* New York: HarperCollins.

Pearce, W. B., & Littlejohn, S. W. (1996). *Moral conflict: When social worlds collide.* Thousand Oaks, CA: Sage.

Rosenberg, S., & Gara, M. A. (1985). The multiplicity of personal identity. In P. Shaver (Ed.), *Self, situations, and social behavior* (pp. 87–114). Beverly Hills, CA: Sage.

Seibold, D. R., & Spitzberg, B. H. (1982). Attribution theory and research: Review and implications for communication. In B. Dervin & M. J. Voight (Eds.), *Progress in communication sciences* (Vol. 3, pp. 85–126). Norwood, NJ: Ablex.

Senge, P. M., Kleiner, A., Roberts, C., Ross, R. B., & Smith, B. J. (1994). *The fifth discipline fieldbook.* New York: Currency Doubleday.

Snyder, M., & Gangestad, S. (1981). Hypothesis-testing processes. In J. H. Harvey, W. Ickes, & R. F. Kidd (Eds.), *New directions in attribution research* (Vol. 3, pp. 171–196). Hillsdale, NJ: Erlbaum.

Spitzberg, B. H. (in press). The status of attribution theory *qua* theory in personal relationships. In V. Manusov & J. H. Harvey (Eds.), *Attribution, communication behavior, and close relationships.* Cambridge: Cambridge University Press.

Wegner, D. M., & Vallacher, R. R. (1977). *Implicit psychology: An introduction to social cognition.* New York: Oxford University Press.

Wegner, D. M., & Vallacher, R. R. (Eds.). (1980). *The self in social psychology.* New York: Oxford University Press.

Weick, K. (1978). The spines of leaders. In M.W. McCall, Jr., & M. M. Lombardo (Eds.), *Leadership: Where else can we go?* (pp. 37–61). Durham, NC: Duke University Press.

Wheatley, M. J. (1994). *Leadership and the new science.* San Francisco: Berrett-Koehler.

Zurcher, L. A., Jr. (1977). *The mutable self: A self-concept for social change.* Beverly Hills, CA: Sage.

Building Motivation

Self-Assessment: Indicate the degree to which you agree or disagree with the following statements, using the following scale.

Scale		
0 = Disagree (*D*)	**1** = Neutral (*N*); neither agree nor disagree	**2** = Agree (*A*)

BELIEFS ABOUT SELF

D	*N*	*A*	
0	1	2	**1.** I must be loved by others in order to like myself.
0	1	2	**2.** If I am anything less than perfect, I am not worthwhile.
0	1	2	**3.** If I do something wrong, I deserve the blame for it, regardless of why.
0	1	2	**4.** I have no control over my happiness or unhappiness.
0	1	2	**5.** I worry about how things might go wrong.
0	1	2	**6.** I prefer to avoid difficult situations rather than face them.
0	1	2	**7.** I prefer to find someone stronger than myself to rely on.
0	1	2	**8.** My present is entirely a product of my past.
0	1	2	**9.** For all communication problems there is a single correct or best solution.
0	1	2	**10.** If I think I might make a mistake, I choose not to do something.
			TOTAL SCORE:

BELIEFS ABOUT OTHERS

D	*N*	*A*	
0	1	2	**11.** I often worry about what others will think of me.
0	1	2	**12.** I think others are watching me to find fault with me.
0	1	2	**13.** When others criticize me I feel terrible for a long time afterward.
0	1	2	**14.** I am nervous when I have to perform a complicated task in front of others.
0	1	2	**15.** When in a group situation, I focus on how the other members view me.
0	1	2	**16.** I am constantly thinking about what kind of impression I am making.
0	1	2	**17.** I would be more outgoing if I weren't so worried about what others think of me.
0	1	2	**18.** Even when I know they can't make a difference, I am anxious about others' opinions of me.
0	1	2	**19.** Other people's impressions of me make more of a difference than my own impression of myself.

D	N	A	
0	1	2	**20.** When in social situations, I can't help but wonder what others are thinking of me.

TOTAL SCORE:

FEELINGS

D	N	A	
0	1	2	**21.** I get nervous in a new social situation.
0	1	2	**22.** I am anxious when meeting new people.
0	1	2	**23.** I worry about making a fool out of myself when I have to speak in public.
0	1	2	**24.** I am nervous in group situations.
0	1	2	**25.** I can't seem to relax when I have to make a good impression on others.
0	1	2	**26.** I lack confidence in public speaking situations.
0	1	2	**27.** I am generally afraid to speak up in group meetings.
0	1	2	**28.** I get tense when I'm about to introduce myself to someone.
0	1	2	**29.** I can't stop shaking when I communicate in public.
0	1	2	**30.** I am nervous when conversing with someone for the first time.

TOTAL SCORE:

Interpreting Your Scores: The statements here are divided into sections—"Beliefs About Self," "Beliefs About Others," and "Feelings." Total the scores for each section.

"Beliefs About Self" refer to beliefs you may have that create unrealistic expectations for yourself. The more irrational beliefs you have about yourself, the more difficult it is for you to develop a competent self in interacting and communicating with others. The score for this section ranges between 0 and 20. A score of 15 or greater indicates that you agree with half or more of these beliefs, and you should examine the reason you perceive yourself and the situations you face in these ways.

The "Beliefs About Others" score reflects the extent to which you fear others' opinions and attitudes. The more concerned you are about others' evaluations, the more anxious you will be and the less competence and confidence you will be able to display in interactions with others. The score for this section varies between 0 and 20 and any score of 15 or greater indicates that you are overly concerned with what others think. If you have scored above 15, reexamine why your opinion of yourself depends so much on others' opinions.

Finally, the "Feelings" section measures your anxiety level in communication situations. To the extent that you score 15 or greater, you perceive communication situations as threatening. If so, pay close attention to the motivation chapters throughout this textbook, and perhaps talk to your instructor to see if there are classes in the curriculum devoted to students with communication anxiety.

CHAPTER 4

Learning Objectives

After studying this chapter, you should be able to:

1. Define language and describe its rule-guided and symbolic nature.
2. Discuss the roles of constitutive and regulative rules in the construction of language.
3. Explain the arbitrary nature of symbols and the role that signifiers and signifieds play in understanding the meaning of symbols.
4. Outline the functions that language plays in people's ability to notice things, in limiting and liberating actions, and in the ability to coordinate actions.
5. Demonstrate how the Ladder of Abstraction influences language choice.
6. Describe how language communities are created and sustained.
7. Explain how clarification, showing, and comparison questions can help in the understanding of others' language.
8. Describe how understanding the context in which people are speaking can help anticipate how language will be interpreted.
9. Discuss the major challenges to language and the strategies for overcoming those challenges.
10. Demonstrate how indexing and the use of I- and we-messages can help others understand your language.

Language

Ernesto is enrolled in an introductory communication course. That semester, all students in the university are given email accounts and the communication professor decides to take advantage of this new resource to teach the course. Prior to each class, he will email a discussion question to all the students and have them email their answers back to him. The professor thinks this will help guide the students' reading and prepare them to participate productively in the in-class discussion.

On Monday evening, Ernesto downloads the following message when he opens up his mailbox:

> Date: 2 October 00 09:12:18 AM
> From: Professor Bateux <bateau@univ.edu>
> Subj: ASSIGNMENT FOR OCTOBER 9, 2000
> To: Comm 101<comm101@univ.edu>
>
> The reading for next Monday is on language. Please consider the following question for our class discussion next Monday: How can language marginalize certain groups of people and perpetuate their minority status?
>
> I need your responses by Thursday night no later than 9 p.m. Because I want your original thoughts on this question, please do not consult with your classmates to write your responses. You will have the opportunity to discuss this in class next week. Please do not ask me for help on this question until class time on Monday.

Ernesto scratches his head and asks himself, "What in the world is Professor Bateux asking for?" To help sort out the question, he decides to call one of his classmates, Sylvia, for some assistance.

"Sylvia? Hi, this is Ernesto. Did you get the discussion question from Professor Bateux for our communication class next week?"

"Yeah, I did. It looks pretty easy. I just finished my response a few minutes ago."

"Easy? I didn't see it that way. Why don't you tell me what you wrote about?"

"Sure, Ernesto. What I basically said is that sometimes minority groups like African Americans, Hispanics, and gays and lesbians develop their own jargon and use it to talk among themselves. Because they are the only ones who use the language, they set themselves up as different and exclude others from participating in their discussion. I mean, if you don't know the slang, how can you talk with them?"

"So you think when the professor uses the term *minority* he means a minority like an ethnic group?"

"Of course. Isn't it obvious?"

"Well, I don't know, Sylvia. In my psychology class we talked about something called 'minority opinion.' That's when a small number of people in a large group have opinions different from the majority of the group. I think Professor Bateux wants us to talk about how people who are in the minority according to their opinions use language—not ethnic minorities."

"Well then, why did you call me if you already knew the answer? Go ahead and send that one in—but I can already tell you that it's wrong!"

Ernesto decides to email his answer to Professor Bateux. In the next class, he and Sylvia sit together, anxious to find out who's right. Professor Bateux walks into the classroom, organizes his materials on the podium, and opens the lecture by saying, "I was very intrigued by all your responses to the question. What really pleased me was how each of you picked up on the notion that there are multiple meanings for the term *minority.* So let's start there and discuss how you all used the term *minority.*" Ernesto and Sylvia looked at each other in confusion. Why wasn't the professor going to give them the correct definition and meaning of the word *minority?* •••

Perhaps you have experienced situations in conversation with someone when you didn't really understand what that person was saying, and asked, "Could you say that again? I'm not sure what you mean." or "Could you rephrase that? I didn't quite catch what you said." You felt the need to ask such questions because you didn't know what specific words meant, and thus you didn't know how to respond. In the vignette, Ernesto called Sylvia because he was unclear about the meaning of the word *minority.* He recognized that the word could have multiple meanings ranging from ethnic minorities to minority opinions. Until Ernesto could grasp what the word *minority* meant to him as well as what it meant to Professor Bateux, he was unable to formulate a response to the professor's question. Our ability to make sense of the meaning of words is critical to our ability to participate in conversations with others. Without an understanding of words' meanings, no coherent and coordinated conversation is possible.

However, making sense of someone else's words can be difficult because of the complexity of language. Words mean different things to different people and they mean different things in different situations. For Sylvia, the word *minority* referred to a minority status based on ethnicity, religion, or sexual orientation. For Ernesto, the word *minority* referred to a small group of people with a set of opinions different from those of the majority group. Both meanings are entirely appropriate depending on the context. When talking about race relations within the United States, the word *minority* may take on the meaning associated with race, ethnicity, or religion. When talking about decision making in organizational work teams, the word *minority* may be more closely associated with a difference of opinion. The meaning of words and language is fluid and changes depending on the situation.

This chapter focuses on the complex nature of language and the challenges it presents. Competent communicators recognize that words take on different meanings depending on how they are used in specific contexts, as well as who utters them. Competent communicators have an ability to make sense of words in ongoing conversations that occur at specific times and in particular places. They spot the unique meaning of a word as it is being used in a particular situation, and in light of that meaning, they determine the most appropriate and effective language choices.

What Is Language?

One of the challenges we face as human beings is choosing what to say and how to say it when asked for our opinion. This challenge is particularly difficult when we feel that expressing our true thoughts and opinions may hurt other people's feelings. For example, when a couple has just brought their new baby home from the hospital, they typically want to show off their pride and joy. Although you may like to believe the myth that all children are beautiful and precious in their own right, in reality some babies are not overly attractive! The dilemma you face is what to do when the enthusiastic parents present their "unattractive" child and ask you what you think. Do you say what you really think ("That is an ugly child!") or do you lie ("What a beautiful child!")? A creative solution to such a situation is to say enthusiastically, "Now that's a baby!" The proud parents usually happily agree.

This example highlights the kinds of linguistic choices we make when interacting with other people. Language can be used both to reveal and to disguise our feelings. Language can be used to clarify or to hide our thoughts and feelings. The phrase, "Now that's a baby!" is sufficiently ambiguous that the parents can draw their own conclusions. In fact, people who use phrases like this are counting on the complexity and ambiguity of language to manage the situation.

If language is complex and can be used to mask as well as reveal our thoughts and opinions, how do people know what particular words or phrases mean in conversation and what to do with them? To answer this question, we need to understand more about the nature of language. As you saw in Chapter 1, **language** is a rule-guided system of symbols that allows us to take messages and utterances, in the form of words, and translate them into meaning.

LANGUAGE IS GUIDED BY RULES

The idea of language as a rule-guided activity can explain how we determine what something means and what we should say in response. People use rules to help sort out what certain words or phrases mean, as well as to determine what they should say next in an ongoing conversation. The former kind of rules may be called constitutive and the latter regulative (Cronen, [illegible])

Constitutive rules help us understand what certain words or phrases "count as" or mean. Constitutive rules take the basic content of the message, its words, and tell us what they mean and how we are to make sense of them. Consider, for example, the following words and phrases. What do they have in common?

"Hi!"	"What's happening?"
"How are you doing?"	"Haven't seen you in a while."
"Hello!"	"It's good to see you!"

You probably have heard these different words and phrases millions of times and interpret these words and phrases as greetings uttered by one person when he or she encounters others. Whether consciously or unconsciously, you apply constitutive rules to words and phrases to determine their meaning and function in conversation.

Once you have applied constitutive rules to interpret another person's words and phrases, **regulative rules** help you determine the appropriate response. Regulative rules usually take the form, "If X happens, then Y follows." These rules are based on the assumption that language has a moral force and creates feelings of obligation. Your interpretation of what particular words and phrases mean influences the kind of response you are obligated, permitted, or prohibited from performing. What is your response when someone comes up to you in the hallway extending his or her hand and says, "Hello"? You more than likely interpret this message as a greeting. As a result, you feel strongly obligated to respond with some type of greeting. The way this person has used language creates a sense of obligation—you must respond in kind. At the same time, a wide range of possible responses is available. You might return the greeting with a robust "Hello!" or say "Hi!" or "It's good to see you." You may also be prohibited from saying certain things. For example, when someone greets you by asking "How are you doing?" you are prohibited from insulting him or her: "Listen you idiot, I don't have to tell you!" or challenging him or her: "What's it to you? You don't really care." Regulative rules are moral in the sense that they tell you what you should or shouldn't do during an interaction. They create opportunities for action—what we can do—as well as constraints for our actions—what we can't do.

Knowledge Link

What is the difference between constitutive and regulative rules?

To understand language you need to understand how regulative and constitutive rules work together. Figure 4.1 shows how constitutive and regulative rules help us understand how we use language when we greet one another. Constitutive rules take the string of words "How are you doing?" and tell us that these words count as a greeting in the context of a greeting situation. Once we have assigned the meaning "greeting" to the words, in most cases regulative rules obligate us to respond with a greeting in kind that we can phrase in a variety of ways. At the same time, we are prohibited from insulting or ignoring the person after the initial greeting. What language means and how we are to structure our language use can be understood through the use of constitutive and regulative rules. Constitutive rules help us assign meaning to words and phrases; regulative rules help us know how to respond given our interpretation.

LANGUAGE IS A SYSTEM OF SYMBOLS

A **symbol** is a sign or word used to define a person, idea, or object. For example, we use the symbols *male* and *female* to distinguish between the two biological sexes. Symbols like *chair* and *table* distinguish between different types of furniture. We also use symbols to assign qualities to people, ideas, and objects. We use adjectives such as *good* or *bad* when describing ideas, and we use verbs such as *running* and *sleeping* to describe actions.

The symbols we use every day in speech are arbitrary—they are not inherently connected to the things they represent. For example, why does the *American Heritage*

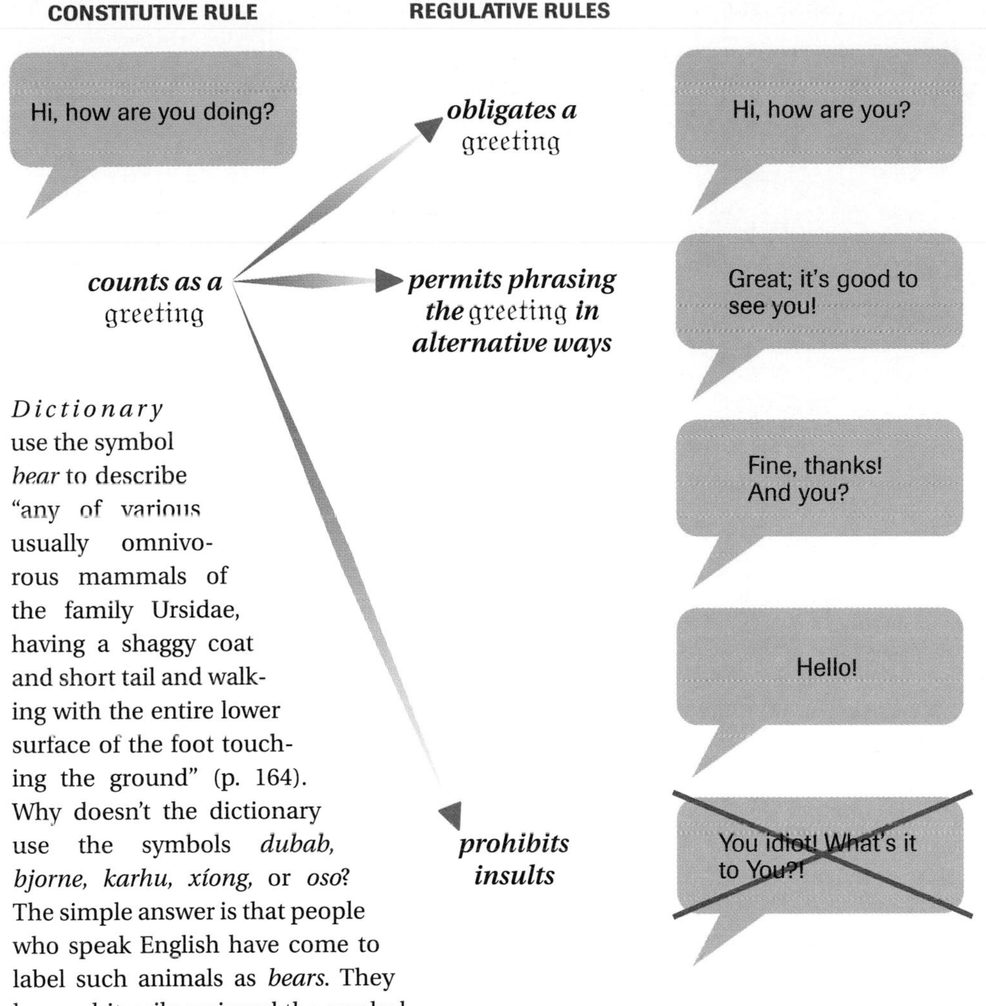

FIGURE 4.1
The Rule-Guided Nature of a Greeting

Constitutive rules help us interpret words and phrases; regulative rules guide our response. In this case, the phrase on the left is interpreted as a greeting and four out of the five responses on the right are judged as acceptable. The last response is inappropriate because the regulative rule prohibits insults.

Dictionary use the symbol *bear* to describe "any of various usually omnivorous mammals of the family Ursidae, having a shaggy coat and short tail and walking with the entire lower surface of the foot touching the ground" (p. 164). Why doesn't the dictionary use the symbols *dubab, bjorne, karhu, xíong,* or *oso*? The simple answer is that people who speak English have come to label such animals as *bears.* They have arbitrarily assigned the symbol *bear* to that animal; just as Arabic speakers call "bears" *dubab,* Danish speakers *bjorne,* Finnish speakers *karhu,* Mandarin Chinese speakers *xíong,* or Spanish speakers *oso.* For English speakers, we have arbitrarily assigned the term *bear* to describe this furry four-legged creature. None of these symbols have anything to do with the animal.

The arbitrary relationship between words and the objects they represent has been called the relationship between a signifier and a signified. A **signifier** is the actual word, or symbol, we associate with an object or phenomena and the **signified** is the object or phenomena itself (Cilliers, 1998; de Saussure, 1974). Returning to our example, in the English language, the word *bear* is a signifier arbitrarily connected to a living being with a shaggy coat, a short tail, a member of the family Ursidae, the signified. Over time, people in a community create a set of agreements that specify the relationship between signifiers, or symbols, and signified, or phenomena. New speakers entering into the community are socialized into that set of agreements. Part of understanding a language, therefore, is grasping the set of arbitrary connections between signifiers and signifieds. Figure 4.2 illustrates just how the relationship between a signifier and a signified is arbitrary. The relationship between the signified object, a four-legged creature belonging to the family Ursidae, and the signifier changes depending on what language is spoken within the community.

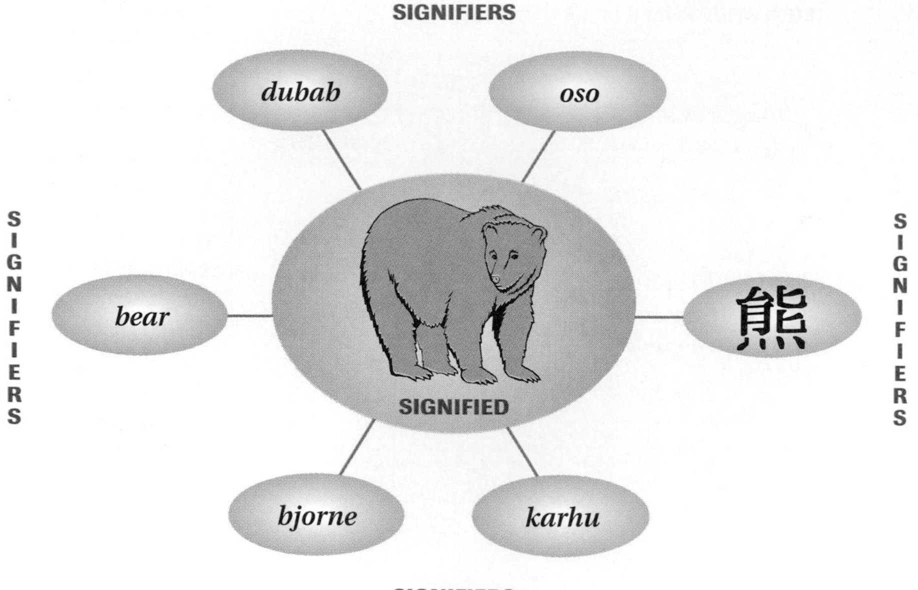

FIGURE 4.2
The Arbitrary Relationship Between Signifiers & the Signified

The words *dubab, bjorne, karhu, oso, xíong*—the Chinese character for bear—are signifiers that signify the animal English speakers call a bear. These words are assigned arbitrarily to represent the animal and are shared by communities that have agreed to use those particular symbols for the animal we call a *bear*.

Is learning a language simply understanding the set of connections among signifiers and signifieds? The answer is "no." To understand what a word means in a language, you need to understand the entire symbol system. A **symbol system** includes the set of relationships among signifiers and the objects they represent, as well as the set of relationships among signifiers. If you are to understand what a signifier means, you also need to look at other signifiers associated with it at a specific time and place (Derrida, 1978). Take, for example, the signifier *bear* in the English language. If we stopped our understanding of the meaning of the word *bear* with the relationship between the signifier and signified, we would only know that the word *bear* is associated with a specific kind of animal. However, much more is associated with the word *bear*—perceptions, feelings, and attitudes. The only way to grasp the various perceptions, feelings, and attitudes associated with *bear* is to explore the other words linked to it. Figure 4.3 illustrates how different signifiers associated with *bear* are interrelated. In the English language, the signifier *bear* has become linked with the words *wild animal* and *ferocious.* At the same time, English speakers associate the word *bear* with the qualities *strong* and *protective* because bears often attack humans and other animals if they perceive them as threatening their cubs. Finally, we may also think of *endangered species* because many types of bears, such as pandas and North American grizzlies are in danger of becoming extinct. In sum, the meaning of the word *bear* is not only revealed by its link to an object or phenomena, the signified, but also through its connections to other signifiers.

Examining the relationships among signifiers is important because even when people within a community agree on the arbitrary relationship between a signifier and a signified, they still may hold different meanings for that signifier because they associate it with other, different signifiers. Returning to the opening vignette, consider the meaning of the word *minority* that Ernesto called into question. For Sylvia, the word *minority* meant a subgroup of people with particular ethnic and cultural characteristics; for Ernesto *minority* meant a subgroup of people who held a common point of view. Both students appear to understand the meaning of *minority* the other is using. However, Ernesto and Sylvia may have differing meanings for these terms even though they agree on the relationship

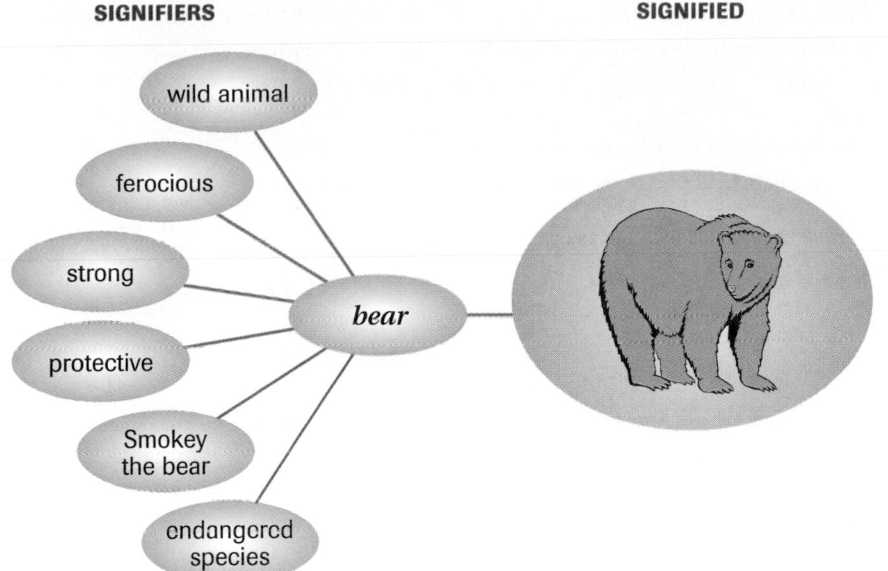

FIGURE 4.3
Relationship Among Signifiers

The words *wild animal, strong, ferocious, protective,* and *endangered species* are signifiers that may be related to the word we use in English to signify the animal we call a bear. The signifier *bear* takes on slightly different meanings when associated with each of the words *wild animal, strong, ferocious, protective,* and *endangered species.*

between the signifier and the signified. For example, Sylvia may associate *minority* with the following words:

minority
Mexican American
injustice
intolerance
oppression

When Sylvia places the word *minority* in relation to the words just listed, *minority* may mean a group of people who are somehow different from the majority of people in a larger community, and this group is treated unfairly and unjustly by the majority based on this difference. Sylvia's notion of *minority* encompasses the problems and frustrations of membership in a "minority group." Yet if Ernesto was asked what words he associated with Sylvia's idea of "minority" as ethnic difference, he might have responded by listing the following words: *pride, diversity, richness,* and *contribution.* Thus Ernesto's meaning for the word *minority* emphasizes the unique contributions that ethnic *minorities* can make to a diverse culture. Understanding a symbol system involves understanding the web of relationships among signifiers and signifieds because even if people agree on the relationship between the signifier and the signified, they may have radically different meanings for that signifier because they associate it with other signifiers.

Why Is Language Important?

Language plays an important role in our lives by helping us create our social worlds and labeling the meanings we ascribe to people, issues, and events. As you saw in Chapter 1, communication is a form of community building—communication creates communities and the ways in which people communicate create different kinds of community. Language plays a key role in defining who we are and how we perceive reality. In the 1950s, Edward Sapir and Benjamin Lee Whorf developed the **Sapir-Whorf hypothesis.** This theory was based on a form of linguistic determinism—language determines what we see in the world and how we think. The word *snow* was used to explain the hypothesis. In some cultures, such as the United States, people use only one word to describe the white fluffy form of condensation that typically falls from the sky in winter temperatures below 32°F, and that word is *snow*. However, other cultures, those with long cold winters, have developed dozens of words to describe types of snow from the heavy wet snow that sticks to trees to the light dry snow that drifts like sand in the wind. Snow skiers who are concerned with the qualities of snow have developed a whole vocabulary around snow such as *powder*, *packed powder*, and *corn* to describe different consistencies of snow. As a result, people in northern cultures with a number of words for snow notice far more differences in the qualities of snow than do people in cultures that use only one word for snow. The words we use influence what we notice about any phenomenon.

Many contemporary theorists and researchers incorporate the Sapir-Whorf hypothesis in their work, based on an approach to communication called **social constructionism,** which states that language creates our perceptions of reality, as well as the kinds of relationships we enter into with one another. By organizing our experience, language exercises a powerful influence in our lives (Volonishov/Bakhtin, 1973). The language you use helps you make sense of people and events in certain ways and guides how you interact within situations. Consider what happens when you choose to label a situation or a person as a "problem." In most cultures, once we label something as a problem, we are then moved to take actions that "fix the problem" and assign blame to a person or persons for that problem. Take the following words:

Knowledge Link

How does language construct our perceptions of reality?

low self-esteem	authoritarian	externally controlled
repressed	depressed	burned out
stressed	paranoid	obsessive-compulsive
bulimic	sadomasochistic	midlife crisis
identity crisis	anxious	antisocial personality
anorexic	seasonal affective disorder	voyeuristic
kleptomaniac	self-alienated	psychopathic deviate
post-traumatic stress disorder		

These words focus on the problems that many people face in their personal lives. **Deficit language** focuses our attention on people's deficiencies and problems (Gergen, 1991). When you use deficit language to organize your experience of people and events, you tend to analyze the causes of the problem, assign blame to events or people who "created" the problem, and then strive to find the one best solution to solve the problem. But if you did not use deficit language to describe people and events, what would you notice? Instead of noticing people's deficiencies, you would probably focus on their strengths and abilities and talk about ways to develop this potential.

People have traditionally viewed language as an important vehicle for getting a point across and expressing thoughts and ideas. However, language has a much greater importance in that it organizes how you see the world and how you interact with others. The Austrian philosopher of language Ludwig Wittgenstein (1953) says, "The limits of my language mean the limits of my world." Thus unless you have a word to label a particular experience, you don't see that experience as a part of your life. Until we bring an experience into language, it doesn't exist. Once we bring it into language, the words and language we choose to characterize our experience not only help us make sense of a situation, they also foreshadow future ways of acting. Think about what happens when you label a set of feelings you are experiencing as the emotional state of being "angry." Labeling your feelings as "anger" not only helps you make sense of your feelings, it also provides you with clues as to how to subsequently act. For example, "angry" people may be expected to show their anger through yelling and attacking others verbally. Angry people may have some latitude to say things in the heat of the moment that they normally wouldn't say. The language we choose to characterize a person or an event provides us with a way to continue the interaction. If we are unable to put our understanding of the event or person into language, we are limited in our ability to coordinate our conversation with others.

Functions of Language

Language does much more than simply reflect our inner thoughts, emotions, and feelings or describe people, issues, and events. Language is an active force in our lives that shapes the way we live together as human beings and the kinds of communities in which we live. Language is a doer, a maker, and a producer. Language constructs, shapes, and forms our lives together. Language performs four key functions: It (1) makes us notice things, (2) creates opportunities and limitations, (3) constructs identity, and (4) facilitates social coordination.

Language Makes Us Notice Things

Imagine you are a building engineer and have been called in to consult with hotel management. The hotel manager says, "We have been getting a lot of complaints from our guests about how slow the elevators are. They feel they wait far too long before an elevator gets to their floor." What recommendation would you make to the hotel manager? You might recommend they replace the elevators' motors with faster ones. You might recommend that they build more elevators. However, both of these options are quite expensive and disruptive to implement. When this event actually happened, the consultant recommended placing mirrors on each floor by the elevators, and miraculously the guests stopped complaining (Mitroff, 1978). Although the wait was just as long, the mirrors gave the guests something to do as they waited. They could fix their hair, adjust their clothing, and so on. This simple, inexpensive solution took care of the problem without overtaxing the hotel management's budget.

What does this sign make you notice that you otherwise might not have?

This example illustrates language's power to make us notice things. The hotel manager's problem, complaining guests, could be labeled as a "mechanical problem." If the consultant had used this kind of language to label the problem, what would be noticed: how many elevators are in operation, how fast the elevators travel up and down, or the pattern of the elevators (do some elevators only go to floors one through ten and others ten through twenty?). When the word *mechanics* is used, it makes people think of solutions based on altering the elevator mechanics.

In this case, the consultant didn't talk about the problem as rooted in the elevators' mechanics, but rather as rooted in people's psychology. By labeling the problem as a "people issue," the consultant noticed what the guests were (or weren't) doing as they waited for the elevator. Labeling the issue as a "people issue" as opposed to a "mechanical issue" led the consultant to a different and better solution.

Language organizes our perceptions of people, events, and issues by playing an active role in making us notice things and directing our attention to certain aspects of situations. When we use language to label an event in a certain way it focuses our attention on certain aspects of the event, as in the case of the consultant. Wittgenstein's (1953) statement "A drop of grammar and an ocean of meaning" reflects the power of language to focus our attention: When we use a word, it is associated with a whole set of other words and meanings. For example, write the words *minority status* on a piece of paper. Then write down all the words you associate with minority status. Did you write down words like *Hispanic Americans, African Americans, Jewish people, Catholics, gays* and *lesbians* as Sylvia in the opening vignette might have done? Or did you write down words like *opinion, Democrats, libertarians, Reform party* as Ernesto might have? By using the word *minority status,* you notice all the other words and meanings associated with them.

Words provide a compass for making sense of our social worlds. The words we use to characterize people, events, and situations not only direct our attention to particular aspects regarding those people, events, and situations, but also inform our understanding of what those behaviors mean. Moreover, the words we use to label a situation highlight certain possible actions that are appropriate to take in the future. Words not only tell us how we make sense of a situation (what we view as important) but also how we will act in the future (where we need to go).

LANGUAGE CREATES OPPORTUNITIES & LIMITATIONS

As you saw earlier, language is a system in which constitutive and regulative rules guide how we come to know what certain words mean and how we use those words in conversation. These two sets of rules guide and shape our behavior.

To understand how language can create opportunities as well as constraints, take the example of what it means to be "just friends." Let's say you have developed a close relationship with someone. When people ask you about your relationship, you both reply, "We're just friends." If you label your relationship with this person as "just friends," what opportunities does that create for you in terms of what you say to and do with one another? Some of the regulative rules that offer opportunities might look like this:

- If we are "just friends," we can talk about our personal lives—including our love lives.
- If we are "just friends," we can offer advice and counsel to the other person when he or she is having difficulties.
- If we are "just friends," we can do things together like go to a party or have dinner.
- If we are "just friends," we can call each other late at night if we need help.

Though the status of "just friends" creates certain opportunities like the ones just listed, it also prohibits certain actions. Some of the regulative rules that impose limitations may look like this:

- If we are "just friends," we should not make any sexual advances.
- If we are "just friends," we should not lie to each other.
- If we are "just friends," we should not reveal each other's personal confidences to others.

The language we use to characterize our relationship influences what we can say and do with one another as well as what we cannot say and do.

This idea that language creates opportunities and limits possible actions underscores the important role it plays in our communication as well as in our relationships. As you can see, you need to take great care in how you use language because it can obligate you toward certain courses of action while closing off different courses of action. Once you label an event or person in a particular way, the labeling opens up and closes off certain ways of positioning yourself in that situation. For example, political leaders involved in a heated dispute with leaders of another country may make this claim: "We have exhausted the possibilities for talk." By labeling the situation in this way, what are the political leaders permitted to do based on the limitations of this language? This kind of language creates "permission" for the country's political leaders to move beyond rhetorical and nonviolent means of influence to waging war to resolve the dispute. This is an example of **rhetorical exhaustion,** by which a party decides that it has exhausted all avenues for talk as a means to settle disputes (Artz & Pollock, 1997). For example, in 1991 the Bush administration successfully used rhetorical exhaustion to appear legitimate in launching the Persian Gulf War. By buying into this language, the American public understood Bush's rationale for the attack and supported the Persian Gulf War. The likelihood that a country's citizens will support and view as legitimate military interventions such as the war in Kosovo or air strikes against Iraq depends on how the country's leadership uses language. The language of rhetorical exhaustion can successfully convince the public that all rhetorical means for resolving the conflict have been exhausted, leaving no other alternatives but violent intervention.

Knowledge Link

When politicians use the language of rhetorical exhaustion, what kinds of actions become legitimate?

LANGUAGE CREATES IDENTITIES

The language we choose to use is significant to communication because language creates our sense of identity. Recall how self-image and identity are created through language as discussed in Chapter 3. As children, we are not only socialized into particular value systems and sets of traditions, we also develop beliefs about who we are and how we should act. Language plays a crucial role in the development of the self as well as the social self. Identity and communication are involved in a reciprocal relationship. The patterns of communication you engage in shape your identity and in turn, your identity affects your subsequent communication. This connection between communication and identity can be seen in three types of language: politically correct language, hate speech, and gender communication.

Politically correct language, also called "PC" language, refers to words and phrases that attempt to remove or compensate for any traces of sexism, racism, ageism, and heterocentrism or any potentially derogatory meanings that might offend a group of people. The 1991 *Random House Webster's College Dictionary* was the first to deal with PC language (Birnbaum, 1991). As a result some of the following words were given entries to deal with various forms of "discriminatory language":

Heightism, weightism: Recognizes discrimination against short and fat people
Herstory: Distinguishes the study of women's affairs from the generic, all-inclusive history
Waitron, wait-person: Gender-neutral term for waiter
Womyn: Alternative spelling to avoid the suggestion of sexism perceived in the sequence m-e-n. (Birnbaum, 1991, p. 51)

Although such language has been included in the official lexicon, many people who hear these words used by others label them PC. Being PC has come to be viewed negatively, as overcompensating for others' sensitivities. In fact, politically correct language was routinely lampooned and satirized during the 1990s.

Yet one of the primary reasons for the emergence of politically correct language was an attempt to eliminate or compensate for discriminatory language. Consider the shift in our language from *chairman* to *chair*, *fireman* to *firefighter*, *stewardess* to *flight attendant*, and *policeman* to *police officer*. Such a shift in how we use language counters the idea that certain positions are filled by a particular gender and highlights the fact that such positions are open to the participation of both men and women. On the one hand, women can construct self-images that include positions and professions previously considered "male," and on the other, men can include a more gender-neutral self-image of other professions typically considered "female." Although politically correct language may be easy to satirize and ridicule, its original intent is to use language in ways that do not constrain people into limiting their self-image.

The idea of politically correct language is closely connected to the relationship between language and gender identity. Language can also shape identity through **gender role socialization,** the process in which girls and boys receive explicit and implicit messages that tell them how females and males are expected to act in a given culture. Girls and boys receive subtle but different kinds of messages as they grow up:

- Parents discuss emotions more with girls than with boys.
- Mothers with daughters focus on the daughter's emotional state itself, whereas mothers with sons focus more on causes and consequences of the son's emotional state. For example, if a girl falls down and skins her knee, the mother may ask, "How much does it hurt?" But if a boy gets hurt, she may focus on the action rather than the emotion and ask, "Did you fall down and go boom?"
- Parents encourage girls to be more socially oriented.
- Girls receive rewards and reinforcements to be nurturing and obedient; boys are pressured to be independent and self-reliant. (Adapted from Guerrero & Reiter, 1998, p. 325)

As a result, girls and boys are socialized into different sets of experiences. Girls are socialized into more cooperative forms of interaction and develop identities that sensitize them to the importance of forming and maintaining relationships. Boys are socialized into more competitive forms of interaction and develop identities that are rooted in assertiveness and accomplishing tasks.

This initial set of socializing experiences creates gender roles that move girls and boys toward certain patterns of language use. In general, girls use language to gain approval and reinforce intimacy, and boys use language to maintain or increase their status and establish independence (Sagrestano, Heavey, & Christensen, 1998). This pattern of language use subsequently reinforces each gender's sense of identity. If girls prove successful in using language that creates approval and intimacy, they create and maintain an identity that emphasizes cultivating close personal relationships. But if their language patterns are challenged, they may create a different identity, one that is more "masculine" in nature—emphasizing accomplishing tasks and being independent.

During the 1990s, sadly, North Americans continued to witness numerous instances of **hate speech**, which involves speech attacks on other people on the basis of race, ethnicity, gender, religion, and sexual orientation that incites the assault, ambush, terrorization, wounding, humiliation, or degradation of the targets of such speech (Calvert, 1997). An example of such speech occurred in March 1999 when Washington, DC, radio shock jock the "Greaseman" Doug Tracht made the following racist remark:

> Noting that the Grammy ceremony was scheduled for that evening, he [Tracht] played a portion of a song by Lauryn Hill [a young R & B artist], who later won five Grammy awards. . . . Then he commented, "No wonder people drag them behind trucks." The reference was to the murder of James Byrd, Jr., a black man decapitated when he was dragged behind a pick-up truck in Jasper, Texas. ("Radio DJ," 1999, p. 19)

The murder of James Byrd, Jr., highlights the potential consequences of hate speech. Hate speech has the power to shape people's personal identities in ways that perpetuate negative stereotypes and feelings of inferiority in the targeted group.

CloseUp on Diversity

Reducing Bias in Language

POLITICALLY CORRECT SPEECH has been criticized and parodied over the last decade. Being politically correct, or PC, has been described as going to ridiculous lengths to rid language of any potential bias due to gender, sexual orientation, race or ethnicity, disability, or age. Using PC language, the term *physically handicapped* becomes *physically challenged, short* becomes *vertically challenged,* and *manhole cover* becomes *street-hole cover.* Critics of PC language attribute the creation of such new terms as an excess of sensitivity to the feelings of particular classes of people. Yet, if language does create identity, then we need to take seriously the notion that the words we use may perpetuate negative stereotypes and demeaning attitudes about certain classes of people. The reality that language creates identity makes it important for you to master linguistic strategies to avoid recreating biases in your language.

Style manuals for writing essays and reports have provided a wealth of information on how to reduce bias in your writing and how you speak (see Gibaldi, 1999; *Publication Manual of the American Psychological Association,* 1994.) One of the best manuals for learning how to avoid bias in language is the *Publication Manual of the American Psychological Association,* 1994. It provides a number of useful suggestions to make sure that individuals and groups are treated fairly in the ways in which we write and speak about them. Here are some examples:

Describe individuals and groups at an appropriate level of specificity:

1. Describe all human beings as *man* or *mankind* is not as precise as using the phrase *men and women.* When describing the sexual orientation of a group of men and women, the term *gay* can be interpreted to refer to men and women or only men. To provide a greater specificity, use the phrase *gay men and lesbians.*

2. Be sensitive to labels: Classes of people may have preferences for what they prefer to be called, and these preferences change over time. For example, the term *Hispanic* covers a number of people from Central or South America. Using terms such as *Mexican American* or a *person of Columbian descent* may be more specific and appropriate. When in doubt, ask people what designation they prefer.

3. Avoid labeling people: Using labels deprives people of their individuality and objectifies them. When you make statements about the *handicapped,* the *elderly, youth,* and so on, your language labels them in terms of one characteristic they possess, not as individuals. In the case of labels such as *handicapped, mentally retarded,* and so on, this language equates the condition with the person. Strategies to counter the use of labels include placing the descriptive adjective in front of a noun (handicapped people, elderly man, young woman) or "put the person first" followed by a descriptive phrase (people with AIDS).

4. Avoid using one group as a standard against which others are judged: When you portray one group as superior or "normal" and use this group as the standard to judge others, your language creates bias and possibly justifies discrimination. The following statements contain some level of judgment that can breed bias:

- When African American student scores are compared to those of the general public . . . (Are African American students not part of the "general" public?)
- The comparison between lesbians and normal women . . . (Are lesbians not "normal"?)
- Women are not as competitive as men . . . (Is being "competitive" a desired standard to achieve?)
- Each of these statements implicitly or explicitly contains an idea that one group sets the standard for other groups. Using words that emphasize difference as opposed to level of sophistication or progress ("Women are different from men . . . ") or using a more even-handed comparison ("The comparison between lesbians and heterosexual women . . .") will help reduce this bias.

The following is a list of problematic and preferred language regarding gender, sexual orientation, race, ethnicity, and disability. It is taken from the *Publication Manual of the American Psychological Association,* 1994, pp. 54–60.

CHARACTERISTIC	BIASED LANGUAGE	PREFERRED LANGUAGE	RATIONALE
Gender	man, mankind	people, humanity, human beings, humankind, human species	Use words that explicitly include both genders.

CHARACTERISTIC	BIASED LANGUAGE	PREFERRED LANGUAGE	RATIONALE
Gender (cont'd)	to man a project	to staff a project, to hire personnel, to employ staff	Specific nouns reduce the possibility of stereotypic bias and often clarify discussion.
	man–machine interface	user–system interface, person–system interface, human–machine interface	
	manpower	work force, personnel, workers, employees, human resources	
	woman doctor, lady lawyer, male nurse, woman driver	doctor or physician, lawyer, nurse, driver	Specify sex only if it is relevant to the discussion.
Sexual orientation	Most homosexuals feel . . .	Most gay male adolescents feel . . . Most lesbians feel . . .	Avoid a general use of homosexual, and specify gender. Use *gay* to refer to men and *lesbian* to refer to women.
	Some gays think . . .	Some gay men . . . Some lesbians . . .	
	the gay designer, the lesbian mechanic, the homosexual activist	designer, mechanic, activist	Avoid specifying the sexual preference of people where it is irrelevant. Avoid lumping all gays and lesbians together. As with anybody, many gays and lesbians do not necessarily share the same opinions simply because they are gay or lesbian.
Racial and ethnic identify	black person, Hispanic	African American, Mexican American, Latino/Latina, Nicaraguan, Peruvian	As appropriate, provide additional information about national or racial origin.
	American Indian	Choctaw, Hopi, Navajo, Seminole	
	the Jewish lawyer, the African American doctor, the Mexican farm worker	the lawyer, the doctor, farm worker	Avoid noting a person's race, ethnicity, or religion when it's not relevant to the discussion. This can signal a perceived "exception" or a stereotype.
Disabilities	disabled person	person with (who has) a disability	Put people first, not their disability.
	defective child	child with a congenital disability child with a birth impairment	
	mentally ill person	person with mental illness	

CloseUp cont'd

CHARACTERISTIC	BIASED LANGUAGE	PREFERRED LANGUAGE	RATIONALE
Disabilities (cont'd)	depressives	people who suffer from depression	Avoid equating the person with the disability by separating the two concepts.
	epileptics	individuals with epilepsy	
	AIDS patient	person with AIDS (or HIV), a person who is HIV positive	
	retarded adult	adult with mental retardation	

Whether it is radio shock jocks making racist and sexist remarks, white supremacist groups verbally attacking ethnic minorities, neo-Nazi groups demeaning Jews, Catholics, African Americans, and Hispanics, or rap music artists advocating the killing of cops or the rape and brutalization of women, hate speech has become a part of our social fabric. On some college campuses, university administrators have gone so far as to create speech codes that spell out what types of speech are protected on campus and what types are not in order to constrain hate speech (Lee, 1997).

Although many people believe the freedom of speech is a civil liberty guaranteed by the Constitution, hate speech is viewed negatively and as an exception to the Bill of Rights. One explanation for this is that the effects generated by hate speech are overwhelmingly negative. Hate speech can produce negative emotions in the aggressor, hurt feelings in those targeted, and changes in the victims ranging from psychological to physical, brought on by severe emotional distress. Hate speech solidifies the aggressor's identity by reinforcing hateful attitudes and beliefs that make it almost impossible to overcome these attitudes and beliefs. As a reaction, the targets of hate speech internalize a negative image of themselves as individuals and as a group (Calvert, 1997). As racial, sexual, and religious epithets are directed toward groups of people, an atmosphere of inequality is perpetuated.

Moreover, hate speech constructs intolerance—the culture targeted by such language is not viewed as worthy of existence. Hate speech directed at certain groups of people labels them as inferior and deserving of hate crimes directed toward them, justifying the words and actions of the aggressors. Although, devil's advocates may argue that hate speech simply makes people "feel bad," it has much more widespread effects. It dehumanizes the target in the eyes of the aggressor and incites and justifies violence toward a group of people. This, in fact, was what Tracht was doing—he began by mocking R & B music, proclaiming it as inferior, and used this judgment of a predominantly black music form to justify Byrd's murder. Such language affects people's actions and creates a type of community where some people and activities are viewed as inferior and deserving of violent words and actions aimed at eliminating those people and activities.

Politically correct language, gender communication, and hate speech are only three ways in which language creates identities. As you can see, our choice of language does so much more than mutually describe people and events. It is a powerful tool that can, for better or worse, construct our sense of identity, as well as influence the identities of others.

LANGUAGE FACILITATES SOCIAL COORDINATION

The final key function of language is that it can be used to coordinate people's actions and abilities. The way you use language can either enhance or hurt your ability to work with others. As you just saw, when you use language that is sexist or racist, you reduce your ability to coordinate with others because people may become offended by your speech and refuse to cooperate. Language that helps promote coordination does not insult or demean others, or place them in a defensive position. Your ability to coordinate with others also depends on the level of abstraction that you adopt in your language. Coordinating your actions with others requires you to select language that is appropriately clear and direct for the situation. Using this language will give others in the situation adequate information to coordinate with you to achieve desirable outcomes.

One way to evaluate the clarity and directness of your language is to place it on Hayakawa's **Ladder of Abstraction**. S. I. Hayakawa (1964), a noted linguist, placed language on a continuum from the very concrete to the more abstract. He devised a Ladder of Abstraction on which he placed the most concrete words on the lower rungs and arranged words on the upper rungs as they increased in abstraction. (See Figure 4.4 for an example). Low-level abstractions or descriptions of concrete phenomena, placed on the lowest rung of the ladder, are the most descriptive and clear because they refer to specific instances and behaviors. The middle rung of the ladder is more abstract because it includes words that draw general inferences about a person or situation based on con-

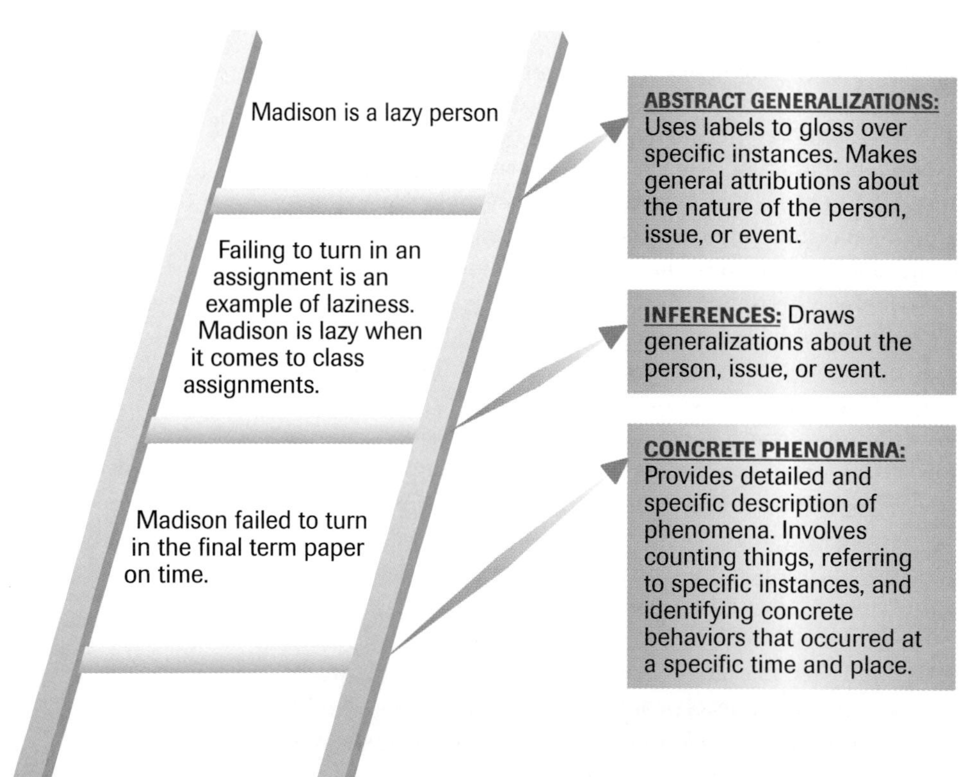

FIGURE 4.4
Hayakawa's Ladder of Abstration

The Ladder of Abstraction moves from concrete language such as "failing to turn in the final term paper on time" on the lowest rung to inferences on the next rung "Madison is lazy when it comes to class assignments," with abstract generalizations on the top rung, "Madison is a lazy person."

crete phenomena. Finally, the highest level includes abstract generalizations about the person, issue, or event that gloss over specific instances.

Looking at Figure 4.4, at the lowest rung and lowest level of abstraction, the concrete description of the behavior is that Madison did not turn in the final term paper on time. On the middle rung of the ladder, an inference is drawn about Madison's behavior in this specific context: "Madison is lazy when it comes to class assignments." At the highest level of abstraction, the inference is generalized across situations and used to label Madison's behavior as lazy in general.

If you wanted to improve Madison's performance, you would use language that is low in abstraction and more concrete: "You failed to turn in the final term paper by Friday at 5 P.M. when it was due." Stating a problem with concrete language that explicitly describes the performance difficulty clearly indicates the specific actions necessary to remedy this problem. Telling Madison "You are a lazy person and must stop that," however, is very ambiguous. Madison may not understand what is prompting you to make this assessment, nor what now needs to be done so as not to be viewed as lazy. In this situation, language at a low level of abstraction is viewed as more accurate and clear, and as a result, it is more effective.

Can we assume that concrete specific language is always the best language to use? Indeed, in some situations using concrete language is very useful in helping people coordinate their actions such as the previous example. Using more abstract language is useful in some cases. For example, consider a new manager who wants to test her employees' planning skills. She may ask her employees to develop a written plan for a particular project. The manager could use very concrete and specific language to describe the assignment: "I want you to develop a five-page plan for this proposed project. First, make sure you overview the project with an introduction. Second, I want a section that highlights your analysis of why we have embarked on this project. Third, I want a solutions section in the report. Finally, I want a description of the criterion and benchmarks for assessing the success of your proposed solution." This request uses very concrete and specific language, but does it meet this manager's needs? By outlining the length and format for the project proposal, the manager clearly specifies what she wants, and in doing so, she reduces her chances to assess her employees' planning abilities. She could have made her request more ambiguous: "Please develop a proposal for this project. I don't want to tell you too much more, because I don't want to limit your creativity." Although this language is more abstract, it does not limit the employees in how they develop the proposal. As such it may give the manager better insight into how each employee thinks and plans.

Our example illustrates that people need to make choices regarding the level of abstraction they select to use in their language. How, then, do you determine which level of abstraction to use in language? Consider the following three factors: First, what is the speaker's intent? Second, what are the other person's expectations? Third, what is the nature of the situation? The manager wanted to test the planning abilities of her employees and viewed the project as an appropriate means of achieving this. At the same time her employees may want specific and detailed instructions for performing the task. How do you manage the competing needs of the manager to be ambiguous to test employee planning abilities and the employees' desire to be given a concrete task to better coordinate their actions with the manager's? One possible answer is found in the ambiguous request itself. To test her employees' ability to plan, the manager kept the request ambiguous; yet she explained why she was being ambiguous to meet the employees' need for structure. This type of answer should allow her to coordinate her actions with her employees' effectively. Her employees have enough information so they can perform their task, and the manager has structured the task so she can assess her employees' planning abilities.

Determining what you want to accomplish, what your audience expects, and what the situation requires can help you choose the appropriate level of abstraction in your language. Choosing the appropriate level of abstraction in your language enables you to create situations where you can coordinate your actions with others.

Challenges to Language

As you've read so far, language is a complex process that influences what we notice and drives how we interact. In addition to the complexities of the process, the fact that we all belong to different language communities adds to the difficulty of using language effectively and appropriately. A **language community** is a group of people that has developed a common set of constitutive and regulative rules which guide the meaning of words and the appropriate reactions based on interpreting those words. Even within the same "language," such as English, there are many different language communities: Some of these are based on work, gender, religion, race, ethnicity, political affiliation, and so on. Although the language we use may be very understandable to others within a particular language community, it may be incomprehensible to those outside that language community—and those people may interpret our language in ways other than we intend. Luckily, people's language communities frequently overlap, making it possible to communicate with one another. However, even if there is overlap between language communities, we may interpret language through the filter of those communities that are not shared, resulting in misunderstanding. Our ability to use language with others in effective and appropriate ways faces two key challenges: (1) we may belong to different language communities, and (2) even if we share a similar language community, we may interpret language through the filter of those communities that are not shared.

Take, for example, the case of gender. Many researchers argue that men and women are socialized into two separate language communities based on gender. Girls are socialized to be "quieter, more peaceful, concerned with harmonious relationships, and more cooperative"; boys are socialized "to be athletic, assertive, focused on [the] self, and more competitive" (Meyers, Brawshers, Winston, & Grob, 1997, p. 23). If men and women are indeed socialized into two different cultures, how might this influence how they interpret lan-

Men and women belong to different language communities.

BIZARRO ©1994 by Dan Piraro. Reprinted with permission of UNIVERSAL PRESS SYNDICATE. All rights reserved.

guage? For example, given the difference in socialization, women may differ from men in the linguistic styles they choose to express themselves. Women in small groups tend to ask more questions than men do (Meyers et al., 1997). Because women value connections and relationships with others more than men, they view this way of expressing themselves as appropriate. Do men use the same linguistic style in group situations? Probably not. Given that men are socialized to be assertive and competitive, they may view language that is more tentative and accommodating to others as a sign of weakness and incompetence. For men, language used to make strong statements within a group is seen as more appropriate.

The challenges associated with using language are even more complex because people belong to multiple language communities simultaneously. As you saw in Chapter 3, we have multiple identities that come into play according to the situation. Bonnie Dow (1997), a feminist critic, describes the difficulty of multiple language communities very clearly. She was attending a lecture by a famous African American feminist critic and theorist who talked about other academics' hostility to her research. Given that they were both women and feminist critics, Dow had encountered some of what she interpreted as the same hostility to her own work. She then asked a question about how this presenter was able to channel her anger in productive ways. To her surprise, the theorist responded, "See? This is the kind of thing white women do to me all the time—they call me 'angry' so they don't have to deal with what I am saying" (Dow, 1997, p. 241). Dow thought she had asked a supportive question, and the theorist interpreted it as a racist reaction.

Why might the lecturer have had this reaction? One way to answer this question is to look at the language communities the two women share and the language communities they don't (see Figure 4.5). According to Dow (1997), when we speak and listen to people, we need to consider a person's social location and social commitments to understand what language communities they belong to. **Social location** refers to the place we occupy according to race, ethnicity, class, gender, sexual orientation, and so on. **Social commitments** refer to the values and political positions we hold. If we revisit our example, both Dow and the lecturer share two language communities because of their social location (gender) and social commitment (feminism). However, they don't share an important language community based on social location (race)—the lecturer is African American and Dow is white. Although the lecturer and Dow shared two language communities, it was the language community they didn't share—race—that may have caused the disconnect between the two women when Dow asked her question.

In conclusion, language is challenging to speakers and listeners for two reasons. First, we may belong to different language communities that may not overlap, which makes it difficult for people to communicate because there is no shared language. Second, even if there is some overlap between the language communities we belong to, we may simultaneously belong to separate language communities, which may govern how we produce and interpret language. This is a real challenge to language use because it makes it difficult to predict how people will interpret your language. All these challenges aside, we can use language in ways that help move us forward and accomplish desirable goals. How do we meet these challenges that language communities erect in the path of communication and use language competently and constructively to facilitate social coordination?

FIGURE 4.5
Shared and Distinct Language Communities

Dow and the African American lecturer share the two language communities based on social location: They are both women and academics. They also share one language community based on their social commitments: They are both feminists. However, they belong to different language communities based on racial identity: Dow is white and the lecturer is African American. It is these language communities that promoted a misunderstanding between the two women.

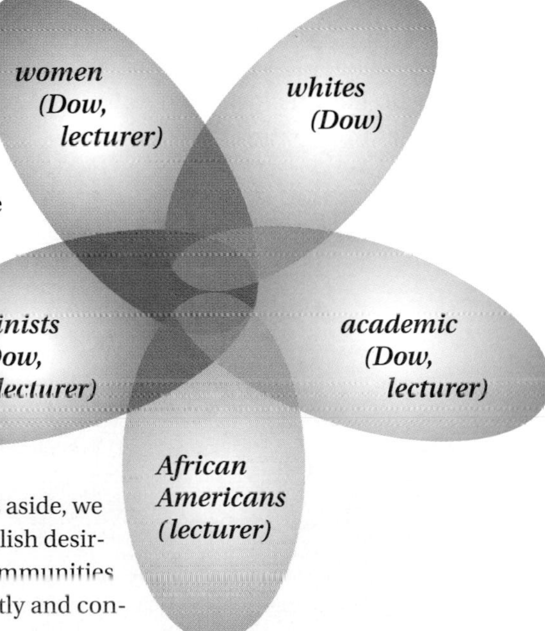

Overcoming Challenges to Competence

As you saw at the beginning of the chapter, using language competently involves developing abilities that allow us to make sense of the unique characteristics of a situation and determine the most useful language choices. Such abilities involve being sensitive to a situation, the people involved and their expectations, and adjusting our language to fit the situation. Three strategies are very useful in developing these abilities: (1) inviting curiosity about the meaning of words, (2) anticipating possible interpretations before we speak, and (3) trying different phrasing possibilities.

BE CURIOUS ABOUT THE MEANING OF WORDS

As the B.C. cartoon illustrates, different words have different meanings in different contexts. For a musician a *gig* is positive, but for a frog a *gig* means having a metal spike inserted into the brain stem to scramble the brain. Similarly, as we mature, we may develop personal meanings for words that differ from others'—given our unique background and experiences. Yet we sometimes forget this simple fact and assume that others have the same meaning for words. And if they do have different meanings for words, we may judge their meanings as "wrong" because ours are superior. This leads to ethnocentric communication (Pearce, 1989). **Ethnocentric communicators** recognize only their own meanings for words as valid and reject alternative meanings as wrong. When we acknowledge the existence of a number of different, valid meanings for words, in contrast, we become **cosmopolitan communicators**. Cosmopolitan communicators recognize that the meanings they have created for certain words are unique to them and not shared by others. They draw out the unique meanings that people have for words to understand the meaning of a word or turn of phrase from others' perspectives.

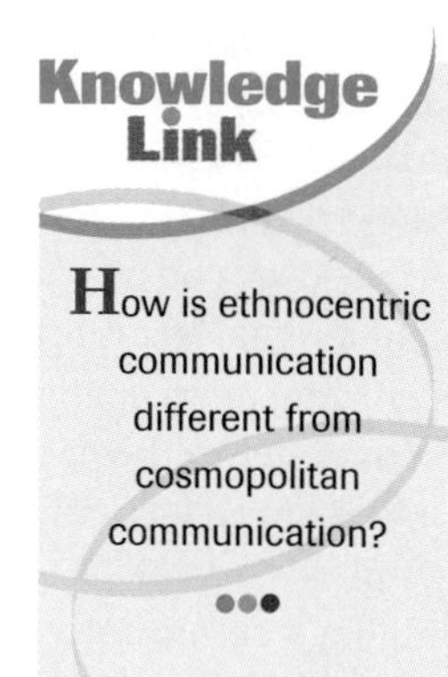

You need to be curious to draw out the unique meanings people have for words. If you have a closed and rigid opinion about the "right" meaning for words you might miss out on the meaning of the other person's message and fail to coordinate your behavior with that person.

What are some strategies that you can use to invite curiosity? The most basic way is to ask questions. Although many strategies are available, three types of questions are most useful: clarifying questions, showing questions, and comparison questions. A **clarifying question** invites the other person to elaborate on his or her meaning for the language he or she uses. Returning to the opening vignette, how might you use clarifying questions to

A word's meaning depends on context.

By permission of Johnny Hart and Creators Syndicate, Inc.

explore the meaning of *minority* for Sylvia and Ernesto? Common clarifying questions are "What do you mean by that?" or "What does *minority* mean?"

A second strategy is to ask **"showing" questions,** which are based on the idea that the meaning of words are revealed by how they are used and the kinds of actions associated with them (Wittgenstein, 1953). "Showing" questions may include questions like "How does minority opinion reveal itself?" or "If minority opinion was expressed in a group, what would it sound like?" Asking "showing" questions invites the respondent to focus on specific actions or activities that comprise the word.

Finally, **comparison questions** invite the respondent to point to words that are similar in meaning to the word in question as well as to list words that carry different meanings. Comparison questions that explore similarity include the following: "What is a synonym for *minority*?" or "What other words do you associate with *minority* opinion?" Comparison questions that highlight differences include "What is the opposite of what you mean?" or "What words are antonyms of *minority*?" By understanding how the word or phrase you have in mind differs from other words or phrases, you can begin to gain a better understanding of its meaning (Derrida, 1978).

Imagine you are in a group meeting and one of the group members accuses you of "slacking off." You are shocked because you feel that you have performed at a high level and contributed to the group. After you work through your initial reaction, what kinds of questions could you ask to clarify this statement? If you are curious about your colleague's criticism, you might ask the following kinds of questions:

Clarifying Question: "What exactly do you mean when you say I am 'slacking off'?"

"Showing" Questions: "When I 'slack off,' what does that look like?" "How does my 'slacking off' show itself?" "How might someone outside of the group notice that I was 'slacking off'?"

Comparison Questions: "What other phrases could you use besides 'slacking off' to describe my performance?" "If I wasn't 'slacking off,' what words would you use to describe my performance?"

By asking questions such as these that come from a genuine curiosity, you can begin to fully understand what people mean in their language, and avoid miscommunication.

ANTICIPATE POSSIBLE INTERPRETATIONS BEFORE YOU SPEAK

Businesses and corporations spend large amounts of money to craft eye-catching television commercials. Think of the television commercials that have caught your attention. Did you include the Taco Bell Chihuahua commercials, the Nike "Just Do It" commercials, the Gap clothing commercials set to familiar songs, or the Lotus Notes commercial with people holding signs that say "I am . . ." as the music in the background plays: "I am Superman. I can do anything"? In television commercials as well as other kinds of persuasive messages, producers spend a great deal of time anticipating the meanings their potential consumers will draw from their message. At a minimum, advertisers try to construct coherent and understandable messages that will capture the viewers' attention and persuade them to buy the product or service. By anticipating how consumers will interpret and respond to advertising messages, successful marketers can create messages that consumers will hear and accept.

Similarly, competent communicators need to anticipate how others might interpret their messages so they can better construct messages that are coherent and understandable. If you were to give a speech advocating gun control, how would you articulate your message? Because there are numerous ways to articulate and present the message, how do you know which one to choose? How you organize and present your message depends on the audience you are addressing. For example, if the audience is strongly in favor of gun control, you may anticipate little resistance to your position and simply outline the plan you are advocating. But if your audience is firmly against gun control and concerned that gun control laws will ultimately violate Americans' constitutional right to bear arms, you will probably anticipate opposition to your position. In this case, you would change your strategy for presenting the need for gun control legislation because failing to recognize and address the needs of your audience will hurt your ability to be heard and understood. In such situations, anticipating how others may interpret your messages allows you to identify possible obstacles to being heard and understood and develop ways to overcome them.

Whether you are in an interpersonal, group, or public speaking situation, to communicate competently you need to anticipate how people will make sense of your language. Three strategies anticipate how people may interpret your language: examining your wording from different perspectives, understanding the larger context, and exploring the historical background for the message.

The first strategy involves examining your wording from the multiple perspectives of different audiences. What are the different audiences to whom you are presenting your message? How might each audience interpret your language? Do they hold similar or different interpretations of your message? If different audiences have different interpretations, you have to develop a message that evokes a common set of meanings across the different audiences. Or you'll need to state your message in several different ways to ensure that all of your listeners interpret the message correctly.

The second strategy is to examine the larger context in which the message occurs. Three contexts are of particular importance: (1) episodes, (2) relationships, and (3) culture. Messages occur within the context of episodes between people within a larger cultural system. An **episode** is a sequence of messages that has a clear beginning and end, and a set of constitutive and regulative rules. For example in greeting episodes, we know that statements such as "Hi, how are you?" count as greetings and we are expected to respond with a similar message (see Figure 4.1). However, the phrase "Hi, how are you?" may be interpreted differently if it occurs in a gossip episode where the initiator of the conversation wants to obtain information about your private life. This message may not function as a greeting, but as an attempt to collect information. In this context, the message may put recipients on the defensive because they perceive the source of the message as snooping into their private lives. Understanding the episodic context of your message helps you anticipate how people will interpret your message.

The *relationship* also serves as an important context for anticipating how your message may be interpreted by others. What relationship do you have with your audience? How does that relationship influence how your audience may interpret your message? For example, if your boss said, "I am disappointed in your performance," you may interpret the message as a criticism or warning. If a co-worker uttered the same message, you might interpret it as sarcasm or a joke. Understanding how your relationship with the receiver of the message influences their perception of the message will help you anticipate how he or she will make sense of your language.

Messages also occur in a cultural context. As you'll recall from Chapter 1, culture refers to the set of beliefs, values, and norms held by a social group.

The term *partner* takes on a meaning equivalent to *spouse, husband,* or *wife* in the gay and lesbian community. Terms such as *marriage* have become the center of conflict because language communities outside of the gay and lesbian community reserve the term for heterosexual couples.

We can have group cultures, organizational cultures, national cultures, ethnic cultures, and so on. Examine the cultural context in which your message is sent. How does that influence audience interpretation? For example, what does it mean to introduce someone as your partner? In the United States, introducing someone as your partner typically refers to a business relationship you have with that person. However in European countries and gay and lesbian subculture, the term *partner* means you are romantically involved with that person. It becomes important to understand that your audience may interpret the word *partner* differently than you intend depending on its culture.

Examine the historical background to your message. Messages and language are communicated over time. What happened in the past before you spoke? How might these events influence the language that you use? For example, if in the past a manager has been criticized by his employees for "not giving clear directions" then he would likely avoid using high-level abstract language to communicate to his employees.

PLAY WITH POSSIBLE PHRASINGS

Have you known a person so well that you knew how to phrase things in ways that could tease and provoke that person or make that person laugh? The language we use can help steer people toward acting in particular ways. When we use language, we open up certain possibilities for behavior and close off others at the same time. By phrasing things in ways that provoke anger in a person, you are probably closing off the possibility of telling a joke and making that person laugh. Using language competently not only involves anticipating your audience's interpretations of what you are saying but it also entails steering its behavior in ways you prefer. Playing with phrasing your messages can shape people's interpretations and actions. Indexing and experimenting with pronouns are two strategies for playing with your phrasing.

Indexing uses language that places an issue, event, or person in a specific time or in a specific context. For example, if you were to index according to time, instead of saying, "Dr. Smith is a poor teacher," you would say, "When I had Dr. Smith four years ago, I thought he was a poor teacher." If you were indexing to place a person in a particular context, you would say, "When we discussed affirmative action, I found Kwan's views offensive" instead of "Kwan is offensive." By highlighting the time and circumstances under which certain events occur, indexing uses language that is lower in abstraction. Part of playing with phrasing involves sorting out the situations in which indexing may be appropriate. Indexing may be appropriate when you want to be specific and clear in your communication, when the person you are talking to requires specificity and clarity to understand your communication, or when the successful completion of a task requires clear, specific language.

Experimenting with pronouns is another way to play with different phrases and see how they work within a situation. Consider the following three statements:

1. You are angry.
2. I think you are angry.
3. We are angry with one another.

What differences can you detect among these messages? All messages use different pronouns to describe anger. The first message is called a **you-message,** a statement that labels another person and involves some evaluation of that person's behavior. The second message is an **I-message,** a statement that labels the speaker's own behavior. The third message is a **we-message** that labels and describes the joint behaviors of two or more people. These messages are different in terms of where they place the anger emotion. Message 1 locates the anger in the other person, and message 2 identifies the anger as the speaker's perception of anger. Message 3 places the anger in the relationship shared by two people.

Using different pronouns in language opens up different ways of talking (Harre, 1989, in Pearce, 1994). For example, when you use a you-message you imply that the other person is acting a certain way. You-messages can put people on the defensive because they are evaluative and imply the person needs to change. As a result, the subsequent conversation in this example may become focused on the target of the message denying the label "angry." But when you use an I-message you own the statement and acknowledge it as your perception of the other person's behavior. In this way, the subsequent conversation can focus on why you perceived the person as "angry" and whether or not the perception is accurate without labeling the person. Finally, when you use a we-message the emphasis is on what you and the message receiver have done jointly to create the situation. Responsibility is not placed on one individual or the other, but on both. The conversation subsequent to the we-message is in many cases the most constructive of all because it focuses on how both parties can deal with the situation instead of debating the label or the perception.

To communicate competently, you need to anticipate how the receiver will respond to your use of you-, I-, or we-messages. Will the person you're talking to view a you-message as an accusation or as an accurate description of his or her behavior? Will your use of I-messages be viewed by others as an honest attempt to acknowledge that your perceptions may be faulty or will it be viewed as condescending? Will the use of a we-message be interpreted as a justified call to share the responsibility for an event, or will it be construed as an attempt to shift the blame? Playing with different phrasings to understand how others may respond contributes to your grasp of the uniqueness of the situation and person you are addressing and, in turn, overcoming challenges to competence in using language.

Ludwig Wittgenstein once referred to the power of words with the following statement: "Uttering a word is like striking a note on the keyboard of imagination." Language can focus our attention on certain phenomena; it can bring into the foreground certain ideas, ways of thinking and feeling, as well as highlight the importance of particular actions. The language we use can open up new horizons in our experiences both in our communication with others and with ourselves.

Chapter Summary

This chapter discussed the nature of language and offered guidelines for how you might use language competently. Language is a rule-guided system of symbols that allows you to take words and phrases and translate them into meaning. Constitutive rules help determine what particular words mean and regulative rules help you decide how you will respond given the meaning you have assigned a word or phrase. The meaning of a symbol is determined by the arbitrary relationship between a signifier (the word) and the signified (the object being represented) as well as the signifier's relationship with numerous other signifiers (words).

Language plays an important role in our social worlds. It defines who we are and how we perceive our reality. This notion of language began in the 1950s with the Sapir-Whorf hypothesis, which suggested that our world is linguistically determined: Our language shapes how we see the world and what we perceive as real. This hypothesis has been incorporated into a contemporary approach to communication known as social constructionism, which maintains that language constructs our perceptions of reality and the kinds of relationships we create with one another.

Because language is an active force in creating our social worlds, what key functions does it serve? First, language makes us notice things. The words we use and the way we phrase things direct our attention to particular aspects of our social worlds and away from others. Second, language creates opportunities and limitations. How we label events and people opens up certain lines of action while closing off others. Third, language creates our identities. The way we talk and relate with one another creates our gender identity, racial identity, among many others. Some forms of communication such as hate, racist, or sexist speech are problematic because they have the potential to create negative images and identities. One challenge for competent communicators is using language that is unbiased and avoids the pitfalls associated with hate, racist, or sexist speech. Fourth, language facilitates social coordination. This is achieved by selecting language that does not make people defensive and manages the level of abstraction so others can understand your language and coordinate their actions with you.

Language also presents many challenges to competent communication. In contemporary society, we belong to a great number of language communities that are defined according to profession or vocation, gender, race or ethnicity, sexual orientation, and so on. Each language community may have a unique way of using language. One of the challenges is finding ways to express yourself that connect you with people from a different language community and allow you to be heard. Because we belong to multiple language communities at once, determining which language community is dominant for the person that you are talking to at a particular moment will help you to connect with that person's language community.

Competent communicators can develop several strategies for overcoming these challenges to language: (1) inviting curiosity about the meaning of words by using clarification, showing, and comparison questions; (2) anticipating possible interpretations before you speak by examining your wording from different perspectives, understanding the larger context in which your message occurs, and exploring the historical background for your message; and (3) playing with possible phrasings through the use of indexing and pronoun use. Indexing allows you to place an issue, event, or person in a specific time or context to make your communication more specific and avoid labeling. Experimenting with pronouns enables you to use you-, I-, and we-messages to better understand how your audience will respond to the phrasing.

Key Terms

- language
- constitutive rules
- regulative rules
- symbol
- signifier
- signified
- symbol system
- Sapir-Whorf hypothesis
- social constructionism
- deficit language
- rhetorical exhaustion
- politically correct (PC) language
- gender role socialization
- hate speech
- Ladder of Abstraction
- language community
- social location
- social commitment
- ethnocentric communicators
- cosmopolitan communicators
- clarification questions
- "showing" questions
- comparison questions
- episode
- indexing
- you-message
- I-message
- we-message

Building Knowledge

1. Why is it important to see how words or signifiers relate to other words or signifiers? For example, why is it important to know whether the word *execute* relates to words like *computer* and *program* as opposed to *prison* and *justice*?
2. Describe a situation in which the language someone used caused you to notice something about the situation that you might not normally have noticed. What language did the person use to focus your attention on that aspect of the situation?

3. In what ways do language and labeling create opportunities or constraints? Give an example of language that does both.
4. Is clear language always the best language to use? Under what conditions is it competent to use clear language? Under what conditions might it be better to use ambiguous language?
5. Recall a situation in which you used very abstract language that may have caused a misunderstanding. Using the Ladder of Abstraction, what could you have said that would have been more concrete and facilitated understanding?
6. If you are not sure of the meaning of what a person is saying, what kinds of questions would you ask to help make sense of his or her meaning?
7. Consider a situation in which you felt your language was misunderstood by another person. In what other ways could you have phrased your message in order to be better understood?

Building Skills

Individual Activities

1. Write down as many bumper sticker messages as you can recall. Next write a list of the different kinds of people you know. How would each of them interpret the meaning of each bumper sticker?
2. Consider the following kinds of conversations: job interview, greeting a friend, greeting a professor, and asking someone out for a date. For each conversation write down as many constitutive rules as you can. For each constitutive rule, try to draw a regulative rule using Figure 4.2 as a guide. How can understanding the rules of language make you a more competent communicator in each type of communication?
3. Take a word and place it in the center diagram here. List five words associated with that word. For each of the five words you generate, list four words associated with each word. What does your diagram tell you about the related nature of words? What would happen to the meanings of the other words if you change one of the words in your diagram?
4. The three major national political parties in the United States have Web sites: American Reform Party (**http://www.americanreform.org/**); Democratic Party Online (**http://www.democrats.org/**); Republican National Committee (**http://www.rnc.org/**). Look at each Web site and examine the language used to describe the party that sponsors the Web site. What kind of language is used to describe the views of opposition parties? How do the words and phrases used to describe the parties differ?

Group Exercises

1. Form groups of 4–5 students. Using the following list of words, compare what the words mean to each member of the group. Discuss how the meaning of a word changes depending on the language community to which a group member belongs.

   family values — family planning
   happiness — freedom
   liberal — success
   welfare

DIAGRAM (QUESTION 3)

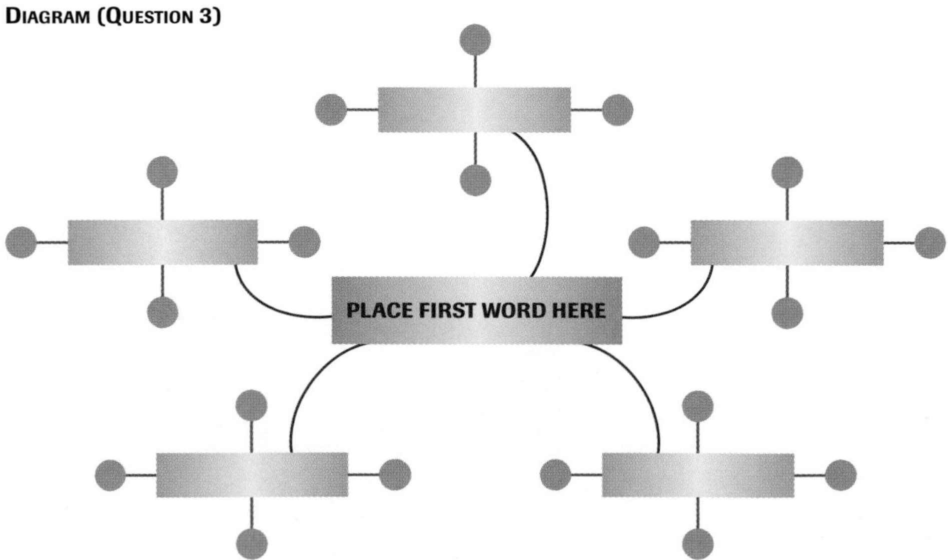

2. Form groups of 4–5 students. Have one of the group members answer the following question: "What does it mean to be a good friend?" Each group member then asks a question of the first person that adds to the understanding of the meaning the first person has for "good friend." After each question has been asked and answered, go to the next person. Repeat this process for each person in the group. Discuss the kinds of questions that help you understand the meanings that people have for words.
3. Form groups of 4–5 students. Each person should select one of the following terms:
   African American communication
   Asian American communication
   Gay/lesbian communication
   Gender communication
   Latino (Hispanic) American communication
4. Using *Infotrac College Edition* each person should look up the term they have selected. Print the citations of the articles that have been retrieved. In the group, compare and contrast the citations for each term. Are particular kinds of language communities more researched than others? If so, what do you think might account for these differences? What are the themes that characterize the articles for each group? In what ways are the themes similar or different?

References

Artz, B. L., & Pollock, M. A. (1997). The rhetoric of unconditional surrender: Locating the necessary moment for coercion. *Communication Studies, 48*(2), 159–173.

American Psychological Association (1994). *Publication manual of the American Psychological Association* (4th ed.). Washington, DC: Author.

Birnbaum, J. (1991, June 24). Defining womyn (and others). *Time,* p. 51.

Calvert, C. (1997). Hate speech and its harms: A communication theory perspective. *Journal of Communication, 47*(1), 4–19.

Cilliers, P. (1998). *Complexity and postmodernism.* London: Routledge.

Cronen, V. E. (1999). Coordinated management of meaning: Practical theory for the complexities and contradictions of everyday life. In J. Siegried (Ed.), *The status of common sense in psychology* (pp. 185–207). Norwood, NJ: Ablex.

Derrida. J. (1978). *Writing and difference.* Chicago: University of Chicago Press.

de Saussure, F. (1974). *Course in general linguistics.* London: Fontana.

Dow, B. J. (1997). Politicizing voice. *Western Journal of Communication, 61*(2), 243–251.

Gergen, K. (1991). *The saturated self: Dilemmas of identity in contemporary life.* New York: Basic Books.

Gibaldi, J. (1999). *MLA handbook for writers of research papers* (5th ed.). New York: Modern Language Association.

Guerrero, L. K., & Reiter, R. L. (1998). Expressing emotion: Sex differences in social skills and communicative responses to anger, sadness, and jealousy. In D. J. Canary & K. Dindia (Eds.), *Sex differences and similarities in communication* (pp. 321–350). Mahwah, NJ: Erlbaum.

Hayakawa, S. I. (1964). *Language in thought and action* (2nd ed.). New York: Harcourt, Brace, and World.

Lee, J. J. (1997). Understanding hate speech as a communication phenomenon: Another view on campus speech code issues. *Communications and the Law, 19*(2), 55–77.

Meyers, R. A., Brashers, D. E., Winston, L., & Grob, L. (1997). Sex differences and group argument: A theoretical framework and empirical investigation. *Communication Studies, 48*(1), 19–41.

Mitroff, I. I. (1978). Systemic problem solving. In M. M. Lombardo & M. W. McCall, Jr. (Eds.), *Leadership: Where else can we go?* (pp. 129–144). Durham, NC: Duke University Press.

Pearce, W. B. (1989). *Communication and the human condition.* Carbondale: Southern Illinois University.

Pearce, W. B. (1994). *Making social worlds.* New York: HarperCollins.

Radio DJ. (1999, March 22). *Jet,* p. 19.

Sagrestano, L. M., Heavey, C. L., & Christensen, A. (1998). Theoretical approaches to understanding sex differences and similarities in conflict behaviors. In D. J. Canary & K. Dindia (Eds.), *Sex differences and similarities in communication* (pp. 287–302). Mahwah, NJ: Erlbaum.

Voloshinov, V. N./Bakhtin, M. M. (1973). *Marxism and the philosophy of language* (L. Matejks & I. R. Titunik, Trans.). Cambridge: Harvard University Press.

Wittgenstein, L. (1953). *Philosophical investigations.* Oxford: Blackwell.

CHAPTER 5

Learning Objectives

After studying this chapter, you should be able to:

1. Define nonverbal communication and compare it to language.
2. Understand the important role nonverbal messages play in communication.
3. Outline and discuss the four functions of nonverbal communication.
4. Describe the role of physical appearance and first impressions, body communication, touch, voice, and time and space in nonverbal communication.
5. Discuss the major challenges to nonverbal communication.
6. Outline strategies to overcome challenges to nonverbal communication.

Nonverbal Communication

Bookstore cafés are popular meeting places, particularly for college students. One Saturday afternoon a few days before the beginning of the fall semester, Samantha went to one of the bookstores near her new campus to look over the course reading lists and pick up a few novels. She wanted to see who else was on campus, with the hope of meeting other students who might be taking some of the same fall classes.

For this excursion, Samantha decided to wear a conservative tweed jacket and turtleneck with a nice pair of jeans. Because she was still a little new to the campus, she wasn't familiar with the unofficial dress code for a casual Saturday afternoon, and she didn't want to wear the trendier clothes that were so popular at her previous college.

Upon arrival at the bookstore café, Samantha spotted Justin having a café latte. Justin's clothes, hairstyle, and even personal mannerisms were hip and casual. At first glance, Samantha decided she liked how he looked and acted. He appeared relaxed yet in control—leaning back in his chair with books strewn in front of him. Samantha grabbed a book and a latte and sat down at a table near Justin. Finding Samantha attractive despite her tweedy clothes, Justin moved over to her table and struck up a conversation.

As Samantha became more attracted to Justin, she changed how she communicated through her subtle nonverbal cues. Her voice became a little softer and lower and she leaned toward Justin, smiling and making direct eye contact. Justin was surprised to discover how much he immediately liked Samantha despite her conservative appearance. He had seen her the day before in the registration office on campus, but today she seemed far more engaging. As their conversation continued, Justin sat up taller and spoke with a little more authority in his voice.

After a second round of lattes, Samantha glanced at her watch and suddenly remembered she had plans for a movie that afternoon. Noticing that cue, Justin leaned across the table, touched Samantha lightly on the arm, and asked if she would like to see him again. She agreed to a date the next week, and Justin said he would pick her up at her apartment at 7 P.M. sharp on Friday night. As she left the bookstore, Samantha wondered how she might control her tendency to arrive late for absolutely everything. She was about to miss a movie date and she was already worried about being ready at seven when Justin arrived. If she wanted him to know she was really interested in him and valued the time she spent with him, she would have to manage her time better than she had in the past. ●●●

During this first meeting, Justin and Samantha reacted to all the nonverbal cues that play a critical role in shaping people's first impressions of one another. At first glance, Samantha appeared conservative because of what she was wearing and Justin appeared more casual and hip both in terms of clothing and behavior. However, both students overcame these differences by using nonverbal communication to enhance their conversation as they got better acquainted. In any interaction, in addition to the actual words being exchanged, the people involved continually read and react to many nonverbal cues. The effectiveness and appropriateness of nonverbal communication, in addition to what is said verbally, adds to the competence of the communication.

This chapter addresses nonverbal communication and helps you (1) heighten your awareness of nonverbal communication, and (2) learn how to improve your competence as a nonverbal communicator. The first step to achieving competence in nonverbal communication is to be motivated to pay attention to the vast number of nonverbal cues that surround each of us every day. Not only is self-knowledge of how we use nonverbal cues, intentionally or unintentionally, significant in understanding nonverbal communication, it is also important to be knowledgeable about the different ways other people communicate nonverbally. These differences result from individual preferences, gender roles, and cultural rules, norms, and prototypes. Finally, competence in nonverbal communication depends on the skill with which nonverbal messages are sent and received. To begin to build a foundation of knowledge, this chapter first defines nonverbal communication and then compares it to language.

What Is Nonverbal Communication?

Nonverbal communication is an evolving area of study. An early definition described nonverbal communication as "all communication other than words." To date, there is still no complete consensus on exactly what nonverbal communication includes. However, nonverbal communication can be understood and defined by first distinguishing between a nonverbal behavior, which contains no intentional meaning, and a message-bearing nonverbal cue.

Defining Nonverbal Communication

Any human behavior or artifact becomes a **nonverbal cue** and communicates a nonverbal message, if meaning is intentionally assigned to it by a sender, a receiver, or a social group (Burgoon, Buller, & Woodall, 1989). The behaviors of scratching your head or furrowing your brow may tell others you're puzzled or confused. If you wear a unique piece of jewelry or a conservative, tailored tweed jacket like Samantha, it may become a nonverbal cue, if someone assigns meaning to what you are wearing. A wink or casual glance in someone's direction may become a nonverbal cue and communicate to that person your desire to get better acquainted (O'Neil, 1998b). The assignment of meaning to a nonverbal behavior or artifact is what creates nonverbal communication.

Taking this approach, **nonverbal communication** includes all behaviors, attributes, and objects of humans—other than words—that communicate messages and have shared social meaning. This includes any aspect of physical appearance, body movements, gestures, facial expressions, eye movements, touching behaviors, the voice, and how people use time and space to communicate. It does not include, however, gestures that signify words, such as American Sign Language (ASL), or the written word or words transmitted electronically.

COMPARING NONVERBAL COMMUNICATION TO LANGUAGE

Nonverbal communication often takes place simultaneously with verbal communication, yet it is not language. So how do nonverbal communication and language differ? Some researchers claim that human beings used nonverbal communication before they developed language, and language actually emerged out of humans' ability to use nonverbal cues (Brook, 1997). Whether you agree with this evolutionary notion or not, the two types of communication differ in several ways compared to language, nonverbal communication is continuous, is more ambiguous, is better at communicating emotion, uses multiple channels, and sometimes operates unconsciously.

Nonverbal communication is continuous, whereas language is discrete. Most of us don't speak continuously, but the minute you walk into a room, before you even say anything, you begin to send nonverbal messages. You may finish your turn speaking, but even while listening, you continue to send nonverbal messages.

Part of the continuity of nonverbal messages is our ability to send them in multiple ways at the same time. You cannot speak more than one word or sentence at one time. However, you can send nonverbal messages through multiple channels simultaneously: through the clothing you wear, your facial expressions and eyes, your body movement and gestures, and so on.

Nonverbal messages are frequently more ambiguous than verbal messages because of the multiple channels through which they are communicated and the numerous possible meanings for any one nonverbal cue. The meanings assigned to nonverbal cues vary culturally, which can introduce even more ambiguity when communicating cross-culturally. Therefore you need to consider the cultural context in which the nonverbal cue is used, as well as your own feelings and perceptual biases.

In addition to its ambiguity, nonverbal communication frequently operates at a lower level of awareness than language does. Most people are aware when speech is taking place, but they are often much less conscious of nonverbal cues. Sometimes, we unintentionally send nonverbal messages or react unconsciously to the nonverbal messages of others, which allows ample room for misunderstandings.

Finally, in comparison to verbal communication, nonverbal communication is more often used to convey emotions and the relationship part of a message. People use language and verbal communication to convey ideas, facts, and opinions, and nonverbal communication to communicate feelings (Burgoon, 1994). We tell people what we think with words, but to convey feelings, we touch, we smile, and we move closer to one another.

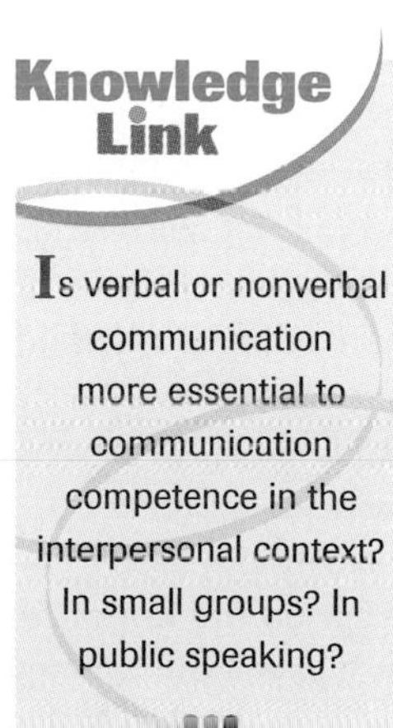

Given these characteristics of nonverbal communication, communicating competently involves being aware that you are continuously sending and receiving nonverbal messages, often at an unconscious level. It is crucial to be aware of the multiple nonverbal cues you are sending as well as your reactions to others' nonverbal cues. Reduce the potential for ambiguity by clarifying the meaning of nonverbal cues as much as possible.

Why Is Nonverbal Communication Important?

The importance of nonverbal communication is demonstrated in a famous story about President Franklin D. Roosevelt. The president was greeting people in a receiving line at the White House. People were walking by, shaking hands with the president, saying, "Good evening, Mr. President, how are you?" Nonverbally, Roosevelt answered as anyone would expect. He was polite, smiling and nodding, while he replied, "Fine, thank you, but I just murdered my mother-in-law." Amazingly, nobody noticed what he said! People paid attention to Roosevelt's nonverbal cues, not his verbal message.

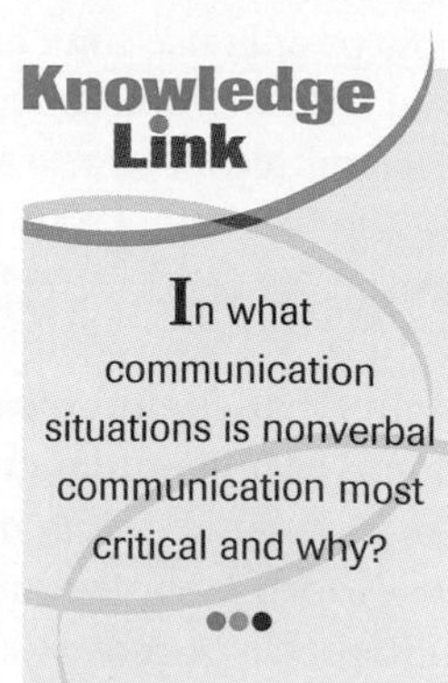

The Roosevelt anecdote has been retold so often that it's hard to know if it happened in exactly this way. However, we do know that people tend to pay attention to and place a lot of importance on nonverbal messages. An early benchmark study of the comparative importance of verbal and nonverbal messages inferred that human communication is mostly nonverbal (Mehrabian & Ferris, 1967). According to this study, up to 93% of the emotional meaning of a message is communicated nonverbally. This leaves only 7% of the meaning in the actual words that are spoken, which is a powerful claim.

More recently, the findings of this benchmark study were challenged based on how the researchers conducted the research project (Lapakko, 1997). The original study involved only 37 female undergraduate psychology students. Obviously, it would be inaccurate to generalize about how most people of both genders communicate based on 37 college women. That said, a subsequent summary of various studies on the importance of nonverbal communication found that a more realistic 65% of the meaning of conversational messages comes from nonverbal cues, leaving only 35% to verbal communication (Philpot, 1983). Figure 5.1 highlights this dominance of nonverbal communication. This research shows that nonverbal communication is essential to competent communication and building mutual understanding.

Further research demonstrates that children who lack the ability to communicate nonverbally develop fewer friendships and often have feelings of incompetence, resulting in depression and negative feelings about themselves (Duke & Nowicki, 1995; Nowicki & Carton, 1997). For adults, the effective use of nonverbal cues contributes to satisfying intimate and romantic relationships (Manusov, 1995) and helps reduce stress in life (Ryan, 1995). Students who receive training and practice in nonverbal communication increase their confidence and speaking performance (Costanzo, 1992). Professionally, good nonverbal skills help lawyers win cases in court, and psychologists interact better with their clients (Hall, Harrigan, & Rosenthal, 1995; Klein, 1995).

Given the importance of nonverbal cues in communication, as well as their frequency of use, developing competence in nonverbal communication will help you communicate better in many situations in your life. Let's now consider how we use nonverbal cues to accomplish various functions in our everyday lives.

FIGURE 5.1
The Dominance of Nonverbal Communication

How much of a message is communicated nonverbally? A summary of research studies finds that a surprising 65% of the meaning of conversational messages is communicated using nonverbal cues.

Adapted from Philpot (1983).

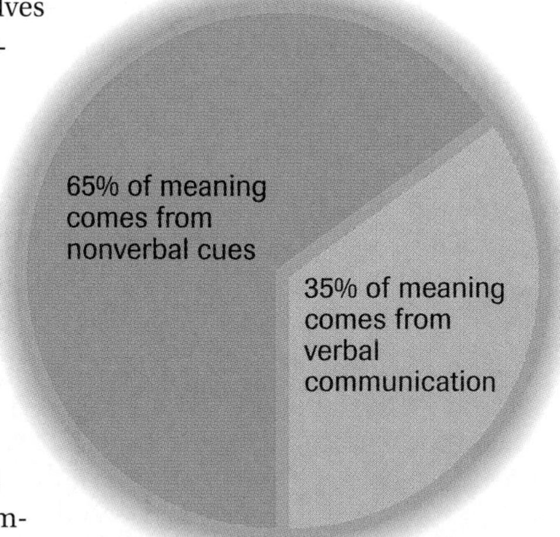

Functions of Nonverbal Communication

As with language, people use nonverbal cues to accomplish a variety of communication goals. We communicate nonverbally to tell others whether we like them, just as Justin and Samantha did in the chapter opening vignette. We use nonverbal cues to make statements about who we are and what we believe. We even use nonverbal communication to conceal the truth. Nonverbal cues fulfill the following functions: They substitute for and repeat words, complement and accent words, regulate verbal interactions, and contradict words.

Knowledge Link

How might you use nonverbal messages to enhance communication competence in interpersonal and group communication and public speaking?

Substituting for & Repeating Words

People use nonverbal cues to take the place of a word or a spoken message. An **emblem** is a nonverbal cue that has meaning for a certain cultural group and substitutes for a word and translates almost directly into a word phrase (Ekman & Friesen, 1969). For example, in North America, people hold up a hand with the palm turned outward to say stop where you are. Although an emblem such as this has a meaning agreed to by a majority of people in North America, it can convey a different meaning in other cultures. For example, the same gesture of the palm held up and outward is considered an insult in Greece.

In addition to substituting for a word, emblems are also used to repeat a spoken word or verbal message. If you're giving someone directions, you would use words to tell him or her that a street is three blocks away. But at the same time, you might repeat the spoken message by pointing toward the street to show the direction or holding up three fingers to indicate it's three blocks away.

Complementing & Accenting Words

Nonverbal cues can also enhance and enliven spoken messages. An **illustrator** is a nonverbal cue that complements and accents the verbal message (Ekman & Friesen,1969). People use illustrators such as tone of voice and rate of speech, facial expressions, and gestures to bring their spoken words to life. Rubbing your stomach and leaning back when saying "I'm full" or scratching your head while saying "Let me see if I can remember" are examples of illustrators. Good public speakers use gestures as illustrators to add excitement to speeches.

Certain cultures use illustrators more frequently than others to add life to their speech. Most Americans make extensive use of illustrators when they're excited or emotionally aroused or when they need to explain a difficult concept or idea. People from Mediterranean cultures and South America often use illustrators even in mundane and simple speech.

Regulating Interactions

People can use nonverbal cues to manage the flow of conversations. A **regulator** is a nonverbal cue that helps regulate and coordinate communication interactions among people (Ekman & Friesen, 1969). For example, regulators are used when one person wants to ask for a turn in a conversation or yield a turn to the other person. If you want to ask for a turn to speak, you might lean forward toward the speaker and use direct eye contact. You can let the other person know it's his or her turn to talk by sitting back and slightly bowing your head in the listener's direction, lowering the tone of your voice, or by stopping speaking altogether. If someone is about to interrupt you, you can suppress the interruption by speaking faster and avoiding pauses.

In the opening vignette, Samantha's glance at her watch served as a regulator that sent the message "I need to end this conversation." Justin responded by setting a date for their next meeting and concluding their conversation.

CONTRADICTING WORDS

On some occasions, a nonverbal message doesn't repeat, illustrate, or regulate the verbal message; rather, it contradicts the verbal message. When a nonverbal cue contradicts a verbal message, you send what is called a **mixed message**. For example, if Samantha is so disorganized that she has to postpone her date with Justin, or if she makes him wait for half an hour, she may communicate a lack of interest in seeing him. Even if she greets him with "It's great to see you," Justin may give more weight to her nonverbal cues.

When a person's nonverbal and verbal messages contradict one another, we do tend to believe the nonverbal message (Knapp & Vangelisti, 1992). An extreme example is that of telling a lie. If when trying to deceive, your nonverbal cues reveal feelings of guilt, nervousness, or any sort of discomfort, the other person is more likely to believe your nonverbal cues over your spoken words.

In fact, research on deception has identified a set of nonverbal cues that people frequently display when they lie. Some liars make fewer hand movements; others tend to look away from the person they're lying to (Feeley & deTurck, 1998; Vrij, Akehurst, & Morris, 1997). Liars' voices also give them away; they make more speech errors and shifts in pitch and hesitate more often than truth tellers (Feeley & deTurck, 1998). They may try to control their voices, which leads to sounding overcontrolled or lacking in control, indi-

"I knew the suspect was lying because of certain telltale discrepancies between his voice and non verbal gestures. Also his pants were on fire."

Nonverbal cues often serve as indicators of deception—even if they are not as drastic as the liar's pants being on fire!

© 2000 Robert Mankoff from cartoonbank.com. All rights reserved.

cating anxiety or possibly deception (Anolli & Ciceri, 1997). Despite these potential clues in nonverbal behavior, most people fail miserably when tested for their ability to detect deception (Goode, 1999). A review of 120 research studies on deception found only two in which subjects scored higher than 70% accuracy at detecting deceit. The people who stood out as expert lie detectors didn't rely on any single cue, like a lack of eye contact; rather, they noticed and interpreted clusters of verbal and nonverbal cues.

Types of Nonverbal Messages

Because people use nonverbal cues to accomplish many different functions in life, they have learned to communicate nonverbally in a variety of ways. The types of nonverbal messages that people send and receive range from physical appearance to body communication, touch, voice, and how people use time and space to communicate.

> **Knowledge Link**
>
> Which type of nonverbal message plays the biggest role in competent communication in interpersonal and group contexts and in public speaking?

PHYSICAL APPEARANCE & FIRST IMPRESSIONS

Physical appearance includes everything you notice about a person including how attractive or unattractive the person is to you, the person's race, gender, height, weight, body shape, clothing, and even how the person smells. Based on this physical appearance, you form a first impression about the person's education level, social status, economic background, trustworthiness, and even moral character. As discussed in Chapter 3, when you attribute these characteristics to others, you may be biased and therefore incorrect in the impressions you form. Furthermore, the first impressions you form impact how you continue to perceive the person thereafter.

Based on first impressions, interviewers claim to know within 1 to 2 minutes whether a job applicant is a winner; and people decide in 30 seconds if a blind date will be a success, mostly based on reacting to nonverbal cues (Berg & Piner, 1990). When Samantha noticed Justin in the bookstore café, her reaction to him was typical of how quickly people form first impressions. Moreover, when Justin attributed characteristics to Samantha because of her tweed blazer, his attributions were incorrect.

One aspect of physical appearance that sends powerful nonverbal messages is clothing and personal artifacts, which include hairstyle, jewelry, and any other personal adornments. Our clothes and artifacts make personal statements about our status, position in life, and even our beliefs and values. For instance, many college students choose to distinguish themselves by wearing particular sweatshirts, T-shirts, baggy jeans, or adornments like jewelry, body piercing, or tattoos.

> **Knowledge Link**
>
> Might nonverbal cues and first impressions represent a great challenge to communicating competently because of the nature of the postmodern self?

In addition to making personal statements, clothing also is used to identify people as belonging to a particular social or cultural group. Many inner-city gangs identify themselves by what they wear. For example, Eric Harris and Dylan Klebold, who were responsible for the 1998 shootings at Columbine High School in Littleton, Colorado, wore long black trench coats as a symbol of their membership in a gang called the Trench Coat Mafia.

Although communication experts do not recommend that you manipulate your appearance, which would be unethical, it is important to be aware of how physical appearance shapes first impressions. If, for example, you are interviewing for a job, remember how quickly you may be judged based on nonverbal cues such as your appearance, alone. Furthermore, when judging others, be sensitive to how their physical appearance affects your reactions to them.

Body language can be used to communicate a message clearly and emphatically.

© The New Yorker Collection 1987 Jack Ziegler from cartoonbank.com. All rights reserved.

BODY COMMUNICATION

In addition to appearance and the clothing and artifacts draped over the body, the human body itself sends strong nonverbal cues. Body communication, or **kinesics**, focuses on how people communicate through movement and posture, gestures, and the face and eyes.

Body Movement & Posture

How people hold themselves, stand, sit, and walk communicates strong nonverbal messages. Whether you intend to send a message or not, every move you make potentially communicates something about you to others. Body movement and posture, also called body language, communicate three things in any situation: how people see power operating, how they feel about themselves in the situation, and how they feel about the topic of discussion. If you feel powerful in a situation, you may communicate that power nonverbally by expanding your body into the space around you or gesturing more expansively. When you feel self-confident, you communicate a sense of immediacy and involvement by facing people directly, sitting in an erect but relaxed posture, and maintaining an open body posture. You communicate positive feelings about a topic of discussion by sitting up fairly straight and looking at or leaning toward the speaker.

Like most types of nonverbal messages, researchers have identified gender differences in the use of body language (Wood, 1994). When men feel in control, they are more likely to expand into the space around them, sometimes tipping their chairs back and spreading their arms out—much like Justin in this chapter's opening vignette. An open body posture, using both the arms and legs, is used by men to communicate power (Cashdan, 1998). By comparison, women are less expansive. In fact, when they feel they have less power, women may constrict the amount of space their bodies take up and tilt the head in deferential positions.

Knowledge Link

Do you agree or disagree that body communication, or "body language," is important to communication competence in contemporary life?

The weak use of body language affects how others perceive women, particularly at work. One study found that a woman executive's intelligence and competence would be overlooked if she communicated weakness through her body language (Mindell, 1996). Weak nonverbal cues include slouching, sitting with stooped shoulders, and clutching the arms around the torso. Based on the results of this study, some female executives are watching videotapes of themselves to identify postures and gestures they can change to communicate more power through kinesics.

Suggestions for using body movement and posture competently include the following:

- Be aware of how you stand, sit, walk, and take up space to make statements about power relationships with others and your own self-esteem.
- Be mindful of how other people use these subtle cues—consciously and unconsciously.
- When appropriate, modify your body language to be sure you are sending the message you intend.

Gestures

Another important aspect of body communication is **gestures**—large and small movements of the hands and arms that communicate meaning within a society or culture. These nonverbal cues are used differently depending on the culture (Samovar & Mills, 1998). People from Mediterranean cultures tend to use large gestures that are more animated than the gestures of people from the British Isles and East Asia.

Gestures are so effective that public speakers such as politicians are now being trained in their use (Ratcliffe, 1996). Even more impressive is a study which found that when blind children speak, they use gestures at precisely the same rate as those who can see (O'Neil, 1998a). Interestingly, blind and sighted children use gestures at the same rate, even when told that the person listening to them is blind.

Used appropriately, gestures can enhance the verbal message, but they also can detract from it (Brittan, 1996). Negative gestures like fidgeting or self-touch let others know that a speaker is nervous. A public speaker who fiddles with a pencil or plays with the buttons on a jacket communicates a lack of confidence, no matter how well informed he or she may be. A lack of gesturing on the part of a speaker may communicate a lack of enthusiasm for the presentation topic. Speakers who don't gesture at all—who keep their hands in their pockets or clasped together in front or back—seem insecure and uncertain, which can damage the speaker's credibility.

Here are a few suggestions for using gestures positively and competently:

- Be sure your gestures match your verbal message. If you're talking about an expansive or important topic, use more expansive gestures. If you're involved in a quiet discussion, avoid big gestures that would seem out of place.
- When speaking, gesture freely and naturally with both hands. Don't clasp your hands together nervously or leave them in your pockets while speaking.
- Don't allow another person's gestures to divert your attention from the message.

Facial Expressions

Movements of the face—facial expressions—are used to convey feelings and the emotional meaning of messages. Facial expressions, also called **affect displays**, communicate six universal and basic emotions that the human face is capable of displaying: sadness, anger, disgust, fear, surprise, and happiness. Surprise and happiness are usually communicated in the eyes and lower face; fear and sadness primarily in the eyes; anger in the lower face, brows, and forehead; and disgust is shown in the lower face (Ekman & Friesen,

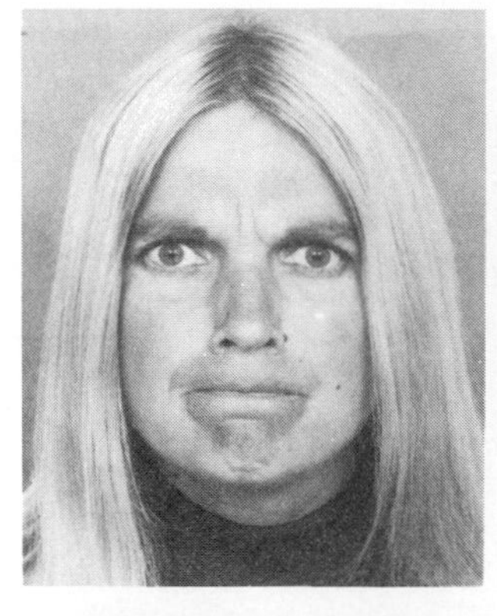
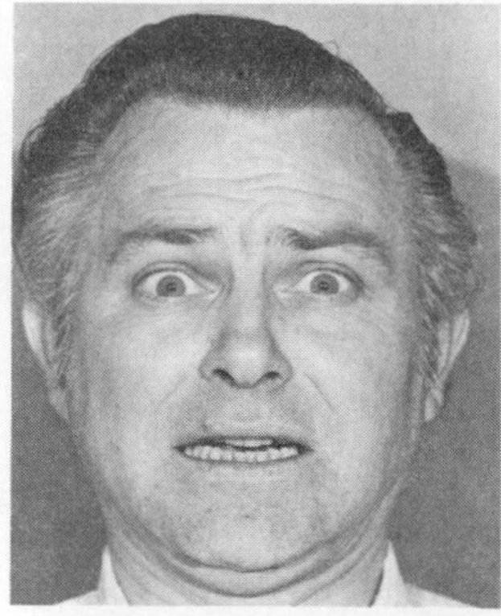
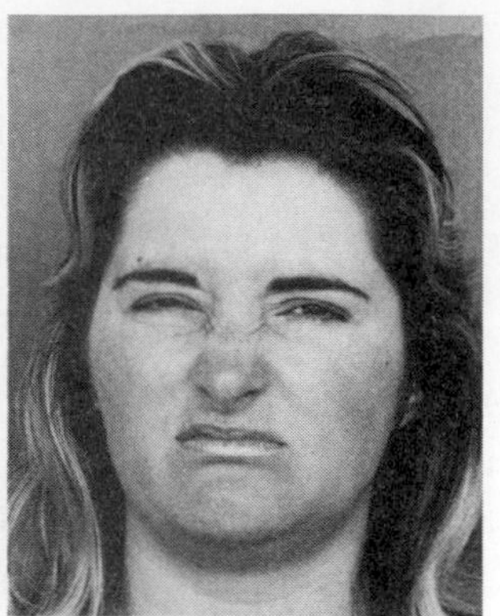
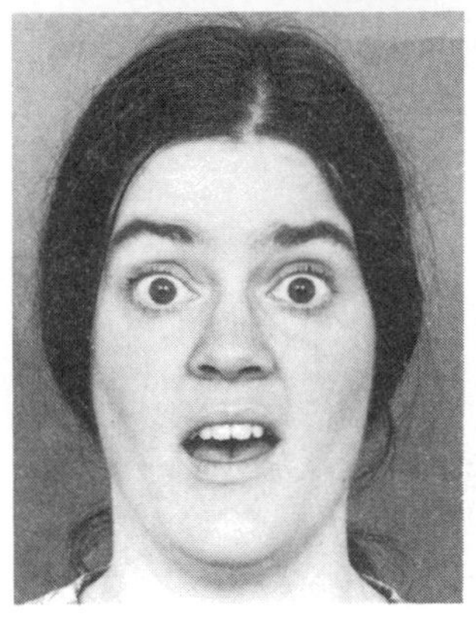

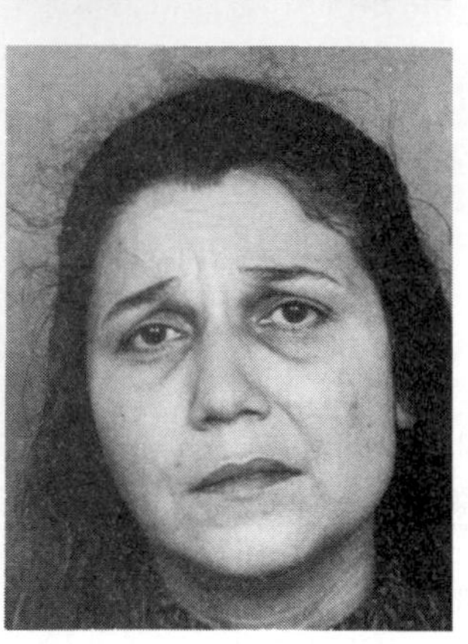

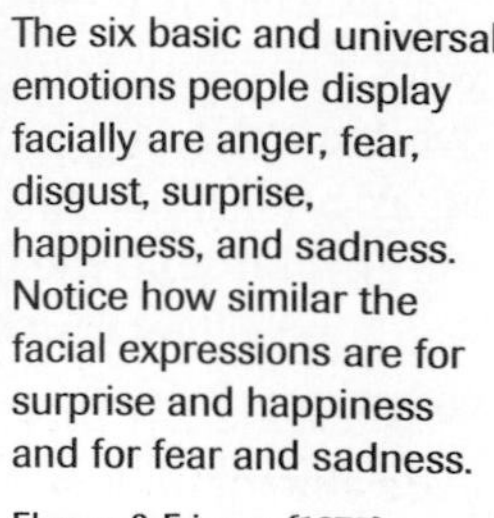
The six basic and universal emotions people display facially are anger, fear, disgust, surprise, happiness, and sadness. Notice how similar the facial expressions are for surprise and happiness and for fear and sadness.

Ekman & Friesen (1975).

1975). Frequently, people blend two or more of the affect displays into one facial expression, resulting in what is called an **affect blend**. Typical affect blends are fear/anger and surprise/happiness.

Researchers have studied the kinds of judgments people make about others, based on their facial expressions. Not only do we judge emotions, we also make attributions about a person's interpersonal traits, such as their tendency toward dominating behaviors—harshness and directness—or affiliative behaviors—kindness and warmth—all based on facial expressions (Knutson, 1996). We perceive a person with a relaxed facial expression as more powerful than someone who has a nervous look (Aguinis, Simonsen, & Pierce, 1998).

Accurately identifying emotions based on facial expressions alone is not always easy (Fernandez-Dols, Sanchez, Carrera, & Ruiz-Belda, 1997). Although people usually know when they are reacting to someone's expressions, sometimes they react to a **micro-momentary facial flash**—an expression that flashes across the face so quickly it is imperceptible. When you have an intuitive sense that something is wrong, you may be reacting to a micro-momentary facial flash.

To confound matters, how people use facial expressions varies based on gender and cultural background (Samovar & Mills, 1998; Wood, 1994). In North America, women tend to be more facially expressive and smile more than men, even when they are not genuinely happy. Men tend to display less emotion on the face and smile less. The Chinese and Japanese don't show emotion freely on their faces in public. In fact, in these cultures, the face is sometimes used to conceal rather than reveal feelings. By contrast, people from Latin American and Mediterranean cultures often display their emotions on the face more freely.

Here are a few suggestions for communicating through facial expressions:

- Be aware of what your face is communicating, particularly in a heated discussion. Sometimes it's appropriate and effective to let others know your feelings; at other times—when negotiating a problem—it can negatively affect your competence.
- Avoid a *deadpan* expression, which can happen when you're involved in a situation of little interest to you. In these situations, others look to your facial expressions to determine whether you're paying attention.
- Be alert and sensitive to differences in how people use facial expressions as a result of individual, gender, or culturally based differences. Although the six affect displays are universal, the timing and appropriateness for different facial expressions varies by culture. If you have any doubt about what someone is feeling, postpone judgment until you can clarify the person's intentions and feelings.

Eye Contact

The eyes as an integral part of the face also send potent nonverbal messages. The appropriate and effective use of eye contact, also called **oculesics**, favorably affects whether you're perceived as credible, dynamic, believable, likable, and persuasive (Aguinis, Simonsen, & Pierce, 1998). People generally use eye contact to accomplish two goals: to communicate interest and intimacy and to express dominance, power, and control. The person with the most power engages in less eye contact and looks away from the other person. The person with less power tries to maintain eye contact and watches the dominant person more closely in order to figure out what that person is thinking and feeling.

At an interpersonal level, we communicate sincerity, trustworthiness, and friendliness using eye contact. When two people are intimately involved, their degree of intimacy is communicated through prolonged gazing at one another. In team situations, we use eye contact to communicate understanding and build a sense of community in the group. Effective public speakers make frequent eye contact with the audience, and good listeners demonstrate interest and respect by maintaining eye contact with the speaker.

To use and interpret this nonverbal cue competently, be aware of variations in the use of eye contact, based on gender and culture. Women engage in more frequent and sustained eye contact than men and are generally more visually attentive than men (Bente, Donaghy, & Suwelack, 1998). Both sexes signal interest and involvement with others by making eye contact, but men also use it to challenge others or to assert their status and power. In Western cultures, like North America and western Europe, direct eye contact communicates interest and respect and indicates that the channels of communication are open. In contrast, people in many Asian, Native American, and Latin cultures are made uncomfortable by too much eye contact. In Japan, people may look away from another's eyes almost completely, and in China, Indonesia, and rural Mexico, the eyes are lowered to communicate deference (Samovar & Mills, 1998).

Consider the following suggestions for using eye contact competently:

- Use eye contact to communicate interest and attention, but don't stare a person down. Remember that some people are comfortable with direct eye contact, but most people are made uncomfortable by staring.
- Because eye contact can be misunderstood, be sure your intentions are clear and watch the other person's response to avoid misunderstandings.
- Because gender and culture affect how people use eye contact, pay attention to any unspoken rules and adapt your behaviors accordingly.

Touch

Touch, tactile contact among people, is another powerful form of nonverbal communication, which social scientists call **haptics**. Touching behaviors and physical contact are considered essential to human social development and to facilitating communication in a variety of situations (Jones & Brown, 1996; McDaniel & Andersen, 1998). Humans need to be touched and offer support to one another with a warm touch on the shoulder or a friendly hug. In fact, one research study on interpersonal communication found that touching a person encourages self-disclosure and makes people far more cooperative (Remland & Jones, 1994).

How does touch play a role in developing self-concept and expressing the self to others, as referenced in Chapter 3?

In addition to facilitating interactions, touch is also used to make statements about relationships. If you recall from the opening vignette, Justin leaned across the table and touched Samantha lightly on the arm when he asked her for a date, a nonverbal cue that marked the beginning of their relationship. Defense lawyers in court use touch to express the nature of their relationships with clients. An attorney might purposefully touch a client to send a message to the jury that the person is likable and not repellant to the touch.

Finally, people use touch as social ritual saying hello and goodbye with handshakes, hugs, and kisses. Social and cultural groups have unique forms of ritualistic touching. In North America, if two people agree or are excited about something, they'll hold a hand up in the air, palm forward, and clap it against the other person's upraised hand. This salutation originated with the African American use of "Gimme five!" and then permeated North American culture as the "high five." However, the high five is now considered dated by hip-hop culture and has been replaced with the "knuckle to knuckle" fist bump greeting shown in the photo here. This greeting has become popular in the sports world and will probably move to mainstream North American culture.

The amount of touching that occurs among people varies culturally. In a benchmark study of touching behaviors, the researcher observed adult couples in coffee shops in different cultures for a one-hour period (Jourard, 1966). During one hour, couples touched each other 180 times in San Juan, Puerto Rico; 110 times in Paris, France; two times in Gainesville, Florida; and zero times in London, England. Similar results were found in a more recent study comparing touching behaviors in low-contact cultures of northern Europe and high-contact cultures of southern Europe (Remland, Jones, & Brinkman, 1995). Italians and Greeks involved in casual conversations touched far more than the English, French, and Dutch. People with a Jewish cultural background touched a great deal; touching was less common among Chinese and Japanese. In addition to knowing how much touch is appropriate in any culture, it's also essential to be aware of culturally based touching taboos. Muslims in Arab cultures, for example, eat and engage in public and socially acceptable touching with the right hand, but reserve the left hand for use in the toilet. Therefore, to touch an Arab Muslim with the left hand is considered a social insult (Samovar & Mills, 1998).

The knuckle-to-knuckle fist bump, a quick one-move greeting, has replaced the high five among members of hip hop culture and athletes.

Marin (1999).

Finally, gender differences in touching behaviors also exist (Wood, 1994). Women are more likely to hug and use touch to express support and affiliation. Men use touch to assert power or express sexual desires; and men tend to touch females more than females touch males. Interestingly, higher status individuals, regardless of gender, touch lower status individuals more than vice versa (Hall, 1996).

Here are a few suggestions for using touch to communicate with competence:

- Be sure the touching behavior is appropriate to the relationship and the situation. What is appropriate with a good friend may not be appropriate at work, and what is acceptable at home may not be acceptable in public.
- Realize that your intention in touching someone could be misunderstood, not just by the person being touched, but also by others observing you.
- Pay attention to how the other person reacts to being touched. Individuals vary in their preferences for touching. If a person reacts negatively, acknowledge their feelings and apologize.

VOICE

The quality of the voice itself adds a significant nonverbal dimension to communication. **Paralanguage**, also called *vocalics*, includes all the nonverbal elements involved in using the voice. To examine the importance of the voice, one research study compared the influence of vocal intensity and touch on getting people to cooperate (Remland & Jones, 1994). The researchers used what they called a "bogus postcard technique" and asked strangers to mail a postcard for them. In one situation, while asking a person to mail a postcard, the person was touched on the forearm. In another situation, there was no touch but vocal intensity was varied, either soft, medium, or loud. Increased vocal intensity was most effective in getting people to mail postcards.

Knowledge Link

Does rate, pitch, or intensity play the greatest role in how you react to a speaker in the interpersonal contexts, in groups, and when listening to a public speech?

The elements of your voice that contribute to communication competence are rate (the speed at which you talk), pitch (highness or lowness of your voice), and intensity (volume). Most communication instructors agree that variety in the use of these elements is essential to being perceived as persuasive, competent, and dynamic. By speaking louder and without hesitation, within reason of course, you will be perceived as more confident, as well as more attractive (Kimble & Seidel, 1991; Zuckerman & Driver, 1989).

Besides vocal variety, the absence of voice, or silence, communicates nonverbal messages. In an age where we are surrounded by constant sound and stimulation, the absence of sound or brief pauses can send powerful messages (Leira, 1995; Martyres, 1995). A silent pause can underscore the importance of a remark and allow listeners to reflect on what was said. Furthermore, using silence effectively will help you avoid filled pauses or **nonfluencies**, the frequent use of distracters and interrupters that slip out when you speak, particularly when you're nervous (uh, um, y'know, and OK). A study of radio talk show "ummers" (people who use lots of "ums") found that too many "ums" had a negative influence on what audiences thought of the speaker (Christenfeld, 1995). This may be because listeners assume a speaker who uses lots of "ums" is either anxious or unprepared.

As with other types of nonverbal communication, people use paralanguage in different ways as a result of gender (Wood, 1994). In general, women use a softer pitch, lower volume, and more vocalic inflection when they speak, as Samantha did in the café when talking to Justin. Men use their voices to be assertive and take command of a conversation, which results in a lower pitch, more volume, and somewhat less inflection. If a woman wants to project power, she could make more use of the men's vocalic behaviors; and similarly, a man could borrow from women's vocalic style to build consensus and encourage cooperation.

Not surprisingly, culture affects the use of vocalics (Samovar & Mills, 1998). Members of cultures that have strong oral traditions, such as African Americans and Jews, value speech and tend to speak with more gusto and enthusiasm. Italians and Greeks also are noted for talking more and using more volume, whereas the Thai and Japanese may speak with quieter voices. In many Asian cultures, where politeness is valued, people talk less and appreciate silence more.

Here are some suggestions for using paralanguage competently:

- Use vocal variety to reinforce meaning, to add emotion to what you say, and hold your listeners' attention.
- Incorporate more silent pauses at strategic points in conversations and control filled pauses that distract listeners from your message.
- When communicating with a person from another culture, anticipate differences in paralanguage and modify your vocalics accordingly.

TIME & SPACE

"Time is money." "Don't keep me waiting ." "Give me some space." "I feel crowded by this relationship." These expressions call attention to a final set of nonverbal cues that you may not consider nonverbal communication. People can exchange meaningful messages with one another using time—the clock—and space—the environment and distance.

The Clock

The intentional and unintentional use of time to communicate is called **chronemics**. How people structure and use time communicates messages about the importance of time in a society as well as how the people value time, how they value each other, and the status and power of those communicating. In a society where a high value is placed on time, such as North America, people try to accomplish as much as possible within a given amount of time. Again, when time is considered a precious commodity, respect for others can be communicated by not "wasting" their time and by arriving on time for appointments. Finally, in such time-sensitive cultures, people with higher status and power control the use of time by deciding when meetings will take place. Status and power are also communicated by making those with less status wait, as their time is considered less valuable.

Chronemics is complicated because its use varies significantly from one culture to the next and from one person to the next. An expert on chronemics points to time values as one of the best ways to get to know the people of a culture (Levine, 1997). Culture, however, is not the only determinant of chronemics. Each individual has his or her own pace and rhythm of time independent of cultural chronemics (Levine, 1997). In fact, partners in troubled relationships might merely be suffering from a temporal mismatch. Revisit the opening vignette; Samantha was aware that her tendency to be late might have a negative impact on her relationship with Justin.

In societies that place a high value on time, people sometimes find themselves rushing from one task to the next, driven by constant deadlines, appointments, and other commitments.

When people from one chronemic culture interact with people from another, problems can arise (Samovar & Mills, 1998). People from the United States, Germany, and Switzerland place a high value on time and avoid "wasting" it, which often results in rushing, multitasking, impulsiveness, and making quick decisions. By contrast, people from Mexico, Japan, China, and Korea favor a slower pace, taking their time and giving full attention to the moment, which results in more reflection and less impulsiveness. As you can imagine, a business meeting attended by people from both types of chronemic cultures could suffer from poor coordination of the group's activities. Participants from clock-bound societies would strive to move quickly to solve the problem at hand; those from less clock-bound cultures would favor a more deliberative approach to problem solving. If the participants fail to acknowledge and coordinate these differences, communication problems would result.

Here are some suggestions for communicating competently using chronemics:

- Be aware of how powerful chronemic messages are, and make sure your use of time matches your intentions. If a friend or colleague values punctuality, the message you send by arriving late for your meetings or not returning phone calls or emails is a negative one.
- When communicating with someone whose culture values and uses time differently, be aware and tolerant of these differences and respect their chronemic behaviors and preferences.
- Understand that a person of higher status, such as a supervisor, may show his or her authority by controlling your time.

Knowledge Link

In what ways might you use time and space to shape the perceptions and impressions that others form of you, as mentioned in Chapter 3?

The Environment

In addition to time, people send nonverbal messages through their use of space. One aspect of space that communicates nonverbally is the physical environment, the actual place in which communication occurs. Physical environments affect how people feel and therefore how they communicate. In an early experiment on motivation, employees evaluated their feelings toward work in three different work environments: ugly, average, and attractive (Maslow & Mintz, 1956). Not surprisingly, the attractive environment made them feel better and more motivated to do a good job.

Architects and home builders are well aware of how the physical structure of an environment affects communication. Designed communities and public buildings contain communal gathering spots for people to meet, such as club rooms and recreation facilities. Private homes have conversation pits and, in a recent trend, larger and open kitchens to encourage conversation while entertaining.

Every environment reflects its designer or inhabitant and provides insights into what the person likes and is like. In one research study, student subjects were able to describe people's personalities accurately based only on interior and exterior photos of their homes (Sadalla, 1987). Two elements in any environment that significantly affect communication are spatial arrangement and the use of artifacts.

Spatial arrangement is the way spaces are laid out and relate to one another, as well as how objects and furniture are placed in those spaces. The positioning of rooms and furniture in rooms can promote or hinder communication. For example, in homes, communication is encouraged by positioning couches and chairs at slight angles to one another and at a comfortable distance apart. Furthermore, if the furniture itself is comfortable, people are more likely to relax and chat.

In the workplace, spatial arrangement sends a message about the power of the employee in question. Upper level executives often sit in corner offices with two walls of windows, and high-ranking vice presidents or managers occupy the offices right next door. The physical proximity of higher level managers to the boss allows them access to him or her, which may often be denied to lower level employees. This proximity allows for increased communication between executives and their management team.

The layout of the office itself also communicates nonverbal messages. In a closed-office design, the executive's office is isolated from subordinates' cubicles and guarded by a secretary's desk. The executive may be seated behind a desk facing visitor chairs, thereby communicating formality and status. By contrast, in an open-office design, individual

Sometimes altering the spatial arrangement of the office doesn't equalize differences in power.

DILBERT reprinted by permission of United Feature Syndicate, Inc.

offices are created within an open space using semipermanent partitions. The furnishings in each office are positioned so the occupant may receive visitors in a chair facing them. Such use of space communicates more accessibility and equal status and encourages open communication.

Artifacts are the objects in an environment that make nonverbal statements about the identity and personality of their owner. These include furniture, wall hangings, books, houseplants, art, or any other items used for utilitarian or decorative purposes in a living or workspace. Artifacts make statements about status and position in life and reveal what the inhabitant of the room thinks is important or attractive. Of course, because money impacts what a person can buy and own, artifacts are not always accurate indicators of personal taste. Rather, they may only indicate what a person can afford at the time.

In addition to artifacts reflecting their owners, there is increasing interest in a practice that suggests artifacts have unique powers when arranged in a certain way in a room. **Feng shui** (pronounced *fung shway*), a 3,000-year-old Chinese approach to spatial arrangement and the use of artifacts, is gaining popularity in North America and around the world. Practitioners of feng shui claim to be able to impact many facets of people's lives, simply by rearranging their homes and offices (Too, 1996). They believe blessings and good fortune result from the correct positioning and use of artifacts like furniture, plants, mirrors, or lighting. Feng shui experts advocate arranging artifacts and space to encourage the flow of energy in an environment, claiming that when energy flows freely, communication will as well.

Distance

How much space you take up, how close you stand to someone else, and even how you identify your personal territory, communicates as loudly as words. **Proxemics** is the study of how people move around in and use space to communicate. Proxemics includes **personal space**, which is how people distance themselves from one another, and **territoriality**, which involves how people stake out space for themselves.

Anthropologist Edward T. Hall (1969) stated that people prefer to maintain comfortable distances from others based on how they feel about them, the situation they're in, and what they're trying to achieve. According to Hall, we choose different distances to communicate with others depending on our relationship, the context, our goals for communicating, and the topic of discussion. Each person is at the center of a bubble in which he or she is surrounded by intimate, personal, social, and finally public space. Figure 5.2 illustrates Hall's concept of how people make use of the space surrounding them.

Intimate space starts at the skin and extends out to 18 inches around you. Typically, we only allow those with whom we have intimate relationships to get this close and usually only in private. An exception is professional situations where close contact is appropriate, such as with doctors, dentists, and hairdressers. Beyond intimate space, personal space extends outward, from 18 inches to 4 feet. The closer part of personal space is reserved for people we know fairly well. When someone you don't know well moves into your closer personal space, you may feel a little uncomfortable. Samantha and Justin in the opening vignette were most likely seated within the farther reaches of personal space, because they had only just met. Social space extends beyond personal space, from 4 feet to about 12 feet. More formal interactions occur within this space, and most conversations at work take place at this distance. Beyond social space is public space, which extends outward from 12 feet and beyond. Teachers and public speakers maintain this amount of distance from students or audience members.

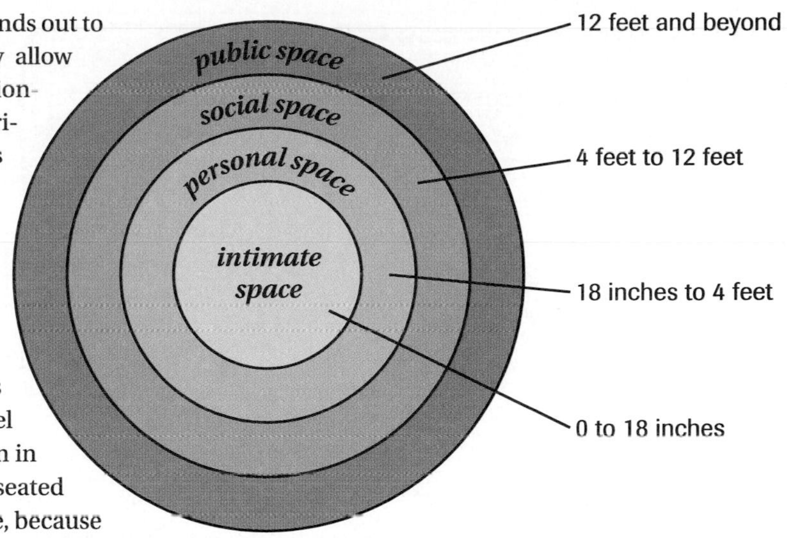

FIGURE 5.2
E. T. Hall's Concept of Space

Each of us is at the center of a space bubble that extends outward from our bodies. We are each surrounded by intimate, personal, social, and then public space. When someone invades our intimate or personal space, it makes us uncomfortable.

Adapted from Hall (1969).

Individual ideas about appropriate distances for interactions result from personal preferences, as described by Hall, but culture also plays a role. In any culture, unspoken norms and rules dictate the amount of space people need and how closely they should interact (Samovar & Mills, 1998). These norms reflect the culture's values and shape how people interact and communicate.

In eastern European, Middle Eastern, and Latin cultures, people tend to sit and stand closer together than in North America or northern Europe. In the United States, people feel comfortable with more personal space, and when this distance is intruded on, cultural norms are violated. When a person from a culture requiring less personal space sits or stands "too close" to a North American, in contrast, he or she may interpret the North American's discomfort or avoidance as hostility, unfriendliness, disinterest, or disrespect.

How people use personal space can make nonverbal statements about status, privilege, and power. Powerful people are usually given more personal space and are allowed to encroach on the personal space of those lower in status. For instance, in the United States, the tendency to give less space to women and ethnic minorities and to invade their space more readily assigns them lower status (Wood, 1994). Nonetheless, invading a person's personal or intimate space isn't always a mistake. In the opening vignette, when Justin moved to Samantha's table, the intrusion into her personal space was welcome.

Closely linked to the idea of personal space is the concept of territoriality. Whereas personal space refers to the space around your body, territoriality relates to fixed space, such as a room, a house, a city, or even a country and its borders. Because people become uncomfortable when their personal space is invaded, they stake out and mark what they consider to be their territory using permanent or fixed markers as well as movable ones.

Fixed markers include fences around houses or a regular seat at the dinner table, as well as the borders that mark where one country ends and another begins. Movable markers are the things you take with you into public spaces such as clothing or books. In the library or at the beach, you spread out your belongings to stake claim to the territory. You may leave your jacket on the seat at a movie theater or a water bottle on the floor at your aerobics class to send the same message.

A sunbather with an exaggerated sense of personal space.

Different people have different needs regarding personal space. We use movable markers to stake out our territory.

Cowles Syndicate, Inc. © 1987.

At an extreme, people encroaching on others' territory can result in a fight or even a war. Gangs expect their territorial boundaries to be respected and countries react with hostility when their territories are invaded. Closer to home, if you're in the library and someone sits down in your territory, you can just pick up your books and move if you feel crowded.

Suggestions for using environment and space to communicate competently include the following:

- Be sensitive to how the environment, spatial arrangement, and artifacts affect how you and others react and communicate.
- Respect other people's personal and cultural preferences for distance, and try to become aware of any unspoken rules for using personal space.
- Respect the territory of others and understand why others may unintentionally invade your territory.

Challenges to Nonverbal Communication

As you can see by now, nonverbal communication is as important as verbal communication, and sometimes more so. Nonverbal communication can be an effective way to communicate, but it also presents challenges to competence. These challenges stem from the quantity and constancy of nonverbal messages and people's low level of awareness of nonverbal cues, as well as from differences in how people communicate nonverbally.

QUANTITY, CONSTANCY, & AWARENESS OF NONVERBAL MESSAGES

First of all, we communicate through so many different nonverbal means and media that we find ourselves dealing with a huge quantity of messages. The sheer quantity of nonverbal messages people send and receive makes accurate interpretation difficult and increases the potential for misunderstanding. Second, nonverbal communication takes place constantly, even when we try *not* to communicate, as long as someone decodes the nonverbal cue as a message. This constant flow of nonverbal cues creates even more potential for misinterpretation. Finally, nonverbal communication operates at a low level of awareness. As a result, we are less aware of nonverbal offenses than when we offend someone verbally. Without awareness, the potential to be misunderstood or viewed as less than competent is great.

Because of the challenges of quantity, constancy, and low awareness of nonverbal messages, the probability of committing critical errors in perception is greatly increased. The process by which we perceive and interpret messages about people, events, and situations becomes far more challenging simply because we are overloaded with or unaware of nonverbal messages. Because our perceptions influence how we respond to situations and to other people, errors in perceiving nonverbal messages can impact our relationships and interactions negatively.

INDIVIDUAL, GENDER, & CULTURAL DIFFERENCES

Although we all encounter challenges of quantity, constancy, and awareness, another set of challenges results from the many differences in how people communicate nonverbally, already discussed throughout this chapter. These differences arise from who we are as individuals, our gender, and various cultural factors.

At an individual level, each of us sends and receives nonverbal messages in our own unique way. Just as each person's way of speaking is unique, each person attributes meaning to nonverbal messages differently. If a friend seems distracted or checks the clock while listening to your problem, you may interpret these nonverbal cues as a lack of caring or disinterest in your friendship. In reality, your friend may be late for an appointment or feel awkward about the confidence. In situations like this, the probability of making attribution errors is great. When you try to determine another individual's motives for behaving in some way, based solely on his or her nonverbal cues, attribution errors are likely to occur.

Gender also plays an influential role in how people send and interpret nonverbal messages. All of the gender-based nonverbal differences related to body communication, touch, and voice represent challenges to communication and can lead to misunderstandings. If a female worker spreads her belongings out on a conference table or speaks at a lighter intensity at a meeting, her nonverbal cues may be mistakenly interpreted as aggressive. The same nonverbal cues would be interpreted as appropriate or simply assertive if displayed by a male worker.

Misinterpretations of nonverbal cues such as these can result from gender-based stereotypes and expectations of what is appropriate nonverbal communication behavior for men and women. When a man or a woman's nonverbal messages appear to violate these stereotypical expectations, his or her communication may be judged as wrong or inappropriate. Take a look at the CloseUp on Gender for a discussion of one possible explanation of why gender differences in nonverbal communication exist.

Finally, cultural differences in nonverbal communication can, at best, result in receiving the wrong message, or, at worst, offend the receiver of the message. Unfortunately, many people are unaware of the cultural rules and expectations for nonverbal communication in cultures outside of their own. When travelers visit foreign countries, they know to bring dictionaries to translate words, but hardly anyone consults a guide to nonverbal communication. This lack of knowledge of culturally based nonverbal differences can present a real challenge, especially as people try to create a community with others from different cultures.

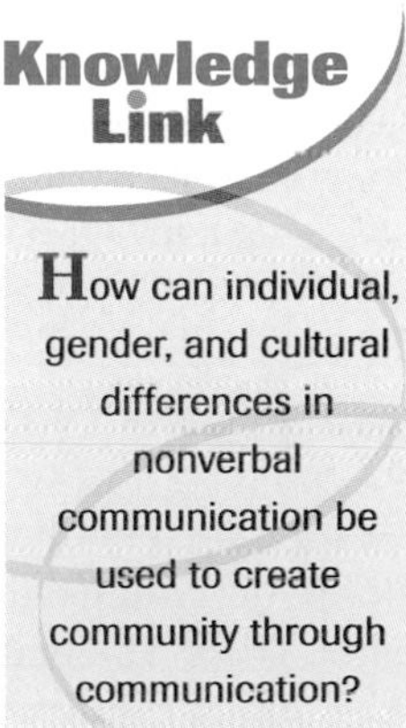

CloseUp ON GENDER

Female & Male Nonverbal Communication—Nature or Nurture?

RESEARCHERS HAVE FOUND that when women communicate, they engage in very different nonverbal communication behaviors than men. They make more frequent and sustained eye contact and they smile and nod their heads in agreement, more than men do. They lean forward and toward the person talking and make affirmative sounds of agreement, all of which indicate they are more relationally oriented than men. Men don't exhibit as many of these supportive nonverbal cues, which researchers say indicates they are less concerned with the relational aspect of communication and more with the content of the communication. Observing these gender differences, you may ask whether these nonverbal behaviors are the result of social learning or an innate, biological sex trait. The question of whether human behaviors that send nonverbal messages are a result of nurture–sociology and psychology–or nature–biology and genetics–is a good one.

According to sociologists, we're conditioned to use the nonverbal cues that our society deems appropriate for our gender. We learn to communicate nonverbally based on observing what other people do in society and modeling the behaviors of male and female role models in families and the social world. Another group of researchers, take a different view of this question The field of sociobiology studies how evolution shapes behavior in animals, as well as in humans. For example, sociobiologists studying human courtship behaviors base their research on primal behaviors, such as the instinct that drives the search for a mate with the best qualities for procreation to ensure the survival of the species. According to the sociobiological approach, men value women who display a variety of nonverbal cues that reflect fertility–full lips, clear skin, lustrous hair, a bouncy, youthful gait, and animated facial expressions, most of which are associated with youth and health. Women value men based on their physical size and strength, and on nonverbal cues that communicate they are ambitious, dependable, stable, and in good health, all traits that suggest a potential good provider for a family. Opponents to sociobiology state that this approach to understanding human behavior discounts the impact of the environment.

Can sociobiology be used to explain human communication behaviors? McCroskey (1997), a prominent communication scholar, argues that people have innate predispositions to communicate in certain ways as a function of biology; however he doesn't rule out the influence of learning on communication. According to McCroskey, genetics (nature) and learning (nurture) interact to influence how we communicate. Based on our neurobiology, we are born with genetically based traits or predispositions to communicate in certain ways, such as some people being more "naturally" shy or apprehensive about communicating than other people. However, life's experiences and situational effects reinforce or restructure these predispositions to communicate in a certain way. Simply stated, nature and nurture are inextricably intertwined in terms of how people communicate nonverbally, and moreover, how men and women use nonverbal cues. Given this perspective, to communicate effectively, we need to understand and value our predispositions in certain ways of communication. It's equally important to examine how we can effectively and appropriately adapt our communication behaviors in various life situations.

We don't yet know which of these factors–nature or nurture–has the most influence on communication behaviors. But we do know that nothing is true of all of the people all of the time. So when researchers say women tend to communicate in one way and men another, these generalities should be construed as just that–generalizations that aren't true of all people all of the time.

SOURCES: Buss (1994), Kenrich & Trost (1998), McCroskey (1997), and Walsh (1995).

As described in Chapter 1, a significant goal of communication is the creation of community. Communication as community is about coordinating actions to bring about desired goals. The inability to communicate nonverbally with persons of other cultural backgrounds can limit how well people coordinate their activities, from something as simple as getting directions to a restaurant in a foreign country to determining appropriate seating arrangements at an international meeting. If people of different cultural backgrounds misinterpret each other's nonverbal messages, the ability to engage in joint actions as a community will be thwarted, no matter how simple the action.

Overcoming Challenges to Competence

Despite how daunting these challenges may seem, a competence approach can provide a framework for becoming a more effective and appropriate nonverbal communicator. You want to be motivated to become more mindful of the nonverbal cues and messages you send and receive using multiple channels. You need to be knowledgeable about and respect the different ways people communicate nonverbally based on individual, gender, and cultural differences. Finally, you need to develop the skills for sending and receiving nonverbal messages, appropriately and effectively, and integrating verbal and nonverbal communication.

Be Mindful of Nonverbal Messages

Because we constantly send and receive many nonverbal messages, it is essential to notice and interpret them accurately. Competence starts with mindfulness of the messages you send, which involves an awareness of all the different nonverbal cues you send with your face, eyes, gestures, body movement, and so forth. After determining what nonverbal messages you are sending, check to be sure you aren't sending any contradictory messages and that your nonverbal messages correspond with your verbal ones. A lack of coordination may send listeners the wrong message or undermine the message you seek to convey.

Being mindful of the nonverbal cues you receive from others involves awareness without overreacting or giving too much weight to any one message. Instead, look for similar messages that are expressed through various nonverbal channels. If you become aware that the same message is repeated in several different ways, then you can more safely assume you're interpreting the message correctly. Finally, remember that some nonverbal messages are unintentional. If they conflict with the speaker's verbal message, avoid jumping to conclusions, ask for clarification, and listen to what the speaker is saying with an open mind.

Respect Differences

Because individual preferences, gender, and culture can introduce differences in nonverbal communication, to communicate competently, learn as much as possible about these differences. As you learn about individual differences, avoid judging other people's nonverbal cues as wrong, and don't expect the other person's nonverbal messages to mirror yours. When sending nonverbal messages, be sensitive to the effects your own individual nonverbal behaviors might have. Be careful that your messages don't offend the other person or overstep boundaries because there is always the potential that nonverbal messages will be misconstrued.

If you are uncertain about what nonverbal cues are appropriate, exercise restraint and avoid nonverbal behavior that could be misinterpreted. For example, do not assume camaraderie or closeness with people you barely know by entering into their personal or intimate space, especially because such behaviors may be construed at best as rude and at worst as sexual harassment. Most important, give everybody respect, regardless of the nonverbal behaviors they exhibit.

When communicating with men or women, avoid attributing specific nonverbal behaviors to the person based on gender stereotypes. Such stereotyping could predispose the other person to demonstrate stereotypical nonverbal behaviors and limit everyone's options in terms of nonverbal behavior, thus derailing communication. Don't assume that you can accurately interpret the other person's motives for communicating based on stereotypes of what men or women can or should do nonverbally.

If you anticipate an interaction with someone from a culture different from yours, educate yourself about that culture's customs, including nonverbal behavior. Being aware of and sensitive to such differences is the first step toward understanding and respecting differences. If anything unexpected occurs during your communication, remain flexible. If someone is late by your standards, stands too close for your comfort, or avoids looking you in the eye, don't take it personally. Remember that the behavior most likely has nothing to do with you and simply reflects cultural differences in nonverbal communication. See these differences as opportunities to expand your own horizons.

INTEGRATE VERBAL & NONVERBAL COMMUNICATION

As you've seen throughout this chapter, nonverbal messages are continuously sent and received, which means they are often communicated simultaneously with verbal messages. Many of the challenges just discussed arise when verbal and nonverbal messages are not effectively or appropriately coordinated. To communicate competently, it's essential that verbal and nonverbal cues work together to complement one another.

Examples that illustrate this effective and appropriate coordination include sports, where coaches are trained to motivate and encourage players by reinforcing their verbal statements with body language (Simon, 1995). Furthermore, therapists are trained to use nonverbal communication to complement their verbal dialogues with clients (Mohacsy, 1995). Similarly, people communicating through electronic media feel the need to integrate nonverbal cues into verbal messages. When using email, they introduce nonverbal cues into email messages, which resemble interpersonal conversations, using symbols that represent basic facial expressions. You'll learn more about these computerized attempts to integrate verbal and nonverbal messages in Chapter 7.

One way to integrate seemingly contradictory verbal and nonverbal messages effectively is to bring the nonverbal message to a verbal level. When a person's verbal and nonverbal messages seem to contradict one another and there is potential for misunderstanding, ask the speaker to clarify the message instead of guessing what the speaker means. This process of clarification will introduce mindfulness and respect for the communicators involved and effectively integrate the verbal and nonverbal messages.

Nonverbal communication, when used effectively and appropriately, helps build understanding and create communities in which people work together to accomplish common goals and participate in mutually beneficial and rewarding relationships. In the opening vignette, Justin and Samantha used nonverbal cues effectively and appropriately to communicate their interest in one another. When Samantha realized that she found Justin attractive, she sat at a table near him. When they began to talk, she lowered her voice, leaned toward Justin, smiled, and made direct eye contact. As a result of these nonverbal cues, as well as her quick glance at her watch, Justin leaned forward, touched Samantha gently on the arm, and asked her for a date. Like Justin and Samantha, you can improve your communication competence by the mindful use of nonverbal cues, by respecting differences in how people communicate nonverbally, and by skillfully integrating verbal and nonverbal communication.

Chapter Summary

Nonverbal communication includes all behaviors, attributes, and objects of humans—other than words—that communicate messages and have shared meaning. When compared to language, nonverbal communication is more continuous and ambiguous, it operates at a lower level of awareness, uses multiple channels, and conveys the emotional and relational part of a message. In fact, 65% of the meaning of conversational messages comes from nonverbal cues, signaling nonverbal communication is crucial in people's personal and professional lives.

People use nonverbal cues to substitute for and repeat words, to complement and accent words, to regulate interactions and conversations, and to contradict words. The types of nonverbal messages that achieve these four functions include physical appearance, body communication, body movement and posture, gestures, facial expressions and eye contact, touch, voice, and time and space.

Physical appearance, which includes clothing and artifacts, significantly impacts first impressions. Body movement and posture communicate how people see power operating, how they feel about themselves, and how they feel about a discussion topic. Natural gestures that match the verbal message enhance it, but negative gestures, such as fidgeting, or the lack of gestures detract from the message. Facial expressions, including the universal affect displays of sadness, anger, disgust, fear, surprise, and happiness, convey the emotional meaning of messages. The effective and appropriate use of eye contact impacts credibility and communicates sincerity, trustworthiness, friendliness, and intimacy. Touch is used to communicate support, power, and affiliation, as well as the intimacy level of the relationship. Vocal variety, or paralanguage, is achieved by varying rate, pitch, and intensity, and using silence effectively. The use of silence and avoiding vocal distracters or nonfluencies is also part of paralanguage. How people use time communicates messages about their value of time itself, their value of one another, and the status and power of the people communicating. How people use and fill up space also sends important nonverbal messages.

Challenges to nonverbal communication include the quantity and constancy of nonverbal messages, the low level of awareness of nonverbal cues, and individual, gender, and cultural differences in how people communicate nonverbally. These challenges can be overcome by being more mindful of nonverbal messages, learning about and respecting differences in nonverbal communication, and integrating verbal and nonverbal messages skillfully. Overcoming these challenges is one way to build understanding with others and create communities through effective and appropriate nonverbal communication.

Key Terms

nonverbal cue
nonverbal communication
emblem
illustrator
regulator
mixed message
kinesics
gestures
affect displays
affect blend
micro-momentary facial flash
oculesics
haptics
paralanguage
nonfluencies
chronemics
spatial arrangement
artifacts
feng shui
proxemics
personal space
territoriality

Building Motivation

See Self-Assessment on page 143.

Building Knowledge

1. Discuss the four functions of nonverbal communication as they relate to the three levels of communication. For each level of communication, decide which function you think is most important and explain why.
2. Explain to someone from another planet who has just landed on earth why humans have two communication systems, verbal and nonverbal.
3. Misunderstandings can result from cultural differences in the use of nonverbal cues. Discuss both the advantages and the disadvantages of those differences and what can be done to transform a potential communication problem into a positive experience for individuals from different cultures.
4. Of the various types of nonverbal messages, which is the most powerful and meaningful in North American culture? Offer a description and examples to support your choice. If you are familiar with another culture, describe which types of nonverbal messages are most important in that culture.
5. If you had to do without most types of nonverbal communication but could choose one type of nonverbal message to use, which type would it be and why?
6. Which type of message is most important in using nonverbal communication to build a sense of community with others? Explain your answer.
7. Knowing how to use nonverbal cues more effectively could give people an unfair advantage and help them manipulate, mislead, or deceive others. What ethical implications are inherent in becoming a better nonverbal communicator?

Building Skills

Individual Exercises

1. On the internet, visit the *Nonverbal Communication Research Page* at **http://socpsych.lacollege.edu/nonverbal.html**. To get a better idea of the scope of nonverbal communication studies, follow links on that site to the home pages of journals, organizations, and researchers who study nonverbal communication.
2. On a single sheet of paper, list the types of nonverbal messages described in this chapter. Next to each type of message, describe how competently you use it. Indicate how you could improve your use of each of the types of nonverbal cues.
3. Go to *Exploring Nonverbal Communication* on the internet at **http://zzyx.ucsc.edu/~archer/intro.html**. Using the photos at that site, determine how good you are at identifying emotions displayed on the face and the meaning of gestures from different countries.
4. Observe several environments in which you communicate: on campus, at work, and at home. How does the spatial arrangement in those environments affect communication? Are there unspoken rules about space and how it is used?
5. If you are using *InfoTrac College Edition,* enter nonverbal communication as the search topic of a subject search. You'll find periodical articles on subjects like eye contact and even hugging. Choose a type of nonverbal communication and read what's available in *InfoTrac* about it. Write a short paper summarizing what you've learned and how to communicate more competently using the particular nonverbal cue.
6. Using *InfoTrac College Edition,* go to an article entitled "Speech class" in *Time,* March 8, 1999, V153 (9), p. 21. Three public speaking experts evaluate the nonverbal cues of five national political figures. Do you agree with the opinions of the experts? Why or why not?

Group Exercises

1. Form small groups of 4–6 students. Select two students to act out either of the following scenarios for about 5–10 minutes. Both verbal and nonverbal communication can be used to role play the scenarios. The others in the group should observe the role-play and take notes about how the two actors use nonverbal cues to substitute, repeat, complement, accent, or contradict words, and regulate their interactions. Observe the types of nonverbal messages the pair uses and then discuss the role play with the student actors.
   - Scenario 1: A student asks a professor to change a grade on an essay exam. The student first approaches the professor right after class, and a second discussion takes place during the professor's office hours.
   - Scenario 2: One student approaches another to ask for a date, either in the school cafeteria, in the library, or in a bar.
2. Form a group of 6 students. Write each of the six basic emotions on a piece of paper and have each student choose a slip of paper from a hat. Each student should

demonstrate the selected emotion for the other group members to guess which emotion is being portrayed. Note if there is any difficulty in identifying the emotions that are part of affect blends.

3.  With a partner, visit a Web site called *The Nonverbal Dictionary of Gestures, Signs, & Body Language Cues* at **http://members.aol.com/nonverbal2/diction1.htm**. Test each other to see how many of the definitions of different nonverbal cues you know.

References

Aguinis, H., Simonsen, M., & Pierce, C. (1998). Effects of nonverbal behavior on perceptions of power bases. *Journal of Social Psychology, 138*(4), 455–470.

Anolli, L., & Ciceri, R. (1997). The voice of deception: Vocal strategies of naïve and able liars. *Journal of Nonverbal Behavior, 21*(4), 259–285.

Bente, G., Donaghy, W., & Suwelack, D. (1998). Sex differences in body movement and visual attention: An integrated analysis of movement and gaze in mixed-sex dyads. *Journal of Nonverbal Behavior, 22*(1), 31–58.

Berg, J., & Piner, K. (1990). Social relationships and the lack of social relationships. In S. W. Duck & R. C. Silver (Eds.), *Personal relationships and support* (pp. 104–221). London: Sage.

Brittan, D. (1996). Talking hands. *Technological Review, 99*(3), 10.

Brook, D. (1997). On nonverbal representation. *British Journal of Aesthetics, 37*(3), 232–246.

Burgoon, J. K. (1994). Nonverbal signals. In M. L. Knapp & G. R. Miller (Eds.), *Handbook of interpersonal communication* (2nd ed., pp. 229–285). Thousand Oaks, CA: Sage.

Burgoon, J. K., Buller, D. B., & Woodall, W. G. (1989). *Nonverbal communication: The unspoken dialogue.* New York: Harper & Row.

Buss, D. M. (1994). *The evolution of desire.* New York: Basic.

Cashdan, E. (1998). Smiles, speech, and body posture: How women and men display sociometric status and power. *Journal of Nonverbal Behavior, 22*(4), 209–228.

Christenfeld, N. (1995). Does it hurt to say um? *Journal of Nonverbal Behavior, 19*(3), 171–186.

Costanzo, M. (1992). Training students to decode verbal and nonverbal cues: Effects on confidence and performance. *Journal of Educational Psychology, 84*(3), 308–313.

Duke, M., & Nowicki, S. (1995). Children who don't fit in need help. *The Brown University Child and Adolescent Behavior Letter, 11*(4), 1.

Ekman, P., & Friesen, W. (1969). The repertoire of nonverbal behavior: Categories, origins, usage and coding. *Semiotica, 1*, 49–98.

Ekman, P., & Friesen, W. (1975). *Unmasking the face.* Englewood Cliffs, NJ: Prentice-Hall.

Feeley, T. H., & deTurck, M. A. (1998). The behavioral correlates of sanctioned and unsanctioned deceptive communication. *Journal of Nonverbal Behavior, 22*(3), 189–204.

Fernandez-Dols, J., Sanchez, F., Carrera, P., & Ruiz-Belda, M. (1997). Are spontaneous expressions and emotions linked? *Journal of Nonverbal Behavior, 21*(3), 163–178.

Goode, E. (May 11, 1999). To tell the truth, it's awfully hard to spot a liar. *New York Times*, F-1.

Hall, E. T. (1969). *The hidden dimension.* Garden City, NY: Doubleday.

Hall, J. A. (1996). Touch, status, and gender at professional meetings. *Journal of Nonverbal Behavior, 20*(1), 23–44.

Hall, J., Harrigan, J., & Rosenthal, R. (1995). Nonverbal behavior in clinician-patient interaction. *Applied and Preventive Psychology, 4*(1), 21–27.

Jones, S. E., & Brown, B. C. (1996). Touch attitudes and behaviors, recollections of early childhood touch, and social self-confidence. *Journal of Nonverbal Behavior, 20*(3), 147–163.

Jourard, S. (1966). An empirical study of body accessibility. *British Journal of Social and Clinical Psychology, 5*, 221–231.

Kenrich, D. T., & Trust, M. R. (1998). Evolutionary approaches to relationships. S. Duck (Ed.), *Handbook of personal relationships* (pp. 151–177). West Sussex, UK: Wiley.

Kimble, C. E., & Seidel, S. D. (1991). Vocal signs of confidence. *Journal of Nonverbal Behavior, 15*, 99–105.

Klein, R. B. (1995). Winning cases with body language: Moving toward courtroom success. *Trial, 31*(7), 82.

Knapp, M. L., & Vangelisti, A. L. (1992). *Interpersonal communication and human relationships* (2nd ed.). Boston: Allyn & Bacon.

Knutson, B. (1996). Facial expressions of emotion influence interpersonal trait inferences. *Journal of Nonverbal Behavior, 20*(3), 165–182.

Lapakko, D. (1997). Three cheers for language: A closer examination of a widely cited study of nonverbal communication. *Communication Education, 46*, 63–67.

Leira, T. (1995). Silence and communication: Nonverbal dialogue and therapeutic action. *Scandinavian Psychoanalytic Review, 18*(1), 41–65.

Levine, R. (1997). *A geography of time.* New York: Basic Books.

Manusov, V. (1995). Reacting to changes in nonverbal behaviors: Relational satisfaction and adaptation patterns in romantic dyads. *Human Communication Research, 21*(4), 456–477.

Marin, R. (1999, September 9). Hug-hug, kiss-kiss: It's a jungle out there. *New York Times Sunday Styles,* Sec. 9, pp. 1–4.

Martyres, G. (1995). On silence: A language for emotional experience. *Australian and New Zealand Journal of Psychiatry, 29*(1), 118–123.

Maslow, A. H., & Mintz, N. L. (1956). Effects of aesthetic surroundings. *Journal of Psychology, 41,* 247–254.

McCroskey, J. C. (1997). *Why we communicate the way we do: A communibiological perspective.* The Carroll C. Arnold Distinguished Lecture. Presented at the annual convention of the National Communication Association, Chicago, IL.

McDaniel, E., & Andersen, P. (1998). International patterns of interpersonal tactile communication: A field study. *Journal of Nonverbal Behavior, 22*(1), 59–75.

Mehrabian, A., & Ferris, S. (1967). Inference of attitudes from nonverbal communication in two channels. *Journal of Consulting Psychology, 31,* 248–252.

Mindell, P. (1996). The body language of power. *Executive Female, 19*(3), 48.

Mohacsy, I. (1995). Nonverbal communication and its place in the therapy session. *Arts in Psychotherapy, 22*(1), 31–38.

Nowicki, S., & Carton, E. (1997). The relation of nonverbal processing ability of faces and voices and children's feelings of depression and competence. *Journal of Genetic Psychology, 158*(3), 357.

O'Neil, J. (1998a, November 24). Thinking with a wave of the hand. *New York Times,* F- 8.

O'Neil, J. (1998b, December 8). That sly 'don't-come-hither' stare. *New York Times,* F-7.

Philpot, J. S. (1983). *The relative contribution to meaning of verbal and nonverbal channels of communication: A meta-analysis.* Unpublished master's thesis, University of Nebraska.

Ratcliffe, M. (1996). Gesture, posture and pose: Everybody's acting nowadays. *New Statesmen, 26,* 41.

Remland, M. S., & Jones, T. S. (1994). The influence of vocal intensity and touch on compliance gaining. *Journal of Social Psychology, 134,* 89–97.

Remland, M., Jones, T., & Brinkman, H. (1995). Interpersonal distance, body orientation, and touch: Effects of culture, gender, and age. *Journal of Social Psychology, 135*(3), 281–298.

Ryan, M. E. (1995). Good nonverbal communication skills can reduce stress. *Law Office Management, Trial, 31*(1), 70.

Sadalla, E. (1987). Identity and symbolism in housing. *Environment and Behavior, 19,* 569–587.

Samovar, L., & Mills, J. (1998). *Oral communication: Speaking across cultures.* Boston: McGraw-Hill.

Simon, M.A. (1995). The unspoken language of motivation. *Scholastic Coach, 64*(6), 68–70.

Too, L. (1996). *The complete illustrated guide to feng shui.* Rockport, ME: Elements Books.

Vrij, A., Akehurst, L., & Morris, P. (1997). Individual differences in hand movements during deception. *Journal of Nonverbal Behavior, 21*(2), 87–102.

Walsh, A. (1995). *Biosociology: An emerging paradigm.* Westport, CT: Praeger.

Wood, J. T. (1994). *Gendered lives: Communication, gender, and culture.* Belmont, CA: Wadsworth.

Zuckerman, M., & Driver, R. (1989). What sounds beautiful is good: The vocal attractiveness stereotype. *Journal of Nonverbal Behavior, 13,* 67–82.

Building Motivation

Self-Assessment: Rate each of the eight communication situations described here, indicating your own typical level of nonverbal competence. Rate each situation for motivation, knowledge, and skills. Use the 1–4 scale, with 1 minimal competence and 4 high competence. Rate one component (motivation) all the way through for all eight situations, then rate the next component (knowledge) and then the third (skills).

Motivation	Knowledge	Skills
1 = Distracted, disinterested, or simply no motivation to be competent	**1** = Completely inexperienced and ignorant about what to do and how to do it	**1** = Completely incapable of behaving competently
2 = Somewhat distracted/ disinterested, but motivated to be competent	**2** = Minimal experience and sense of what to do and how to do it	**2** = Barely capable of behaving minimally competent
3 = Somewhat interested and motivated to be competent	**3** = Somewhat experienced and knowledgeable about what to do and how to do it	**3** = Fairly capable of behaving competently
4 = Highly interested and motivated to be competent	**4** = Highly knowledgeable about all aspects of what to do and how to do it	**4** = Highly capable of behaving competently

Communication Situations:	Motivation	Knowledge	Skills
1. Visiting a foreign country for the first time			
2. Going on a blind date with a person from a different culture			
3. Meeting a homeless person and chatting for a few minutes			
4. Accompanying a close friend to a therapy group discussion about drug abuse			
5. Presenting a project to a work team at your job or to your class at school			
6. Presenting the commencement speech at your school graduation			
7. Discussing a problem with your boss who is of the opposite sex			
8. Attending a party by yourself where you know hardly anyone			
TOTAL SCORES			

Interpreting Your Scores: Total your score separately for each component (motivation, knowledge, and skills). The possible range of the score per component is 8–32. If your total score for any of the three components is 14 or less, you see yourself as less competent than you should be. A score of 15–28 means you are average at sending and receiving nonverbal messages. A score of 29–32 indicates you have a high level of nonverbal competence.

CHAPTER 6

Learning Objectives

After studying this chapter, you should be able to:

1. Distinguish between listening and hearing.
2. Define listening and describe the listening process.
3. Describe competent listening.
4. Understand the benefits of listening.
5. Describe the three types of listening.
6. Identify and describe physical, psychological, and interaction barriers to listening.
7. Understand receiving, constructing meaning, and responding competence and use related skills.
8. Understand and use feedback and paraphrasing.

Listening

Aisha and Jesse met in the computer lab where they worked while going to school. They went out on a date the first day they met and spent plenty of time together from then on. Because they were students on the same campus, they had much in common, enjoying the same activities and becoming close friends—going to parties and sporting events and studying together every weekend.

When they first met, they were curious to find out more about one another and engaged in lively conversations. They would hang on each other's every word, listening attentively and tuning in to the other person's verbal and nonverbal messages. Aisha had a tendency to get excited and talk fast, leaving out a lot of details, but this was not a problem for Jesse. After listening closely to what Aisha said, he would try to figure out what she meant and decipher her message. Then he would explain his perception of what she said and ask her to clarify any misunderstandings. Similarly, when Jesse told Aisha about his shift in the computer lab, she would listen carefully to every detail, expressing genuine interest in even the most mundane of his daily activities.

However, as time went on Aisha and Jesse became less enamored with one another. During this cooling-off period in the relationship their excellent listening skills faded proportionally. In contrast to the early days of their friendship, there were times when they didn't listen to each other at all. Jesse would be lamenting the unreasonable demands and amount of study time required by his calculus professor, and Aisha found her attention wandering from Jesse's problem to matters more important to her. When Jesse would ask for advice on how to approach the professor, Aisha faced the listening dilemma of having no answer to his question, because she hadn't even listened to Jesse's description of the problem. As a result, poor listening skills began to have a negative influence on what had been a good relationship. •••

Have you ever found yourself in a similar situation? A common *listening dilemma* is not paying attention when you're supposed to be engaged in a discussion. Your conversational partner is talking away and suddenly asks a question or looks for a response from you. You have nothing to say because you weren't really listening. Your mind was far away. What can you do in a situation like that? You could admit you haven't a clue about what was just said, but you would almost certainly put yourself in an awkward position. Or you could make an evasive comment such as "How interesting! Good point! You know, I never looked at it in quite that way!" If you experience listening dilemmas more often than you care to admit, you're not alone. They happen to all of us, in interpersonal conversations, in small group discussions, and frequently when listening to a professor, a politician, or a business leader.

Interpersonally, we tend not to listen when it's most important to do so, during heated arguments with another person. In fact, it's most important to listen when you most strongly disagree with another person. However, our natural tendency during a disagreement is to busy our minds planning a clever remark to counter the other person's argument.

As a member of a small group, listening is one of the best contributions you can make to the group process. Only after you listen to the ideas of other group members, can you evaluate the discussion and offer your best thinking. Unfortunately, instead of listening to other people's opinions, we tend to listen for an opening in the group discussion for a chance to present the best idea: ours!

You probably already know that not all presenters are great public speakers. In fact, you've probably sat through more than your share of tedious lectures, daydreaming and waiting for class to end. Your attention easily wanders from a dull speech and the listening dilemma kicks in. But if the content of the lecture is going to be on the next exam, applying competent listening skills will help you retain the lecture content and save you time later.

We can apply the model for communication competence presented in Chapter 2 to developing listening competence. Based on that model, competent listening involves motivation, knowledge, skills, and sensitivity to the particular context and listening situation. This chapter explores listening from the vantage point of those components of competence, beginning with knowledge and understanding.

What Is Listening?

o begin to understand listening, we will first differentiate between hearing and listening and then examine the listening process.

LISTENING COMPARED TO HEARING

Hearing is an automatic process that involves the physiological reception of sounds (Schnell, 1995). By contrast, **listening** is a learned communication skill, so it implies much more than just hearing. It is a psychological process in which you receive the message, assign meaning to it, and send feedback to the speaker. Hearing, in contrast, frequently takes place unconsciously. When you're sitting in a room and the heater turns on and off, you hear it physiologically, but you are not involved in the psychological process of listening. People who live on busy streets in big cities or next to highways tune out the noises they hear every day. In contrast, when you choose to pay attention to a message and assign meaning to it, that's listening—a highly important component of communication competence.

Knowledge Link

How can competent listeners become more sensitive to those occasions when they are hearing what is said but not really listening?

THE LISTENING PROCESS

The first step in competent listening is developing a better understanding of what it is and how it works. This includes defining and understanding listening as a three-step process. The following definition of listening reflects the best thinking to date of leading researchers and experts in the field: "Listening is the process of receiving, constructing meaning from, and responding to spoken and/or nonverbal messages" (International Listening Association, 1995).

Three key steps in the listening process are identified in the definition just cited: *receiving, constructing meaning,* and *responding.*

Receiving means tuning in to the entire message, including both its verbal and nonverbal aspects, and consciously paying attention. This calls for knowing when you're paying attention and when you're not, which isn't as easy as it may sound. Most people's attention span is very short, ranging from 2.3 to 20 seconds depending on the circumstances. As a result, we are constantly paying attention to some things and ignoring others (Wolvin & Coakley, 1996).

Chapter 3 discussed the perception process, referring to it as *mindfulness*—when you pay attention—and *mindlessness*—when you don't. For example, if you're engaged in a long phone conversation with a friend or sitting through an hour-long lecture, you may slip into mindlessness and not listen to what's being said. Or your attention may wander and you may listen selectively, attending to some things but not others.

Constructing meaning involves how listeners attribute and assign meaning to a speaker's message and mentally clarify their understanding of it. Remember that the meanings listeners assign to messages reside in the people involved, not in the words spoken (Bohlken, 1995).

Chapter 1 referred to meaning as an individual's personal and unique interpretation of a message. Because each listener constructs his or her own interpretation of any message, you need to be sensitive to how other people construct meanings. If you're attending a lecture, your interpretation and understanding of the message may differ from what the speaker intends as well as from the meaning that other listeners construct.

Responding, which completes the interaction between the listener and speaker, is the process the listener uses to let the speaker know the message has been received and to clarify his or her understanding of it. Responding calls for remembering what was said, so the response can include appropriate verbal and nonverbal feedback to the speaker. When listeners nod their heads and look interested in what a speaker is saying, they're responding to the message nonverbally. When they ask questions to clarify or better understand a message, they're responding verbally. Figure 6.1 illustrates the three steps that make up the listening process.

Knowledge Link

Using the three steps in the listening process, how might a listener use communication to create community—as described in Chapter 1?

If you review the listening dilemma at the beginning of this chapter, you'll see that Aisha followed a process opposite to these three steps. She not only failed to pay attention and receive Jesse's message, she tuned him out almost completely. She couldn't construct any meaning out of his message because she had hardly listened and remembered

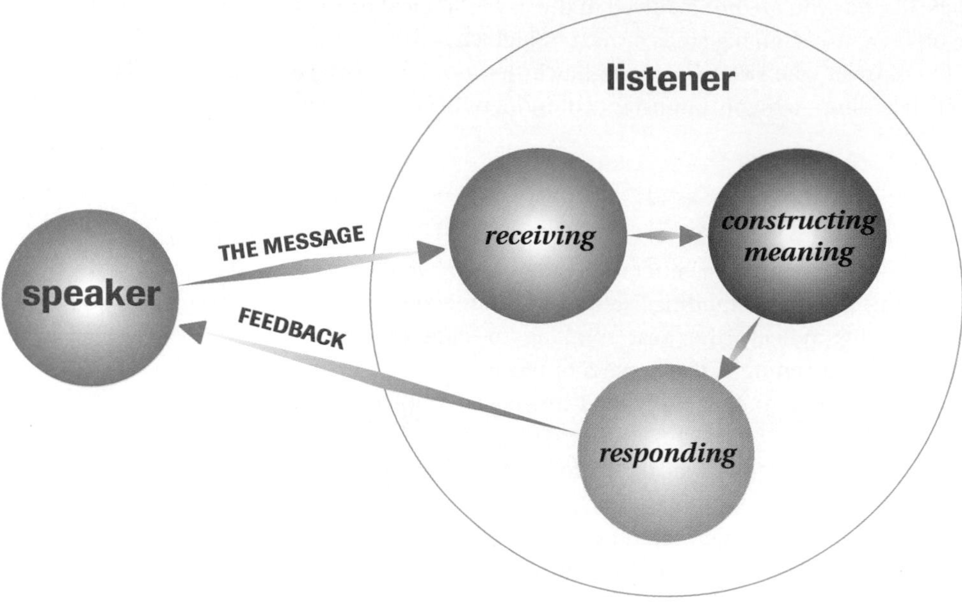

FIGURE 6.1
Listening: A Three-Step Process

The listener receives the message in the first step of this process. During step 2, the listener constructs meaning out of the message that is received. In step 3, the listener responds to the speaker.

so little of it. So Aisha found herself with several choices for responding to Jesse: to guess what he said, fake a response, or admit to not listening.

By contrast to this situation, Aisha and Jesse could have taken a competence approach to listening, which begins with an understanding of how skillful and competent listening differ.

A COMPETENCE MODEL FOR LISTENING

Competent listening is not the same as skillful listening. A **skillful listener** understands the listening process, possesses a set of listening skills, and is able to choose among and use those skills. Skillful listening may sound sufficient; however, national experts explain competent listening somewhat differently (Roberts, 1998; Wolvin & Coakley, 1994). They say that in addition to the characteristics of skillful listening, competent listening includes the *willingness to listen in a variety of different situations.* They describe a **competent listener** as someone who:

- Wants to listen effectively in a variety of situations.
- Knows what to do to listen effectively in a variety of situations.
- Demonstrates the ability to listen effectively in a variety of situations.

Given this description, two elements transform skillful listening into competent listening: the motivation to listen effectively and the ability to do so across a variety of situa-

Knowledge Link

Which level of context—interpersonal, group, or public speaking—represents the greatest challenge to a competent listener's willingness to listen and why?

tions. According to the experts, most people think they listen well, but in reality they are not motivated to listen well in a variety of situations. As you may have experienced, it is easy to listen in some situations, when you like or admire the person who is speaking, or the person is communicating information you want or need to know. Going beyond those situations, a competent listener is motivated to listen even when the situation is not personally appealing or intriguing.

What do you do when a distant relative begins to reminisce about the good old days? Do you tune in or tune out? Are you inclined to listen when a co-worker complains about a problem at work that doesn't affect you directly? If you are a competent listener, you are motivated to listen even when you'd rather not. You listen without knowing ahead of time what's in it for you. Of course, competent listening is not possible all of the time. That would be like a jogger running at top speed continuously (Roberts, 1998). A competent listener discriminates between times when it's essential to listen and times when it's not.

A competence model for listening calls for the listener to apply motivation, knowledge, and skills to the three steps in the listening process—receiving, constructing meaning, and responding (International Listening Association, 1995). A diagram of this model is presented in Figure 6.2.

Knowledge Link

Which step in the listening process challenges communication competence the most, and during which step, is listening ineffectively most likely to occur?

FIGURE 6.2
A Competence Model of Listening

Motivation, knowledge, and skills are essential to competence at each step in the listening process.

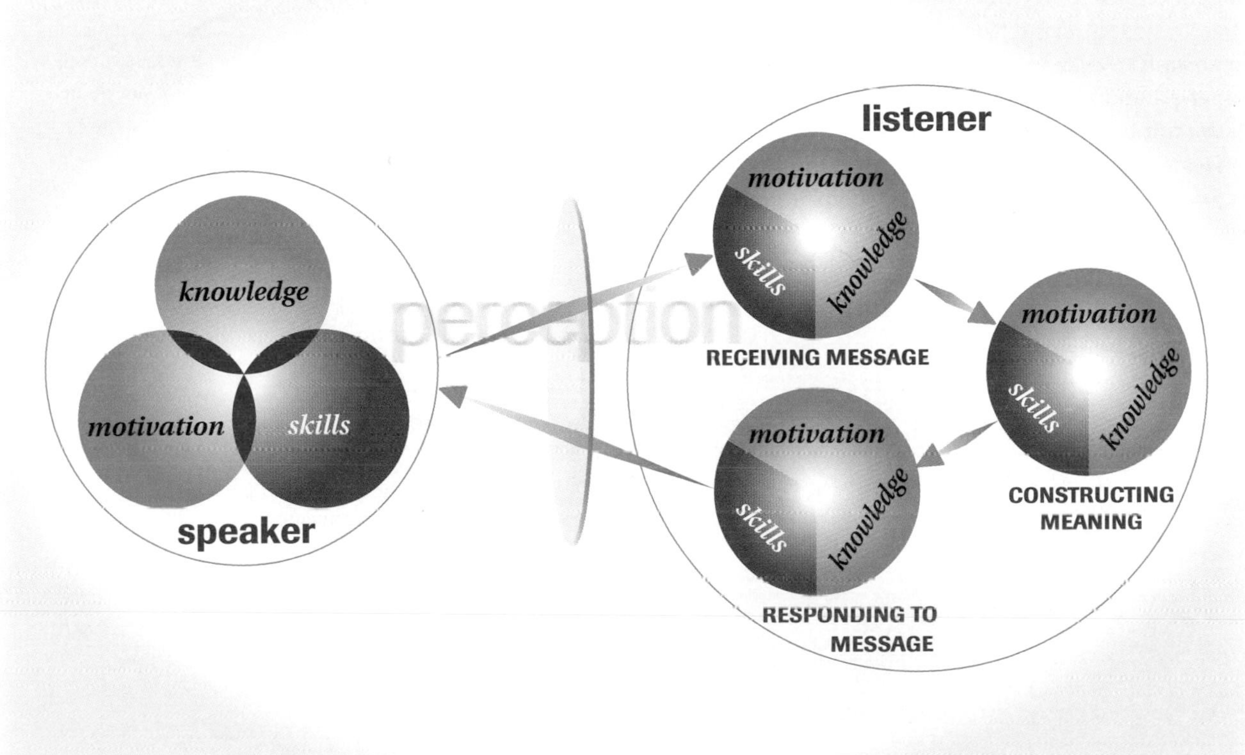

Why Is Listening Important?

Most people, including college students, spend more time listening than using any other communication skill. The results of a benchmark study of how college students spend their communication time illustrate this surprising fact (see Figure 6.3). The researchers found that students spend 53% of their communication time listening, compared to 17% reading, 16% speaking, and 14% writing (Barker, Edwards, Gaines, Gladney, & Holley, 1980). These percentages suggest that listening is the communication skill we use most often in all situations.

If we spend most of our communication time listening, it makes sense to listen well. But, most people are poor listeners. In one study, only 31% of employers indicated that their recently hired employees listen effectively. Another study shows that classroom listening is not as good as it should be; students only recall about half the content of a 10-minute lecture immediately afterward, and one quarter of it two weeks later (Roberts, 1998).

Although this information seems discouraging, there is a bright side. A classic study conducted by pioneers in the field of listening established the value of listening training for college students (Nichols & Stevens, 1957). Students who received instruction in listening displayed a 25% to 40% increase in actual knowledge in various subject areas over students who did not receive such training. Moreover, those listening skills learned in college are transferable to the workplace and to relationships and society.

Given the amount of time people spend listening and the benefits of listening well, why is it most people are not good listeners?

IN COLLEGE & AT WORK

In light of how much time you spend listening, you'll benefit in college by listening more effectively. Improving listening skills helps develop critical thinking abilities, which are important to everything you do as a college student—synthesizing information, writing papers, and taking tests (Hunsaker, 1991). By becoming a better listener, you'll become a better thinker and a better student.

Listening and critical thinking are equally important at work, regardless of your career or job. In today's workplace, all jobs involve communication in some form—speaking, lis-

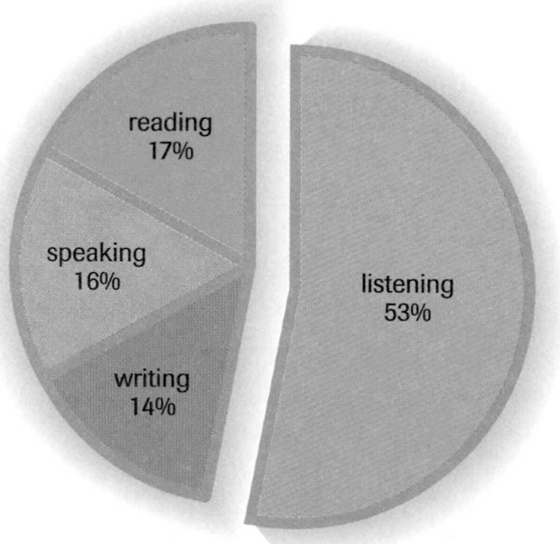

FIGURE 6.3
Communication Activities of College Students

Although college students spend the majority of their communication time listening, listening skills are often overlooked.

SOURCE: Barker, Edwards, Gains, Gladney, & Holley (1980).

tening, writing, and handling information—and a large portion of that time involves listening. In the United States, both employees and executives spend more than half of every workday engaged in listening (Wolvin & Coakley, 1991).

Leaders in a variety of fields, from corporate trainers to teachers and doctors, have related the power and importance of listening to success on the job (Campbell & Inguagiato, 1994; Graves, 1995; Harris, 1997). One study in a large corporation found that listening skills played a central role in how organization members evaluated each other's overall ability to communicate (Haas & Arnold, 1995). Listening skills accounted for approximately one third of the workers' evaluation of the overall communication competence of their co-workers. Those who listened well were perceived as more competent.

IN RELATIONSHIPS & SOCIETY

Not only can improving your listening abilities help you achieve success in college and at work, competent listening also can help you build and maintain more satisfying personal relationships and contribute to a healthier society. Listening builds rapport with others, which enhances relationships, and better relationships result in a more cohesive and functional society.

How does this work? When you listen to people who disagree with you, it demonstrates that you respect them. However, when you disagree, the usual tendency is to tune the other person out and not listen. When you make a conscious choice to listen, the other person appreciates it and respects you more as a result. Thus listening promotes understanding among people and a respect for differences of opinion. Moreover, when people listen to one another, they are often able to see the argument from the other person's perspective, thereby lessening potential disagreements in the future. An internationally recognized linguist and educator expressed this idea well: "As human beings we tend to respect the intelligence of, and eventually to like, those who listen attentively to our ideas, even if they continue to disagree with us" (Hayakawa, 1997).

The heartfelt plea of a student for someone to *just listen* (in Figure 6.4) calls attention to the importance of listening in relationships, no matter where those relationships occur in society. The student, who suffers from a paralysis of the vocal mechanism that limits her ability to speak and articulate words clearly, read the poem "Could You Just Listen" in a public speaking class. She presented the poem on the very first day of class because she wanted her classmates to relate to her as a person and listen to her speeches regardless of the halting and stammering nature of her speech. After listening, her classmates reacted to the poem with a resounding round of applause and repeated the applause every time she gave a speech in class. By the time she presented her last speech at the end of the semester, she had no problem getting the other students to listen to her. Her classmates had learned to take listening seriously and, as a result, had built special relationships with other class members.

In addition to improving relationships, listening competently helps you gain power and influence in society by expanding what you know (Reiss, 1994). Knowledge and information are important commodities in the information age, and the phrase "information is power" accurately reflects the fact that those who acquire more knowledge frequently find themselves in powerful positions in different spheres of society. In fact, competent listening not only provides the listener with knowledge, it also enhances the person's credibility and thereby contributes further to that person's power and influence.

The International Listening Association's Web page (**http://www.listen.org**) provides resources on listening and links to other Web sites, all of which further emphasize the

COULD YOU JUST LISTEN . . .

When I ask you to just listen to me, and you start giving me advice,
you have not done what I have asked.
When I ask you to listen to me and you begin to tell me
why I shouldn't feel that way,
you are trampling on my feelings.
When I ask you to listen to me and you feel you have to do
something to solve my problem,
you have failed me, strange as that may seem.

LISTEN!

ALL I ASKED WAS THAT YOU LISTEN!

NOT TALK TO . . . DO . . . JUST HEAR ME!

Advice is cheap. 20 cents will get you both Dear Abby and Billy Graham
in the same newspaper.
I can do that for myself. I am not helpless,
maybe discouraged and faltering, but not helpless.
When you do something for me that I can and need to do for myself,
you contribute to my fear and inadequacy.
But when you accept as a simple fact that I do feel what I feel,
no matter how irrational, then I can quit trying to convince you,
and get about the business of understanding my own irrational feelings.
When that's clear, the answers are obvious and I don't need advice.
Irrational feelings make more sense when we understand what's behind them.
So, please, just listen and just hear me.
And if you want to talk, wait a minute for your turn.
And I'll listen to you.

FIGURE 6.4 Could You Just Listen . . .

A college student made this plea to her classmates to just listen to her speeches.

SOURCE: Author unknown. Personal records of Sherwyn P. Morreale.

importance of listening in many life situations. Understanding the types of listening, as well as how to integrate them, will help you learn how to listen competently in a variety of contexts.

Types of Listening

Listening can be categorized according to the listener's purpose (Wolvin & Coakley, 1996). People listen for any one of three reasons: to learn and comprehend, to evaluate and critique messages, and to empathize and understand others (see Table 6.1).

Knowledge Link

Is any one of the three types of listening more valuable than another for understanding others as described in Chapter 3? Which type of listening and why?

LISTENING TO LEARN & COMPREHEND

Listening to learn and comprehend involves a search for facts and ideas and a quest for information. This type of listening often occurs during public presentations or when technical subjects are explained or new information is presented. The listener's purpose is to receive a message that is as similar as possible to the speaker's intended message. With this type of listening, people listen because of a need to know something, such as the meaning of facts, figures, or events, or because they want to keep up with the world.

A good example of listening to learn is the classroom lecture, like Jesse's calculus class described at the beginning of this chapter. In a classroom situation, the professor's purpose is that as many students as possible receive and understand the message he or she

TABLE 6.1

Types of Listening

Each of the three types of listening encompasses a particular set of challenges. The solutions to each challenge are shown in the right-hand column.

LISTENING TYPES	DESCRIPTION	CHALLENGES	SOLUTIONS
To learn and comprehend	• Involves searching for facts, ideas, and information	• Large amount of information available • Complexity of information	• Discriminate among available messages • Attend to message carefully
To evaluate and critique	• Focuses on critically assessing and analyzing the speaker's message	• Speaker biases • Listener biases	• Be open-minded • Postpone judgment
To empathize and understand	• Entails concentrating on the speaker's feelings and attitudes	• Disagreement with speaker • Discomfort talking about feelings	• Try to understand the message • Respect the speaker

intends. In a work situation, a training seminar is another context where listening to learn and comprehend is crucial. Attendees need to know the material inside and out to perform their jobs, which is accomplished by concentrating on the speaker's message.

A challenge to listening to learn and comprehend is the vast amount of information that bombards us through broadcast, print, and electronic media. Although you might not think of reading computer-mediated messages as a form of listening, the steps of receiving, constructing meaning, and responding apply to email and chat room conversations. By carefully selecting what messages to attend to and then giving them your full attention, you can listen to learn and comprehend more effectively, both in traditional settings and on the internet.

LISTENING TO EVALUATE & CRITIQUE

In addition to understanding a message, **listening to evaluate and critique** calls for critically analyzing the meaning and merits of a speaker's message. Evaluative listening is more than listening to learn and understand, in that the listener's purpose is to evaluate the speaker's facts, opinions, and assumptions. When Jesse told Aisha about the problems he was experiencing in his calculus class, he was looking for her to listen evaluatively and give him some advice about managing the workload in the course.

As you may suspect, because listening to evaluate involves analyzing the speaker's message, it entails critical thinking: examining the speaker's reasoning processes and logic, sifting through the ideas and evidence presented, and forming your own conclusions of what was said. However, listening to evaluate is not a negative process; critical evaluation is thoughtful and reflective. It's important to remain positive and open-minded while listening to evaluate and critique and postpone judgment until you've listened to the entire message.

Evaluative and critical listening skills are developed gradually. As people mature, they learn to listen critically and objectively. A good example of evaluative and critical listening is what takes place in a court of law. The judge and the jurors listen evaluatively and critically to all the evidence presented and make decisions based on their objective analysis.

Although not as serious as legal cases, you will encounter and experience many situations in your life in which evaluative listening skills are crucial. You may find yourself attending an important presentation in a corporate boardroom or at a civic meeting. At the end of the presentation, you will be expected to comment thoughtfully and provide feedback to the speaker. Or you may be listening to a political figure's presentation on an issue of vital importance to you and your neighbors. In each of these situations, like a judge or jury, you first listen to the evidence and information presented, giving it your full attention. Then you thoroughly analyze and critically evaluate it, before formulating your opinion or decision.

As a juror, your most important task is to listen to evaluate and critique, no matter how emotional the defense, prosecution, or defendant become. Every juror's duty is to cut through all distractions and focus on the very important task of listening.

The main challenge to evaluative and critical listening involves biases, both your own and the speaker's. These biases act as a form of psychological noise and affect how you perceive a message, as well as how the speaker presents it to you. So while listening to evaluate, it's crucial to be aware of your own biases on the topic and how they may affect the steps of constructing meaning and responding to the message. Furthermore, if the speaker appears biased in a way that influences how the message is presented to you, try to separate these biases from the message itself. If the message is intended to persuade, or if the speaker has considerable emotional involvement in the topic, the likelihood of personal bias is increased. By remaining open-minded and postponing judgment, and above all, by listening evaluatively and critically, you can sidestep any tendency toward bias.

LISTENING TO EMPATHIZE & UNDERSTAND

Listening to learn and listening to evaluate concentrate on the content of the message. By contrast, **listening to empathize and understand** entails focusing on the speaker's feelings and attitudes while gaining information. However, when listening empathically, you're not trying to gain information for your own purposes or to form judgments of what is said. The interests, opinions, and feelings of the other person supercede your own. The empathic listener's purpose is to see and feel the world as the other person does and to offer understanding and support or to get to know the person better. Returning to the vignette at the beginning of this chapter, when Jesse shared his woes about the calculus class, he was asking Aisha to listen empathically and understand his frustration with the heavy workload, which she didn't do.

Because empathetic listening helps you understand other people, it's a useful skill in building and maintaining healthy relationships as well as helping other people. If a friend or a partner comes to you with a serious problem, or if you have a relationship problem, listening to empathize is crucial to understanding the other person's point of view. Listening empathically without judging or providing unsolicited advice, then reflecting your impressions of the speaker's feelings and attitudes back to him or her, not only helps your friend feel better, it also strengthens your relationship. This type of feedback plays an essential role when listening to empathize.

One of the main challenges to empathetic listening is having to listen without evaluating or criticizing even when you disagree with the speaker. Overcoming this challenge involves suppressing the desire to argue or debate what the person is saying. Although more positive, jumping in to offer solutions prematurely also hinders empathic listening. Instead, try to just listen to what the speaker has to say and use nonverbal and verbal feedback to let him or her know that you understand and respect the message. Then if asked for advice, you can provide it; however, be careful that your advice is really wanted, it is correct, and the person requesting it is open to listening to it.

Another challenge to empathic listening is how comfortable people feel talking about feelings and emotions. Although this level of comfort differs from person to person, many researchers say that gender is a factor, with men disfavoring discussions about emotions and women favoring such talk. An overwhelming number of women report they can talk more openly and freely with other women about emotional matters than with men (Hite, 1987). Furthermore, women often express dissatisfaction with the listening behaviors of their male partners when it comes to discussing emotional topics (Borisoff & Merrill, 1992).

Whether you are male or female, different communication situations call for different types of listening. Read the CloseUp that describes how gender affects how you listen, and how it may predispose you to one type of listening over another.

INTEGRATING THE TYPES OF LISTENING

Considering the three types of listening as separate, discrete, or unconnected to one another is misleading. There are times when you may want to use more than one type of listening during the same communication situation. Suppose you're talking with a good friend about an important life decision, such as deciding whether to change careers or become engaged and get married. Should you only listen to empathize in interpersonal communication situations like these? Not necessarily. In addition to empathizing with how difficult some decisions in life can be, you may also want to listen critically to evaluate your friend's choices and offer advice if it is requested.

Similarly, if you're participating in a small group discussion to prepare a group presentation, listening to learn and to evaluate critically other students' ideas are both equally important. But if your classmates start worrying aloud about not liking the assignment or about how much time it may take, listening to empathize may be helpful.

Suppose you're participating in a campus organizational meeting to protest the firing of a popular professor. You could listen to empathize with the other students regarding their feelings about the professor in question. However, if the students are planning a protest or a demonstration, it's crucial to listen critically to the other demonstrators, so you can work together toward a common goal. Listening to learn might also play a role when planning the demonstration, to help you learn from others' experiences and plan strategies objectively.

Challenges to Listening

As we discussed earlier in this chapter, competent listening benefits you personally. You'll learn more, have better relationships, and improve your career opportunities and be more successful on the job. Given these benefits, why haven't we all become better listeners already? The reason is that every day we encounter challenges to competent listening: physical barriers, psychological barriers, and interaction barriers.

Knowledge Link

How might a competent communicator use language or nonverbal communication to overcome barriers to listening?

PHYSICAL BARRIERS

The world in which we live and communicate is full of **physical barriers** to listening. This set of barriers includes interferences from the physical environment and distracting characteristics or behaviors of the speaker or the listener.

CloseUp ON GENDER

Gender-Based Stereotypes & Expectations for Listening

TO LEARN TO LISTEN more competently, a good place to start is with an awareness of your own listening style. You may find it surprising, but how you listen is influenced by your gender.

Have you ever noticed that when men listen to a message, they tend to focus more on its content? For this reason, men are sometimes called action-oriented listeners. Women, in contrast, consider content but tend to attend more to the relationship and personal aspects of what is said. Women are sometimes referred to as people-oriented listeners. Imagine a couple discussing a problem. Typically, the man listens for an opportunity in the conversation to offer advice to solve the problem—to take some action. The woman, listens to empathize and understand the feelings of the speaker in order to offer support, not just solutions. Because men listen to offer solutions, they may tune out what they can't solve right away. Or they may not bother listening if there isn't a problem to solve. Because women tend to listen empathetically, they develop relationships more quickly. Two women can meet casually at a social event and sound like life-long friends within minutes.

Cynthia Langham, a listening instructor at the University of Detroit, says that men fall short at remembering details of personal conversations, and women may not be as good at remembering facts. This might explain why a man may forget a discussion about a planned social event but recall all of the details of a major news event. When asked why these gender differences exist, Langham points to socialization. Other communication researchers like Deborah Borisoff and Lisa Merrill agree. They say that society predisposes men and women to use gender-based communication behaviors. What they mean is that society imposes expectations based on gender stereotypes for appropriate behaviors on both men and women, and people tend to conform to those expectations.

Although it sounds like these gender-based expectations may present a challenge to listening, they can be handled effectively by a competent listener. First, remember the three types of listening—listening to learn and comprehend, to evaluate and critique, and to empathize and understand. Gender-based expectations suggest that men more frequently listen to learn and evaluate, and women more frequently listen to empathize. Gender aside, there is actually a time and place for each type of listening. A competent listener, whether male or female, should consider the listening situation he or she is experiencing and decide which type of listening is most appropriate.

Sometimes listening to learn is the right thing to do. For example, you want to listen for content and details at work when you're getting instructions for operating a new computer program or being briefed about new corporate goals. If a candidate for a position in student government or for public office wants your vote, you'll need to listen critically, evaluate the facts, detect biases, and then form your opinion. And when a friend or significant other speaks to you about a concern in your relationship, listening to understand the other person's feelings and viewpoints is the right thing to do. Despite the fact that some researchers say men listen for facts and women for feelings, a competent listener adjusts his or her listening style to the demands of the situation and the needs of the other person.

SOURCES: Ivy & Backlund (1994). Borisoff & Merrill (1992)

Environment & Noise

An environment does not have to be loud to be distracting. Any sounds or noises however minor, can become obstacles to listening. Even mild distractions such as voices from a nearby discussion or traffic in the street outside can become barriers to competent listening. An uncomfortable chair, a bad view of the speaker, or a hot and stuffy room can easily distract you from listening.

Speaker & Listener Characteristics & Behaviors

The physical characteristics or behaviors of a speaker can also put up a physical barrier to listening. A slight accent, a lisp, or even nervous tics or pacing on the part of a speaker may be enough to distract a well-intended listener. In her plea (Figure 6.3), the vocally challenged student asks her classmates to overcome any physical barrier that her speech impediment may cause. Physical barriers can also exist in listeners. Feelings of physical fatigue, hunger, thirst, or even uncomfortable clothing can easily distract listeners. Other physiological limitations, such as hearing problems, also act as physical barriers.

Imagine it's late spring and you're sitting in your first class of the day. It's already 75°F, but the air conditioning hasn't been turned on yet. The instructor asks you to open the window right behind you. Fresh air, sounds of traffic, and the roar of the first lawn mowing of the season waft in through the open window. Nevertheless, you're determined to listen and learn, because the professor made clear that the day's lecture material will be on the final exam. You wish you had left your best friend's birthday party a bit earlier than 2 A.M. the night before. As you try to concentrate on the lecture and listen for main points, you notice that the professor keeps tapping a pencil and shuffling through lecture notes. Slowly, your mind drifts away from the lecture and the information on which you will be tested.

Obviously, this is a worst case scenario for listening. Physical barriers to listening like those just described are common, however, so you want to plan ahead to be ready to listen. Whenever possible, try to avoid opening yourself up to physical distractions in the environment. For example, arrive early and take a seat near the front of the class. At an interpersonal level, if you and a friend need to have an important conversation, choose a quiet restaurant, not a noisy bar. If you are to attend an important meeting or lecture, be as well rested as possible.

Psychological Barriers

Closely linked to physical barriers are **psychological barriers** to competent listening. This set of barriers resides within the listener and includes mental and emotional distractions to listening such as boredom, daydreaming, or thinking about personal concerns. If you're not interested in the topic of a message or if some aspect of it offends you, you may succumb to psychological distractions. Rather than listening, you daydream about a more appealing idea or person. You become inattentive at best, or opinionated and closed-minded, at worst. In the case of Jesse and Aisha, Aisha was already losing interest in Jesse when she succumbed to psychological distractions while listening to him talk about his problems with calculus.

Psychological barriers to listening may cause even competent listeners to become distracted.

PEANUTS reprinted by permission of United Feature Syndicate, Inc.

Psychological distractions to competent listening also frequently occur as a result of two other factors: the difference in speaking and listening rate and message overload and complexity.

Speaking Versus Listening Rate

How slowly people speak contrasted with how fast they can listen causes a psychological distraction. People can listen at least four times as fast as most speakers can talk. According to Ralph Nichols, a pioneer in listening research, the average rate of speech for most Americans is 125 words per minute (Nichols & Stevens, 1957). However, experiments show that people can do a good job of listening to words spoken much faster than the average person talks. In fact, it has been found that people can understand messages that are spoken as fast as 300 words per minute, without significant loss of comprehension.

Taking an average of the findings from different studies, people now talk at approximately 200 words per minute and can listen at about 500 to 600 per minute, a vast difference (Wolvin, personal communications, 1999). This wide discrepancy between the two rates leaves considerable mental *downtime*, during which the mind wanders and psychological barriers like daydreaming begin to occur.

Message overload is a challenge to competent listening in today's information-intensive workplace.

Message Overload & Complexity

Two other causes of psychological distractions are **message overload**—the sheer quantity of messages—and **message complexity**—the extent to which messages are detailed and complicated. Most people spend a large amount of time listening to all kinds of messages and, as a result, they experience message overload. Who wouldn't tire of listening, given the amount of messages we are exposed to every day? We find ourselves listening to teachers, friends, salespeople, and even radio and television personalities. When we sit down at our workstations, we sift through piles of mail, voice mail, and email. In today's fast-paced world, people frequently check their email and voice mail at the same time, or take a phone call and continue to check email, even with someone waiting for a turn to talk at the door. Message overload, discussed in Chapter 7 as information overload, has a serious impact on competent listening.

Message complexity adds to message overload, contributing to psychological barriers and causing even more listening problems. We tend to tune out messages we perceive to be too complex or complicated, particularly if we think we can't figure them out. Have you ever attended a lecture that was hard to understand or contained an overwhelming amount of complicated new information? In such situations, even the best listeners become distracted and, as a result, they lose interest and begin to daydream.

Psychological barriers present even more of a challenge than physical barriers, because they often go unnoticed and unconsciously divert our attention from listening (Roberts, 1998). Furthermore, when your attention wanders, you may deny that a psychological barrier has affected you. When a friend chides you for not listening and being a million miles away, how do you react? Rather than acknowledging why poor listening occurred, most people tend to deny the negative listening behavior.

One remedy for overcoming the psychological obstacles of message overload and complexity is to listen more selectively and attentively. Consider your typical day as a college student. If a lecture at your school is an hour and fifteen minutes long and you attend three or four lectures a day, by the end of the day you may experience message overload and complexity. In addition, you spend some time every day reading and replying to email and listening to friends and family. It's not surprising that your attention wanders and you find yourself not listening competently. Out of all of these messages, you need to make decisions about which are important to attend to and which to ignore. Once you consciously decide to listen to a message, do it with full attention and concentration.

INTERACTION BARRIERS

Although physical and psychological barriers primarily involve ourselves, other obstacles to listening result from interactions with other people. **Interaction barriers** arise in communication situations with others, as a result of engaging in verbal battles and using inflammatory language, or because of cultural differences between the speaker and listener.

Verbal Battles & Inflammatory Language

When people become involved in heated arguments, they often fail to listen to one another. In a variety of situations—at home, school, or work—discussions that begin as conversations about opinions and preferences frequently spiral into disagreements and verbal battles. Unfortunately, these conflicts can easily get out of hand and result in the exchange of inflammatory language, which only makes matters worse. When a discussion escalates to conflict and verbal attack, little or no listening occurs. While one person is speaking, the other is preoccupied with planning a counterattack, rather than listening. We assume we know what the other person thinks and we tend to anticipate and prejudge what he or she will say. As a result, we hardly listen to the speaker's message. When a message isn't listened to, it cannot be responded to fairly and competently.

During verbal battles, speakers often use **trigger words** or phrases that cause emotional reactions, intensify conflicts, and further discourage competent listening. Such words or phrases, particularly in a heated discussion, stop competent listening and foster prejudgment. Suppose one of your co-workers brings up a controversial issue such as affirmative action. And suppose that word acts as an emotional trigger, unleashing strong reactions on both sides of the issue. As the conversation continues, you may fail to listen to your co-worker's viewpoints and he or she may fail to listen to the reasons for your beliefs.

Listening is an excellent way to overcome interaction barriers between good friends.

© Watterson. Reprinted by permission of Universal Press Syndicate, 1993.

Because these interaction barriers can cause emotional reactions in all of us, you can address this obstacle to listening by making a conscious effort to control your own use of inflammatory language and trigger words. However, avoiding these tactics yourself may not be enough to control verbal battles and inflammatory language. You also have to learn to handle such language when you're on the receiving end of it. When you realize you're reacting to a trigger word or phrase and a verbal battle is intensifying, try to refocus the discussion on how you and the other person can communicate more competently. This method of stepping outside the conversation and focusing on the process of communication is often used to diffuse and deal with conflict.

Cultural Differences

A final interaction barrier to competent listening can occur when communicating with people from other cultures and cultural subgroups—sometimes referred to as co-cultures. Recalling the definition of culture from Chapter 2, cultures and co-cultures can encompass characteristics such as race, ethnicity, gender, and age.

Culture becomes an interaction barrier to listening in two ways. Cultural differences in how people engage in listening are a reality, so you need to recognize and respect such culturally based differences in listening styles. Also, people from other cultures may speak or communicate messages in ways that are different than what you're accustomed to. This means you need to listen more competently, despite the fact that the different speaking or presentation style may create a barrier that distracts you from listening.

According to an expert in intercultural communication, the general rules for communication that are learned and respected in a culture result in members of that culture favoring particular listening styles (Wood, 1998). For example, in Nepal, it's considered impolite to make vocal sounds of any kind while listening. On the contrary, in the United States and other Western cultures, sounds like "um-hmm" are used to indicate the listener is paying attention. In Western cultures, it's considered polite for the listener to make frequent, but not constant, eye contact with the speaker. By contrast, in some Eastern and Middle Eastern cultures, it's considered disrespectful for a listener to look directly at a speaker. In some Asian cultures, periods of silence during conversations are considered desirable opportunities to reflect on key ideas being discussed, whereas in most Western cultures, if the speaker pauses, the listener may rush to fill the silence and thereby avert awkwardness.

Although you need to respect and adjust to culturally based differences in listening styles, don't pretend to prefer the listening style of another culture because it may appear condescending. However, you can communicate respect for the speaker if you're aware of and honor cultural differences. If you're listening to a person from a culture that disfavors direct eye contact, avert your gaze. If the other person's culture disfavors any sound from the listener while the speaker is talking, or similar nonverbal cues like head nodding, try to minimize these behaviors. But if a person from another culture is listening to you, don't expect them to display the listening styles of your culture.

Just as listening styles differ, how people send and present messages differs from culture to culture. A competent listener is aware of and sensitive to cultural differences in how messages are presented and adjusts his or her listening behaviors to the speaker's style, by putting aside his or her own cultural expectations for how messages should be presented. Chapters 4 and 5 discussed cultural differences in how people send and receive verbal and nonverbal messages. To listen competently, be patient with how the other person communicates. Make an extra effort to attend to the message and avoid

TABLE 6.2

Challenges to Listening

CHALLENGES TO LISTENING	BARRIERS	CAUSES OF BARRIERS
Physical Barriers	• Environment and noise	• Peripheral conversations, uncomfortable furniture, bad view, crowds, heat, cold, noise
	• Distracting speaker characteristics	• Accent, lisp, pacing, tics, unusual clothing
	• Distracting listener characteristics	• Fatigue, hunger, thirst, uncomfortable clothing, hearing problems
Psychological Barriers	• Speaking versus listening rate	• Boredom • Daydreaming • Worry about personal concerns
	• Message overload and complexity	• Quantity of messages • Message delivery in multiple media • Complexity of messages
Interaction Barriers	• Verbal battles and inflammatory language • Cultural differences	• Trigger words and phrases • Emotional reactions • Different cultural listening styles • Different cultural speaking styles

being distracted by cultural differences. Table 6.2 provides a summary of the three barriers to listening and their causes.

Overcoming Challenges to Competence

All the barriers to listening may seem overwhelming. However, adopting a competence approach will help you overcome the challenges of physical, psychological, and interaction barriers. Let's refer back to the model for listening competence introduced earlier in this chapter (page 149) and examine listening competence at each step in the listening process—receiving, constructing meaning, and responding. Table 6.3 shows how the competent listener makes use of motivation, knowledge, and skills in each step.

RECEIVING COMPETENCE

Receiving competence means the listener is motivated, knowledgeable, and skilled tuning in to the speaker's message and attending to it. When Jesse told Aisha about his problem, she did not receive his message competently—she tuned him out and failed to pay attention. A competent listener demonstrates motivation by being open and receptive to the message and by showing a willingness to adjust his or her listening style to the speaker. If the speaker's use of language is unfamiliar or his or her use of nonverbal cues is distracting, the competent listener remains motivated to overcome these physical barriers and willing to bridge the differences.

A competent listener also demonstrates knowledge and understanding of the various factors that influence how a message is received. These factors include the many ways in which the listener and the speaker may differ—such as their cultures, values,

TABLE 6.3

The Listing Process

MOTIVATION	KNOWLEDGE	SKILLS
Receiving Competence		
A competent listener is motivated to • be open and receptive to the message • adjust his or her listening style to the speaker • overcome physical barriers and bridge differences	A competent listener understands the influence on receiving of • culture, values, communication styles and preferences • speaking and listening rates • message overload and complexity	A competent listener • prepares to listen • clarifies the purpose for listening • identifies barriers and eliminates distractions • focuses attention on listening • postpones evaluation of the message
Constructing Meaning Competence		
A competent listener is motivated to • respect differences in perceptions between speaker and listener • acknowledge that biases distort how meaning is attributed to the message	A competent listener understands the influence on constructing meaning of • perceptual differences of meaning on the message • personal experiences, opinions, and attitudes • personal biases	A competent listener • sets aside biases and prejudices • listens impartially • represses emotional or negative responses • analyzes the message objectively
Responding Competence		
A competent listener is motivated to • show interest and respect for what is said • avert misunderstandings by clarifying the message	A competent listener understands the influence on responding of • feedback and paraphrasing • verbal and nonverbal feedback • interrupting the speaker	A competent listener • identifies and remembers main points • provides verbal and nonverbal feedback • clarifies meaning by asking questions • paraphrases the message • controls interruptions

communication styles, and communication preferences that would serve as interaction barriers as well as differences in how the message is prepared and presented. As we mentioned earlier, the difference in speaking and listening rates, and message overload and complexity, also influence the receiving of any message.

In addition to motivation and knowledge, skills are essential to the competent reception of a message. Have you ever had the experience of attending a lecture and taking notes, only to find that later you don't remember any of the presentation you listened to? Even if you have the motivation and knowledge to receive a message, without skills you cannot receive that message competently. Here are some receiving skills to help you become a more competent listener:

- Prepare yourself to listen mentally, physically, and emotionally. Be well rested and well fed (but not too well fed!).
- Clarify your purpose for listening—to learn, evaluate, or empathize. Set a specific but flexible listening goal for yourself in a given situation. Decide exactly what outcome you hope to achieve by listening to the speaker.

- Identify barriers to listening and eliminate distractions, so you can concentrate on the message.
- Focus your attention on listening in the moment. Concentrate on the speaker and the message, not on your own thoughts and feelings.
- Postpone evaluation of the message until the speaker has finished.

CONSTRUCTING MEANING COMPETENCE

Constructing meaning competence calls for the listener to be motivated, knowledgeable, and skilled when it comes to assigning meaning to a speaker's message. Aisha was not able to attribute meaning to Jesse's message, primarily because she had failed to even receive it. A competent listener demonstrates motivation by realizing that his or her perceptions of the meaning of a message may differ from the speaker. This involves overcoming interaction barriers by setting aside any personal biases that might distort how you attribute meaning to the message as you listen to the speaker.

A competent listener demonstrates knowledge and understanding of the various factors that influence constructing meaning from a message. Competent listeners realize their interpretations of a message are filtered through their own experiences, opinions, and attitudes, and that personal biases affect understanding of the message as well as what the speaker says. *Real meaning*—objective meaning—is not in words, but is individually constructed by both the speaker and the listener.

In addition to motivation and knowledge, certain skills are necessary to construct meaning competently. Suppose you are involved in a conversation with a close friend who is trying to tell you how your behavior has hurt him or her. In this situation, to construct meaning competently, you would need to pause, quiet your own reactions and rebuttals, and construct meaning based on the speaker's perspective and experience. Only when you construct meaning from the message accurately, can you offer a worthwhile response. Here are some constructing meaning skills that will help you listen more competently:

- Set aside personal biases and prejudices as you attribute meaning to the message: Make a conscious effort to listen as impartially as possible before you decide what the message means.
- Repress any tendency to respond emotionally or negatively to the message: Don't overreact or listen for flaws in the message. Set aside your emotional reactions until you've listened to the entire message and clarified your perception of it.
- Analyze objectively what the speaker is saying: Listen for both the global meaning of the message and the speaker's evidence or argument. Mentally construct a picture of the speaker's message and examine and evaluate its meaning and worth, based on its own merits.

RESPONDING COMPETENCE

Responding competence means the listener is motivated, knowledgeable, and skilled when communicating to the speaker that the message has been received and understood. Returning to the opening vignette, Aisha was unable to respond competently to Jesse because she had failed to both receive and construct meaning out of his message. A competent listener demonstrates motivation by showing interest in and being responsive to what is being said. By responding, competent listeners demonstrate respect for the speaker's opinions and ideas and show a desire to take responsibility for averting misunderstandings by clarifying their interpretations of the message.

Feedback is essential to listening competently

LUANN reprinted by permission of United Feature Syndicate, Inc.

Competent listeners demonstrate knowledge and understanding of the importance of feedback and paraphrasing for overcoming psychological barriers to listening. This includes recognizing the role of both verbal and nonverbal feedback as tools to encourage the speaker and clarify the message. Competent speakers also recognize the potential negative effects of interrupting the speaker. Here are some responding skills you should use as a competent listener:

- Identify and remember the main points of the message: Use memory devices such as taking notes to help you retain an accurate picture of the message.
- Demonstrate interest in the speaker's message by providing appropriate verbal and nonverbal feedback: Provide verbal feedback to clarify your understanding of and reactions to the message. Let the speaker know you're listening by using nonverbal cues.
- Strive to understand and clarify the meaning of the message by asking questions: As appropriate, clear up any aspects of the message that are unclear to you.
- Paraphrase the message to achieve full comprehension and clarity: Describe the meaning you have attributed to the message, without evaluating it or presenting your point of view.

Feedback and paraphrasing are central to competent listening. These two processes are described in more detail next.

Feedback & Paraphrasing

Feedback is the process a listener uses to communicate to the speaker, his or her understanding of the message, reactions to it, and any effects it may have had on the listener. Feedback, which can be sent verbally and nonverbally, is the listener's way of informing the speaker of the success or failure of the reception of the message.

Paraphrasing is a technique used to provide verbal feedback to the speaker in which the listener summarizes and restates the meaning of the speaker's message in his or her own words. Because the verbal and nonverbal aspects of a message are both important, listeners may need to paraphrase both. To provide such feedback, you would summarize the content of the message—the speaker's opinions, ideas, and attitudes—and how the speaker appears to feel about the message. For example, Aisha could have paraphrased her impression of Jesse's calculus situation in this way: "I think I heard you say that you're having a real problem keeping your head above water in the calculus class, and that seems to be very upsetting to you. Am I correct?"

In a group meeting at work, paraphrasing can clarify your understanding of a new concept or solution to a problem being presented. Paraphrasing allows the speaker and

Knowledge Link

Is verbal or nonverbal feedback more essential to communication competence? Which is more valuable for expressing the self to others?

other group members to know what you have understood as well as what you haven't, and it gives the speaker a chance to clear up any misconceptions. In addition to paraphrasing, a verbal technique, you could send nonverbal feedback to the speaker in the group by nodding your head in agreement or smiling in reaction to the presentation. Or you might furrow your brow or shake your head in disagreement, if you don't think the idea is a good one.

An important key to paraphrasing and sending feedback competently is the use of language that establishes your ownership of the response. In the case of paraphrasing, you are communicating only your perception of the message and not the actual message itself. You want to indicate this in the way that you word the response. To do this, you can begin the paraphrase statement with an "I" statement and end it with a perception-checking statement. "I think that I heard you say *this or that.* Am I correct? Is that what you meant?" This ownership of your perception of the message is critical because you may not be correct in your perception. The perception-checking question gives the speaker an opportunity to clarify his or her message if, in fact, it has been misunderstood.

Despite the value of feedback and paraphrasing in interpersonal and small group communication situations, these skills should be used cautiously in intimate relationships. Recent research suggests that using paraphrasing to check understanding and express empathy isn't always as effective as previously thought (Gottman, Coan, Carrere, & Swanson, 1998).

Paraphrasing first became popular as a technique psychologists and therapists used to communicate with their clients. The subject of discussion was usually a third party, someone other than the therapist or the client. So the feedback message would invariably be about something a third party had said or done and represent an attempt to clarify some of the details of that secondhand experience. In contrast, in intimate relationships, you may be paraphrasing what the other person just said or your perception of something the person has done. Gottman and other researchers have found that hearing this kind of feedback too often from an intimate partner can become annoying and actually have a negative effect on the discussion. Given these findings, use paraphrasing when there is an obvious and genuine need to clarify your perception of what the other person says, but avoid providing feedback continuously or too often during an intimate discussion.

Paraphrasing and feedback help intimate relationships thrive when those skills are used appropriately.

This caution aside, feedback and paraphrasing can be important skills for a competent listener to use, based on the following guidelines:

- Feedback should be fairly immediate. The sooner feedback is provided to the speaker, the more valuable it is, because people pay more attention to information about recent events.
- The paraphrased message should represent your honest impression and feelings, without being unnecessarily cruel. To avoid offending the other person, preface negative feedback with positive feedback, like a compliment. The positive message predisposes the other person to pay attention to the negative feedback.
- The feedback you provide to the speaker should be clear, informative, and unbiased. Think through what you intend to say to make sure it's a fair and unbiased interpretation of the speaker's message. Then be open to corrections to your feedback.

In summary, competent listening involves the use of three sets of competencies that relate to the three stages in the listening process. In the vignette at the beginning of this chapter, if Aisha had used these listening competencies, she would have avoided a listening dilemma. If she had received Jesse's message and accurately assigned meaning to it, she would have been able to respond and provide feedback to him.

The next three main parts of this book focus on interpersonal communication, small group communication, and public speaking. The motivation, knowledge, and skills necessary for competent listening discussed in this chapter are essential to competence in each of those three communication contexts.

Chapter Summary

Listening is the process of receiving, constructing meaning from, and responding to spoken and/or nonverbal messages. Receiving is tuning in to the speaker's verbal and nonverbal message; constructing meaning involves assigning meaning to the message; and responding is the process the listener uses to let the speaker know the message is received and understood. Hearing, in contrast, is the automatic physiological reception of sounds. Listening is a psychological process; hearing is physiological.

It is essential to go beyond skillful listening and become a competent listener. A skillful listener understands the listening process and possesses and is able to use a set of listening skills. By contrast, a competent listener is highly motivated to listen well across a variety of situations.

Although we spend a large part of our communication time listening, studies show that most people are not good listeners. Therefore, achieving competence in listening is crucial—in college, at work, as well as in relationships and society.

Listening can be categorized based on the listener's purpose. Listening to learn and comprehend involves a search for facts and ideas and a quest for information. Listening to evaluate and critique focuses on critically analyzing the meaning and merits of a speaker's message. Listening to empathize and understand entails concentrating on the speaker's feelings and attitudes.

Challenges to listening competence result from physical, psychological, and interaction barriers. Physical barriers include distractions in the physical environment and distracting characteristics or behaviors of the speaker or the listener. Psychological barriers include mental and emotional distractions to listening, and can result from the discrepancy between speech and listening rates and from message overload and complexity. Interaction barriers arise when people engage in verbal battles and use inflammatory language, or because of culturally diverse listening or speaking styles.

A competence model for listening calls for the listener to apply motivation, knowledge, and skills to the three steps in the listening process and thus overcome the challenges to listening. A competent listener is motivated, knowledgeable, and skilled when it comes to tuning in to the speaker's message, assigning meaning to it, and letting the speaker know the message is received and understood. Feedback is used to communicate the listener's understanding and reactions to the speaker's message, as well as effects it may have had on the listener. The listener uses paraphrasing to restate verbally the meaning of both the verbal and nonverbal content of the speaker's message.

Key Terms

hearing
listening
receiving
constructing meaning
responding
skillful listener
competent listener
competence model for listening
listening to learn and comprehend
listening to evaluate and critique
listening to empathize and understand
physical barriers
psychological barriers
message overload
message complexity
interaction barriers
trigger words
receiving competence
constructing meaning competence
responding competence
feedback
paraphrasing

Building Motivation

See Self-Assessment on page 171.

Building Knowledge

1. If listening improves the quality of life in society, what can be done to encourage more people to listen better?
2. Which of the three steps in the listening process (receiving, constructing meaning, responding) is most important and why? Which step do you think causes the most misunderstandings? Explain.
3. Of the three types of listening (to learn, to evaluate, and to empathize), which do you find most difficult to do and why? How can you address that challenge?
4. Of the three types of barriers to listening (physical, psychological, and interaction), which causes you the most problems as a listener? Why? What can you do about it?
5. If listeners think and understand faster than people speak, should we all just try to talk faster? Why or why not?
6. Motivation to listen in a variety of communication situations is important to competent listening. What can you do to become more motivated?
7. Research suggests that paraphrasing and feedback in intimate conversations can be annoying, but we know it helps prevent misunderstandings. How can we provide feedback in the most acceptable way to the speaker?

Building Skills

Individual Exercises

1. Find out how good a listener you are by taking the *Top 10 Listening Habits Profile* on the internet at http://www.listencoach.com/LHProfile.html.
2. Identify a communication situation in which it's important to listen to learn. List the reasons for that importance. Then identify communication situations in which listening to evaluate and listening to empathize are crucial and list the reasons why.
3. At the beginning of the next lecture at school or meeting you attend at work, identify the possible barriers to listening in the particular situation. Decide how you can overcome these barriers and listen more competently. Set a goal to listen attentively throughout the lecture or meeting. Afterward, do a self-check to see if you retained more information than you usually do.
4. On the internet, go to http://www.listen.org/pages/quotes.html, an award-winning site containing many quotations about listening. Choose several quotations that particularly appeal to you and write a short explanation of why they are meaningful.
5. Watch an interview on television, perhaps one of the late night talk shows, and observe the listening skills of the interviewee and interviewer. Critique each person's listening, feedback, and paraphrasing skills. Who is the better listener and why?
6. If you are using *InfoTrac College Edition*, enter *listening* as the initial search topic of a "subject search" . In over a dozen periodical sources, you'll find a variety of hints for improving listening skills. Review the sources and prepare your own list of things to do to become a better listener.
7. Use the skills grid on page 168 to analyze a listening situation in which you were recently involved and use the results of the analysis to develop and refine your listening skills.

Group Exercises

1. Form a small group and have each group member think of a person who is a good listener. Each member should write a description of what that person does and why he or she is considered a good listener. Compare the descriptions and discuss the different characteristics of a competent listener.
2. In a small group, have each group member list several trigger words that can provoke an emotional reaction. Share the words in the group and try to come up with alternative words that won't trigger an emotional response. Compile a list of trigger words and their alternatives and share them with other groups.
3. Form groups of four with people you don't already know. Each group member should choose a number, from 1 to 4. For three minutes, person 1 tells person 2 about herself or himself. Then for another three minutes, person 2 tells person 1 about himself or herself. Persons 3 and 4 observe. Then person 1 paraphrases and provides feedback to person 2 about what was said. In the same way, person 2 paraphrases and provides feedback to person 1. Give each person a chance

Listening Competence Skills Grid

To help you understand how to use this grid, the skills displayed by Aisha and Jesse in the opening vignette of this chapter have been analyzed below. Examine that analysis and then think about a recent listening situation and what you could have done more competently. First, describe the context of the listening situation in the spaces provided. Next, analyze your listening skills based on the skills explained in this chapter for each step in the listening process. In the first column,

ANALYZING AISHA AND JESSE'S LISTENING SKILLS

Context

CULTURE: College campus in the United States

TIME: Evening after work and school

RELATIONSHIP: A girlfriend and boyfriend in an intimate relationship

PLACE: At the home of one of the two students

FUNCTION: To exchange information about each other's experiences of the day

LISTENING SKILLS	LESS COMPETENT	MORE COMPETENT
RECEIVING SKILLS	Aisha tuned Jesse out completely, and her attention wandered from what he was saying to matters of more personal importance to herself.	Jesse needs to talk to Aisha at a time when she is more ready to listen. Aisha should eliminate any barriers to listening that are distracting her, so she can focus her attention on what Jesse has to say.
CONSTRUCTING MEANING SKILLS	Because Aisha failed to receive Jesse's message, she was unable to accurately assign meaning to it.	Aisha needs to analyze Jesse's messages objectively, listening for his global meaning.
RESPONDING SKILLS	Aisha was unable to respond competently because she had neither received nor constructed meaning out of Jesse's message.	When Aisha realized that she had not listened to Jesse, she could have responded honestly and asked him to repeat his concerns and problem, perhaps at another time.

briefly describe and give examples of how your skills may have been less than competent. Using these less competent skills as a point of comparison to fill in the second column, describe the skills you think would have been perceived as more competent in the particular context. With practice, you will find you can use this grid to help develop your listening skills for future listening situations, as well as to analyze listening situations you have already experienced.

ANALYZING YOUR LISTENING SKILLS

Context

CULTURE:

TIME:

RELATIONSHIP:

PLACE:

FUNCTION:

LISTENING SKILLS	LESS COMPETENT	MORE COMPETENT
RECEIVING SKILLS		
CONSTRUCTING MEANING SKILLS		
RESPONDING SKILLS		

to speak, listen, and observe. Neither person should interrupt the other while the paraphrased message is being presented. The observers (persons 3 and 4) should comment on how accurate the feedback was. Finally, persons 1 and 2 are given time to clarify any misunderstandings. Switch pairs so persons 3 and 4 speak and listen while persons 1 and 2 observe.

References

Barker, L., Edwards, R., Gaines, C., Gladney, K., & Holley, F. (1980). An investigation of proportional time spent in various communication activities by college students. *Journal of Applied Communication Research, 8,* 101–109.

Bohlken, B. (1995). *The bare facts about the listener's responsibility in understanding semantic meaning.* Paper presented at the annual meeting of the International Listening Association, Little Rock, AR.

Borisoff, D., & Merrill, L. (1992). *The power to communicate: Gender differences as barriers* (2nd ed.). Prospect Heights, IL: Waveland.

Campbell, T., & Inguagiato, R. (1994). The power of listening. *Physician Executive, 20*(9), 35.

Gottman, J., Coan, J., Carrere, S., & Swanson, C. (1998). Predicting marital happiness and stability from newlywed interactions. *Communication Education, 60,* 5–22.

Graves, D. H. (1995). Teacher as listener. *Instructor, 105* (2), 36.

Haas, J. W., & Arnold, C. L. (1995). An examination of the role of listening in judgments of communication competence of co-workers. *Journal of Business Communication, 32,* 123–139.

Harris, R. M. (1997). Turn listening into a powerful presence. *Training & Development, 51*(7), 9.

Hayakawa, S. I. (1997). In L. M. Shilling & L. K. Fuller (Eds.), *A dictionary of quotations in communications* (p. 136). Westport, CT: Greenwood Press Hite, S. (1987). *Women and love: A cultural revolution in progress.* New York: Knopf.

Hunsaker, R. A. (1991). *Critical listening—a neglected skill.* Paper presented at the annual convention of the National Communication Association, Atlanta, GA.

International Listening Association. (1995, March). An ILA definition of listening. *ILA Listening Post, 53,* 1–4. Milwaukee, WI: Alverno College.

Ivy, D., & Backlund, P. (1994). *Exploring genderspeak: Personal effectiveness in gender communication.* New York: McGraw-Hill.

Nichols, R. G., & Stevens, L. A. (1957). *Are you listening?* New York: McGraw-Hill.

Reiss, R.(1994, November). Listen up. *Incentive,* p. 102.

Roberts, C. (1998, March). *Developing willing listeners: A host of problems and a plethora of solutions.* Paper presented at the International Listening Association Convention, Kansas City.

Schnell, J. (1995). *Effective listening: More than just hearing.* (ERIC Document Reproduction Service No. ED 379 691)

Wolvin, A., & Coakley, C. (1991). A survey of the status of listening training in some Fortune 500 corporations. *Communication Education, 40,* 152–164.

Wolvin, A., & Coakley, C. (1994). Listening competence. *Journal of the International Listening Association, 8,* 148–160.

Wolvin, A., & Coakley, C. (1996). *Listening.* Dubuque, IA: Brown & Benchmark.

Wood, J. (1998). *Communication mosaics.* Belmont, CA: Wadsworth.

Building Motivation

Self-Assessment: Rate each of the following eight communication situations described here, indicating your own typical level of listening competence. Use the 1–4 scale, with 1 minimal competence and 4 high competence. Rate one component (motivation) all the way through for all eight situations, then rate the next component (knowledge) and then the third (skills).

Motivation	Knowledge	Skills
1 = Distracted, disinterested, or simply no motivation to be competent	**1** = Completely inexperienced and ignorant about what to do and how to do it	**1** = Completely incapable of behaving competently
2 = Somewhat distracted/ disinterested, but motivated to be competent	**2** = Minimal experience and sense of what to do and how to do it	**2** = Barely capable of behaving minimally competent
3 = Somewhat interested and motivated to be competent	**3** = Somewhat experienced and knowledgeable about what to do and how to do it	**3** = Fairly capable of behaving competently
4 = Highly interested and motivated to be competent	**4** = Highly knowledgeable about all aspects of what to do and how to do it	**4** = Highly capable of behaving competently

Communication Situations:	Motivation	Knowledge	Skills
1. Listening to a person from a culture very different from your own			
2. Listening to a distant relative who you have not met before at a family wedding			
3. Visiting your elderly grandmother and spending the afternoon with her and her friends			
4. Attending a training session at work to learn about a new software program you won't use frequently			
5. Attending a public lecture with a friend on a topic you don't find very interesting			
6. Attending a class taught by a lecturer who overestimates what you know about the complex topic			
7. Participating in a lengthy group discussion about a class project			
8. Becoming part of a guided tour of a gallery displaying art you find unappealing			
TOTAL SCORES			

Interpreting Your Scores: Total your scores separately for each component (motivation, knowledge, and skills). The possible range of the score per component is 8–32. If your total score for any of the three components is 14 or less, you see yourself as less competent than you should be. A score of 15–28 means you think you are an average listener. A score of 29–32 indicates you think you have a high level of competence.

CHAPTER 7

LEARNING OBJECTIVES

After studying this chapter, you should be able to:

1 Explain the nature of and differences between richness and openness.

2 Compare and contrast mediated communication and unmediated communication.

3 Explain how media sensitivity is related to communication competence.

4 Understand how the components of motivation and knowledge apply to mediated communication environments.

5 Discuss and give examples of mediated communication skills (attentiveness, composure, coordination, expressiveness).

6 Identify the ways in which culture, relationship, situation, and function influence mediated communication.

7 Define technophobia, identify its causes, and describe ways in which people can overcome it.

8 Identify the ways in which developments in communication technology are changing society and the role of the individual in society.

Mediated Communication Competence

Sloane had heard how much fun chat rooms could be. Given her interest in the television show *The X-Files* in which two FBI agents attempt to solve cases related to extraterrestrials and the paranormal, a chat room seemed a natural way of keeping up with the current buzz of the show. However, she had also heard that women tend to be in the minority in such chat rooms and, as a result, get hit on by geeks and lonely guys who can not meet people any other way. She decided to enter the chat room under an assumed male identity, Ted, and went by the nickname of "Chupacabra" after one of the episode's mysteries.

Sloane immediately found the daily chats to be exciting and informative. She even found Chad, nicknamed "Twilight Time," whose conversation she particularly enjoyed. As their online relationship developed they began to leave the chat room and email each other directly, disclosing more and more personal information about their past, their beliefs, and their values. Sloane and Chad were responsive to each other, rarely letting a message go more than a few hours without some type of response. They started developing their own code names for the ideas they came up with during discussions of *The X-Files*. They found they had much in common, and that they intended to attend the same X-Con in San Francisco soon. In a matter of weeks, Sloane felt herself strongly attracted to Chad, but faced the dilemma of having deceived him all this time about her actual identity while she wanted to start an honest and trusting relationship with him.

Sloane followed her motivation to join a chat group and used her knowledge of *The X-Files* and computer communication. She soon found herself developing a relationship with someone she knew only from words on a screen. Her interpersonal skills translated well to the medium, but she also found that she had created a deception early on which was now difficult to unravel without betraying the trust that had rapidly evolved. She had let the medium dictate many of her choices, and was now faced with the dilemma of how to manage the consequences. What would your advice to Chupacabra be? •••

In this chapter, we examine how the model of communication competence applies to the emerging context of mediated interpersonal communication. In Sloane's case, The model accounts for the role of motivation, both in Sloane's initial interest in *The X-Files* and her later motivation to pursue an online relationship. The model also reveals the importance of her knowledge: Her expertise with *The X-Files* gave her credibility in the chat room and the ability to impress the others in the digital space of the interaction. Finally, the model illustrates the importance of her computer-based communication skills. Sloane was expressive with her disclosures about much of her private life, coordinated with her responsiveness, composed with her expertise, and attentive with her display of interest in what Twilight Time had to say. But the model needs further development to make complete sense of this particular environment. The technology introduces a variety of unique characteristics into the interpersonal communication context. This chapter applies the model of communication competence to this emerging context.

What Is Mediated Communication Competence?

Today, most of us think of mediated communication as **computer-mediated communication (CMC),** which refers to any human symbolic interaction through digitally based technologies. The word *mediated* comes from the term *medium,* which in Latin means *middle.* It refers to the means through which one person's message is conveyed to an audience. Computers in one way or another act as the channels or intermediaries through which messages travel from one person to others.

Computers are technological media, contrasted with **natural media**, those that send and translate symbols using only our bodies and minds. Natural media include face-to-face media such as spoken words, gestures, posture, and all the other verbal, nonverbal, and listening processes we examined in the previous chapters. **Technological media** are those devices that translate, amplify, or otherwise alter the information in these natural media. Technological media include letters, now often called "snail mail," telephones and teleconferencing, videophones, and videoconferencing, email, computer-assisted interactions, such as telemarketing, group-decision support systems, computer chat lines, and multiuser domains, and some virtual reality systems.

This chapter focuses on computer-mediated communication (CMC). The most commonly used forms of CMC are email, the World Wide Web (WWW), chat lines, and videophone communication via the computer. Although left in the shadow of email and other online communications, telephone communication is still obviously vital to society (Fischer, 1992; Hopper, 1992), and we compare it to CMC throughout this chapter.

Characteristics of Computer-Mediated Communication

Unquestionably computer media are rapidly changing the pace and volume of communication. Who can open a newspaper or magazine or turn on a television without encountering the topic of how technology is changing how we communicate? However, it remains to be seen if media are changing the fundamental nature of our communication.

For example, hikers are now commonly going deep into wilderness areas to enjoy nature, armed with cell phones. So as one person is admiring the view of a forest valley, the person five feet away is talking to a friend or family member on a cell phone describing the view. Media are altering both our relationships to society and the world (Inose & Pierce, 1984; Meyrowitz, 1985; Pavlik, 1998), as well as our own sense of who we are (Negroponte, 1995; Turkle, 1995). Some of these changes are superficial, but others may be transforming our basic way of understanding the world (Chesebro, 1995).

The nature of computers makes certain characteristics of communication more important to competence than others. Two basic characteristics of CMC are important in understanding competence: richness and openness.

Richness

When you sit and talk with people face-to-face, you see them, hear them, and perhaps even touch and smell them. Such natural media are very rich in information. **Media richness** is the extent to which a medium recreates or represents all of the information available in the original message. It is also called "telepresence" or social presence, which is the extent a medium allows communicators to feel like they are in the physical presence of another. So if a medium is richer, it permits more feedback, with greater immediacy, more types of verbal, visual, and audio cues or information, more tailoring of messages to particular individuals, and more use of everyday language (Schmitz & Fulk, 1991; Trevino, Daft, & Lengel, 1990). For example, a videophone offers you more sense of presence than just a telephone, and a telephone offers you more interactivity than sending letters back and forth through the mail. The concept of richness is the foundation of all current theories of mediated interpersonal communication.

Several characteristics—speed, interactivity, and completeness—determine the richness of a medium. "Poor" or "lean" media lack these characteristics. **Speed** is the lag between the production of a message, the sending of the message, and the receipt of that message. Letters are now known as snail mail because compared to email they are relatively slow in the time they take to reach the receiver. Both email and snail mail are slow in production time compared to the telephone, which translates thoughts to words almost instantaneously without the need to type or write. Generally, the more rapid the production, sending, and receiving are in a medium, the richer the medium is.

Interactivity is the extent to which the parties interacting through a medium can communicate simultaneously and respond to each other's messages. It is related to time, but involves the added element of including the production, sending, and receiving ability of the other persons in the communication situation. Standard email, for example, is not very interactive because a writer must complete an entire message, send it, and wait for switching systems to download the message to the recipient's mailbox, which may itself only inform the recipient every five minutes or so of incoming mail. Many chat rooms, in contrast, are more interactive because they allow a recipient to see the other person's message as it is being typed, and permit interruptions in midsentence almost like a face-to-face conversation. The more interactive the medium, the richer it is.

Completeness is the extent to which the medium represents the nonverbal and emotional content of messages. For example, people think of the telephone as a fairly limited medium. Yet it reflects a wide range of vocalic information of speaker intent and emotion that letters and email are more limited in revealing. All of these media are poor compared to video-telephony, which includes verbal content and vocalic and facial nonverbal information. Yet, even video-telephony only presents a fairly flat, two-dimensional, fixed picture of the other person. The more complete the medium, the richer the medium.

Speed, interactivity, and completeness permit communication to simulate the richer environment of face-to-face conversation. Some media are considered richer than others by the very nature of their technology. Figure 7.1 displays a traditional way of organizing media in terms of their richness. Some of the media in this figure, such as virtual reality, videophones, chat rooms, and group-decision support systems, were not even topics for discussion in 1990, but are either currently used extensively or on the immediate horizon of technological development.

A common assumption is that the richer media are more competent at communicating than poorer media. If more of a message is reproduced, others are more likely to understand the meaning of the message. This assumption is too simplistic because it does not take the context or message into account. Competence in CMC is a combination of media richness, context, and message. For example, if you are in a hurry to inform a large number of people of something simple such as a deadline for homework, sending out a brief email, which is relatively poor, quick, efficient, and perfectly acceptable. Further, it may not be a message that requires deep considerations of people's feelings or depends greatly on their feedback on how the basic message needs to be adapted. In such cases, a leaner rather than richer medium is most competent.

HIGH
face to face
virtual reality
video-phone
telephone
chat rooms
group-decision support systems
electronic mail
letter
note/memo
special report
flyer, bulletin
LOW

FIGURE 7.1
Media Richness Continuum

Media vary in their ability to represent both verbal and nonverbal information in communication. Those that are higher in richness incorporate more of both verbal and nonverbal information.

Adapted from Trevino, Daft, & Lengel (1990) by permission of the author.

Openness

One of the reasons that Sloane and Chad began leaving the chat room and interacting directly with each other via email was because they wanted more privacy in their messages. In addition, interacting with someone directly rather than through a group chat room develops a one-on-one relationship with the particular person, rather than simply relating as part of a group. This use of privacy involves the openness of a medium. **Openness** is the extent to which the messages sent through the medium are public. Erving Goffman, a famous sociologist, argues that people have two areas of action, front stage and backstage. Front-stage behavior is public and accessible to all present to observe the action. Front-stage action is high in its openness. When you give a speech to a class of students, it is front stage. When you ask someone out on a date, it is front stage. However, when you are home by yourself and you belch, it is backstage behavior. When you change your seating to get a better look at the person you intend to ask out on a date, the behavior is more backstage than front stage.

Computers permit a wide range of front-stage and backstage action. Email, for example, permits you to forward messages to entire address lists, and these address lists can be public or hidden. Thus, if Chris asks you out to a party on email, you can reply just to Chris, you can reply and copy both Chris's and your response to a mutual friend who will be at the party with your friend's address publicly displayed, or you can copy the same messages to your friend while concealing the friend's address. Further, you could copy Chris's message and your response onto a public chat line or even post it on a publicly accessible Web page, assuming you had some reason to treat such a personal exchange as public in nature.

Knowledge Link

What is the nature of media richness and media openness, and how do they differ?

To some extent, computer-based communication media have begun to blur the lines between private and public communication. Virtually everything sent by email is

Measuring Your Media Sensitivity

RATE THE APPROPRIATENESS AND EFFECTIVENESS of using each medium in each situation, using a rating scale from 1 Inappropriate/Ineffective to 5 Appropriate/Effective. There are no right or wrong answers. For appropriateness, consider how the message fits the situation described. Will it offend others or be perfectly legitimate? For effectiveness, consider whether the medium will best permit you to achieve what you want to achieve.

SITUATION	FACE-TO-FACE		TELEPHONE		LETTER/MEMO		EMAIL	
	APP	EFF	APP	EFF	APP	EFF	APP	EFF
You need to fire a friend								
You want to ask someone out on a date								
You need to inform a large number of people of an upcoming concert								
You want to chat with a friend who lives in another state about how his or her week went								
You need to get student group members together for an immediate meeting								

Interpretation: Media sensitivity implies making choices about when using one medium is more competent than using another. Thus the greater the difference between your ratings across media and contexts, the more media sensitive you are. In contrast, if you rated one medium as best for all contexts, you probably need to reexamine the competence of that medium across those contexts. Generally, the more personal and potentially emotional the purpose of the encounter, the more important it is to use face-to-face media, whereas the more the purpose of the message is to inform and the larger the audience, the leaner and colder the medium can be.

recorded somewhere. Unlike letters that can be burned, voice mail that can be erased, and telephone and face-to-face conversations that are rarely recorded, computer-based messages are commonly copied, manipulated, forwarded, and reproduced for many eyes to see. The fact that messages often take on a life of their own on computer-based networks is one of the many features any communicator needs to consider when choosing to send a message.

Decisions to move your CMC backstage rather than front stage or to choose a richer medium to send a romantic message illustrate sensitivity to the advantages and disadvantages of using various media for communication. Such decisions involve media sensitivity.

MEDIA SENSITIVITY

Media sensitivity is the awareness that different media possess different characteristics that systematically affect their appropriateness and effectiveness in different communication contexts. Because the competence of a medium depends on the context, competence in CMC depends not only on the richness or openness of the medium, but also on sensitivity to when and why one medium should be chosen over another in any given context

Consider the situations described in the CloseUp on Technology. Four different media are presented for five different contexts. You are media sensitive if you vary your ratings from one situation to the next. If, however, you think that one particular medium is most competent for all contexts, you are not sensitive to context. Firing a friend or asking someone on a date by email seems inappropriate. Email is too cold and impersonal a medium for communicating in such emotional and relational situations. In contrast, using email to call a group meeting or inform people of a deadline or upcoming event is generally considered a very acceptable and efficient use of the medium. Further, most people consider telephone and voicemail channels as most competent for meeting the other person's needs compared to meeting the sender's needs (Westmyer, DiCioccio, & Rubin, 1998). Written messages are viewed as too impersonal to please others entirely.

So why should you be concerned about your sensitivity to which media you use or the richness of the media? Because the world is about to leave those who are concerned with neither in its digital dust.

The Importance of Computer-Mediated Communication

Historians typically point to certain revolutions that have transformed how humans relate to the world and to each other. The Dark Ages gave way to the Renaissance and Age of Enlightenment. The invention of the printing press made the transfer and accumulation of generalized knowledge far more accessible than ever before. The industrial revolution gave way to the service economy. Most contemporary observers believe the microchip and computer have ushered in the next revolution, which stands to alter the way we interact with the world around us.

THE EXTENT OF MEDIATED COMMUNICATION

Current trends reveal the extent to which society depends on computers and the extent to which some groups may be threatened by such dependency. Take a moment and read over the information regarding CMC in society in Table 7.1. Then ask yourself what this information means to you personally, and how a person from a village in a developing nation that has only two or three telephones might view the trends.

The trends are both exciting and frightening. It is often difficult for people today to fully comprehend the pace of change. The first programmable computer, named ENIAC (for electronic numerical integrator and computer) was unveiled in 1946. It was 10 feet tall, 150 feet wide, and cost millions of dollars. It executed about 5,000 operations per second. Today's personal computers execute millions of operations per second using microchips the size of salad crackers. Many people now routinely do banking, investing, calculations, scheduling, and shopping on devices that are self-contained and held in the palms of their hands. However, all this computing power is potentially useless, or worse, counterproductive, if a person has no access, no motivation, no knowledge, and no skills to use it.

TABLE 7.1

••• CMC in Society •••

Computers are integrated into most of our society, and their role is becoming increasingly important to everyday life in a wide variety of ways and contexts.

The Prevalence of Technology

- Computing power has been doubling every year and a half for the past 30 years.
- The total amount of published materials in the world doubles every three years.
- Three quarters of the world's telephones exist in only 8 countries.
- There are 32 personal computers for every U.S. citizen, about one third of U.S. households has a personal computer, and about 23 million Americans use a computer every day.
- Almost half of all U.S. teenagers report having a home computer.
- Over 100 million people in over 160 countries use the internet.
- The World Wide Web (WWW) grew over 1,700% in 1994, and over 440,000% in 1993.
- By 2005, as many as a billion people may connect to the Web.
- As much as 80% of the world's population has no current access to the information technology society.

The Business of Communication Technology

- About 4 million American homes telecommute or rely on information technology to work from home, and this is increasing about 20% annually.
- By 2002, as much as $300 billion of electronic commerce among businesses may be conducted.
- About 7.5 million Americans work in the information technology sector, earning an average of $46,000 a year compared to an average of $28,000 for the rest of the economy.
- Information technology companies are growing at double the rate of the rest of the economy, comprising over 8% of the gross domestic product and contributing over 25% of real economic growth over each of the last 5 years.
- About 6 million Americans are monitored by computer by their employer.

The Personal Dimension of Technology

- A survey of internet users showed the average respondent spent 19 hours a week on the internet.
- This same survey showed that the average respondent experienced at least 10 signs of interference in their quality of life (such as sleeplessness, failure to manage time, depression, etc.).
- According to one survey, about 55% of Americans express some degree of technophobia, or fear of technology. Another survey, however, found that 65% of respondents claimed to like computers, and 42% perceived computers as providing users with more rather than less control over their lives.
- Computer users read more books and newspapers, watch more television, and engage in more sports and recreational activities than people who do not use computers.

SOURCE: Adapted from Brenner (1997), Cochrane (1995), Hudson (1997), *San Diego Union-Tribune* (1995), Times Mirror Center for People and the Press (1994), and U.S. Department of Commerce (1998).

Another sign of the pace of change is that even if the publication dates for the information sources for Table 7.1 seem recent, they are already outdated by the time you read this sentence. New communication products are brought to market daily, requiring new competencies, new program languages, and new hardware support. Each new product anticipates a large market of new users, all of whom differ in their own individual abilities to use the technology. Some trends continue to catch society, as well as the experts, by surprise. Although palm-sized computer-based organizers took a while to catch on, they are joining the cell phone as indispensable for today's technologically competent.

INFORMATION HAVES & HAVE-NOTS

Recently, much has been made about who may or may not be left behind in the information revolution. The information haves, those who have access to computer resources and the skills to use them, will have enormous advantages compared to the information have-nots. The stakes of this digital divide could be enormous. CMC gains importance as society becomes increasingly dependent on mediated forms of communication. In the near future, those with no access to and no competencies with media will become increasingly dependent on others, which will result in lower status, lower economic potential, and perhaps even greater powerlessness in society (Ronfeldt, 1992). Looking back at Table 7.1, notice that people employed in the information technology sector make almost 65% more than those in other sectors of the economy. This part of the U.S. economy is growing at twice the rate of other sectors, accounting for a quarter of the nation's economic growth over the past five years.

Some trends suggest the gap between the haves and the have-nots is narrowing. With each passing year computer power consistently becomes cheaper, and programs with greater and greater user friendliness are developed. The public may find that access to and knowledge of the media are easier to acquire. As a result, fewer and fewer people will be left behind. However, having access and knowledge do not necessarily imply media sensitivity and competence in using these technologies.

If you now feel like you've got it made because you have media access and some level of competence in using such media, don't be fooled. There is a dark side to this brave new world. Just as some people think technology will create utopia, others envision the opposite: dystopia, a vision of a world in which everything has gone wrong. A technological

Knowledge Link

How does a technological dystopia relate to the postmodern self discussed in Chapter 3?

Computer-mediated communication raises new types of problems in communicating with others.

Garry Trudeau, June 21, 1998, *Doonesbury,* Universal Press. Syndicate. Reprinted by permission.

The Dark Side of a Mediated Interpersonal Society

HERE IS A SELECTED SET of true stories that have shown up in the news about CMC abuses. Although not necessarily common, they illustrate some of the potential problems that can arise with technological advances in our communication abilities.

- In Arizona, a married couple separates. As one of his last acts before moving out, the husband sets up a new computer system for their daughter. In the coming weeks, through telephone conversations with her estranged husband, the mother realizes the father has knowledge of details of the daughter's home life that he should not have access to. The suspicious mother gets the help of a computer expert only to find that the husband has set up the computer as an audio and text monitoring system. Any time it is turned on, he can listen into, tape, or download whatever is said near the computer or processed with the computer.
- A recent sting by New York state police netted arrest of 31 individuals accused of trafficking in child pornography over the internet.
- Recent cases illustrate the potential for pedophiles to lure innocent children and teenagers exploring the internet into threatening situations. In 1994, a 51-year-old man was arrested in New York after traveling from Seattle to meet a 14-year-old girl he met through computer connections. In another indication of the risks, a reporter for the magazine *Computer Life,* pretended to be a 15-year-old cheerleader on the internet. He received over 30 email messages with sexual content.
- Surveys continue to report frequent experiences of "flaming" episodes, in which people online engage in outrageous and seemingly unedited insults and criticism. The use of **bold**, CAPITALIZED, underlined, exclamation!!!, escaLATION, parallelism ("you stupid, ignorant, useless . . ."), and other such creative uses of type color the message without other nonverbal cues that might soften or contextualize the message.
- Further, it is often assumed that because of the lack of face-to-face communication online, insults and criticisms are easier to communicate because there is less nonverbal basis for empathy, and little chance for the offended party to reach out and slap or choke the sender! Finally, sarcasm may not translate well on email because it is basically communicated as a verbal message that is contradicted by nonverbal information.
- Many people blissfully assume their email messages are private, only accessible to those to whom they send their mail. Increasingly, however, organizations routinely monitor email. Most organizations maintain permanent records of email correspondence, which may become important evidence in future legal proceedings.
- Increasingly, any purchases of items on the internet results in a "cookie," or information tracking program, being deposited in your computer. This cookie monitors your purchasing habits so that future marketing by that company can target your personal spending habits more precisely.
- The possibility for revenge is greater than ever on the internet. Ex-partners can dump prior correspondence on your system or on public sites. Incriminating photographs can not only be loaded on to the internet but sent to thousands of people at the push of a button. Pictures can even be fabricated: Recent Hollywood stars have been embarrassed to find photos of their faces digitally attached to someone else's naked body on celebrity internet sites.
- Finally, as you saw in the opening vignette to this chapter, many people are learning to engage in elaborate deception on the internet. Men pretend to be women and women pretend to be men. Straight people pretend to be gay or lesbian, and same-sex preference persons pretend to be straight. Normal upright citizens may create alter egos of wild and perverted identities on the Web, whereas most frighteningly, deviants may pretend to be normal upright citizens.

dystopia, therefore, is a world in which technology works to the detriment of humanity. A world of constant surveillance, technological dependence, and manipulation is envisioned as a technological dystopia. Even the popular image of the information highway is suggestive of a problem: Either get on with everyone else or get left behind or run over (Berdayes & Berdayes, 1998). The next CloseUp on Technology reveals just a few of the problems the new communication technologies are introducing to our social and work environments. This dark side is also illustrated in the Doonesbury cartoon. Not only is the online dater negatively stereotyped for using the computer to meet women, but then he discovers his online relationship may not be with a woman after all.

Media sensitivity and competence in the future will increasingly consist of being able to recognize people's deceptions in such media and being more selective in choosing the media appropriate for specific messages. Let's apply the communication competence model as a framework for understanding the computer-mediated environment.

The CMC Competence Model

Recall that the basic model of communication competence consists of motivation, knowledge, skills, context, and outcomes. Communication is competent when it is perceived as appropriate and effective, and it is more likely to be perceived as competent to the extent that a person is motivated, knowledgeable, and skilled in a given context. These same components apply to situations in which media are used to exchange messages.

The model in Figure 7.2 shows how the basic model of communication competence applies to the CMC environment. As you saw in Chapter 2, the three components central to the individual are motivation, knowledge, and skills. The middle components of the model represent the context in which the media are used and the characteristics of the

FIGURE 7.2
The Model of Mediated Communication Competence

The more motivated, knowledgeable, and skilled a communicator is in selecting and using CMC for a given type of message in a given context, the more likely the communicator is to achieve competent outcomes.

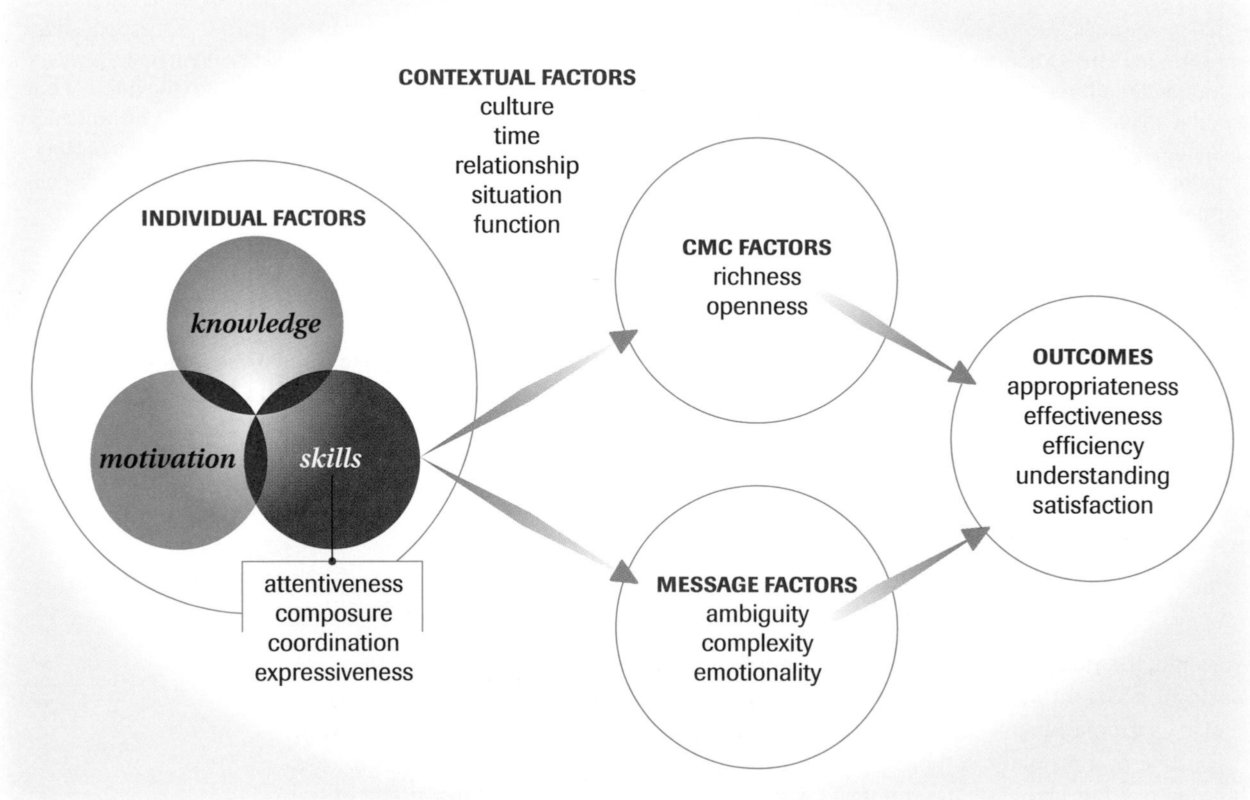

media and messages. Recall from Chapter 2 that context defines the functions and situations of communication. The same types of context, such as culture and relationship, apply to this CMC model. However, because CMC involves specific media, more components are added to the message aspects of the model. The final component of the model represents the outcomes that help define a mediated interaction as competent or incompetent.

MOTIVATION

As you saw in Table 7.1, a majority of U.S. citizens have some degree of anxiety about technology. These people experience difficulty getting motivated to use computers for everyday communication. As we discussed in Chapter 2, motivation is the energizing force of communication. Communicators are much more likely to make a positive impression on others to the extent they are motivated to communicate competently.

Motivation in the mediated world has two sides to it: positive and negative. Positive motivation in mediated communication is the feeling or belief that a given medium can enhance preferred outcomes. If you believe a presentation given through PowerPoint rather than using a chalkboard or flip charts will be much more likely to land a big contract or motivate your sales force, you are positively motivated to use that software in a computer-based medium. But if you think such a presentation might overwhelm your audience or complicate your message, you might decide simply to do a face-to-face presentation with few or no visual aids.

Negative motivation in the mediated context is the feeling or belief that you are incapable of using a given medium competently. The fear of incompetence in CMC is **technophobia.** As indicated in Table 7.1, many people suffer from technophobia. In societies like the United States in which technology is common, technophobia generally afflicts older generations rather than younger generations. The United States and Japan are currently preparing to connect all educational institutions to the internet and supply every student with computer access. The average eighth grader may well know more about computers than his or her parents. Such familiarity makes the younger generation more comfortable and less afraid to use and experiment with the technology.

KNOWLEDGE

One of the reasons people are afraid of technology is because they don't know how to use it. There are several ways in which people learn to use communication media. Some people use formal ways such as taking classes or working through menu-driven tutorials. Other people use more informal ways such as having a friend show them how to use a new program or product. It seems that for most people the last way they ever learn about a new technology is by actually reading the manuals written for the technology. Increasingly, set-up videos, menu-driven programs, on-screen instructions, in-store demonstrations, and workshops are designed to make adopting media easier. These are more formal means of knowing. More informal ways of gaining knowledge about media include tinkering and interpersonal means.

Tinkering is an approach that involves experimenting and trial and error (Turkle, 1995). It is similar to what is referred to as "hunt and peck" typing, which involves scanning a keyboard visually until you find the letter you are looking for, using only two index fingers, typing that key with one of your index fingers, and then repeating the process. Similarly, trial and error in media use is simply pushing buttons, exploring drop-down window menus, and trying options until you find something that seems to get you one step closer to what you want to do or may someday want to do.

Many people tinker only to accomplish an immediate task, never straying too far into other possibilities the medium has to offer. Reviewing the competence grid introduced in Chapter 2, these people are engaging in a sufficing approach, doing only the bare minimum, that is, only what is necessary to get by. Others enjoy the process of learning, and hunt and peck their way into features they may never use, but some of which they use "because they can."

Interpersonal means of learning about the computer are often the most relaxed and comfortable.

Interpersonal means of learning involve one-on-one instruction. Although this type of learning may occur with a help desk or help-line, a common source of interpersonal learning is having a knowledgeable friend or acquaintance show you how to use the medium. People generally feel more comfortable asking a friend to explain a technical feature than an impersonal company technical support staff. Although learning through these more informal ways may seem more natural than formal learning, interpersonal means of learning also often end up skipping important areas of knowledge that may seem insignificant at the time. Most people do not know what to do when they have inadvertently deleted a file or when an LCD projector does not project in the middle of a presentation because they only learned how to use the technology in the best possible situation when everything was working the way it should.

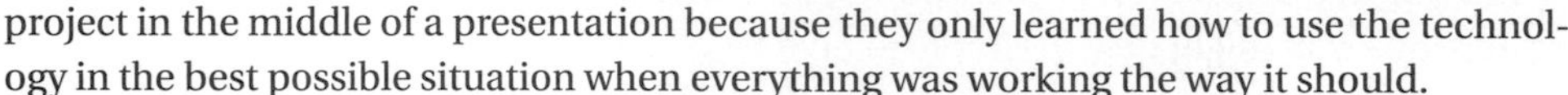

Knowing what to do and being able to do it are two different things. You can know the rules of chess, yet not know the best strategies to beat a given opponent. Likewise, you can know how media are supposed to operate, but not actually know when and where to best use them. In other words, what you know about how you communicate and how you *actually* communicate are often quite different. This difference reveals the importance of developing your skills in CMC, to make sure that what you think you are doing appears to others as you intend.

Skills

Skills, as we explained in Chapter 2, are the repeatable, goal-oriented behaviors used to communicate. Skills are goal oriented in the sense that the behaviors are enacted to accomplish something. For example, we sometimes send email messages to people just to maintain contact—to let them know we are thinking of them—but not for any particular reason. Skills are repeatable, which means you have learned what is needed to accomplish something. You may have been working hard to figure something out, and accidentally find you solved it, only to realize that you don't know *how* you solved it. In these cases, you don't have the skill because you can't repeat it. In the mediated context, specifically the computer-mediated context, skills are displayed in four ways: attentiveness, composure, coordination, and expressiveness.

Attentiveness

One of the most important features of any communication situation is making others feel they are part of the process. People need to feel that their presence and ideas matter. Even in public speaking events, one of a speaker's most prized skills is the ability to make each person in the audience feel as if he or she is being addressed individually. When communicating through computer media, generally a much colder and more impersonal medium than face-to-face or telephone communication, it is often difficult to make a warm or personal connection with the other parties.

When communicating on a local area network of computers (LAN) in which an entire organization is interconnected, for example, and a memo needs to be sent to a given department, committee, or group, it is easy to treat each person in the group as undifferentiated. That is, rather than addressing a collection of unique individuals, messages are often impersonally worded or boilerplate task-based messages.

Attentiveness is the ability to show interest in, concern for, and attention to others when communicating. As you know, this is often difficult to achieve in mediated contexts. Many qualities of CMC make attentiveness difficult. More often than not, you cannot see the other person directly, message replies are delayed, and messages are often sent to groups of people rather than just to one person. Even so, there are many ways of being attentive even when communicating by computer.

Attentiveness on the computer consists of adding a personal touch to a message. This personal touch in a traditional business letter consists of directing questions to a particular recipient, displaying awareness of past correspondence and revisions, and so on. To show interest, you might begin a business email memo with a question or pleasantry about the recipient's recent business trip. Helping a member solicit solutions to a problem placed on the agenda by a group shows concern for the individual as well as the group. As with natural media, responding rapidly and relevantly to someone's computer-mediated message shows attention. You cannot lean toward the recipient or reach out and touch him or her when using CMC, but the medium does allow you to show interest and concern. The medium may alter the way in which attentiveness is shown, but not its importance.

Composure

Composure is the ability to display comfort with, control of, and confidence in communication. In the mediated environment, composure reflects a mastery of both the medium and your communication behavior within that medium. Composure reflects a lack of technophobia as well as a confidence and assertiveness with media.

Composure often goes hand in hand with knowledge. As you've seen, technophobia is often based on unfamiliarity with a medium. Such unfamiliarity leads to uncertainty regarding the ability to perform competently within the medium. A person who knows more about a medium is generally perceived as more composed. Knowledge promotes confidence.

Composure in a computer-mediated environment is displayed in a variety of ways. A person who accepts and meets the challenges of new programs, new techniques, and new technologies displays confidence. Some people go out of their way to learn how to scan images and soundwaves and set up their own Web pages. In contrast, more reluctant users simply remain on the barest minimum platform from which they send and receive email. Thus adoption of innovation reveals a person's composure with electronic communication media.

Composure is also reflected in a person's language choices. Consider two opening statements for a hypothetical email memo:

1. "I'm not sure if you will get this or not, but if so, please respond to the following message."
2. "Please respond to the following message."

The latter displays greater confidence and composure, although the author of the second opening might be as unsure of the technology as the author of the first message. The very fact that the first opening statement does not make much sense detracts from composure.

Composure reveals a communicator's sense of comfort with a medium's complexities and a sense of self-control over his or her own messages. Such comfort and control permit greater management of interactions with a given recipient. This improved management, in turn, facilitates the coordination of the interaction process.

Coordination

Coordination in the computer-mediated environment is the management of time and relevance. Management of time concerns the extent to which messages are sent and received when they should be, and the extent to which they are not too long or dense to process. Management of relevance means that messages are about what they are supposed to be about.

If you have ever sent an urgent message by email requesting an answer to a question, only to get a response a few days later that does not respond to the original question, you have experienced the sender's poor coordination. The response is uncoordinated in two senses. First, it was not topically connected with the message to which it was supposed to respond. Second, it did not respond immediately to a message labeled "urgent." Further, in the process of attempting to repair this uncoordinated interaction, both communicators are likely to risk even more problems of wasting time and creating frustration and blame as they dance around the issue of how to get back on track.

Coordination requires that you respond to messages in a timely fashion. Timeliness obviously varies from message to message and from relationship to relationship. If Sloane is cautious about exploring a personal and romantic relationship with Chad, she might slip in a few hints in a longer message about their meeting at *The X-Files* convention. For example, she might suggest, "I know a really great restaurant, but it's so popular that reservations would need to be made almost immediately if you were interested." If this were inserted into a longer message about various activities and discussions of *The X-Files* news, Chad might easily either overlook it in his response, or decide that he doesn't want to risk sending an awkward response. Chad might respond to other issues in the message while simply not mentioning the dinner suggestion. In doing so, he has chosen not to coordinate on an issue both in terms of topical relevance and timing, since the issue requires fast action to make it relevant. Thus coordination requires both responding in a timely fashion as well as responding with a message appropriate to previous and future messages in the relationship.

Expressiveness

As you've read previously, many communication media are relatively poor in telepresence. As the words are typed on this page, they appear cold, uniform, and colorless. Do they arouse images in your mind? Do they get you to remember similar experiences you have had with computers? Can the words do a better job of getting the intended meanings across? All of these are issues of expressiveness.

Expressiveness in the computer-mediated environment is the vividness of the message, or how alive and animated it is. A message is vivid to the extent that it possesses multiple dimensions or characteristics. If you think of the evolution of movie theaters over the last 50 years, black and white gave way to color, then color got richer, screens got wider, sound systems got louder and more dynamic, mono went to stereo, which went to digital sound, and so forth. The progress of film has been toward greater expressiveness.

Similar changes have occurred in CMC. When, for example, email first became popular for day-to-day communication, people soon realized how limited they were in expressing emotions through this medium. As a solution, people invented **emoticons,** or whimsical

TABLE 7.2

CMC Emoticons

Emoticons are used in casual CMC to indicate moods or facial expressions and add a nonverbal element to an otherwise very verbal medium.

EMOTICON	MEANING	EMOTICON	MEANING
:-)	smile	:-	anger
:-(	frown	:X	my lips are sealed
:'	cry	:P	sticking out the tongue
;-)	wink	:Q	smoking
:D	laughter	:*	a kiss
:-0	yell	%-)	confusion

SOURCE: Pavlik (1998).

icons that communicated the emotion underlying a verbal statement. Others began to develop acronyms and abbreviations for phrases to make messages more efficient, as well as help frame the meaning of the message that precedes or follows the phrase. New terms that began as inside lingo were spread from one person to a chat room and then extended into the popular vocabulary as they were adopted by literally thousands of other people. As a final example, people developed symbolic figures to add to their email signatures. Even while using an impersonal medium, such personalized features offer a mark of individuality to enhance the expressiveness of messages. Table 7.2 shows some of the more common emoticons. Look at Table 7.3 for some popular acronyms and new terms to illustrate various efforts to enhance the expressiveness of such a cold medium. People display a rather obvious desire to find more and more ways to express themselves, regardless of the relative coldness and leanness of the medium (Markus, 1994). A list of thousands of dictionary-style definitions of computer emoticons and symbols can be

TABLE 7.3

CMC Acronyms

People have created acronyms as shorthand for emotions or actions that would be visible in face-to-face interactions to add expressiveness to CMC.

ACRONYM	MEANING	ACRONYM	MEANING
BTW	by the way	LOL	laughing out loud
F2F	face-to-face	LOLIGAG	laughing out loud so hard I gag
FAQ	frequently asked question	MEGO	my eyes glaze over
FWIW	for what it's worth	OTOH	on the other hand
IJWS	I just want to say	TMOT	trust me on this
IOW	in other words	TPTB	the powers that be
IRL	in real life	WADR	with all due respect
JADP	just another data point	YMMV	your mileage may vary

SOURCE: Adapted from Higgins (1996).

found at http://www.astro.umd.edu/~marshall/smileys.html, and http://www.ascusc.org/jcmc/vol7/issue2/bechar.html.

CONTEXT

Recall from Chapter 2 that context has the levels of culture, time, relationship, situation, and function. Mediated communication primarily affects the situational level of context, but the other levels also play important roles in competent communication through media.

As Table 7.1 made clear, some cultures are not very media based in their communication. It is so easy for North Americans to take computer-mediated communication for granted, that they are often surprised that much of the world's population has never even made a telephone call! It can be rude to presume that a person has access to a computer, much less that this person understands the lingo of computers or the acronyms and words illustrated in Tables 7.3 and 7.4. Furthermore, some cultures value ambiguity or politeness, which runs counter to the tendency for people to engage in online flaming. Flaming is the term used to describe people's tendency to be more aggressive online than face-to-face, perhaps because the medium seems more impersonal, and thus, permits less empathy with the receiver. Other cultures, such as the Japanese, value a more leisurely development of trust in business relationships prior to the actual discussion of possible contracts. This runs counter to the impersonal feel of email relative to face-to-face interactions. Culture can influence a variety of decisions regarding the choice of communication medium as well as how it is used.

The relationship and time levels of context are extremely important to the choice and use of media (Walther, 1995). Sloane faced a delicate problem in defining her relationship with Chad and then attempting to "redefine" it once she became attracted to him as more than just a chat room friend. Furthermore, as you saw in Table 7.1, many people find the amount of time they spend on the internet takes time away from their relationships that are not primarily maintained via computers.

Email encourages rapid development of relationships, at least in terms of disclosure of personal information. In much the same way that flaming is thought to occur because of the emotional distance involved in email, people may disclose more because they cannot see the reaction of the recipient to their disclosures (Turkle, 1995). In addition, writing on a computer may feel like disclosure to a mechanical diary rather than to another person. However, it is not yet known whether such disclosure and relational development through computer media promotes normal and healthy relationships when compared to face-to-face paths of development (Walther, 1996).

Another dimension of the relational level is **status,** the level of respect and power a person, or a person's position, is given by those who interact with that person. Which medium you choose to communicate a message, and what you choose to say in that medium, depends in part on the relative status of the person(s) to whom you are sending the message. The difference between the sender's status and the receiver's status is called the **status ratio.** A high status ratio means the recipient has a much higher status than the sender. A low status ratio means the receiver has a much lower status than the sender. In general, we might expect that the higher the status ratio, the more a message should be formal, respectful, and task based. Furthermore, the higher the status ratio, the more the sender should attempt to choose the medium that the receiver prefers, rather than the medium the sender prefers. A summer intern should avoid sounding too informal or demanding when sending an email to his boss, who in turn must show the same type of concern when composing a message regarding this matter to her boss. In con-

TABLE 7.4

••• CMC Jargon •••

Many words we commonly use in conversation and writing today began as CMC jargon, such as *browser, Web, download, hyperlink,* and *hit.* Soon, the jargon in this table may be as commonplace and widely accepted.

JARGON	MEANING
Beepilepsy	The bizarre spasms and facial expressions people go through when their pagers go off.
Betamaxed	When something makes something else obsolete, as in "That new accounting system just betamaxed an entire department."
Blowing your buffer	When people lose their train of thought or simply lose track.
Cobweb	A WWW site that is never updated.
Meatspace	The physical world, as opposed to the digital and virtual world (also "carbon community," "facetime," F2F, and RL, or "real life").
Square-headed boy/girlfriend	A personal computer.
Treeware	Manuals, documentation.

SOURCE: Adapted from Higgins (1996).

trast, a CEO can afford to choose between either formal or informal means of expression through email.

The culture, time, and relationship levels of the CMC context reflect ways of defining the context. In contrast, the situation of mediated communication is obviously different by virtue of the physical medium itself. Two specific aspects of the technological environment particularly important to competence are media access and distance. Consider **media access,** which is the extent to which CMC technologies are available to your intended audience. In attempting to coordinate a family reunion, it makes little sense to operate strictly through email if only a fraction of the extended family uses or has access to email. The second important aspect of the situation is distance. If the recipient is literally two doors down the hallway, it probably makes more sense to walk the 20 steps and chat with the person instead of sending an email message. Competence in CMC depends on being sensitive to adapting the medium to the context.

The functional level of the context refers to the purpose and pressures of the communication. One of the most common pressures that influences the choice between face-to-face and mediated forms of communication is time pressure (Sitkin, Sutcliffe, & Barrios-Choplin, 1992). When a message has to get out to people immediately, a communicator often simultaneously uses multiple media—sending email and leaving voice mail at the same time, for example. The use of pagers and cellular telephones illustrates the paramount importance of speed and efficiency for contact with others. Even though overnight express mail takes only a day to reach the recipient, more and more people choose to attach files to an email message instead because it is even faster than sending hard copy overnight. The greater the time pressure for the receipt of a message, the more that faster media are needed for competent communication.

The context of computer-mediated communication involves people's culture, time, relationship, situations, and function. Together these factors play a significant role in determining what will and will not be competent as a choice of medium. As you saw previously, choosing a poorer, leaner medium to send more emotional messages tends to be a mistake. Similarly, overlooking the recipient's cultural characteristics and relational level often leads to a less competent choice of communication medium. However, context is not the only factor to consider in media choice. Like the frame of a painting, the context shows you what is and what is not part of the picture, but it is not the picture itself. The picture itself is the message, which represents what the artist intended to communicate. Competence in CMC requires attention to the message as much as the context.

In many cultures, closing a deal, launching a business relationship, or resolving a conflict is best achieved through face-to-face communication. Furthermore, the higher status level of the person, the less likely he or she is to use email or other CMC and therefore, the less appropriate it is to convey such business messages through a poorer, leaner medium.

MESSAGE FACTORS

One of the factors involved in competent communication is the content of the message. Media influence *how* a message appears. The writer Marshall McLuhan claimed the medium *is* the message. That is, the medium influences a message so much that the meaning of the message changes as a result of the choice of media. To some extent, seeing the Bosnian conflict on the evening news created a very different experience of the war than if it had only been reported by radio or newspaper. The medium made the war emotionally hot, real, and explosive. Seeing the faces of refugees as they poured forth in lines miles long from the burning rubble of their former villages created an immediacy that made the war more real and terrifying than mere words ever could. Furthermore, these images spoke for themselves. They often did not need words to convey their message.

The medium is certainly part of the message, just as a frame becomes an important part of a painting. However, the message itself is at least as important. A competent communicator needs to pay attention to both the medium and the message communicated through this medium. The competence of mediated communication is influenced by the ambiguity, complexity, and emotionality of messages.

Message ambiguity is the extent to which a message has either unknown or multiple meanings. Most people assume that ambiguous messages are incompetent. But this is not true. Every day of our lives we get through conversations, group decisions, and public presentations by relying on ambiguity (Spitzberg, 1993, 1994). Most people are more likely to vote for political candidates who speak about ambiguous and vague concepts like freedom and democracy than for candidates who speak only in concrete terms about issues like the cost of reforming health care and the need for campaign finance reform. When a friend asks what you think of his new haircut and you say, "It's . . . interesting," you are using ambiguity. Once Sloane decides that she is attracted to Chad, she may create messages that are more ambiguous about her gender rather than specifically refer to herself as a guy. Rather than recounting a story about a former "boyfriend," which might lead Chad to assume her sex, she might use terms such as "special friend" or "significant other." This preserves her options for claiming that she was not deceptive, while allowing her to avoid ending the relationship with an abrupt disclosure of her deception. She may see it as a way of easing Chad into the eventual disclosure of her true gender.

Generally, CMC increases the possibility of ambiguity because it is a poorer medium. When it is almost impossible to include nonverbal information in the message, the receiver has more options of how he or she interprets the message. Although this may sound useful, it can backfire in unintended ways. Sarcasm and humor, for example, may not translate well on email precisely because the intended meaning is lost because there is no accompanying nonverbal information. As a result, a statement written as criticism but intended as a joke is lost in the medium when it travels from sender to receiver. This is why many people characteristically follow their sarcastic or joking statements with an emoticon :-) or ☺ to communicate that the intent is not malicious or angry, but humorous.

Message complexity refers to the amount of detail, density, and integration of information in a message (Sitkin et al., 1992). More meanings can be derived from messages that have a large amount of information and details. Furthermore, with more information, various parts of the information can be interpreted and viewed in light of other bits of information in ways not intended by the sender. Generally, highly complex messages are difficult to communicate in face-to-face interaction. There are too many opportunities for listening to fail, for interruptions to derail the message, and for details to be confused. Highly complex messages may benefit from media that permit both careful production of the entire message and then careful review by the recipient. For example, many email messages are now sent routinely with an introductory comment by the sender followed by text, visual, video, or sound attachments. Such a message offers more information, but also permits the receiver to review it as completely as needed to comprehend its content.

A characteristic that affects the selection of the medium is **message emotionality,** the extent to which a message attempts to communicate the sender's feelings. These feelings can be part of the message content, such as when you say "I love you," or they can be more nonverbal or implicit, such as when you simply say "I've been thinking about you." Some messages have almost no emotional content, whereas others are almost entirely emotional in nature.

Messages with a strong emotional component are likely to require different media than messages that are emotionally lean. Despite the convenience of breaking off a relationship over the telephone, by letter, or by email, most receivers would probably consider the choice of such media incompetent for such an emotionally serious message. As McLuhan suggests, there are times when the medium actually becomes part of the emotional message. For example, the sending of a postcard may be as important as what the postcard says, because it shows that the sender thought of the recipient. In general, however, the more emotionally based the meaning of a message is, the more competent a richer medium will be to send it.

MEDIA FACTORS REVISITED

Sometimes, the medium is the message, or at least, a significant part of the message. Earlier in this chapter, we examined some of the more important characteristics of media including richness and openness. These same factors were discussed in the various ways in which context and message content are influenced by the medium itself.

When research first examined CMC in the 1980s, media were viewed as essentially richer or poorer. This view, however, did not take the unpredictable and creative human element into account. When faced with relatively poor media, people invented emoticons and used more humor to add an emotional and expressive touch to a relatively lean medium. When faced with the vast openness of the World Wide Web, people invented ways of stripping personal address information, deleted cookies (the secret marketing monitors deposited in people's files after access to certain Web sites), and developed more securely encrypted transactions. When faced with overly technical DOS-based computer systems, we invented user-friendly icon-based programs. As you can see, humans attempt to make mediated forms of communication more like face-to-face forms of communication. Progress in virtual reality systems reflects this ongoing trend.

Indeed, research indicates that computer-mediated relationships may, in fact, be quite similar to nonmedia-based relationships in many ways (Parks & Floyd, 1996). As media in general become richer, the lines between face-to-face and mediated communication will blur. Although much of the world's population does not own a telephone, in most of North America the telephone is so omnipresent that people barely even view it as a medium at all. For better or worse, telephone conversations are now routine on buses, in restaurants, and even in movie theaters. In the future, computer-based forms of communication may indeed enter the same league as the telephone. Indeed, new-generation telephones are becoming interlinked and even merged with computers to serve many of the same functions. People can now be linked to information, and each other, as never before.

OUTCOMES

Competence cannot be achieved in a vacuum. As you saw in Chapter 2, messages, behaviors, and media are not competent or incompetent by nature. Instead, communication is competent in its use in a given context based on the outcomes of the communication.

The appropriateness and effectiveness of outcomes determine the competence of the communication and medium. Recall from Chapter 2 that a message is effective if it accomplishes preferred goals and appropriate if it is acceptable to the participants in the context. The outcomes in the mediated context are not really different from those in the face-to-face context. They may, however, depend on somewhat different factors. Instead of a recipient evaluating the appropriateness of the message in a face-to-face encounter, the recipient in a technologically mediated encounter is also likely to evaluate the competence of the choice and use of the medium. If you send an emotionally rich message that carries important consequences through a poor medium, you risk being perceived as less competent. The medium should be chosen so that it optimizes the appropriateness and effectiveness of the message.

CMC makes it easy to achieve satisfaction for ourselves and for others. An email greeting or announcement is easily accessible and instantaneously gratifying for a large group of people.

Mediated messages produce outcomes other than appropriateness and effectiveness. Businesses view efficiency as an important standard of quality. **Efficiency** is the amount of resources such as people, time, and money relative to the benefits (profits, public awareness, etc.) achieved through that investment. Efficiency has taken on great importance in the corporate world, where time is money, and computers are cheap and very fast at distributing information. However, appropriateness and effectiveness should still serve as the key touchstones of competence. It may be efficient to fire an employee through an email message, but hardly appropriate and probably not effective for the long-term interests of the organization.

TO BRIAN
A Valentine for You

You Have My Seal of Approval,
Happy Valentines Day!
—Lena

From: Lena@xxxx
[sender]

As discussed in Chapter 2, understanding is another common standard for evaluating competence. Sometimes your goal simply may be to get information or a message across to someone else. If you want to meet someone for dinner or a movie at a particular place or time, the most important aspect of the message is that the other person clearly understands the meeting place and time. Again, however, understanding can be achieved in more and less appropriate and effective ways. Telling someone not to be late by as much as five minutes or you'll go on without that person is hardly the most appropriate way of achieving understanding.

Finally, sometimes the most important purpose a message serves is to make people feel good about it. You send many messages because you are part of a relationship or with the primary purpose of making the other person smile. In short, we often seek satisfaction for ourselves as well as for others through communication (Spitzberg & Hecht, 1984). Satisfaction is a feeling that desired outcomes have been achieved. Many people routinely send jokes, greeting cards, humorous video clips, and other "feel good" messages to their address lists of friends. Sloane and Chad conducted much of their email correspondence for the sole purpose of feeling good, for the satisfaction of sharing a worldview with someone else. The digital medium has made it convenient to share such feelings with others.

Challenges to Mediated Communication

Communication technology is changing so rapidly that it is difficult to know how it will affect society. However, given that much of the economy, and therefore your own livelihood, will depend significantly on how competently people use these evolving media, it is vital to have a road map to navigate the technological jungle. The model of CMC competence gives some directions for more competent communication in this mediated world. However, challenges to competent communication still remain. The most significant challenges to competence are access and mastery.

Access is the extent to which different types of media and many types of options in these media are available. **Mastery** is the extent to which a user understands how to use the media. Clearly it is difficult to have mastery without access. However, access alone is not enough to achieve mastery. The model of CMC competence presented in this chapter demonstrates that mastery results from motivation, knowledge, and skills, adapted to context, message, and media factors. Understanding the challenges to achieving both access and mastery is key to reaching competence in CMC.

Access

As you are probably aware by now, not everyone has access to high-technology communication media. Most of the world does not and a majority of Americans have yet to enter the digital realm of networked communication. Many children now use pagers and cellular phones, but may have no computer of their own, or only outdated computers. However, the challenge of access is more than not being able to touch a keyboard physically.

Access has both depth and breadth dimensions. **Breadth** concerns the number of different communication media to which a person has access. You can own a pager and a computer, but not be able to afford a cell phone and its fees. You may have a computer and internet service provider, but only one telephone line, so you can only access one mode of communication at a time. **Depth,** in contrast, refers to access to the various options available within a medium. You may have an internet service provider, but too limited a modem to have full access to the content available on the network. You may have a computer, but no sound card to enjoy the audio portions of messages or internet pages.

Both the depth and breadth of access may sound like purely economic issues that can be addressed by making more money to purchase newer hardware and better software. However, competence depends not only on using state-of-the-art equipment and upgrades, but also on mastery. Even if people recognize the value of improving their depth and breadth of access, they may not feel capable of mastering the technology.

MASTERY

As mentioned earlier, mastery is the extent to which a person is able to use the full potential of a medium. Mastery in CMC depends, in turn, on three factors: technophobia, information overload, and the pace of change. As technology changes more and more rapidly, many people feel as if their knowledge and skills cannot keep pace with new technologies. Further, as communication technology gives people greater access to more information, information overload becomes an ever-increasing threat. As the pace of change and level of information overload increase, more and more people may begin to experience technophobia as they feel overwhelmed by the challenge of learning new and complex technology. This, in turn, affects mastery as people find it increasingly difficult to feel like experts on systems that change every two years.

With new CMC technologies comes the convenience and the potential of information and access overload.

As with any area of change, people are afraid of new technologies and overwhelmed at the idea of using them. As we mentioned earlier, this fear of technology is called technophobia. The typical characteristics of technophobia are feelings of inadequacy in the areas of knowledge and skills when faced with a technology. With such feelings of ignorance and inadequacy, a technophobic person avoids unfamiliar technology so as not to face his or her own incompetence or appear incompetent to others.

The fear of technology is made worse to the extent that technology changes rapidly. The sheer pace of change is a major cause of technophobia, affecting many people's perception of their ability to use communication media. The sense that a system or software package is antiquated within less than two years of its purchase illustrates this rapid pace of change. Deciding whether to purchase the ability to "burn" (record onto) CDs, an internal DVD drive, or whether to move to flat-screen display represent just a few of the decisions that are now routine for any computer user. Imagine how intimidating it seems to someone who has never gotten online to consider buying a computer, much less becoming expert at it. This, and the fact that the options made available to the consumer change so rapidly, leave many behind in the information revolution.

The technology you know today will be obsolete within a few years of its creation; the computer you write your term papers on this semester may have already reached the limits of its capacity and technological life. Compare current computer technology with the typewriter in the 1960s and 1970s. The typewriter easily had a life span of a decade. Thus, in the new millennium, technologies are not only changing rapidly, but the *rate* of change is increasing as well. As a result, even when people overcome their fear of technology and actively participate in the world of communication media, they may soon find their old fears confirmed when they cannot keep up with learning about the next generation of technology.

A common complaint is that communication technology is creating **information overload** (Melody, 1994), the feeling of being overwhelmed because of having more media content and access to and from people than can be processed meaningfully. Information overload is caused, in part, by the greater access people have to each other through more channels such as cell phones, pagers, email, and voicemail systems. Given the increase in storage capacity and the greater affordability and availability of such technologies, it is increasingly difficult to achieve privacy. You may go on a long weekend vacation only to return to 40 to 50 email messages, 20 or 30 voicemail messages, a stack of snail mail, on top of several pages and cellular telephone calls during the vacation. The capacity of communication media to store messages means that messages which once simply never reached the recipient must now be answered. There is little escape short of becoming a cave dweller. Such overload presents the challenge of devoting equal attention to all messages. People have less time to compose their thoughts, much less their mediated response to messages.

Overcoming Challenges to Competence

Just as computers and communication media create challenges, they also offer solutions. There are no easy answers to becoming more competent with media in general and computer media in particular. As our society and other societies increasingly become hardwired in schools and homes, and as children are increasingly brought up on computers, the more the access problems will be overcome.

With increasing access and mastery of media, technophobia is likely to be less of a problem. As with so many fears, the best protection is familiarity and expertise. When personal computers first became widespread, people viewed them much as large calculators that needed very specific rule-based programming skills to use. Increasingly, we are becoming a nation of explorers who tinker with our computers to find out what we can do. In the process of tinkering, we forge a personal relationship with the computer that ultimately teaches us more about how to use the computer than any manual of instructions. According to one study of African American students, the students found a classroom multiuser email system much easier to use than they expected, once they started tinkering with it (Griffin & Anderton-Lewis, 1998). Such tinkering is both a useful practice, and a useful attitude, to help overcome technophobia.

Selectivity in both media production and consumption are important if we are to avoid drowning in information. Overload is best overcome by increasing sensitivity and competence with media. Media sensitivity permits people to make more informed choices.

Computer-mediated communication may present as many solutions as problems.

Copyright, Los Angeles Times Syndicate. Reprinted by permission. 1999.

Media sensitivity also facilitates interpretation of mediated messages, so that less time and effort is expended. Asking yourself before sending a message who it needs to go to, whether the medium you are using is the most competent for the context, and whether you have the motivation, knowledge, and skills to use that medium competently can go a long way to avoid overload. Just because a message *can* be sent to someone (or hundreds of people) doesn't mean it *should* be sent.

Chapter Summary

Media and computers are rapidly changing our world. Computer-mediated communication is defined as any human symbolic interaction through digitally based technologies. Two basic features of media affect our relationships with each other and society in this digital context. Media richness is the extent to which a medium recreates or represents all of the information available in the original message. Openness is the extent to which messages are public, as opposed to private, in a given medium of communication.

The extent to which these factors affect our competence also depends on our motivation, knowledge, and skills with communication media, the context in which the communication occurs, and the nature of the message itself. Motivation depends on focusing on positive reasons to use CMC, as well as minimizing technophobic or negative motivations regarding media. Knowledge depends on access to interpersonal sources of expertise as well as the ability to tinker with technologies and media. The skills of communication covered in Chapter 2, attentiveness, composure, coordination, and expressiveness, are relevant to mediated communication.

The contextual levels that frame communication, culture, time, relationship, situation, and function, are also relevant to the mediated environment. In mediated communication, culture affects not only how someone communicates, but also whether a person is able to communicate in that medium. Relationship includes factors such as the types of emotions expressed and the status ratio of the communicators. The situational level includes access and distance. Finally, the functional level context involves the message's intent, task ambiguity, task complexity, and time pressure.

The message itself can also influence the competence of mediated communication. Messages vary in their ambiguity, complexity, emotional content, and consequences.

Communication, whether face-to-face or mediated, is intended to produce an outcome, even if it is only satisfaction as opposed to understanding or efficiency. The extent to which mediated communication is efficient, understood, and satisfying significantly influences the competence of the message(s), although even these outcomes are only competent to the extent they are appropriate and effective.

Two significant challenges to achieving CMC competence are access and mastery. Access consists of both the breadth or number of different media available to a person, as well as depth, which is access to the various options available within a medium. Mastery is the extent to which a person is able to use all of the potential of a medium. Mastery depends, in turn, on a person's technophobia, the level of information overload facing that person, and on the pace of technological change.

Overcoming these challenges involves both formal forms of instruction as well as a spirit of tinkering that can enhance a user's sense of mastery over time. Overcoming information overload requires prioritizing media use according to one's media sensitivity. Becoming more selective regarding which media are used for what purposes and with which audiences is an essential ingredient of competence in overcoming the challenges to mastery and access.

Key Terms

computer-mediated communication
natural media
technological media
media richness
speed
interactivity
completeness
openness
media sensitivity
dystopia
technophobia
tinkering
emoticons
status
status ratio
media access
message ambiguity

message complexity
message emotionality
efficiency
access
mastery
breadth
depth
information overload

Building Motivation

See Self-Assessment on page 202.

Building Knowledge

1. How have communication media and computers changed your everyday interactions and relationships? Create a table with three columns. List the changes in a first column, and then in the next two columns indicate if there are any positive or negative consequences for each change. Do you think these changes are common to everyone, or are they unique to you? Why or why not?
2. Some people think that media are changing the fundamental way we relate to one another. Others say we are simply transforming our media into something more like face-to-face interaction, and thus no big changes are likely to occur. Do you think these changes are fundamental or only superficial? Why?
3. Where do you feel most comfortable relating to people, online or in "real life" (RL)? Why? Does it depend on the type of situation, and if so, in what ways?
4. Take a moment and think about where communication technology seems to be going in our society. What changes do you think media will bring to the way we relate to one another 10 years from now, if any? If you see changes occurring, will these changes be mainly positive or negative?
5. How competent do you think you are in relating to people in various communication media (telephone, letter, email, chat rooms)? How competent do you think others think you are when you communicate using these media?
6. Look up and read the following articles on *InfoTrac College Edition*: Jeff Minerd in *The Futurist*, in 1999, Article #A53889568, "Pathological internet use," *U.S. News & World Report*, September 1, 1997, article #119703501. On balance, do you see CMC as an improvement of, or as a detriment to, communication in society? Why?
7. Cyber-Nicks. Go to the following WWW site: **http://www.ascusc.org/jcmc/vol1/issue2/bechar.html**. You should find an article authored by Haya-Bechar-Israeli, published in the electronic *Journal of Computer Mediated Communication* on the development of nicknames in CMC. After browsing the article, come up with a nickname for yourself, or, if you have one already, come up with a new one. Speculate on how nicknames help you communicate more competently with others in CMC.

Building Skills

The exercises here assume you have access to computerized networks of some sort. If not, gain access through your educational institution, or locate someone with access who will allow you to participate in the activities here.

Individual Exercises

1. Examine the differences between search engines such as Yahoo, Altavista, Lycos, Excite, Hotbot, or Infoseek. Search engines are programs that match key words or phrases with words in Web site descriptions. Choose a topic on which you will prepare a speech or paper in this course, and enter the same terms into three different search engines. Note the differences in the sites located and the order in which they are listed. Which engine did a better job? In what sense was it better? Did it present the information in more usable form, or did it simply list the most relevant sites before the less relevant sites?
2. Find out more about computer-mediated communication using the World Wide Web. Enter *computer-mediated communication* into the search engine you prefer from Exercise 1. Among other links, you should find an entire journal devoted to the study of this phenomenon: *Journal of Computer-Mediated Communication*. Search this journal's Web page for particular topics of interest. For example, do you think it's true that computer-mediated communication is dominated by men more than women? If yes, why?
3. Six degrees of separation? Find out how many computer links are needed for you to connect with someone famous or someone with whom you have never communicated but would like to. For

example, if you know a science fiction fan (first link), who engages in CMC with a sci-fi conference organizer (second link), who corresponds through CMC with a Hollywood agent (third link), who works for a talent agency manager (fourth link), who sends emails to the secretary (fifth link) of the talent agent (sixth link) for Gillian Anderson (who plays the character Dana Scully), then you are six degrees of separation from engaging in CMC with the star of *The X-Files.* Technology may have reduced the number of "degrees" you need to contact someone. Now search for information on the Web about yourself using all the search tools available to you. This is referred to as "ego surfing." How accessible are you to others because of technology? How much privacy do you have, and do you need more or less?

4. A recent study found that the more time people spent on the internet, the fewer people they had in their social network, and the more depressed and lonely they became (Kraut et al., 1998). Keep a diary or log to track your communication activities, similar to the one shown below. Over the span of a week, at the end of each day note in your log every medium you used directly and indirectly. Direct use refers to a technology that you used to send or receive a message. Indirect use means you send or receive or are influenced by a message through someone else's use of a medium. For example, you ask someone else to send a fax to you, or one of your friends receives a page in your presence. At the end of the week, tabulate the number of different media that affected you, and note whether direct or indirect influences were more significant. How media competent are you, based just on the number of different media you use? How dependent are you on media and how comfortable are you with this level of dependence? Are your friends and acquaintances more or less media connected than you? Why?

Group Exercises

1. Form a group of 4–5 people and discuss and decide which of the following types of encounters would be best transmitted through which media:

   Encounter/Message
   - Informing people of an upcoming party
   - Asking someone out on a date
   - Criticizing someone for a careless comment to you
   - Lifting the spirits of a friend who is feeling depressed
   - Introducing yourself to other employees in your organization who do not work in your department

   Medium
   - face-to-face, interpersonal
   - face-to-face, group or public context
   - Letter (snail mail)
   - Email, interpersonal
   - Email, chat room, or group virtual environment
   - Bulletin board announcement
   - Allow gossip or rumor to work its way to someone else

Weekly Diary (Question 4)

F2F = Face-to-face
PH = Telephone
CF = Cell phone
FAX = Fax
LTR = Letter
CMC = Computer

	Direct						Indirect					
	F2F	PH	CF	FAX	LTR	CMC	F2F	PH	CF	FAX	LTR	CMC
Monday												
Tuesday												
Wednesday												
Thursday												
Friday												
Saturday												
Sunday												

2. Form groups of 4–5 people to compare group computer assignments with those accomplished face-to-face and by telephone. At some point in the semester, you are likely to have one or more group assignments. Try to arrange one assignment entirely over the computer or telephone, and compare it to group projects that make more use of face-to-face interactions. Analyze the differences, if any, in the way each member related to others and how each felt about the experience.
3. Form teams of 4–5 people to debate utopia and dystopia. Recall that utopia is a world in which everything meets an ideal sense of what is best. A dystopia is a world in which everything is disastrous or dysfunctional. Each team will either be arguing for a utopian vision or for a dystopian vision of communication technology. Each team will have a set amount of time to research the topics. Allow each team 15 minutes for presenting their arguments, 10 minutes for the rebuttal. Based on the in-class group presentations, which vision seems more realistic, and why?
4. Complete the following items below as individuals first. Then form groups of 5–6 members, and identify the group's average preferences by tallying how many people in the group chose each answer.

   For the following situations, check the *best* answer for each statement. For each situation, assume that all the listed media are available to both (or all) of the parties mentioned and all concerned know how to use them. To what extent did your answers differ from those of the other group members? Why do you think this is?

Situations (Question 4)

a. If you needed to talk to a friend about feeling depressed, which medium would you most likely use?

_____ face-to-face
_____ Rumor or talk through "friends of friends"
_____ Letter or memo
_____ Email
_____ Telephone/voice mail

b. If you needed to inform a department's employees of an upcoming retirement party, which medium would you most likely use?

_____ face-to-face
_____ Rumor or talk through "friends of friends"
_____ Letter or memo
_____ Bulletin board posting
_____ Email
_____ Telephone/voice mail

c. If you needed to reprimand an employee for his or her attitude problems, which medium would you most likely use?

_____ face-to-face
_____ Rumor or talk through a "friend of a friend"
_____ Letter or memo
_____ Bulletin board posting
_____ Email
_____ Telephone/voice mail

d. If you wanted to express your romantic interest in an employee in another department, which medium would you most likely use?

_____ face-to-face
_____ Rumor or talk through a "friend of a friend"
_____ Letter or memo
_____ Bulletin board posting
_____ Email
_____ Telephone/voice mail

e. If you had a complicated conflict with a boss over a project you were working on, which medium would you most likely use to work it out?

_____ face-to-face
_____ Rumor or talk through a "friend of a friend"
_____ Letter or memo
_____ Email
_____ Telephone/voice mail

f. If you had a complicated conflict with a subordinate over a project you were working on, which medium would you most likely use to work it out?

_____ face-to-face
_____ Rumor or talk through a "friend of a friend"
_____ Letter or memo
_____ Email
_____ Telephone/voice mail

(*Continued*)

g. If you were a member of a small task team to improve workplace safety, which medium would you most likely use to reach a set of recommendations for the organization?

_____ face-to-face

_____ Rumor or talk through a "friend of a friend"

_____ Letter or memo

_____ Email

_____ Telephone/voice mail

h. If you had an announcement you needed to make to an entire department, which medium would you most likely use?

_____ face-to-face

_____ Rumor or talk through a "friend of a friend"

_____ Letter or memo

_____ Bulletin board posting

_____ Email

_____ Telephone/voice mail

References

Berdayes, L. C., & Berdayes, V. (1998). The information highway in contemporary narrative. *Journal of Communication, 48,* 109–124.

Brenner, V. (1997). Psychology of computer use: XLVII. Parameters of internet use, abuse, and addiction: The first 90 days of the internet usage survey. *Psychological Reports, 80,* 879–882.

Cheseboro, J. W. (1995). Communication technologies as cognitive systems. In J. T. Wood & R. B. Gregg (Eds.), *Toward the twenty-first century: The future of speech communication* (pp. 15–46). Creskill, NJ: Hampton Press.

Cochrane, P. (1995). The information wave. In S. J. Emmott (Ed.), *Information superhighways: Multimedia users and futures* (pp. 17–33). San Diego: Academic.

Fischer, C. S. (1992). *America calling: A social history of the telephone to 1940.* Berkeley: University of California Press.

Gergen, K. K. (1991). *The saturated self: Dilemmas of identity in contemporary life.* New York: Basic Books.

Griffin, F. W., & Anderton-Lewis, L. (1998). Enhancing connections between students and instructors: African-American students' use of computer-mediated communication. *Business Communication Quarterly, 61,* 9–19.

Higgins, B. (1996, November). How email changed everything. *San Francisco Focus,* 59–67.

Hopper, R. (1992). *Telephone conversation.* Bloomington: Indiana University Press.

Hudiburg, R. A. (1995). Psychology of computer use: XXXIV. The computer hassles scale: Subscales, norms, and reliability. *Psychological Reports, 77,* 779–782.

Hudson, H. E. (1997). *Global connections: International telecommunication infrastructure and policy.* New York: Van Nostrand Reinhold.

Inose, H., & Pierce, J. R. (1984). *Information technology and civilization.* New York: Freeman.

Kraut, R., Patterson, M., Lundmark, V., Kiesler, S., Mukophadhyay, T., & Scherlis, W. (1998). Internet paradox: A social technology that reduces social involvement and psychological well-being? *American Psychologist, 53,* 1017–1031.

Markus, M. L. (1994). Finding a happy medium: Explaining the negative effects of electronic communication on social life at work. *ACM Transactions on Information Systems, 12,* 119–149.

Melody, W. (1994). Electronic networks, social relations, and the changing structure of knowledge. In D. C. Crowley & D. Mitchell (Eds.), *Communication theory today* (pp. 254–273). Stanford, CA: Stanford University Press.

Meyrowitz, J. (1985). *No sense of place: The impact of electronic media on social behavior.* New York: Oxford University Press.

Negroponte, N. (1995). *Being digital.* New York: Knopf.

Parks, M. R., & Floyd, K. (1996). Making friends in cyberspace. *Journal of Communication, 46,* 80–97.

Pavlik, J. V. (1998). *New media technology: Cultural and commercial perspectives* (2nd ed.). Boston: Allyn & Bacon.

Rice, R. E. (1993). Media appropriateness: Using social presence theory to compare traditional and new organizational media. *Human Communication Research, 19,* 451–484.

Ronfeldt, D. (1992). Cyberocracy is coming. *The Information Society, 8,* 243–296.

Computers keep on multiplying. *San Diego Union Tribune,* Wed., April 26, 1995, p. E-3.

Schmitz, J., & Fulk, J. (1991). Organizational colleagues, media richness, and electronic mail: A test of the social influence model of technology use. *Communication Research, 18,* 487–523.

Schrage, M. (1990). *Shared minds: The new technologies of collaboration.* New York: Random House.

Sitkin, S. B., Sutcliffe, K. M., & Barrios-Choplin, J. R. (1992). A dual-capacity model of communication media choice in organizations. *Human Communication Research, 18,* 563–598.

Spitzberg, B. H. (1993). The dialectics of (in)competence. *Journal of Social and Personal Relationships, 10,* 137–158.

Spitzberg, B. H. (1994). The dark side of (in)competence. In W. R. Cupach & B. H. Spitzberg (Eds.), *The dark side of interpersonal communication* (pp. 25–49). Hillsdale, NJ: Erlbaum.

Spitzberg, B. H., & Hecht, M. L. (1984). A component model of relational competence. *Human Communication Research, 10,* 575–599.

Steuer, J. (1992). Defining virtual reality: Dimensions determining telepresence. *Journal of Communication, 42,* 73–93.

Times Mirror Center for People and the Press. (1994, May). *The role of technology in American life.* New York: Author.

Trevino, L. K., Daft, R. L., & Lengel, R. H. (1990). Understanding managers' media choices: A symbolic interactionist perspective. In J. Folk & C. Steinfield (Eds.), *Organizations and communication technology* (pp. 71–94). Newbury Park, CA: Sage.

Turkle, S. (1995). *Life on the screen: Identity in the age of the internet.* New York: Simon & Schuster.

U.S. Department of Commerce. (1998). *The emerging digital economy.* Washington, DC: U.S. Department of Commerce (http://www.ecommerce.gov./digital.htm).

Walther, J. B. (1995). Relational aspects of computer-mediated communication: Experimental observations over time. *Organization Science, 6,* 186–203.

Walther, J. B. (1996). Computer-mediated communication: Impersonal, interpersonal, and hyperpersonal interaction. *Communication Research,* 23, 3–43.

Westmyer, S. A., DiCioccio, R. L., & Rubin, R. B. (1998). Appropriateness and effectiveness of communication channels in competent interpersonal communications. *Journal of Communication, 48,* 27–48.

Building Motivation

Self-Assessment: Computer-Mediated Communication (CMC) includes all forms of email and formal/informal computer-based networks (World Wide Web, chat rooms, electronic bulletin boards, multiuser domains, terminal-based video-telephony, etc.) for sending and receiving written messages. Here you'll see 38 statements about your activities and your impressions of various communication media. Using the following scale, indicate the degree to which you agree or disagree with each statement.

Scale

1 = Strongly Disagree
2 = Mildly Disagree
3 = Neither Agree Nor Disagree
4 = Mildly Agree
5 = Strongly Agree

MOTIVATION TOTAL ____
(3–15, midpoint = 9)

1 2 3 4 5 **1.** I enjoy communicating through computer media.

1 2 3 4 5 **2.** I never get nervous using CMC.

1 2 3 4 5 **3.** I like tinkering with options to make my CMC messages more effective.

KNOWLEDGE TOTAL ____
(3–15, midpoint = 9)

1 2 3 4 5 **4.** I am very knowledgeable about computer-based communication techniques.

1 2 3 4 5 **5.** I am familiar with email and communication networks.

1 2 3 4 5 **6.** I feel quite comfortable when communicating through computer-mediated media.

SKILLS

Coordination TOTAL ____
(3–15, midpoint = 9)

1 2 3 4 5 **7.** When I receive a message from someone, I generally reply within a day.

1 2 3 4 5 **8.** I always reply to all the aspects of someone's message.

1 2 3 4 5 **9.** I manage CMC interactions skillfully.

Expressiveness TOTAL ____
(3–15, midpoint = 9)

1 2 3 4 5 **10.** I am very articulate and vivid in my CMC messages.

1 2 3 4 5 **11.** I use emoticons when appropriate in my CMC messages.

1 2 3 4 5 **12.** I try to use humor when appropriate in my CMC messages.

Attentiveness TOTAL ____
(3–15, midpoint = 9)

1 2 3 4 5 **13** I adapt my words and writing style to the person I'm corresponding with.

1 2 3 4 5 **14.** I ask a lot of questions of the other person in my CMC.

1 2 3 4 5 **15.** I am skillful at showing concern for and interest in others when using CMC.

Composure TOTAL ____
(3–15, midpoint = 9)

1 2 3 4 5 **16.** I have no trouble expressing my opinions forcefully when using CMC.

1 2 3 4 5 **17.** I use the first-person pronoun ("I") frequently in my CMC messages.

1 2 3 4 5 **18.** I am skillful at revealing self-confidence in my CMC interactions.

CONTEXTUAL FACTORS

Culture TOTAL ____
(1–5, midpoint = 3)

1 2 3 4 5 **19.** I consider the culture of the recipient when I write messages on CMC.

Relational Context TOTAL ____
(1–5, midpoint = 3)

1 2 3 4 5 **20.** CMC messages are opportunities to work on relationships as well as tasks.

Status TOTAL ____
(1–5, midpoint = 3)

1 2 3 4 5 **21.** I adapt my messages, such as using more or less formal language, based on the status of the person I'm sending them to.

Distance TOTAL ____
(1–5, midpoint = 3)

1 2 3 4 5 **22.** I tend not to use CMC messages for people I could communicate with face-to-face.

Media Access TOTAL ____
(1–5, midpoint = 3)

1 2 3 4 5 **23.** I have access to a variety of media for communicating with others.

Time Pressure TOTAL ____
(1–5, midpoint = 3)

1 2 3 4 5 **24.** Computers give me time to prepare drafts of my messages.

MESSAGE FACTORS

Message Ambiguity TOTAL ____
(1–5, midpoint = 3)

1 2 3 4 5 **25.** I try to be as specific as possible in all my task-related CMC messages.

Message Complexity TOTAL ____
(1–5, midpoint = 3)

1 2 3 4 5 **26.** The more technical a message, the more selective I am in who I send it to.

Message Emotionality TOTAL ____
(1–5, midpoint = 3)

1 2 3 4 5 **27.** The more emotional a message, the less likely I am to use a computer to send it.

MEDIA FACTORS

Richness TOTAL ____
(1–5, midpoint = 3)

1 2 3 4 5 **28.** I choose media (CMC, mail, phone, or face-to-face) based on how lively the interaction and feedback need to be.

Access TOTAL ____
(1–5, midpoint = 3)

1 2 3 4 5 **29.** I choose media (CMC, mail, phone, or face-to-face) based on how much access others have to the particular medium.

OUTCOMES

Understanding TOTAL ____
(1–5, midpoint = 3)

1 2 3 4 5 **30.** I get my ideas across clearly when I use CMC.

Efficiency TOTAL ____
(1–5, midpoint = 3)

1 2 3 4 5 **31.** I am more efficient using CMC than other forms of communication.

Satisfaction TOTAL ____
(1–5, midpoint = 3)

1 2 3 4 5 **32.** My CMC conversations are often more pleasant than my face-to-face interactions.

Appropriateness TOTAL ____
(1–5, midpoint = 3)

1 2 3 4 5 **33.** I avoid saying things I shouldn't on CMC.

Effectiveness TOTAL ____
(1–5, midpoint = 3)

1 2 3 4 5 **34.** I generally get what I want out of my CMC interactions.

Interpreting Your Scores: Each heading represents a component of the CMC competence model. For each component, add your responses to the items (for single items, your score is whatever rating you replied with), and then compare to the range and midpoint specified in the parentheses. Generally speaking, scores below the midpoint suggest you need to work on your competence, and scores above the midpoint suggest that you consider yourself fairly competent in that component.

CHAPTER 8

Learning Objectives

After studying this chapter, you should be able to:

1. Identify the difference between signs and symbols.
2. Distinguish between content and relationship levels of messages.
3. Identify the characteristics of interpersonal communication.
4. Identify the components of interpersonal communication competence.
5. Describe the stages of relationship evolution.
6. Define the three dimensions of interpersonal motivation and the types of motives they classify.
7. Define relational dialectics, and explain their relationship to interpersonal communication motives.
8. Locate the motivations of interpersonal communication on a map of motives.
9. Define and describe the major challenges to interpersonal competence.
10. Discuss methods of overcoming the challenges to interpersonal competence.

Introducing Interpersonal Communication

Although Konrad thought this day would be pretty much like any other day, he was especially looking forward to the evening. He had a couple of morning classes to attend, and he was anticipating seeing his girlfriend for lunch to discuss the fraternity party they were going to this evening. Feeling upbeat and confident, he strolled over to the café next to campus, walked up behind his girlfriend, put his hands over her eyes and asked, "Guess who?" When she turned around, one look at her face and the first sound of her voice told him that his day had just taken a turn for the worse.

Leane's reply was "Konrad, we need to talk." Within the span of a few moments, Leane explained that she didn't feel the relationship was going in the direction she had hoped it would, and she wanted to break up. Even though they had only been dating for a few months, she had been thinking about the relationship a lot lately, and simply did not feel it was going to work out. She felt they should be further along in getting to know each other's "deeper selves," and started discussing how exclusive and how serious they should be. She continued by saying that she just didn't feel they were going to get serious, and although she wasn't looking to get married at the moment, she did want to date people with whom she felt there was a possibility of marriage. Konrad had seen none of this coming, and although he tried to find a way to discuss the possibility of giving the relationship another chance, Leane's decision seemed firm.

Konrad no longer felt like attending the party, but it was his fraternity and he was an organizer. He had to be there, and he was. All evening he kept replaying his earlier conversation with Leane in his head; scenes from their two-month relationship passed before his eyes. He kept trying to figure out what he had done wrong, why he hadn't seen this coming, and he realized how upset he was, how much he had begun to fall for this woman. He really did care for Leane, but he hadn't realized he was beginning to think about a future with her.

Throughout the evening friends and strangers began conversations with Konrad, and each time, Konrad was listless, distracted, and uninterested in making the usual small talk. He occasionally overheard acquaintances saying things like "What's up with Kon?" "I don't know—he's just being antisocial tonight" or "Konrad's really not himself." Konrad got the distinct impression that the few strangers who tried to strike up conversations with him left with a negative impression of him, but he didn't care. He was feeling lonely and rejected and didn't see the point in trying to get into a partying mood, meet people, and make a good impression. He left the party early and went for a long walk to contemplate what had happened.

After a while, he decided he would call Leane, ask to have a talk the next day over coffee, and tell her how serious he was about the relationship. He decided to tell her that he wanted to make it an exclusive relationship and apologize for not discussing the relationship and where they wanted it to go. He believed he could persuade her to give their relationship another chance, and this time, he would make it work. It was late, but when he got back to his room, he gave Leane a call. His voice was sincere, his words calm and focused, and his desire to reestablish the relationship was clear. As they talked, Konrad was able to articulate the importance of the relationship, and asked for a second chance to show Leane that he was ready to make it work. As the conversation unfolded both Konrad and Leane expressed their needs and desires, each listened, and eventually, they felt closer and more attracted to one another. The conversation reminded them of just how well they connected when they made the effort. They decided to give the relationship another try. •••

Normally Konrad is a popular, socially skilled person. But at the party he had no interest in trying to be competent. That is, he had the knowledge and skills to make positive impressions on others, but he lacked the motivation to do so. Furthermore, as one relationship ended (in behavior, if not in his memory), he faced the possibility of beginning new relationships. But again, he was not motivated to pursue those potential relationships. He didn't care much about the first impressions he made on strangers or, for that matter, what his friends thought about him. He was, in short, not managing his interpersonal communication very competently. However, once he assessed what was really important to him, reestablishing his relationship with Leane, he was able to formulate plans and engage in a bold communication strategy to achieve his goals. In short, he was motivated to make a competent impression on Leane, if not his friends and acquaintances. His communication behavior reflected this motivation.

Most of our daily communication is interpersonal. Face-to-face conversations, telephone calls, chat room discussions, and correspondence by email and letters are all forms of interpersonal communication. So are chats over lunch, brief interactions with classmates, arguments with romantic partners or parents, discussions with the boss, requests from a sales clerk, and peek-a-boo games with an infant. Interpersonal communication is the stuff of which relationships are ultimately made. We may develop a sense of knowing celebrities or our favorite rock star, but if there is no interpersonal communication, the relationship is at most a substitute for actual social interaction.

Assumptions About Interpersonal Communication

You communicate interpersonally virtually every day of your life. You learn to communicate interpersonally when you are so young that you don't even remember how you first learned many of the lessons of communicating. It may seem that interpersonal communication is something you simply and naturally "do" with competence. So take a moment to see how naturally competent you are by testing your assumptions about interpersonal communication.

Test your assumptions

INSTRUCTIONS: Read each of the following statements. Circle the answer that you think best reflects each statement.

TRUE	FALSE	**1.** I can simply "be myself," regardless of the relationship or context I'm in.
TRUE	FALSE	**2.** I can read my partner "like a book."
TRUE	FALSE	**3.** I can tell when my partner is lying.
TRUE	FALSE	**4.** I can tell instantly if someone likes me or not.
TRUE	FALSE	**5.** I communicate every day of my life—I'd know if I had a problem communicating.
TRUE	FALSE	**6.** I can put myself in someone else's shoes if I want.
TRUE	FALSE	**7.** Relationships become easier the more intimate they become.
TRUE	FALSE	**8.** There wouldn't be conflicts if people simply communicated better.
TRUE	FALSE	**9.** I only need a couple of good relationships—all the others are relatively unimportant.
TRUE	FALSE	**10.** If I am motivated enough to accomplish something, I can make it happen.
TRUE	FALSE	**11.** Effective communication is always clear and unambiguous.

Answers: 1: F; 2: F; 3: F; 4: F; 5: F; 6: F; 7: F; 8: F; 9: F; 10: F; 11: F

The assumptions listed represent common beliefs people have about interpersonal communication. Taken literally, each of the assumptions in the Test Your Assumptions box is false. As you saw in Chapter 3, people are complex and display different aspects of their selves in different situations and relationships (assumption 1). Because of the complexity of multiple selves, we generally cannot read others as accurately as we think we can (assumption 2). As we often form positive and negative impressions of others without letting them know what we think, they, in turn, don't always give us accurate feedback, making us unaware of our own communication limitations (assumption 5). For this reason, we frequently don't know whether or not others are telling the truth (assumption 3) or whether they like us (assumption 4). Furthermore, given that people possess many different selves and we can't always read their feelings accurately, we can't really see the world the way they do (assumption 6). Relationships reflect this complexity as well. As intimacy increases between two people so does their interdependence on one another, which often makes relationships harder to manage (assumption 7). Indeed, communicating clearly and accurately provides as many opportunities to discover your differences as your similarities. These opportunities lead to *more* opportunities for conflict (assumption 8). As troublesome as your relationships may be, you do need many different types of relationships in your life. Your relationships with acquaintances and casual friends have a significant impact on how you feel and act (assumption 9). Finally, as important as motivation is to communication competence, motivation alone cannot guarantee you will achieve your communicative goals (assumption 10). As you've see, communication competence depends on motivation, knowledge, skills, and the context in which you are communicating.

This chapter introduces interpersonal communication and the motivations that underlie it. Chapters 9 and 10 explore the other components of interpersonal communication competence, knowledge and skills, in greater detail. The first step to understanding competence in interpersonal communication is defining interpersonal communication.

What Is Interpersonal Communication?

Interpersonal communication is the process of exchanging signs or symbols that create meaning in an interactive context of few people. This definition incorporates several characteristics of interpersonal communication that distinguish it from other contexts of communication. Thus interpersonal communication is a transactional process, it involves signs and symbols, it creates meaning, it occurs in an interactional context, it involves a few people, it is relational, it creates relationships, and it evolves in stages.

INTERPERSONAL COMMUNICATION IS A TRANSACTIONAL PROCESS

As you saw in Chapter 1, communication is a transactional process. For interpersonal communication this means the communicators involved are both senders and receivers. Interpersonal communication is also a process, which means the communicators influence one another as they communicate. If a partner's message doesn't influence your thoughts, feelings, or behaviors at all, then you would be hard-pressed to claim that communication has actually occurred. Interpersonal communication, then, requires that two-way communication occurs, with the potential for feedback messages sent and received by all persons.

INTERPERSONAL COMMUNICATION INVOLVES SIGNS & SYMBOLS

As with all communication, interpersonal communication involves the exchange of signs and symbols. Recall from Chapter 4 that signs are actions or representations that bear a direct relation to the thing to which they refer. Symbols, in contrast, stand for or refer to something else. For example, you are eating at a restaurant and you see someone unable to breathe or speak, begin to turn blue, and raise both hands to her throat. This person is not intentionally attempting to formulate a message. Instead, she is simply choking. Her actions are signs of physical distress, and her hands around her throat refer directly to the problem. Yet you assign meaning to these actions and receive the message that this person needs immediate assistance. If, in contrast, she hurriedly writes CHOKING! on a napkin and shows it to her dining partner, or if she merely points to her throat rather than grabbing it, the writing or pointing are symbols, intentionally used to refer to something other than the symbols themselves.

INTERPERSONAL COMMUNICATION CREATES MEANING

For symbols and signs to be important at all, they must be vehicles of meaning. Meaning is the essential basis of communication. Without meaning, there is no communication. As you saw in Chapter 1, meaning is the interpretation a person assigns to a message. Remember that these interpretations are not contained in the message itself. Instead, interpersonal communicators play an active role in making sense of messages, based on each other's culture, sense of time, relationship, purpose, and the situation in which the message is perceived.

The attribution of meaning, like communication, is a process. It involves both cognitive and emotional types of interpretation, and these interpretations evolve over time. The first time you hear "I love you" in a developing relationship leads you to make a variety of cognitive interpretations regarding where the relationship is and is expected to go. This phrase is also interpreted at the emotional level: You might feel excited, anxious, hopeful, or joyful. A month later the meaning of this phrase may be quite different. You may come to conclude that the other person's meaning for being in "love" is quite different from your own.

INTERPERSONAL COMMUNICATION OCCURS IN AN INTERACTIONAL CONTEXT

For interpersonal communication to occur, signs or symbols must serve as the medium of meaning. However, meaning is an element of all communication. What makes this meaning *interpersonal* is the fact that it occurs in an interactional context. An **interactional context** is simply one in which there are opportunities for all participants to engage in the process. If communication is interactional, the interactants must be able to send and receive messages. Email interaction, for example, is considered interpersonal communication because the participants can both send and receive messages, even though responses are often delayed.

INTERPERSONAL COMMUNICATION INVOLVES FEW PEOPLE

What makes communication interpersonal rather than group or public? The definition of interpersonal communication specifies it involves few people. The distinctions between interpersonal communication, which involves a few persons, small group communication, which involves a small number of persons, and public speaking, which involves many people, are subtle. For example, you saw in Chapter 7 that new technologies are now allowing people to chat with hundreds, perhaps thousands of others, but also permit communicators to shift to one-on-one exchanges. Is a chat room interpersonal, group, or public communication? Most scholars have concluded there is no absolute difference between contexts. Instead, the distinctions among these three contexts of communication reflect tendencies for interpersonal communication to involve few people, group communication to involve a moderate number of people, and public speaking to involve one to many people.

Although there may be no precise number of participants to distinguish contexts, the number of participants clearly makes a difference to communication. Several trends occur as more and more people communicate in a given context. First, more people introduce greater coordination problems. For example, determining whose turn it is to talk becomes more complex. Second, there is a greater likelihood of misunderstanding. The more people involved in the communication, the more ways a message can be interpreted. Third, there tends to be less opportunity for any given person to influence the entire episode of communication because more voices compete in a given amount of time. Thus, in order for communication to occur between *persons,* that is, for *interpersonal* communication to occur, it is essential that each communicator be able to treat the other as an individual. This can only happen in contexts of a few people.

Traditionally, interpersonal communication has implied transactional communication with only a few people. But in this situation, interpersonal communication can occur over email, chat room, teacher-student interaction, and student-student interaction. But is this type of communication also group and public communication?

INTERPERSONAL COMMUNICATION IS RELATIONAL

There are two key aspects by which someone understands the meaning of a sign or symbol in interpersonal communication: content and relationship. The **content dimension of messages** refers to the "what" of communication. The ideas, the meanings of the words or behaviors, the dictionary definitions of the utterances, represent the content of a message. The **relational dimension of messages** refers to the way communicators define their relationship to one another (Watzlawick, Beavin, & Jackson, 1967). Messages have implications for how people see themselves as connected to each other.

Knowledge Link

How does the relationship type of context discussed in Chapter 2 relate to the dimensions of content and relationship?

•••

The relational aspect of communication has many dimensions, but as you saw in Chapter 2, the most important are affiliation and power. Affiliation is whether and how you want to be close to someone, spend time with that person, develop a relationship with that person, and so forth. Konrad clearly wanted a certain type of affiliation with Leane. Power is the level of respect you command from a person, or vice versa. It concerns who is higher, lower, or similar in status and respect. Leane clearly tried to assert her power in defining the relationship.

The meaning of any interpersonal communication can be understood in large part by its content and relational implications. Consider the following interchange between intimate partners:

DANA: Honey, get me a glass of water while you're up, will you?
LEE: Get it yourself! I'm in the middle of something.

Several things are going on here. At the content level, Dana's message is merely a request for a drink of water. But at the relationship level, it implies several other things. The word *honey* implies an intimate relationship (affiliation). Yet the message that follows is a request for Lee's compliance. Dana and Lee are in a relationship in which they can request things from each other. Such a request is apparently not unusual given prior requests. Further, the message implies that Dana has the right to make such requests and Lee has the right to refuse them. Otherwise, the message might be phrased in the form of a simple command. Finally, it seems that Lee feels put upon by the request and has equivalent status in the relationship to refuse the request. So although the words have simple content meanings, they also carry implications for how the communicators define their relationship.

Content and relationship dimensions sometimes get confused. Dilbert interprets the message in the context of his understanding of his status and affiliation relative to meeting his new boss. His relationship status is subordinate to his new boss, so the message *content* "Neal" is mistakenly interpreted as the *relational* command "Kneel."

DILBERT reprinted by permission of United Feature Syndicate, Inc.

INTERPERSONAL COMMUNICATION CREATES RELATIONSHIPS

If the meaning of any message has implications for the content of the message, as well as how you relate to the message sender, then messages create relationships. A **relationship** is an ongoing, interdependent process of interaction between two or more people. For people to be in a relationship, it has to exist over a period of time, or be ongoing. Onetime encounters, such as with a salesperson or a stranger asking the time, do not constitute relationships. Furthermore, a relationship involves interdependence. To obtain your goals you depend in part on the other person's actions, and vice versa. A child depends on a parent for survival, learning, and development. But parents depend on the child for achieving their goals of having a family and passing their hopes on to the next generation. Neither can achieve their goals without the other's cooperation.

Relationships come in many different types. In Chapter 2 we examined relationship as a type of context. A context can vary in terms of how intimate or close the people are. Your relationship is likely to be more interdependent (1) the more frequent your interaction, (2) the more your actions influence each other, (3) the more different types of interaction you have with each other, and (4) the longer you interact with each other over time (Berscheid & Peplau, 1983). A parent and child, therefore, are likely to feel a strong sense of closeness, whereas an employee may only feel slightly acquainted with someone in a different department at work.

Relationships tend to be "going somewhere," even if that somewhere is nowhere. That is, relationships take paths. These paths sometimes reflect a relationship moving toward greater intimacy and closeness, and sometimes toward dislike or an ending. Because relationships exist over time, they often seem to have a life of their own. People speak of their "relationship" as if it is an organism that is doing well or poorly, going in a good direction or a bad direction, or perhaps, just not going anywhere at the moment. If asked about your relationship with someone you broke up with, you might respond, "We don't *have* a relationship," meaning you no longer have a pattern of interaction that is going anywhere. These relationship paths represent one of the primary functions of interpersonal communication: to establish, maintain, and manage relationships with others. Not all interpersonal communication leads to a relationship, certainly not a close relationship, but all relationships require interpersonal communication.

INTERPERSONAL COMMUNICATION EVOLVES IN STAGES

Interpersonal communication evolves in the sense that it changes and develops over time. At the conversational level, interpersonal communication develops from greetings to endings. It makes little sense to say goodbye to someone when you first see that person. At the daily level, if you see someone several times a day, you are more likely to exchange more formal and elaborate greetings the first time you encounter him or her than the last time (Goffman, 1971). Your communication evolves from a more complete "Hi. How are you doing? How was your weekend?" to later simply giving a simple nod of recognition as you pass each other in the hallway. At the relational level, communication changes in a variety of ways as the relationship progresses. Clearly people don't behave the same way on a first date as they do on their 100th date.

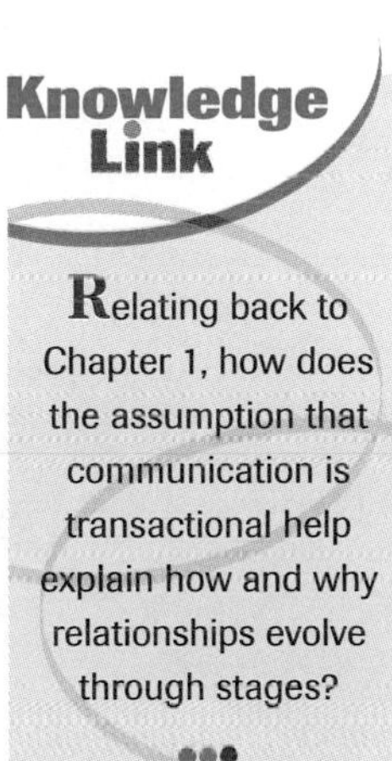

Every relationship you ever develop with another person is unique. No relationship with a particular person happens exactly the same way with anyone else. Yet most relationships develop in ways that we recognize as "typical" or "appropriate." Somehow, despite the uniqueness of every new relationship, we find familiar aspects to how the relationship unfolds. This process by which relationships unfold is called **social penetration,**

the communicative pattern by which two persons pursue a mutual relationship. This pattern can be understood at both a general and a specific level.

At the general level, as shown in Figure 8.1, relationships typically unfold through four stages: acquaintance, development, decline, and dissolution (Hinde, 1997). These stages represent the extent to which two people are moving closer to or further from intimacy. Intimacy here does not mean romance. Instead, it refers to how well you know someone and how important the relationship is to how you view yourself. Each stage represents movement, even if that movement is toward stabilizing the relationship.

The first relationship stage is **acquaintance,** the point of first contact between people. You come into contact with others for a wide variety of reasons. Some of the most common reasons are how closely you live or work to others, what hobbies or activities you share, commonality of values and communication styles, and whether you find one another attractive. **Development** is the stage in which people pursue a mutual definition of the relationship. You may be developing a friendship, or a collegial task-oriented relationship, a romance, or even a kinship relation with a new sibling. Regardless of the definition, you interact to find the type of relationship you desire. This interaction establishes a manner of communicating appropriately to the kind of relationship you are both pursuing. **Decline** represents the stage in which communication reveals increasing tensions or struggles in maintaining the desired relationship definition. Communication is most likely to show conflicts, apathy, or avoidance during this stage. Finally, **dissolution** is the stage where communication actually negotiates an end to the relationship. This end may

FIGURE 8.1
The Stages of Social Penetration

Most people pursue relationships through a typical set of stages, as shown in this figure. In each stage communicators may decide to maintain the relationship at that particular stage. At times, stages can be skipped altogether or the relationship can revert to an earlier stage.

Adapted from Knapp, & Vangelisti (1996).

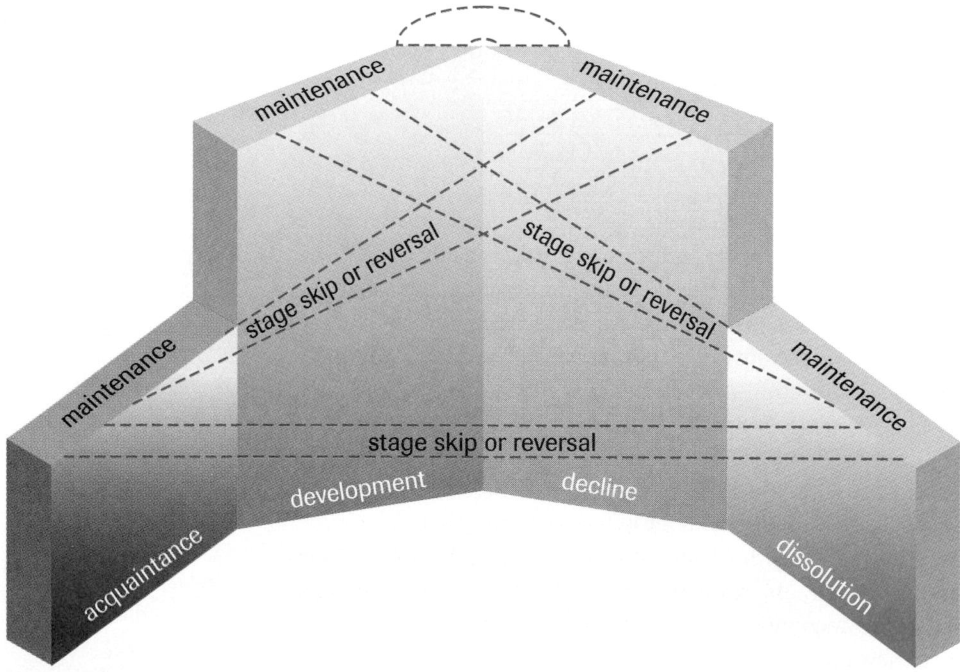

signal the end of interaction or merely provide a transition to a new type of relationship in which the stages begin again, albeit from a different starting point. For example, in the opening vignette, Leane ended her relationship with Konrad, and yet they found a way of reestablishing their relationship. People not only sometimes shift back to other relationship stages, but they can also skip stages. "Love at first sight" may be rare, but it suggests people's belief in the possibility of skipping acquaintanceship altogether. On the other end of the spectrum, people on a blind date may decide to call it quits at the front door before acquaintance has even begun.

In each stage, as illustrated in Figure 8.1, interactants may reach a state in which the relationship reaches the stage they believe is appropriate. At such points, interactants are likely to try and maintain the relationship. **Relational maintenance** is the use of communication to sustain preferred relationships. You attempt to keep a friend friendly, an enemy distant, a romantic partner romantic, and a marriage together. Relationships are never static, but we often try to maintain a certain desired state of relationship.

Knowledge Link

How will computer-mediated communication, as discussed in Chapter 7, alter the stages of social penetration?

●●●

At a more specific level, each of these stages is made up of a variety of communication behaviors. For example, in the typical movement of a future romantic relationship from the acquaintance stage to the maintenance stage, you would expect the following types of behaviors: meet for the first time at a party, class, or club; ask for the other's phone number or email address for later contact; engage in small talk about school, jobs, hobbies, and so on; engage in joint activities and spend informal time together; engage in deeper and broader self-disclosure; go on a formal date to dinner or movie; show some physical affection such as a hug, holding hands, or kissing; make other-oriented statements about attraction and love; discuss commitment to relationship and future; and finally consider cohabitation or marriage (Honeycutt, Cantrill, & Green, 1989).

Conversely, parties in this same relationship, in moving from maintenance of the development stage to the decline stage, could be expected to communicate in the following ways: express intimate feelings verbally and nonverbally less often; use more negative communication such as arguments, disagreements, fights, and criticisms; decrease mediated and face-to-face contact; reevaluate the relationship through talks about where the relationship is going, analyzing what's wrong, talking to mutual friends for advice, and considering options for changing the relationship; spend more time with friends or outside interests, possibly dating others; and finally, discussing the end of the relationship (Honeycutt, Cantrill, & Allen, 1992). In short, the relationship stages consist of, and are defined by, evolving interpersonal communication.

A Model of Interpersonal Communication Motivation

A high school boy spends half an hour rehearsing how he will ask a girl from his history class out on a date. The words are simple. They are no different than words he speaks every day of his life to his friends, family, teachers, and acquaintances. Words like *would, you, like, to, go, out, with, me* don't present a challenge when viewed individually. Yet when strung together, in this particular context, he will find these words difficult to say competently, perhaps even too intimidating to say at all. His attraction to the girl makes his goals very clear, but it also makes him very nervous. He is experiencing a conflict of positive and negative *motivation* that challenges his competence in this interpersonal context.

A recent college graduate goes to her first job interview with a major consulting firm. She, too, is experiencing conflicting motivations. She wants a job offer very much, yet feels extremely nervous about the interview. Still, she manages to control her nervousness and goes into the interview. However, once there, she quickly finds she is ill prepared. She cannot answer many questions about why she wants to work for the company. She does not know much about the particular job duties of the position for which she has applied. She has not thought through answers to questions such as "Where do you see yourself in five years?" or "What is your managerial philosophy?" A week later she receives the letter informing her that the job has been offered to another candidate. She realizes that her competence was greatly challenged by her lack of *knowledge* in the context.

A young couple is discussing whose family to visit for the Thanksgiving holiday. A brief conversation ensues:

DANA: I suppose we ought to figure out whose parents we visit for Thanksgiving.

LEE: I was rather hoping we might visit my parents, since we visited yours last year.

DANA: I don't know . . . every time we go to your parents' house, I have to listen to your dad talk politics like he always does. We always get into such big arguments. Can't we go to my folks again this year?

LEE: What an insensitive thing to say. I never insult *your* parents!

DANA: Okay, I'm sorry, but we really do need to decide . . .

LEE: You don't *sound* like you're sorry.

DANA: Look, I said I was sorry and I am. Now can we talk about . . .

LEE: You *still* don't sound like you mean it. If you seriously think that way about my father, then why haven't you said anything before?

DANA: I don't feel that way about your father. Can we just drop it?

LEE: You *really* don't seem to care about my feelings. You just keep trying to change the subject. If you really cared, you wouldn't have said something so hurtful in the first place, let alone apologized so insincerely.

This dialogue suggests that Dana was motivated to make a decision. Dana viewed this decision as the appropriate goal of the conversation. Dana was knowledgeable about Lee and about the subject area under discussion. However, Dana's opinion was expressed as an attack, which made the following apology sound insincere. The conflict escalated, and Dana got into more and more trouble in the encounter. In short, Dana had motivation and knowledge, but lacked the *skill* to deliver a contrite apology.

Although these three examples offer different situations, different communicators with different objectives, they share several things in common. First, in each of the situations, the eventual outcomes of the interpersonal encounter depend on the communication competence of the interactants. Second, in each situation, the interactant was keenly aware of the importance of being competent in the situation. Third, in each case, one of the components of competence (motivation, knowledge, or skill) rendered the communication unsuccessful.

The components of motivation, knowledge, and skill represent the basic ingredients of communication competence in any context, including the interpersonal communication context. Sometimes a communicator needs to be strong in all three areas. At other times a communicator may achieve competence by showing strength in only one or two of the areas. For example, when engaging in small talk with a friend over a cup of coffee, it may not be vital for a communicator to strive for his or her most competent performance.

However, a key assumption of the model of communication competence is that *in general, the more motivated, knowledgeable, and skilled a communicator, the more likely it is that this person will communicate competently.* In the case of the high school boy, he had adequate positive motivation, but his negative motivations of anxiety interfered with his competence. In the case of the interviewee, had she known more about the communication context, she might have gotten the job. And in the case of the young couple, had Dana been more skilled at communicating emotions, the conflict might have been managed more productively or even avoided in the first place. Motivation, knowledge, and skills play a significant role in any interpersonal communication, influencing where a person's actions are placed on the spectrum of competence.

These basic components of communication competence that you saw in Chapter 2 are displayed in Figure 8.2 applied to an interpersonal context. The model depicts a context in which two people bring their own motivation, knowledge, and skills to a mutual encounter. Their motivation activates their use of knowledge to produce communication behavior through their skills. Their skills are the only components of communication each interactant experiences directly. These communicators' skills interact in a transactional process, which produces certain outcomes for both interactants. During this process, each interactant achieves certain goals, experiences certain feelings, and forms impressions, both of the self and the other. These outcomes, in turn, feed back into each communicator's ongoing motivation, knowledge, and skills in the encounter.

A few principles of the model will help you interpret it. First, people only interact through their skills, which consist solely of their behaviors. Technically, you cannot interact directly with another person's motivation or knowledge, which are internal to the person. Motivation and knowledge can only be displayed through skills, that is, through the *inter-action* of each person's communication. For example, in the case of the couple mentioned earlier, ultimately the outcomes did not depend on whether Dana was actually sincerely sorry or not. The resolution of the situation depended on Dana's ability to *express* sincerity in the apology. In any interpersonal encounter, *you* know what you feel and mean, but all the other person sees is how you behave, and how you behave is revealed entirely through your communication skills.

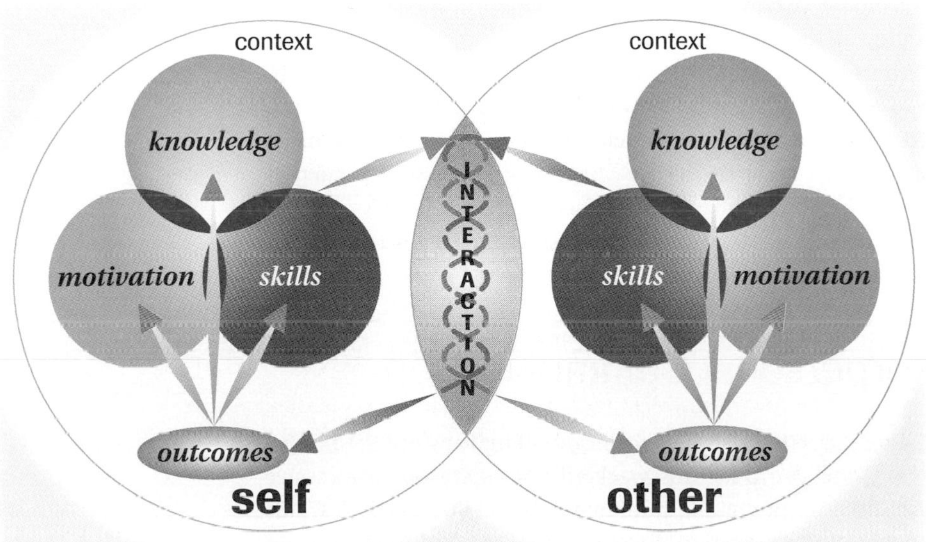

FIGURE 8.2
Model of Interpersonal Communication Competence

Motivation and knowledge provide the basis for the communication skills used in the interaction process in a given context. This interaction produces outcomes, which feed back into the process of communication.

A second principle of the model is that the components are interdependent. Skills depend on motivation and knowledge. In the opening vignette, Konrad's communication skills varied as a direct function of his motivation. When he thought his relationship was over, he didn't particularly care about chatting competently at the fraternity party. You may have considerable communication skill, but if you are not motivated or knowledgeable in an interpersonal context, you aren't likely to employ these skills. Likewise, motivation and knowledge depend on each other. The young woman interviewing for a job experienced difficulties both because she was nervous and because she had not done her homework. However, after a dozen more job interviews, she is likely to show much more confidence in her interviews and know a lot more about what to expect in such situations.

Third, contexts are flexible in the sense that they change in form and function as people interact and define them. For example, when Konrad first walked up behind Leane and placed his hands over her eyes, he was defining the context as one of joyful reunion. Leane's reaction quickly redefined the context as one in which there was bad news to deliver. Likewise, Dana and Lee began the conversation by defining it as a decision-making task of determining where to spend Thanksgiving. As the conversation progressed, Dana first viewed it as a context in which to air opinions about Lee's parents and then tried to redefine the context as one of decision making. On the other hand, Lee quickly defined the conversation as a relational discussion about the couple's views of family. Although the couple's interaction occurred in the same actual time and space, the context and what it meant to each person was quite different.

Fourth, interaction always functions to influence communicator outcomes, and these outcomes influence not only the communicators, but ongoing and future interactions as well. Looking back at the model in Figure 8.2, this principle is displayed by the arrows from the outcomes to the communicator's motivation, knowledge, and skills components. For example, if the high school boy were to ask the girl out and she agrees to go out with him or if the interviewee gets a job offer, these outcomes can give the communicators greater confidence. Such confidence, in turn, can motivate these communicators to seek out similar interpersonal encounters in the future, which leads to greater knowledge and skill. Even within a given episode of interpersonal communication, interaction outcomes influence the ongoing encounter. In the job interview, if the interviewer smiles in response to the interviewee's answers and talks about how impressive her résumé looks, she may feel more comfortable and consequently apply more of her interpersonal skills.

In these examples, motivation is the force driving how people interact and whether their outcomes are achieved competently. Although a process does not have a true beginning or ending, motivation is often the most intuitive way of understanding how communication events start. In everyday interaction it is natural to consider questions of communication motivation, such as why a person says what he or she says or why a person even decides to talk to one person rather than another. A comprehensive understanding of motivation in interpersonal communication is essential to understanding competence in both conversations and relationships.

Motivation & Interpersonal Communication

In the cartoon, the character faces the "real-life adventure" of figuring out the motive behind the question: "Say, are you busy this weekend?" Despite our impressive minds, other people's motives often remain quite mysterious, even when it seems they should be simple. Understanding motivation, therefore, is an essential step toward interpersonal communication competence.

Motives in Interpersonal Communication

Recall the general discussion of communication motivation in Chapter 2. When examined more specifically, and in relation to interpersonal communication, motivation reveals a complex nature. Sometimes we say or do something just because we *feel* like it. Our emotions get the best of us and we scream at someone, or laugh at a joke, or seem sad. Like Konrad at the party, sometimes our interpersonal communication merely expresses our feelings. At other times, we communicate a message that we have thought about or something we intend to say or do in particular. In their first conversation of the day, Leane had thought about what she wanted to say to Konrad. In these instances, interpersonal communication is used to achieve a particular task or objective. So interpersonal communication is sometimes motivated by very expressive or emotional reasons; at other times it is motivated by cognitive or instrumental reasons.

Another way in which motives differ is their value. Value in this sense concerns whether the motive is moving toward something, against something, or away from something (Horney, 1945). Is the reason for communicating to do good for the self or the other, to hurt the self or others, or simply avoid something or someone?

A third way in which motives vary is who the messages are intended to benefit. Interpersonal communication can benefit the self or it can benefit others. You can say something to obtain information you need, such as asking someone the time. You can also adapt your communication to the other person, such as when you give the time to someone who has just asked you for it. Even messages that seem self-serving, for example, can be intended to benefit others. In fact, research shows that the most common reasons for deceiving someone are to benefit the person being deceived (O'Hair & Cody, 1994). For example, in the opening vignette, Konrad's friends might tell him that they think it's "for the best" that Leane broke up with him, even if they thought she was a good partner for him. They intend to comfort him in the process of concealing their true feelings. Thus interpersonal communication can be self-oriented or it can be other-oriented.

By now, you have probably concluded that there are many motivations for human behavior in general, and for communication behavior in particular. It can be difficult to comprehend how all these motives relate to one another as well as to interpersonal communication. A simpler way of organizing motivations is to view them according to the three basic dimensions: positive versus negative, affective versus cognitive, and self- versus other-oriented.

The **affective/cognitive dimension of motives** can be defined as the degree to which interpersonal communication is motivated by emotions, or by intentions. Does the message purely express emotions, such as laughter or anger, or is it a product of mental thought and planning? The **positive/negative dimension of motives** refers to the impact of the interpersonal communication on others. Is the message helpful or hurtful, does it build consensus or cause division, does it benefit or exploit others? The **self-oriented/other-oriented** dimension concerns whether an interpersonal message was generated to meet the self's needs or to meet someone else's needs. Is the message strictly to benefit yourself, such as making up an excuse to get out of trouble, or to benefit others, as in making up an excuse to get someone else out of trouble? These three dimensions are mapped in Figure 8.3, along with some of the most common interpersonal communication motives that can be described by these dimensions.

The motives underlying any message can be very complex and difficult to determine.

REAL LIFE ADVENTURES © 1997. GarLanco. Reprinted with permission of United Press Syndicate, Inc. All rights reserved.

The remarkable computer called the human brain is capable of playing out multiple scenarios in milliseconds.

FIGURE 8.3
Model of Interpersonal Communication Motives

Interpersonal communication motives can be understood along three interdependent dimensions: affective and cognitive motives, positive and negative motives, and other-oriented and self-oriented motives. Locating your motives on one of the two cubes can help you understand what type of communication is taking place.

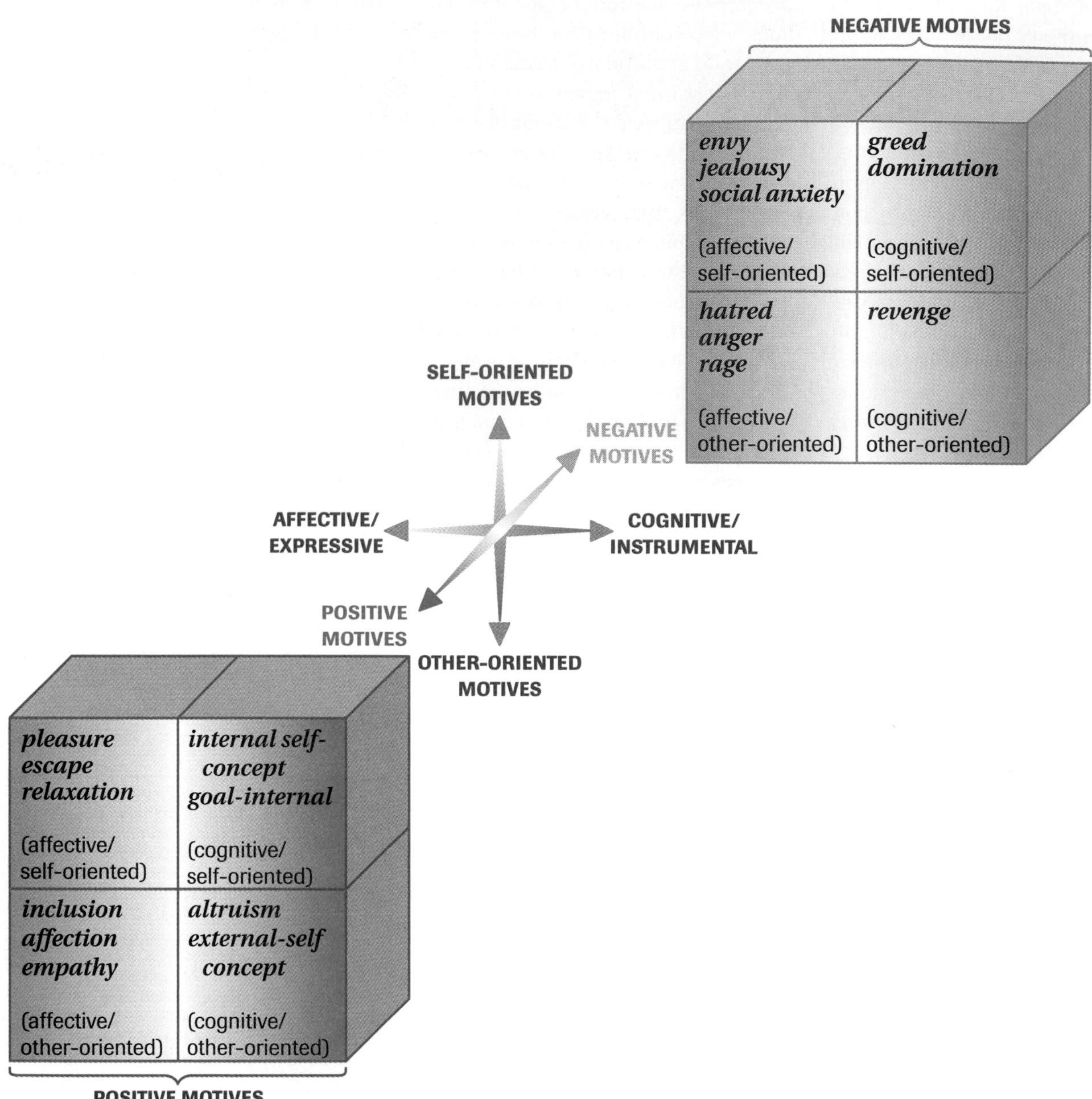

Positive Motives in Interpersonal Communication

Motives such as pleasure, escape, and relaxation represent positive emotions that are primarily oriented toward self-gratification (Rubin, Perse, & Barbato, 1988). Inclusion is largely a positive motive that reflects the emotional or affective feeling of connection with other(s) (Schutz, 1966). People sometimes communicate emotional support or empathy, which tends to be a positive, affective, and other-oriented motivation (Davis, 1994). Communicators who do or say things primarily to help someone else in a planned way, such as giving a surprise birthday party or offering to help someone with homework, are communicating for positive, other-oriented, and cognitive reasons. Likewise, fulfilling someone else's expectations by trying to say all the "right" things when a friend asks you for advice regarding a possible career decision is a positive, other-oriented, and cognitive motive (Burleson, 1994; Daly & Kreiser, 1994). Similarly, external self-concept motivation is the desire to be liked and approved of by others (Barbuto & Scholl, 1998).

In contrast, internal self-concept motivation is the need for interpersonal communication to be consistent with one's "ideal" self (Barbuto & Scholl, 1998). If you see yourself as a "good friend," and your prototype of a "good friend" is someone who does favors for friends, then you are likely to do favors for your friends when asked. Communicators who construct their messages to fulfill their visions for themselves are pursuing positive, self-oriented, and cognitive motives (MacKinnon, 1994). Finally, people who try to control others or seek instrumental outcomes may be responding to either positive or negative purposes, but are likely to rely more on cognitive bases for their actions (Cody, Canary, & Smith, 1994).

Negative Motives in Interpersonal Communication

Less is known of the darker, negative motives people use when communicating. Recently, scholars have become much more interested in how interpersonal communication serves these "darker" motives in interactions (Cupach & Spitzberg, 1994) and close relationships (Spitzberg & Cupach, 1998). Motives and emotions such as deception, manipulation, jealousy, envy, anger, intentional embarrassment of others, revenge, and conflict are increasingly recognized not only as common in everyday interpersonal communication, but also as even sometimes competent in the ways in which they are expressed (Andersen & Guerrero, 1999). Most people who admit to deceiving their friends, family, or romantic partners claim to have done so for largely positive or altruistic reasons (Camden, Motley, & Wilson, 1984). For example, your best friend tells you how he or she is nervous before giving a speech and expects everything to go wrong. You might well tell this friend, "Come on now, I'll bet everything's going to be fine!" whether you believe it or not. Your motive is to build your friend's confidence, even though your message might not reflect your true level of confidence.

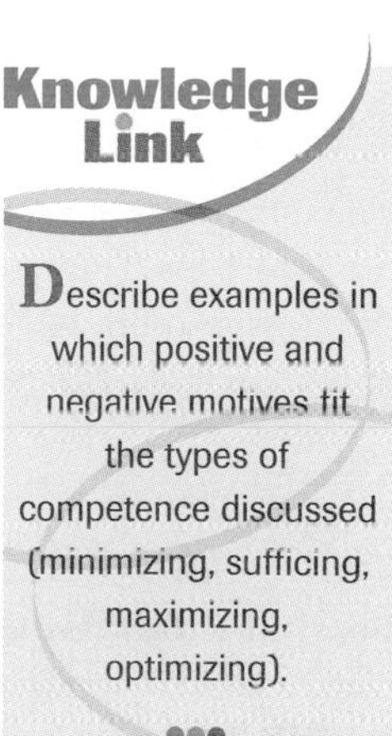

Negative motives are a fact of social relationships. For example, people communicate out of envy, to satisfy a desire for someone else's partner. A person might befriend someone whose romantic partner he or she wants to "steal away" from the new "friend." This behavior reflects a self-oriented motive of desire and an affective motive. Others communicate out of hatred, anger, and rage. In the heat of argument, people sometimes resort to pushing, shoving, slapping, name calling, and screaming (Spitzberg, 1997). Such behavior reflects negative, affective, and other-oriented motivation because it is an unintentional expression of frustration and anger, both negative emotions, as well as a reaction to the other person's actions. If, in contrast, a person uses violence just to control another person, the underlying motivation is more about dominating that person, and therefore would be considered cognitive and instrumental. Sometimes, people are motivated by revenge, which is a negative, largely planned, cognitive, and other-oriented process. Finally, many messages are designed to exploit or obtain resources from others, such as money, property, or favors. Unscrupulous salespeople, fraudulent investors, and thieves are all people who communicate out of simple greed or selfishness. Such motives are self-oriented, generally negative, and cognitive in nature because the resulting actions tend to involve planning and preparation in the pursuit of a tangible goal or outcome.

Goals in Interpersonal Communication

People are not motivated solely by needs or emotions. A need is a deficit term. A car that *needs* gas is running low on gas. A person who is in *need* of love is likely to be feeling a lack of it. Another way of thinking of motivation is in terms of goals. Communicative goals, as discussed in Chapter 2, are the outcomes, objectives, or purposes being sought through communication. They represent "some desired state in other people" (Berger, 1997, p. 19). Goals are the specific outcomes a person intends to bring about through his or her interpersonal communication.

Goals are particularly relevant to communication competence because they are a way of assessing effectiveness. An interpersonal communicator who achieves his or her goals is effective and, therefore, more competent. Goals, in turn, help guide communication behavior. It is much easier to know what to do and how to do it if you are clear about the social goals you intend to bring about. To simply describe yourself as "needing to be loved" is to describe a state of existence. This need can be translated as follows: "I want and intend to develop a romantic relationship." When articulated this way, the need is transformed into a goal that can be met through a series of steps, which can be then formulated into a plan.

Goals can also help an interpersonal communicator visualize the connection between motivation and specific communication situations. In the opening vignette, Konrad needed to regain control of his life, realize what was most important to him, and make a plan to win back Leane. Revisiting the other examples, the high school boy wanted more intimacy with his classmate, and to achieve this goal he needs to make plans to ask her out. The college graduate needed to gain control of her fear of communicating in new situations, and to do this she must make plans to better prepare for and conduct herself competently in job interviews. Finally, Dana needs to separate unconnected issues and focus more on the decision-making task at hand, and Lee needs to learn not to rise to the bait and also focus on the task at hand. Goals, relative to needs, represent more future-oriented and potential-fulfilling forms of motivation.

MOTIVES IN INTERPERSONAL RELATIONSHIPS

The motives of interpersonal communication reveal a complex set of reasons why we create messages. The motives of specific messages, however, are different from the motives we pursue more generally in relationships. Most motives that operate within relationships can be understood as contradictory processes.

The Dialectics of Interpersonal Communication in Relationships

Recall the relationship stages that bring people closer to or further from intimacy. You might think that a relationship involving intimacy with another person is pursued separately from autonomy. Intuitively, you may believe people pursue intimacy at one time in a relationship and autonomy at another time. However, people generally pursue both intimacy and autonomy simultaneously, even though these motives conflict with one another. Such contradictory tension between motivations is referred to as a **dialectic,** a see-saw tension between opposing goals or needs, such that pursuing one goal tends to preclude the other.

Dialectical theories portray human relationships, especially close relationships, as a combination of these contradictory motivations (Baxter & Montgomery, 1996). We want to be close to someone, but we also want to preserve our own space and privacy. We want to share our thoughts and feelings with others, but we don't want to disclose too much about ourselves. We look for predictability in our partners and relationships so that we can enjoy security and stability; however, we also value spontaneity and surprises so the relationship does not become boring.

Any given relationship revolves around many possible dialectics. However, research shows that most relationships move back and forth among at least three major dialectics (Baxter & Montgomery, 1997): autonomy-connection, closedness-openness, and predictability-novelty. The **autonomy-connection dialectic** is the tension between the desire to be unconstrained and independent in your actions and thoughts, and the desire to be intimate and coordinated with another person. You may find that you want to share intimacy and feel connected to another person while wanting to be yourself and free to do what you want when you want. The **closedness-openness dialectic** is the contradiction between the desire to preserve your privacy and wanting to share your life's stories with another person. We guard our innermost thoughts, feelings, and fears; however we also need to reveal ourselves to others. The **predictability-novelty dialectic** refers to the tension between seeking stability and pattern in relationships while thriving on a degree of unpredictability and surprise at the same time. Stability gives a sense of control over the future, but surprise contributes significantly to the excitement of any relationship.

These three major relationship dialectics are displayed in Figure 8.4. These dialectics reflect conflicting motives that drive relationships and help make sense of the more basic motives for interpersonal communication discussed in Figure 8.3, such as affective versus cognitive, positive versus negative, and self-oriented versus other-oriented motives. On the one hand, we want to be included, feel pleasure, fulfill self-oriented goals, and be altruistic. But when we fear losing intimacy, we feel jealous. When our partner does

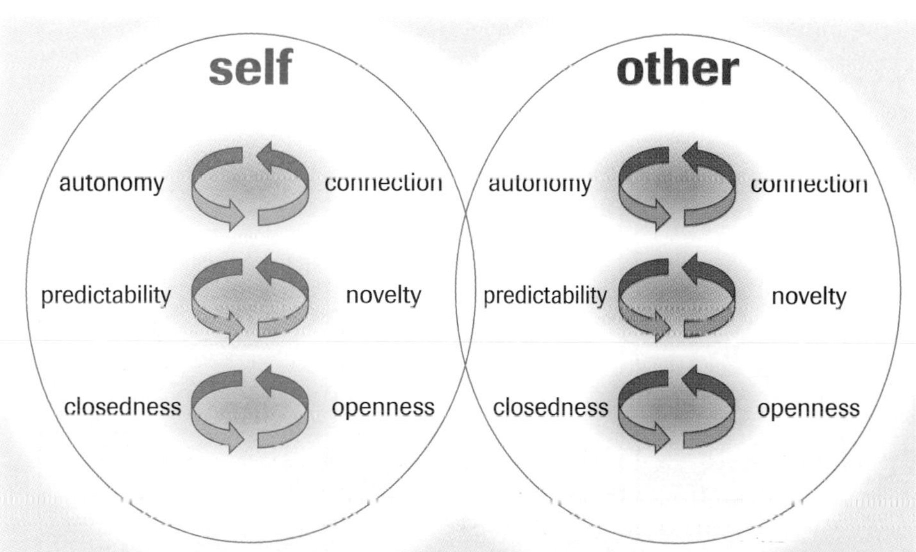

FIGURE 8.4
Relationship Motives—"Dialectics"

People pursue their relationships along three ongoing dialectical motives, each of which influences the other dialectics, the dialectics of the other person, and thus the relationship.

something we don't like, we feel anger, which often drives our partner away, increasing our autonomy but decreasing our intimacy. We want to exert control in the relationship so things will be predictable. In other words, we pursue our interpersonal communication in ways that increase autonomy at the cost of intimacy, or predictability at the cost of novelty, and so on. As we pursue relationships we are pulled by these dialectics, balancing the tensions of our own motives with the other's. Every message we send in the context of the relationship pulls in the direction of one or more of these dialectics, thereby influencing the evolution of the relationship. Furthermore, because interpersonal communication is a transactional process, we are constantly "negotiating" these dialectics through our interactions with others to achieve desired motivations.

Consider, for example, two people who have known each other casually for months who become attracted to each other and start dating. In the early weeks and months, the relationship grows fast, and the couple begins spending almost all their free time together, making plans for the near future, even talking about vacationing together, meeting family, and so forth. However, in the midst of the growing relationship, one of the partners says, "We need to have a talk," and expresses a "need for some space."

In the beginning of this relationship, both partners were motivated to pursue their intimacy needs, which at the time were unfulfilled. However, as they began meeting this intimacy need, one of the partners began feeling his or her autonomy needs surface. As intimacy increases in a relationship, the need for intimacy no longer dominates a person's behavior, and other needs surface. Furthermore, as intimacy increases, the more interdependent two people are, and the harder it is to feel autonomy needs are being fulfilled.

So why did only one of the partners feel his or her autonomy needs were not satisfied? Dialectical theory suggests that people vary not only in their levels of motives, but also in the way they resolve their dialectical motives, both individually and relationally. For some people, relationships rarely get to the point of committed intimacy because they perceive their autonomy motives threatened by such commitment. For others, however, the right type of intimate relationships may enable their autonomy motives. For example, your ideal situation might be having a close relationship with someone with whom you can share intimacy, but who also understands your need to pursue your own interests. If this is how the relationship has been defined, then separate vacations, solitary hobbies, or time alone contributes to the intimacy of the relationship.

In summary, motives are the driving force for communication, and as such, are critical components of interpersonal communication competence. Although there are many types of motives and people communicate for many reasons, most of these reasons can

In what ways might a dialectical motive, such as autonomy versus connection, be more competent in some cultures and less competent in other cultures?

Sometimes we are motivated by love, but our knowledge and skills can't quite match the motivation.

LUANN reprinted by permission of United Feature Syndicate, Inc.

be summarized according to any of the three basic dimensions discussed earlier: affective/cognitive, positive/negative, and self-oriented/other-oriented. These dimensions assist not only in helping make sense out of your own motivations, but also the motivations of others. Further, by better understanding the role of motivations in communication encounters, you will be better able to specify goals and make plans to interact more competently.

One of the most common and important reasons people benefit from competent interpersonal communication is that it permits them to develop love and liking in their relationships with others. Incompetent interpersonal communicators are likely to experience difficulty in establishing loving relationships and friendships, whereas competent interpersonal communicators are likely to develop much more satisfying relationships (Spitzberg & Cupach, 1984).

Love & Liking in Relationships

Konrad, the would-be lover, is clearly motivated to increase his intimacy with Leane. But his motivation is not easily translated into competent knowledge and skills. Such intimacy motivations play a large role in the motivations surrounding love, one of the most complex affective states. **Love** is a positive emotional state regarding another person, consisting of three basic dimensions: intimacy, passion, and commitment (Sternberg, 1986). **Intimacy** is warmth, closeness, caring, and feeling connected. Spending time with someone, offering to help that person, putting your arm around that person's shoulder, asking about that person's day, and disclosing a personal experience are all expressions of intimacy. Friends, lovers, young and old couples, and parents and children can experience intimacy in their relationships. **Passion** is the arousal, sexual and otherwise, associated with interpersonal attraction. Although some friendships attain strong feelings, passion is most commonly associated with the sexual motivations in romantic relationships. **Commitment** is the decision to maintain a relationship over a period of time. The decision to get engaged and the actual marriage ceremony are perhaps the most common expressions of commitment, but even decisions to date exclusively, to be "best" friends, or to promise to "always be there" for one another represent forms of commitment.

The type of love someone experiences can be characterized by the dominance of one or more of these dimensions. For example, "liking" can be viewed as intimacy, without passion or commitment. Love in which you are passionate, but lack intimacy and commitment, is "infatuation." To make a commitment to someone in a relationship in which there is neither intimacy nor passion is considered "empty" love. In contrast, "romantic" love requires passion and intimacy, but not commitment. Intimate and committed love without passion are "companionate" or "platonic" love. Love in which you are passionate and make a commitment, but in which there is no intimacy, is "foolish" love. Finally, love that is intimate, passionate, and committed is a "complete" type of love. Love is certainly more complex than these three dimensions. But these dimensions also reveal much of the subtlety that distinguishes the motives associated with affection, intimacy, and inclusion. Table 8.1 shows Sternberg's taxonomy of love based on these three dimensions.

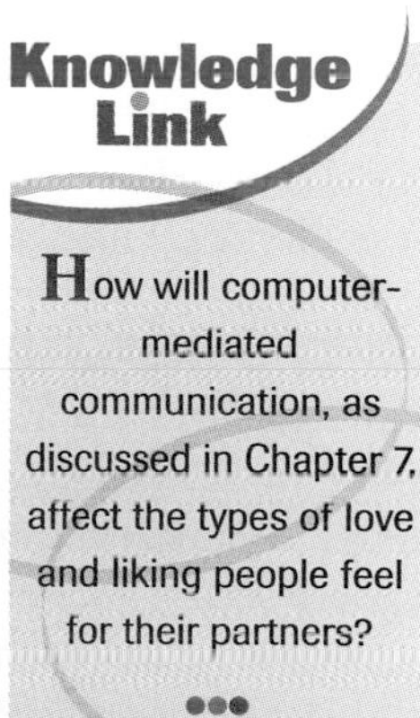

The fact that we are strongly motivated by both autonomy and intimacy may seem ironic. After all, if we pursue intimacy with someone, doesn't that reduce our autonomy? Intimacy implies greater interdependence with another person, thereby reducing our control of our own actions and rendering us more susceptible to control by someone else. And, to the extent that we pursue autonomy, don't we have to sacrifice intimacy? Perhaps "no one is an island," but the extent people try to take control of themselves and others makes it difficult to develop true, interdependent intimacy with others.

TABLE 8.1

The Types of Love

You can determine the type of love you have for someone by analyzing the types of motives you feel toward the person. Each check mark indicates that you feel or experience that dimension. For example, if you commit to someone you feel no passion for nor have any intimacy with, it is an empty kind of love.

	INTIMACY	PASSION	COMMITMENT
Nonlove			
Liking	✓		
Infatuated love		✓	
Empty love			✓
Romantic love	✓	✓	
Companionate love	✓		✓
Foolish love		✓	✓
Complete love	✓	✓	✓

SOURCE: Adapted from Sternberg (1988). Reprinted by permission of Robert Sternberg.

The examination of motives in interpersonal communication and relationships reveals a complex set of reasons for why people pursue interaction with others. Managing these diverse motives to become a competent interpersonal communicator requires understanding several specific challenges to competent motivation in interpersonal communication and relationships.

Challenges to Interpersonal Competence

As you've seen earlier, what we say and do in the interpersonal context is based on a complex interplay of motivations. When our interpersonal communication is incompetent, it is often due to the challenges involved in managing our motivations. Three challenges to motivation interfere with competent interpersonal communication and relationships: social anxiety and shyness, goal complexity, and oversimplifying the self and other.

SOCIAL ANXIETY AND SHYNESS

The most common challenge people face in any communication context is anxiety. Virtually everyone has experienced communication anxiety in public speaking contexts. However, anxiety in interpersonal situations is very common as well. **Social anxiety** is the real or imagined fear of interacting in an interpersonal encounter. Fear is the result of a perceived threat. Most social encounters do not threaten your personal safety, but recall how communication and social interaction are inextricably connected to self-concept and a sense of well-being. Social situations can be very threatening to self-concept because we derive so much of our self-concept from what we think others think of us. Thus social anxiety occurs not only during actual communication situations, but also in anticipation of an actual situation, or even when imagining a situation. The high school boy anticipating asking the girl out on a date, in our earlier example, experienced anxiety just thinking about the conversation.

CloseUp ON DIVERSITY

Diversity & the Culture of Love

LOVE IS OFTEN CONSIDERED a universal experience. However, the concept of romantic love is relatively contemporary. A millennium ago, people rarely pair-bonded on the basis of love, and instead were paired by parents or their tribe on the basis of what the elders considered a good match, what could be traded for a mate, or for the practical consideration of putting food on the table. Even now, love may be universal as a feeling, but it is far from universal in how it is defined. Nicotera (1997) conducted research on relatively small samples of college students in several cultures. She asked students to "list at least 10 characteristics of a mate-type (dating, romantic) relationship." Here are some of her findings, showing how often certain traits were listed in each culture. The "Total" column shows how often each trait was listed *across* cultural groups.

	North American Whites		*African Americans*		*Caribbeans*		
	%M	*%F*	*%M*	*%F*	*%M*	*%F*	*Total*
Trust	57	72	33	31	60	75	328
Love	50	56	17	54	70	67	314
Honesty	43	56	50	46	50	58	293
Communication	36	44	17	54	30	50	231
Caring	36	28	17	38	50	33	202
Friendship	50	56	0	23	30	42	201
Understanding	7	17	33	32	30	50	168
Respect	7	22	17	23	20	58	147
Humor	14	33	0	23	10	25	105
Physical attractiveness	21	17	17	15	10	8	88
Intelligence	7	17	17	23	0	8	72
Sexual attractiveness	14	6	0	23	10	0	53

Indeed, when college students from these cultures were asked to indicate the typical stages that romantic relationships go through, there were some similarities and differences as well, as shown here.

Whites	*African Americans*	*Caribbeans*
Occasional date Regular date	Dating	Dating
Exclusive date Sexual partners	Lover	Lover
Cohabitation	Engaged	Long-term couple
Marriage	Marriage	Marriage

As you can see from this research, people in different cultures do not define love and relationships in some universal sense. These differences can occur in every cultural sense. For example, Nicotera also found that the deaf culture perceives these same traits and relationship stages somewhat differently than these ethnic groups. The implication for competence is that you may be operating with one definition of love and expectation for its stages, whereas your partner may be operating with quite a different definition. What is competent to display in one relationship to inspire love, for example trust or friendship, may be a priority for you but not your partner, because these characteristics vary by both ethnicity and gender. Furthermore, you may think there is a stage of regular dating before exclusive dating, and your partner may be expecting exclusive dating to be the first stage. The motives of love and liking are complex and require careful consideration if they are to be negotiated competently.

Generally speaking, the more formal, the more unfamiliar, the larger the audience, and the more important the goals are, the more nervous people become. Most people would feel more nervous interacting with their state's governor than their best friend because of the formality of the situation. Likewise, most people would experience more anxiety interacting with their family on a televised talk show than in their living room because of the unfamiliarity of the situation and size of audience. Even though it only involves one person in a situation with which most of us are familiar, a first date can cause anxiety because the outcome of finding a potential life partner is potentially so important to us.

When anxiety is experienced across a wide variety of social situations over an extended period of time, it generally results in **shyness,** a tendency to withdraw from social activities. Shy people may not appear very different from others in a given situation, but they are less likely to initiate or actively participate in conversation. It is important to remember that some cultures such as many Asian cultures value unassertiveness and seem shyer than others. In these cultures, the conversational shyness of members does not necessarily reflect incompetence. On the contrary, in their cultures, "nonassertiveness and nonargumentativeness are probably more socially desirable" (Kim, 1999, p. 62), making shyness in interpersonal communication competent within that particular culture. However, it is possible to be shy even by the standards of a relatively unassertive culture. Thus shyness can be a challenge to competence regardless of a communicator's culture.

Shy people may show lower levels of both verbal and nonverbal involvement when in conversation with others.

Social anxiety and shyness challenge interpersonal communication competence by making it more difficult for people to meet their needs and goals in interactions. Generally speaking, you don't get a date if you don't ask or accept, you don't get a job if you don't interview for a job, and your partner doesn't know how much you love him or her if you don't somehow communicate this. If you are anxious about such activities, it is difficult to fulfill your needs and goals.

GOAL COMPLEXITY

Another challenge people face is that some communication situations involve multiple and competing goals (Spitzberg, 1993, 1994). Reviewing the discussion of relationship dialectics, remember that sometimes we want to meet needs and accomplish goals that are not entirely compatible. In turning someone down for a date, for example, you generally want to keep the person from feeling bad, but you also want to preserve your own autonomy. That is, you need to communicate clearly that you aren't interested in dating but you also want to help the other person save face. The more clearly you turn the person down, the more face threatening your message becomes. On a larger scale, it may be difficult to sort out your goals if a choice has to be made between career and relationship. For example, do you move to another state to pursue a job opportunity or attend graduate school, or stay in the same place because your partner is still in school or has a good job? The conflict increases between autonomy and connection as our social world becomes more complex.

Goals can interfere with communication competence not only because they are incompatible, but also because most situations involve multiple goals. Some contexts are relatively straightforward. For example, the college graduate in the job interview discussed earlier wants one thing: a job. However, this goal links to other goals in her life. If she is offered the job, what are some of the other goals she must consider? Does the job pay well? Will it allow advancement in the organization? Will she feel good about herself by taking the job? Will the job allow her to acquire new skills? Does the work lead to a career or is it just a job? Will she like working with her colleagues? These are the multiple goals relevant to her motivation to get the job. The more goals she has, the more difficulty she experiences determining how to communicate competently with the interviewer.

OVERSIMPLIFYING SELF & OTHER

In Chapter 3 you saw that the self is a very complex concept. If the self alone is complex, then the relationship between *two* selves is clearly much more complex. Furthermore, when relationships are recognized as evolving along dialectics, which are by definition contradictory, it's clear that competent interpersonal communication can be very challenging indeed. One of the reasons for this is that we tend to develop overly simple models of the self and other. We tend to think that when we say something it has one meaning, serves one motive, and the other person's response similarly has one meaning and one motive. As you saw in Chapter 4, this is not the case. Meanings are in people, not in words.

By viewing the self and other as having coherent and consistent motives, much of the subtlety of interpersonal communication and relationships is lost. By missing such subtlety, we overlook the opportunity to develop more competence in our interpersonal communication. For example, in a developing relationship it is easy to interpret a partner's message of "I need some space" as meaning that this person is trying to end the relationship. Such an interpretation is probably an oversimplification of the tensions the partner is coping with. Rather than wanting to end the relationship, the partner may be working through complex dialectical tensions and balancing the multiple goals and needs that the relationship serves. You have probably experienced such a tension before in your relationships, yet it is easy to reduce a partner's message to a single meaning.

When we are filled with such contradictions and multiple goals, needs, and meanings, it is tempting to view our selves and others as single, consistent entities. For example, it is simpler for you at times to see your instructor as only that: a teacher. Likewise, it is easy for the instructor to view you as just a student. Yet our self, who we are, fulfills many roles and is itself interdependent with others' selves. Treating another person as having a single, simple self oversimplifies that person and that person's interpersonal communication. This oversimplification contributes to the challenge of communicating competently.

Overcoming Challenges to Interpersonal Communication Competence

Overcoming the challenges to more competent motivation in interpersonal encounters depends significantly on increasing your awareness of the factors and processes that influence motivation. There are three areas in which such awareness is likely to enhance your motivational competence in interpersonal encounters: managing negative motives, managing communication goals, and managing dialectics.

MANAGING NEGATIVE MOTIVES

One important step to overcoming challenges to motivation in interpersonal interaction is managing negative emotions. As you saw earlier in the map of communicator motives, negative motives are those emotions, needs, and goals that function to harm, exploit, or inhibit the self or others. Although managing all negative motives is important, the most common challenge to interpersonal communication competence is social anxiety. There are many approaches to managing social anxiety, some of which we discuss in relation to the other contexts of communication later in this textbook. One of the approaches most effective for managing social anxiety in the interpersonal context is belief restructuring.

Knowledge Link

How does belief restructuring relate to self-fulfilling prophecies, as discussed in Chapter 3?

Belief restructuring, or cognitive modification, is the process of systematically using thought to overcome beliefs about your self-concept that impair your competence. For example, if you believe you are unlovable, you are likely to be nervous about asking someone out for a date, as that person will surely see you are unlovable and reject you. If you believe you are basically unprepared for the job market, then it will be difficult to show confidence in a job interview.

Belief restructuring involves identifying all the irrational or self-critical beliefs you have about a type of social situation that makes you nervous, and then rationally refuting or qualifying each belief. You should always be able to identify at least some aspects of yourself that are special, positive, and, therefore, respectable. Continuing the second example, although you may not have experience in a given industry, you most likely have developed talents and experiences that make you a good risk for a prospective employer. In the process of pinpointing how your self-critical beliefs are unrealistic or irrational, you can begin to unlearn the beliefs that make you feel threatened by social situations.

Many students embarking on a job search visit the university's career office. Researching their vocational values and goals helps guide students in selecting a career that best utilizes their talents, accomplishments, and relevant experience for prospective employers.

MANAGING GOALS

Another approach to overcoming the motivational challenges of interpersonal communication competence is to manage your goals in interactions. Sometimes we are acutely aware of our goals, whereas at other times we find them particularly difficult to articulate. If someone asks you what your specific goals are in having a chat with a friend over coffee, you might be at a loss for words. Konrad had to spend considerable time and effort determining what his goals were regarding his relationship with Leane. He had to consider issues such as how important she was to his goals and how he should communicate these goals to her.

The extent to which the interactants haven't articulated or prioritized their goals presents a challenge to competent communication. The key to overcoming this challenge is to incorporate goal analysis as part of your everyday communicative strategy. Goal analysis involves a heightened awareness of the goals of an anticipated communication situation beforehand, analyzing goals in terms of their relative importance and connections, and determining the steps needed to fulfill these goals. Surprisingly, people seldom even attempt such goal analysis. How often, for example, do you specify your goals in going out on a date or interviewing for a job? And even assuming you have articulated your goals for these situations, how often do you try to determine which are most important, and how they are related to one another? Taking these actions doesn't guarantee you will succeed in achieving your goals; however, you will likely improve your chances simply by becoming more aware of what you are attempting to accomplish.

MANAGING DIALECTICS

Because interpersonal communication involves at least two people, it requires a consideration of both the self and other. However, as you've seen, relationship dialectics make the consideration of the self and other in interpersonal communication more complex. But dialectics make relationships more interesting. Overcoming the challenge of oversimplifying the self and other requires that communicators develop richer understandings of the dialectics of relationships (Spitzberg, 1993). A richer understanding consists of reinforcing two relational beliefs: appreciating contradictions and appreciating cooperative progress (Baxter & Montgomery, 1996).

Appreciating contradictions involves recognizing that people often cope with multiple conflicting motives simultaneously when they communicate. A fulfilling relationship permits both connection as well as autonomy. You may feel better about your own achievements when you have an intimate relationship with someone with whom you can share those accomplishments. Appreciating contradictions permits you to develop a better understanding of the other's messages, and therefore permits you to better adapt your messages in response.

Appreciating cooperative progress means moving forward toward a better relationship *with* the other person rather than on your own. You may experience the pull of relationship dialectics, but so does the other person. In any conversation, therefore, competence depends on recognizing that person's contradictions as well as your own, and attempting to find ways in which *all* dialectics can be satisfied. Once Leane clearly articulated her needs for greater connectedness and dating people who shared the same goal of marriage, Konrad realized just how important this connection with Leane was to him. Not only had he not managed his internal dialectics, he hadn't really managed the relationship's dialectics well either. In this case, the solution might be for Konrad to acknowledge and try to understand the tensions Leane and even he himself are wrestling with, as well as their multiple goals. Potential solutions need to address both persons' dialectical challenges.

People are pulled in many directions by the complexities of interpersonal communication. Developing greater confidence and a richer understanding of the dialectical forces influencing people's communication and relationships can help you overcome the motivational challenges to competence in interpersonal communication.

Ethics & Interpersonal Communication

As you saw earlier, we are motivated by a variety of goals, needs, and dialectics in our interpersonal communication and in relationships. Whenever we communicate, however, the competence of our behavior is judged in terms of the criteria of appropriateness and effectiveness. Regardless of the motives a communicator pursues, competence requires this person's behavior be perceived as appropriate and effective. However, the criteria of appropriateness and effectiveness are not always compatible. This incompatibility often raises ethical questions. That is, effective communication may be ethically inappropriate, and appropriate communication can be ethically ineffective. If Leane's reason for wanting to end the relationship was because she was actually seeing someone else, telling Konrad "The relationship just isn't working out" may be effective, but Konrad would likely consider such deception ethically inappropriate. Conversely, had Leane decided to continue the relationship just to be appropriate and not hurt Konrad's feelings, this would be ineffective in terms of her own goals of honesty. Effectiveness and appropriateness are not always sufficient for competent interpersonal communication; it requires an additional consideration of ethical concerns. Such ethical concerns can be considered through three steps: self-examination, examination of the other, and compatibility analysis.

First, through careful self-examination, you can determine what your basic motives are in a given interpersonal communication situation. Recall the dimensions of motivation to clarify what is at stake in any given interpersonal encounter. Remember that a communicator's motives can be affective or cognitive, self-oriented or other-oriented, and positive or negative. These distinctions can help illustrate ways of distinguishing ethical concerns in interpersonal communication. If self-examination causes you to discover that your motives are entirely self-oriented rather than other-oriented, or negative rather than positive, you need to reconsider them in terms of their ethics. Expressing jealousy or anger is not necessarily unethical or incompetent. But recognizing selfish motivations provides a better appreciation of how such expressions will be viewed by others. For example, many people consider deception to be unethical. However, deception is viewed as more unethical when it is self-oriented than when it is other-oriented (O'Hair & Cody, 1994). Telling a friend that a ridiculous outfit looks really good on him or her in the hope your friend will go out and make a fool of himself or herself generally would be viewed as more unethical than if the motive were to boost your friend's confidence.

Second, apply the dimensions of motivation to other persons involved in the interpersonal context. They have motives as well. If you attempt to pursue motives that violate others' motives, it will often create ethical problems. For example, if one person is involved in a romantic relationship merely for pleasure and escape and the other is in it for inclusion, love, and internal self-concept, this suggests the first person may be exploiting the other. The person with the relationship motives of pleasure and escape may leave as soon as a more pleasurable opportunity comes along, but the person who sees the relationship as fulfilling his or her self-concept is less likely to envision any other relationship as acceptable. This callousness to the other's motives may well be viewed not only as unethical, but it may unfavorably color the first person's entire communication history in the relationship.

Finally, honestly identify the compatibility of your motives with the other person's motives and determine if there are ways of fulfilling both. Because competence involves both effectiveness and appropriateness, it is vital that the other person's motives be taken into account. Fulfilling only your own motives assures your effectiveness, but may jeopardize your appropriateness, especially from the other person's perspective. In most situations, this means working toward the positive end of the motive dimensions, working to balance self-oriented motives with other-oriented motives, and seeking to fulfill the appropriate cognitive or affective motives as they apply to the context.

Many of the ethical questions surrounding compatibility represent the classic ethical questions people have asked throughout history. How would you feel if the other person's communication was motivated by the same motive as your communication? What would it be like if everyone communicated with the same motive? Does the value of the motive of your interpersonal communication justify the form of interpersonal communication you intend to use? There are no simple or right answers to such questions, but if these questions are not asked *before* we communicate, we are often faced with larger ethical dilemmas *after* we communicate.

Chapter Summary

Interpersonal communication is the transactional process of exchanging signs or symbols that create meaning in an interactive context of few persons. Like all communication, it is best viewed as a process in which all aspects of the communication experience can affect one another and in which communication changes over time and across contexts.

Interpersonal communication occurs in an interactional context; involves few people, which distinguishes it from small group and public speaking contexts; is relational; and creates relationships. Relationships are created through a constant interplay of both the content dimension and the relationship dimension of messages. In defining and redefining relationships, these messages enable the unfolding of relationships across stages of evolution. These stages reflect a process of social penetration, in which interpersonal communication achieves acquaintance, development, decline, and dissolution in our relationships with others, as well as the maintenance of these stages.

Competence in interpersonal communication is facilitated by motivation, knowledge, and skills. Motivation can be analyzed on two levels: the motives of interpersonal communication and the motives of relationships.

Interpersonal communication is motivated by a person's needs and goals. These motives can be organized according to three basic dimensions: affect-cognition, self-other orientation, and positive-negative.

People go into relationships with these motives, but as they interrelate their motives with those of another person, the relationship is best understood as a set of dialectics. Dialectics are simultaneous but conflicting motives. Most relationships revolve and progress or digress along three primary dialectics: autonomy-connection, predictability-novelty, and closedness-openness. As these dialectics are managed in relationships, intimacy, passion, and commitment develop to determine whether and what type of love is experienced.

There are three major challenges to competent interpersonal communication: People often suffer from social anxiety in communicating interpersonally; communicators often don't know how to pursue their goals due to their complexity; and people tend to oversimplify others as having single, coherent selves.

Overcoming these challenges involves managing negative motives, especially anxiety; managing goals; and managing dialectics. Belief restructuring, the identification and refutation of irrational beliefs that interfere with the ability to cope with a communication situation, can help manage negative motives. In addition, managing motives also involves assessing the compatibility of goals in a given context. Finally, overcoming the challenge of oversimplifying the self and other requires understanding the concept of the multiple self, accepting the complexity of the interpersonal communication process, and the motives and dialectics that influence our relationships with others.

As in many communication contexts ethical issues influence interpersonal communication. These ethical issues concern whether a person is communicating in a way that preserves the rights and integrity of the other communicators involved. If you are only communicating for self-oriented and/or negative reasons, then you may be judged as unethical. Ethical interpersonal communication requires that people reflect on their own motives for communicating, decipher the motives of others' communication, and consider the compatibility of these motives.

Key Terms

- interpersonal communication
- interactional context
- content dimension of messages
- relationship dimension of messages
- relationship
- social penetration
- acquaintance stage
- development stage
- decline stage
- dissolution stage
- relational maintenance
- affective/cognitive dimension of motives
- positive/negative dimension of motives
- self-oriented/other-oriented dimension of motives
- dialectic
- autonomy-connection dialectic
- closedness-openness dialectic
- predictability-novelty dialectic
- love
- intimacy
- passion
- commitment
- social anxiety
- shyness
- belief restructuring

Building Motivation

See Self-Assessment on page 235.

Building Knowledge

1. What assumptions do people usually make about interpersonal communication, and how can these assumptions influence their competence?
2. What is an interactional context? Give several examples of interactional contexts.
3. Distinguish between the content and relationship levels of interpersonal communication, giving examples.
4. What are the dimensions of relational communication? Draft a brief dialogue and analyze it in terms of these dimensions.

5. What is a relationship? What is the connection between interpersonal communication and relationships?
6. What are the stages of interpersonal relationships? Describe their connection to the concept of social penetration.
7. What are the three major dimensions of interpersonal communication motives? What are some common motives described by these dimensions?
8. What is a dialectic? List the three major dialectics of relationship motivations. Describe how one of these dialectics has created difficulties in a recent relationship.
9. Define social anxiety. What is the difference between social anxiety and shyness?
10. Describe some of the characteristics of interpersonal communication goals.
11. Explain an approach to managing social anxiety. Describe an interpersonal context in which you would like to feel more confident and discuss how you could apply this approach.

Building Skills

Individual Exercises

1. Think of a recent problematic social encounter you have experienced. Describe it briefly in writing to recall some of its details. Identify the motives of the interactants involved according to the motive map discussed in this chapter. Next, map these motives according to the motives map, designating motives in terms of yourself (S) and the others (O) involved. How similar are the motives involved? What role might these motives have played in making the situation problematic?
2. In the situation just described, consider the ethics involved based on your analysis of motives. Was everyone ethical? Why or why not?
3. Think of a close friend of yours. Take a moment to think about this person's characteristics, your history with this person, your recent interactions, and any problems you may have encountered in your relationship along the way. Under the assumption that interpersonal communication creates relationships that evolve in stages, how has your communication with this person changed over time? Be specific. What do these changes tell you about interpersonal communication?
4. Think of a close romantic partner you have had. Take a moment to think about this person's characteristics, your history with this person, your recent interactions, and any problems you may have encountered in your relationship along the way. Under the assumption that interpersonal communication creates relationships that evolve in stages, how has your communication with this person changed over time? Be specific. What do these changes tell you about interpersonal communication? Are these changes similar to the changes that occurred with your close friend (question 3)? If so, how?
5.  Look up the article by Cynthia G. Wagner (1998) entitled "Cures for Social Phobia," in *The Futurist, 32,* available on *Infotrac College Edition* under the search term *shyness.* In this article, psychiatrists are cited as identifying shyness as a significant problem in the adult U.S. population. Compare this article to one by Michelle Cottle entitled "Selling Shyness" in *The New Republic* (August 2, 1999) at **http://www.thenewrepublic.com**. In it, the author argues that the problem of shyness has been exaggerated by a medical establishment that needs such epidemics to make their own profession necessary. Based only on these two articles and the material covered in the chapter, which position do you think is right and why? Once you have articulated your answer and reasons, compare your answers with those of another student in class.

Group Exercises

1. Form small groups of 3–5 people. Individually, take 5 minutes to list and rank-order, from the most uncomfortable to the most comfortable, the types of social situations that make you nervous. Once everyone in your group has finished, compile a master list, and combine rankings to develop a "group" ranking of those situations a majority of the group members listed. How, if at all, did the group's ranking, and list, differ from your own? What factors led your list to be different from the group's? Discuss each member's outcomes and identify some of the causes of individual anxiety.
2. In the group formed for question 1, select the two to three most uncomfortable situations listed in the activity. As a group come up with all the possible goals that could be pursued in those situations. After a few minutes, take a moment to look over the list. What goals would you not have thought of individually, and why? Does awareness of these additional goals change your outlook on your motivation in these situations? If so, how? If not, why not?
3. In the chart on page 233 are several situations and goals that may or may not apply to the situations.
   a. First, simply check the first column provided if you think the goal typically applies to the situation.

Situations/Goals (Question 3)

	Friendly Chat		Job Interview		Romantic Date		Compliant/ Criticism		Class-room	
Goal 1—Being accepted by others										
Goal 2—Having fun										
Goal 3—Maintaining self-esteem										
Goal 4—Seeking help or reassurance										
Goal 5—Getting to know others										
Goal 6—Influencing others										

	Friendly Chat	Job Interview	Romantic Date	Compliant/ Criticism	Class-room
Goal 1—Being accepted by others	80%	78%	81%	<65%	<65%
Goal 2—Having fun	92%	<65%	100%	<65%	73%
Goal 3—Maintaining self-esteem	65%	85%	80%	81%	<65%
Goal 4—Seeking help or reassurance	63%	<65%	<65%	< 65%	<65%
Goal 5—Getting to know others	68%	<65%	93%	<65%	<65%
Goal 6—Influencing others	80%	<65%	<65%	90%	<65%

b. Now, compile a group percentage by calculating the total number of members who checked a given goal for a given situation and dividing by the number of students in your group. Write this number in the second column. Compare your answers to your group members' answers.

c. Compare your group's answers to those from a study (shown upside down in the box below the chart) that was conducted by Argyle, Furnham, and Graham (1981). Which situations appear to have the most goals? Why? Which goals appear to be most relevant across situations? Why? What similarities and differences occurred between your ratings and those of these researchers' findings?

4. • Using *InfoTrac College Edition*, enter *communication ethics* as a search term, and locate the article entitled "Teaching communication with ethics-based cases" by Betsy Stevens (1996) in *Business Communication Quarterly, 59* (3), (article A18728272). Read the two cases described, and as a group reach consensus on the questions asked at the end of each case. What were the key issues involved in determining the ethics in each case? What role might competence in communication have played in resolving these issues so that ethical concerns might not have been so controversial in these cases?

References

Andersen, P. A., & Guerrero, L. K. (Eds.). (1999). *Handbook of communication and emotion.* San Diego, CA: Academic Press.

Argyle, M., Furnham, A., & Graham, J. A. (1981). *Social situations.* Cambridge: Cambridge University Press.

Barbuto, J. E., Jr., & Scholl, R. W. (1998). Motivation sources inventory: Development and validation of new scales to measure an integrative taxonomy of motivation. *Psychological Reports, 82,* 1011–1022.

Baxter, L. A., & Montgomery, B. M. (1996). *Relating: dialogues and dialectics.* New York: Guilford.

Baxter, L. A., & Montgomery, B. M. (1997). Rethinking communication in personal relationships from a dialectical perspective. In S. Duck (Ed.), *Handbook of personal relationships* (2nd ed., pp. 305–350). New York: Wiley.

Berger, C. R. (1997). *Planning strategic interaction.* Mahwah, NJ: Erlbaum.

Berscheid, E., & Peplau, L. A. (1983). The emerging science of relationships. In H. H. Kelley et al. (Eds.), *Close relationships* (pp. 1–19). New York: Freeman.

Burleson, B. R. (1994). Comforting messages: Features, functions, and outcomes. In J. A. Daly & J. M. Wiemann (Eds.), *Strategic interpersonal communication* (pp. 135–162). Hillsdale, NJ: Erlbaum.

Camden, C., Motley, M. M., & Wilson, A. (1984). White lies in interpersonal communication: A taxonomy and preliminary investigation of social motivations. *Western Journal of Speech Communication, 48,* 309–325.

Cody, M. J., Canary, D. J., & Smith, S. W. (1994). Compliance-gaining goals: An inductive analysis of actors' goal types, strategies, and successes. In J. A. Daly & J. M. Wiemann (Eds.), *Strategic interpersonal communication* (pp. 33–90). Hillsdale, NJ: Erlbaum.

Cupach, W. R., & Spitzberg, B. (Eds.). (1994). *The dark side of interpersonal communication.* Hillsdale, NJ: Erlbaum.

Daly, J. A., & Kreiser, P. O. (1994). Affinity seeking. In J. A. Daly & J. M. Wiemann (Eds.), *Strategic interpersonal communication* (pp. 109–134). Hillsdale, NJ: Erlbaum.

Davis, M. H. (1994). *Empathy: A social psychological approach.* Boulder, CO: Westview Press.

Goffman, E. (1971). *Relations in public.* New York: Basics.

Honeycutt, J. M., Cantrill, J. G., & Allen, T. (1992). Memory structures for relational decay: A cognitive test of sequencing of de-escalating actions and stages. *Human Communication Research, 18,* 528–562.

Honneycutt, J. M., Cantrill, J. G., & Greene, R. W. (1989). Memory structures for relational escalation: A cognitive test of the sequencing of relational actions and stages. *Human Communication Research, 16,* 62–90.

Horney, K. (1945). *Our inner conflicts: A constructive theory of neurosis.* New York: Norton.

Kim, M-S. (1999). Cross-cultural perspectives on motivations of verbal communication: Review, critique, and a theoretical framework. In M. E. Roloff (Ed.), *Communication yearbook 22* (pp. 50–89). Thousand Oaks, CA: Sage.

Knapp, M. L., & Vangelisti, A. L. (1996). *Interpersonal communication and human relationships.* Boston: Allyn & Bacon.

MacKinnon, N. J. (1994). *Symbolic interactionism as affect control.* Albany: State University of New York Press.

Nicotera, A. M. (1997). *The mate relationship: Cross-cultural applications of a rules theory.* Albany: State University of New York Press.

O'Hair, H. D., & Cody, M. J. (1994). Deception. In W. R. Cupach & B. H. Spitzberg (Eds.), *The dark side of interpersonal communication* (pp. 181–213). Hillsdale, NJ: Erlbaum.

Rubin, R. B., Perse, E. M. , & Barbato, C. A. (1988). Conceptualization and measurement of interpersonal communication motives. *Human Communication Research, 14,* 602–628.

Schutz, W. C. (1966). *The interpersonal underworld.* Palo Alto, CA: Science & Behavior Books.

Spitzberg, B. H. (1993). The dialectics of (in)competence. *Journal of Social and Personal Relationships, 10,* 137–158.

Spitzberg, B. H. (1994). The dark side of (in)competence. In W. R. Cupach & B. H. Spitzberg (Eds.), *The dark side of close relationships* (pp. 25–49). Hillsdale, NJ: Erlbaum.

Spitzberg, B. H. (1997). Violence in intimate relationships. In W. R. Cupach & D. J. Canary (Eds.), *Competence in interpersonal conflict* (pp. 174–201). New York: McGraw-Hill.

Spitzberg, B. H., & Cupach, W. R. (1998). Introduction: Dusk, detritus, and delusion: A prolegomenon to the dark side of close relationships. In B. H. Spitzberg and W. R. Cupach (Eds.), *The dark side of close relationships* (pp. xi–xxii). Mahwah, NJ: Erlbaum.

Sternberg, R. J. (1986). A triangular theory of love. *Psychological Review, 93,* 119–135.

Sternberg, R. J. (1988). *The triangle of love: Intimacy, passion, commitment.* New York: Basics.

Watzlawick, P., Beavin, J. H., & Jackson, D. D. (1967). *Pragmatics of human communication: A study of interactional patterns, pathologies, and paradoxes.* New York: Norton.

Building Motivation

Self-Assessment: Indicate the degree, using the scale provided, to which each of the statements either does, or does not, describe you.

Scale		
0 = Strongly disagree **1** = Mildly disagree	**2** = Neither agree nor disagree; undecided	**3** = Mildly agree **4** = Strongly agree

	1. I get nervous when I know I'm going to meet new people.
	2. New situations make me anxious.
	3. I often feel like people are evaluating me in social situations.
	4. I worry about what kind of impression I'm making on others.
	5. I get uncomfortable when interacting with people I don't know.
	6. I get inhibited in social situations.
	7. I feel nervous when interacting with people who are higher in status than I am.
	8. I often wish I had greater confidence in social situations.
	9. I feel anxious around people who are very different from me.
	10. I am tense at parties and social gatherings.
	10. I am generally reluctant to speak up in group conversations.
	12. I feel tense when meeting new people.
	13. I feel nervous when I have to keep a conversation going.
	14. I often feel awkward in social interactions.
	15. I am shy when it comes to interacting in groups of people.

Interpreting Your Scores: Add your responses across all items. Scores range from 0 to 60. Generally speaking, if you scored 45 or over, you are very anxious about interpersonal interaction.

CHAPTER 9

Learning Objectives

1 Explain the difference between knowing "what" and knowing "how" to communicate.

2 Describe the similarities and differences among repertoires, scripts, and rules.

3 Describe how goals influence communicative plans and subplans.

4 Identify the factors that can interfere with action assembly of communicative behavior.

5 Explain the role of prototypes in the perception of competence.

6 Explain the role of positive and negative expectancies in the perception of competence.

7 Explain the ways in which mindlessness and mindfulness can challenge competent communication.

8 Define self-centeredness in communication.

9 Describe how self-monitoring, empathy, and perspective taking assist in learning how to be a competent communicator.

10 Describe how information-gaining strategies assist in learning how to be a competent communicator.

Interpersonal Relationships: Building Knowledge

Eliah was a young, attractive college student, tending bar in the campus pub. Preston, a recent graduate, was visiting with his friends, Greg and Jeff. They had decided to meet at the pub to discuss their recent job-finding experiences and catch up with each other. After some discussion, one of them mentioned how attractive he found Eliah. All three guys agreed, and the conversation turned to discussing how awkward it is to ask someone out for a date. They talked about various ways of introducing themselves to women, various pickup lines they had used, and the general strategies of directness and indirectness, serious and humorous approaches, and so on. After some heated discussion about their respective "theories" about pick up lines, Preston excused himself for a moment while Greg and Jeff continued debating the merits of their favorite approaches to the initial courtship ritual. A few minutes later, Preston returned to the table and announced that he was able to get Eliah's number and she would be expecting a call from him the following week! Thoroughly surprised, Greg and Jeff asked how he had managed to get her number. Preston explained that he had approached the bar with a big smile on his face, placed his calendar book on the bar, and asked her which day she would like him to call her. At first she had seemed a little flustered, but having regained her composure, gave him the excuse of a busy schedule. Preston realized that Eliah experienced some embarrassment about being put on the spot, so he made small talk about how busy the bar looked, sympathizing that she must have a lot of responsibility at work. He then suggested he would adapt his schedule to hers, and asked if there was any time on his schedule that would work for her. After the initial awkwardness had been smoothed over by chatting with her, she looked over his appointment book and wrote her number on a date on which Preston had nothing scheduled. Greg and Jeff looked at each other in disbelief, and after a long moment passed, Jeff simply said, "There goes *my theory*." ●●●

This situation illustrates several important features about the role of knowledge in interpersonal communication. First, people often have theories about how things are supposed to work, and what things work better than others. These theories are based on all types of notions. In the vignette, notice that Preston, Greg, and Jeff were operating on the assumption that men are supposed to do the asking. Greg and Jeff assumed further that the asking should be ornamented or disguised as a strategy.

Second, people's theories are not always correct in a given situation. It is possible that any of Greg's, Jeff's, or Preston's strategies would have worked. However, there are several other possibilities. Eliah may already be in an exclusive relationship. She may only go out with people of a given religion or ethnic group. Eliah might be a lesbian. She might even prefer to do the selecting and asking, rather than letting the man do it. In short, people's working theories of communication are just that: theories. They may do a fair job of accounting for things much of the time, but they are rarely right in all cases.

Third, sometimes people overanalyze. While Greg and Jeff were debating the fine points of their strategies, Preston acted. His action was based on creativity and knowledge, and he had the same chances of being as competent or incompetent as Greg or Jeff. But rather than thinking through the situation in all its possible variations, Preston took the chance and acted on his instinct and experience. It is possible to overanalyze communication, and often the best solution is to follow your instincts.

This chapter examines the role of knowledge in the development of relationships. When you interact with someone, you are developing a relationship. Over time, you come to consider a person a "stranger," "acquaintance," "friend," "best friend," "lover," "colleague," "sibling," "parent," "kin," or even an "enemy." All of these labels represent mental models of who these people are in your world, and how you are supposed to behave toward them. These labels suggest a type of relationship with someone, and they all imply that you have interacted, or might interact, with this person. How any of these relationships unfold, whether they are successful or unsuccessful, brief or enduring, depends in large part on how you use your knowledge of communication to influence the course of the relationship.

Knowledge underlies all communication. Yet most of the time you are unaware *how* you know what to say and do. You simply "know" or you "don't know." In order to communicate more competently, it is important to understand the mystery of what we know and how we know it. The first step is to understand the difference between the two basic types of communicative knowledge introduced in Chapter 2: content and procedural knowledge. As you recall, content knowledge is *what* you know, and procedural knowledge is knowing *how* to use content knowledge.

Content Knowledge: Knowing What to Communicate

Superstars are often asked what makes them so much better than their peers. Whether in science (Stephen Hawking), sports (Serena Williams), acting (Anthony Hopkins), writing (Toni Morrison), or another field, such stars often are unable to answer this question. Of course they study under good teachers or coaches, work hard, and use established methods of their trade. But their peers can claim the same. So what makes these superstars more successful?

This is one of the enduring mysteries of knowledge. We often know something without really knowing how we know it. For example, how do you know how to engage someone in a conversation over coffee? How do you know whether someone is being friendly or being flirtatious? When the other person says something, do you take time to interpret each word separately and then add up all these meanings, based on your knowledge of syntax, or do you just have an instinctive sense of the person's overall meaning? Do you reflect back on all of the similar statements you have ever heard, run through all the possible responses you have learned, select one, and then decide how to perform it with a particular style of inflection and nonverbal nuance? There may be situations in which you do, but in general, conversation simply happens with relatively little conscious attention to how it is happening.

We send many signals when we communicate, but are we always sure of what those signals are and how they are interpreted? Are any of the people in the picture flirting, or are they merely being friendly? How do you know? What cues do you use to determine whether these people are flirting or being friendly?

Understanding how communicative knowledge works first requires an understanding of how we build a mental library of concepts. This library of our mind is a repository of what we know. It is our content knowledge, the "what" of knowledge. It represents the ideas and words we use to construct messages. A recipe first lists the contents needed to make a dish before it tells you what to do with the contents. Likewise, when you tell a joke, the content knowledge is the actual words or lines of the joke. You know the contents of the joke, that is, the ingredients that make up the joke.

In a large bookstore, the books are organized in two very different ways. In the sales tables or bins, books are often shelved with no attention to type of book, author, or subject matter. On the retail shelves however, books are typically arranged according to subject matter. Fiction is divided into adventure, romance, suspense, science fiction, and horror. Nonfiction may be divided into reference, travel, current events and politics, social sciences, self-help, and so forth. Although you may doubt it at times, our minds are almost never organized like the sales bins.

To be useful, knowledge must be organized, and to be organized, it must be categorized. Like books, knowledge is rarely generic. There is little you could say that is equally relevant to all situations. In the cartoon, the suitor finds himself at a loss for what to say in a first date situation, and instead of locating appropriate topics in his store of communicative knowledge, he thought bringing notes along would help guide his conversation. Of course, his lack of knowledge is displayed in several ways. First, by bringing notes at all, he displays his lack of knowledge of small talk topics. Second, by being unable to locate the notes, he displays his lack of organization and memory. Third, by being

Doonesbury BY GARRY TRUDEAU

Competent communicative knowledge is not always as accessible as it seems it ought to be.

Reprinted by permission of Universal Press Syndicate.

unaware of how incompetent he looks for not even being able to make small talk without notes, he all but seals the fate of the date.

Three categories of communicative knowledge comprise the library of the mind: repertoires, scripts, and rules. Because these categories represent the contents of communication knowledge in any context, they have been discussed elsewhere in this textbook. Here we explain them specifically in relation to knowledge in the interpersonal communication context.

REPERTOIRES

A **repertoire,** discussed briefly in Chapter 2, is the set of all roles a person is capable of playing or enacting and the set of behaviors or actions that comprise the role. **Roles,** in turn, are the patterns and style of lines and behaviors a person is able to perform across contexts. Thus a repertoire consists of the various characters, or persons, you can play, or perform. The idea of a repertoire is derived from the world of acting. In their careers, most actors play many different roles with many different characters and plot lines. Similarly, you may have a repertoire of many different roles in your everyday communication with others. As you saw in Chapter 3, the concept of the postmodern self is about being able to play many different roles in life. To one person you're a friend, to another a classmate, to another a sibling, to another a person who stops to help change a tire, to another an employee, and to still another a romantic partner. When registering for classes, you are a student, and the person behind the counter is an administrator. But if you and the administrator meet later at an intramural baseball game and go to a celebration after the game, you both engage in a completely different set of activities that in part define who and what you are to each other and what behaviors are viewed as competent.

Repertoires vary in both breadth and depth. Breadth is the number of different types of roles a person can play. The actors Robert DeNiro and Meryl Streep have played very different types of roles. Streep, for example, is known for her ability to adopt any number of dialects and display various types of social class and background as her role demands. Most Elvis impersonators, in contrast, probably only know one role—Elvis. Depth is the level of familiarity a person has with any given role in a repertoire. A typical singer may know a few Elvis songs, but a professional Elvis impersonator is likely to know all of them.

Roles imply a set of behaviors that can be chosen to enact the roles. Any given role may have an almost infinite number of behaviors, but most roles imply a particular set of appropriate behaviors. For example, consider the nonverbal behaviors listed in Table 9.1. The behaviors in the second and third columns reveal that the appropriate behaviors differ slightly from one role to another, depending on whether the person intends to play the role of flirt, friend, or seducer. Most people prefer to have all three roles in their repertoire and to be expert in them all. In other words, it is generally advantageous to have both breadth and depth in one's repertoire.

In general, the broader and deeper a communicator's repertoire, the higher a communicator's competence level. Broader repertoires allow a person to select from a wider set of roles and achieve the most competent enactment in a given situation. Greater depth in a repertoire results from greater experience and expertise in performing any given role.

Repertoire breadth can complicate choosing the most appropriate role, or may encourage the awkward blending of roles that don't belong together. For example, sometimes people choose the role of teasing another person, thinking this role will lighten the mood or create a sense of playfulness. This role can easily backfire, however, when the other person believes the context calls for seriousness. The recipient of the teasing is playing a different role.

TABLE 9.1

Repertoires of Behaviors in Different Types of Roles

Different roles require different types (breadth) and amounts (depth) of behavior, as illustrated by the roles of friendly, flirtatious, and seductive communication.

Channel	FRIENDLY	FLIRTATIOUS	SEDUCTIVE
Kinesics (use of body)	Small amount of smiling; body relaxed	Moderate amount of smiling; head tilted; open mouth/pout	Frequent amount of smiling; body relaxed; exposed skin
Haptics (use of touch)	Little/no touch	Moderate touch (arm, shoulder)	Touch hand/leg
Proxemics (use of space)	Farther away from each other while talking	Moderately close; cross legs toward each other	Very close
Oculesics (use of eyes)	Little/moderate eye contact	Moderate eye contact with occasional glances downward	Constant eye contact
Vocalics (use of voice)	Neutral voice tone; less fluency/more silences	Animated voice tone; decreased silences/latencies	Intimate voice tone: greater fluency/fewer silences

SOURCE: Adapted from Koeppel et al. (1993). Reprinted by permission of Liana Koeppel.

Likewise, having too much depth in a role may limit a communicator's choices. Being too familiar with a role often leads a communicator to fall back on that role rather than find the most appropriate role. A lawyer who lapses into legalistic styles of arguing with her spouse may find that her lawyerly role is inappropriate in that context. In the opening vignette, Eliah may get approached for a date so often in her role as an attractive bartender that her rejection routine may become second nature to her. Clearly, however, there may be times when she needs to resist the familiar routine and consider the merits of the person making the approach. Thus, as the breadth and depth of a communicator's repertoire increase, this person is more likely to communicate competently, but only up to a point. Beyond that point, breadth and depth are likely to limit this person's competence.

Knowledge Link

What is the relationship between a person's repertoire and the various selves constructed in our postmodern life discussed in Chapter 3?

SCRIPTS

A repertoire is comprised of various roles. Roles, in turn, imply scripts to read. A **script** is a sequence of actions intended to achieve some form of narrative sense. In essence, a script is a story that needs to occur in a given sequence. If the actions are taken out of sequence, the story falls apart. Roles and scripts are related, yet distinct. In the opening vignette, Eliah plays the role of bartender. Within this role, she may occasionally need to enact the script of dealing with difficult patrons who flirt with her, or being a good listener when someone wants to talk about personal problems, and so on. However, when she goes out with Preston, she will need to play a different role and use a different script than being a bartender. Furthermore, Preston's role of pursuing a relationship with Eliah started with one script of getting her to say yes to a date. Once on their date, there are many different scripts he could play to get her attracted to him. Roles and scripts are distinct concepts, and yet neither is fully defined without the other.

Scripts are rarely exact in social interaction. Wedding vows, greeting rituals, and some teasing routines become highly scripted. Most scripts, however, take the form of general sequences of types of actions. For example, Table 9.2 illustrates typical scripts for the

TABLE 9.2

••• Scripting the Story of Romantic Relationships •••

Research has shown that different stages of relationships represent different scripts for what behavior should occur and the sequence in which it should occur. In the table, sex differences are noted by italics type. In later stages of the relationship, there are few consistent sex differences in how behavior unfolds in the relationship.

ACQUAINTANCE: GETTING A DATE

WOMAN'S SCRIPT	MAN'S SCRIPT
notice other person	*initiate mutual notice*
get caught staring at other person	get caught staring at other person
smile	smile
find out about other person from friends	find out about the other person from friends
manipulate ways to "accidentally" run into other person	manipulate ways to "accidentally" run into other person
get introduced by a friend	get introduced by a friend
say "hello"	*begin the conversation*
attempt in conversation to find common interests	attempt in conversation to find common interests
	ask for phone number
	phone later to ask person out
	make arrangements by beginning "small talk"

DEVELOPING: DATING

WOMAN'S SCRIPT	MAN'S SCRIPT
groom and dress	*leave to pick up date*
feel nervous	*pick up date*
be picked up by date	*meet date's parents/roommates*
introduce date to parents/roommate	*pick up friends*
"courtly behavior" (e.g., date open doors)	discuss to confirm plans
leave	talk, joke, laugh
discuss to confirm plans	go to movies, show, party
get to know/evaluate date	eat, drink
talk, joke, laugh	*initiate sexual contact*
go to movies, show, party	*make out*
eat, drink	*take date home*
talk to friends	*ask for another date*
have something go wrong	*initiate kiss goodnight*
be taken home	go home
be asked for another date	
told by date that date will call	
respond to kiss goodnight	

DEVELOPING: BECOMING MORE INTIMATE

COUPLE'S SCRIPT

meet for the first time (party, class, bar, etc.)
ask for other person's phone number and call later
small talk (discuss weather, school, etc.)
show physical affection (kiss, hug, touch, etc.)
date formally (dinner, movie, etc.)
self-disclosure of intimate information
overcome relational crisis (jealousy, uncertainty)
meet parents
talk about future plans as a couple
express love verbally
bonding rituals (give gifts of flowers, jewelry)
commit verbally (stating a desire for an exclusive relationship)

TABLE 9.2 (cont'd)

sexual intercourse
cohabitation (living together)
other-oriented statements (stating interest in each other's goals)
marriage

DISSOLUTION: DECLINE AND DISSOLUTION

COUPLE'S SCRIPT

display lack of interest
notice other people
act distant
try to work things out
increase physical distance/avoidance
display lack of interest
consider breaking up
communicate feelings
try to work things out
notice other people
act distant
date other people
get back together
consider breaking up
break up
move on and recover

SOURCES: Adapted from Battaglia et al. (1998); Honeycutt, Cantrill, & Greene (1991); Pryor & Merluzzi (1985); Rose & Frieze (1993).

relationship stages discussed in Chapter 8. Several characteristics of scripts are apparent from these stages.

First, scripts vary in their complexity and detail. As shown in Table 9.2, some steps of developing a romantic relationship, such as getting to know one another, involve a wide variety of specific communication activities, including self-disclosure, asking questions, storytelling, and so on. Women reveal somewhat more complex date scripts than men, and they view the man's actions as part of their script. In contrast, men show somewhat simpler scripts, which are entirely made up of the actions they initiate.

Second, scripts can vary according to role and context. In the first study in Table 9.2 there are some sex differences because dating in our culture is still influenced by traditional gender stereotypes, such as who should plan and initiate the date. However, in the relationship dissolution stage, gender is less relevant to the roles that partners enact. These scripts might be quite different for elderly people's dates, same-sex dates, or for dating in a culture where courtship is regulated by the partner's parents.

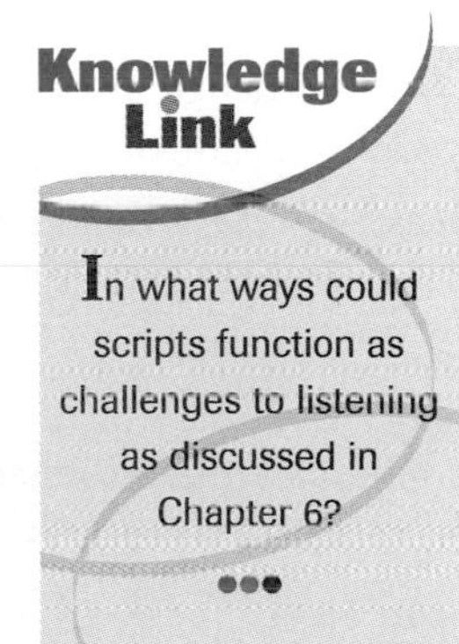

Third, scripts are flexible. In Table 9.2 the breakup script reveals several loops in which the partners rekindle the relationship and then leave it again. Apparently relationships, and therefore their scripts, are relatively fluid and often get several chances for recirculating. Scripts are relatively precise and locked into a particular set of moves. But many of these script elements would not make sense if they occurred out of sequence. Obviously it makes no sense to "pick up date" in the middle of a date. More subtly though, "date other people" makes less sense early in a relationship decline than later, although in happening before the declining stage, it could cause dissolution.

Scripts give coherence and meaning to what would otherwise be random strings of people's actions. Scripts cannot generally go in any direction or tell any story people want them to. Scripts, like virtually all communication, are constrained by social preferences known as rules.

Rules

Rules are followable prescriptions for behavior in a given context. They are followable in the sense that a person must be capable of behaving successfully in accordance with the rule. It must be possible to avoid violating the rule. It makes no sense to make a rule that is not followable. "Defy gravity" or "Recite the entire Constitution of the United States off the top of your head" are not followable and therefore make no sense as rules. But "Don't use foul language when referring to the other person" or "Don't yell or raise your voice when having an argument" specify behaviors most of us can avoid.

Rules are prescriptions. They specify what behavior is or is not allowable. "Be nice" is advice many people give, but it is not a rule because it is not clear what it means in any particular situation. In contrast, "When having an argument, let the other person finish what he or she is saying before starting to speak" is a prescription that is specific. Prescriptions can indicate what to do or what not to do, and sometimes both. For example, the rule just stated is really another way of saying "Don't interrupt the other person when having an argument." In both instances the rule specifies what is allowable or what is not.

Finally, rules are context specific. "Don't interrupt" is in fact not a very useful rule in all communication contexts. Many interruptions are actually appropriate. Many of them signal involvement, for example when you excitedly give reinforcing feedback, such as "yeah," "OK," or "no kidding." Other interruptions involve helping the speaker, such as filling in a desired word when the speaker can't think of the right phrase. However, in given contexts, interruptions are highly inappropriate, such as in many conflict encounters when they signal a lack of respect for the other's position or right to express a position.

Together, repertoires, scripts, and rules constitute the content knowledge of communication. They provide a communicator with a sense of what can and should be communicated. But when you tell a joke, only part of your competence is in knowing what to say. Much of the competence of the joke is *how* you tell it, which involves procedural knowledge.

Knowledge Link

How might rules relate to the creation and maintenance of community discussed in Chapter 1?

Procedural Knowledge: Knowing How to Communicate

From the time you are an infant, you add more and more behaviors, roles, scripts, and rules to your content knowledge. But like a library, merely *having* such knowledge does not mean it is useful to you as a communicator. For this knowledge to be useful, you need to know *how* to access and use it. Knowing how to use communication knowledge involves two processes—planning and action assembly. Planning is the process of anticipating and formulating possible strategies for achieving some goal or goals (Duran & Spitzberg, 1995). Action assembly is the process by which you put behaviors together in an actual performance in the pursuit of those goals.

Planning

A **plan** is an intentional description of the actions involved in achieving a goal. A plan intends to accomplish some outcome(s). However, it does not have to be entirely conscious. When you eat a meal, you may be fulfilling the plan to satisfy your goals of decreasing your hunger and eating something tasty, but you may be unaware that you are

CloseUp ON CULTURE

Conversational Rules

RULES HAVE BEEN DESCRIBED as context-specific prescriptions for behavior. Given that culture is one of the main types of context, it follows that rules are often culturally specific. Violating rules increases the likelihood of being seen as incompetent, so following rules is one of the more important ways of communicating competently. But how do you know what rules to follow when interacting with someone whose cultural rules may be different from your own?

Some rules are likely to be fairly common across cultures. For example, rules regarding behaving politely, such as being courteous, speaking the appropriate language, being considerate of the other, and listening to the other, are likely to be important regardless of the other person's culture. However, certain other rules may vary from one ethnic interaction to another. In one study, for example, African American, Mexican American, and European American college students were asked to recall recent conversations that were either appropriate or inappropriate. The conversations recalled were also either with an "acquaintance" of the same cultural group or a person from one of the other cultural groups identified. When the recollections were analyzed, certain rules were found to be relevant to competence throughout the conversations (Collier, 1988):

- Politeness: Speaking proper English, being verbally courteous, using appropriate nonverbal style, asking for feedback, listening actively.
- Roles: Acknowledging ethnic identity, avoiding stereotyping, behaving consistently with gender role, following job or student roles.
- Content: Using proper reasoning in statements, staying relevant to the conversation topic, keeping criticism constructive.
- Expressiveness: Speaking assertively without violating other person's rights, being open-minded, speaking directly to the point.
- Relationship: Expressing appropriate dominance or submissiveness, expressing appropriate friendliness or hostility, feeling comfortable, seeing other's behavior as predictable, showing trust.
- Goals: Gaining information, achieving personal goals.
- Understanding: Being appropriately empathic, being understood.
- Self-validation: Confirming each other's statements, feeling good about the self.
- Cultural validation: Feeling pride in one's own cultural identity, avoiding embarrassment.

Collier found that politeness and following rules were fairly commonly identified as important across interactions. In contrast, content, expressiveness, and relationship rules were not often recalled by interactants as causes of appropriateness or inappropriateness. European Americans tended to emphasize politeness and roles more when interacting with other European Americans than when interacting with African or Mexican Americans. Mexican Americans recalled conversations being affected by relationship rules more among themselves than when interacting with European Americans. African Americans tended to recall interactions as affected by roles when interacting with European Americans more than when interacting with each other.

These kinds of differences may help explain why somewhat different characteristics of communication are viewed as satisfying by different ethnic groups (Hecht & Ribeau, 1984). Research indicates that, compared to European and African Americans, Mexican Americans tend to be most satisfied in conversations in which the look on the other person's face indicates the interactants want the same thing, and that neither is "talking down" to the other. African Americans, compared to Mexican and European Americans, were more satisfied when there was no misunderstanding in the interactions.

Culture also affects what interactants consider the most competent way to repair or improve conversations when rules are violated. One study (Martin, Hecht, & Larkey, 1994) shows that both European and African Americans try to avoid inappropriate topics or ignore rule violations and involve the other person more in the conversation. African Americans are more likely to use strategies that involve the other person in the conversation or avoid unpleasant topics, whereas European Americans are more likely to not go along with what the other person is doing or saying or expect the other person to apologize. In other words, African Americans tend to engage in more relational-focused forms of conversational repair, and European Americans tend to use more individual-focused forms of conversational repair.

All cultures value competent conversation. Indeed, many of the rules that guide conversation are common across cultures. Nevertheless, when interacting with someone from another culture or ethnicity, knowledge of possible rule differences may be essential to being viewed as competent.

also fulfilling your more overarching goal of survival. Similarly, when you flirt with someone, you may be fulfilling a plan to initiate a romantic relationship, but you may also be facilitating a larger plan to get married someday. For example, in the opening vignette, Preston's first goal was getting Eliah's phone number, which in turn was a step in getting a first date, which in turn is a step in the plan of achieving an intimate relationship.

These examples reveal that most plans are made up of smaller plans, or **subplans,** which are the steps that need to be taken to achieve a given stage of the larger plan. You may not want to get married right now, but you realize that at some point you may meet the right person and flirtation with a person now is part of the same step that will eventually lead to meeting the right person. You are unlikely to get married without flirting with someone, so flirting to establish a romantic relationship becomes a subplan to the larger "parent" plan of getting married, even if the parent plan seems far off.

Plans are oriented toward goals. Goals, like plans, have subgoals. A subgoal, like a subplan, is a goal formulated as part of defining and achieving a larger goal. If flirting is a subplan, establishing a romantic relationship is this subplan's goal. But this goal is a bridge to the larger goal of getting married. At the same time, if this relationship doesn't lead to marriage, it is not necessarily viewed as a loss, because the subgoal itself can be viewed as a desirable goal itself.

As you saw in Chapter 8, goals are an essential part of communication motivation. They also serve to activate knowledge processes. Communicators do not spend all their time thinking through every possible message they could be communicating at any point in time. Such an overload of information processing would be disabling. Instead, communicators process information efficiently by selecting what they will think about. They make these choices based on their communicative goals.

Goals, like the process of communication discussed in Chapter 1, are very transactional. Goals are interdependent with the goals of others. They evolve over time. In the opening vignette, Preston did not know he would be pursuing the goal of flirtation when he went to the pub to meet his friends. Indeed, had his discussion with Jeff and Greg not ventured into the topic of flirtation, he might never have thought to attempt his bold move. But the context provided the right opportunity for him to redefine his goals in that encounter. Specifically, the topic of conversation is flirtation, he sees an attractive woman with whom he can strike up a conversation, and he has friends to whom he can show off. So he began the interaction with goals of reacquainting with his friends, but soon found himself pursuing a completely different goal.

When Preston returned to talk with his friends, they eventually got back to becoming reacquainted. Preston had achieved a flirtation goal by asking Eliah out and a reacquainting goal by talking to Greg and Jeff. Both goals were achieved, but not simultaneously. Preston had the ability to manage multiple goals efficiently.

This illustrates a key to the process of communicative planning. Planning is generally efficient. **Efficiency** refers to the amount of effort invested in developing and performing a plan. Given two plans to get a date with someone, assuming both plans would succeed, people generally choose the plan that requires less effort to think through and enact. To achieve efficiency in plans, communicators tend to process plan-based information according to certain principles.

The first principle of plan efficiency is the **competence principle.** Plans are selected on the basis of their efficiency in competently achieving the goals to which the plans are directed. Efficiency generally serves the major concerns of appropriateness and effectiveness. Given two plans equal in efficiency, communicators tend to choose the one most likely to be viewed as competent. Furthermore, given two plans that differ in their efficiency, but that are different in their impact on competence impressions, communicators are likely to look for the most efficient plan that achieves the most competence. In the opening vignette, Preston's immediate goal was to get a date with Eliah. One plan would be to start small talk with her, try to achieve some rapport, and leave a good first impression so that at some later time he could come into the pub and continue the conversation and ask her out. Another plan would be to make the bolder approach that he used. The second plan was far more efficient. But a plan is very inefficient if it fails, and in this case, Preston was betting that the more efficient plan would not be seen as so inappropriate that it would make him look incompetent in Eliah's eyes. Communicators want to accomplish their goals, but only rarely do they choose the most efficient plan if that plan also happens to make them look incompetent. Goal accomplishment is most likely to occur when behavior is appropriate to the context in which the goal is being pursued.

The second principle of planning efficiency is the **prior success principle:** Plans are based on previous plans when previous plans seem effective and apply to the present situation (Berger, 1997). When a goal arises for a communicator, the communicator could spend an enormous amount of energy analyzing the roles, rules, and script options of the context. Or the communicator may realize that he or she has already faced this goal context before and was able to achieve the desired goal by using a plan available from memory. A question many interviewers ask during a job interview is "What are your weaknesses?" This question throws many an interviewee into a panic, but a person who has been asked this difficult question previously will have thought through plans on how to answer such a question more competently, and the job seeker should be able to recall it and deliver it fluently in the future.

The third efficiency principle is the **simplicity principle:** All things being equal, communicators are likely to simplify their plans rather than complicate them, or make only slight alterations to their plans (Berger, 1997). If a communicator can think of two plans to achieve a goal, the simpler one tends to be chosen. Furthermore, once a person has begun enacting a plan, changes tend to be made sparingly rather than shifting radically to an alternate plan. People generally don't want to "change horses in midstream." Such major alterations of plans involve a radical shift of behavior and may appear too wild and unpredictable to observers.

Communicators highly experienced in a given area are likely to develop more complex plans over time because they understand all the factors involved. For such knowledgeable communicators, producing more involved plans is efficient because they expend less effort analyzing how to employ a plan in the situation. A good salesperson has heard all the reservations that potential customers may have. With this experience, this salesperson is likely to have developed not only a wide variety of responses, but also a complex set of plans of how to combine these responses in the most persuasive ways. This combining of plans results from the process of action assembly.

ACTION ASSEMBLY

Action assembly is the mental process of putting behaviors together in the pursuit of goals. When Preston opened up his calendar planner in the opening vignette and asked Eliah for a date, from where did this action originate? Had he performed this tactic before? If not, how did he know how to enact it? What vocal inflection should he use? Should he be smiling or not? Should he ask it as a teasing command? Should he try and seem shy while asking his bold question, or should he act assertive and confident? Preston resolved all of these questions and many more in a split second. He did not entirely know what he would say or do—but when he got to the bar it all fell into place almost as if it had been planned.

How did Preston assemble the actions involved in asking Eliah for a date? The cognitive process by which such communicative episodes are enacted is referred to as action assembly (Greene, 1993). Action assembly is a cognitive process activated when a particular goal becomes relevant to a communication context. This goal stimulates a mental search of a person's repertoire of applicable roles, scripts, and rules. These action sequences can be viewed as packets of behaviors and their associated goals.

Action assembly starts with a goal. The goal is sometimes presented by a situation, such as when Preston saw Eliah in the pub. At other times a person generates the goal that leads to the situation, which would happen if Eliah decides where Preston and she should go on their first date. Presented with the goal, a communicator then searches his or her memory for examples of similar situations and goals to see if certain communication behaviors have worked before to achieve a goal similar to the one currently being pursued. It may be that Preston had previously used this particular approach, or something similar, and decided it might work again. If there are no previous examples of the present goal or situation in memory, the communicator searches for those situations and goals that are *most* similar, and then searches for communication behaviors that worked for those situations and goals. Preston may not have tried to flirt with a bartender before but he may have flirted with a waitress, and he views the situations and goals as similar. Having located situations and goals that are similar, the communicator then examines what behaviors were used in those situations and which behaviors most competently achieved the goals. Here the previous principles of efficiency help the communicator choose the particular behaviors that will be assembled for performance.

Once a set of behaviors has been mentally collected, they must be assembled in a way that makes sense in the context. In some cases this means applying memories of role, script, or rule information. For example, Preston probably realizes it is generally the male's role to be the one who asks for the woman's telephone number. Although the normal cultural script is to spend some time conducting small talk before asking for the person's number, Preston perceives that this script may not apply when the other person is engaged in work activities and has only a brief amount of time to talk. Finally, among the rules that would guide the assembly of action in this situation is to avoid being too pushy or aggressive.

Research has shown that 40 to 50 behaviors or behavior sequences may be associated with flirtation in American culture (Egland, Spitzberg, & Zormeier, 1996). Although a person may have all of these behaviors in repertoire memory, it is not likely that he or she will remember them all as equally competent. Furthermore, as a flirtation episode unfolds there may be flirtation routines called from memory that are specifically considered more effective when the other person seems disinterested, distracted, or interested but reluctant, and so forth. We not only store actions, but also their consequences, in our memory.

There are a variety of ways in which the action assembly process can fail. You may lack the motivation necessary to engage in an adequate search and assembly process. If you are physically exhausted, you may not care if you appear competent, and thus you may not go to the trouble of searching out the most competent actions for a given situation. You may have the actions in memory, but lack the appropriate plan or knowledge of the role, script, or rules for combining the actions. While Preston walked right up to Eliah and asked her out, his friends Greg and Jeff were still wondering how to best go about such an approach.

Further, a communicator may have the actions in memory, but not make the connection to the present context because he or she had previously used the actions in another type of context. If you meet someone who had been a friend years earlier, you may continue to search only for friendship actions rather than flirtation actions, even though under the present circumstances the latter may now be relevant.

Finally, people may activate less competent actions because these actions are more available because of recent use and familiarity or because they seem to be the best match at the time. You may occasionally find yourself in the midst of saying something even while you realize that you could be saying something else much more appropriate to the situation. You probably simply went with what first came to mind, which means it had the best initial match, even if it wasn't the most competent action to call forth.

Thus far we have examined what communicators know how to say and do, and how they organize this knowledge. Throughout we have considered some of the ways in which this knowledge is processed to increase, and occasionally decrease, a person's communication competence. Competence depends not only on the knowledge, but also on how that knowledge is perceived when applied. For full understanding of the role of knowledge, we need to discuss the relationship between knowledge and others' impressions of competence.

Knowing How to Be Competent

In the process of attempting to be competent, we sometimes find ourselves unable to figure out what we should be doing. Furthermore, sometimes when we have been perfectly competent, we second-guess our knowledge of the rules of the situation.

Competence is indeed a fragile achievement. It can be difficult to gain and easy to lose. One moment you can make a remark that makes you seem like a genius. A moment later in the same conversation, with the same people, you can make an awkward comment that completely embarrasses you. As you saw in Chapter 2, competence is an impression, and not in the behavior itself. It is not enough to be motivated, knowledgeable, and skilled. Ultimately, your competence is decided by your peers, that is, by other communicators. Although being motivated, knowledgeable, and skilled may not guarantee you will be viewed as competent, it does make it more likely. These components make it more likely that your actions will fit the ideal characteristics by which you and others define a competent performance.

Prototypes

As you saw in Chapter 3, this ideal performance is known as a prototype, the ideal case or example of something. The first process involved in determining whether a person's communication is competent or incompetent involves comparing the actual performance and what you consider an ideal performance. Figure 9.1 shows the concept of a "skilled person," broken down by levels of cognitive prototype. If someone asked you what you think a skilled person is, you would first need to categorize the type of skilled person on the individual level. You could then identify the context in which you are evaluating the person. It doesn't make much sense to judge a carpenter by the same standards of behavior as you would a writer, although there may be some similarities of behavior across some contexts. Both a carpenter and a writer might need patience, for example.

Once you know the context in which you are evaluating a person, you associate a small group of behaviors with competent performance in that context. This group includes behaviors that you have learned to associate with appropriateness and effectiveness over time. Once your mental library shelves are stocked with these repertoires of behaviors,

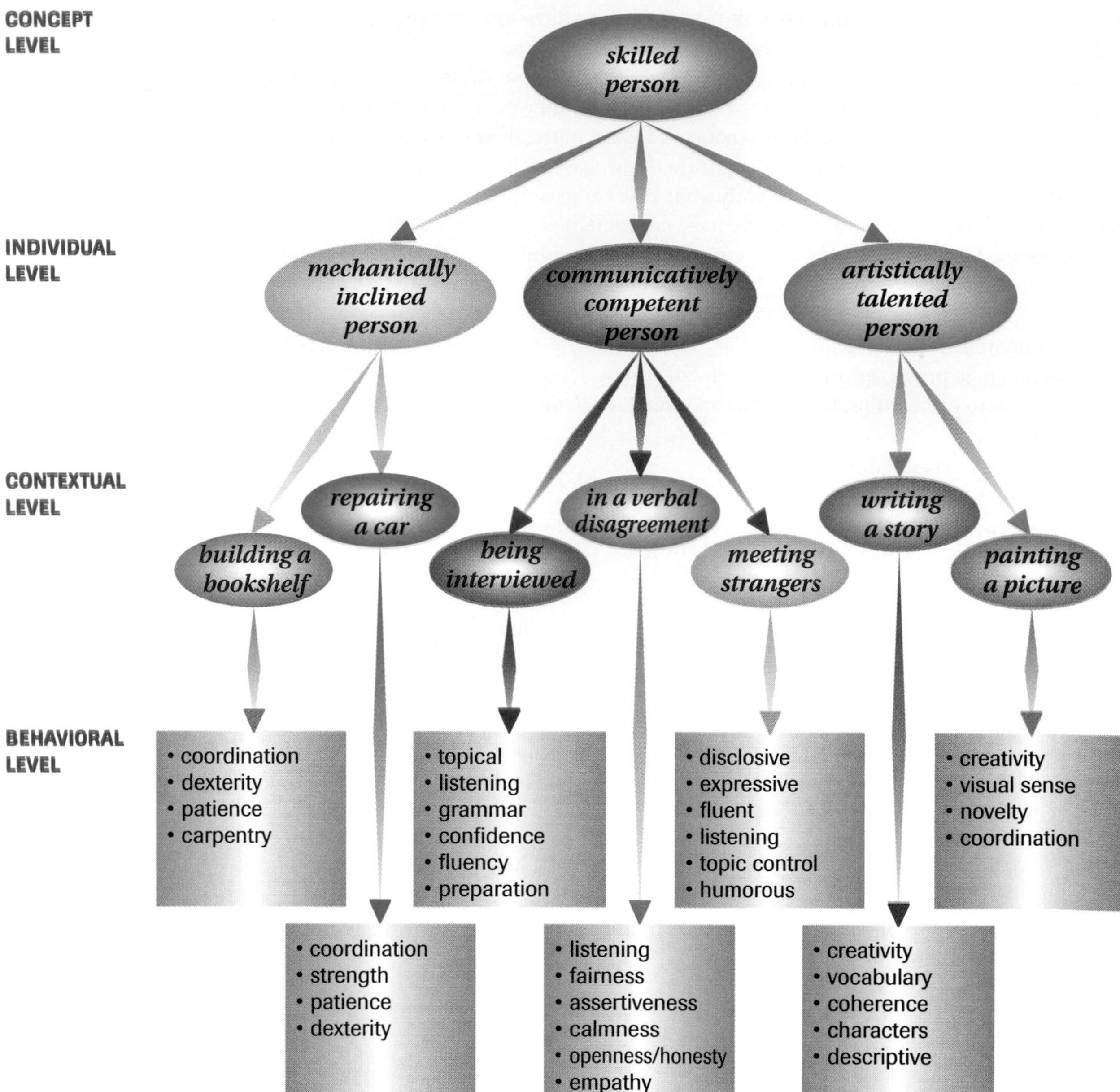

FIGURE 9.1
The Skilled Person Prototype

Behavior is related to mental concepts of competence and vice versa. You can infer a person is a competent communicator by observing his or her actions first and then concluding that they fit your idea of a competent communicator, or by identifying your mental ideal of a competent communicator and looking for a communicator's behaviors that are consistent with that ideal.

Adapted from Pavitt & Haight (1985).

repeated experience allows you to connect these behaviors to their relevant roles, scripts, rules, and goals.

Thus far, the perception of a communicator's competence has been described as a process in which you observe the person's behavior, compare this behavior to your prototype, and then evaluate the behavior's fit to the prototype. This is a **bottom-up process** in which you start at the level of specific behaviors and work up to a general evaluation of competence. This process of competence evaluation can move in the other direction as well. If you are asked to define a competent communicator your knowledge search is a **top-down process.** You start with a general evaluation of competence and work down to the specific behaviors that comprise this evaluation. If you were asked, "What kind of person do you hope to marry?" or "What makes a comedian funny?" you would start with your prototype of an ideal spouse or ideal comedian and then search your prototype for the behaviors that define the prototype.

Looking back at Figure 9.1, a top-down process starts with determining the concept, identifying the type of individual involved and the context in which the individual is communicating, and then listing the most typical competent behaviors for that concept. However, in everyday life people are not likely to ask you to articulate your definition of competence. Instead, you tend to use bottom-up processing in which you observe a person's communication behavior and then assess the behavior: Was that a competent performance? Your processing of information now goes from bottom-up. You compare the person's behavior to the repertoires of behavior for various contexts, match it to the context in which the behavior was performed, and then to the individual type.

If the person's behavior does not fit your prototypes for behavior or context, you are likely to conclude this person is not very competent. In contrast, if the person's actions match up with many of the behaviors in your competent person prototype, you are likely to view this person as competent. Research has shown that for many people in North American culture, the prototype of a competent communicator is someone who is intelligent, articulate, confident, outgoing, well dressed, and listens well (Pavitt & Haight, 1985). But again, as illustrated in Figure 9.1, which of these behaviors is most prototypically competent depends on the context and type of communicator being judged.

Knowledge Link

How might prototypes contribute to the formation of stereotypes as discussed in Chapter 3?

Expectancy Fulfillment

Both the top-down and the bottom-up forms of perceiving competence imply that you compare behavior you observe in others to a mental concept. But you rarely enter a communication context with absolutely no idea of what to expect. In other words, your expectations concerning the context are also likely to influence which prototypes you apply to a situation. These expectations, in turn, influence how your prototypes determine your perceptions of your own and others' competence.

Expectancy fulfillment is the process by which communication outcomes are evaluated in regard to anticipated outcomes. We expect certain communication behaviors or behavior outcomes to occur in a situation. At some point we evaluate the extent to which our expectations are met by these behaviors or outcomes. By the time most people are in college, they have experienced a wide variety of communication situations and developed expectancies for these situations. Once you know what prototype to apply to a situation you can assess what constitutes competent behavior in that situation.

Most communication situations involve some level of prior expectancy. Some of the most typical contexts include casual social encounters, administrative encounters, conflicts, expertise encounters (for example, therapy, teaching, etc.), activity-based encounters (for example, playing a sport or game), and romantic encounters (Argyle, Furnham, &

TABLE 9.3

Relationship Rules

Research reveals that communicators are aware of many rules in two common interpersonal contexts.

Rules of Friendship	
Exchange:	Share news of success with the other
	Show emotional support
	Volunteer help in time of need
	Strive to make other happy while in each other's company
	Repay debts and favors
Intimacy:	Trust and confide in the other
Third Parties:	Stand up for the other person in his or her absence
	Be tolerant of the other's friends
	Don't criticize each other in public
	Keep each other's confidences/secrets
	Don't be jealous or critical of the other's relationships
Coordination:	Don't nag the other
	Respect each other's privacy
Rules for Conflict	
Understanding:	Say you're sorry when you have transgressed
	Support and praise other when he or she deserves it
	Listen to the other
	See the other's viewpoint
	Be honest and say what is on one's mind
	Look at each other
Rationality:	Don't get angry
	Don't raise voice
	Avoid combative issues
	Don't lose temper or be aggressive
	Try to remain calm and not get upset
Conciseness:	Get to point quickly
	Be specific; don't generalize
	Be consistent
	Keep to the main point
	Avoid rash judgments
Consideration:	Don't talk too much
	Don't make other feel guilty
	Don't push your view as the only view
	Don't mimic the other or be sarcastic
	Don't talk down to the other

SOURCE: Adapted from Argyle & Henderson (1984); Honeycutt, Woods, & Fontenot (1993).

Graham, 1981). No two experiences in these contexts are identical, and yet within these types of contexts interactions tend to share certain similarities. Every conflict encounter is unique, and yet, you intuitively know a conflict is a different context than small talk. For example, as shown in Table 9.3, many relationship contexts are recognizable by their rules, and therefore, the expectancies you have for them.

Competent communication is largely about matching performance with expectation in a given context (Burgoon, 1995; Spitzberg & Brunner, 1991). You might think that fulfilling people's expectancies for a given encounter would be the most competent thing to do. However, this intuition is wrong! Expectancies can be either positive or negative. If you have had great experiences on first dates, and the person on a particular first date fulfills your positive expectancies, then you are likely to view this person as competent. However, if you have had nothing but terrible experiences with first dates, and this is what you expect, it would hardly be competent for your date to fulfill these expectancies! Consequently, you would view this person as competent as a result of fulfilling positive expectancies and violating negative expectancies. In the opening vignette, Eliah may have experienced a lot of insincere or manipulative pickup lines and was pleasantly surprised when a simple and direct line was used creatively. These expectations are part of the way we use our knowledge of competent communication.

Competent communication requires a complex interplay of knowledge. We have to coordinate our knowledge of repertoires, scripts, and rules through processes of planning and action assembly. Having coordinated all these processes, we then are subject to other people's comparisons of our behavior to their expectancies and competence prototypes. Given the complexity of these processes, it is hardly surprising that there are a number of ways in which our knowledge can lead us astray in the pursuit of competent communication.

Challenges to Competence in Relationships

Competent communication does not occur out of thin air like a magic trick. People learn how to be competent over long periods of time, and this learning process is represented in the communicator's knowledge. But knowledge is not always as useful or as accessible as we need it to be. Several processes make our knowledge of communication less competent than it needs to be. This section examines some of the specific challenges that knowledge presents to competent performance.

Plan Adjustments

The principles of plan efficiency help communicators select from among their plans. However, even efficient plans can fail. Therefore, competent communicators learn how to adjust to plan failures. **Plan adjustment** is the process of changing elements of plans after receiving feedback that indicates opportunities for plan improvement. Plan adjustment is a challenge to interpersonal communication competence because most people are reluctant to change their plans or else they change them in ways that make the situation worse. When plans fail repeatedly over time, communicators are likely to use increasingly less appropriate plans (Berger, 1997). Because communicators seek efficiency in their plans, they are often reluctant to make the kinds of changes to their plans that might be required to overcome obstacles. Many people, for example, pursue dating relationships over the internet rather than through everyday social interactions. Such an approach is viewed as efficient because it allows a person to search many possible partners for several types of desired characteristics. However, the person may be lacking in the more complicated skills of social interaction and flirtation that would be required to initiate a successful relationship in a face-to-face context.

When situations don't go as planned, it is often difficult to find an appropriate plan to substitute for the situation, and embarrassment can often result as you fumble through the encounter.

The best laid plans often go astray

Reprinted by permission of Universal Press Syndicate (1994).

Plans that fail are often painful, produce anxiety, and can interfere with the planning process. Communicators whose plans continually fail may begin to doubt their ability to plan. Such a lack of self-confidence often leads to relying on increasingly simple plans that cannot take into account the complexity the goal requires. In the cartoon, Cathy realizes that her initial plan was not as important as knowing what to do if the initial plan failed.

Mindlessness

Often when we say something we regret, we ask ourselves, "What in the world was I thinking when I said that?" This question assumes that thinking before communicating makes us more competent, whereas mindlessness makes us incompetent. This assumption is far from accurate. **Mindlessness** is a state of engaging in activities without consciously monitoring the operations or process of that activity. If you commute using a given route to school each day you may occasionally arrive at your destination only to realize that you don't remember *how you got where you are!* This is an example of mindless activity. You drove, biked, or walked a route, changed your pace, made turns, saw traffic go by, and generally reached your destination without mishap. Yet you may not recall a single specific perception of the trip itself.

So was your commute incompetent? Not really. Mindlessness is truly a double-edged sword. Learning a new skill or concept for the first time is a very mindful process. We make mistakes. We have difficulty achieving competent performance. For example, in learning a foreign language or how to drive, the early learning stages are extremely difficult because, among other things, they are extremely mindful. The mind is limited in the number of things it can focus on at once. In learning to drive, for example, at first you try to pay attention to everything: the speedometer, the gas pedal, the break, the steering wheel, the cars to the sides, front, and rear, the signs on the roadside, and so forth. Furthermore, with a new set of concepts, there are no procedural rules or prototypes from which to work. However, over time, with practice and experience the mind becomes so fluent at calling forth the required actions that it has forgotten how it knows to do these things. If you have tried to explain to someone how to drive a car you recognize the difficulty of putting your knowledge into a form the other can use. Your knowledge of how to drive is so deeply embedded in your mind, you find it difficult to articulate what you know.

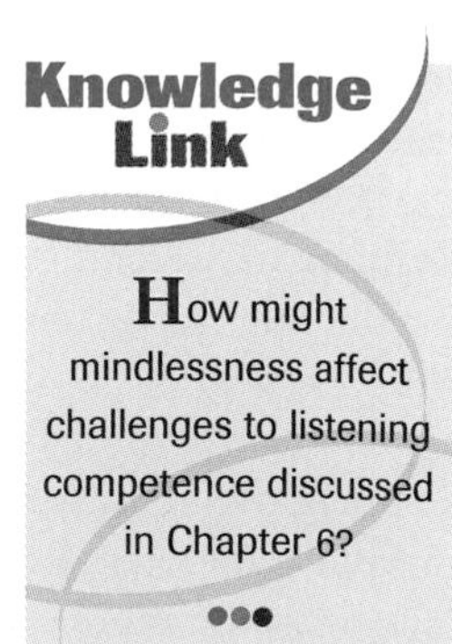

Knowledge Link

How might mindlessness affect challenges to listening competence discussed in Chapter 6?

Mindlessness occurs because it is efficient. If you had to think about every single action you ever performed, you would be completely debilitated. For example, looking straight ahead rather than at your hands, place your hands on a flat surface in front of you. Now use your fingers tapping on the surface to "type" the following sentence: "Mindlessness is a double-edged sword." Not having the keyboard to touch, you probably experienced some difficulty. You may not have been as fluent as you ordinarily would be at a keyboard. That is because you became mindful of the activity that you ordinarily perform mindlessly.

As efficient as mindlessness is, it creates challenges for interpersonal communication competence when you rely on it too much in situations in which your ordinary ways of doing things don't work. The challenge therefore is that you need to become mindful of what you are doing wrong and how to improve your competence. However, once you have the appropriate knowledge, this knowledge needs to become relatively mindless in its application to achieve competence. This communication course, therefore, may occasionally make you feel less competent in the process of trying to improve your communication competence. This is because communication routines that were mindless in the past will have become mindful. Although mindless routines are efficient, they are not necessarily competent. We often continue with them not because they are competent, but because it would involve effort, and perhaps temporary incompetence, to change them. In addition, given that these routines are mindless you may not even realize you are doing them incompetently.

Mindlessness can be particularly problematic in ongoing relationships with others. You develop routines and rituals of interaction, ways of greeting each other, typical arguments, and patterns of bickering. To change your behavior would involve a great deal of conscious reflection in situations that demand spontaneity. Over the short term, a person trying to communicate more competently in his or her relationships may seem awkward or even manipulative. This person may need to pause, reflect, experiment with new behaviors, and generally respond with less fluency than before. But over time, if the new behaviors become routine and therefore mindless, and if the new routines are selected on the basis of their appropriateness and effectiveness, their mindlessness is likely to benefit competence.

SELF-CENTEREDNESS

Few characteristics have been so consistently attributed as a challenge to interpersonal communication competence as self-centeredness. **Self-centered communicators** think primarily of their own goals, needs, communication behaviors, and ways of doing things. Any attention they pay to the other person in the interaction tends to focus on their own needs and how to get that person to do what they want. Self-centered people are more likely to pursue topics of conversation they find interesting, direct the conversation to their own topics of interest, and interrupt others' topics of conversation. Furthermore, self-centered communicators often tend not to see things from the others' perspective, resulting in overly simplistic ways of thinking about the world. This is because they believe their way of doing things is best or because they aren't open to other alternatives.

Self-centeredness prevents interpersonal communication competence in several ways. By not including the other person in the conversation, he or she tends to view you as narcissistic or uncaring. In other words, the other person is likely to view your behavior communication as inappropriate. Further, if your effectiveness depends on getting the other person to do what you want, that person is less likely to comply to the extent that he or she views you as incompetent or only interested in yourself. Finally, a large part of what makes a relationship is the sharing and the caring that the people develop. If you are self-centered in your communication, you do not get the benefit of what the other person has to offer to you and the relationship.

As you saw in Chapter 3, the creation of the social self allows people to develop an ability to view themselves from the perspectives of others. In Chapter 4, we described the self as becoming increasingly social as people begin to view themselves as objects of perception. Self-centered people rarely develop a mature social self. A certain degree of self-centeredness can be valuable, given that effectiveness in interpersonal communication depends on an awareness of a person's interests and goals in a situation. But appropriateness relies significantly on sensitivity to others' perspectives, which requires a concerted effort to "see the world from their point of view," the primary function of the social self.

Overcoming Challenges to Competence

Plan adjustment, mindlessness, and self-centeredness represent biases in the way we use communicative knowledge. These biases challenge our competence in interpersonal communication by making us inattentive to others or unable to search our knowledge for the most competent ways of adapting to the situation. In order to develop more competent knowledge, it is important to engage in more monitoring of the communication situation, to experience the communication situation more from the other person's point of view, and to learn how to develop more useful knowledge of the communication situation.

Self-Monitoring

Mindlessness often results from a divided, or lack of, attention. At the level of communicative knowledge, attention is best viewed as a form of **self-monitoring,** a tendency to focus on the social environment for cues that are relevant to your own competence in that context (Snyder, 1987). In other words, it is an activity of monitoring your situation so you can use the information available to formulate the most competent responses to the situation.

Self-monitoring involves balancing the context that is outside yourself with the context of yourself as an object of perception. If you spend too much time focusing on the context or yourself, it is likely to show in your behavior. Excessive attention to the context can make you unaware of how you are being perceived. It can also lead you to conform to whatever the context calls for rather than attempting to represent your most competent self. Too much conformity can cause a loss of others' respect because you come across as simply agreeing with everyone or having no opinions of your own.

The key to self-monitoring is to strike a balance between attention to your environment and your own motivation, knowledge, and skills. Ideally, such a balance is a part of your natural orientation toward interaction with others. This balancing is accomplished by developing mental routines in which you remind yourself to pay attention. One of these techniques is keeping a diary of your interpersonal communication encounters so you start noting what interactions are about and the factors that make a difference in these conversations. Another technique is to play guessing games with yourself about what an encounter you are anticipating is going to be like. Afterward, you can compare your actual experience with your guesses. Such techniques are designed to make you more aware of the factors in interpersonal interactions that influence competence. Such techniques seem simplistic, and may even seem awkward at times, but before long they can become routine tools for enhancing attentiveness in conversations.

EMPATHY & PERSPECTIVE TAKING

Empathy is the ability to experience the feelings similar to or related to those of another person. It is often confused with sympathy but is quite different. Sympathy is a desire to offer support for another, generally when that person is in a predicament. Empathy does not imply that you feel sympathy and vice versa. If you see a person on the news who just lost a loved one in a home fire, you may sympathize by feeling sorry for that person, but you may not *feel* what that person is feeling by wanting to cry or feeling depressed. If you see an expectant father in a hospital waiting room, you may feel excitement for him even if you have never been a father, and there may be little reason for you to feel sympathy in this context.

In contrast to empathy and sympathy, **perspective taking** involves seeing the world as the other person sees it. In the examples just described, you may not feel the loss or the excitement but you can visualize what the people are experiencing, the thoughts they might be thinking, and you can imagine what it might be like to lose a loved one or be about to gain a loved one. So empathy is primarily concerned with emotions, whereas perspective taking is concerned with thoughts and perceptions.

Both empathy and perspective taking are important methods to overcome some of the challenges of competent interpersonal communication. As you saw in Chapter 8, dialectical theory shows that successful relationships allow people to achieve independence along side of interdependence. Empathy and perspective taking facilitate interdependence by allowing you to adapt your behaviors to the other person's needs. In the process these factors also help you coordinate your actions with each other so you can better achieve your own objectives. Empathy helps you feel the other person's joys and sorrows, moods and rages, and even quiet reflections. It promotes sympathy, and perhaps more importantly, gives credibility to offers of sympathy and support. Perspective taking lets you see the world from another person's point of view and discover another way of thinking. It helps you anticipate the other person's actions and adapt your own behaviors accordingly. Both empathy and perspective taking therefore take you out of your self-centeredness and allow you to be mindful of the other person and the effects of your own behaviors on the feelings of others. They also facilitate plan adjustment by providing better information about how the other person would react to changes in your communication plans.

Considering again the Chapter 3 concept of the postmodern self, is perspective taking becoming more or less difficult? Why?

KNOWLEDGE-GAINING STRATEGIES

Not all knowledge is based strictly on emotional and mental processes. One of the ways people acquire knowledge is through active and interactive **knowledge-gaining strategies** (Berger & Bradac, 1982), which are behaviors a communicator uses to obtain information about others. The most common strategies for gaining information relevant to interpersonal communication are questioning, contextual alteration, and self-disclosure.

Questioning is the explicit or implicit use of verbal or nonverbal behavior to request information from another person. If you need more information about someone, one of the best ways to get it is to ask the person or ask someone who knows the person. Instead of assuming that Patricia would like to be called "Pat" or "Patty," you can simply ask her. The same strategy can also be applied less directly, such as when you ask someone else for information about that particular person. For example, you can ask a friend or associate of Patricia whether or not she likes to be referred to by a nickname.

Contextual alteration involves changing something about a situation to see how a person reacts. The person's reaction can reveal a lot about that person's personality or thought process. For example, in a roommate situation you may clean up the other person's mess because it is bothering you. But having altered the environment, if the roommate does not notice you cleaned up his or her mess, it tells you something about how attentive this person is.

A third strategy, self-disclosure, is somewhat counterintuitive. As discussed in Chapter 4, self-disclosure is generally used as a strategy for making oneself known to others. But by making yourself known to another you also tend to make it easier to know the other. As a relationship progresses people tend to reciprocate each other's disclosures. As you disclose information about yourself the other person tends to disclose similar amounts and types of information. This reciprocity of self-disclosure means that by disclosing information to others, you are creating a context in which that person feels safer disclosing about himself or herself.

Chapter Summary

Most people know how to communicate interpersonally. They do so every day of their lives. But people generally do not know *how* they know what they know, and they generally do not know how to communicate in optimally competent ways. This chapter identified some of the ways in which we know what we know, and how this knowledge can be improved.

Communicative knowledge comes in two forms: content and procedural. Content knowledge involves knowing what to say and do communicatively. Procedural knowledge involves knowing how to say and do things communicatively. Content knowledge includes the ideas and words that we use to construct messages. This knowledge in turn needs to be stored in our minds in usable ways. We store knowledge in the form of repertoires, scripts, and rules. Repertoires are the various roles that we perform in interpersonal interaction. Scripts are the sequences in which we learn to enact behaviors, and rules are the guidelines that help us discern what communication is appropriate and inappropriate in given contexts.

Procedural knowledge refers to understanding how to implement our content knowledge. We understand the procedures of interpersonal communication when we are able to engage in planning and action assembly. Planning is the anticipation and intentional description of actions that can achieve a goal. Action assembly is the process of putting these planned actions into a complete package that can be performed.

Knowing what and how to communicate help you perform competently in interpersonal interactions. But performance is half the equation. The other half is how others perceive your performance. The perception of competence is based on prototypes and expectancy fulfillment. Prototypes are ideal mental models of competent performance. Expectancies are anticipations of how communicative encounters are likely to unfold. If positive expectancies are fulfilled or negative expectancies unfulfilled by interpersonal communication, that performance is likely to be perceived as competent.

Despite the fact that most people communicate interpersonally every day, there are a variety of challenges to communicative knowledge. Communicators often make plans but fail to adapt them to changes in the situation. Furthermore, because it is efficient to communicate mindlessly, people often fail to attend to the situation. Finally, because most communicators are attempting to achieve some personal goal, they tend to be self-centered in their communication and therefore inattentive to the needs of other interactants.

These challenges are best overcome by enhancing self-monitoring, empathy, perspective taking, and knowledge-gaining strategies. Self-monitoring is the ability to pay attention to cues and information in the interaction context that can help guide communication. Empathy is the ability to feel similarly to another person's feelings. It is distinct from perspective taking, which is being able to see the world as another person sees it. Empathy is based on emotions, and perspective taking is based on ideas and thoughts. Together, empathy and perspective taking allow you to avoid self-centeredness and mindlessness, and to engage in better adapted planning. A final way of improving communicative knowledge is to use knowledge-gaining strategies such as questioning, altering the context to observe people's reactions, and self-disclosure.

Key Terms

- repertoire
- role
- script
- rules
- plan
- subplans
- efficiency
- competence principle
- prior success principle
- simplicity principle
- action assembly
- bottom-up process
- top-down process
- expectancy fulfillment
- plan adjustment
- mindlessness
- self-centered communicators
- self-monitoring
- empathy
- perspective taking
- knowledge-gaining strategies
- questioning
- contextual alteration

Building Knowlege

1. Of the two types of knowledge, content and procedural, which one are you least likely to be aware of? Why?
2. Identify a situation that you think is relatively well scripted. How flexible is that script? What factors might influence changes in that script? Why?
3. Identify a situation that you think has a lot of rules associated with it and a situation that has very few rules associated with it. What is different about these situations?
4. Explain the influence of positive and negative expectancies on impressions of competence. Are there encounters that you have had that illustrate both types of expectancies? Explain.
5. Think of a recent interpersonal communication encounter in which you did something differently than you usually do. Describe the action assembly of your behavior by identifying what similar situations you may have used to draw your actions.
6. What is your prototype of a competent teacher? Of a competent student? How prominent is communication in these prototypes? How well does your teacher fulfill the communication portion of your prototype? How well do you fulfill your communication prototype of a competent student? Did you use bottom-up or top-down processing to reach these evaluations?
7. What kinds of activities do you think you engage in most mindlessly? Which do you think you engage in mindfully? What is the difference between these types of activities, if any? How might you overcome your mindlessness?

Building Skills

Individual Exercises

1. The following six problems concern familiar or everyday scripts. Answer each of them, and do not read any further until you do so.
   a. If you had only one match, and entered a room in which there was a kerosene lamp, a wood-burning stove, and a gas fireplace, which would you light first?
   b. How many outs are in an inning of baseball?
   c. A patient is wheeled into the emergency room and the surgeon, looking at the patient, says, "I can't operate on this patient—he's my son!" The surgeon is not the patient's father. How is this possible?
   d. You have a dime in an otherwise empty wine bottle. The bottle is corked. How do you get the dime out without removing the cork or damaging the bottle in any way?
   e. How many animals of each species did Moses take aboard the ark with him?

f. Connect the following 9 dots using only straight lines, without removing your pen from the paper.

These questions seem simple enough. But people often answer them incorrectly, or cannot answer them at all. This is in part because each of them leads you to expect a script that is not actually the appropriate script, or because each leads you to focus on the wrong part of the script. In each case, discuss what led you to apply the wrong script. What scripts in everyday communication encounters might you experience in which you could apply the wrong script? Answers:

a. The match. We are led to think of lighting the sources of warmth, rather than the item we use to light these sources.

b. Six. We tend to think of baseball in terms of how many outs there are for our team. But there are two teams.

c. The surgeon is the patient's mother. We still tend to think of surgeons as men.

d. Push the cork in. We tend to think of wine bottles only in terms of removing the cork.

e. None. What was *Moses* doing on the ark? We see the terms "animals" and "ark," and the remaining script is overlaid onto the question, despite the fact that the word "Moses" is staring us in the face.

f. Follow along as illustrated. This problem tends to frustrate people because they think the 9 dots form a square. We are accustomed to seeing squares, and therefore think "inside the box." The only way to solve the problem is to think "outside the box."

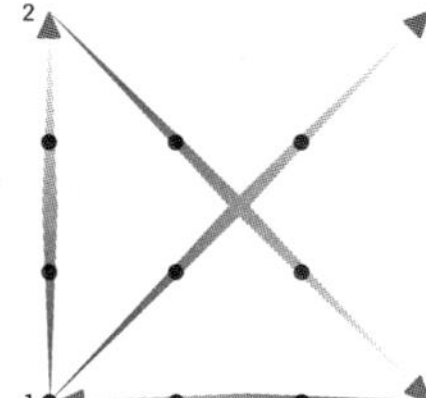

2. Think through some of the situations you have experienced (e.g., student-professor discussion about a grade, job interview, negotiating the price of a car, etc.). Choose one and write out the script for this situation. What factors might influence changes in that script? How rigid is this script? Why? How detailed is your script compared to those identified in this chapter?

3. The chart on page 261 identifies several types of behaviors and several types of situations. In the spaces provided, rate, using the scale, the appropriateness of each behavior for each situation.

4. For a week keep an interaction diary. After each conversation over 10 minutes long, whether face-to-face or mediated, take notes on the following aspects: When did it occur? Where did it occur? How long did it last? What was your relationship with the other person(s)? What were the main themes or topics of the conversation? What were your goals in the conversation? What rules would you say were most important in the situation? What cues best informed you of how to behave in the conversation? How competent were you and the other person? After the week of diaries has been completed, look them over for patterns. Compared to before the diary assignment, how well did you self-monitor your conversations? To what extent did you find yourself self-monitoring differently as you got more accustomed to making diary entries? How can self-monitoring improve your interpersonal competence in everyday conversation?

5. Think of an important conflict you have had with another person. Remember it in as much detail as you can. Go to the International Online Training Program on the Intractable Conflict Web site at **http://www.colorado.edu/conflict/peace/**. On their menu bar of topics, under "Conflict Problems" click on "Communication." Review the types of communication problems the site identifies. Return to the menu bar and under "Treatments" click on "Communication." You will see a list of strategies for "Treating Communication Problems." Review the techniques listed, occasionally clicking on any technique that seems particularly relevant to the communication problems you may have experienced in the conflict encounter you have recalled. How might you have behaved differently in the conflict in order to be a more competent interpersonal communicator, using the conflict management techniques discussed in this Web site?

6. In *InfoTrac College Edition*, enter the key term *communicator competence*. Retrieve and review the following article: Communication Quarterly, Spring 1995 v43 n2 p142(13). The funny people: a source-orientation to the communication of humor. Melissa Wanzer; Melanie Booth-Butterfield; Steven Booth-Butterfield. The competency of being humorous requires two types of communicative knowledge. First, humor requires content knowledge, that is, the joke or humorous idea. Second, humor requires procedural knowledge, or the way in which the humor needs to be delivered. Identify procedural types of knowledge needed to be competent at being humorous. Which of these types of knowledge do you think are most important? Why?

Situations/Goals (Question 3)

APPROPRIATE: 1 : 2 : 3 : 4 : 5 : INAPPROPRIATE

	CLASS-ROOM	FIRST DATE	INTERVIEW	ELEVATOR	OWN ROOM	TOTAL
Talk						
Kiss						
Argue						
Cry						
Laugh						
TOTAL						

If you add across each row, and then down each column, you will get a number ranging between 5 and 25. The higher the row sum, the more rule bound the behavior. The higher the column sum, the more rule bound the situation. What is it about these behaviors and situations that make them differ in terms of their rules?

Group Activities

1. One of the indirect ways we know how to communicate is by learning to play roles. We often look to others to tell us what role we should play. These persons are role models. Our role models include mothers, fathers, movie stars, rock stars, and historical figures such as Mother Teresa or Amelia Earhart. One way of developing your knowledge in any given situation is to imagine what your role models would do in that situation. List the three problematic communication situations you have experienced recently, and list the role model you would most want to follow as an example for how to behave in that situation. What would the model's response have been in each situation? Now compare your list of situations, role model, and responses to those of another classmate. What are the similarities and differences between your lists? Discuss what factors you think may have led to these similarities and differences.

2. Form groups of four students. Each member should write down three strategies each for gaining information on a first date. There should be one question, one contextual alteration, and one self-disclosure strategy for each member. Compare your list to those generated by the other members in the group. How competent do you think these strategies would be? Would any of them violate the rules or the scripts of the first date situation? Why?

3. Form a dyad with someone in your class you don't know very well.

   a. The chart on page 262 list several questions. Conduct a get acquainted conversation, making sure you don't ask the other person any the questions listed in the chart directly. After the conversation each member of the dyad should provide answers to questions, even if they are guesses.

   b. Compare your answers to your partner's answers regarding you. How accurate are they? How much can you expect to get to know a person from casual conversation?

4. Form groups of 3–5 students. Identify an interpersonal communication context of interest to the group. For example, your group might select an intimacy situation in which you ask someone to marry you, a confrontation situation in which you try to get a roommate to change a personal habit, a negotiation situation in which you are bargaining for a better deal on a car or computer system. Each member of your group should then individually construct his or her personal prototype of the competent person involved (for example, a potential mate, roommate, negotiator, etc.). The prototype should have a concept, individual, contextual, and behavioral level (see Figure 9.1). As a group, compare, discuss, and combine your answers to construct a group prototype. To what extent did other members come up with similar elements of the prototype? To what extent and in what ways is the group prototype more complete than your individual prototype? Why?

5. Using the same situation developed in question 4, individually identify the rules of the situation. Then, as

GETTING ACQUAINTED CONVERSATION (QUESTION 3)

a. What is the person's religious affiliation, if any?	**f.** Are/were the person's parents divorced?
b. Does the person have/want to have children?	**g.** Is the person in a satisfying romantic relationship?
c. Is the person basically happy most of the time?	**h.** Is this person a political liberal, conservative, independent, or politically disinterested?
d. Where would the person most like to visit/travel?	**i.** What is this person's favorite food or cuisine?
e. Would the person rather go to a formal ball or a casual party at someone's apartment?	**j.** What career does this person want after college?

a group, discuss, compare, and combine your answers to construct a group list of rules for the situation. To what extent did other members come up with similar rules for the situation? To what extent and in what ways is the group list of rules more complete than your individual list? Why?

References

Argyle, M., Furnham, A., & Graham, J. A. (1981). *Social situations.* Cambridge: Cambridge University Press.

Argyle, M., & Henderson, M. (1984). The rules of friendship. *Journal of Social and Personal Relationships, 1,* 211–237.

Battaglia, D. M., Richard, F. D., Datteri, D. L., & Lord, C. G. (1998). Breaking up is (relatively) easy to do: A script for the dissolution of close relationships. *Journal of Social and Personal Relationships, 15,* 829–845.

Berger, C. R. (1997). *Planning strategic interaction: Attaining goals through communicative action.* Mahwah, NJ: Erlbaum.

Berger, C. R., & Bradac, J. J. (1982). *Language and social knowledge: Uncertainty in interpersonal relations.* London: Edward Arnold.

Burgoon, J. K. (1995). *Interpersonal adaptation.* Cambridge: Cambridge University Press.

Collier, M. J. (1988). A comparison of conversations among and between domestic culture groups: How intra- and intercultural competencies vary. *Communication Quarterly, 36,* 122–144.

Duran, R. L., & Spitzberg, B. H. (1995). Toward the development and validation of a measure of cognitive communication competence. *Communication Quarterly, 43,* 259–275.

Egland, K. L., Spitzberg, B. H., & Zormeier, M. M. (1996). Flirtation and conversational competence in cross-sex platonic and romantic relationships. *Communication Reports, 9,* 105–118.

Greene, J. O. (1993). An action assembly perspective on social skill. *Communication Theory, 3,* 26–49.

Hecht, M. L., & Ribeau, S. (1984). Ethnic communication: A comparative analysis of satisfying communication. *International Journal of Intercultural Relations, 8,* 135–151.

Honeycutt, J. M., Cantrill, J. G., & Greene, R. W. (1991). Memory structures for relational escalation: A cognitive test of the sequencing of relational actions and strategies. *Human Communication Research, 16,* 62–90.

Honeycutt, J. M., Woods, B. L., & Fontenot, K. (1993). The endorsement of communication conflict rules as a function of engagement, marriage, and marital ideology. *Journal of Social and Personal Relationships, 10,* 285–304.

Koeppel, L. B., Montagne-Miller, Y., O'Hair, D., & Cody, M. J. (1993). Friendly? Flirting? Wrong? In P. J. Kalbfleisch (Ed.), *Interpersonal communication: Evolving interpersonal relationships* (pp. 13–32). Hillsdale, NJ: Erlbaum.

Martin, J. N., Hecht, M. L., & Larkey, L. K. (1994). Conversational improvement strategies for interethnic communication: African American and European American perspectives. *Communication Monographs, 61,* 236–255.

Pavitt, C., & Haight, L. (1985). The "competent communicator" as a cognitive prototype. *Human Communication Research, 12,* 225–241.

Pryor, J. B., & Merluzzi, T. V. (1985). The role of expertise in processing social interaction scripts. *Journal of Experimental Social Psychology, 21,* 362–379.

Rose, S., & Frieze, I. H. (1993). Young singles' contemporary dating scripts. *Sex Roles, 28,* 499–509.

Snyder, M. (1987). *Public appearances, private realities: The psychology of self-monitoring.* New York: Freeman.

Spitzberg, B. H., & Brunner, C. C. (1991). Toward a theoretical integration of context and competence inference research. *Western Journal of Speech Communication 56,* 28–46.

CHAPTER 10

Learning Objectives

After studying this chapter you should be able to:

1. Distinguish among skills, abilities, and behaviors.
2. Explain the link between skills and impressions.
3. Identify key behaviors involved in the skill of coordination.
4. Identify key behaviors involved in the skill of composure.
5. Identify key behaviors involved in the skill of expressiveness.
6. Identify key behaviors involved in the skill of attentiveness.
7. Describe a way of balancing flexibility with selectivity.
8. Describe a way of balancing adaptability with consistency.

Interpersonal Relationships: Developing Skills

Dipak, an international student from India, roomed with Chad in an apartment near campus. They had met in a political science class, and when they realized they both needed a new place for the coming semester, they arranged to find an apartment together. Although they had developed a friendship in class, once they moved in together it became clear before long that they had quite a few differences in their lifestyles.

One Sunday morning, after a particularly busy weekend preparing for upcoming papers and exams, Dipak woke up and walked into the common space to brew a pot of coffee. The chaos of their living area shocked him. He had difficulty seeing the floor because every square inch of it, as well as all the tables, chairs, countertops, and surfaces, were covered by books, wadded-up papers, empty pizza boxes, soda cans, blankets, and potato chip bags. Chad was sprawled out on the sofa covered by an old sleeping bag. As Dipak tried with little success to clear a path through the mess to get to the kitchen, in frustration he yelled "This place is a disaster zone!" waking Chad from his two hours of sleep.

Chad groggily made some excuses about having an exam the next day and having invited some friends from class over to study after Dipak had gone to bed. The exchange quickly spiraled into a shouting match, and Dipak said he couldn't live like this—the place is like a pigsty. Chad continued to make excuses and say it is only temporary. Dipak countered that it is a mess all the time. Escalating the argument, Chad inquired, "Are you implying I'm a pig?" Furious, Dipak replied, "Yes, that is exactly what I am implying!" "Well, what would you know of pigs, given your crazy religion that worships every reasonable source of meat because it might be your dead uncle?" Chad angrily accused. Dipak began to shake visibly. "At least I believe in *something!* You're nothing but a typical godless American with no values and . . ." Chad interrupted midsentence: "You don't like the way I am? Find someone else crazy enough to live with you someplace else. Just get out of my face and let me get some sleep for once." •••

Conflicts and arguments often bring out the worst in people (Spitzberg, Canary, & Cupach, 1994). But why? There are many reasons, but one of them is that many of us have never learned or had the opportunity to refine competent skills for managing conflict. Both Dipak and Chad are generally nice, well-intentioned people who are usually socially skilled and polite most of the time. However, they come from family backgrounds and cultural contexts that gave them different schemas for handling conflict. Dipak has learned to conform when possible or otherwise avoid conflict. Chad has learned to be competitive and internalized the belief that to withdraw from conflict is a sign of weakness. Dipak's style of conflict management works well when the issues are not too serious or ongoing, but it leads him to bottle up his dissatisfactions. In this confrontation, they boiled over and he exploded. Chad's style of conflict, in contrast, leads him to refuse to let someone else "win," which in turn leads him to try to always get the last word in. Dipak's and Chad's styles of conflict did not allow for a competent resolution of their differences. However, these were the only conflict management skills that Dipak and Chad had available to them. The concepts of rational argument, clarifying each other's concerns and interests and calmly discussing possible solutions, simply did not occur to either of them.

This chapter examines interpersonal communication skills as they play a role not only in any given conversation, but as these conversations create, maintain, and cause problems for our relationships. As you saw in Chapter 9, ultimately all we know of any relationship partner is what he or she shows us through behavior. Because we cannot know exactly what a relationship partner thinks or feels, our only choice is to infer these things from his or her behavior. This behavior, in turn, is a reflection of this person's communication skills.

The Nature of Communication Skills

Most of us feel like we are enrolled in a beginner's class in relationships at least some of the time. We often find ourselves complicating relationships or simply making them worse even though we want them to go smoothly. We understand how different behavior could improve our relationships. In other words, we are generally motivated and knowledgeable about our communication in relationships. Yet we often communicate in ways that are less than competent. Why does this happen? First, we need an understanding of the nature of skills.

CHARACTERISTICS OF SKILLS

A skill is a repeatable, goal-oriented action sequence enacted in a given context. As you saw in Chapter 2, skills are behaviors directed toward the achievement of preferred outcomes in a given context. Several key concepts are involved in understanding this simple notion.

Skills Are Actions

First, **actions** are the behaviors performed by a person. You do not enact all the behaviors you are able to perform. You select which behaviors to enact on the basis of motivation and knowledge. If you are highly motivated, you search your knowledge for the best possible skills. If you are highly knowledgeable, you have a broad and deep repertoire of behaviors from which to select. Finally, if you are skilled, you have enacted and refined this knowledge over time so your actions can be carried out appropriately and effectively.

In many ways, every relationship is a beginner's class.

By permission of Creators Syndicate, Inc.

Skills are the link between motivation and knowledge on the one hand and actions on the other. You may be able to follow a recipe. But are you *skilled* at following the recipe? The word *skilled* implies a sense of quality about your ability and suggests the behaviors used to follow the recipe will be performed in a way that reflects this quality. In other words, can you cook well enough to get by, or are you a great cook? This sense of quality is vital to the notion of skill.

To say that someone is skilled therefore implies at least two things. First, the person is able to perform certain behaviors involved in accomplishing some goal, and the person enacts these behaviors at a certain level of quality. These two meanings of the concept of skill are often confused. For our purposes, we reserve the first meaning for the concept *skill,* and the second for the concept *competence.* Thus, to say that someone is skilled is to say this person is able to perform a series of behaviors in pursuit of a goal. To say this person is "competent" is to say that these behaviors are performed in a high-quality manner, that is, appropriately and effectively.

Knowledge Link

Recalling Chapters 2 and 8, what role do goals play in linking motivation with skills?

Skills Are Goal Oriented

A skill is a set of behaviors directed toward achieving some particular outcome. These outcomes are the goals that communicators are attempting to achieve. As you saw in Chapter 2, goals are a key feature of defining a communicator's effectiveness, and thus competence. The more of your goals you achieve through your communication, the more effective you are. Goals generally define the skill itself. For example, *conflict skills* refer to achieving your goal of resolving conflict. *Assertiveness skills* refer to the goal of asserting your rights. *Argumentation skills* refer to the goal of constructing arguments. So skills achieve some outcome. The quality with which they achieve these outcomes determines the quality of the skill itself, and in large part, your effectiveness. Dipak and Chad displayed rather poor quality conflict management skills because neither seemed to achieve their desired goals.

Skills Are Repeatable

A third characteristic of skills is that they are repeatable. Returning to the cooking example, a person might follow a complex recipe very competently by luck at least once. We cannot say this person is a skilled cook, however, because he or she may not be able to repeat this cooking task as desired. Similarly, you might tell a joke with all the right inflections and delivery one time, but not the next. Such subtleties can make all the difference in telling a joke, and the skill of telling it is in the ability to perform it the same, or better, as the context calls for that performance.

Skills Are Sequential

As you saw in Chapter 9, most of what we know about communicating can be formulated into scripts. Scripts, in turn, are always sequential; that is, certain behaviors need to occur before others for the action sequence to be competent. Skill sequences may have great flexibility, but they always have at least some sequential order. This can be illustrated simply at the level of the sentence. Consider the following sentences.

> "Dipak and I had a big argument last night about the neatness of the dorm room."
> "The neatness of the dorm room was the basis for a big argument between Dipak and me last night."
> "Last night, I had a big argument with Dipak regarding the dorm room's neatness."

Each of these statements communicates roughly the same idea, using similar words. Each of these sequences works. However, consider an alternative sequence for the first sentence:

> "A about and argument big Dipak dorm had I last neatness night of room the the."

This sentence actually has a clear sequence. The words are arranged alphabetically. But this sequence is neither grammatical nor sensible. So not just any sequence will be skilled. Only sequences that provide a possibility for accomplishing a contextual goal are skilled.

Skills Are Contextual

Skills are also contextual, in that they depend on the context in which they are performed. Skills are contextual because the goals to which skills are directed are contextual. Recall that goals are the preferred outcomes or objectives that a person seeks through interaction. Recall also that one of the types of context is the function of the communication. A person seeking social or emotional support is performing communication in a different context than a person seeking to persuade someone to clean the dorm room. The goals in these examples define different contexts to which the communicators' skills are directed.

Some goals are virtually universal. For example, people generally try to achieve the goal of feeling good about themselves and being polite to others. But even these goals can change depending on the context. People with low self-esteem sometimes select friends who reinforce that low self-esteem even though the low self-esteem is unpleasant (Robinson & Smith-Lovin, 1992). Other people will be rude to others if provoked enough. In fact, most of our everyday communicative goals are fairly specific to a given context.

ABSTRACTNESS OF SKILLS

Skills exist at many different levels. These levels reflect an **abstraction dimension** of skills. Some communication skills are very specific and objective. Such skills are **molecular skills.** Just like molecules make up larger substances, molecular skills are the ingredients of broader types of skills. Molecular skills include such behaviors as gestures, eye contact, smiling, vocabulary, articulation, vocal variety, and so forth. Other communication skills are broader and more general in nature. These skills are **molar skills.** Molar skills represent the assembly of molecular skills to create the performance of molar skills such as assertiveness, self-disclosure, social support, conflict management, deception, and wit.

If molecular skills are the bricks and mortar, molar skills are the actual rooms built from the bricks and mortar. But these rooms serve different purposes. Living rooms are different from kitchens. So gestures and vocabulary are used in most conversations, but in different ways depending on the goals of that situation. You might use animated gestures in an argument with a roommate as well as in telling a joke. You are using the same molecular skill but for different molar skills in different contexts. Much of communication competence depends on selecting the right molecular skill for the relevant molar skill. Thus if you use loud volume to express how "serious" you are about the context, but do so in offering social support to a friend at a funeral, the molecular skill of volume is not well adapted to the molar skill of support. Later in this chapter we identify the molar skills of interpersonal communication competence along with the types of molecular skills that comprise those more abstract skills.

IMPRESSIONS & SKILLS

One of the most common misconceptions about competence is that skills *make* you competent. As you saw in Chapter 2, motivation, knowledge, and skills make you more *likely* to be viewed as competent, but they do not guarantee your competence (Canary & Spitzberg, 1990). Competence is the impression that skills have been performed appropriately and effectively. Over time, communicators learn how to refine and adapt their skills so that most of the time their communicative actions are viewed as at least maximizing or sufficing in competence. However, in any given context, a communicator may use the skills he or she has always used competently in that context, only to be viewed by someone as minimizing in incompetence. You may have offered apologies and said "I'm sorry" many times in ways that were perceived as competent. You performed the skill of apology. In any given context, however, your apology turns out to have been repeatable, but not competent in the eyes of the person to whom you are communicating. You were still "skilled," but not competent in this context. Optimizing competence will require you find the skills that will achieve the perception of appropriateness and effectiveness you desire, or else conclude the other person's view of your competence is no longer important.

This distinction between impressions and behaviors is central to the model of interpersonal competence. As you've seen, a given set of behaviors comprises a skill. A skill can then be repeated until it becomes efficiently and confidently performed. But its competence still depends on how it is perceived, interpreted, and evaluated. Fortunately, such impressions are rarely arbitrary. In a given culture certain types of skills and behaviors are more likely to be viewed as competent than are others. The question then is which skills are most likely to be viewed as competent. The following section addresses this question.

Knowledge Link

How does attribution theory help explain the relationship between impressions of competence and communication skills?

Types of Interpersonal Skills

If competence varies from context to context, how can you hope to develop a set of skills that helps you communicate competently across these contexts? Even though contexts differ widely, certain molar skills, and the molecular skills that comprise them, are important across these varied contexts. The rules of sports differ widely, but most still require eye-hand coordination, fast reflexes, endurance, and so forth. Similarly, even though communication contexts vary considerably, certain skills are important across these contexts.

The communication skills discussed here represent four molar skills that are useful in all interpersonal contexts. The molecular skills discussed within each molar skill can be viewed a bit like building blocks. A box of building blocks may give you pictures of basic models you can build from the pieces, but you are actually able to build an infinite number of models from the blocks provided. Similarly, the skills of coordination, composure, expressiveness, and attentiveness discussed here are pictures of key models you can build from the building blocks of interpersonal skills (Spitzberg, 1994b), but you should not limit yourself to only these models or the illustrations within each molar skill.

Coordination

Coordination is the skill of managing the flow of the interaction. It is involved in regulating whose turn it is to speak, developing topics for discussion, maintaining the conversation, and entering and exiting conversations. The skill of coordination generally is considered competent when interactants engage in conversation that is "smooth" rather than awkward. Smoothness, at least in North American cultures, implies that uncomfortable silences in which people are wondering what to say next or whose turn it is to speak are rare.

Smooth conversation also implies that interactants don't interfere excessively with each other's efforts to contribute to the interaction. You might, like most people, think this means avoiding interrupting others. In fact, this belief is so widespread it is often restated as a general communication rule: Don't interrupt others when they are speaking. However, this rule's inaccuracy illustrates just how fallible people's intuitions about communication can be. When everyday conversations are studied word by word and turn by turn, interruptions are both complex and common. They also tend not to be disruptive; on the contrary, they are even considered competent most of the time (Kennedy & Camden, 1983).

Interruptions occur in many forms. The two most common forms are talkovers and deep interruptions. **Talkovers** are instances in which you say something during someone else's turn to talk. Most of these interruptions are reinforcers in which the listener provides feedback to the speaker that his or her words are understood and/or need clarification. As you saw in Chapter 6 in the discussion of responding skills, expressions such as "Hm-hm," "yeah," "uh-huh," "Really?," "You're kidding," and so on, are common expressions inserted while another person is speaking to display listener involvement. Other types of talkovers are competent forms of assistance, such as when the listener supplies the right word that allows the speaker to continue speaking. These types of talkovers are competent when the speaker struggles to find the right word, and thereby risks introducing an uncomfortable pause in the speech.

Deep interruptions are interruptions that take over a speaker's turn in the middle of a speaker's statement. This is what most people mean when they warn not to interrupt when others are speaking. However, even deep interruptions are sometimes neither disruptive nor incompetent. In lively group interactions, members are often so excited by the topic of conversation and working toward a common goal that they build on each others' thoughts before the speaker is even finished expressing the idea. Some couples, especially many family members who share an extensive history, find that they carry on conversations for hours rarely finishing a statement. Yet they evaluate such conversations as highly competent because the interruptions signal how attuned they are to each other rather than how much they only care about their own opinions.

© 1995 Watterson/Dist. by Universal Press Syndicate

Even if conversations aren't contests, people often treat them as if they were.

CALVIN AND HOBBES © Watterson. Reprinted with permission of UNIVERSAL PRESS.

Although talkovers and deep interruptions are considered competent in most contexts, there are contexts in which they are less likely to be perceived as such. Situations in which interruptions seem less competent include more formal situations, situations where the speaker has higher status than the listener, when the speaker is expending considerable effort to keep focused on his or her speech, and when the speaker clearly knows far more about the topic of conversation than the listener.

One of the reasons for interruptions is that silences, even extremely short silences, are the doorways through which people generally get to take a turn in conversation. Because deep interruptions occur less often than talkovers, and are more likely to be viewed as incompetent, most people try to avoid deep interruptions. One way to avoid them is by paying close attention to possible conversational openings. Most communicators don't need much of an opening to take a turn at speaking. One of the world's foremost scholars of conversation claims that any pause of 1 second or more is likely to represent some kind of problem in the conversation (Jefferson, 1989). This seems to be a universal principle. As a result, most of us are quite skilled at jumping in when such an opening presents itself.

If silences and interruptions are ways in which we manage silence, the activity we use to avoid silence is the conversation itself. Avoiding silence implies that the communicators are able to find a topic to talk about. This reflects the skill of **topic initiation,** introducing topics for discussion. Competent topic initiation typically involves the development of topics relevant to both or all interactants as well as to the context at hand. Such topics permit all interactants to participate in the conversation. Competent topic initiation also continues threads of topics from previous conversations, adding a dimension of cohesiveness. This cohesiveness of topics over the course of conversation is highly flexible. You may frequently find yourself in conversations where you wonder how you got from the beginning topic of the conversation to the topic you are currently discussing. Yet, if you were to trace the turn-by-turn shift of topics, you would see that each turn represents a reasonable and relevant extension of the previous topics.

Composure

In the Quigmans cartoon, fear of intimacy is shown as both a tangible reaction to social anxiety and shyness, but also as a self-fulfilling prophecy. The characters in the cartoon may fear intimacy, which is why they have signed up for the class; however, they are behaving in ways that almost guarantee they will never discover any rewards from intimacy either.

When fears are expressed in behavior, they often lead to the very things that make you afraid.

Copyright Los Angeles Syndicate. Reprinted by permission. 1999.

Recall the discussion of social anxiety and shyness in Chapter 8. Anxiety and shyness also influence social behavior. That is, negative motivation affects people's interpersonal communication skills. Most people are familiar with these effects and experience at least occasional fears associated with social and communication contexts. Being interviewed for a desirable job, discussing the dissolution of a relationship, asserting yourself in front of others, and other such difficult communication contexts often provoke fears in us. These fears, in turn, often deter us from doing and saying what we prefer, or interfere with how well we communicate.

The behaviors resulting from negative interpersonal motivation are probably familiar to most of you. Avoiding eye contact, fidgeting, tripping over words, speaking quietly with a quavering voice, initiating speaking turns less often, and displaying an impression of nervousness are all behaviors that result from negative motivation. On the other hand, positive motivation is associated with confidence and assertiveness. People who are strongly motivated and knowledgeable tend to be more forceful and charismatic in their communication style. Such people are more fluent, speak with a steadier vocal tone and louder volume, use more confident and expressive gestures, and engage in eye contact. Positively motivated communicators initiate more speaking turns, spend more time talking, and appear more in control of their behavior as well as the course the conversation takes.

The communication skills that manage negative motivations and show positive motivation reflect the molar skill of composure in conversation. **Composure** is the skill of displaying control and confidence. A lack of composure typically produces an impression that a communicator is anxious, nervous, shy, or apprehensive. A person skilled at projecting composure is more likely to be viewed as competent, confident, focused, motivated, and assertive. Specifically, the skill of composure can best be understood in terms of its more competent form of performance: assertiveness. When composure occurs in excess, it is more likely to appear as aggressiveness. When composure is lacking, it is more likely to appear as passiveness.

Knowledge Link

Looking back at Chapter 8, what is the impact of negative motivation on a communicator's composure skills?

Assertiveness is the skill of expressing one's rights or views without violating another's rights or views. Assertiveness is the ability to "give voice" to your interests, position, needs, desires, and opinions in a way that is appropriate to the context. Assertiveness is different from its alternatives of passivity and aggression. **Aggressive communication** is the expression of your rights or views in a way that violates other's rights or views. It generally represents an excess of composure in that all you care about are your own motives. Finally, **passive communication** is the avoidance of self-expression or the accommodation to others' concerns over your own. It generally represents a lack of composure. In the opening vignette, when Chad made an excuse about the mess being due to late-night studying, it was a passive attempt to deal with the accusation and implications that it should have been cleaned up. When the interaction degraded into name calling, it became more aggressive. Neither Chad nor Dipak found a more assertive manner in which to discuss the issue of the neatness of their shared space.

To better differentiate these three concepts, consider the following situations:

1. You have been standing in line for hours to buy tickets to a popular concert, and several people walk up to someone they know in line in front of you and start up a conversation as if they are now part of the line.
2. You are up studying late for a final exam to be held the next day. The people in the apartment next to yours are partying and playing loud distracting music at 1 A.M.
3. You are at a family dinner, meeting your romantic partner's parents and siblings for the first time. Your partner's father expresses an opinion that you find offensive, and no one at the table seems to take notice of the comment as anything unusual.

In each of these situations, you have an opinion you would express in an ideal world. Indeed, if you found yourself in these situations you probably would have a planned response. Interestingly, however, the research is clear that most people "think" a better game than they actually play (Spitzberg & Cupach, 1984). That is, in the abstract it's easy to believe you would actually say something in these situations, but most people don't. People are often nervous about causing trouble or disrupting the situation. Many think that if they assert themselves, they will be seen as rude or aggressive. Indeed, when assertiveness is performed with abruptness and intensity, it is often interpreted as aggressive.

Returning to the opening vignette, consider how the interaction might have unfolded differently. Instead of Dipak aggressively yelling, "This place is a disaster zone!" he could have awakened Chad gently and assertively said, "Chad, I know you had a study session last night. But on several occasions I have cleaned our shared space only to find it later messed up by you and your friends. I have also asked you several times to clean up after you make such messes. This is my space too, and I think it's unfair of you to take advantage of my rights in this situation. Please wake up and clean things up." Similarly, Chad passively tried to avoid the issue by claiming that he had a study session the night before. Instead, he could have asserted, "Dipak, you're right that the place is a mess. But I don't think it's fair to expect me to have it clean early in the morning after a study session. I'll clean it later today."

Composure is important, but it can be demonstrated in very different ways. Typically the most competent form is **empathic assertion,** the attempt to recognize and grant legitimacy to others in a situation while simultaneously expressing your own rights or views. In our examples, the assertive responses first attempt to acknowledge the other people's reasons for their actions (i.e., "I know you are all having fun, but . . . ,"), but then assert your position in the situation. In doing so, you are not invalidating their rights in the process of trying to achieve your own. In essence, it is an attempt to be effective while simultaneously trying to be appropriate.

Knowledge Link

Given your understanding of empathy discussed in Chapter 9, how does empathy help make assertive behavior more competent?

EXPRESSIVENESS

Expressiveness is the skill of animating verbal and nonverbal communication. Expressiveness makes communication behavior lively, varied, and colorful. It serves as the primary avenue for displaying affect and emotion in interaction, as well as getting across particular shades of meaning and intention. Expressive communication relies heavily on facial displays, gestures, vocal variety, and word choices. If you have experienced someone with an emotionally flat vocal tone, or who is extremely monotone, you quickly realize that such a voice detracts from the communication.

As you saw in Chapter 5, the voice provides an important window into expressiveness (Scherer, 1986). The voice has three basic forms of expressiveness: wide-narrow, tense-lax, and full-thin. The **wide-narrow dimension** describes a range from lower frequency tones produced by a relaxed vocal tract to higher frequency tones produced by tense vocal tracts. Generally, people using wider voices are viewed as more competent and those with narrow voices as less competent. The **tense-lax dimension** refers to a range from the harshness of a metallic or piercing voice to a continuous more muffled and relaxed voice. Generally, people using lax voices are viewed as more competent than those using tense voices. Finally, the **full-thin dimension** of vocal expressiveness describes a vocal range from deep and forceful resonance, voices that communicate strong energy to more rapid and shallow resonance and low-energy voices. Generally, people with fuller voices are viewed as more competent than those with thin voices.

The skill of expressiveness is also evident through nonverbal messages sent though facial expressions and eyes. The face, particularly the eyes, is considered a window into a person's true feelings. Despite this assumption, we learn early in life to control or edit our facial expression so as not to reveal feelings we don't want others to see. This interpersonal skill of managing facial expressions becomes vital to competent communication in a variety of situations. Many situations call for polite responses that mute true feelings. For example, a friend may ask you what you think of her new hairstyle. Although it may make you want to laugh out loud, you are more likely to express a more toned-down response. When negotiating, the other side may make an exciting offer, yet cautious approval or neutrality often constitute a more competent response as opposed to revealing your delight at the offer to the other party. Rather than deceptive, these situations are representative of the nature of social interaction and the roles we play, and the roles that society requires of us to function smoothly.

Aside from the ability to control facial expressions, the range of facial expressiveness is also important to competence. In most contexts, people who are more facially expressive are perceived as more competent and attractive (Sabatelli & Rubin, 1986), and the resulting interactions are judged as more satisfying (Friedman, DiMatteo, & Taranta, 1980). Even something as simple as a smile can positively impact people's impressions of a communicator (Harwood & Williams, 1998). In short, facial expressiveness generally enhances a communicator's competence.

Collectively, the expressiveness skills of using your voice and face have a great influence on whether people find you interesting or not. However, there are other things that influence others' interest. One way of thinking about the value of expressiveness is to think of how you might describe a boring communicator. Boring communicators are passive, tedious, sometimes distracting, unemotional, self-focused, and seem to engage only in small talk or trite sayings (Leary, Rogers, Canfield, & Coe, 1986). Every one of these characteristics refers to some aspect of expressiveness. If a lack of expressiveness leads to boredom, it follows that expressiveness in communication leads to excitement, all other things being equal. Indeed, communicating in an animated style has a powerful effect on people's tendency to remember you and view you as competent (Norton, 1984).

ATTENTIVENESS

Expressiveness is largely about revealing the self to others. As such, it is a largely self-oriented skill. The skill of attentiveness, however, is more an other-oriented skill. **Attentiveness** is the skill of showing interest in, concern for, and attention to the other person or persons in the interaction. Attentiveness is the ability to involve the person with whom you're communicating in the interaction and to demonstrate your own involvement with that person and his or her contribution to the conversation.

Knowledge Link

Considering the discussion of listening in Chapter 6, what is the connection between listening and attentiveness?

Attentiveness significantly overlaps with listening, the topic of Chapter 6, but is also distinct in many ways. The goal of attentiveness is not to decode exactly what the other person is saying; rather it is to behave in ways that involve the other person in the interaction. This involvement can take many forms, only some of which include listening skills.

Two closely related aspects of attentiveness that can greatly improve or impair the skill of attentiveness are topic development and time management. **Topic development,** which typically is used after topic initiation, is the management of the subject under discussion in a conversation. Topic development progresses in two basic ways: topic shifts and questions. A topic shift is illustrated in the following example:

> MARY: My summer place has been such a blessing this year.
> JOHN: I know, I sure would like a place like that, the way I've been feeling, but I've got to earn the bread first, you know?
> MARY: Yeah.
> JOHN: I figure that if I work enough this year and next, I'll be able to check out that place in Vermont again and maybe . . ." (Derber, 1979, p. 26)

Here John develops the topic into an area of interest to himself. This skill, when used carefully, can actually show competence because it requires careful attention to the topic of the other person in order to make the transition smoothly. However, most people want to talk about a topic of interest to themselves, and this is where the second skill of topic development is relevant: questioning.

Questions invite the other person to determine where the topic goes. But you can also influence that topical development through the types of questions you use. Questions come in two forms. **Open-ended questions** permit the other person wide discretion in how to answer. They are contrasted with **closed-ended questions,** which give the respondent very limited options in answering. For example, "What's your major?" and "Where were you born?" are closed ended. They generally call for one-word answers and do not supply topical materials for the respondent to elaborate on. In contrast, consider the following questions: "What got you interested in your major?" and "What, if anything, do

CloseUp on Conflict

Conflict, Assertiveness, & Competence

As YOU'VE SEEN before, Cathy and Irving are motivated and knowledgeable about how to engage in disagreements and conflicts. However, they lack the skills to apply their motivation and knowledge. One of the reasons is that conflict tends to bring the worst out in people. Conflict is difficult to manage in part because it pits the key competence dimensions against one another. You are trying to be effective by achieving your goals. However, the other person considers these goals inappropriate. Thus, in the attempt to pursue your effectiveness, you are likely to be perceived as inappropriate, and the other person's attempts at keeping you from achieving your goals will in turn seem inappropriate to you. In a conflict situation, the extent to which the other person is effective, you are likely to be ineffective. In short, it is very difficult for people involved in a conflict to be competent, that is, both appropriate and effective.

Research on competence in conflict has identified three molar conflict skills. *Avoidance skills* function to displace conflict. You postpone the conflict to another time or place to avoid dealing with the issue at a particular moment, or you sidetrack the interaction so it is forgotten or redirected. Avoidance often involves shifting the topic of discussion, postponing the discussion until later, or simply leaving the situation when the conflict seems ready to get out of hand. In the opening vignette, Chad could have asked to talk with Dipak later that morning, or Chad might have started talking about how his exam was coming up soon and how he had to get ready. Avoidance is commonly assumed to be an incompetent approach to conflict, but some classic research showed it sometimes helps communicators avoid the type of escalating conflict that enveloped Dipak and Chad (Raush, Barry, Hertel, & Swain, 1974).

The second conflict skill is distributive interaction. *Distributive skills* attempt to divide, that is, distribute the outcomes of the conflict so that you win more than the other person. It is a maximizing and aggressive approach to communication. Deception, persistent argumentation, yelling, criticizing, complaining, and refusing to admit fault are all forms of distributive communication. Although we generally don't think of these as "skills" of conflict management, some communicators are clearly better than others in using these skills. Furthermore, generally speaking, the more communicators use these skills, the more incompetently they are perceived (Spitzberg, Canary, & Cupach, 1994). Certainly Dipak and Chad engaged in their share of distributive communication in the opening vignette and viewed each other's approaches to the disagreement as incompetent.

The final conflict skill is integrative communication. Whereas distributive skills attempt to divide the outcomes of the conflict, *integrative skills* attempt to bring your goals and the other person's goals together so both of you can achieve what you want. It involves careful interaction that uncovers both persons' goals, clarifies the importance of these goals, identifies possible options, and tries to

Being motivated and knowledgeable in conflict management is not enough if you don't also have the skills to manage conflict.

CATHY © 1994 Cathy Guisewite. Reprinted with permission of Universal Press Syndicate. All rights reserved.

CloseUp cont'd

develop a plan that achieves everyone's interests. Had Dipak and Chad calmed down, and discussed ways in which Chad might get the room cleaned up if Dipak gave him another 24 hours until after the exam, it would illustrate more of an integrative approach to the conflict.

Research on conflict has made three things clear about these skills (Spitzberg et al., 1994). First, in any given situation or context, any one of these skills *can* be competent. Sometimes it is best to avoid a conflict rather than let your anger loose (Canary, Spitzberg, & Semic, 1998). Sometimes distributive skills are the only way to escape being exploited by someone who is determined to be distributive, such as in negotiating for the best price on a car.

Second, it is the competence with which you engage in these skills that determines the impact of these behaviors on your relationship with the other person. It is not as important *which* skill you use, so much as how competent the skill is perceived to be in the context in which you use it. Thus, if distributive skill is viewed as the most competent form of conflict in a given relationship, then it will tend to lead to a satisfying, trusting, and likable relationship. If, in contrast, avoidance skill is viewed as most competent, then it is the behavior most likely to lead to a satisfying and trusting, relationship.

Finally, across most situations, competing behavior, particularly aggressive competitive behavior, tends to be viewed as relatively incompetent. Conversely, across most situations, collaborative behavior tends to be viewed as competent.

you miss about where you were born?" These concern the same topics as the closed-ended questions, but direct the respondent to become much more involved in the process of developing the topic.

The second aspect of topic development that can improve or impair attentiveness is **time management,** the skill of balancing the relative proportion of time each communicator gets to speak during a conversation. Achieving the right balance between speaking time and attentiveness is crucial to competent communication. On the one hand, the skill of expressiveness involves taking time in a conversation to reveal your feelings and interests. On the other hand, the skill of attentiveness involves allowing the other person to express himself or herself and showing interest through listening and openness. Research shows that people are perceived as more competent the more time they spend speaking relative to the other person, but only up to a point. When someone begins talking 70%, 80%, or 90% of the time rather than letting others take their turn at conversation, this person tends to be viewed as less competent (Wheeless, Frymier, & Thompson, 1992). Communicators who dominate topic development to such extremes tend to be viewed as egotistical and manipulative, and thus incompetent.

The discussion of time management demonstrates just how subtle the relationship is between skills and competence. Too little of something, such as talk time, tends to be viewed as incompetent. But too much of the same thing, in this case, talking all the time in a conversation, is also likely to be perceived as incompetent. This subtle relationship suggests several challenges to managing interpersonal skills in relationships.

Knowledge Link

What kind of context is created by a communicator who speaks too much of the time versus too little of the time?

Four molar skills of interpersonal communication competence have been identified. These molar skills are comprised of smaller, more molecular skills. Some of these molecular skills, like building blocks, are used to construct more than one molar skill. To illustrate these concepts, Figure 10.1 shows how certain molecular skills obviously comprise more than one molar skill. Expression of personal opinions, for example, is clearly an aspect of a communicator's expressiveness. In addition, expressing personal opinions also reveals a person's sense of composure and confidence in speaking up for himself or

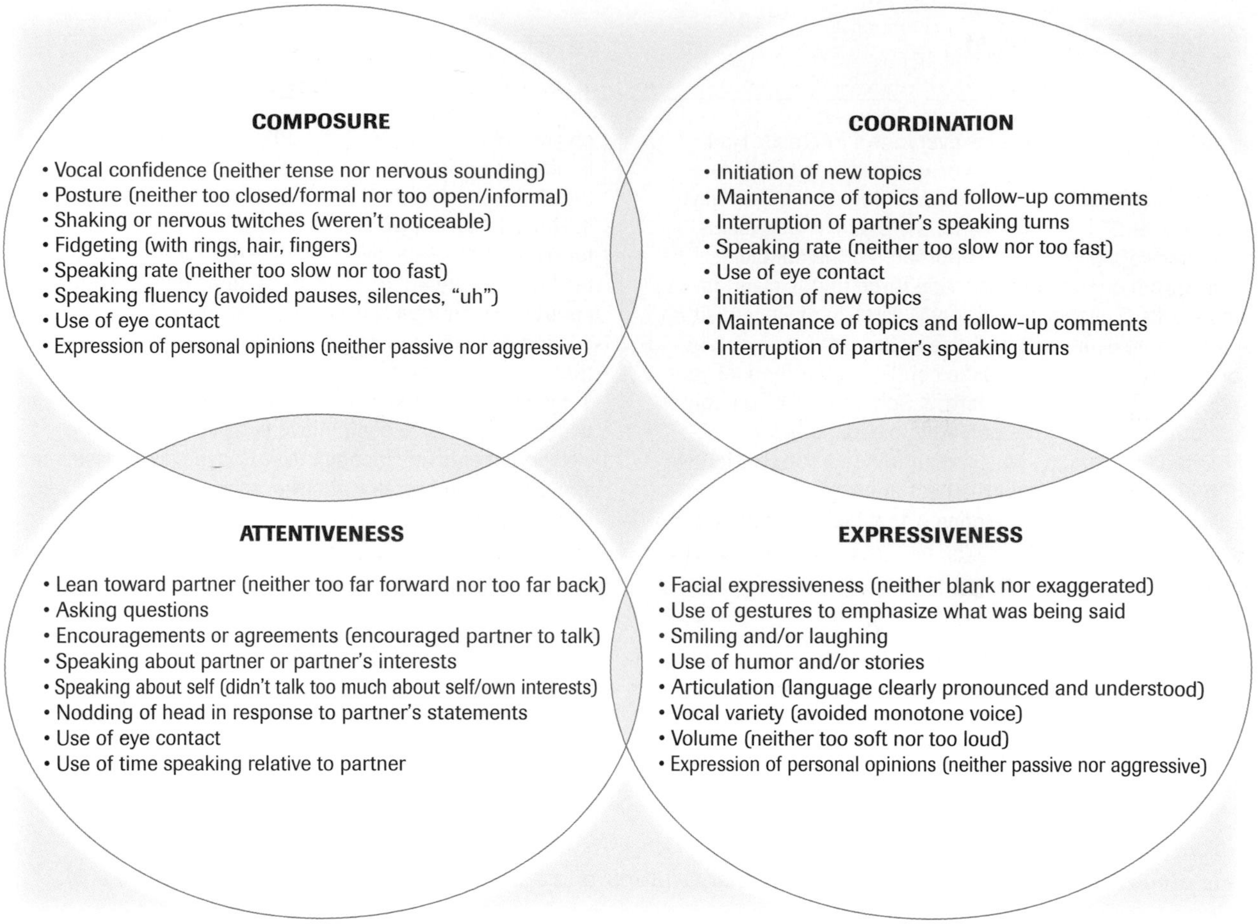

FIGURE 10.1
The Four Molar Skills

The four basic molar skills of interpersonal communication are made up of smaller molecular skills, some of which make up more than one molar skill.

herself. Although seeing the skills displayed so straightforwardly may make them seem simple, there are many challenges to their competent use.

Challenges to Managing Interpersonal Skills in Relationships

We use four molar communication skills in all our interpersonal interactions. Each one of these skills is comprised of many more molecular skills. In every instance of interpersonal communication, we attempt to manage these skills so we effectively achieve our goals in a way that is appropriate to the context. Given the number, subtlety, and complexity of these interpersonal communication skills, it is not surprising that we face several challenges to our competence. The three major challenges are managing habit and routine, balancing the amount of our skills, and balancing self-interests versus other-interests in our communication.

HABIT AND ROUTINE

In Chapter 9, we defined mindlessness as engaging in activities without consciously accessing or monitoring the operations of those activities, learning something so well that it becomes second nature. When an action becomes mindless, you don't need to think about it any longer. In fact, when a skill has been overlearned, thinking consciously about it can make your performance more *in*competent. However, overlearning can present a challenge to competent interpersonal communication. Once a skill is overlearned it becomes harder to recognize when the actions no longer work. When skills become overlearned, they become habitual and routine.

Habit and routine make your behaviors seem effortless. For most of you, many of the skills discussed in this chapter have become second nature, so you seldom purposefully think of them. When was the last time, for example, that you thought about the expressiveness of your voice? Unless you're an acting major, you probably spend little time reflecting on whether your face is depicting the emotion you're feeling. These routines are so deeply ingrained in your normal everyday communication that you no longer think about them. Like most of your communication behaviors, they seem entirely natural. And yet these communication skills are precisely what everyone around you uses to interpret your competence. If you are communicating routinely and mindlessly, and you are being perceived as incompetent, you may well be the last to know.

Habit and routine are very efficient means of getting through life. However, they also let you run on auto pilot until something goes very wrong. We often don't become aware there is anything wrong with our communication until we violate a social rule. Routines call attention to everything *except* our own skills. Thus when something in our communication does go wrong, we are often left wondering what possibly could have caused it. Consequently, we cannot neither accurately monitor feedback nor adapt our behavior to changes in the communication situation.

Knowledge Link

Referring back to Chapter 3, does mindlessness always result in habit and routine, and why or why not?

BALANCING THE AMOUNT OF SKILLS

Interpersonal skills are performed in amounts. You engage in eye contact a certain proportion of the time in a conversation. You ask a certain number of questions. Managing the amount of interpersonal communication skills is an ongoing challenge. Managing the amount of skills performed translates simply to "too much of a good thing is bad." Consider each of the following examples for the skills discussed in this chapter: coordination, composure, expressiveness, and attentiveness. Some communicators are too coordinated. If you have ever been approached by professional salespeople or telemarketers, they often practice the skill of coordination to the detriment of all others. They speak in clichés and jargon that seem like they have been repeated thousands of times, and they are too quick to offer immediate canned answers to all of your responses. In this way, their communication lacks spontaneity and genuineness because they come across as too smooth and practiced.

Some communicators are too composed. They display a brash overconfidence and an air of unflappable self-control. In any social situation, things could go wrong in an almost infinite number of ways. A display of composure that seems disconnected to such risks can appear out of touch with the actual situation. Furthermore, overly composed people may be so caught up in their own goals that they may not adapt their behavior to others. Finally, it is often a thin line between extreme confidence and aggressiveness or arrogance.

Other communicators are overly expressive. Perhaps you have known someone who is excessively expressive. Every emotion is a flood of expression. In other words, when the context seems to call for one expression, the person provides a much more extreme version of that expression. When the situation calls for a grin, the person displays a smile. Instead of a smile the person lets out a loud laugh. When a loud laugh seems appropriate, this person bellows in a fit of outrageous laughter. Every facial expression is made as if on a stage, and every vocalization made as if the recipient needs an exaggerated version of the emotion being expressed. Such excesses of expressiveness can create a sense of insincerity, can exhaust the senses of the recipients, and leave little room for interpreting subtleties that certain messages may require.

Finally, attentiveness, when overdone, can lose its competence as well. As much as we like to feel attended to, in the extreme it can become unnerving. Too much attentiveness forces you into the spotlight by placing the responsibility of the entire conversation on your shoulders. Too much attentiveness may also detract from a person's competence, as he or she may be perceived as lacking anything to say.

In short, much of the challenge of using interpersonal skills competently is finding the optimal balance for producing those skills in a given context. For the most part, in most situations, displaying coordination, composure, expressiveness, and attentiveness will enhance the impression of competence that others have of you. However, each skill has its breaking point, such that producing more of that skill will detract from your competence. Too much of a skill is often just as incompetent as too little of that skill.

Balancing Self-Interests & Other-Interests

Some skills are directed toward satisfying your goals, whereas other skills are directed toward satisfying others' goals. Balancing the pursuit of self and other goals is a key challenge to competent interaction. Too much self-satisfaction becomes narcissistic, whereas too much satisfaction of others becomes ingratiating.

Composure and expressiveness are largely self-focused skills. They are oriented to managing your own behavior consistent with your own goals. When applying the skill of composure, you are primarily trying to manage your own behavior to attain your own goals. Composure is the control of your own behavior. When you engage in expressiveness skills, you are giving voice to your inner experience, your feelings, and your thoughts. Extremes of these behaviors risk conversational narcissism, which is the appearance in your communication of caring only about yourself (Vangelisti, Knapp, & Daly, 1990). **Conversational narcissism** is displayed through self-aggrandizing or defensive statements, interruptions and other attempts to control a conversation, minimal uninvolved responses to others' statements, overly lengthy and frequent speaking turns, excessive self-disclosure, and showy or exhibitionist behavior (Leary, Bednarski, Hammon, & Duncan, 1997).

In contrast, coordination and attentiveness are more other-focused skills. Coordination depends on adapting one's own actions with those of another person. Successful coordination requires orienting toward the other's actions so your collective behavior meshes smoothly. Attentiveness, in turn, is a skill almost entirely focused on the other person. However, extremes of these skills can appear ingratiating. **Ingratiating communication** behavior in interaction appears only interested in seeking favor from the other person. Frequent compliments, offering of favors, constant agreement, and ongoing attention focused on the other person all reflect forms of ingratiating behavior.

Consequently, one of the challenges of interpersonal skills is not just applying each skill in the right amount, but in balancing all four of the skills. If you concentrate too much on expressiveness and composure, you may appear narcissistic or self-focused. But if you display the skills of coordination and attentiveness too much, you may be perceived as lacking individuality. Indeed, this is the challenge of relationships in general, which are a constant balance of managing self versus other needs and interests (Baxter & Montgomery, 1996; Hinde, 1997).

We have examined several challenges to interpersonal skills in relationships. So what can be done to avoid excessive use of skills, unbalanced use of skills, and habitual inattention to our skills? There are no simple answers, but becoming aware of such challenges is the first step. Once you become aware of the challenges, you can use the methods described in the following section to overcome these challenges.

Overcoming Challenges to Competence

Interpersonal communication is deceptively difficult. Most of the time we feel as if our communication is going relatively well, and thus we seem relatively unaware of the challenges to our competence. Yet there is always room for improvement. Most of the time, however, we don't feel pressed to strive for this improvement. It follows, then, that overcoming the challenges to our competence requires us to become aware of some methods of managing these challenges. Three methods are discussed in the following section: identifying ways of balancing adaptability and consistency, signal monitoring, and balancing appropriateness and effectiveness.

Balancing Adaptability & Consistency

We rely on habit and routine for a reason. It is efficient and the resulting behavior is something we become very practiced and comfortable with. However, as we saw earlier, habit and routine sometimes lead to a lack of adaptability and competence. In order to overcome this challenge, people need to balance adaptability with consistency in their communication skills (Spitzberg, 1993, 1994a). **Adaptability** is the ability to alter skills appropriately as contexts and conversations evolve and change. **Consistency** is maintaining similar ways of behaving across contexts and conversations. Although these skills are the opposite of one another, they are both essential to interpersonal communication competence.

Knowledge Link

Examining Chapter 3 again, in what way does the skill of adaptability help explain the postmodern self?

We rely on others to be at least somewhat predictable. We trust that people generally speak the truth as they know it; they will respond to our statements with statements that aren't always "just what we want to hear"; and, if they have generally been outgoing or shy, they are likely to continue to be so. This consistency in our conversational partner's communication skills permits us to concentrate on conversational goals without second-guessing every aspect of the encounter. In other words, because we predict certain things about each interaction, we are able to concentrate on those aspects that are not predictable and the content and goals of the conversation itself. If nothing were predictable, every interaction would involve a huge amount of effort just to coordinate basic communication activities.

To a large extent, therefore, each new communication context brings with it a variety of old and a variety of new behaviors and experiences. Competence in interaction involves a constant balancing of adaptability and consistency, in which a communicator portrays a performance consistent with his or her past performances while simultaneously altering his or her behaviors to be appropriate to the situation at hand. Competence, in short, involves changing your behaviors against a backdrop of constancy. In order to overcome the challenge of habit and routine, communicators need to self-monitor, as discussed in Chapter 9, and take opportunities to assess whether or not changes in current communication skills are called for. In the opening vignette, had either Dipak or Chad taken a moment to self-monitor, they might have recognized that their current escalation of conflict needed to be deescalated by a shift to less expressive, more composed and attentive communication.

SIGNAL MONITORING

When people drone on and on in a conversation, never letting you say anything, or boring you with talk of things in which you have little interest, how do you behave? If you are like most communicators, you remain minimally polite and appropriate, but you also send certain signals that this is less than ideal conversation. The other person just does not seem to be monitoring your signals. **Signal monitoring** is similar to self-monitoring, as discussed in Chapter 9, but specifically looks for signals that interaction is not going well because too little or too much of a skill is being performed.

Generally speaking, people reciprocate signals they want to see increased and compensate for signals they want to see decreased. **Reciprocation** is responding with behavior similar to what you are seeing in the other communicator. If he or she smiles, you smile. If he or she asks questions, you ask questions. Reciprocation is a signal that invites continuation or increases in such behavior. **Compensation** is behavior that is a reversal of another behavior. If you smile, the other person frowns. If you lean closer, the other person leans back. If you ask questions, the other person doesn't ask questions, and instead offers assertions (Andersen, 1998).

Signal monitoring scans the conversational partner's behavior for signals that more of certain behaviors are invited and certain other behaviors are being enacted excessively. If your eye contact is too direct and intense, you can expect to see the other person compensate by decreasing eye contact. This is a signal that you may need to adjust your amount of eye contact. Conversely, if you follow up a person's statement with a topically related statement, and they do the same for your comment, then it's an invitation to continue engaging in that pattern of behavior. Attention to such reciprocal and compensatory behaviors in conversations help alert you when you are engaging in too much or too little of a behavior.

BALANCING APPROPRIATENESS & EFFECTIVENESS

Much of everyday communication brings with it the challenge of balancing self- versus other-interests. In the opening vignette, Dipak decided to place priority on his own interests, to the detriment of Chad, and Chad likewise chose self-interests over the interests of Dipak. Balancing self- and other-interests is a challenge overcome by an attention to another balancing act: managing to balance appropriateness and effectiveness.

As you've seen in the model of communication competence and throughout this book, appropriateness and effectiveness play a significant role in competent communication. These elements of competence become much more important to the perception of competence than in the enactment of skills. Every behavior, every nuance of one's performance in communication, is at risk of failure. This failure can be in the form of not achieving the intent of the behavior or in the form of offending someone else's sense of appropriateness. As discussed in Chapter 2, optimizing competence is communication that is simultaneously both appropriate and effective.

Revisiting the competence grid from Chapter 2, overemphasizing other-interests leads to sufficing communication. In most contexts, both of these types of communication reflect an excessive concern for appropriateness as perceived by the other person, leading to the neglect of your own best interests. Your own goals and agendas in conversation are achieved through effectiveness. However, as you've seen in this section, you will seldom find yourself in a situation where you can simply ignore the other person's concerns or goals in the process of pursuing your own. This pursuit of effectiveness at the risk of appropriateness, or maximizing behavior, can threaten your very relationship with that person. If you destroy that relationship by ignoring appropriateness, then you are also ineffective in achieving all the goals you hope to accomplish within that relationship. In the opening vignette, Dipak's initial interest in the short-term effectiveness of getting a clean apartment runs the risk of destroying the relationship he has with Chad. Similarly, Chad needs to consider a balancing of appropriateness in his responses to Dipak's anger. If they each need the other's rent to stay in that apartment, then it is to their advantage to consider a more competent approach to resolving their differences. As you can see, effectiveness in communication doesn't rule out the need for appropriateness.

If we return to the skills examined in this chapter, composure and expressiveness tend to be most directed toward self-interests, and therefore, effectiveness. Composure is oriented to self-control and inner-directed goals of managing your behavior. Looking calm, confident, assertive, and "in control" typically reflect an interest in self. Similarly, expressiveness is a tendency to let out what is inside. Expressiveness gives voice to your emotional states, your wishes, and your intentions. If you think or feel it, express it. In contrast to these more self-interested and effectiveness-oriented skills, coordination and attentiveness tend to be other-interested and appropriateness oriented. Coordination can only be accomplished in concert with, and in response to, another person. To coordinate is to follow the other person's leads and moves. Attentiveness involves listening to, focusing on, and showing interest in the other person. These skills emphasize appropriateness more so than effectiveness.

If the skills of composure and expressiveness tend to emphasize effectiveness, and the skills of coordination and attentiveness emphasize appropriateness, it follows that overcoming the challenge of balancing self- and other-interests requires the competent performance of all four skills. Only an attention to both appropriateness and effectiveness is likely to produce optimizing communication. Thus you need to practice and refine all four of the skills examined in this chapter if you hope to achieve a consistently optimizing type of communication competence.

Chapter Summary

Communicative competency depends on our skills. It is often enough to be motivated and knowledgeable. But being motivated and knowledgeable is rarely enough to be optimal. Optimizing our performance requires the use of interpersonal skills. The use of these skills has been found to make a difference in the quantity and quality of relationships, and these relationships in turn affect every aspect of a our psychological, emotional, and physical well-being.

Skills are repeatable, goal-oriented actions. Skills vary along a dimension of abstraction, from molecular skills, such as gesturing or giving a compliment, to molar skills, such as being supportive or engaging in conflict. Skills are important, but they do not guarantee competence. Competence is an impression of the quality of a performance. Consequently, the use of certain skills makes it more likely that a communicator will be seen as competent, but in any given encounter, the participants involved might not view the performance as competent. Thus skills are distinct from the impressions made about them, and competence is one of these impressions. Four interpersonal skills make competence impressions likely.

The first skill area is coordination, the skill of managing the flow of conversation. This involves starting and stopping conversations and individual speaking turns, developing the topic of conversation, and managing interruptions. The second skill area is composure, the skill of regulating behavioral anxiety and displaying confidence and assertiveness. This involves being neither too aggressive nor too passive in expressing oneself. The third skill area is expressiveness, which involves the animation of verbal, vocalic, facial, and bodily actions. Finally, attentiveness is the skill of showing interest in, concern for, and attention to the other person or persons in the interaction. Specific skills that enhance attentiveness include listening, topic development, and questioning.

There are three common challenges to the competent use of these skills. The first is avoiding excessive habit and routine in communication skills. The second challenge is balancing the amount of skills that we perform to avoid engaging in too little or too much of any given behavior. The final challenge to competent communication is balancing self-interests versus other-interests in communication.

Overcoming these challenges involves complex and delicate balancing acts. In order to avoid excessive habit and routine, a communicator needs to balance adaptability with consistency of communication skills. The challenge of balancing the amount of skills enacted in communication requires careful attention to signal monitoring, in which you reciprocate preferred behaviors and compensate for behaviors that are excessive. Finally, the challenge of balancing self-interests versus other-interests is overcome by balancing appropriateness with effectiveness through the balancing of composure and expressiveness on the one hand, and coordination and attentiveness on the other.

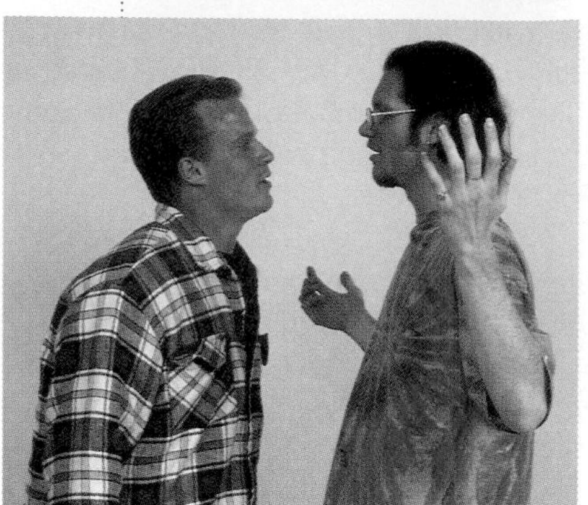

Key Terms

- actions
- abstraction dimension
- molecular skills
- molar skills
- coordination
- talkovers
- deep interruptions
- topic initiation
- composure
- assertiveness
- aggressive communication
- passive communication
- empathic assertion
- expressiveness
- wide-narrow dimension of voice
- tense-lax dimension of voice
- full-thin dimension of voice
- attentiveness
- topic development
- open-ended questions
- closed-ended questions
- time management
- conversational narcissism
- ingratiating communication
- adaptability
- consistency
- signal monitoring
- reciprocation
- compensation

Building Knowledge

1. What are the relationships and distinctions among skills, abilities, behaviors, and impressions of competence?
2. How are molar skills (e.g., empathy, assertiveness, etc.) related to molecular skills (e.g., facial expressiveness, asking questions, etc.)?
3. How can conversational interruptions be competent?
4. What are the four major skill areas of interpersonal communication competence? How do they differ from one another? Give examples for each type of skill.
5. In what ways do the four skill areas of interpersonal communication competence relate to self-concern and other-concern?
6. Distinguish among assertive, aggressive, and passive communication behavior.
7. Explain reciprocity and compensation in relation to signal monitoring.

8. Describe the process of balancing adaptability with consistency.
9. Describe the process of balancing appropriateness with effectiveness.

Building Skills

Individual Exercises

1. Listed in the chart below and on the next page are some skills grouped together by skill area examined in this chapter. Select one skill in each skill area, describe the skill you have chosen, and define five levels of competence for each skill. The first two skill areas have been completed as examples.
2. Go to the Conflict Resolution Network, in their component on the "twelve skills" of conflict management, at **http://crnhq.org/twelveskills.html**. Think of two communication situations you have faced recently, one in which you responded too aggressively, and one in which you responded too passively. Briefly describe the contexts: who were you talking to, what was your relationship with that person, where were you, and so on. Then, as accurately as you can remember the conversation, write down a statement or response you provided that was too aggressive in the first situation and too passive in the second situation. Now, using the information in this Web site's description of "I statements," reformulate your statements to be more appropriately assertive. To what extent could these "I statements" help resolve conflicts in which you find yourself in everyday encounters? Why?
3. Following are several potentially problematic situations. For each situation, describe an aggressive, a passive, and an assertive response.
   a. A week ago you and your steady dating partner of a year broke up. You still have strong feelings for this person, but you need to move on. A week later, your best friend calls and says, "Guess what? I'm going to a party with your ex-partner. I hope you don't mind."

Skills/Levels of Competence (Question 1)

	LEVELS OF COMPETENCE
VOCAL CONFIDENCE A display of vocalic firmness, calmness, forcefulness, and steadiness of expression	1. Vocalizations are almost constantly nervous, shaky, breaking in pitch, or equivocal in tone or volume 2. Vocalizations are frequently nervous, shaky, breaking in pitch, or equivocal in tone or volume 3. Vocalizations are occasionally nervous, shaky, breaking in pitch, and/or equivocal in tone or steadiness of volume 4. Vocalizations are generally calm and/or forceful, firm, and composed 5. Vocalizations are consistently calm and/or forceful, firm, composed, and assertive
FACIAL EXPRESSIONS A facial display of a range of emotion, animation of face, and normal facial expressions compatible with verbal content and partner statements	1. Constant display of blank, uninterested, or hypnotic gaze, or highly exaggerated, cartoonish expressions, and/or expressions inconsistent with verbal content of discussion 2. Frequent display of blank, uninterested, or hypnotic gaze, or highly exaggerated, cartoonish expressions, and/or expressions inconsistent with verbal content of discussion 3. Occasional display of blank, uninterested, or hypnotic gaze, or highly exaggerated, cartoonish expressions, and/or expressions inconsistent with verbal content of discussion 4. General display of variation in facial emotion consistent with subject matter and partner 5. Consistent displays of variation in facial emotion consistent with subject matter and partner

ATTENTIVENESS Leaning toward partner Eye contact Asking of questions Use of time speaking	
COORDINATION Speaking fluency Topic initiation Topic maintenance Interruptions of partner	
COMPOSURE Posture Nervous twitches Expression of personal opinion Volume	
EXPRESSIVENESS Speaking about self Vocal variety Use of gestures Smiling/laughing	

b. Despite having agreed to buy food separately to avoid disputes over who can eat which snacks, you come home to find your roommate eating the last of your microwave popcorn.

c. Someone you have been dating exclusively for a while says, "I think we're getting a little stale. Maybe we should start seeing other people for a while."

d. You take someone you have been dating exclusively to a local pub. Soon after arriving, you go up to the bar to order something, and when you turn around, you see your partner flirting with someone else.

4. Here are several situations in which you might find yourself. For each situation, write three possible statements you might make to open up conversation.

   a. You are at the veterinarian and you see another person with a pet like yours.

   b. You are discussing an essay with a professor in his or her office.

   c. You are at the park watching people throw a Frisbee and an elderly person sits next to you on the bench.

   d. You see a friend at a shopping mall.

   e. You are at a party and an attractive person asks you what time it is.

5. Here are some examples of closed-ended questions. For each question, write three open-ended questions that are related to the same topic area.

   a. Where are you from?

   b. How long have you been in/out of school?

   c. What is/was your major?

   d. Where do you work? What is your position?

   e. What are your hobbies?

   f. Where do you live?

Group Activities

1. Here is a list of terms and topics. In this activity you will be asked to show creativity in topic development. Form dyads. The first person to volunteer should select a topic from the list, and make a comment related to the topic. For example, if the first topic selected was "gun control," you might start by saying something like "I can't believe the government hasn't banned assault rifles yet." The person to the right of the person who went first will then select another topic from the list and make a statement that is topically relevant to both the topic selected *and* the previous statement made by the other person. Thus, following our example, if the next topic was "abortion," the next person's statement might be something like "Yeah, if they don't start controlling guns better, they'll keep having these nuts go out and attacking abortion clinics, or whatever else they disagree with." Each person sequentially to the right of the person who spoke before in the group continues by making a comment that is topically relevant to both the previous comment as well as the next topic he or she selects from the list. Continue until all topics have been exhausted. See if you can continue without the list once you have finished all its topics.

   Topics

Equal rights	Auto safety
Terrorism	The economy
Welfare	AIDS and HIV
Drunk driving	Foreign language education
Hunting and poaching	Media violence
Sports	Genetic engineering
Separation of church and state	Sex education
Right to die	The environment
Family values	Illegal aliens

   When the conversation ends, discuss the skill of topic maintenance and development. What distinguished competent from incompetent follow-up comments?

2. • Go on *Infotrac College Edition* and enter the search term *interpersonal skills*. Among the entries you will find an article by Virginia Anderson, Janet Reis, and Yvonne Stephens on interpersonal skills and sexual coercion, published in the journal *Adolescence* in 1997 (Article A196119422). In this article the authors examine how confident adolescents are in asserting themselves in sexual situations. Form a dyad and discuss the items in Table 1. Are there situations college students face that were not identified in this list? What are they? Are college students more competent at asserting themselves in these situations than high school students? Why? Finally, which molar and molecular interpersonal skills would be helpful in these kinds of situations?

3. Form a dyad with someone you don't know very well. Conduct a get-acquainted conversation. For the first 3-5 minutes, both parties should engage in zero eye contact. For the next 3-5 minutes, both of you should engage in total eye contact. For the final 3-5 minutes, engage in conversation as you normally would. Afterward, discuss the three conditions (no eye contact, total eye contact, normal eye contact) in terms of how they made you feel, how they affected the conversation, and what they suggest about the role of eye contact in conversation management.

4. Form a dyad with someone you don't know very well. Conduct a get-acquainted conversation. Throughout the conversation, both parties should wait 5 seconds before responding to the other's previous statement. You can do this by mentally counting off the seconds before saying anything. After about 10 minutes, discuss the effects of the delays in affecting the flow of the conversation.

Interpersonal Communication Competence Skills Grid

To help you understand how to use this grid, the skills displayed by Dipak and Chad in the opening vignette of this chapter have been analyzed below. Examine that analysis and then think about a recent interpersonal communication situation and what you could have done more competently. First, describe the context of the interpersonal communication situation in the spaces provided. Next, analyze your interpersonal communication skills based on the skills explained in this chapter for each step in the listening process. In the first column,

ANALYZING DIPAK AND CHAD'S INTERPERSONAL COMMUNICATION SKILLS

Context

CULTURE: An Indian and North American student in a U.S. apartment

TIME: Weekend morning

RELATIONSHIP: Roommates, friends, and fellow college students

PLACE: In a shared apartment

FUNCTION: Dipak: to get Chad to clean up the apartment

MOLAR SKILL	LESS COMPETENT	MORE COMPETENT
ATTENTIVENESS	Accusing the other person; using insulting language (e.g., "pigsty" and "disaster zone"; giving ultimatums (e.g., "Find someone else . . . .")	Describing the situation; using more neutral language (e.g., "very cluttered" or "messy"); being flexible (e.g., "Can we find some way to resolve this?")
COMPOSURE	Aggressiveness (e.g., "Find someone else . . . ."); passiveness (e.g., making excuses when you are to blame); escalating unnecessarily by yelling back.	Empathetic assertiveness (e.g., "I think you may want to consider finding another roommate"); responsibility (e.g., "I will clean it up later today"); remaining calm
COORDINATION	Interrupting the other person in midsentence; waking someone by yelling	Letting the other person finish his or her turn speaking; waiting until a person is ready to talk to begin conversation
EXPRESSIVENESS	Exaggeration (e.g., "pigsty" and "typical godless American"); yelling louder and louder	Reasonable description (e.g., "The room is a mess" and "I don't see what you believe in"); speaking in an animated but not screaming voice

briefly describe and give examples of how your skills may have been less than competent. Using these less competent skills as a point of comparison to fill in the second column, describe the skills you think would have been perceived as more competent in the particular context. With practice, you will find you can use this grid to help develop your skills for future interpersonal communication situations, as well as to analyze situations you have already experienced.

ANALYZING YOUR OWN INTERPERSONAL COMMUNICATION SKILLS

Context

CULTURE:

TIME:

RELATIONSHIP:

PLACE:

FUNCTION:

MOLAR SKILL	LESS COMPETENT	MORE COMPETENT
ATTENTIVENESS		
COMPOSURE		
COORDINATION		
EXPRESSIVENESS		

5. Select five emotions from the list here. List them in the blanks provided. Form a dyad, making sure neither person can see the other's list. Take turns expressing each of the five emotions on your lists. First express the emotion using only your face. Then express the same emotion by using only vocalics, by saying the phrase: "We take these truths to be self-evident, that all people are created equal." After each facial expression, and each vocal expression, have your partner write down that emotion from the list he or she thinks you are expressing. Afterward, compare the emotions you intended to express to those that your partner thought you were actually expressing. Discuss the implications of the results for being interpersonally competent.

Emotions

Anger	Happiness
Anticipation	Hate
Attraction	Hopefulness
Confidence	Hopelessness
Depression	Impatience
Despair	Love
Disgust	Pessimism
Eagerness	Sadness
Embarrassment	Solitude
Excitement	Surprise
Fatigue	Tension
Fear	Terror

References

Baxter, L. A., & Montgomery, B. M. (1996). *Relating: Dialogues and dialects.* New York: Guilford.

Canary, D. J., & Spitzberg, B. H. (1990). Attribution biases and associations between conflict strategies and competence outcomes. *Communication Monographs, 57,* 139–51.

Derber, C. (1979). *The pursuit of attention: Power and individualism in everyday life.* Cambridge, MA: Schenkman.

Friedman, H. S., DiMatteo, M. R., & Taranta, A. (1980). A study of the relationships between individual differences in nonverbal expressiveness and factors of personality and social interaction. *Journal of Research in Personality, 14,* 351–364.

Harwood, J., & Williams, A. (1998). Expectations for communication with positive and negative subtypes of older adults. *International Journal of Aging & Human Development, 47,* 11–33.

Hinde, R. A. (1997). *Relationships: A dialectical perspective.* East Sussex, UK: Psychology Press.

Jefferson, G. (1989). Preliminary notes on a possible metric which provides for a "standard maximum" silence

Emotions (Question 5)

EMOTIONS EXPRESSED	PARTNER'S INTERPRETATION

of approximately one second in conversation. In D. Roger & P. Bull (Eds.), *Conversation: An interdisciplinary perspective* (pp. 166–196). Philadelphia: Multilingual Matters.

Kennedy, C. W., & Camden, C. T. (1983). A new look at interruptions. *Western Journal of Speech Communication, 47,* 45–58.

Leary, M. R., Bednarski, R., Hammon, D., & Duncan, T. (1997). Blowhards, snobs, and narcissists: Interpersonal reactions to excessive egotism. In R. Kowalski (Ed.), *Aversive interpersonal behavior* (pp. 111–131). New York: Plenum.

Leary, M. R., Rogers, P. A., Canfield, R. W., & Coe, C. (1986). Boredom in interpersonal encounters: Antecedents and social implications. *Journal of Personality and Social Psychology, 51,* 968–975.

Norton, R. (1984). *Communicator style: Theory, applications, and measures.* Beverly Hills, CA: Sage.

Raush, H. L., Barry, W. A., Hertel, R. J., & Swain, M. A. (1974). *Communication, conflict, and marriage.* San Francisco: Jossey-Bass.

Robinson, D. T., & Smith-Lovin, L. (1992). Selective interaction as a strategy for identity maintenance: An affect control model. *Social Psychology Quarterly, 55,* 12–28.

Sabatelli, R. M., & Rubin, M. (1986). Nonverbal expressiveness and physical attractiveness as mediators of interpersonal perceptions. *Journal of Nonverbal Behavior, 10,* 120–133.

Scherer, K. R. (1986). Vocal affect expression: A review and a model for future research. *Psychological Bulletin, 99,* 143–165.

Spitzberg, B. H. (1993). The dialectics of (in)competence. *Journal of Social and Personal Relationships, 10,* 137–158.

Spitzberg, B. H. (1994a). The dark side of (in)competence. In W.R. Cupach & B.H. Spitzberg (Eds.), *The dark side of interpersonal communication* (pp. 25–49). Hillsdale, NJ: Erlbaum.

Spitzberg, B. H. (1994b). Instructional assessment of interpersonal competence: The Conversational Skills Rating Scale. In S. Morreale, M. Brooks, R. Berko, & C. Cooke (Eds.), *Assessing college student competency in speech communication* (1994 SCA Summer Conference Proceedings, pp. 325–352). Annandale, VA: Speech Communication Association.

Spitzberg, B. H., Canary, D. J., & Cupach, W. R. (1994). A competence-based approach to the study of interpersonal conflict. In D. D. Cahn (Ed.), *Intimates in conflict* (pp. 183–202). Hillsdale, NJ: Erlbaum.

Spitzberg, B. H., & Cupach, W. R. (1984). *Interpersonal communication competence.* Beverly Hills, CA: Sage.

Vangelisti, A. L., Knapp, M. L., & Daly, J. A. (1990). Conversational narcissism. *Communication Monographs, 57,* 251–274.

Wheeless, L. R., Frymier, A. B., & Thompson, C. A. (1992). A comparison of verbal output and receptivity in relation to attraction and communication satisfaction in interpersonal relationships. *Communication Quarterly, 40,* 102–115.

CHAPTER 11

Learning Objectives

After studying this chapter, you should be able to:

1. Define small group communication and explain how perception, interdependence, and communication relate to groups of three or more people.
2. Outline the four assumptions underlying small group communication.
3. Discuss why communicating in small groups is important.
4. Explain how motivation, knowledge, skills, and context influence competence in small group communication.
5. Understand how people, task, needs, and personal traits influence an individual's motivation to join and participate in small groups.
6. Recognize challenges to competence in small groups arising from coordination issues and multiple motivations among group members.
7. Propose strategies to overcome challenges to competence in small groups arising from coordination issues and multiple motivations.
8. Outline how the concepts of people, objectives, environment, and time can be used to develop ethical behavior within small groups.
9. Understand the need to communicate ethically in small groups and develop methods to foster ethical behavior.

Small Group Communication: Getting Motivated

Graham was entering the final day of examinations for the fall semester at his university. He woke up early that morning looking forward to completing his last exam for his political science course and going home for the holidays. He quickly brewed a cup of coffee, poured it into a travel mug, and raced across campus to meet some classmates for some last-minute studying before the political science final. They met in a quiet corner in the student union, as they had done the entire semester before each class, and reviewed for the test. Graham attributed much of his success in political science to his study partners—they had provided much needed motivation, intellectual stimulation, and emotional support.

After reviewing for the examination, Graham and his study partners walked over to their classroom to take the test. The test was given in a large auditorium because the class had over 250 enrolled students. In fact, the class was so large the professor had changed the class to lecture rather than discussion format. The size of the class not only influenced how the professor taught the class, it also influenced how Graham interacted with other students. Outside of his study partners, Graham didn't know anyone else from class. Every day throughout the semester, Graham had simply walked into class, taken his seat, and written notes on the professor's lecture without talking to anyone else. Graham was not alone—the pattern was the same for almost all of the students in the class.

After the final, Graham went to the computer lab and logged on to the computer to relax. He was a regular participant in a university listserv that discussed the relationship between church and state. He downloaded his email and found a couple of new postings that looked interesting. One was made by a close friend whom he had known since high school. The other was from someone he did not know; in fact, Graham thought this might be the first time this particular person had posted to the listserv. He responded quickly to both, wished them a happy holiday, logged off, and went to his campus job.

Graham had a work study position in the library where he worked behind the reference desk. He worked regularly with two other students who had the same shift. They had nicknamed themselves the "Elders" because they felt they had wisdom and knowledge about the library that other students did not. Because it was the last day of examinations, few students needed help with their library research. The Elders mostly talked about their plans for the holiday, complained about how the library policies sometimes hindered their ability to help students effectively, and made plans for approaching their supervisor regarding some possible changes in existing policies.

When the library closed, Graham went to catch a bus home. On the way to the bus stop, Graham ran into Kennedy, a close friend. They quickly talked about how their finals had gone and made a promise to get together for lunch the next semester. When he arrived at the bus stop, five other people were also waiting. Graham didn't know any of them; nevertheless, he said "hello" as he walked up. They made small talk with each other for about five minutes until the bus pulled up. Once he got on the bus and sat down, Graham began thinking about his family. He was looking forward to this holiday in particular, as this would be the first time in five years that all his brothers and sisters would be home for the holidays. •••

In our daily lives, we constantly move in and out of relationships with people. We move in and out of deeply personal relationships with individuals we care about such as friends and loved ones. We move in and out of somewhat superficial relationships with people such as the clerk at the corner store or the server at a frequented coffee shop or café. The kinds of relationships we move in and out of during our daily lives are not restricted to single individuals. We also move in and out of relationships with collections of people such as bands, gatherings, and crowds. In the vignette, Graham moved in and out of relationship with a several collections of people including his study partners, his political science class, his listserv, and his work team.

Do all of these collections of people have the same relationships? Probably not. Graham's study circle had met the entire semester, whereas the people at the bus stop met for the first and probably last time. The political science class that Graham was enrolled in was so large that people didn't know one another, whereas the Elders knew each other quite well and talked to each other often during work as well as outside the library. Graham's study partners met face-to-face during the semester whereas his contact with members of the listserv was mediated through the internet. The Elders were a group of people with the purpose of achieving specific work-related tasks, running the library reference desk; Graham's family was primarily concerned with cultivating good relationships and having fun. As you can see, how long or short collections of people last, how well they know one another, what channel they use to communicate, and the purpose for the collection's existence vary greatly.

This chapter focuses on a specific collection of people known as a small group. Small groups have a set of distinctive qualities that separate them from other collections of people. In this chapter, we explore what makes a small group. Using the competence model, we look at the steps you can take to become a motivated and competent small group communicator.

What Is a Small Group?

In the chapter-opening vignette, Graham encountered and engaged with several collections of people throughout his day. Which of these collections of people would you characterize as a small group? Do you view Graham's family as a group? Do you consider the people at the bus stop a group? List the criteria you used to decide which collections of people qualified as a group and which did not. How many criteria did you generate? Although a great many criteria exist for classifying a collection of people as a group, four criteria determine a small group: (1) the collection must be made up of three or more people, (2) every group member must have the perception of belonging to this particular group, (3) each group member's behaviors and goals must be interdependent and the group must be interdependent with its larger context, and (4) there must be communication between group members. Using these four criteria, a **small group** can be defined as three or more people who perceive themselves to be a group, who are interdependent, and communicate with one another.

INVOLVES THREE OR MORE PEOPLE

Using the criterion that small groups must consist of at least three people, Graham's study partners, his political science class, the Elders, the five people waiting for the bus, and his family would be considered groups, and his relationship with his friend Kennedy would not. What is so important about the number three for small groups? When you move from a dyad to a group of three or more people, possibilities for majority rule, minority opinion, coalitions, and voting emerge. For example, consider a committee of faculty members that is deciding whether to increase or decrease enrollment at their university. Once you have more than three people, several committee members can formulate a majority opinion by agreeing on the need for an enrollment increase. It is also possible that a few committee members may hold a minority opinion that enrollment should be decreased and actively try to build a coalition with undecided members to overturn the majority opinion. However, if you have a dyad where each member has equal power and one member wants to increase enrollment and the other does not, there is not a possibility for majority rule, minority opinion, or coalition building.

Being physically present in the same space is not enough for a collection of people to be called a group. Belonging to a group involves communicating with three or more people who perceive themselves as a group, who possess a common goal, and who are interdependent.

If the lower bound for any small group is three people you may wonder, "How large can a group be and still be called a *small* group?" Do you consider Graham's large lecture class of 250 people a small group? You'll find that most people would respond "no," but what is the criterion we use to distinguish small groups from large groups? One way that has been used historically to distinguish a small group from a large group is the possibility for group members to have some reaction about each of the others as an individual person even if only to recall that the other was present (Bales, 1950, p. 33). This suggests that the ability to be aware of all the other people in a group and to recall what a particular group member was like or what he or she did sets the upper limit for people in a small group. It is highly unlikely that all the members of Graham's political science class made an impression on him, and even less likely that he would recognize them as members of the class if he ran into them elsewhere on campus. Therefore, his political science class would not be considered a small group.

INCLUDES SHARED PERCEPTION

If you asked the collection of people standing with Graham at the bus stop if they thought they belonged to a group, how do you think they would answer? You might assume correctly that their answer would probably be "no." This was a random group of people assembled at a bus stop to get transportation to go home, to work, or to some other location. They didn't know one another because they had never met before. If you asked Graham's circle of study partners if they were a group, they would probably answer "yes." They had been together for a semester united in a common purpose—to master the material in the political science course.

People can be said to belong to a group if they perceive themselves as belonging to a group. If they label themselves as group members, then they have met the second criterion. Using this perception criterion, it is likely that Graham's study partners, the members of the listserv, the Elders, and Graham's family would consider themselves a small group. Why is someone's perception of membership in a group important for determining whether the small group exists? It is crucial to the definition of a small group because people can be gathered and interacting but not be members of a group. The people at the bus stop are waiting together and they interact with one another, but they would not perceive themselves as belonging to a small group. It is even possible for people who have worked together over a long period of time to not view themselves as members of a small group. For example, suppose one of the members of Graham's work team, the Elders, did not perceive herself as a member of the team. Can we then classify the Elders as a group if some members do not perceive themselves as members of this group? Given the difference of opinion, we would have to say that the majority of people in the work team classify themselves as a group and that a minority does not. The criterion of perception is important for defining small groups because it cautions us to avoid the mistake of thinking that people who interact with each other necessarily form a group.

EMPHASIZES INTERDEPENDENCE

The third criterion for a small group is interdependence. Three or more people who are interdependent make up a small group. **Interdependence** means that two elements are related to and mutually affect one another. Small group interdependence can appear in three ways: (1) goal interdependence, (2) behavioral interdependence, and (3) context interdependence. The forms of interdependence are not mutually exclusive; they can be simultaneously present within a small group.

The first way in which group members can be interdependent, **goal interdependence,** is accomplished by sharing goals. Goals are the ends to which effort is directed. For example, consider the goals of Graham's study partners. What about the people participating in the listserv? The Elders? The goal of the circle of study partners is to master political science course work. The goal of those individuals participating in the listserv is to discuss issues regarding the separation of church and state. The goal of the Elders is to help keep the library running smoothly by assisting students with their research. Although the goals of each group is different, each group has a primary goal that all members share. When individuals share a common goal, they can be said to be interdependent.

A second form of interdependence is **behavioral interdependence,** which means that an individual's messages affect and are affected by other people's messages. Consider the following conversation from a small group:

> RASHEED: What do you think we should do for our class project?
>
> MEI: That's a good question. I think we should do something that the professor would like.
>
> AL: I agree. It's best to choose a topic that Professor Barge would like. When he lectured on small group decision making, he became much more animated and passionate. I think he really loves that topic. What about doing something on small group decision making?
>
> MEI: That's an excellent idea! I also noticed that he cited a lot of his own research when he discussed decision making. Let's do something on decision making for the project.

In the conversation, you can see how each message incorporates some piece of information from the message immediately preceding it. Behavioral interdependence is characterized by a flow of messages where each message is influenced by the messages preceding it and affects the messages following it.

Finally, group members can be interdependent through context. **Context interdependence** occurs when a group's environment affects and is, in turn, affected by a group's actions. Groups and group members do not exist in a vacuum; they exist in a web of relationships with other stakeholder groups in a larger environment. In the chapter-opening vignette, the group known as the Elders is also affected by an environmental influence—the library's preexisting policies. These library policies affect how each group member interacts with each other and the students. At the same time, it may be possible for the work team to influence the environment, in this case by recommending new procedures or strategies to help deliver better service to the students.

Knowledge Link

What are the differences among goal, behavioral, and context interdependencies?

REQUIRES COMMUNICATION

As you saw earlier, communication is a process of managing messages and meaning in ways that build community. The last criterion for a small group to exist is that three or more people need to communicate with one another. All the collections of people in the opening vignette would be considered groups using this criterion because they all communicate with one another. Recall, however, that the channels they use to communicate with one another vary. Graham's study circle met face-to-face whereas Graham's participation in the listserv on church and state issues was through email. As you know, communication may occur through a nonmediated channel such as face-to-face communication or through a variety of mediated channels such as audioconferencing, teleconferencing, and email. The influx of communication technologies has opened up a wide variety of ways for group members to communicate with each other. Group members no longer need to be face-to-face to collaborate; they can be physically located in different geographic regions or on different floors in an office building and be linked by communication technologies. Regardless of what channel of communication they use, in order to be considered a group, members need to communicate with one another.

To summarize, a collection of people can be classified as a small group if (1) it includes three or more people; (2) the people perceive themselves as belonging to a group; (3) the people share a set of goals and their actions are interdependent with one another; and (4) they communicate with one another. These criterion help distinguish small group

CloseUp ON TECHNOLOGY

Technology & Small Group Communication

MOST DEFINITIONS OF small group communication during the 1950s and 1960s typically included the criterion of face-to-face communication. However, most contemporary definitions of small group communication no longer emphasize face-to-face communication. Why? The simple answer is that the explosion of communication technologies through which people exchange messages has altered the ways in which group members communicate. They no longer have to be physically present in the same room to communicate in a small group context. Think of the various ways communication technology can be used to connect group members. You can now use the intranet, the internet, desktop videoconferencing, computer-based messaging, and teleconferencing to exchange messages. You can also employ computer software that helps group members keep track of communication such as Lotus Notes or assists them in making decisions such as VisionQuest.

How does communication technology influence how group members communicate? To answer this question, let's examine one of the most heavily researched areas regarding communication technology—computer-mediated communication (CMC). As you may recall from Chapter 7, CMC represents a wide range of communication technologies that serve as a medium through which people exchange messages by computer. In small groups, members communicate through computers to perform key decision-making tasks such as analyzing the problem, generating solutions, and evaluating solutions. Several researchers investigating group CMC have focused on how technology influences communication among group members (see Scott, 1999; McLeod, 1996). The results suggest there are several misperceptions of technology's influence on group communication:

Misperception 1: Computer-mediated communication increases task-oriented communication while decreasing relational communication.
Misperception 2: Computer-mediated communication always increases group member participation.
Misperception 3: Communication technology allows the equal participation of all group members.
Misperception 4: More information is exchanged by groups using computer-mediated communication than face-to-face.

The research in these areas has been equivocal. Some research shows that CMC increases group member communication, and other studies demonstrate that it decreases communication. Similarly, some studies suggest that CMC can equalize participation among group members, and other research suggests that it creates unequal participation.

What are the consequences for the competent group communicator? Competent small group communicators need to pay attention to four issues when they use technology to coordinate group activities. First, they need to determine whether they are achieving an appropriate balance between working on the task at hand and maintaining relationships. Second, they need to consider whether they have enough participation from group members to accomplish the task. Third, are all group members participating equally or are some dominating the discussion? Fourth, they need to assess whether the group is exchanging all the relevant information in order to accomplish the task at hand. The solutions to these issues depend on the unique circumstances of the group situation. For example, when decisions need to be made quickly, task communication may be more important than communication that maintains group member relationships. When certain group members have more expertise in a particular topic area, they may need to dominate the discussion. When using technology, competent group communicators need to assess the context they are operating in and make informed judgments about the kind of communication that is required, how much group member participation is needed, whether it's effective for group members to participate equally, and whether the necessary information is made available during discussion.

communication from interpersonal and public communication as well as collections of three or more people who are randomly put together. Given these four criterion for small groups, how many of the collections of people in the chapter-opening vignette are small groups? The answer is four: Graham's study circle, the church and state listserv, the Elders, and his family.

Assumptions About Small Group Communication

Small group communication occupies a complex terrain comprised of multiple stakeholders, people both inside and outside the group who are concerned about the group's activities and who may have conflicting motivations and expectations. The terrain is complex also because a wide variety of communication channels and strategies are available to the small group communicator. Navigating group life requires an awareness of some of the central landmarks that characterize the terrain. When using an actual map, individuals can begin to orient themselves by understanding what important sites dot the landscape. The landmarks in the terrain of small group communication are the core assumptions most, if not all, researchers make about small group communication. What are some common assumptions that most researchers make about small group communication? Take a minute or two and complete the self-test here.

Now that you have finished the self-test, note your responses and let's examine which small group assumptions are true and which are false.

Test your assumptions

INSTRUCTIONS: Please read each of the following statements. Circle the answer that you think best reflects each statement.

TRUE	FALSE	**1.** Groups are more productive when the roles and responsibilities of group members are clearly defined.
TRUE	FALSE	**2.** Making decisions is the only kind of work that small groups do.
TRUE	FALSE	**3.** Dissenting opinions in small groups should be encouraged.
TRUE	FALSE	**4.** Leadership in small groups should be centralized in one or two people.
TRUE	FALSE	**5.** Effective groups are highly cohesive.
TRUE	FALSE	**6.** Good group members should conform to the wishes of the group even if it goes against their personal code of ethics.
TRUE	FALSE	**7.** Effective groups follow an orderly set of stages when developing.
TRUE	FALSE	**8.** To make an effective group decision, a group must first define the problem, then create criteria for selecting among solutions to the problem, evaluate possible solutions, and finally select a solution.

Answers: 1:T 2:F 3:T 4:F 5:F 6:F 7:F 8:F

SMALL GROUPS FACILITATE TASK ACCOMPLISHMENT

Is making decisions the primary work that groups perform? The correct answer to statement 2 is false. Groups perform a wide variety of task activities. A **task activity** is an assigned piece of work that prescribes certain duties and responsibilities that group members should perform. Table 11.1 shows the variety of groups that we may belong to. Each group is distinguished by a task activity that needs to be performed. For example, familial groups typically perform tasks such as caring for and supporting children, socializing children into the larger community, and nurturing one another's development. Recreational groups focus on playing games, competing against other teams, and providing fellowship. Occupational groups perform work. Each of these groups may make decisions, but they also perform a wide variety of other functions such as providing social support, performing work, providing leisure outlets, and so on. Earlier literature on small group communication tended to focus on decision making as the key function in groups, although recently researchers have begun focusing on a variety of other group functions (Frey, 1996a).

SMALL GROUPS INVOLVE RESPONSIBILITIES & ROLES

When people enter a small group, they begin to negotiate with the other members about the roles they will assume in a group. What kinds of roles have you played in groups? Have you been the person who keeps the group on track? Have you been the person who plays

TABLE 11.1

Type of Groups by Activity

Groups can be categorized according to the task or activity they perform. A person can belong to more than one of the groups. How many do you belong to?

ACTIVITY	SMALL GROUPS
Commercial	Consumer groups, food cooperatives, investment groups, real estate boards
Educational	Work groups in preschool, ability-level groups in elementary and secondary school, study groups in college and graduate school, occupational-training groups
Familial	Immediate family, extended family, orphanages, foster-care groups, day-care groups, communal-living groups, assisted living home groups, senior residential-facility groups, convents, rectories, abbeys
Health and welfare	Therapy groups, support groups, rehabilitation groups, residential-care facility groups
Occupational	Quality circles, management teams, research-and-development teams, committees, corporate boards of directors, work teams
Political/civic	Zoning boards, planning boards, political party committees, protest groups, boards of directors for charities, civic leagues
Recreational	Sports teams, fraternal associations, lodges, scout troops, musical bands, choirs
Social	Friendship groups, groups of acquaintances, gangs, clubs
Spiritual	Church groups, Sunday school classes, synagogues, mosque congregations, cults, covens

SOURCE: Socha (1996), p. 14.

devil's advocate? Are you the person who leads the group? Are you first to tell a joke to relieve tension in the group? Although many possible roles may be created in small groups, it is important for small group members to define their roles clearly. Defining roles and responsibilities clearly allows groups to coordinate their activity more successfully. The answer to statement 1 therefore is true.

An important role within small groups that helps coordinate a group's activity is that of the leader. Whether leadership is best performed by one or two people in a group is open to debate. Robert Bales (1950) argued that the function of leadership in small groups is so complex, it should be performed by two people in a group. One person's role should be that of the task leader with a focus on keeping the group on track in accomplishing its task. The second leader would act as the socioemotional leader and help construct and maintain a positive group climate. Bales argues that because each task is complex and time consuming, separate leaders should perform these roles.

However, recent research shows that leadership may not be limited to two people. In fact, the nature of the task determines who acts as a leader. If the task is fairly simple, one or two leaders may be all a group requires. However, if the task is complex, all members of the group may need to share leadership responsibilities. Leadership may become shared as various people perform the leadership role in the group over time (Barge, 1996). More people may need to assume leadership positions within the group as the task becomes more complex. Therefore, the answer to statement 4 is false.

SMALL GROUPS DEVELOP A CULTURE

Group culture is the values, norms, and beliefs that guide a group. Revisiting the opening vignette, Graham's study circle group culture included the values of hard work, the norms of showing up to study at prearranged times, and the belief that this hard work would lead to good grades. The creation of a group culture tells group members what is important to the group and offers rules that define how they should act and respond to each other. Groups with strong cultures have members who accept and maintain the existing group culture. As a result, such groups tend to be highly cohesive; their members feel psychologically close to one another.

Does a high level of cohesion make for more effective groups? The answer to statement 5 is false. Effective groups are those that have a productive level of cohesion. If a group's cohesion level is too low, the group exhibits scarce agreement about how members should act together and little consensus around what is important. As a result, the group is disorganized and, at times, may fall into conflict. This conflict emerges because group members struggle over which values are important and how the group should be organized. When groups become too cohesive, however, members may fail to voice dissenting opinions from the majority as well as fail to vigorously question and debate the group's decision and the assumptions that led to the decision (Janis & Mann, 1977). This means that groups need to have enough cohesion to reach consensus on the group's goals and tasks but not so much cohesion as to prevent a rigorous examination and evaluation of alternatives that could be taken to solve a group problem or achieve a task.

When groups have too much cohesion, group members may fail to voice dissenting opinions even if the group's decision goes against their better judgment and personal code of ethics. Although it may be difficult, group members need to voice their concerns even if they don't conform to the wishes of the group, especially if they feel the group has not adequately explored all alternatives. Bringing up different viewpoints and perspectives can improve group decision making. At the same time, group members need to be aware that by voicing unpopular views and challenging the majority group opinion, they run the risk of being ostracized from the group. Therefore, the answer to statement 6 is false.

SMALL GROUPS MUST MANAGE THEIR DEVELOPMENT

No matter what their purpose, all groups must make choices. These choices involve the kinds of task activities the group wishes to pursue, the types of roles and responsibilities members will assume, and the values, norms, and beliefs that will drive the group interaction. Groups also make choices about how the group will develop and how it will accomplish decision making. As you saw in the opening vignette, Graham's study group made choices about how often to meet to study for their political science class. The Elders made decisions about how they would provide service to library users—when to pay attention to library policies and when to conveniently ignore them.

You might think that group development and decision making are orderly, rational processes, yet the answer to statements 7 and 8 are false. It seems intuitive that groups should go through an orderly set of stages. Tuckman and Jensen (1977) suggest that all groups go through the following phases as they develop: (1) forming, (2) storming, (3) norming, and (4) performing. During the forming stage, group members meet each other, often for the first time, and orient themselves toward each other and the task they must perform. During the storming phase, group members argue and debate the nature of the task at hand and fall into conflict over their role relationships and ways to organize the group. The norming phase signals the end of the storming phase as group members forge a consensus on the nature of the task and how best to achieve it as well as their respective roles. The last phase is the performing phase when the group performs the work it was assigned.

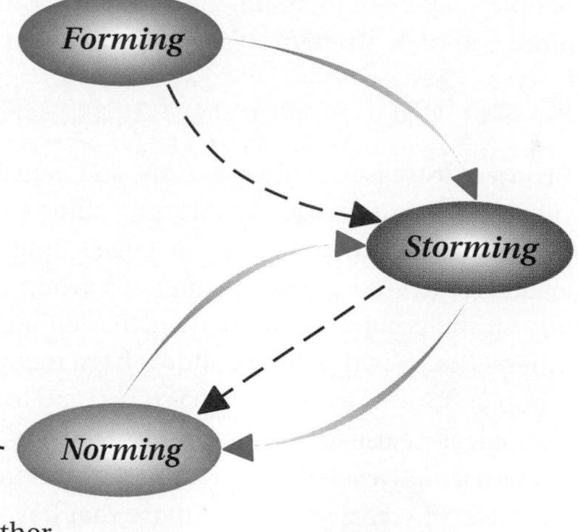

FIGURE 11.1
Group Phases

To see the order of phases in Tuckman and Jensen's Model, start with the forming phase and follow the dashed red lines. To see an example of the phases and sequences in Poole's model, start with the performing phase and follow the solid blue lines.

Do all groups go through these phases in a precise order? Some groups do and they are able to develop in an orderly fashion and make high-quality decisions. However, an increasing amount of evidence suggests that groups do not develop as neatly as Tuckman and Jensen (1977) and other similar models suggest. M. Scott Poole and his associates (1996) argue that groups can go through this process in a variety of different combinations of phases and even experience each phase any number of times. It is possible that a group may start off with the forming stage but cycle repeatedly between storming and norming without ever getting to the performing stage. In this case, endless heated discussions about how to organize the group may prevent the group from performing. The differences between Tuckman & Jensen and Poole's Model can be seen in Figure 11.1. Given that groups may cycle through any number of any phases in any given order, does this mean that good group development and quality decision making are rare? As we explore in Chapter 12, the key to quality decision making is in fulfilling basic functions such as defining the nature of the task, setting criteria, generating alternatives, and evaluating alternatives. The performance of these particular functions rather than the order in which they are performed is critical to quality decision making.

Why Small Group Communication Is Important

Mastering small group communication is important for several reasons: (1) we find ourselves communicating in many small groups and cannot help but communicate in small groups in every aspect of our lives, (2) constructive small group environments can generate higher creativity and push people to surpass their individual performance, and (3) small groups can also negatively influence people. Given the prevalence of small groups and the positive and negative effects they can have on your life, sharpening one's small group communication skills is central to becoming a competent communicator.

WE FIND OURSELVES COMMUNICATING IN MANY SMALL GROUPS

Take a moment and list all the groups you belong to—social clubs, sports teams, study groups, work groups, and so on. You will probably find that you have created a fairly long list. This is not surprising because we are increasingly creating groups to help us manage our work and personal lives. The use of small groups or work teams in business organizations is on the rise. Given the complexities of organizational life, business strategies such as dispersing decision making and increasing flexibility have emphasized the use of teams (Scott, 1999). Because small groups play an increasing role in business and personal spheres, learning to manage group dynamics and developing team skills will become even more valuable in business. Educators increasingly use small groups in the classroom to enhance learning through a method known as *cooperative learning* in which students help others master the class material in a group structure (Cooper, Robinson, & McKinney, 1994; Gamson, 1994). Group work is expanding in the important field of mental health as well. It is estimated that 40% of the U.S. population, 75 million people, currently belong to some type of support group that meets regularly (Wuthnow, 1994). You can safely anticipate that you'll be an active participant in any number of small groups in different arenas during your lifetime. Thus learning how to communicate competently in this setting can enhance your professional and personal development.

SMALL GROUPS CAN MOTIVATE CREATIVITY & HIGH PERFORMANCE

In addition to enriching a professional and personal life, certain types of small groups have great potential to create an environment that encourages personal performance and generates high creativity in decision making. Research and development teams in organizations depend on creating environments that allow group members to be creative and develop innovative new products. In fact, the results of work teams in such organizations as Microsoft, Apple, Volvo, and W.I. Gore demonstrate the promises of unleashing creativity and high-level performance. Local chapters of nonprofit organizations such as the Red Cross, American Heart Association, and Muscular Dystrophy Association routinely assign committees the task of developing new fund-raising activities. Such groups emphasize brainstorming creative fund-raising projects and events to support the organization. Even support groups for addictions such as alcohol, drugs, and smoking provide encouragement and motivation to their members. These groups provide opportunities for members to share their success stories, provide new and creative ideas for coping with addiction, and offer encouragement.

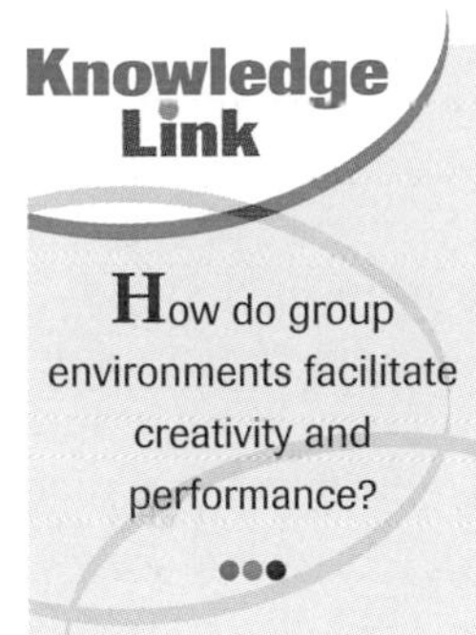

The idea that small groups have the potential for stimulating higher levels of performance among their members has been recognized for over a century (Triplett, 1897). **Social facilitation** maintains that individuals increase their level of effort on a task in the presence of others. Small groups are thought to motivate people to perform their very best and are, for this reason, used to harness this motivational power. Moreover, small groups are thought to generate more high-quality decisions and engage the creativity of group members (Jarboe, 1999). For example, one of the benefits of Graham's study group in the opening vignette was that each group member was motivated by friendly competition. The presence of others in the study group motivated each member to master the material and demonstrate his or her knowledge. To fall behind in the reading and fail to offer constructive input during group meetings would be neither appropriate nor effective.

SMALL GROUPS CAN ALSO NEGATIVELY INFLUENCE PEOPLE

The power that small groups wield can also take on a negative dimension. Small groups can lead to poor decision making and even cause harm and destruction. For example, highly educated engineers involved in the decision to launch the space shuttle *Challenger* in 1986 ignored clear signs of a disaster due to negative influences from the group. Perhaps even sadder are the tragic deaths of group members in cults such as Jonestown in Guyana, the Branch Davidians in Waco, and Heaven's Gate in San Diego. These cult tragedies provide sobering examples of how small groups can pose personal peril by eroding people's individuality and causing them to act as they normally would not. In

Sometimes people try to disguise the negative effects of groups.

DILBERT reprinted by permission of United Feature Syndicate, Inc.

each of these cults, the group had created such a strong culture that each member lost his or her individual identity and was unable to challenge the group. When members are strongly socialized in the values, attitudes, and beliefs of a group, they may begin to lose their sense of personal identity and think of themselves only in terms of the group (Keyton, 1999). Strong socialization caused the tragedies in all of these cults. In the Heaven's Gate cult, for example, all the members dressed in the same way and ate the same food at the same time; in short, they manifested outward signs of loss of their individuality. This conformity led to their tragic decision to commit suicide to join the "mother ship" following the Hale-Bopp comet in 1997. Not one member spoke out against this fatal plan.

Thus small groups hold both promise and peril for those who participate. They can challenge us to reach higher levels of performance and generate creative ideas and arrive at high-quality decisions. At the same time, groups present the risk of erasing our sense of individuality. Pressure to conform to a group agenda can diminish critical thinking ability and may decrease the ability to make good decisions. Still, small groups are an important environment in which communication takes place. You not only will belong to a large number of small groups during your lifetime, but you also have the ability to make choices that will influence the quality of your small group communication. You can make choices that lead to an empowering group life or you can make choices that disempower you and lead to poor choices. Learning about competent communication in small groups will facilitate the positive effects groups can bring to your life and minimize the negative effects.

A Model of Small Group Communication Competence

Small group communication competence is an impression formed by you and other people that you have acted in ways that are appropriate and effective in the small group. As you'll recall, three factors influence your ability to communicate competently: (1) motivation, (2) knowledge, and (3) skills. When a member of a small group is highly motivated, knowledgeable, and possesses the necessary skills, he or she is more likely to be perceived as a competent communicator in the context of the small group. Competent communication takes place when the circles of motivation, knowledge, and skills in the model intersect and produce perceptions of communication competence. The greater the overlap among these three circles, the more likely the small group communicator will be perceived as a competent communicator. Let's now return to the specific components—motivation, knowledge, and skills—of the communication competence model as it applies to the small group context shown in Figure 11.2.

MOTIVATION

Motivation refers to a person's desire to engage in small groups and to interact with the other members. But what determines the level of one's motivation to participate in a small group? For example, what motivated Graham to participate in his study circle? Perhaps he was motivated to participate because he enjoyed spending time with the people who were in the group. Or perhaps he was motivated to join and participate in the group because he needed to complete a task. Perhaps he felt that studying political science in a small group would gain him a high grade in the course. Or maybe Graham is simply one of those people who are joiners, people who sign up for everything that is offered. Graham may have joined the study circle for any one of these reasons.

Each of these explanations highlights a different motivation for joining a small group. In fact, four factors motivate individuals to join and participate in groups: (1) people, (2) task, (3) need fulfillment, and (4) personal traits. **People factors** refer to an attraction to the people who are members of the group. For example, groups of friends or social clubs are small groups where the primary motivator to join is an attraction to the people. **Task factors** refer to an attraction to the specific task, activity, or goal that the group performs or hopes to accomplish. Examples of groups motivated by task factors include study groups, work groups, and sports teams. An individual's personality may influence how motivated he or she is to join and participate in a group. **Need fulfillment** occurs when an

FIGURE 11.2
The Model of Small Group Communication Competence

Small group communication competence depends on your level of motivation, knowledge, and skills. Communicating competently in small groups depends on your ability to interact in ways that are appropriate and effective given the context.

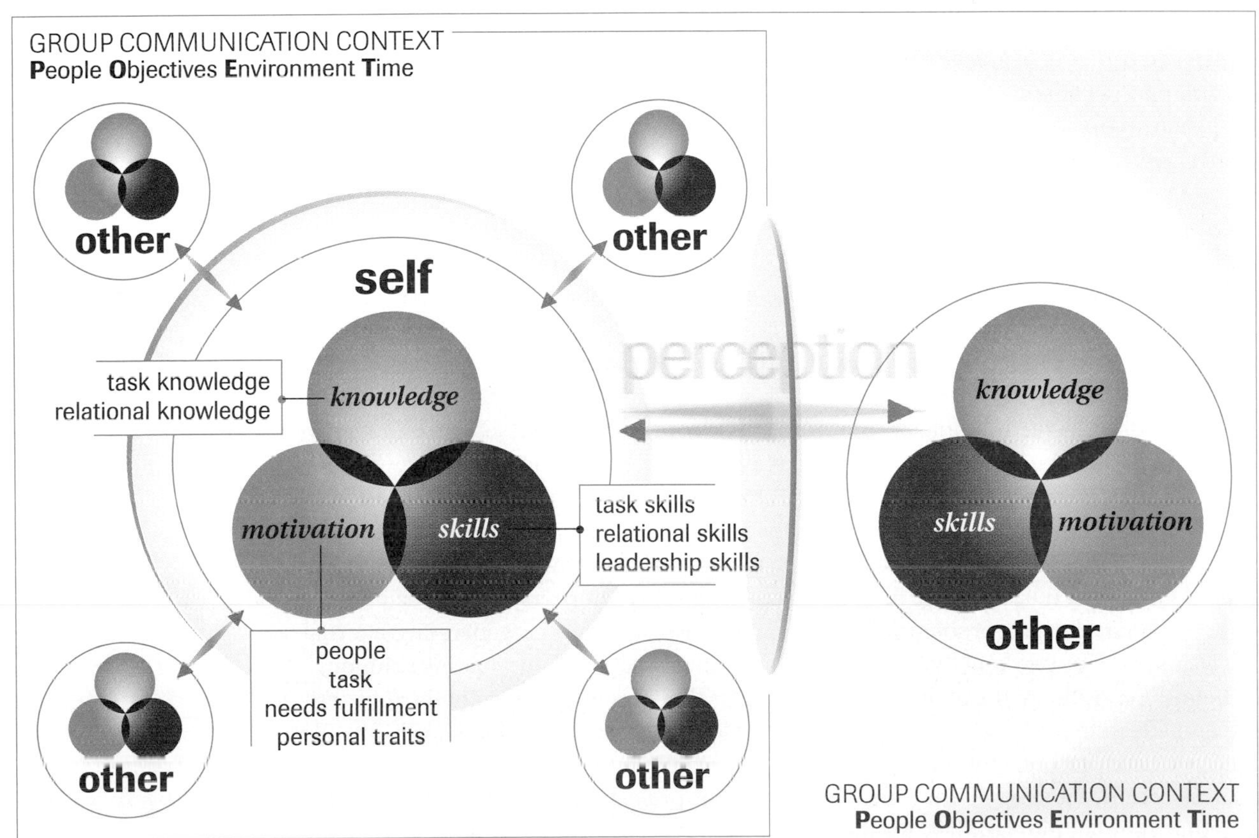

individual joins and participates in a group based on his or her personal and social needs. People may join a Neighborhood Watch group in order to meet their safety needs or they may join groups such as Weight Watchers or SmokeEnders to improve their self-image. **Personality traits** are cognitive and social qualities inherent in a person that affect the level at which he or she joins and participates in groups. For example, extroverted people have personalities that lead them to join small groups; introverts do not. Although each of these factors influences the level of motivation to join and participate in groups, some are more dominant in some situations than others. For example, an individual may be so attracted to the people in the group (people factors) as to overcome his or her ambivalence toward the group task.

KNOWLEDGE

What does a person need to know in order to participate competently in a small group? To be a competent small group communicator, you need to have knowledge about the task at hand and managing relationships. The former, called **task knowledge,** is knowledge about how to perform a particular group activity and how to make decisions appropriate to the task. For example, in the opening vignette, Graham's task knowledge about his study partners included knowing how to share information about the class readings and how to challenge and critique the ideas of his study partners.

The latter, called **relational knowledge,** is knowing how to manage social relationships among group members, build positive group environments, and manage potential conflict. Small groups such as Graham's study group encounter a variety of challenges as they go through a variety of stages in their life. In Graham's group, the members initially needed to orient themselves to each other and to the task they were undertaking. As they worked together over the semester, they created roles for each group member to perform and developed a set of agreements about of how they would interact with one another. As a result they became a highly productive group. Knowing how to create a constructive role in a small group and being aware of the various strategies that you can use to develop productive working environments facilitates creating and maintaining positive relationships.

SKILLS

Similar to the knowledge component of the small group communication competency model, the skills component includes task and relational skills. **Task skills** are associated with decision making, selecting among competing alternative courses of action and ideas. In traditional small group theory, task skills include the ability to communicate messages that define and analyze the problem, identify criteria for solutions, generate and evaluate solutions to the problem, and maintain task focus. Imagine that you chair a committee for a service club at your college or university that is charged with coordinating the club's semester schedule for social service projects. To chair such a committee, you would need the task skills of articulating the purpose of performing these social service projects (defining the problem), identifying challenges to performing these social service projects (analyzing the problem), brainstorming possible projects (generating alternatives), and selecting among the particular projects for the schedule (evaluating solutions).

Relational skills are the ability to send messages that promote and maintain appropriate and effective working relationships among group members. Relational skills include managing conflict and maintaining positive group climate. As you chair the social service project committee, people may disagree over what projects should be included in the schedule and fall into conflict. Relational skills will help you work through these differences of opinions, manage the input so everyone gets a voice, and direct the interaction to remind group members of the task at hand and the value of each member's contribution. Both skills and knowledge work together to facilitate communication competence. The primary focus of task knowledge and skills is decision making and problem solving, which we cover in depth in Chapter 12. Relational knowledge and skills center on conflict management and leadership. We will cover these functions in depth in Chapter 13.

Context

As you've seen thus far in this chapter, as well as in your own experiences, groups do not exist in a vacuum. They function as social units in a world of people with different intentions and expectations. In addition to mastering the components of motivation, knowledge, and skills, to be a competent communicator you must be aware of the context in which the small group communication is taking place so you can communicate in a way that is appropriate and effective for others. As discussed in Chapter 2, context refers to culture, function, place, and time. These four factors provide a general starting place for understanding the group context. However, the small group context is unique and can be better understood by considering **P**eople, **O**bjectives, **E**nvironment, and **T**ime (POET).

"People" refers to the individuals who have an interest in the group's activities. "People" may include members inside the group and individuals or stakeholders external to the group. For example, a city council may want to annex property adjoining the city. To make an effective decision, the city council must take into account the expectations of the people who live in the proposed area to be annexed as well as the current city citizens. People may hold certain expectations and preferences for particular kinds of behavior. Not only may they want the group to act in a certain way, but they may also hold certain ideas of what each group member's behavior in the group should be. Therefore, to communicate competently, group members must learn to anticipate the expectations that others within and outside the group may have for their behavior.

The second way to characterize small groups is by objectives. Any variety of groups exist, and one of the ways to define them is by the activity they perform and the objectives driving these activities. The group's objectives determine the types of activities valued by the group. An objective is an endpoint or destination toward which effort is directed. Groups can have many objectives. For example, some objectives may focus on the aspects of a task and include completing it within a given time frame, performing it to meet certain criteria of excellence, or even performing the task to include all group members and build consensus. Other objectives may focus on the interpersonal relationships between group members, rather than the task at hand. Such objectives may include minimizing conflict in the group, establishing friendships that will outlast the group, and establishing high levels of group cohesion. Objectives create benchmarks for evaluating a group member's behavior. Competence in small group communication, then, involves recognizing the group's objectives and performing in ways that meet these objectives.

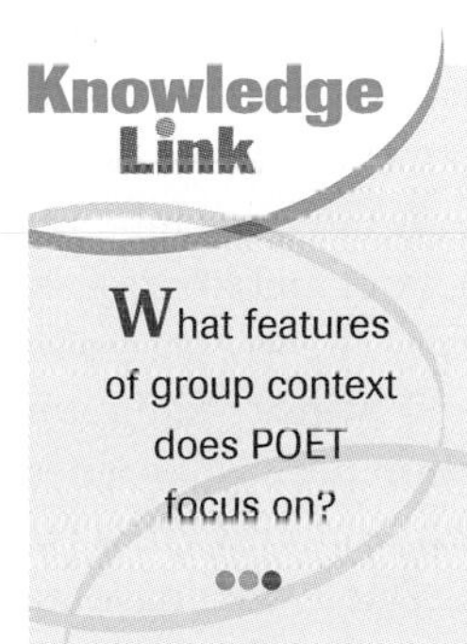

The context is also described in terms of the environment created among group members. The **group environment,** informed by group members' feelings and emotions, is the climate in which group members communicate. Group environment can be described as friendly, supportive, hostile, encouraging, and so on. Recognizing the environment of a group allows a competent communicator to select messages that either affirm constructive feelings and emotions or transform negative, hostile environments into more positive and open environments.

Finally, the last context factor is time, or the developmental phase of the group. Just as humans experience different developmental phases throughout their lifetimes, groups also go through phases similar to human development. As you saw earlier, these stages are forming, norming, storming, and performing. Each group phase carries with it certain expectations and norms for competent behavior. Imagine you are the city manager for the city council, which has decided to annex property adjoining the city. One of the reasons you were hired is to manage the city more proactively. On your executive staff team, a particular manager does not agree with your philosophy and subtly undermines your authority. What do you do? Most people's instincts would lead them to reprimand or even terminate this person. Although it may be tempting to fire this individual, doing so in the forming stage of this group could backfire—you have just assumed your position, and you have only begun the process of developing relationships with other employees and building trust. If you fire an employee almost immediately after assuming your position, you may jeopardize this very important stage in the development of your group. Such a move might be viewed as appropriate in a later stage of the group's development, once you have established yourself and gained some experience with the group. As you can see, the time factor, or the phase of the group, influences how you act and how your actions are perceived.

What Motivates You to Join & Participate in Groups?

What motivates you to join small groups? Do you join because you like the people? Is there something about the task itself that you find attractive and want to participate in? As you saw in the opening vignette, numerous attractors motivate people to join and participate in groups. Consider Graham's possible motivations for participating in different groups: He joined the study circle group to get an "A" in his political science class; he participated in the listserv because it concerned a topic he was highly interested in; he was highly motivated to go home for the holidays to renew his friendships with his family. These can be grouped into four major attractors: (1) people, (2) task, (3) need fulfillment, and (4) personality traits. We previewed these factors earlier when discussing a model of competence. We look at them in depth now.

People

On most college campuses, a number of formal and informal social organizations, such as fraternities and sororities, dorm groups, and groups of friends, provide opportunities for people to be together and socialize. In the larger community there are any number of social service or charity groups as well as sports teams, investing clubs, dinner clubs, and theater groups you can participate in to pursue personal and professional interests. What motivates people to join such groups? A common reason for most people is that they simply like the people who already belong to that particular group. Such attraction can be based on a variety of factors such as similarity of experience and background, physical attractiveness, common values, and similar beliefs and interests. For example, people join alumni clubs of colleges and universities because they attended that particular school and like to keep in contact with people who shared the same educational experience. People join advocacy groups for the homeless, the economically disadvantaged, and at-risk children because they share a common set of values. People join particular churches, synagogues, and mosques because the people who already belong to such institutions share a common set of religious and cultural beliefs.

Our attraction to other people is influenced by how we are introduced and become acquainted with them. When people are told about another person and discover that this person has a very different set of beliefs and values from themselves, they are typically not attracted to that person. But, if they first have a conversation where they discover similarities and then subsequently discover they have different beliefs, they are still likely to be attracted to the person. For example, with the goal of fostering constructive conversation, a group of therapists brought together people with opposing viewpoints on controversial issues such as abortion (Chasin et al., 1996). The therapists set up an initial meeting to have people from both sides of the issue get to know each other. In these get-acquainted conversations, the participants were told not to reveal their positions on abortion but simply to get to know one another, sharing their hobbies, their family experiences, and so forth. By preceding the discussion of the controversial topic with conversations that stress similarities, opponents experience more interpersonal attraction and trust, which, in turn, created a space for more constructive conversation of the debated issue.

TASK

People often join groups because of their attraction to the task. People are interested in many kinds of tasks, including political activity, hobbies, social service projects, and religious activities.

We may be attracted to some groups more than others based on the activities or task they perform. **Task attraction** involves a particular task a group performs and the goals it pursues that motivate people to join and participate in a group. You may find yourself attracted to groups such as the Republicans, Democrats, Reform Party, Greenpeace, National Eagle Forum, and the Sierra Club for the kinds of political beliefs they pursue and the agenda they advocate. You may want to join groups because they can further your own personal interests and hobbies. Theater groups, singing groups, athletic clubs, wine-tasting clubs, and hobby clubs, such as coin collecting, Beanie Babies, or antiques, represent groups that perform tasks we enjoy. For example, in the opening vignette, Graham joined the listserv group because he was attracted to the particular topic the group was engaged with.

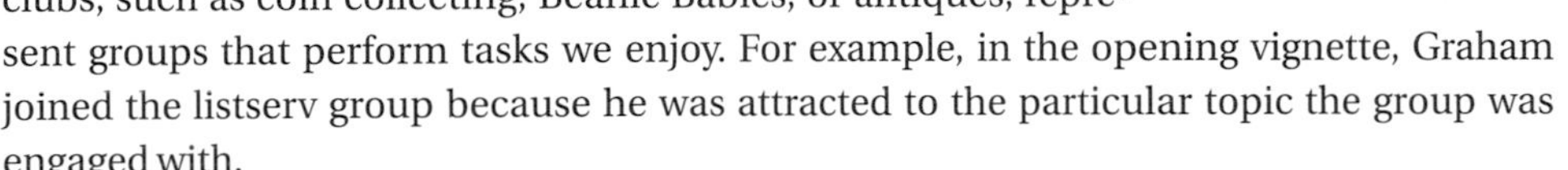

NEED FULFILLMENT

Small groups serve an important social function in that they help us meet our personal and social needs. In fact, it is impossible to achieve personal and social needs without the help of others. Therefore, a primary motivator for joining and participating in small groups is that they facilitate fulfilling our needs. One of the major theories that classify and explain human needs is Alfred Schutz's interpersonal needs typology.

Schutz (1960, 1966) argues that people have three primary needs: (1) the need for inclusion, (2) the need for control, and (3) the need for affection. Schutz also theorized that the way we express these needs to others may vary from the ways we want others to express them to us.

The **need for inclusion** is the need to maintain satisfactory relationships and associations with others. Individuals who have high needs for inclusion want to be involved in relationships, friendships, and associations with other people. Such people may express this need to others by asking to join groups and inviting others to join them in activities. These people may also participate more in group discussions. On the contrary, people who have low inclusion needs don't feel the need to issue invitations to join and tend to participate little in group discussions.

The **need for control** is the amount of power an individual needs in a relationship. People with a high need for control typically express this need to others and may assume a position of leadership or power within the group. Such people have a strong need to guide and direct the activities of others. In contrast, people with a low need for control may actually invite others to lead and control their actions. Such people may feel more comfortable in a subordinate position within the group.

The **need for affection** is the need for receiving and giving warmth and positive regard to others. People who have a high need for affection typically seek warmth, support, and positive regard from others; people who have low needs in this area do not.

Schutz argues that the needs for inclusion, control, and affection have two dimensions. The first dimension is what people want others to express to them. For example, people who have high inclusion needs typically want to be invited to participate in activities and included in relationships. People who have high control needs prefer to direct their own behavior. The second dimension is what a person expresses to the group. For example, a person who is high in inclusion needs may express to the group that he or she wants to be included in group activities. A person who is high in control needs may express an interest in leadership to the group.

It would be easy to assume that to understand motivation for joining and participating in a group all you would have to do is to assess someone's needs for inclusion, control, and affection. What makes this difficult is that although a person may want one thing, he or she may express the opposite. For example, a group member may desperately want to be included in group activities, yet he or she may express the opposite to others. Similarly, a person may want to take control of a group and yet express to others that he or she doesn't mind assuming a more submissive position. To understand people's motivations for joining and participating in a group, it is important to understand what they want others to express to them as well as what they express to others.

PERSONALITY TRAITS

Personality traits are tendencies to think, act, and feel in certain ways. Personality traits influence our tendency to participate or to be assertive, shy, or anxious in small groups (Frey, 1996b, p. 69). One personality trait that influences how you work within small groups is whether you hold an individualistic or collectivistic orientation. If you hold an **individualistic orientation,** you tend to stress individual

Test your cultural orientation

Are you more individualistic or collectivistic? Complete the scales to see where you fall.

INSTRUCTIONS: The purpose of this questionnaire is to help you assess your individualistic and collectivistic tendencies. Respond by indicating the degree to which the values in each phrase are important to you on a scale of 1 to 5: "opposed to my values" is 1, "not important to me" is 2, "somewhat important to me" is 3, "important to me" is 4, and "very important to me" is 5.

_____ **1.** Obtaining pleasure or sensuous gratification

_____ **2.** Preserving the welfare of others

_____ **3.** Being successful by demonstrating my individual competency

_____ **4.** Restraining my behavior if it is going to harm others

_____ **5.** Being independent in thought and action

_____ **6.** Having safety and stability for people with whom I identify

_____ **7.** Obtaining status and prestige

_____ **8.** Having harmony in my relations with others

_____ **9.** Having an exciting and challenging life

_____ **10.** Accepting cultural and religious traditions

_____ **11** Being recognized for my individual work

_____ **12.** Conforming to social norms

_____ **13.** Being self-directed

_____ **14.** Being benevolent (and kind to others)

_____ **15.** Having power

_____ **16.** Being polite to others

_____ **17.** Being ambitious

_____ **18.** Being self-controlled

_____ **19.** Being able to choose what I do

_____ **20.** Enhancing the welfare of others

Answers: To find your individualism score, add all of your numerical responses to the odd-numbered items. To find your collectivism score, add your responses to the even-numbered items. Both scores will range from 10 to 50. The higher your scores, the more individualistic and/or collectivistic you are. Equal scores in both areas reflect a balance between individualist and collectivist tendencies.

SOURCE: Gudykunst (1998), p. 67.

goals and personal achievements over group goals and achievements (Haslett & Ruebush, 1999). For example, North American students of all ages express concern about working in groups because they feel the group grade may not adequately reflect their contributions or that they will be forced to do the majority of the work. Such reactions are common in countries like the United States where the overall culture has an individualistic orientation. A **collectivistic orientation,** which is dominant in cultures like Japan, China, and Korea, is one where group goals take priority over individual goals. People with a collectivistic orientation often find it hard to speak up and offer their opinions in a group setting especially if they are contrary to the group majority opinion. Are you more individualistic or collectivistic in your orientation? Take the self-test on the facing page to find out.

How might an individualistic or collectivistic orientation influence your behavior in small groups? If you hold an individualistic orientation, you may believe:

- individuals make better decisions than groups.
- leaders and not all group members should do the planning.
- rewards should be based on individual performance.
- individuals are motivated to work for themselves.
- competition among group members is healthy.
- the best way to accomplish a task is to work with individuals as opposed to the entire group.
- the purpose of group meetings is to advance the individual's objectives.
- leaders should retain tight control over group meetings. (Beebe & Masterson, 1997, p. 20).

If you held a collectivistic orientation you probably value team meetings because they allow all group members to offer input and make decisions. You may make this assumption because you believe group members work for the team and the team is strongest when consensus is reached in decision making. If you hold a collectivist orientation, you may believe:

- loyalty to the group supersedes individual needs.
- individuals are identified with the groups to which they belong.
- consensus in group decision making is paramount.
- individuals should not stand out and take recognition for group efforts.
- team meetings are valuable because they offer opportunities for all team members to make recommendations.
- the group is strongest when members reach consensus in decision making.

Understanding your predisposition to individualistic or collectivist culture is indispensable to building strong productive groups. In a group of people who hold strong individualistic tendencies, it may be difficult to encourage group members to collaborate with one another. But if a group is comprised of people with a strong collectivist orientation, they may not analyze each others' ideas and opinions critically because they prefer not to disrupt the group harmony. As a result, an uncritical acceptance of information and ideas can lead to poor decision making.

Challenges to Small Group Competence

Two central challenges confront the small group communicator. First, group members may have difficulty coordinating their activity given the large number of possible relationships between people in the group. Unlike an interpersonal relationship where you only have to manage the relationship between you and one other person, in group situations you must manage your relationship with each group member as well as the relationships that exist between other group members. The number of possible relationships within groups that need to be managed can be overwhelming.

Second, people have multiple motivations for belonging to and participating in groups. As we discussed in the previous section, in the United States and other individualistic cultures, people are taught to "go it alone" and "look out for number 1." When people have different reasons for participating in groups, it becomes difficult to encourage collaborative group work.

COORDINATION PROBLEMS

Part of the challenge small group communicators face is the number of interactions they must manage with other group members. In interpersonal communication, there are only two interactions to manage—your interaction with the other person and the other person's interaction with you. In Figure 11.3, when you have 3 people in a group, you have 9 interactions to manage. The number and complexity of interactions increases exponentially as you add more people to the situation (Bostrom, 1970). When you have a group of 4 people, 28 interactions exist. At 8 people, the number of possible interactions jumps to 1,056.

The sheer number of interactions that group members must manage can make it difficult to coordinate group action. For example, in a group of 8 people, the 1,056 interactions you have to manage complicates what you should say during a meeting because you have multiple audiences. How you might explain something to Ming may be very different than how you would explain it to Otis. If you could talk to each person privately, you could tailor your explanation to each audience by using language he or she could understand. However, in a small group setting, how do you get your point across to all the group members? Your ability to coordinate the action of the group is limited by not being able to communicate in ways that each group member will hear equally clearly.

Besides managing multiple interaction possibilities, coordination problems can also arise because of a phenomenon known as **social loafing,** which occurs when people do not put fourth their best effort to complete a task because they believe other group members will pick up the slack to compensate for their lack of effort (Latané & Harkins, 1979; Schultz, 1999). It is not unusual for group members to slack off in performance because they know others will fill in the gap. Social loafing can lead to a variety of coordination problems. On one hand, other group members may pick up the slack but label the loafer as "trouble" and ostracize him or her from future group interactions. Although this may appear to be a good solution to some, it increases the workload for the remaining group members, which may in turn increase stress and fatigue and result in coordination problems. On the other hand, the other group members may refuse to fill in for the loafing member. The risk in this situation is that the work may not get done, hurting the group's productivity. Again, this results in a coordination problem. Social loafing poses a significant challenge for the individual group members as well as the overall group in terms of productivity.

FIGURE 11.3
Complexity and a Three-Person Group

In a three-person group there are nine possible relationships you have to manage. Single relationships are relationships that occur between two people. Double relationships have one person relating to the other two group members. Triple relationships refer to the relationships between a group member and the entire group.

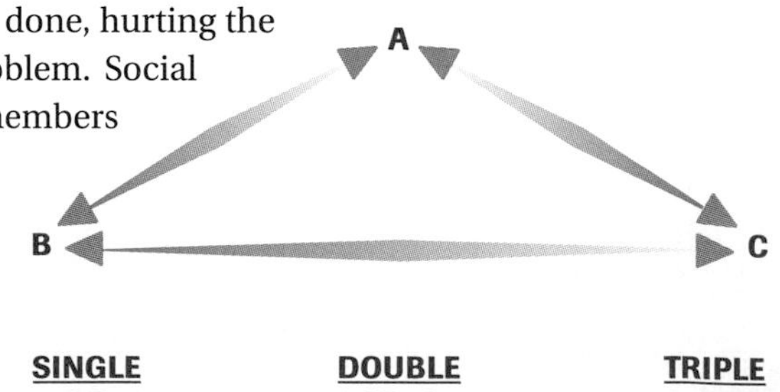

SINGLE	DOUBLE	TRIPLE
AB	AB-C	A-ABC
AC	AC-B	B-ABC
BC	BC-A	C-ABC

MULTIPLE MOTIVATIONS

Some challenges to small group competence emerge from the fact that members have multiple motivations for belonging to groups. A person may have multiple reasons for joining a hiking club. Perhaps this person wants to exercise and lose weight.

Perhaps the person has a genuine love of the outdoors and the environment. It could be that the person joined for the sake of joining a group. Or perhaps the person joined to make new friends and meet a potential mate or partner. How would the president of the hiking club manage the club, given the members' diverse set of motivations? If the president wanted to launch a large-scale environmental conservation project that would involve a lot of effort on the part of the members, this project would appeal only to members genuinely interested in the outdoors—not those using the club for social interaction. Or the president might want to emphasize the social aspects of the club. This emphasis may appeal to people who joined the club to make new friends and develop new love interests, but it may be viewed as a waste of time by those people who are serious about exercise and losing weight. As you can see, the president faces some significant challenges in developing an agenda that will appeal to all of the members.

Managing multiple motivations of group members is difficult because the motivations are not always visible. Group members may sometimes have a hidden agenda for joining and participating in a group. A **hidden agenda** is a motivation for joining a group that is kept secret by concealing the motivation from other group members or by publicly offering a false motivation while keeping the real motivation private. A prime example of the hidden agenda is when a person runs for elected office such as a local school board in order to pursue their own private agenda. They say their reason for running is "helping the kids," but they pursue other ideological goals once elected.

Knowledge Link

How do issues of coordination and multiple motivations pose problems for the competent group communicator?

Overcoming Challenges to Competence

Many of the negative experiences emerging from your group participation can be traced to the challenges arising from the multiple motivations of group members and the difficulty in coordinating multiple relationships within small groups. How do you work through challenges to competence in ways that help the group work productively? You can begin to address these challenges by examining what motivates you to participate in small groups as well as exploring what motivates others to join and participate in small groups. Exploring your personal motivations for joining and participating in small groups as well as those of the other group members provides valuable information that can be used to coordinate the activities of the group. Three strategies are important to exploring motivations and creating group structures that facilitate coordination:

1. articulating personal hopes and motivations
2. exploring others' motivations
3. establishing accountability

Articulating Personal Hopes & Motivations

One strategy for determining what motivates you to join groups is articulating your personal hopes and motivations. The process of articulating your personal hopes and motivations consists of two steps.

First, reflect on the past successes of groups you participated in and the times when you were highly motivated. To get started, answer the following questions:

1. What was the best group you ever participated in? What happened in that group to make it a peak experience?

2. When you belonged to this group, what motivated you most? When were you most motivated to participate? What did other people say or do that motivated you?
3. What was the most important value shared by group members that guided the group?
4. What rules did the group use to help run the group effectively?
5. What was it about the group experience that motivated you to do your best?

Once you've answered these questions, repeat this step for as many groups as you feel necessary. These questions allow you to identify those times when you were highly motivated to participate in a group. Recalling those times when you were highly motivated provides the information necessary to construct a profile of the factors that create and maintain your motivation to participate in small groups.

The second step involves recognizing the factors that influence your motivation. Using the information you collected in the first stage, complete the following phrase: "I am most motivated to participate in a small group when . . ." Provide multiple answers to this phrase if needed. For example, your answer list may look something like this:

I am most motivated to participate in a small group when . . .

- the group's goal is clear.
- everyone pulls their own weight.
- we have clear deadlines for completing our task.
- we have fun.
- the task or problem we face is interesting.

Developing a list like this will help you better understand what your needs, hopes, and desires are for a successful group experience. Once you clarify what you need to have happen in the group, you will then be better able to explain your needs and preferences to other group members and experience a fulfilling group experience. Your ability to articulate your needs and preferences influences the other group members' ability to understand and address the multiple motivations of people within the group.

EXPLORING OTHERS' MOTIVATIONS

Now that you've considered your own motivations for joining small groups, consider what motivates others to participate in groups. Knowledge of your own motivations isn't always enough to overcome challenges to communication in small groups; it is also important to explore and recognize other people's needs. This can be challenging because people may have hidden agendas and disguise their true motivations.

How can you begin exploring someone's motivations and uncover their hidden agenda? The easiest way to accomplish this task is to inquire into their needs and listen to their responses. The method for articulating your personal hopes and motivations can also be applied to sorting out others' motivations. Inquiring into what motivates people can help you articulate other group members' needs and preferences. The listening skills covered in Chapter 6 can also help you identify other people's motivations as you perform this exercise.

ESTABLISHING ACCOUNTABILITY

One of the chief challenges to communication competence in small groups is managing the large number of relationships within the group. As you've seen, the large number of relationships within small groups makes it difficult to coordinate group activity and can lead to social loafing. How can you ensure that group members share the same orientation to the task? How can you keep the activities of group members coordinated and focused on the task at hand? One strategy for overcoming challenges arising from coordination is establishing accountability.

Developing agreements within small groups that hold members accountable for their group responsibilities is one way to overcome differing levels of motivation. Some groups develop agreements about how individual and group performance should be rewarded. For example, each member of a sales team of pharmacy representatives may be assigned the task of selling a new line of drugs within a given territory. Part of each sales rep's compensation is determined by his or her individual level of performance, and part of the compensation is determined by the overall performance level of all reps in the entire district. Such a compensation system holds the sales reps accountable for individual performance levels while fostering collaboration to drive other reps' sales in the region. In small groups, developing incentives for both individual and group performance increases the accountability of group members.

Group members must discuss at the outset how they will handle performance problems and keep people accountable to achieve competent small group communication. For example, a group may agree that if a member fails to execute an assignment the first time, the group meets to tell the low performer of the difficulty and offer advice on how to correct it. The second time this person fails to perform an assigned task, the group may decide that the person should be assigned additional responsibilities to make up for the lack of performance. The third time it occurs, the group may agree to terminate the group member's relationship with the group. In this example, through establishing accountability the group has created guidelines for discussing and remedying performance issues caused by members who are unable or unwilling to perform in the small group context. Establishing accountability early on in a group's life can prevent the problems associated with multiple motivations.

ETHICS & SMALL GROUP COMMUNICATION

Imagine you are the lead person on a team designing a new video game for a recently formed computer game company. The new video game is based on the idea that a high school has been taken over by supernatural demons and monsters who have trapped the students in the school. The player in the game then fights his or her way out of the school by killing the demons and monsters. Although the game is fairly violent and the graphics are gory, you are very excited about this project because it represents some of your best work. The financial investors, who took a big risk on providing the start-up capital for the organization, are also impressed with the project and believe it will be a big seller. Just as you are putting the final touches on the game, horrific shootings at a high school occur making national news. Your team calls a meeting to decide whether or not to cancel the project because it may remind people of the sad and horrific events and others preceding it or even send the message that violence in schools can be justified. As the lead designer, what do you say? Do you push for releasing the game or advocate revamping the game and postponing its release?

Small group communication competence involves making ethical choices at two levels: (1) an individual level, and (2) a group level. At the individual level, group members need to make choices about the kinds of messages that are appropriate and effective to the discussion at hand. Considering our example, should the lead designer in the video game team suggest the game be released or canceled? At the group level, making ethical choices involves how the group as a whole will respond to its environment. For example, because there has been intense scrutiny of violence in video games due to recent school shootings in the United States, is it an ethical response to the environment for the group to release the video game? The individual and group levels are interrelated. How you choose to respond as an individual within a group depends on how you think the group needs to respond to its larger environment. Similarly, how the group chooses to respond to its environment depends on the kinds of messages the group members exchange.

Although we cannot identify specific behaviors or universal principles that are either inherently ethical or tell us what counts as ethical behavior, we can identify a process to help you formulate ethical group responses to various situations. First, assess the four POET factors—people, objectives, environment, and time. Begin by asking the following questions:

1. Who will be affected by my messages? How would they perceive my messages? (People)
2. What are the key objectives? (Objectives)
3. How would I characterize the climate of the group? Is it supportive or hostile? (Environment)
4. Where is the group in terms of development? Is it still in the forming phase? Has a group culture been established? (Time)

The answers to these questions can help you develop a rich description of the situation in which you need to make ethical choices about your communication.

Returning to our example, using POET, how might the lead designer determine what counts as an ethical response? Answering question 1, people who will be affected by the lead designer's message are the other project team members, the financial backers, and the other members of the company. Assuming these people have a vested interest in seeing the product completed and brought to market, arguing for the release of the game would be appropriate and effective. Answering question 2, the key objective is to develop and release a marketable project, which makes arguing for the game's release consistent with the group's objective. Considering question 3, is arguing for releasing the game ethical given the environment of the group? Assume the group has established a supportive yet challenging environment. This means there is a sense of camaraderie and trust among group members. As a result, the lead designer may voice his or her opinion to release the game with the understanding it would probably be challenged by other group members. Given that the group has worked together for a long time on the project, the group has experienced the forming, storming, and norming stages. The resulting group culture makes it permissible for members to voice their opinions, which may indeed reflect a desire to move to the performing stage. Given the assessment of the POET factors, at the individual level, it makes sense for the lead designer to advocate releasing the video game.

But is this position ethical at a group level? Is it ethical for the group to respond to its larger societal environment and release the product? Consumers are the largest audience that will hear the message the company makes by releasing the video game. Given this audience's opposition to school violence, it will likely oppose the release of such a game fearing it would promote copycat shootings at school. The objectives held by many consumers may include providing a safe school environment for children and teenagers. They may feel the release of the game is at odds with their objective of creating a nonviolent school environment. Given the recent spate of school shootings in the United States, a national debate has emerged on the relationship between video game violence and school violence. This debate has created a hostile environment for video game companies that develop violent games.

Finally, at the group level, the timing may be problematic. This would be the new company's first product on the market and represents the beginning of a relationship with the general public. The controversy surrounding the product may generate negative publicity for the company and dissuade consumers from purchasing future products. At a group level, the ethical decision would be to postpone release of the video game.

As you can see, an analysis at an individual and group level may point to different courses of action. If this is the case, you need to determine whether or not you can craft a response that meets these conflicting expectations. It is useful to ask yourself a refocusing question. A **refocusing question** directs your attention toward trying to develop creative responses that meet contradictory needs. A refocusing question may take the following form: "How can I communicate in a way that meets these conflicting needs?" Returning to the preceding example, the lead designer may ask, "How can I communicate in a way that allows us to release the game while being sensitive to consumer concerns?" When answering this question, the lead designer may suggest the game's release be delayed or the setting for the game be changed from a school setting. Such responses may offer a way to balance the two competing actions.

If it is not possible to develop a response that can successfully address these competing needs, you should then determine which of these factors is most important. Which need, if not addressed, would have the most negative influence on the group or individual? Ethical behavior in a group first tries to meet the conflicting needs facing the group. But if it cannot meet those conflicting needs, ethical behavior needs to address the most pressing and potentially damaging influences confronting the group.

Chapter Summary

Four criteria distinguish a small group: (1) it needs to be made up of three or more people, (2) each group member must perceive of himself or herself as belonging to the group, (3) each group member's goals and behaviors must be interdependent, and (4) group members must communicate with one another. Group interdependence includes sharing goals or goal interdependence, behavioral interdependence or a flow of messages that affect and are affected by others' messages, and context interdependence where the group's external environment influences group members' behaviors and vice versa.

Several assumptions guide small group communication. First, small groups facilitate task accomplishment across a wide range of activities such as making decisions, delivering products or services, providing recreational opportunities, and offering social support. Second, small groups involve people performing responsibilities and roles such as leadership. Third, groups develop a culture complete with values, norms, and beliefs that influence group behavior. Fourth, groups must manage their development by making choices about the kinds of task activities the group wishes to perform and the kinds of relationships members forge with one another. Groups typically manage their development by going through phases such as forming, storming, norming, and performing.

Studying small group communication is important for three reasons: (1) we find ourselves belonging to many groups and cannot help but communicate in small groups in a wide variety of settings, (2) constructive small group environments can generate creativity, innovation, and high performance, and (3) small groups can produce negative effects by emphasizing too much cohesion and impairing one's individual decision making. The bottom line is that groups create social facilitation; the presence of others influences our individual performance within the group.

Given the importance of groups in our lives, it is important to develop group communication competency, which involves four components. First, competent small group communicators must be motivated to participate in groups. Several factors influence a group member's level of motivation including people factors such as individuals joining groups because they are attracted to other group members; task factors such as an attraction to the specific task, activity, or goals the group performs; need fulfillment or an attraction to the group based on the belief that the group can help fulfill personal or social wants such as the need for inclusion, control, and affection; and personality traits or cognitive and social qualities that affect the level at which a person joins and participates in groups. People who have personality traits that are more collectivistic versus individualistic are also more likely to join and participate in groups. Second, task and relational knowledge about small groups facilitates competent small group communication. Third, competent small group communicators need to be able to perform task skills such as decision making and relational skills such as conflict management and managing positive group climate. Fourth, competent group communicators are sensitive to and adapt to their context. They pay close attention to situational factors such as people, objectives, environment, and time (POET) that characterize their group.

Two major challenges confront the competent small group communicator. First, the large number of possible relationships among people in the group may make it challenging to coordinate group activity. This is sometimes evidenced by a phenomenon known as social loafing where people do not perform up to their potential because they feel others will pick up their slack. Second, people may have multiple motivations for joining and participating in groups. Not only does the fact that each group member may have a different motivation for joining and participating in the group make coordination difficult, it is also problematic because members may have hidden agendas, making it even more difficult to assess their motivations for participating in the group.

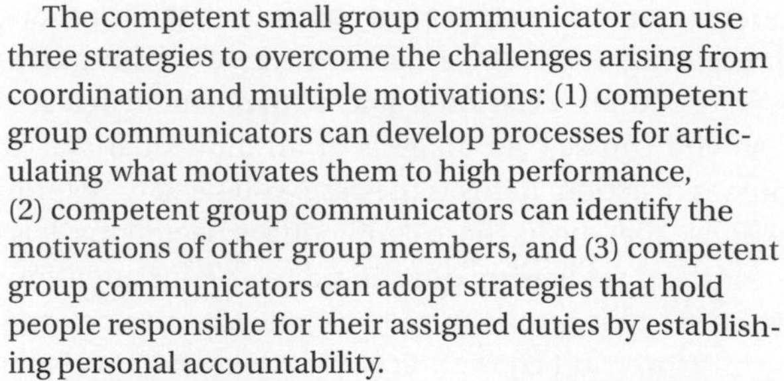

The competent small group communicator can use three strategies to overcome the challenges arising from coordination and multiple motivations: (1) competent group communicators can develop processes for articulating what motivates them to high performance, (2) competent group communicators can identify the motivations of other group members, and (3) competent group communicators can adopt strategies that hold people responsible for their assigned duties by establishing personal accountability.

Competent group communication involves making ethical choices at two levels. First, a competent group communicator needs to make ethical choices in terms of what is appropriate to say or do within group conversation. Second, competent group communicators need to make ethical choices at the group level where they assess the impact of the group's activity on the larger environment. Paying attention to the people, objectives, environment, and time factors (POET) can help persons make ethical choices that will fit with the expectation of those stakeholders in the larger environment.

Key Terms

small group
interdependence
goal interdependence
behavioral interdependence
context interdependence
task activity
group culture
social facilitation
people factors
task factors
need fulfillment
personality traits
task knowledge
relational knowledge
task skills
relational skills
group environment
task attraction
need for inclusion
need for control
need for affection
individualistic orientation
collectivistic orientation
social loafing
hidden agenda
refocusing question

Building Motivation

See Self-Assessment on page 321.

Building Knowledge

1. How do the criteria for classifying a small group (three or more people, perception, interdependence, and communication) connect? Is it possible to have a small group that perceives itself to be a small group where the members do not talk or communicate with one another? Is it possible for two people who perceive themselves as a group, who are interdependent and communicate with one another, to be classified as a group? Why or why not?
2. How do the three forms of group interdependence relate? Can a small group have goal interdependence without having behavioral interdependence? Can a small group have behavioral interdependence without context interdependence?
3. How does technology influence competent small group communication? What misperceptions exist regarding technology's effects on the communication process?
4. What are the advantages of having a strong culture with clearly defined norms and roles? How might you go about creating a strong culture in a group?

5. Is it better for a group member to adopt a single role within a group or to perform multiple roles? What can be gained from members playing multiple roles in a group?
6. How can the presence of others both motivate people to do better and create social loafing? Explain and give examples of groups where both phenomena can occur.
7. What does the acronym POET stand for? How can POET be used to make decisions about what counts as ethical behavior in group situations?

Building Skills

Individual Exercises

1. Ask four or five friends how they define small group communication. Do their definitions of small group communication reflect the four characteristics of small groups: three or more people, perception, interdependence, and communication? Why do you think your friends defined communication in the way that they did?
2. Think of a time when you had a very positive group experience. List all the factors that contributed to making this a positive experience. Using POET, go through the list and label each of the factors as people, objectives, environment, or time factors. Which of these factors were most important to you in creating a positive group experience?
3. Take a sheet of paper and write down the following questions:
   a. What core values do I believe in?
   b. What strong beliefs do I hold about people? In general? In small groups?
   c. What kinds of commitments am I willing to make to people in a group?
   d. What kinds of personal behavior do I view as competent in a small group?

   Using your answers to these questions, develop a personal code of group ethics. Your code of ethics should answer the following two questions: What are the personal standards I use to determine whether my personal behavior or the behavior of others is ethical? What kinds of behavior do I view as ethical in a small group?
4. Think of a group you belonged to that created a supportive environment. Write a dialogue for the group that reflects what people said or did to create this supportive environment. Write the dialogue in script form, identifying each speaker and recording what they said and did. What kinds of communication characterize supportiveness? What kinds of verbal and nonverbal messages do people use to convey support?
5. Using *InfoTrac College Edition*, search for articles in the journal *Small Group Research* that have been published in the last five years. Write a short one-page summary of the various themes that characterize published research about small groups. [NOTE: This exercise can be amended to say "type in the key words 'small group communication' and search for articles that have been published during the last five years.]

Group Exercises

1. In groups of 4–5 people, brainstorm the kinds of typical comments that people make in small groups. For each comment, using Schutz's typology of needs, identify what need that comment reflects. What needs do you see underlying these comments? What needs do you see underlying these comments that are not part of Schutz's typology?
2. As a group of 4–5 people, identify a historical group you would like to investigate, such as the Texas Rangers (**http://www.texasranger.org1**), the Sierra Club (**http://www.sierraclub.org1**), a sports team, a think tank like the Heritage Foundation (**http://www.heritage.org1**), or religious groups such as the Promisekeepers (**http://www.promisekeepers.org1**). Use the internet to locate information about that group. How would you describe the group values and norms of the group you selected?
3. In groups of 4–5 people, brainstorm to produce a list of strategies for motivating the following kinds of groups: (a) a group composed of people who have individualistic tendencies, (b) a group of individuals who have collectivistic tendencies, and (c) a group of individuals who have a mixture of individualistic and collectivistic tendencies. What kinds of strategies can you use to motivate group members? How do they vary as a function of the kinds of people who are in the group?

References

Bales, R. F. (1950). *Interaction process analysis: A method for the study of small groups*. Reading, MA: Addison-Wesley.

Barge, J. K. (1996). Leadership as communication. In L. R. Frey & J. K. Barge (Eds.), *Managing group life: Communicating in decision-making groups* (pp. 201–233). Boston: Houghton Mifflin.

Beebe, S. A., & Masterson, J. M. (1997). *Communicating in small groups* (5th ed.). New York: Longman.

Bostrom, R. (1970). Patterns of communicative interaction in small groups. *Communication Monographs, 37,* 257–258.

Chasin, R., Herzig, M., Roth, S., Chasin, L., Becker, C., & Stains, R. R. (1996). From diatribe to dialogue on divisive public issues: Approaches drawn from family therapy. *Mediation Quarterly, 4*(13), 323–344.

Cooper, J. L., Robinson, P., & McKinney, M. (1994). Cooperative learning in the classroom. In D. F. Halpern (Ed.), *Changing college classrooms: New teaching and learning strategies for an increasingly complex world* (pp. 74–92). San Francisco: Jossey-Bass.

Frey, L. R. (1996a). Remembering and "re-membering": A history of theory and research on communication and group decision making. In R. Y. Hirokawa & M. S. Poole (Eds.), *Communication and group decision making* (2nd ed., pp. 19–54). Thousand Oaks, CA: Sage.

Frey, L. R. (1996b). Individuals in groups. In L. R. Frey & J. K. Barge (Eds.), *Managing group life: Communicating in decision-making groups* (pp. 52–79). Boston: Houghton Mifflin.

Gamson, Z. (1994). Collaborative learning comes of age. *Change, 26* (5), 44–49.

Gudykunst, W. B. (1998). *Bridging differences: Effective intergroup communication* (3rd ed.). Thousand Oaks, CA: Sage.

Haslett, B. B., & Ruebush, J. (1999). What differences do individual differences in groups make? In L. R. Frey, D. S. Gouran, & M. S. Poole (Eds.), *The handbook of group communication theory and research* (pp. 115–138). Thousand Oaks, CA: Sage.

Hewes, D. E. (1996). Small group communication may not influence decision making: An amplification of egocentric theory. In R. Y. Hirokawa & M. S. Poole (Eds.), *Communication and group decision making* (2nd ed., pp. 179–214). Thousand Oaks, CA: Sage.

Janis, I. L., & Mann, L. (1977). *Decision-making: A psychological analysis of conflict, choice, and commitment.* New York: Free Press.

Jarboe, S. (1999). Group communication and creativity processes. In L. R. Frey, D.S. Gouran, & M. S. Poole (Eds.), *The handbook of group communication theory and research* (pp. 335–368). Thousand Oaks, CA: Sage.

Keyton, J. (1999). Relational communication in groups. In L. R. Frey, D. S. Gouran, & M. S. Poole (Eds.), *The handbook of group communication theory and research* (pp. 192–222). Thousand Oaks, CA: Sage.

Latané, B. K., & Harkins, S. (1979). Many hands make light the work: The causes and consequences of social loafing. *Journal of Personality and Social Psychology, 37,* 822–832.

McLeod, P. L. (1996). New communication technologies for group decision making: Toward an integrative framework. In R. Y. Hirokawa & M. S. Poole (Eds.), *Communication and group decision making* (2nd ed., pp. 426–461). Thousand Oaks, CA: Sage.

Poole, M. S., Siebold, D. R., & McPhee, R. D. (1996). The structuration of group decisions. In R. Y. Hirokawa & M. S. Poole (Eds.), *Communication and group decision making* (2nd ed., pp. 114–146). Thousand Oaks, CA: Sage.

Schultz, B. G. (1999). Improving group communication performance. In L. R. Frey, D. S. Gouran, & M. S. Poole (Eds.), *The handbook of group communication theory and research* (pp. 371–394). Thousand Oaks, CA: Sage.

Schutz, W. C. (1960). *FIRO: A three-dimensional theory of interpersonal behavior.* New York: Holt, Rinehart & Winston.

Schutz, W. C. (1966). *The interpersonal underworld.* Palo Alto, CA: Science & Behavior Books.

Scott, C. R. (1999). Communication technology and group communication. In L. R. Frey, D. S. Gouran, & M. S. Poole (Eds.), *The handbook of group communication theory and research* (pp. 432–474). Thousand Oaks, CA: Sage.

Socha, T. (1996). Group communication across the life span. In L. R. Frey & J. K. Barge (Eds.), *Managing group life: Communicating in decision-making groups* (pp. 1–28). Boston: Houghton-Mifflin.

Triplett, N. (1897). The dynamogenic factors in pacemaking and competition. *American Journal of Psychology, 9,* 50–533.

Tuckman, B. W., & Jensen, M. (1977). Stages of small-group development revisited. *Group and Organization Studies, 2,* 419–427.

Wuthnow, R. (1994). *Sharing the journey: Support groups and America's new quest for community.* New York: Free Press.

Building Motivation

Self-Assessment: Rate each of the following tasks associated with group communication competence, indicating the typical level of competence you feel you can or do achieve. Use the scale of 1–4 provided, with 1 minimal competence and 4 high competence. Rate one component (motivation) through all the situations, and then rate the next component (knowledge), and then the third (skills).

Motivation	Knowledge	Skills
1 = Anxious, disinterested, or no motivation to be competent	**1** = Completely inexperienced and ignorant about how to behave	**1** = Completely incapable of behaving competently in the situation
2 = Somewhat nervous, but some motivation to be competent	**2** = Minimal experience and knowledge about how to behave	**2** = Barely capable of behaving minimally competently
3 = Somewhat confident and motivated to be competent	**3** = Somewhat experienced and knowledgeable about how to behave	**3** = Fairly capable of behaving competently
4 = Highly confident and motivated to be competent	**4** = Highly knowledgeable about all aspects of how to behave	**4** = Highly capable of behaving competently

Small Group Communication Competencies:	Motivation	Knowledge	Skills
1. Define and analyze a problem that confronts the group.			
2. Participate in establishing the group goal and identify criteria for assessing the quality of the group outcome.			
3. Generate solutions or alternatives to the problem.			
4. Evaluate the solutions or alternatives identified by group members.			
5. Help the group stay on the task, issue, or agenda item under discussion.			
6. Manage disagreements and conflict among group members.			
7. Provide supportive comments and encouragement to other group members.			
8. Manage the group interaction and invite other members to participate.			
TOTAL SCORES			

Interpreting Your Scores: Total your score for each column (motivation, knowledge, and skills). You should end up with three scores. The possible range of scores per column is 8–32. Scores 8–14 indicate you are minimizing your competence and have significant room for improvement. Scores 15–21 indicate you think you are average in your competence. You may be sufficing or maximizing your competence, and you still have room for improvement. Scores 22–28 indicate you think you are nearing optimizing competence. Although you may still improve, you have a good grasp of the competence process. If your score for the motivation component is lower than you like, pay close attention to the content and suggestions in this chapter; to improve your scores in the knowledge component, study the knowledge sections in both Chapters 12 and 13; and to improve scores in the skills component, read the skills sections in both Chapters 12 and 13.

CHAPTER 12

Learning Objectives

After studying this chapter, you should be able to:

1. Distinguish between group problem solving and decision making.
2. Define questions of fact, conjecture, value, and policy.
3. Highlight which types of communication are important to high-quality decision making maintained by a functionalist approach to group communication.
4. Explain how the criteria of vigilant interaction, decision acceptability, collaboration capability, and personal development can be used to assess decision quality.
5. Outline the conditions when group decision making is preferred to individual decision making.
6. Identify task skills associated with defining the problem, identifying criteria for solving the problem, generating solutions or alternatives, evaluating solutions or alternatives, and maintaining task focus.
7. Explain why groupthink contributes to ineffective decision making
8. Propose procedures and processes that enhance divergent thinking, stimulate convergent thinking, develop reflections, and build a common focus in small groups.

Understanding Decision Making

The Board of Regents at National University asked the president to form a task force to tackle the issue of managing student enrollment. During the last few years, student enrollment at National University has risen dramatically, provoking concerns by students, faculty, and administrators about the university's ability to provide high-quality instruction as well as support the faculty's ongoing research programs. The president of National University appointed a group of students, faculty, and administrators to the task force and charged them with "coming up with a recommendation about what to do." She appointed Eva, a faculty member, to chair the task force.

Eva began the first meeting by providing an overview of the president's charge to the task force. She opened the discussion: "As I understand it, the charge for this committee is to come up with a recommendation to the president regarding how we propose to manage student enrollment in the future. I think there is a concern that our recent growth is causing some problems."

Bob, the vice president for Finance, immediately responded, "What's the problem? More students mean a lot more tuition dollars and revenue for the university. As far as I'm concerned, that isn't a problem. We've got more financial resources than we have ever had. We would have a problem if we decreased student enrollment without finding alternative sources of revenue. We should continue to enroll more students each year."

Sally, the president of the Faculty Senate, jumped in. "You finance people only see student enrollment in terms of dollars and cents. What I hear from faculty is that they are seeing 20% more students in class. Moreover, the overall quality of students has gone down and faculty find they are having to spend a lot more time covering basic material in their classes. Not only has their workload increased in terms of the number of students, but they have less time to cover the required topics because of poorly prepared students. This is a huge problem!"

Nilam, president of the student body, stated, "I can't talk about the quality of students, but I do know there is a lot of overcrowding in the classes and the students don't feel they're receiving enough attention from the faculty." Eduardo, the Alumni Association president, chipped in, "Our alumni have also been quite vocal in their opinions. If we decrease the number of students we admit each year by raising entrance requirements, they worry that some of their kids won't be able to get in. Families that have a long history of attending National are particularly upset."

The discussion quickly erupted into a heated debate with some of the task force members arguing that a decrease in student enrollment would provide better instruction for students. They argued that becoming more selective would limit the number of students admitted each year. Not only would raising entrance standards decrease the number of students accepted at National, it would free professors from teaching basic material because of the higher quality of students admitted. Other task force members contended that increased student enrollment was the only way to bring in enough money to keep the university running. After all, the president had said she wanted to keep tuition low, so significantly decreasing student enrollment while raising tuition was not an option—which left increasing student enrollment at National. Other task force members voiced concern over whether the task force would actually have any voice in this process. They felt a decision had already been made by the Regents and this committee was, in fact, spinning its wheels.

Eva sat there quietly trying to figure out what to do. How had the deliberation degenerated so quickly? There were so many different issues to manage for the task force to make a decision. What could she do to restore order to the deliberation? As she sat there listening to this chaos, she felt a tension headache coming on. When another task force member mused out loud that perhaps this was a time to reconsider the university's mission, since the size of the university depended on its mission, she sighed heavily and knew it was going to be a long afternoon. ●●●

One of the primary tasks small groups engage in is making decisions and solving problems. Decision making occurs within a wide variety of small groups including juries, marketing and management teams, nonprofit boards, support groups, and task forces such as the one in the opening vignette. The quality of decisions ranges greatly from those decisions that are successes such as Dell Computer's decision to market and sell computers over the internet to those decisions which are disastrous such as decisions by construction companies to use lower grade building materials in earthquake-prone countries such as Turkey. The decisions that groups make have short- and long-term consequences for those who belong to the group as well as those outside the group, or external stakeholders. The decision that the task force on enrollment makes will not only have consequences for how each committee member will experience National, but also will have consequences for National's students, faculty, administrators, and alumni.

The key to making effective decisions in groups is communication. The importance of communication can be seen in the following equation (Steiner, 1972):

$$\text{Actual group productivity} = \text{Potential productivity} - \text{Faulty group processes}$$

This equation shows that a group's ability to reach its full potential by making high-quality decisions and solving problems effectively depends on how group members relate, connect, and talk with one another. When small group members are able to communicate in ways that facilitate the sharing of information and pooling of knowledge, when they communicate in ways that permit a rigorous analysis of the problem and critical evaluation of possible solutions, it is more likely the group will make a high-quality decision. In the opening vignette, Eva failed to create a process to facilitate the sharing of information by task force members; instead, members simply broadcast their own views to other committee members without listening critically to the input or insights others had to offer. The group's ability to analyze the problem and evaluate possible solutions quickly became sidetracked when committee members failed to explore each unique perspective.

In this chapter, we explore how decisions are made in small groups and the role that communication plays in making high-quality decisions and solving problems. Part of making high-quality decisions is having knowledge about the general qualities of group tasks and how effective decisions are made, as well as possessing the skill to communicate messages that facilitate defining and analyzing a problem, generating solutions, evaluating solutions, and thereby establishing an effective group process. Figure 12.1 highlights the kinds of knowledge and skills that the competent small group communicator requires to make high-quality decisions.

FIGURE 12.1
Model of Small Group Communication

Competent communicators in small groups need to know about the different kinds of decisions groups must make as well as when it is appropriate for an individual or group to make a decision. The ability to perform communication skills, such as analyzing the problem, also facilitates the likelihood that a group will make a high-quality decision.

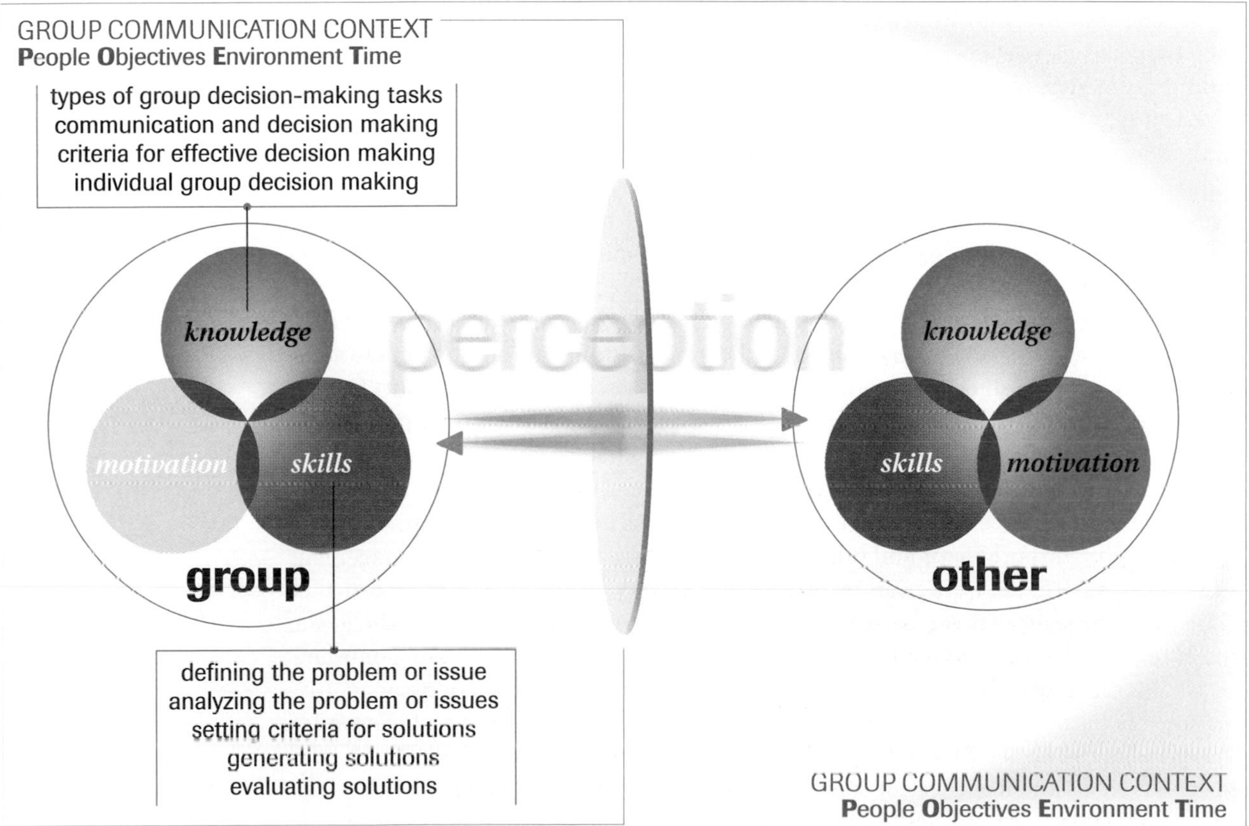

Knowing How to Make Group Decisions

What are some of the major decisions being made in your local community? In your state? In your country? In the world? In your local community, perhaps people are trying to make decisions about how to create affordable housing for low-income families or the local school board is wrestling with how to introduce sex education into its curriculum to reduce the teen pregnancy rate. At the state level, perhaps groups of people are trying to decide the best way to manage the competing needs of furthering economic development while conserving the environment. Perhaps at the national level, political parties struggle with issues related to providing access to health care for all citizens and developing stronger schools. At the international level, groups such as the United Nations or the Red Cross make decisions about how to provide assistance to war-torn countries or countries where natural disasters such as drought, hurricane, or earthquake have decimated the country and denied its citizens basic needs such as food or water. Regardless of where you look, groups of people are making important decisions that influence others.

Competent small group communicators need to be knowledgeable about several areas regarding group communication: (1) the relationship between decision making and problem solving, (2) the types of group decision-making tasks, (3) the process of group decision making, (4) the criteria for high-quality decisions, and (5) when to use groups instead of individuals for making decisions.

DISTINGUISHING PROBLEM SOLVING & DECISION MAKING

Do all decisions involve solving a problem? The simple answer is "no." A **problem** exists when there is a gap between an ideal state and the current state of events. For example, community leaders may feel the need to address developing affordable housing because there is a gap between the number of low-income families that own a home and the national average of home ownership. School board members may find that local teen pregnancy rates are significantly higher than the national average and decide they must develop solutions to reduce this difference. In both of these examples, a gap exists between the ideal state where the group would like to be and the current state of events—where the group currently is.

Groups similar to the ones just described often take steps to resolve problems. **Problem solving** is a group process in which members assess problems and formulate solutions to resolve the problems. Central to the notion of assessing problems is Kurt Lewin's (1951) idea of a **force field analysis,** a process for analyzing the reasons for a problem as well as what is preventing the problem from being eliminated. Figure 12.2 illustrates a force field analysis. The problem—the gap between an ideal and current state of affairs—is at the center of a force field analysis. The key questions in a force field analysis are (1) What is causing this problem? and (2) What is preventing the resolution or management of the problem? The first question focuses on the **drivers,** or the causes of a particular problem, or the sources that create the problem, and the second question introduces the idea of restraining forces, or forces that prevent the resolution of the problem. For example, what is creating the gap between the local and national rates of teen pregnancy? Drivers for this particular problem may include the lack of appropriate sex education for teenagers, low self-esteem on the part of teenagers, poor communication between parents and their children, or a lack of constructive role models for teenagers.

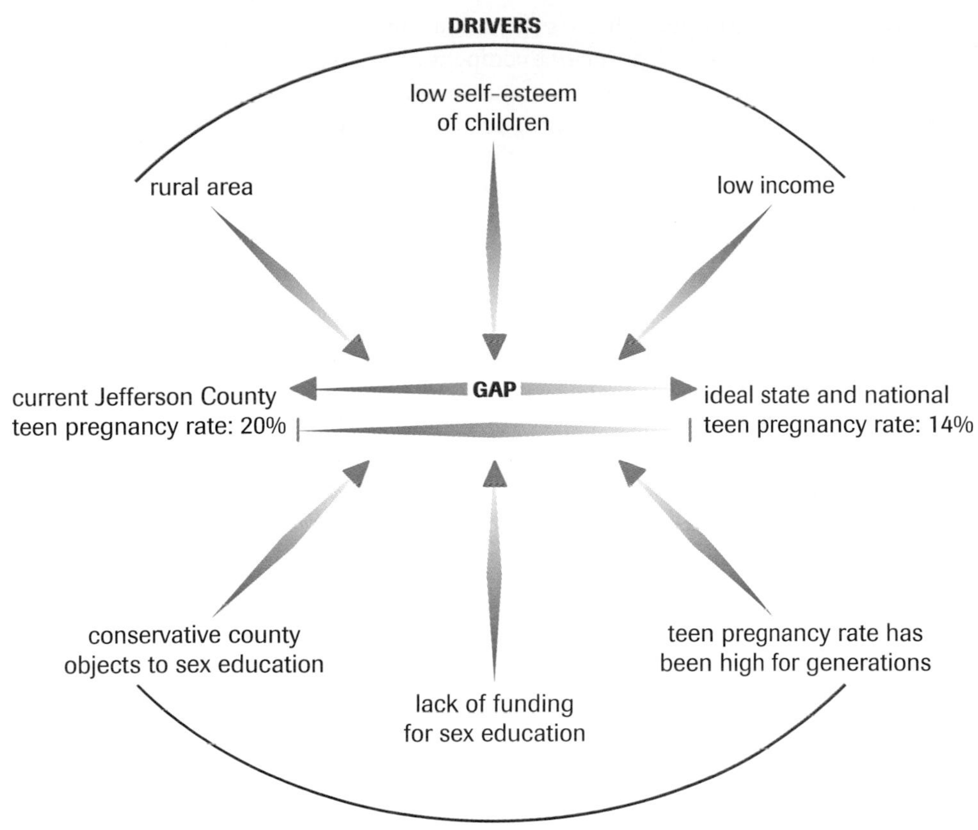

FIGURE 12.2
Force Field Analysis

A gap is the disparity between the actual and ideal state of affairs. In this example, the current state for the teen pregnancy rate in Jefferson County is 20% and the ideal state at the national level is 14%—a gap of 6%. Drivers are the reasons the gap exists in the first place, and restraining forces limit people's abilities to reduce the gap. In this example, geography, low self-esteem of children, and income may be driving the gap and political groups, lack of funding for sex education, and historical factors may be restraining decision makers from making decisions that reduce the gap.

The second question introduces the concept of restraining forces in the force field analysis. **Restraining forces** are those factors that prevent groups from addressing and solving the problem. Conservative lobbyists may try to prevent changes in the sex education curriculum. School board officials may try to squash discussion about the problem because it is such a controversial issue. The state school board may set limits on the content of the sex education curriculum.

In order to understand a problem fully it is important to assess the drivers and restraining forces. Then you can proceed to solve the problem by addressing the drivers and removing restraining forces to close the gap. How might the enrollment task force manage the gap between the current enrollment of National University and where it needs to be? Task force members might begin by asking, "What is driving this gap?" Some possible drivers may include the university's need for tuition revenue dollars, a lack of rigorous admission policies, and a low student to faculty ratio. They may also ask, "What is preventing the problem from being solved?" Possible restraining forces could include the alumni's resistance to making National more selective, a university mission that emphasizes giving access to a wide variety of students, and financial issues. The task force members could propose two solutions: (1) hiring additional faculty to meet student demand, or (2) establishing more selective enrollment policies. The former solution removes a significant driver for the problem, and the latter removes a key restraining force.

Decisions are distinct from problems. A **decision** is the selection among alternative explanations or proposals. Alternatives may be competing explanations for what causes a problem. Is the gap in health care coverage caused by the high cost of health care insurance or by the high costs of medical procedures? Alternatives may include competing proposals for solving a problem. Which alternative is better for reducing health insurance costs—capping fees and charges for selected medical procedures or limiting access to high-cost experimental procedures? Decision making may be used to solve problems, but it is not the same as problem solving. For example, suppose the U.S. Congress has agreed to extend health care benefits to all uninsured children and now must decide on the best way to achieve this. What is the problem they are solving? At this stage of discussion, they are not solving a problem; they are making a decision by selecting one of various action proposals.

Decision making is a group process in which members select among competing alternatives. What kinds of decisions do group members make? How does the decision type influence how the group manages its communication to select among competing alternatives? Different kinds of communication structures and processes may be used when the decision is between two alternatives, such as in court cases (the guilt or innocence of the defendant), or among multiple viable alternatives in policy decisions, such as introducing a sex education curriculum or legislating health care policy. The group may use communication in different ways if the task involves a relatively noncontroversial issue such as increasing home ownership or a politically charged issue such as sex education. The kinds of decisions that a group makes influences the kind of communication the group uses as well as how group members organize themselves and manage their roles and relationships.

DEFINING GROUP DECISION-MAKING TASKS

As you saw in Chapter 11, groups perform a wide variety of tasks such as manufacturing products, providing services, creating strategic plans, developing marketing campaigns, and so on. One way to define a group task is to identify the specific question that a group will discuss. There are four kinds of questions that small groups may discuss: (1) questions of fact, (2) questions of conjecture, (3) questions of value, and (4) questions of policy. To illustrate these different kinds of questions, return to the chapter-opening vignette and imagine you are a member of the task force charged with developing recommendations for managing student enrollment. What kinds of decisions would your committee need to make? The major decision is how many students to admit in an incoming freshman class. But what other kinds of decisions need to be made? List as many possible concerns and issues that require decisions be made by your committee.

Questions of fact focus on whether a particular claim regarding an event is accurate or true. Juries are a prime example of small groups that focus on questions of fact. In jury trials, the prosecution presents evidence and testimony from witnesses to make its case against the defendant. The defense attorneys present information supporting the innocence of their client and attempt to persuade the jury that their client is innocent.

The enrollment management task force may need to consider the following questions of fact:

- What is the optimal number of incoming students given our facilities? Number of faculty?
- Do we have a sufficiently large pool of potential applicants from which to select?
- Is the applicant pool qualified?
- Are our student recruitment strategies attracting a qualified pool of applicants?

Each of these questions of fact may have competing claims, and the enrollment management committee needs to determine which of the claims are more realistic. For example, the optimal number of incoming students may vary depending on how you define facilities.

Questions of conjecture are questions that ask what might happen in the future. Questions of conjecture can be projections about events or possibilities that might occur. For example, private investors in the stock market are continually asking questions of conjecture. What will happen if new companies enter the market? What will happen if the stock takes a dip? Will it bounce back to its former level? These are questions of conjecture because investors are speculating about what might happen in the future. Although their decisions may be informed by statistical evidence, trend data, history, and expert opinion, the decision is ultimately conjecture.

Returning to the enrollment management committee, it may ask a variety of questions of conjecture:

- What will happen to the university if we raise enrollment?
- How will faculty respond to increased numbers of students?
- What are the possible positive or negative consequences of increasing enrollment? Decreasing enrollment?
- How will the culture of the university be influenced if we raise entrance requirements such as minimum ACT or SAT scores? Lower entrance requirements?

Questions of value explore issues of intrinsic importance, worth, utility, and desirability of objects, attitudes, and beliefs. Questions of value evolve around the fundamental questions: Is it important? Is it right? Is it desirable? Is it worthwhile? For example, questions of value occupy center stage when economic and environmental interests conflict. In the Northwest United States, the Department of Forest Services constantly deals with questions of value when it determines land-use policy. What values are important to maintain regarding land use? Should economic values be privileged and the forests and national parks opened to timber and mining development? Should environmental values be elevated and recreational use of the parks be limited to preserve the environment? Value judgments are inherently subjective. Depending on who you ask, you will receive different answers to the question, "Which values should be emphasized?"

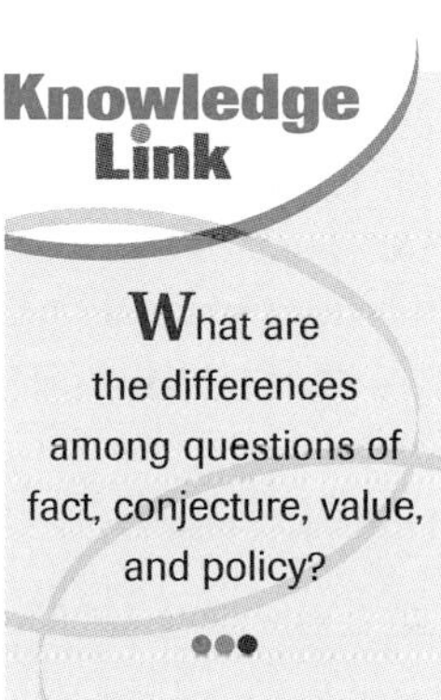

What are some of the key questions of value that might be included in the discussion of enrollment management? Some questions about the kind of community the university would like to create might be included. Questions about who key stakeholder groups are may be important. For example:

- What kind of university community do we desire? What kinds of students best fit the kind of community we would like to create?
- How important is limiting enrollment to us?
- What is most important to us quantity of students or quality of students?
- Are we serving our community if we limit our enrollment?

By sorting through what values are important to the university community, the enrollment management committee may be able to develop a workable enrollment plan that reflects the university's values.

Questions of policy focus on actions that should be taken to solve a problem. Questions of policy include determining what actions need to be taken to decrease illiteracy, what actions may reduce illegal drug use, and what actions can decrease domestic violence. In the example of the enrollment management committee, the central question of policy is, "What actions should the university take regarding enrollment?"

It is rare that any group will make a decision based on the answer to only one question of fact, conjecture, value, or policy. Rather, the resolution depends on making decisions regarding a variety of other issues first. This is called **nested decision making,** which requires decision makers to prioritize the questions they ask. Questions they ask earlier in the process serve as the foundation for subsequent questions, which, in turn, lead to the answer of the major question. In making a nested decision, it is difficult to answer the central question that your group is responsible for without answering those questions that serve as the foundation.

In order to answer the central policy question, "What should the university's policy be regarding enrollment?" the enrollment management committee must answer a number of other questions of fact, conjecture, and value. If the committee is not clear on the factual economic impact of varying levels of student enrollment, it will make a poor policy decision. If the committee has not explored the possible consequences of varying levels of student enrollment on facility issues, again, the decision may be a poor one. Finally, if the committee does not clarify what key values the university and key stakeholder groups maintain, the decision may be inappropriate. The ultimate quality of the policy decision depends on the ability of the group to identify and answer subquestions that are nested beneath the major question, as shown in Figure 12.3.

COMMUNICATION & GROUP DECISION MAKING

If decision making is the process of selecting among alternatives and a group's desire to make high-quality decisions, then it is important for small group members to be aware of those processes associated with high-quality decision making. In the early 1900s, John Dewey (1910), a scholar in philosophy, became interested in the processes that people use to make decisions. He interviewed hundreds of students and asked them to describe the processes they used to make decisions. From the information he gathered in these interviews, he created the **reflective thinking model,** which profiles a series of steps that decision makers follow in order to make high-quality decisions. The steps are as follows:

1. Recognize that a problem exists.
2. Define the scope and nature of the problem and identify factors that cause the problem.
3. Generate a number of solutions that may solve the problem.
4. Develop criteria for choosing among alternative solutions and evaluate those solutions using those criteria.
5. Select the best solution.
6. Assess solution to see if it is the right one.

The reflective thinking model assumes that each of these steps needs to be followed in the prescribed sequence in order to analyze problems logically and make decisions.

Dewey's reflective thinking model has become the basis for a perspective called the functionalist approach. A **functionalist approach** to group decision making assumes that particular decision-making functions can be identified that when performed will lead to high-quality decision making. Dennis Gouran and Randy Hirokawa (1996; Gouran, Hirokawa, Julian, & Latham, 1993), the chief proponents of this approach, argue that four key decision-making functions need to be performed if a group is to make a high-quality decision:

1. Assess the problem situation.
2. Specify the goals of the decision-making process.
3. Identify range of alternatives.
4. Evaluate the alternatives in light of positive/negative consequences.

QUESTIONS OF FACT

- What is the optimal number of incoming students given our facilities? Number of faculty?
- Do we have a sufficiently large pool of potential applicants from which to select?
- Is the applicant pool qualified?
- Are our student recruitment strategies attracting a qualified pool of applicants?

QUESTIONS OF VALUE

- What kind of university community do we desire? What kinds of students best fit the kind of community we would like to create?
- How important is limiting enrollment to us?
- What is most important to us—quantity of students or quality of students?
- Are we serving our community if we limit our enrollment?

QUESTIONS OF CONJECTURE

- What will happen to the university if we raise enrollment?
- How will faculty respond to increased numbers of students?
- What are the possible positive or negative consequences of increasing enrollment? Decreasing enrollment?
- How will the culture of the university be influenced if we raise entrance requirements such as minimum ACT or SAT scores? Lower entrance requirements?

QUESTIONS OF POLICY

- What actions should the university take regarding enrollment?

FIGURE 12.3
A Flow Chart for a Nested Decision

To answer the ultimate policy question regarding student enrollment, the enrollment management task force could start with factual questions for a detailed picture of the current situation. Second, task force members could define their hopes for the future by answering questions of value. After answering questions of fact and value, they are then able to explore questions of conjecture. The answer to their questions of fact, value, and conjecture, in this order, will prepare them to answer their question of policy.

Gouran and Hirokawa contend that groups which fail to fulfill these key functional requisites will make poor decisions. For example, if a group fails to assess the problem accurately, it may generate solutions which do not address that particular problem. Similarly, if group members do not identify a wide range of alternatives and generate only one alternative, a systematic evaluation of alternatives cannot be undertaken and the most appropriate alternative may be overlooked.

What is the role of communication in a functional approach to group decision making? Communication is instrumental; that is, it helps the group perform these key functions. For example, communication can help a group assess the problem situation, the first step involved in decision making. Consider the following situation: You are a member of a committee charged with promoting positive race relations on your university campus. Given what you know about the reflective thinking model and the force field analysis,

Team members at internet or dot.com companies often have unique knowledge and understanding of the group task. One member of the team may be the content expert, one may be charged with design of the Web site, one may be responsible for business development strategies, one with quality control, and one with programming the actual code. When team members have unique knowledge and insights about a task that other members may not, it is critical that they take the time to share their insights.

what kinds of questions might you want to ask during this meeting? Using the reflective thinking model, you may be motivated to ask questions such as these:

"What does it mean that people from different racial backgrounds are not getting along?" (problem definition)

"In what situations on campus are people from different racial backgrounds not getting along?" (scope of problem)

Using the idea of the force field analysis you might ask questions such as these:

"What is causing the need for us to construct more positive race relations?" (identification of drivers)

"What will limit our committee's ability to take actions that will promote more positive race relations?" (identification of restraining forces)

Each of these questions assesses the problem, but in different ways. The questions generated by using the reflective thinking model broadly define the problem and articulate its scope—where it is most noticeable. The questions suggested by using force field analysis more specifically identify the causes of the problem as well as potential forces that may restrain addressing the problem. All of these questions, although they focus on different aspects of the problem, perform the same function—assessing the problem situation. From a functional perspective, the key question to ask about a particular message is "What purpose does it serve?"

For functionalist theorists, it is more important to specify the core decision functions that need to be served as opposed to specifying the kinds of specific messages that need to be sent. From a functional perspective, the nature of the task influences what decision-making functions need to be performed. Some of the key task features that influence the kind of communication required to make a high-quality decision include the following:

Task structure: When the task is very clearly defined and the criteria for selecting among alternatives are agreed on, group members need to spend more time and effort on identifying a range of alternatives and exploring the positive and negative consequences associated with each alternative.

Group member knowledge: When each group member has unique knowledge and understanding of the group task, group members need to share their perspectives with one another when performing these key functions of identifying the problem, specifying the goals of the process, and generating and evaluating potential alternatives.

Evaluation demands: When groups confront a task where there are several possible alternatives, the criteria for selecting among competing alternatives is unclear, and it is difficult to judge the appropriateness of the solutions, group members need to devote time and energy revisiting the goal of the decision-making process and evaluating the positive and negative consequences of alternatives. (Hirokawa, 1988, 1990)

Knowledge Link

How do task features influence which decision-making functions need to be performed?

How do these task features relate to the task force in the chapter-opening vignette? Given that the task and the criteria for solutions are unclear, it is not surprising the task force members spent much of their time analyzing the task they were given and the causes for the student enrollment problem. Similarly, given that committee members were a mix of students, faculty, and administrators, they more than likely had differing perspectives on the problem they were charged with resolving. Therefore, they should have spent more time sharing the unique knowledge and information they possessed. Finally, the task of managing student enrollment has several possible demands; therefore, the task force needs to be prepared to expend energy on evaluating the problem and solutions.

ASSESSING THE QUALITY OF DECISION MAKING

How does a group know if it has made the right decision? Like students getting feedback from their professor about their performance on an exam, it is tempting to say that groups have made the "right" decision when someone from outside the group says it is "correct." However, this assumes that someone is an expert on the issue and there is really an objective answer to the issue much like there is a right answer to a "true/false" question on an objective test. Yet much of group decision making does not lend itself to judging decisions by their correctness. For example, suppose a group of city supervisors is making a policy decision regarding annexing a piece of property adjoining the city in order to manage growth. They won't know if this is the correct decision until they have actually annexed the property, waited 2 or 3 years, and examined whether their decision did or did not control growth. Similarly, when groups make decisions about questions of value, correctness is not a useful criterion. Questions of value, by definition, do not have right or wrong answers. You may think that correctness is the most useful criterion when deliberating questions of fact. However, with some exceptions, even questions of fact are open to debate. In jury trials, jurors are asked to determine a question of fact: Is the defendant guilty or innocent? However, even the answer to this question of fact is not truly about the correctness of facts. Rather, in jury trials, the jurors are instructed to vote "guilty" only if the prosecution's case has been "proven beyond a reasonable doubt." By law in the United States all defendants are innocent until proven guilty. In this case, correctness, although important, is less important than the notion of reasonable doubt.

CloseUp ON ETHICS

When to Use Groups to Make Decisions

USING GROUPS TO MAKE DECISIONS within the public and private sector has grown dramatically over the last 20 years. Federal, state, and city governments increasingly use citizen task forces and committees to help them make decisions about public policy (Forrester, 1999). In the private sector, business and industry are using team-based decision making as a means of improving productivity and effectiveness. Giving team members decision-making responsibility is believed to enhance performance because they are more attuned to the challenges and issues confronting their team than are higher level managers who do not face these issues on a daily basis (Katzenbach & Smith, 1993).

Given this increased use of groups to make decisions, the ethical use of groups to make decisions and create recommendations must be considered. For example, is it ethical for a manager to create a team to make a decision or a recommendation if he or she has no intent of following the team's recommendation? Many of you would answer "No." Yet many teams face the demoralizing situation in which the group makes a decision or recommendation that conflicts with the manager's desires and as a result, he or she ignores the committee's recommendation. Is it ethical to charge a group with making a decision when it is the manager's responsibility? Again, you would probably respond "No." Yet managers sometimes set up committees to make unpopular decisions so they can scapegoat the committee for the decision and avoid taking the blame.

When a group devotes time and energy to making a decision or developing a recommendation that has no chance of being implemented or adopted or when a group is positioned to take the blame for an unpopular decision, we would be inclined to say that using groups to make decisions in these circumstances is unethical. When then is it ethical and appropriate to use groups to make decisions? How can groups be ethically guided to make decisions?

Group leaders have to make decisions about when it is appropriate to use groups to make decisions. There are five considerations to explore when using groups ethically:

1. *Explore your motivation for using a group to make a decision or develop a recommendation.* It is ethical to use groups when you need a diversity of opinions on a particular issue. Bringing in people from a broad spectrum of backgrounds introduces unique insights and experiences into the decision-making process. Conversely, if the motivation for assembling a group is simply to avoid accountability for a decision, it is unethical to use groups.

2. *Determine the scope of the group's responsibility.* It is ethical to clearly specify the scope of the group's task. Is the group simply to serve in an advisory role or does it have the authority to implement the members' suggestions? Is the group to be held accountable if its recommendations produce negative outcomes or is another individual or group accountable? It is unethical to hold a group accountable if members do not have the authority to implement their recommendations.

3. *Clearly communicate the task to the group.* When groups meet for the first time, it is critical for the manager creating the group to provide a clear orientation to the task. He or she must lay out the scope of the group's responsibility so group members fully understand. One strategy for conveying the task is to explain how the group task fits into the overall process, as well as who will consider the final decision. As long as the group knows what its responsibilities are, who will accept or reject its final decision, and how it will be implemented, the manager has ethically appointed this group to the task.

4. *Provide periodic feedback to the group as it performs the task.* Keep in close contact with group members as they are working. A common mistake is to assign the group a task and then never check back with the group until it has come to a decision or completed the task. This can create difficulties for the group if it has gone in a different direction than intended by the manager. By keeping the communication lines open with a group as it completes a task, a manager can keep the group on track and provide new information that might assist the group in achieving its goal. Managers who behave ethically check in with the group periodically to provide information and ensure that group members and the manager have a shared understanding of the group's task.

5. *Provide feedback on the implementation of the group's decision.* Many times, group members make decisions and recommendations to others only never to find out what has been done with their work. Providing feedback on how the work has been used is an important part of the group decision-making process. Not only does this provide the group closure on a project, it also communicates

valuable information about what members may need to consider the next time they are given a group task. If the recommendation has been rejected, for example, they can explore the reasons for the rejection and this information may help them construct future recommendations that may be more likely to be accepted. It is ethical to inform group members of what has been done with their decision or recommendation.

Using groups to make decisions is a trend that will continue in the 21st century. The question, therefore, is not "*Will* we use groups to make decisions?" but rather "*How* do we use groups ethically to make decisions?" Understanding the motivation for using groups as well as providing clear ongoing communication about the task and expectations are strategies that make use of groups ethically.

If correctness is not a standard for differentiating between effective and ineffective decisions, then what is? There are four criteria for evaluating decision-making effectiveness: (1) vigilance, (2) decision acceptability, (3) collaboration capability, and (4) personal development.

First, is the group vigilant in its interaction? **Vigilant interaction** is a process-oriented criterion that involves evaluating whether group members are committed to assessing the problem rigorously, developing goals for the decision-making process, and generating and evaluating alternatives. Underlying the criterion of vigilant interaction is the idea that the group surfaces needed information and subsequently analyzes it in a critical fashion. Remember the discussion in Chapter 3 of the importance of being mindful of one's behavior? Vigilant interaction emphasizes the need for group members to be mindful of performing key decision-making functions. These activities include the following:

- Thoroughly investigating a wide range of alternative courses of action
- Carefully considering the negative as well as positive consequences that could result from each alternative
- Questioning members' statements for hidden or inaccurate assumptions
- Intensively searching for new information to help evaluate each alternative
- Taking new information into account even when it does not support the course of action the group favors
- Basing decisions on accurate and reasonable premises
- Reexamining all the alternatives before making a final decision
- Making detailed plans for implementing the chosen solution, including contingency plans if circumstances change. (Jensen & Chilberg, 1991, p. 37)

Unlike the first criterion, which is process oriented, the next three criteria are outcome oriented: They focus on the consequences of the decision-making process rather than the process itself (Hackman, 1990). **Decision acceptability** reflects the degree to which the decision meets the standards of quality, quantity, and timeliness set by the people who will use or be affected by the decision. Returning to the chapter-opening vignette, will the decision the enrollment committee makes be acceptable to students, faculty, administrators, alumni, and the community the college serves?

Collaboration capability reflects the ability of group members to work interdependently in the future. Decisions that increase the likelihood that members will collaborate in the future and are better able to create a collaborative working relationship are more effective. When group members leave a meeting fired up for the next meeting, the criterion of collaboration capability has been met. Such positive outward signs reflect a positive group experience and a willingness for group members to work together in the future.

The **personal development** criterion refers to decision processes that enhance the personal well-being of group members and facilitate their growth and development. When group members leave a meeting believing they have acquired new skills and abilities that enhance their communication competence, the decision processes have facilitated their personal development.

It is possible for group members to decide that only one or two of the criteria described here are important to determine whether a decision is high quality. However, those decisions that use vigilant interaction, produce a high level of decision acceptability by others, build collaboration capability among group members, and allow individual members to grow and develop are more effective. Such decisions are more effective because they pay attention to the process used to make the decision as well as the consequences of the decision. Last, but not least, they focus on the needs of group members as well as on the needs of people who will be affected by or use the decision.

DETERMINING WHEN GROUPS SHOULD MAKE DECISIONS

Certainly, there are many advantages to having a small group rather than an individual make decisions. Using small groups to make decisions can enhance the amount of information available. When a number of people come together to make a decision they bring a variety of perspectives, information, and expertise to bear on the problem. However, given these advantages of group decision making, there are times when individual decision making is more effective. Consider the following situations. In which would you rather have an individual or the entire group make the decision?

Situation 1
A group of specialized health care professionals are performing a risky and delicate brain surgery on you. Would you want the leading neurosurgeon or the neurosurgeon's entire surgical team including nurses and anesthesiologists to make a life or death decision?

Situation 2
A local community theater is presented with a rare opportunity, but a decision must be made within the next 4 hours. Should the executive director of the community theater make the decision alone or should the entire board of directors convene to decide?

Situation 3
A university task force on how to manage computer usage on campus is deeply divided and lacks cohesion. Would it be better for the committee chair alone or for the entire group to make the decision?

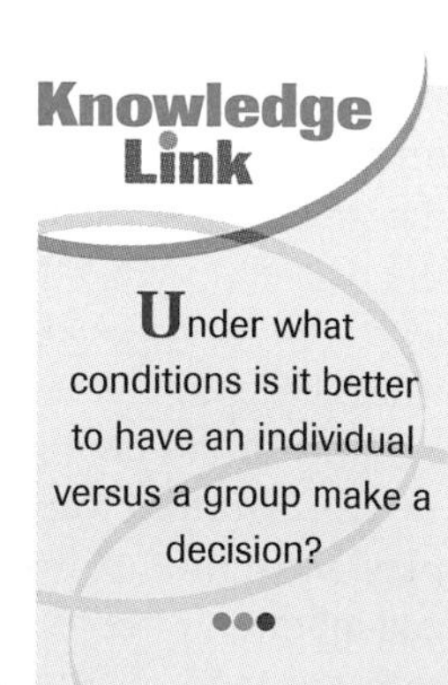

In situation 1, if under the knife you would probably opt for the leading neurosurgeon to make the decision given his or her level of expertise. When an individual group member has expert knowledge not shared by other group members that is highly relevant to the task being performed, the best decision is most likely made by that individual as opposed to the group. In situation 2, the executive director may need to make the decision given the time constraints. In this situation, the logistics of assembling the board of directors and allowing sufficient time for the group to make an informed decision is too difficult. In situation 3, it might be useful to have the committee make the decision as a whole in

TABLE 12.1

Individual and Group Decision Making

When to use individuals and groups to make decisions depends on the nature of the task, the amount of time that the task requires, and the characteristics of the group members.

DECISION REQUIREMENTS	INDIVIDUAL	GROUP
Routine decision: Decision is relatively simple or guidelines already exist.	✓	
Time constraints: Decision needs to be made quickly; extremely negative consequences exist if the decision is not immediate.	✓	
Technical expertise: Decision requires the knowledge or analysis of highly trained specialists.	✓	
Idea generation: Task requires that many creative ideas be generated.	✓	✓
Group commitment: Decision requires group acceptance before it can be successfully implemented.		✓
Integrative tasks: Decision requires knowledge, perceptions, or skills that a single individual is unlikely to have.		✓

SOURCE: Jensen & Chilberg (1991).

order to build cohesion. The group's cohesion would continue to disintegrate if the individual chair made the decision, particularly if the chair is not well liked. The group members may also try to undermine the chair's decision, further eroding group cohesion.

Therefore, factors like the group members' expertise, the time in which the decision needs to be made, and the cohesion of the group determines whether individual or group decision making yields the best results. Table 12.1 highlights the various factors you may want to consider when deciding whether to use individual or group decision making.

Competence in small group communication requires that you know whether a group needs to be formed to solve a problem or make a decision. If a group is selected to solve a problem, the competent small group communicator needs to determine the type of task being performed. Will the group discuss a question of fact, conjecture, value, or policy? Finally, knowledge about the general process of making a decision is required. Yet there are a number of ways to perform key decision-making functions. Knowing that functions such as analyzing the problem or generating solutions are key to decision making is not enough; the competent small group communicator must also be skilled at performing messages that meet these decision functions.

Task Skills for Making Decisions

A **task skill** is a message a person performs that helps the group make a decision. Based on ideas contained in the reflective thinking model, the functionalist approach, and vigilant interaction, five central task skills are key to making effective decisions: (1) defining the problem, (2) analyzing the problem, (3) identifying criteria for solving the problem, (4) generating solutions or alternatives, and (5) evaluating solutions. Using the vignette that opened the chapter, let's explore what kinds of messages may facilitate groups making high-quality decisions.

DEFINING THE PROBLEM

A group's success in making effective decisions is strongly influenced by the ability to define the problem clearly and appropriately. Developing an answer to the question, "What appears to be the problem?" can be difficult. Group members may not want to define the problem clearly or they may want to frame the problem to give them an advantage in the discussion. Group members may want to define the problem ambiguously to prevent the group from fragmenting. For example, a work team may define a problem ambiguously as "low morale" as opposed to specifically defining it as "poor leadership." The team members know that if they define the problem as one of "low morale," they stand a better chance of being able to discuss it with their immediate supervisor as opposed to identifying the supervisor as the problem. Group members may spend a great deal of time arguing over which definition of the problem would benefit the group. For example, much environmental discussion in the United States is focused on what must be given up economically in order to protect the environment. This leads opponents of increased environmental regulation to define the problem as a trade-off between a healthy economy and preservation of the environment. Typically, economics wins and the environment loses. However, when the problem is framed as building both a healthy economy and natural environment, groups on both sides of the issue win.

Despite the difficulty of agreeing on how to define a problem, problem definition is important to the decision-making process. Group members can send many messages to facilitate defining the problem. They include the following:

- Problem statement: Messages that propose a specific definition of the problem.
- Modifying the problem statement: Messages that combine competing definitions of the problem or slightly alter an existing problem statement.
- Detailing assumptions: Messages that examine the assumptions made about the nature of the problem and the people who are either involved in the decision-making process or who will be affected by the group's decision.

One of the first steps that lead to making high-quality decisions is to define the problem.

© Randy Glasbergen. Reprinted with special permission from www.glasbergen.com

- Changing perspectives: Messages that highlight how different people or stakeholders perceive the problem.

Each of these messages further clarifies the definition of the problem.

If Eva, the task force chair, had sent these types of messages, what might she have said during the board meeting? She might have stated the problem this way: "I think our problem is we don't have enough faculty and staff to meet the increased enrollment" or asked each member of the task force for their problem statement: "What do you see as the problem facing National University?" She may have detailed the assumptions regarding the problem statement: "One of the assumptions I make when looking at enrollment trends is that providing high-quality instruction to our students is key to our future success." She may have used other people's perspectives to explore the problem statement: "What do you think our alumni would view as the problem?" or "If some of the town's community leaders were here at this meeting, what might they say is our problem?" In the event that multiple problem statements surfaced during the discussion, Eva might have modified the problem statements: "It sounds as if the problem is both declining revenues *and* limited faculty resources." Group members and leaders who want to facilitate constructing a useful problem definition need to be skilled at performing these kinds of messages.

Knowledge Link

What kinds of messages characterize the five task skills associated with making effective decisions?

ANALYZING THE PROBLEM

The next skill necessary for effective decision making is analyzing the problem confronting the group. Statements that help analyze the causes, obstacles, history, symptoms, and significance of the problem the group is attempting to solve help develop the skill of analyzing the problem. These statements use objective evidence and facts as opposed to subjective opinions. Statements that analyze a problem explore a variety of issues:

- Symptoms: How do we know there is a problem? What signs point to this?
- Drivers: What is driving the problem? What is the basis for the problem?
- Restraining forces: What is preventing us from solving the problem? What forces are restraining our ability to manage the problem?
- Significance: How important is the problem? To whom?
- History: What is the history of this problem? When did it begin? Who was the first to determine it was a problem?

These kinds of statements help flesh out the rich detail inherent in any problem.

To lead the task force, Eva could have asked several questions to analyze the problem: "How do we know there is a problem?", "Who was the first to notice the problem?", and "When did the problem start?" Asking about the symptoms of the problem would allow her to guide the discussion toward exploring the problem's significance and history. For example, she could offer a statement of the significance of the problem: "If we are unable to raise money through increased grant writing by our faculty, we will have to explore other means of generating revenue, including raising enrollment." She may offer an account of what led to the problem: "This problem really began five years ago when we lost our vice president for development. Since then we haven't been able to raise a lot of contributions by alumni and business and industry." In order to set up the discussion for generating solutions, she may guide the meeting into a discussion of drivers and restraining forces. She may have articulated a driver for the problem such as "The reason we've enrolled too many students is that we are not selective enough in our admissions policy" or solicit board members' opinions regarding possible drivers, "What do you think are the major reasons for too much enrollment?" Questions such as "What is preventing us from solving these problems?" or "How can we overcome this problem due to lax admissions policy?" may help the task force identify the restraining forces that prevent solution of the problem.

IDENTIFYING CRITERIA FOR SOLVING THE PROBLEM

Making effective decisions requires groups to establish standards for selecting among competing ideas, solutions, and actions. Establishing standards for comparison can help groups select among competing alternatives. Such standards may take the form of setting criteria or using the group goal to select among alternatives. The task skill of identifying criteria for solving a problem involves making statements to identify criteria for assessing the quality of possible alternatives for solving the problem. The following statements facilitate the establishment of criteria:

- Propose criteria: What are the criteria or standards we need to use when evaluating solutions?
- Modify criteria: How can these criteria be combined to create a useful standard for evaluation? How can we alter a criterion to make it more appropriate in light of the group's task?

For example, the task force members on student enrollment could identify criteria by asking questions or making comments such as, "What criteria do we need to use when selecting among plans for raising tuition?" or "Any action that helps provide high-quality student instruction must take faculty resources into account." Questions and comments that help modify criteria include "I agree that any proposal we put forth must recommend a decrease in admissions, but it also needs to suggest that the Development Office be more involved in generating revenue." or "I understand that we need to decrease student enrollment significantly, but could you quantify what you consider to be an acceptable decrease?" Proposing and modifying decision criteria will enable the group to make higher-quality decisions.

GENERATING SOLUTIONS OR ALTERNATIVES

When making decisions in a group setting, the skill of generating solutions or alternatives is critical. Two types of messages that generate alternatives are solicit solutions or propose a solution. For example, to focus the task force on the issue, Eva could have solicited solution proposals by asking, "What can we do to resolve this problem?" She could have also proposed solutions by providing the group a list of her recommendations. When a solution is proposed, however, it is often modified by other group members. For example, Eva may have proposed higher admissions requirements as a strategy for reducing student enrollment. During the group discussion, another committee member may have introduced exceptions for the children of alumni. This committee member may have offered the rationale that a higher enrollment of children of alumni will encourage their parents to make higher donations. These skills of proposing alternatives and openness to modifying the alternatives help groups make high-quality decisions.

EVALUATING SOLUTIONS OR ALTERNATIVES

One of the central challenges to successful decision making occurs when groups fail to analyze rigorously the proposed alternatives or solutions. Much research concludes that even if groups actively evaluate alternatives, they tend to overestimate the positive consequences while underestimating the negative consequences of a proposed alternative (Gouran & Hirokawa, 1996). Effective solution evaluation involves realistically identifying and assessing the positive and negative consequences of proposed alternatives. How can group members enhance constructive evaluation? Statements and questions that address the consequences and test the appropriateness of particular alternatives can facilitate decision making. Specifically, group members need to investigate the following areas:

- Positive consequences: What advantages are gained from adopting this solution?
- Negative consequences: What disadvantages are created from adopting this solution?
- Problem-solution fit: Does the solution meet the criterion established at the beginning?
- Reality testing: Does the solution make sense? Is the solution possible? Will people support the solution?

Together these areas facilitate a well-rounded analysis of the strengths and weaknesses of various alternatives under consideration by the group.

Returning to the opening vignette, how might Eva have facilitated the committee to look more closely at the opportunities and difficulties of each proposed solution? Certainly she could have asked broad open-ended questions such as "What do we gain or lose if we adopt this alternative?" or made statements to communicate her assessment of the advantages and disadvantages of various alternatives: "If we adopt X, what I am afraid will happen is . . ." Alternatively, she could have tied the discussion of alternatives back to the criterion set by the group and discuss how this solution will work in real life: "How well does this alternative meet our goal of managing student enrollment?" On the other hand, she could have asked a series of questions to help the group test the reality of their solution:

- If we adopted this alternative, what would be the next step?
- Who would be in charge of the next step?
- What would we do if the next step failed?
- Who would be supportive of this alternative? Who would oppose it?
- Given the level of support and opposition, can we realistically expect this solution to work?

In reality testing, Eva would be trying to help the group identify what specifically will need to be done in the future and to examine whether those steps are realistic. As you saw earlier, one way to assess a decision's effectiveness is to determine the degree to which the decision is acceptable to those who will use it. Asking questions that probe the support or opposition of those affected by the decision allows a group to foresee the challenges associated with implementing a decision.

Challenges to Competent Decision Making

What frustrates the decision-making process? If the goal of most groups is to make quality decisions, they must define the task appropriately, survey all relevant information, assess both the negative and positive consequences of their decision, examine all possible solutions, and develop contingency plans if the decision is a poor one. Yet many groups are not vigilant in their interaction and do not rigorously examine the information and logic they use to make decisions. One of the primary explanations for poor decision making is groupthink (Esser, 1998; Turner & Pratkanis, 1998). **Groupthink** occurs when group members establish a norm that makes consensus the highest priority and diminishes the vigilant appraisal of the reasons for and consequences of possible alternatives to their final decision (Janis, 1972, 1982; Janis & Mann,

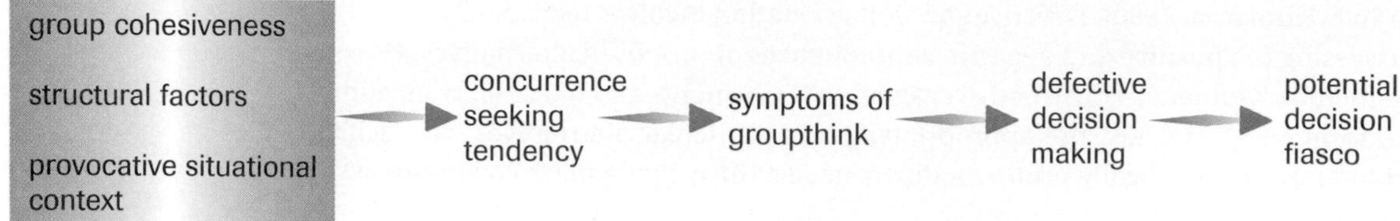

FIGURE 12.4
Janis's Model of Groupthink

The focus of Janis's groupthink model is to explain how potential decision fiascoes are created. Three major preexisting conditions propel groups to seek concurrence regarding an issue: (1) group cohesiveness, (2) structural factors, and (3) provocative situational context. The concurrence-seeking tendency of groups can lead to symptoms of groupthink that can cause defective decision making.

1977). Groupthink results from preexisting conditions that lead to ineffective decision-making behavior, as shown in Figure 12.4.

CAUSES OF GROUPTHINK

Three major preexisting conditions lead to groupthink. First, groups that are moderately or highly cohesive tend to suffer from groupthink. As group members become more cohesive and share similar values, there is a danger that each individual will stop thinking critically to maintain a strong sense of affiliation with other group members and group spirit.

Second, several structural factors may influence a group's likelihood to engage in groupthink:

Insulated group: When groups begin to feel cut off from their larger environment, they are more likely to engage in groupthink. A classic example of insulated groups are cults that are isolated from society at large. In fact, this is one explanation for the tragedy of David Koresh and the Branch Davidians in Waco, Texas.

Lack of impartial leadership: When group leaders express strong opinions about solutions to problems, the group members may be more prone to engage in groupthink. In this situation, group members may try to please the leader by following his or her opinions without evaluating alternatives.

No methodical procedures: Groupthink is more likely to occur when the group does not have procedures in place to encourage a rigorous analysis of the problem and possible solutions.

Members with similar backgrounds: The more people share attitudes, values, and beliefs, the more likely they are to engage in groupthink. Given the similarity of experience, group members may take certain things for granted and neglect to evaluate alternatives.

Third, a provocative situational context may propel groups toward groupthink. Two key situational factors are particularly provocative: stress and self-esteem. High stress is positively linked to groupthink. When group members are placed under pressure, they tend to short-circuit the decision-making process. They may conclude that they do not have enough time to analyze the problem, generate solutions, or evaluate alternatives. Similarly, when group members have low self-esteem they are more likely to engage in groupthink. Members suffering from low self-esteem lack the confidence to articulate an individual viewpoint, particularly one that challenges the larger group.

GROUPTHINK & DECISION MAKING

These preexisting conditions lead to **concurrence seeking,** which is when groups try to achieve a consensus regarding their decision. The tendency for concurrence seeking is not inherently problematic; after all, most groups try to come to a consensus on the actions that need to be taken regarding a problem. However, when this tendency goes too far, it produces symptoms of groupthink and defective decision making.

Here are several symptoms of groupthink:

- Group members possess an illusion of invulnerability. They feel they are invincible and cannot make a poor decision.
- There is an unquestioned belief in the group's inherent morality. As a result, the ethical implications of decisions are not fully explored.
- Members who suffer from groupthink make collective rationalizations or justifications for their decisions. When group members make collective rationalizations, they ignore the warning signs that signal a flawed decision.
- Group members who disagree, raise concerns, or oppose the decision are negatively stereotyped. Those in the minority opinion are often characterized as wrong, weak, unintelligent, or unimportant compared with those in the majority opinion. When opposing group members are stereotyped as not posing a significant threat to majority opinion, their claims or critiques are not viewed as legitimate.
- Direct pressure is applied to group members who dissent from the majority opinion. Groups that suffer from groupthink believe the majority opinion is correct, and those members who disagree are pressured to reconsider their views and conform. Dissenting group members may find their opinions attacked and their positions in the group threatened.
- As direct pressure is leveled against dissenters, other group members may censor their own dissenting opinions. Such members do not even voice minority opinions because the majority opinion forces them to question their own criticisms, second-guess their ideas and positions, and anticipate negative feedback. As a result of self-censorship—the failure of group members to voice dissenting positions—an illusion of unanimity is created.
- Some group members assume the role of protecting the group from dissenting opinions and maintaining the majority argument.

When groups fall prey to groupthink, the decisions they make may have extremely negative consequences. In the case of David Koresh and the Branch Davidians, one explanation for this tragedy is that group members became insulated from their larger environment and failed to question the assumptions and beliefs that informed their decisions.

These symptoms of groupthink lead to defective decision making. The group suffers from informational problems because groupthink prevents it from collecting relevant and necessary information and seeking expert opinion on the issue under consideration. Instead, it suppresses all information that exposes or disconfirms the preferred solution. The group also is hurt by an inability to engage in rigorous and open analysis of the decision. Key objectives are not thoroughly analyzed, the full range of alternatives is not examined, preferred alternatives are not reexamined for pitfalls, and dismissed alternatives are not reexamined. Finally, in the event that the decision is faulty, the group does not create contingency plans.

Overcoming Challenges to Competence

Making effective and appropriate decisions in small groups can be a challenging process. Few people, if any, purposefully set out to make bad decisions in groups. Nevertheless, a variety of factors including group members' low self-esteem, high levels of group cohesion, and members with similar backgrounds may move groups to make poor and ineffective decisions. How can groups overcome these challenges that frustrate high-quality decision making? One answer suggested by the theory of groupthink is that competent small group members need to employ group procedures methodically. A **group procedure** is a process for performing a function that is central to the group. Group procedures serve important functions such as keeping the group focused on central decision-making functions and maintaining a sense of order and coherence within the group (Sunwolf & Siebold, 1999). Group procedures can be used to (1) stimulate divergent thinking, (2) initiate convergent thinking, (3) create space for reflections, and (4) develop a common focus.

STIMULATING DIVERGENT THINKING

One of the major challenges small groups face is failing to explore fully the nature of the problem in depth or generate a number of possible solutions. The first description of the problem or the first solution offered is typically not the most effective or creative; yet small group members tend to latch on to their first problem description or the first solution suggested. **Divergent thinking** involves generating multiple ideas and alternatives about issues, problems, and solutions. Divergent thinking is particularly useful when groups examine the possible causes of a problem or solutions to a problem. In both of these situations, groups need to survey the broad variety of possible causes and solutions to avoid focusing on only one or two possible causes and solutions. Brainstorming and brainwriting are two group procedures that can be used to enhance divergent thinking.

Brainstorming is a group procedure in which each individual in a group generates ideas and adds them to the group discussion. Brainstorming is guided by three rules:

- The "no criticism rule": Group members are not allowed to evaluate the quality of other group members' ideas.
- The "hitchhiking rule": Group members are allowed to develop their ideas based on other ideas from the group. For example, in a discussion on how to address teen violence in a community, one member may suggest developing "boot camps" for first-time offenders. Another member may "hitchhike" off this idea and suggests establishing "activity camps" where kids could learn about art, music, and drama.
- The "quantity breeds quality rule": The first ideas generated are usually the most obvious or simple; by generating lots of ideas, the chances that high-quality and creative ideas will emerge is increased.

Brainstorming is typically done orally within a group with a member assigned to record each of the ideas on a laptop computer or a flip chart.

To use brainstorming effectively, group leaders need to pay close attention to two issues. First, is every group member participating? Group brainstorming works best when each member feels free to contribute ideas. Yet some group members do not feel comfortable volunteering their ideas in large group settings. One way to address this concern

Brainstorming has long been a tool for small group creativity.

THE FAR SIDE © 1998 FARWORKS, INC. Used by permission. All rights reserved.

is to have members first silently brainstorm ideas and then state them out loud in the group. Giving the members some time to prepare an answer silently may make them less anxious about volunteering their ideas. Another way to enhance member participation is to divide the group into two or more subgroups. Each subgroup then can brainstorm and subsequently share the resulting ideas in the larger group. Decreasing the size of the group increases the likelihood that a quieter member would participate in the brainstorming. Moreover, splitting and mixing up group members into smaller subgroups enables each subgroup to generate as many ideas as the larger group might. In fact, when the ideas generated by two subgroups are combined, they generally total more than if the large group had simply brainstormed without splitting.

A procedure known as brainwriting also allows each group member's voice to be heard in the discussion. In **brainwriting**, a written method for brainstorming, a grid is created on a sheet of paper and passed along for each member to contribute an idea while reviewing what previous group members have written (Wycoff, 1995). Brainwriting is used in groups that rely on oral communication as well as adapted for groups whose primary mode of communication is written, such as groups linked through email.

A second issue is the degree to which a group focuses on only one idea as opposed to multiple ideas. One of the drawbacks to brainstorming is that one person's idea may become the base for all subsequent ideas. Group members may be so heavily influenced by one idea that the subsequent ideas they generate are simply variations on the initial idea. For example, if a person had volunteered the idea of boot camps as a solution for dealing with juvenile crime and subsequent ideas only covered different kinds of camps—arts camps, computer camps, sports camps—the range of ideas is limited. Other possible solutions such as after-school programs, tutoring in the schools, and neighborhood youth centers are neglected. The creativity of brainstorming may be preserved if each individual silently generates or initially writes down a few ideas before sharing them with the group. This method prevents group members from being influenced by others in their thinking.

STIMULATING CONVERGENT THINKING

Whereas divergent thinking generates lots of ideas, **convergent thinking** is concerned with evaluating the ideas and narrowing a wide range of alternatives and selecting the one most appropriate to the task at hand. Procedures that narrow the range of alternatives to be considered and explore the strengths and weaknesses of each alternative help promote convergent thinking. Two procedures are particularly useful in stimulating convergent thinking: nominal group technique and fishbone diagrams.

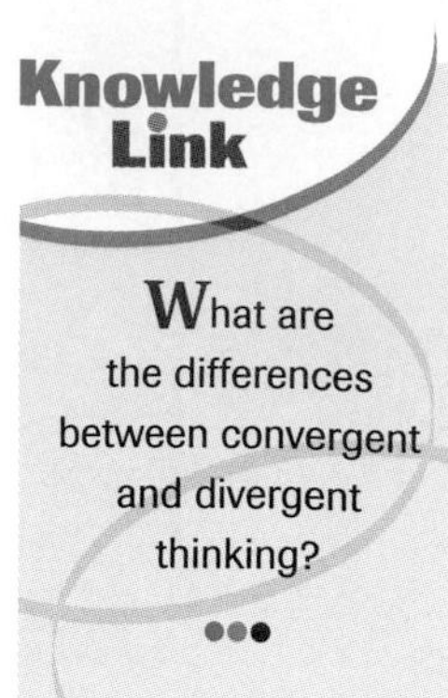

Nominal group technique (NGT) is a procedure in which group members generate ideas individually, share these ideas with the group, and then evaluate them as a group. This technique assumes that idea generation is best done individually and idea evaluation is best done as a group. Nominal group technique uses the following steps:

1. Each member silently generates and writes down as many ideas as possible on the selected topic.
2. Each person volunteers one idea, which is recorded on a flip chart set before the large group. This process is repeated until each member has volunteered all of his or her ideas.
3. Using the list of ideas written on the flip chart, the group then evaluates the strengths and weaknesses of each idea.
4. Group members then individually rank the ideas. Another group member tallies up the individual rankings and produces an overall group ranking of the ideas.
5. The group then selects the most highly ranked ideas (say the top three), and the subsequent discussion focuses on those top ideas.
6. Steps 3–5 are repeated until the group reaches a decision.

Another tool that can help group members examine the strengths and weaknesses of ideas is **fishbone diagrams,** which are visual maps of the important causes and drivers that influence the outcomes group members wish to pursue. At the head of the fish, you write down the desired outcome. Continuing the earlier example, the desired outcome is reducing violent teenage crime. Along the spines of the fish, you note the various causes and drivers that would lead to a decrease in violent teenage crime. Access to after-school teen activities and the presence of adult mentors are influences that may decrease teenage violence. Once groups have generated their fishbone diagram, discussion then centers on which of the "spines," or actions, are most likely to bring about the desired outcome. The fishbone diagram, illustrated in Figure 12.5, allows group members to discuss which of the actions are most important in achieving their goal and to select among these various actions after a discussion of all possibilities.

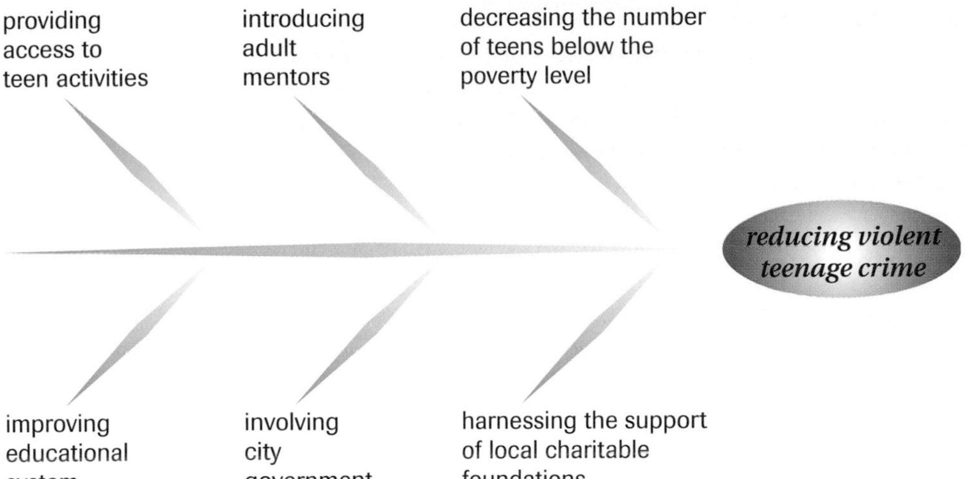

FIGURE 12.5
A Fishbone Diagram

A fishbone diagram can be used to examine causes that lead to an effect. A goal is placed at the "head" of the fish. Activities that will allow the group to achieve the goal are placed along the "spines," with the most important placed closest to the head. In this diagram, decreasing the number of teenagers who live below the poverty line is more likely to decrease violent teenage crime than involving city government.

DEVELOPING REFLECTIONS

Groups that make high-quality decisions are vigilant in their interaction. Yet as the groupthink model illustrates, many times group members fail to be vigilant—they don't examine the problem with a critical eye or carefully review the arguments for or against a particular solution. Being vigilant requires group members to be reflective and aware of the values, assumptions, and interests that guide how they define the problem and evaluate solutions. Developing this reflective approach involves making the values, assumptions, and interests guiding decision making explicit and reexamining the assumption on which the decision is based and revisiting previously dismissed alternatives. Developing this reflective ability can be accomplished through three procedures: (1) devil's advocate, (2) the use of minority reports, and (3) stakeholder analysis.

The **devil's advocate procedure** involves the group assigning an individual to question the assumptions and the processes it uses to make the decision. The devil's advocate challenges the group's thinking by introducing contrasting viewpoints and ideas. The devil's advocate's role in the group is significant in that it introduces minority views to the group. The more that minority opinions are included in the final decision, the higher quality the decision (Schwenk, 1990). Devil's advocate procedure is only effective when group members are open to criticism and value contrasting ideas. If a group is not open to hearing divergent views, no matter how hard the devil's advocate tries, the minority views will not be heard. The devil's advocate will be dismissed as uninformed, a troublemaker, or irrelevant. Even if minority opinion is present in the discussion, if it is not heard or valued by the majority of the group, it will not lead to high-quality decisions.

A second way to create space for the group to reflect on its decision and decision-making process is for it to commission minority reports. **Minority reports** are generated by a subgroup to reflect thinking and ideas that are not shared by a majority of the group members. Minority reports provide an alternative perspective from the majority opinion. In a minority report, group members (1) propose a different solution from the majority, (2) articulate the assumptions that guided their proposed solution, and (3) critique the set of assumptions that guided the majority opinion. A minority report sets up a critical comparison between two points of view—the majority and minority view. Developing a minority report permits a specific analysis of the strengths and weaknesses of both sides. Minority reports help groups develop reflections by having them stop group discussion for a moment and revisit the assumptions and beliefs that are guiding the decision.

Finally, performing a stakeholder analysis can enhance a group's ability to be reflective. A **stakeholder analysis** occurs when a group identifies its key stakeholders—those who will be affected by their decision—and analyzes how each stakeholder would view the group's decision. Many times groups only consider the views of the group members significant. However, these decisions are perceived by and influence the lives of people outside the small group. One way to integrate the views of key stakeholders into the decision-making process is to list all the key stakeholders interested in or affected by the decision. Then, for each stakeholder, ask the following questions:

- "How would this person or group view the problem?"
- "What would they view as an appropriate decision?"
- "What are the implications for this stakeholder group if the current decision stands?"

By thinking through the views and expectations of key stakeholders, a group can incorporate contrasting views into the final decision-making process. Stakeholder analysis allows group members to reflect on their decision from the perspectives of those who will be affected.

DEVELOPING A COMMON FOCUS

To achieve desirable goals, group members must be able to coordinate their activities with one another. One of the lessons from groupthink theory is that for a group to be effective it needs to have members with different backgrounds. At the same time, when people bring different backgrounds and perspectives to a meeting, it can be challenging to focus on the task at hand. They may experience difficulty listening to one another because they may disagree over fundamental assumptions and beliefs regarding the decision to be made. One way to help group members maintain a common focus and accomplish their task is to develop a set of discussion ground rules for how they will interact with each other.

Setting ground rules in a discussion can be invaluable. Such rules help group members know what they are responsible for and how to relate to one another. Ground rules can be established for the following areas:

- attendance ("no interruptions to take phone calls or check email")
- discussion ("everything is open for discussion")
- confidentiality ("the only things to leave this room are what we agree will leave this room")
- analytic approach ("facts are preferred over opinions")
- end-product orientation ("everyone completes assignments")
- constructive confrontation ("no finger pointing")
- contributions ("everyone does real work") (Adapted from Katzenbach & Smith, 1993)

The more that groups can establish ground rules for working together, the more they will be able to keep focused on the task. Ground rules also open up the space for the group to reflect on its decision-making process. When rules such as discussion and confidentiality are established, group members may feel free to actively examine key assumptions and views knowing they are in a safe environment.

Establishing discussion ground rules is very important when groups are going to discuss potentially controversial and sensitive issues. For example, consider a dialogue on race relations. In each discussion group, the following ground rules for discussion could be presented and enforced:

1. Listen with attention.
2. Speak from experience.
3. Don't repeat stories.
4. Respect each other's truth.
5. Share time fairly.

Ground rules for group discussions provide a common understanding of each member's roles and how group members are to relate to one another. For example, if the discussion becomes heated and participants attack one another, the group facilitator could invoke the "Respect each other's truth" rule to refocus the discussion. Ground rules are valuable resources in organizing group activity because they can be called on to restore order and coherence to the discussion anytime a group member violates the rules.

Chapter Summary

Many of the decisions we make in life are not made on an individual basis; rather, they are made in small groups. Small groups are used to make a wide variety of decisions such as governmental policy, the products and services an organization should sell and market, and financial planning by nonprofit organizations. Groups are central to helping get work done by weighing competing alternatives and making informed choices.

First, recognize that group decision making differs from group problem solving. Decision making involves selecting among competing alternatives, whereas problem solving is about reducing a gap between a current and ideal state. Conducting a force field analysis can help you understand what is causing the problem and restraining the problem from being solved. Second, groups make decisions about a variety of issues, using questions of fact, conjecture, value, and policy. Third, groups need to perform particular functions if they are going to make high-quality decisions. Beginning with Dewey's reflective thinking sequence and continuing with functionalist theory, effective groups need to (1) assess the problem situation, (2) specify the goals of the decision-making process, (3) identify a range of alternatives, and (4) evaluate the alternatives in light of positive/negative consequences. Fourth, group members need to determine what will count as an effective decision. Effective decisions are those that are acceptable to key stakeholders, help promote group members' future collaboration, and enhance the group members' personal development. Finally, competent group communicators need to know when to use groups and when to use individuals to make decisions.

Knowing how to make decisions must be paired with task skills for competent small group communication. Five task skills are key to effective decision making: (1) defining the problem, (2) analyzing the problem, (3) identifying criteria for solving the problem, (4) generating solutions or alternatives, and (5) evaluating solutions or alternatives.

The major challenge to effective decision making is groupthink. Groupthink short-circuits the decision-making process by moving group members toward a superficial analysis of the problem and potential solutions. A number of factors can move the group toward groupthink: cohesiveness, structural factors, and provocative situational contexts. Group members in a cohesive group may decrease critical thinking to maintain affiliation. Groups that are insulated from the larger environment, lack impartial leadership and methodical procedures, as well as groups with members who share values, beliefs, and assumptions have a tendency for groupthink. Finally, the situational factors of high stress and low self-esteem among group members can lead to groupthink.

How can this challenge to competent group decision making be overcome? At a minimum, groups can use group procedures to structure the decision making process. Group procedures can help determine whether ideas need to be generated (divergent thinking) or evaluated (convergent thinking), how space can be created for group members to reflect on the process, and how groups can develop a common focus and coordinate their activities. Brainstorming and brainwriting are two procedures that can be used to enhance divergent thinking. Nominal group technique (NGT) and fishbone diagrams are tools that can be used to narrow down competing alternatives in a process called convergent thinking. Developing a reflective ability is accomplished by appointing group members to act as the devil's advocate, commissioning minority reports, and performing a stakeholder analysis. Finally, groups need to develop a common focus by coordinating members' activities and setting ground rules for discussion—two valuable ways to organize group activity and ensure high-quality decision making.

Key Terms

problem
problem solving
force field analysis
drivers
restraining forces
decision
decision making
questions of fact
questions of conjecture
questions of value
questions of policy
nested decision making
reflective thinking model
functionalist approach
vigilant interaction
decision acceptability
collaboration capability
personal development
task skills
groupthink
concurrence seeking
group procedure
divergent thinking
brainstorming
brainwriting
convergent thinking
nominal group technique (NGT)
fishbone diagram
devil's advocate procedure
minority reports
stakeholder analysis

Building Knowledge

1. What are the differences between problem solving and decision making? Is it possible to solve a problem without making a decision or make a decision without solving a problem?
2. Are all decisions nested? Do all decisions inherently involve questions of fact, conjecture, value, and policy? Can you have a question of fact that does not involve a question of value? Can you have a policy question that does not involve questions of fact?
3. What kinds of communication does the reflective thinking model and the functionalist approach to decision making suggest is important for effective decision making?
4. Under what conditions is it best to use groups to make decisions as opposed to individuals?
5. How does groupthink influence decision making? Are there ever times when a group leader may want to encourage groupthink?
6. When should group members engage in divergent and convergent thinking? What strategies can they use to generate and evaluate ideas?
7. What is the relationship between being reflective in a group and effective decision making? How can groups develop a reflective ability?

Building Skills

Individual Exercises

1. Select and interview two or three individuals who participate in small groups. Use the following questions for your interview:
   a. What has been your best experience in group decision making?
   b. What made it such a good experience?
   c. What factors make it possible to make a good decision?
   d. What criteria do you feel should be used to evaluate whether a group has made a good decision?

   Compare the answers you get from your interviews to the material in the chapter. In what ways are your interviewees' answers similar or different from the material in the chapter? Why do you think that is?
2. Brainstorm a list of problems that concern you. Starting with the most important problem, do a force field analysis on this problem. What is the gap that represents the problem? What are the drivers? What are the constraining forces?
3. Imagine you are a member of an organization. You have been assigned to write a memo about effective decision making that will be distributed to all members. What are five rules for effective decision making you would include in the memo?
4. Log on to the internet and search for sites that discuss decision-making procedures. Type in

the keywords *decision-making procedures* and identify two sites that discuss ways to coordinate group decision-making activity. Compare the procedures they highlight to the procedures identified in the chapter that facilitate divergent thinking, convergent thinking, developing reflective ability, and creating a common focus. In what ways are they similar and different to the procedures discussed in the chapter?

Group Exercises

1. Form groups of 4–5 people. Using the following list of group topics, brainstorm the kinds of ground rules you would set up for a constructive discussion on a controversial topic like affirmative action or extending health benefits to partners of gays and lesbians:

attendance	end-product orientation
discussion	constructive confrontation
confidentiality	contributions
analytic approach	

1. As a group of 4–5 people, watch the 1950s movie *12 Angry Men*. Focus on the character played by Henry Fonda. Using Fonda as an example, what is it that allows a person to create effectively the role of devil's Advocate? As a group, generate a list of rules for being an effective devil's advocate.

2.  Using *InfoTrac, College Edition*, look up the article, "Challenge courses can build strong teams," Training and Development, April 1997 v51 n4 p12 (2) by Carol Steinfeld. Read through the article. Using the information contained in the article, prepare a presentation for your class that addresses the following question, "How can challenge courses help develop a common focus for groups?"

References

Dewey, J. (1910). *How we think.* Boston: D. C. Heath.

Esser, J. K. (1998). Alive and well after 25 years: A review of groupthink research. *Organizational Behavior and Human Decision Processes, 73* (2/3), 116–141.

Forrester, J. (1999). *The deliberative practitioner.* Cambridge, MA: MIT Press.

Gouran, D. S., & Hirokawa, R. Y. (1996). Functional theory and communication in decision-making and problem-solving groups: An expanded view. In R. Y. Hirokawa & M. S. Poole (Eds.), *Communication and group decision making* (2nd ed., pp. 55–80). Thousand Oaks, CA: Sage.

Gouran, D. S., Hirokawa, R. Y., Julian, K. M., & Latham, G. B. (1993). The evolution and current status of the functional perspective on communication in decision-making and problem-solving groups. In S. A. Deetz (Ed.), *Communication yearbook 16* (pp. 573–600). Newbury Park, CA: Sage.

Hackman, J. R. (Ed.). (1990). *Groups that work (and those that don't): Creating conditions for effective teamwork.* San Francisco: Jossey-Bass.

Hirokawa, R. Y. (1988, April). *The role of communication in group decision-making efficacy: A task-contingency perspective.* Paper presented at the annual meeting of the Central States Speech Association, Schaumburg, IL.

Hirokawa, R. Y. (1990). The role of communication in group decision-making efficacy: A task-contingency perspective. *Small Group Research, 21* (2), 190–204.

Janis, I. L. (1972). *Victims of groupthink: A psychological study of policy decisions and fiascoes* (2nd ed.). Boston: Houghton Mifflin.

Janis, I. L. (1982). *Groupthink: Psychological studies of policy decisions and fiascoes* (2nd ed.). Boston: Houghton Mifflin.

Janis, I. L., & Mann, L. (1977). *Decision-making: A psychological analysis of conflict, choice, and commitment.* New York: Free Press.

Jensen, A. D., & Chilberg, J. C. (1991). *Small group communication: Theory and application.* Belmont, CA: Wadsworth.

Katzenbach, J. R., & Smith, D. K. (1993). *The wisdom of teams: Creating the high-performance organization.* Cambridge, MA: Harvard Business School Press.

Lewin, K. (1951). *Field theory in social research.* New York: Harper & Row.

Schwenk, C. R. (1990). Effects of devil's advocacy and dialectical inquiry on decision making: A meta-analysis. *Organizational Behavior and Human Decision Processes, 47,* 161–176.

Steiner, I. D. (1972). *Group process and productivity.* New York: Academic Press.

Sunwolf, & Siebold, D. R. (1999). The impact of formal procedures on group processes, members and task outcomes. In L. R. Frey, D. S. Gouran, & M. S. Poole (Eds.), *The handbook of group communication theory and research* (pp. 395–431). Thousand Oaks, CA: Sage.

Turner, M. E., & Pratkanis, A. R. (1998). Twenty-five years of groupthink theory and research: Lessons from the evaluation of a theory. *Organizational Behavior and Human Decision Processes, 73* (2/3), 105–115.

Wycoff, J. (1995). *Transformation thinking.* New York: Berkley Books.

Decision-Making Competence Skills Grid

To help you understand how to use this grid, the skills displayed by Eva in the opening vignette of this chapter have been analyzed below. Examine that analysis and then think about a recent decision-making situation and what you could have done more competently. First, describe the context of the decision-making situation in the spaces provided. Next, analyze your decision-making skills based on the skills explained in this chapter for each step in the decision-making process. In the first column,

ANALYZING EVA'S DECISION-MAKING SKILLS
Context

CULTURE: Task force at a large university in North America

TIME: Weekday afternoon

RELATIONSHIP: Student-faculty, student-administration, faculty-administration

PLACE: At the office

FUNCTION: Eva must facilitate a task force decision regarding strategies for managing student enrollment

DECISION-MAKING SKILLS	LESS COMPETENT	MORE COMPETENT
DEFINING THE PROBLEM	Not defining the problem (e.g., "I'm not sure what we're supposed to do about . . ."); ambiguously defining the problem (e.g., "The problem is in the general area of . . .")	Offering a definition of the problem (e.g., "The President has charged us with . . ."); highlighting assumptions (e.g., "One of the assumptions we are making about student enrollment is . . .")
ANALYZING THE PROBLEM	Defining the problem without using data; not articulating the reasoning behind your problem assessment	Stating causes of the problem (e.g., "One of the drivers for this issue is . . ."); articulating the history (e.g., "The background of the problem is . . .')
IDENTIFYING CRITERIA FOR SOLVING THE PROBLEM	Proposing unrealistic criteria for solutions; proposing ambiguous criteria for adopting solutions	Asking task force members for criteria for evaluating (e.g., "What criteria should we use . . ."); combining two or more criteria into a new criterion (e.g., "If we take these two criteria together, we . . .")
GENERATING SOLUTIONS OR ALTERNATIVES	Suggesting unrealistic solutions; criticizing proposed solutions before brainstorming of ideas is completed	Soliciting task force members for solutions (e.g., "What do you think we can do . . ."); proposing solutions for the problem (e.g., "I think what we can do is . . .")
EVALUATING SOLUTIONS OR ALTERNATIVES	Failing to tie an evaluation of solutions back to a criterion; underestimating negative consequences of solutions while overestimating positive consequences	Stating advantages gained from accepting a particular solution (e.g., "A key benefit of this idea is . . ."); asking whether solutions meet a criterion (e.g., "How does this solution relate to our criterion of . . .")

briefly describe and give examples of how your skills may have been less than competent. Using these less competent skills as a point of comparison to fill in the second column, describe the skills you think would have been perceived as more competent in the particular context. With practice, you will find you can use this grid to help develop your decision-making skills for future decision-making situations, as well as to analyze decision-making situations you have already experienced.

ANALYZING YOUR OWN DECISION-MAKING SKILLS

Context

CULTURE:

TIME:

RELATIONSHIP:

PLACE:

FUNCTION:

DECISION-MAKING SKILLS	LESS COMPETENT	MORE COMPETENT
DEFINING THE PROBLEM		
ANALYZING THE PROBLEM		
IDENTIFYING CRITERIA FOR SOLVING THE PROBLEM		
GENERATING SOLUTIONS OR ALTERNATIVES		
EVALUATING SOLUTIONS OR ALTERNATIVES		

CHAPTER 13

Learning Objectives

After studying this chapter, you should be able to:

1. Differentiate among the orientation, conflict, and emergence phases of group development.
2. Discriminate among task, relational, and ego-centered group roles.
3. Explain how the concepts of interaction, interdependence, and incompatibility inform a definition of conflict.
4. Distinguish among affective, ideational, and procedural conflict.
5. Identify group situations where the accommodating, avoiding, competing, compromising, and collaborating styles of conflict management are superior.
6. Illustrate how the skills of acknowledging and reflecting can help manage conflict and create a supportive group climate.
7. Define leadership and identify types of leadership behavior that facilitate group productivity.
8. Demonstrate how issue framing, making group members' reasoning explicit, and exploring the group's commission can help manage relationships within groups.

Managing Relationships in Groups: Leadership

Rob is the newly hired executive director for the Arlen Arts Company (AAC), a local nonprofit group that sponsors a wide variety of adult and children's theatrical programming. The AAC owns a building that has a ticket booth, a large lobby, dressing rooms, a main stage, a rehearsal room, and a workshop for making theatrical sets. At the time the building was constructed, the main stage was honored as one of the most innovative theater designs in the nation. The theater has flourished over the years, expanding its programming to include a children's theater program and summer productions. During the last decade, however, season ticket sales have plummeted. Moreover, the talent pool of actors and actresses has dwindled and volunteer support for building the sets and helping at the box office has fallen. After interviewing several candidates, the board of directors hired Rob to reverse the pattern of falling ticket sales and to increase community involvement with the theater.

Shortly after Rob was hired, he conducted an analysis of the theater's operating budget and created a set of recommendations for the board of directors to consider. When he presented his ideas to the board a heated discussion in the board meeting erupted. Some board members voiced disagreement with Rob's recommendation and verbally attacked him, calling him "young and inexperienced." These board members had voted for another candidate for executive director and had difficulty accepting Rob as the new executive director. Other board members didn't want to talk about Rob's recommendations at all; they wanted to talk about the problems the theater was having. They had great difficulty moving beyond talking about the theater's financial difficulties to talking about actions that could address the problems. Still other members wanted to talk about the theater's history. They had belonged to the theater for over 20 years and wanted to focus on how good things had been in the past. Any new idea that Rob presented was met with the refrain of "that's not how we've done it in the past." Other board members were open to Rob's ideas and tried to keep the discussion focused on the recommendations. And there were some board members who sat there in silence trying to make sense of the discussion.

Rob had problems leading the discussion. He felt that some board members were "out to get him" and no matter what he said they were going to disagree. He felt other board members "were out of touch" and so focused on the past that they failed to recognize that times had changed and that what worked well in the past doesn't work today. Although he appreciated the efforts of those group members who were receptive to his ideas, he knew they were a minority on the board. He was confused and getting angry. Rob thought to himself, "What do these people want? They hire me to help straighten out the theater, and yet they fight me when I want to make changes."

Just as Rob thought the discussion couldn't get any worse, one of his staff members, the director of the Children's Theater, entered the discussion and criticized Rob's recommendations as not being sensitive to the needs of the Children's Theater. At that point, Rob suggested that the board table his recommendations to the next board meeting, and adjourn. ●●●

What would you do if you were in Rob's position? Would you have adjourned the meeting? One of the chief problems that Rob faced during this meeting was managing the participation of the board members. He had multiple groups of board members each pursuing their own agenda. For some board members, the agenda was to sabotage Rob's recommendations in order to show he was ill-equipped for the executive director position and that the other candidate would have been superior. Other board members wanted to talk about the past, perhaps in order to deny the existence of current problems. Still others never wanted to talk about actions—perhaps because talking about actions would force the group to make hard choices and split the board apart. With such a diverse set of people and goals, it is not surprising that the meeting became chaotic and unproductive.

Is it fair to blame Rob for this meeting's failure? As the formally appointed leader of the group, Rob does share some responsibility for the disintegration of the meeting. Yet the individual board members also made choices about their participation in the board meeting. Some chose to pursue their political agenda and sabotage Rob's authority. Others chose to abdicate their responsibility to think about the future and chose to remain focused on the past. Others chose to work toward making changes in the theater that could lead to increased ticket sales and community involvement. Although it was Rob's responsibility to manage the board of directors, that does not absolve group members of the responsibility to participate constructively. Members of any group make choices, consciously or unconsciously, about how they are going to position themselves during the discussion.

Part of the difficulty that Rob faced during the meeting also emerged from a conflicting set of expectations generated by the board. On one hand, Rob felt quite correctly that he had been hired to change the theater's operations in order to generate increased ticket sales and community involvement. Yet, at the same time, when he tried to be proactive and make recommendations to change the theater, he was met with resistance. This highlights a common dilemma for group leaders. Leaders in groups are commonly charged with creating change and innovation within the group; yet the groups they work

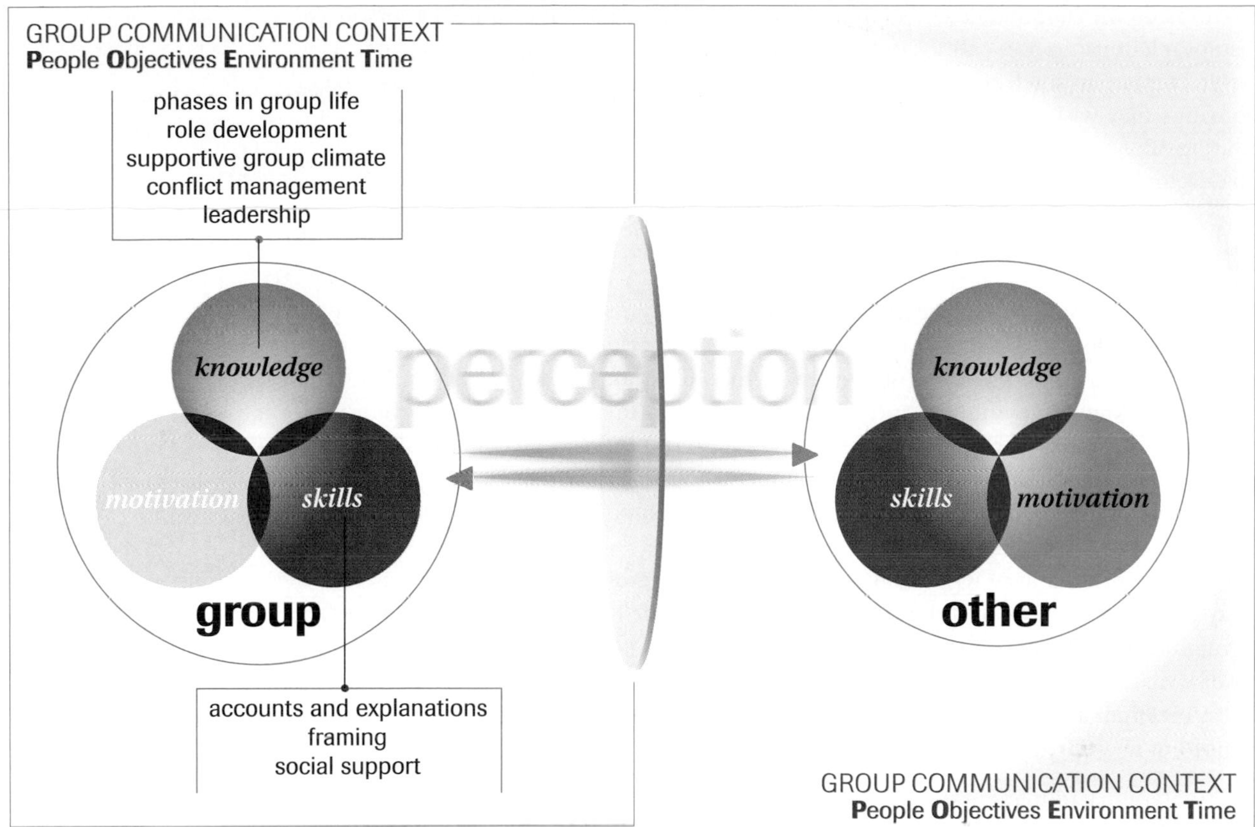

FIGURE 13.1
Expanded Group Communication Competence Model

Competent communicators in small groups need to know about a wide variety of relational processes, such as role development, conflict management, and leadership. Being skilled at giving accounts and explanations, framing, and providing social support also facilitates building high-quality relationships.

with deny that change is needed or desired and resist. How then do leaders institute change in groups? What kinds of strategies can be used to weaken resistance among group members and create constructive change? What are the positive resources that leaders can draw on to manage innovation and change in groups?

This chapter focuses on the issue of creating constructive relationships in small groups. In any group we belong to, we make choices regarding the kinds of relationships we wish to create, and these choices have consequences for how group members work together. We can choose to establish cooperative or competitive relationships with other group members. We can choose to foster conflict and create defensive climates or we can select ways of communicating that manage conflict and create supportive relationships. Figure 13.1 highlights the kinds of knowledge and skills that make up competent group communication. We begin by examining the kinds of knowledge that competent small group communication require to facilitate managing relationships.

Knowing How to Manage Relationships

Think of a current group you belong to and imagine the people who belong to the group. How would you describe the kinds of relationships you have with other group members? How would you characterize your role in relationship to the other group members? At the heart of small group communication is the idea that group members are always in relationship with each other. Even if you decide not to form a close relationship with another group member, you still have a relationship with that person—a distant relationship. You cannot *not* be a in relationship with other group members. As a result, competent small group communicators must make choices about the kinds of relationships they wish to create with other group members. Knowing how to manage your relationships with other group members requires (1) recognizing phases in group life, (2) developing roles, (3) creating a supportive group climate, and (4) managing conflict.

RECOGNIZING PHASES IN GROUP LIFE

Groups are like individuals in that they are born, they live, and ultimately they die. Groups exist along a life span where they are created, perform a task or tasks, and ultimately come to an end. As the Glasbergen cartoon illustrates, how group members initially get to know one another and become oriented to their task is so important that people feel we need to begin the group process at birth! Cultivating constructive group member relationships are important to accomplishing tasks and they evolve and change during the life of a group. The kinds of relationships group members create are determined, in part, by the phase that group is currently in.

What is a group phase? A **group phase** is a stage in the group's life span where there is a clearly defined purpose and theme for the group activity. Just as people sometimes "go through a phase" where they constantly perform some activity, so do groups. Several models that identity phases of group development exist (Bales & Strodtbeck, 1951; Fisher, 1970; Tuckman and Jensen, 1977), yet most share the belief that the following phases are important in group life:

- Orientation: Group members orient themselves to the task and the ways they should relate to one another. Discussion of roles, leadership, and guidelines for interaction characterize the orientation phase.
- Conflict: Group members offer their opinions regarding the task. Typically these opinions polarize the conversation, and disagreement and debate may occur. It is not unusual for members to try to persuade other members to adopt their way of thinking.
- Emergence: Group members offer suggestions on how to perform the task. A collaboration among group members begins to develop a workable solution to the task.

Cultivating high-quality group member relationships needs to begin early in the life of the group.

© Randy Glasbergen. Reprinted with special permission from www.glasbergen.com.

Each of these phases suggests that group members create different kinds of relationships with each other. During the orientation phase, group members do not know one another and have not established relationships with each other. Therefore, it becomes important to have conversation within the group that orients its members to one another and articulates how they will relate to one another and what kinds of roles each will assume. During the conflict phase, relationships among group members have been created, and those relationships are put to the test as group members argue over how the task can best be accomplished. At this stage, group members need to talk in ways that resolve their conflicts and maintain their existing relationships. During the emergence stage, group members feel comfortable with their relationships and focus on the task at hand. They are able to reach a consensus on what solutions should be selected and implemented.

One of the large questions about successful group development has been whether all high-quality groups go through a single sequence of phases. One position argues that groups need to go through a particular set of phases if they are to develop successfully. The **phase hypothesis** states that small groups must go through the phases in a prescribed order in order to be effective and make high-quality decisions (Bales & Strodtbeck, 1951). For example, the phase hypothesis suggests that groups need to go through an orientation phase, followed by a conflict phase, and ending with an emergence phase. Using the phase hypothesis, Rob's difficulty with the board of directors can be explained by the fact that Rob and the board had not gone initially through the orientation phase. Rather than orient the group to the problems at hand and develop solid working relationships with the board members (orientation phase), Rob started by having the group talk about the recommendation with the hope they would approve his recommendations (emergence phase). According to the phase hypothesis, the foundation for high-quality group work had not been laid because the group skipped the orientation phase. This explains why the group discussion was ridden with conflict and was unproductive.

In contrast, some believe that high-quality groups do not go through a single set of phases. Rather, groups may cycle through these phases in any particular order (Poole, Siebold, & McPhee, 1996). For example, a group may start off in an orientation phase and then move to a conflict phase where they explore competing ideas. However, rather than progress to the emergence phase, they may go back to the orientation phase. During the discussion of competing ideas, they may have felt a need to return to a discussion of what the task is and what their responsibility is to each other before entering the emergence phase. Group effectiveness is not determined by the sequence of phases that group members go through; rather, group effectiveness is determined by the amount of energy that group members exert in analyzing and evaluating the issue at hand. As discussed in Chapter 12, when group members actively engage in vigilant interaction, they will be more likely to make quality decisions and bring about desirable outcomes. The energy they devote to fulfilling key task functions is more important than if the group follows a preset order of phases.

Developing Roles

When we are in relationships with other people, we tend to perform particular roles. When we are in a romantic dating relationship, we may assume the role of a lover. When we are in a teacher-student relationship, one person performs the role of teacher and the other the student. When we are in a employer-employee relationship, one person is the employee and the other the employer. The same is true of group relationships. When you are in small groups, you create relationships with other group members, and these relationships have implications for the kinds of group roles you perform. A **group role** is made up of a set of prescribed behaviors that individuals are expected to perform.

There are many kinds of roles that you may perform in small groups. One classic typology of group roles, offered by Benne and Sheats (1948), is based on the type of behavioral function performed by the individuals playing the role. Three general classes of roles are identified:

- Task roles: These roles help the group achieve its task or objective. They include behaviors that orient the group to the task at hand, manage the exchange of ideas and opinions, and encourage the group to complete the task.
- Relational roles: These roles include behaviors that function to maintain the interpersonal climate within the group. They provide harmony to the group, create openness for sharing information, convey the feelings of group members, and help manage the relational environment of the organization.
- Ego-centered roles: These roles emphasize the individual's personality and thereby favor the needs of the individual over the group. Such roles are typically viewed as destructive to a group because they hinder the organization's ability to achieve a task.

Table 13.1 highlights specific examples of these three general classes of roles. For small groups to be effective, it is important for a wide variety of roles to be performed. High-quality groups must pay close attention to accomplishing their task and constructing high-quality group relationships and environments. Therefore, it is important for group members to perform task and relational roles. At the same time, group members need to avoid performing ego-centered roles because they can hinder the group's ability to achieve its task and goals.

It is important to remember that roles are not taken; rather, they are created in collaboration with other group members. How roles are created is similar to how roles are created in improvisational theater. In dramatic productions such as Shakespeare's *Two Gentleman of Verona* or musicals such as *Les Miserables,* actors play particular roles according to a predetermined script. The playwright has determined what roles the characters will perform and what lines they will utter. In improvisational theater, the roles of the characters are created on the spot and depend on how other characters in the production relate to them. Like improvisational theater, group roles are worked out through interaction, negotiation, and feedback from other group members. Feedback is provided by other group members that frames the types of roles an individual can legitimately assume within a group (Bormann, 1975). The relationship between feedback and roles can be summarized as follows:

- If group members give ambiguous feedback to an individual about role performance, the individual will continue to display the behavior until clear approval or disapproval is received.
- If group members give positive feedback or approval to an individual about role performance, the individual will integrate the behavior into his or her role repertoire.
- If group members give negative feedback or disapproval to an individual about role performance, the person will begin to avoid the behavior.

The importance of feedback in creating roles cannot be underestimated. Have you ever been critical of another group member's role and behavior? It is tempting to view this individual's behavior as due to some personal characteristic such as personality, knowledge, or motivation. However, it is just as likely that you and other group members have knowingly or unknowingly given feedback that makes that person view his or her role and

TABLE 13.1

••• Typology of Group Roles •••

There are three categories of group roles: task, relational, and ego centered. Within each category, group members may select among several distinct roles to play.

ROLE	FUNCTION
Task Roles	
Initiator	Provides direction and guidance to a group. Proposes definitions of problems, suggests solutions, gives ideas, and suggests operating procedures.
Information seeker	Recognizes the need for additional information. Requests clarification of ideas and relevant facts about the group's task.
Information giver	Provides relevant facts about the group's task.
Opinion seeker	Solicits people's feelings and views about any aspect of the group's task. Tests for the group opinion.
Opinion giver	Offers personal views and evaluation of the group's work. May comment on the value of certain group procedures, the solutions under consideration, or the nature of the group's task.
Clarifier	Eliminates confusion by identifying points of agreement or restating ideas or viewpoints.
Elaborator/coordinator	Extends information and clarifies relations among various viewpoints, ideas, and solutions within the group.
Problem identifier	Proposes definitions of a problem and its related causes or antecedents.
Procedure developer	Proposes and identifies the procedures a group should use when making a decision; includes setting and proposing an agenda.
Orienter-summarizer	Focuses the group on the task and summarizes its discussion by reviewing the relationships among solutions, facts, and opinions.
Information recorder	Records group discussion.
Tester of agreement	Checks to see how close the group is to reaching an agreement.
Energizer	Motivates the group and prods it toward action.
Relational Roles	
Supporter	Recognizes others' contributions and encourages them to participate.
Harmonizer	Attempts to balance and manage conflict within the group. Serves to maintain and restore a positive interpersonal climate. Includes helping the group express its feelings to relieve tension.
Tension reliever	Through joking and humor, attempts to relieve group stress.
Compromiser	Seeks to maintain group cohesion by compromising his or her own ideas that are in conflict with the group's. Admits error to the group.
Gatekeeper	Manages and directs the flow of communication and participation within the group.
Feeling expresser	Highlights for the group its feelings, emotions, and attitudes. Shares feelings with other group members.
Standard setter	Articulates the standards the group must achieve. Refers to these standards when evaluating the group's progress.
Follower	Accepts the ideas and views of other group members without question.

(Continued)

TABLE 13.1 (Cont'd)

••• Typology of Group Roles •••

ROLE	FUNCTION
Ego-Centered Roles	
Blocker	Inhibits group discussion by refusing to cooperate. Rejects other group members' ideas.
Aggressor	Tries to gain power within the group by criticizing other group members' ideas and competence.
Deserter	Withdraws from group participation.
Dominator	Monopolizes group discussions.
Recognition seeker	Seeks personal recognition and praise from other group members by boasting about past accomplishments.
Confessor	Distracts the group from its task by using the group as a means of solving personal problems.
Playboy	Uses cynicism, humor, and horseplay to distract the group from its task.
Special interest pleader	Pursues a personal agenda or the agenda of an outside group.

SOURCE: Adapted from Benne and Sheats (1948). *Note:* This table appeared in J. K. Barge (1994).

behavior as legitimate. It is how you have defined this person's relationship within the group that may be generating the problem, not the individual's personal characteristics. This highlights the importance of small group members providing quality feedback to group members if they are to construct productive roles in small groups.

CREATING A SUPPORTIVE GROUP CLIMATE

One of the qualities of successful teams is that team members are highly motivated, have clear goals, and are supportive of one another. Whether the group is a team of championship professional athletes like football's Denver Broncos or a high-performing work team like the design group that created the iMac computer, such groups have supportive member relationships. Group members are able to offer support to other members and motivate them to higher levels of group performance. Central to constructing supportive member relationship is the creation of a group environment. As defined in Chapter 11, a group environment is the climate in which group members communicate and is informed by the feelings and emotions of group members. Recognizing a group's current environment allows a competent communicator to select messages that either affirm constructive feelings and emotions or transform negative hostile environments.

Two different kinds of group environments exist (Gibb, 1961). A **supportive group environment** exists when group members collaborate with each other to achieve group goals jointly. The following types of communication are typical of supportive environments:

- Communication that describes, rather than evaluates, situations or feelings.
- A problem orientation, indicating a mutual interest in solving the problem rather than controlling or manipulating other group members' actions.
- Spontaneous openness and honesty, not a preconceived strategy that is disguised as being unpremeditated.
- Communication that conveys empathy and concern, not a neutrality or a lack of concern.

- Equal value assigned to all members and ideas, rather than assigning power, status, and values to a few members and ideas.
- An open give-and-take of ideas rather than an inflexibility about new and different ideas. (Lumsden & Lumsden, 1993, pp. 207–208)

Defensive group environments, in contrast, are characterized by a lack of trust and cooperation among group members. Defensive group environments create competition among group members, arouse negative emotions between group members, and frustrate achieving group goals. Defensive environments are created when group members act in ways that negatively evaluate situations and feelings, manipulate others' actions, use ambiguity to gain control, demonstrate a lack of concern and caring, act as if their ideas are superior to others, and communicate that they are certain they are right in their thinking and others are wrong. Such behaviors are typically viewed as ineffective and inappropriate by other group members.

Competent small group communicators need to understand how constructing supportive group environments can generate positive results. For example, supportive environments can help groups accomplish work by creating feelings of affirmation among group members. On the other hand, defensive environments can frustrate group members from accomplishing their task. Returning to the opening vignette, one reason Rob may have difficulty with the AAC board is that they have created a hostile group environment. Board members acted in ways that conveyed superiority and voiced their opinions in ways that indicated certainty that they know the correct answer. Such communication arouses negative feelings for other group members and feeds the conflict among board members. Transforming defensive group environments into supportive ones depends on how group members are able to manage conflict.

MANAGING CONFLICT

What is conflict? How does conflict differ from having a disagreement? How are conflicts different from having a fight? Although many definitions have been offered, **conflict** is typically defined as interaction among interdependent people who perceive others as opposing their goals, aims, or values and having the potential to frustrate them in achieving these goals, aims, or values (Putnam & Poole, 1987, p. 552). This definition contains the three "I's" of conflict: (1) interaction, (2) interdependence, and (3) incompatibility. It is through *interaction* that people become aware of the differences among their goals, aims, or values and begin to manage these differences. People are not telepathic (at least most of us are not!), and interaction through the exchange of verbal and nonverbal cues is the way we become aware of the differences that separate us. The notion of *interdependence* is central to understanding conflict. Many times we can disagree over a variety of issues. You might vote for a particular political candidate and I might vote for another. You might think the welfare system should be overhauled and I don't. These disagreements, however, are not necessarily conflicts. People can disagree but not be in conflict with one another. Conflict emerges when one party in the conflict can interfere with the realizations of the other party's goals, aims, and interests. For example, if Rob wanted to pursue a particular recommendation for the AAC, and the board does not, Rob and the board are in conflict. Rob's ability to pursue a recommendation depends on the board, and the board depends on Rob to follow the board's wishes. At the heart of conflict is the third "I"—*incompatibility.* There needs to be a real or perceived opposition to one's interest for conflict to exist.

Conflicts emerge over a wide variety of issues within small groups and may be managed in different ways. Competent small group communicators need to understand types of conflict and conflict management strategies.

Types of Conflict

What kinds of oppositions form the basis for conflict in small groups? Reflect on your past group experiences. What kinds of conflicts have you had within groups? What were the conflicts over? Who did you have the conflicts with? Make a list of the various conflicts you have had in groups and the specific topics and people involved in those conflicts. As you can see from your list, there is a great variety of topics and issues that group members may find themselves in conflict about.

Three types of conflict typically emerge in groups. **Affective conflict** involves the interpersonal relationships formed among group members and the group's emotional climate. Affective conflict may occur when two group members don't like one another or there is a power struggle between people. In the former, people who don't like one another may begin sniping during the group meetings and insulting one another. In the latter, two group members may fight over who will be the leader of the group. **Ideational conflict** centers on the arguments and issues regarding decision alternatives. People may have conflict over which alternative is better. They may have conflict over what counts as appropriate data and assumptions to base decisions on. They may have conflict over how they define the problem or which criteria are acceptable. Ideational conflict evolves around conflicts associated with defining problems, generating solutions, setting and applying criteria, and selecting among competing alternatives. **Procedural conflict** regards differences of opinion on what procedures to use during group discussion. Disputes over how to structure the agenda, whether to use a specific procedure such as brainstorming to enhance divergent thinking, or to employ minority reports and stakeholder analysis to create reflections are examples of procedural conflict.

Part of a group's success depends on the ability to manage disagreements and conflict appropriately. By helping the group stay focused on issues rather than personalities and finding ways to blend the talents of group members, group leaders and members can help move a group from being paralyzed by different styles of conflict to using conflict as a resource for greater productivity.

Conflict Management Styles

One way to manage conflict is to adopt a style appropriate for the situation. **Conflict management styles** are distinguishable patterns of behavior that represent different forms of managing disputes. Perhaps the most famous typology of conflict management styles is Kilmann and Thomas's (1977) scheme of five conflict management styles: (1) accommodating, (2) avoiding, (3) compromising, (4) competing, and (5) collaborating. Each of these styles is arrayed along two behavioral dimensions. The first dimension is cooperation. Cooperation is defined as people's willingness to collaborate with others to achieve goals and may range from low to high. The second dimension is assertiveness, defined as a person's motivation to pursue individual goals and agenda. Some individuals are highly motivated to pursue their goals and agenda; others will quickly abandon their goals. Figure 13.2 shows how these two behavioral dimensions combine to form the five conflict management styles.

The **accommodating style** is low in assertiveness and high in collaboration. Such a style may be described as a "win-lose" strategy because people who use an accommodating style want to collaborate so much they are willing to give up their own individual goals. When people adopt this style they may make concessions to others' demands and not argue forcefully for their position.

The **avoiding style** is low in both assertiveness and collaboration. Rather than engage in disputes, conflict avoiders do not want to expend energy to advocate their own view or

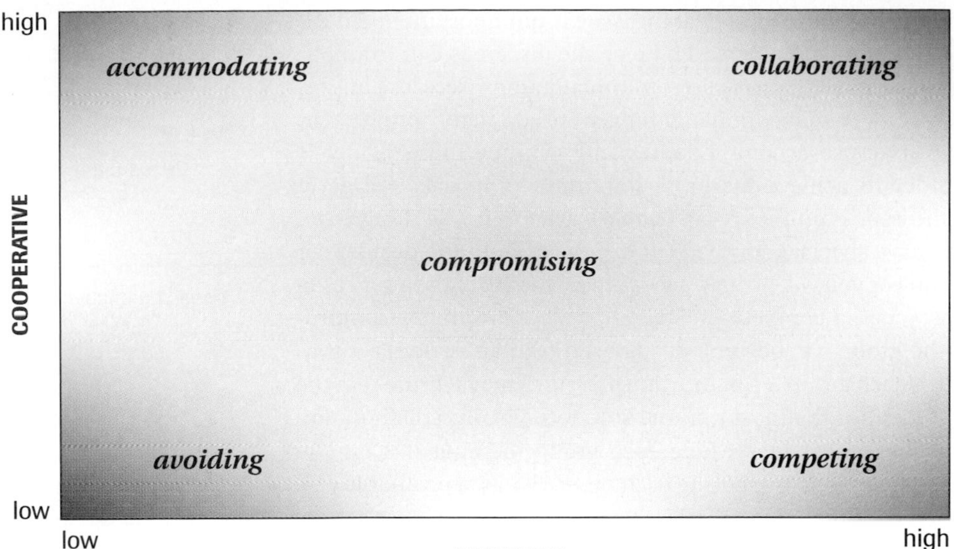

FIGURE 13.2
Thomas & Kilmann's Conflict Management Styles

Conflict management styles are arrayed along two dimensions. The cooperative dimension reflects how willing a group member is to collaborate and work interdependently with other group members. The assertive dimension reflects how much energy and effort an individual will put forth to affirm his or her views.

to collaborate with others. When people say, "I don't want to get into it with you" or "Let it be," they are indicating they don't want to get involved with the conflict.

The **competing style** is a "win-lose" approach to conflict. Group members who employ such a style are high in assertiveness—they want to achieve their goals—and are low in cooperativeness—they are relatively unconcerned if the other disputant achieves his or her goals. The most important goal is to achieve your own goals and needs no matter the cost.

A **compromising** style is a "lose-lose" approach to conflict management. In this style, a disputant is willing to forgo some of his or her personal goals provided the other disputant does the same. Compromise is about finding the middle course with each party agreeing to make concessions to the others.

A **collaborating style** is high in both assertiveness and collaboration. Collaboration necessitates that both disputants be creative in finding ways that allow each to achieve personal goals (high assertiveness) while still allowing the other to achieve personal goals as well (high cooperation). For example, suppose a person is sitting at a library with a friend and asks to open the window in the room. The friend refuses. If these two parties used a collaborating style, they may try to find a way to meet each other's needs. Upon exploring the issue, the person who made the request did so because she was hot and the friend refusing the request did so because she was afraid the draft from the open window would blow their papers around. They collaboratively come up with a solution by opening the door to the room that allows fresh air to enter and cool the room but without a draft (Fisher & Ury, 1991). Collaboration is about inventing creative "win-win" solutions to conflict.

It is tempting to think that collaboration is the best way to manage conflict within a small group. However, each of these styles can be appropriate depending on the situation.

A person may want to use the accommodating style if the issue is unimportant and if the other disputant has the power to punish the person if he or she disagrees. For example, suppose Rob in the opening vignette felt that certain recommendations were less important than others, and these less important recommendations were adamantly opposed by certain board members. Rob may use accommodating and sacrifice these relatively unimportant proposals in order to achieve his more important proposals. Similarly, avoiding may also be used if the issue is unimportant. People learn to agree to disagree.

On the other hand, say you have special knowledge or expertise about the problem or issue that the group is addressing or you will be held accountable for the consequences of the decision. In such circumstances, a competition style may be appropriate. Compromise may be appropriate if the group has become deadlocked over an issue for a prolonged period of time. Although each group loses, the time pressures may require that the group do something—even if it is not the most optimal solution. Finally, collaboration may be very useful when dealing with issues where each group member has unique knowledge and insight about the problem. By sharing each other's ideas, a profitable way to end the conflict may be created. At the same time, it is important to realize that collaboration takes time, and if the group is forced to resolve the conflict quickly a competing style may be most appropriate.

Knowledge Link

What factors may influence your choice of a particular conflict management style?

Knowing How to Lead Groups

When you think of leaders, who comes to mind? Who do you perceive as group leaders? Organizational leaders? Community leaders? National leaders? International leaders? As you look over your list, what characteristics do these leaders share? In Western culture, leaders are typically associated with people who manage crises and problems effectively (Kouzes & Posner, 1995). For example, Martin Luther King, Jr. confronted the problem of racial inequality in the United States. Susan B. Anthony worked with the issue of voting rights for women. Jaime Escalante became an educational leader at East Garfield High School in Los Angeles as he worked to educate lower income children in mathematics and calculus. In each of these cases, the individual was charged with managing a crisis and managing it well.

Although there appears to be some agreement that leadership is associated with managing difficulties and problems, there is much disagreement over what leadership is and what counts as effective leadership. Let's examine three questions regarding leadership: (1) What is leadership? (2) What are the skills associated with leadership? and (3) How can leaders change a group, organization, or community?

Leaders such as Susan B. Anthony are usually associated with managing change and crisis.

UNDERSTANDING LEADERSHIP

What is leadership? This is a difficult question to answer because over 300 definitions of leadership have been recorded (Bennis & Nanus, 1985). Some people associate leadership with formal positions of authority such as a manager in an organization or an elected official; others view leadership as a process involving informal authority. Some people view leadership as directly tied to the personality, physical, and cognitive traits that one is born with, and others contend that leadership can be taught—it is not an innate trait. Still others view leadership as an elite process that can only be performed by certain highly skilled and knowledgeable people; others view leadership as an ability that anyone can possess and develop.

For purposes of our discussion, we define **leadership** as a communication process that helps groups organize themselves to achieve desirable goals. This definition has two important implications.

First, leadership is a communication process. Early leadership research focused on the traits that individuals are born with that enable them to emerge as leaders with groups, organizations, and society (Stogdill, 1948). A variety of traits such as intelligence, motivation, drive, social competence, assertiveness, and communication anxiety were examined to see if they allow individuals to emerge as leaders. However, researchers discovered no uniform correlation between personality traits and leadership. What happened next was that people began to view leadership as a behavioral process. The focus shifted from the question, "What are leaders like?" to "What do leaders do?" This latter question is about communication. How do leaders talk? What do they say? How do they use nonverbal communication to get their point across? Contemporary leadership theory views leadership as a communication process that is directly tied to what leaders say and do.

Second, the terms *leaders* and *leadership* are different. Leadership is about a communication process that involves the give-and-take among leaders and followers. In order to be a leader, you must have people who are willing to follow. **Leaders** are individuals within a group who guide and direct the group's activities. *Leadership* is the process of communication that occurs between leaders and followers. To understand leadership, you need to look at what leaders say and how followers respond as well as what followers say and how leaders respond.

How do positions of group leadership get created? One way is for leaders to be appointed by some external authority to the group. For example, managers are often appointed to be leaders of work teams within an organization. Upper-level managers appoint lower-level managers to guide and direct work teams. Another way that positions of leadership get created in groups is that leaders emerge from the interaction among group members. An individual may emerge as a leader in a group if he or she participates a great deal within the group, demonstrates expertise that other group members do not, and collaborates with other group members (Barge, 1996). Is one way better than the other? No. Both approaches have strengths and weaknesses. Appointed leaders may be viewed favorably by other group members particularly if the people doing the appointing are well respected. Being appointed by high-status people can give a leader credibility. At the same time, if group members do not perceive the process of appointing leaders as legitimate, the appointed leader may be viewed as incompetent or not deserving the position. Leaders who emerge in the course of the group discussion tend to be viewed as more credible. At the same time, individuals who are unqualified may emerge as leaders. For example, people who participate a great deal in the discussion tend to emerge as leaders (Barge, 1996). Other group members take this high level of participation as a sign of commitment and concern for the group and allow this person to emerge as the leader. Yet does talking a lot in a group discussion guarantee that a person has the needed knowledge and expertise to guide the group? The answer is a resounding *no*. Unqualified people sometimes emerge as leaders simply by virtue of their being active in the group discussion.

Leadership also may be shared among group members. Multiple leaders may be present in a group. In fact, having multiple leaders in small groups is one way that people address what has been called the equilibrium problem (Bales, 1970). The **equilibrium problem** is the challenge in small groups to maintain a constructive tension between getting the task done and maintaining a positive group environment. The answer for some groups has been to share the leadership responsibilities, with one person taking primary responsibility for keeping the group on task and another person maintaining a positive group climate. A central issue for small groups, therefore, is how to divide the leadership responsibilities within the group.

Leadership is also about instrumental behavior—behavior that moves groups toward goal achievement. This is not a surprising statement. After all, think about some of the people you listed as leaders. We would be surprised if the people that you listed were not skilled organizers. We would be surprised if the people you listed were not able to perform key functions at critical points in time during the life of the group that got the group moving and focused them in on achieving their goal. The key issue is how leaders go about organizing the group's activities. What are the resources and strategies they can draw on to perform leadership?

LEADING & MANAGING PEOPLE

How do you lead and manage small groups? Do you take the responsibility for making all the decisions and telling other group members what to do? Do you invite all group members to participate in decision making and make the decision collectively? Do you always make the decision individually or collectively? Do you lead the same way in similar situations? These kinds of questions have been the focus of leadership research for a number of years.

Some researchers argue that group leaders need to master particular behavioral styles of leading. For example, many contend that effective leaders are democratic in nature regardless of the situation. **Democratic leadership** involves two-way communication among people with equal power who jointly make decisions. In this instance, leaders and followers have equal status and they collectively determine the direction of the group. **Autocratic leadership** is about leaders having more power than followers and using one-way communication to direct and guide the actions of followers. Autocratic leaders unilaterally make decisions and use communication to command followers to execute their decisions. For many years, leadership researchers have argued that democratic leadership is superior because group members feel more included in the decision-making process and are more committed to adhere to the decisions that have been made. Moreover, having more people participating in decision making brings more diverse views into the process and increases the likelihood of making high-quality decisions. Yet recent research suggests that democratic leadership does not necessarily produce higher levels of productivity; in fact, autocratic leadership is just as likely to produce increased levels of productivity as democratic leadership.

The difficulty of identifying the one best style of leadership has led many researchers to believe that a key skill for leaders is an ability to read a situation and adapt their behavior according to the particular constraints of the situation (Bolman & Deal, 1997; Morgan, 1997). From this perspective, effective leadership is about acting in ways that are appropriate given the situation. What kinds of situational factors influence how a leader should act? Here are some of the key situational factors that influence leadership behavior:

- Task structure: When the nature of the task is very clear and the steps that group members need to take to complete the task are unambiguous, effective leaders need to be supportive and encourage group members to complete the task. When the nature of the task is unclear and there are many ways to complete the task, effective leadership helps clarify the nature of the task and lay out the pathway to achieve the goal.
- Group maturity: If group members have the necessary knowledge or expertise to perform a task and are highly motivated to perform the task, leaders may delegate the task to the group members. If group members are not knowledgeable about how to per-

form a task and are not motivated to learn or perform the task, leaders need to tell group members precisely what to do.
- Group commitment and acceptance: If the ability to implement a decision depends on the commitment and support of the group, it is better to use a democratic style of leadership. If the ability to implement a decision is independent of the group's acceptance, a leader can use an autocratic style of leadership.
- Information requirements: If each group member has unique information and insights about the task, democratic leadership should be used in order to pool the information of the different group members. If all group members have the same level of task knowledge, it may be appropriate to employ autocratic leadership.
- Ambiguity: If the nature of the task is ambiguous, leaders may need to clarify the scope and nature of the task. If the nature of the task is very structured and clear, a leader may need to introduce some ambiguity into the discussion in order to prompt creative thinking.

Knowledge Link

What situational factors should a leader consider when selecting a leadership style?

Effective leaders need to examine the situations and groups they are leading and determine what needs to be done to keep the group moving forward. They need to pay attention to factors such as the task structure and group commitment in order to determine what course of action will best propel the group toward success.

THE LEADER AS AN AGENT OF CHANGE

Perhaps the biggest challenge a group leader faces is creating change within the group. The kind of leadership needed to create change within a group depends on the type of work a group is doing and what kind of work needs to be changed. There are two kinds of work that small group leaders and followers do (Heifetz, 1994). In **technical work,** the problem the group is working on is clearly defined and the solution for the problem and how the solution is to be implemented are also clearly defined. Using a medical example, if a doctor has a patient with an infection, the doctor prescribes an antibiotic to cure the infection. The problem is clear—the patient has an infection—and the solution is clear and easy to implement—the doctor tells the patient to take the antibiotics.

When leaders are involved with technical work, the leader is most responsible for the change. It is up to the leader to tell the group what needs to be done and how to do it. For example, suppose you are a leader of a sales team for a pharmaceutical company and you have been told your team needs to report their sales data to the headquarters in a new way. As the leader, the problem is clear—change the way the data is reported. The solution is clear—you have the new format that the data needs to be reported in to headquarters. You also have the authority to make the change. To implement the change, you simply need to inform the team about the change and ask them to make it.

However, not all group work is technical work with the leader telling the group members what to do. Would you classify the kind of work Rob was doing with the board of directors for the AAC as technical work? Probably not. The problem Rob is dealing with is not clearly defined, nor is the solution and its implementation clearly defined. Such work is better labeled adaptive work. **Adaptive work** has problems and solutions that are not clearly defined and places the responsibility for change on the group members. Given the ambiguity and complexity of the problem, group members need to learn about the nature of the problem and to learn about possible solutions and ways of implementation. In adaptive work, the role of the leader is to facilitate the group's learning so they can make the change. Using a medical example, consider a doctor working with a terminally ill cancer patient. The doctor and the patient know death is imminent. Yet there is a great deal of learning the patient needs to undergo before the death. How do you talk to friends

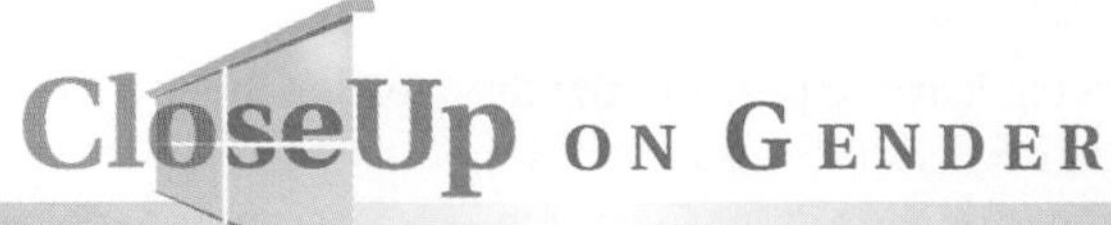

CloseUp ON GENDER

A Feminine Advantage?

WHEN YOU THINK OF THE TERM *leader,* who comes to mind? Are most of the leaders you listed males or females? Historically, leaders and leadership have been viewed as a predominantly masculine activity (Klenke, 1996). Yet recently, with the influx of women into the work force and more and more women occupying leadership positions in the public and private sector, there has been a renewed interest in examining the relationship between gender and leadership. An important question then becomes, "What are the similarities and differences between the leadership performance of men and women?"

Several researchers contend there is a distinct difference between men and women and the way they lead groups and organizations. Consider some of the research findings relating gender and leadership:

- Male leaders are task oriented and female leaders are more relationship oriented.
- Male leaders tend to employ styles that are more directive and autocratic in nature and women utilize styles that more democratic and participatory in nature.
- Male leaders tend to be more competitive and independent and female leaders are more cooperative and dependent.
- Female leaders tend to use motivation strategies that appeal to the heart and intellect of followers and male leaders tend to use rewards and punishments to motivate followers.
- Males tend to evaluate male leaders more highly than female leaders, and female leaders tend to rate female leaders more highly than male leaders.

Such research draws a clear line between the way men and women lead. In fact, people argue that the feminine way of leading with its emphasis on participation and relationship is more effective in today's society (Helgesen, 1995). Given that organizations are increasingly moving to team-based styles of management, it is important for leaders to be able to develop and cultivate strong working relationships among team members.

Yet other researchers argue that no significant and consistent differences exist in the leadership performance of men and women. They claim that men and women use the same kinds of styles to lead (Eagly, Karau, & Makhijani, 1995). There is no behavioral difference in the ways that men and women lead. Rather what influences how a leader performs depends more on the nature of the situation than the gender of the leader.

This split in the research poses a potential problem for leaders: Does my gender make a difference in the way I lead and how I am perceived? To be an effective leader means you have to pay attention to the nature of the situation, and part of the situation is the gender of the leader. Therefore, effective leaders need to answer the following kinds of questions to ensure they have addressed gender issues:

- At what stage of development is the group? If the group is in the early stages of development, group members will evaluate leaders in terms of gender stereotypes (Eagly & Johnson, 1990). This means male leaders are expected to be autocratic, independent, and competitive, and female leaders are expected to be democratic, dependent, and cooperative. At this stage of development, if a leader wants to be viewed as competent, he or she either (a) needs to conform to the stereotypic expectations for male or female leadership, or (b) provide an explanation for why he or she is deviating from these expectations. As groups enter later stages of development, the situation, rather than gender, will be the dominant criterion for evaluating competence.
- What does the situation require of the leader? In more developed groups, the nature of the situation influences the type of leadership required. Issues of task structure, information requirements, and acceptability become important.

Although it is unclear whether gender exercises a significant influence on leadership performance, what is clear is the need for leaders to be flexible in their behavior. The nature of the situation is critical in determining what kinds of leadership behavior are required. The competent leader therefore needs to be able to master both more so-called masculine leadership styles such as being more autocratic and competitive as well as more so-called feminine leadership styles, which are more democratic, participatory, and cooperative in nature.

and family about your disease? Are the finances in order? If the patient has a family, how will they be cared for? These are problems that do not have simple and clear answers. The doctor's role in this instance is to create an environment in which the patient can learn and develop definitions and solutions for the problem. It is the patient who is responsible for the change, not the doctor. In the case of the AAC, as much as Rob wants to change the board, it is up to the board to learn and to make the changes. It is Rob's responsibility to create an environment where the board takes responsibility for understanding the problem and generating solutions.

To help the group begin the process of doing adaptive work, leaders need to create an environment where group members can first investigate what is causing the distress or problem. At this point, leaders need to get the group to engage with questions such as these:

1. What is causing the problem?
2. What perspectives do key stakeholders in the group or organization hold that are now in conflict?
3. What is the history of the problem?
4. How do people respond to the problem?
5. In the past, when has the problem reached a breaking point and people have begun to engage in self-destructive patterns?
6. How have people in the past tried to address the problem?

These kinds of questions focus the group on the tensions that are creating the problem. By focusing on the tensions and their history, the group members can learn about the details of the problem and how the problem has been addressed in the past.

Leaders may then focus the group on the issues that need attention and also discuss why the group tries to avoid working on the problem. What are the issues that we need to focus on in light of our problem analysis? Why do people want to avoid tackling these problems? Which issues are ripe for working with? For example, if Rob had worked with the board of directors on defining the problem, the group may have generated a number of problems ranging from poor audience attendance to unmotivated board members. The group may then decide the issue most ripe for working with and implementing change is the audience attendance issue. They may feel that talking about poor board member motivation may simply aggravate the situation and not help. In the process of discussing these various issues, they may reach an understanding that one of the reasons the board wants to avoid working on the problems is that if they did, they would be forced to confront their lack of motivation.

Relational Skills for Working With People

Managing relationships within groups involves dealing with the personalities, emotions, and feelings of people within the group. When group members become agitated over issues and personally attack one another, it is difficult, if not impossible, to move the group toward a thoughtful consideration of the issues and make high-quality decisions. For example, many group meetings over intense moral issues such as abortion and homosexuality often deteriorate into highly charged polarizing conversations where group members take sides and attack the other. Even though the early discussion is civil, when people discover opposition to their views regarding this moral issue, they soon take sides and argue with one another. Until the emotions and feelings of the group members can be managed in ways to bring about constructive conversation, the opportunity to make high-quality decisions is lost.

One key to creating effective small groups is managing the relationships among people. Three abilities are central to managing small group relationships: (1) giving accounts and explanations, (2) framing, and (3) providing social support.

Giving Accounts & Explanations

Whether you are managing conflict within a group or leading its members, it is important to articulate your viewpoints in ways that are heard and understood by other group members as well as to inquire into the expressed viewpoints of other group members. Part of having constructive conversations within small groups depends on your ability to give accounts and explanations for your viewpoints as well as exploring other members' accounts of their viewpoints. Providing an explanation and using inquiry rest on your ability to delve into the assumptions, values, and beliefs used to form an opinion, explore the data used to arrive at the conclusion, and understand how context influences people's conclusions.

The Ladder of Inference presented in Figure 13.3 provides one way to articulate your position and inquire into other group members' positions in a rich and detailed manner (Senge et al., 1994). The **Ladder of Inference** is a tool that helps people articulate how they arrive at conclusions by examining their assumptions, values, and beliefs, the kind of data they use to form their conclusions, and their process of drawing inferences. This same process helps people explore others' assumptions, values, and beliefs, the data they use to form conclusions, and the inference-making process. Starting at the right-hand side of the figure, the Ladder of Inference suggests there is a wealth of information that

FIGURE 13.3
The Ladder of Inference

The Ladder of Inference can help group members explore the reasoning behind their conclusions. Group members can better articulate their own views and inquire into other group member views using the Ladder of Inference.

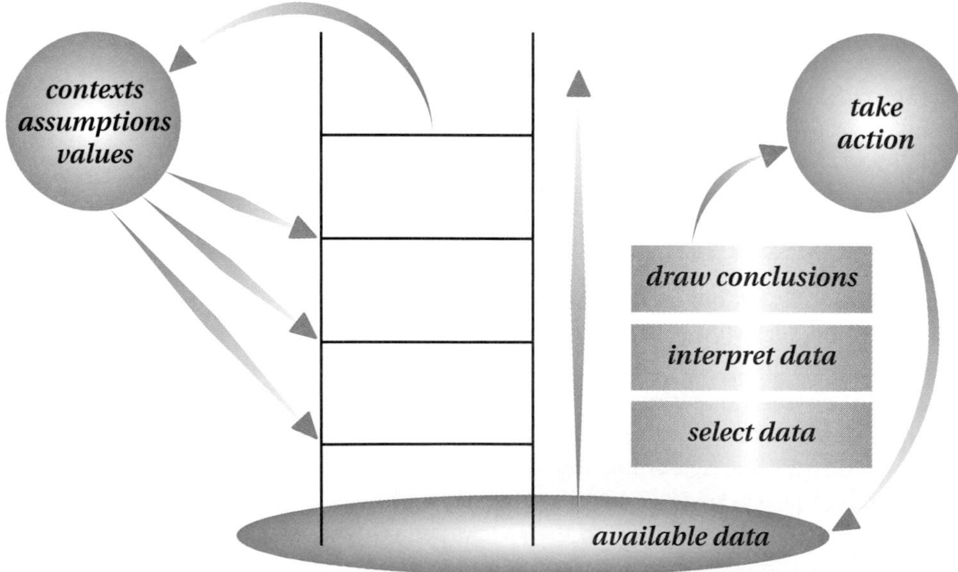

people can draw on when making conclusions. Given the large amount of information, we select only bits of the data and interpret the data. From these interpretations, we draw conclusions that move us toward taking action. For example, suppose you are at a group meeting with a number of people for the very first time. You notice that Jose is talking a great deal. However, one thing that Jose said stands out in your mind: He used some incorrect statistics to make his point. Based on his use of wrong statistics, you interpret that to mean he was not adequately prepared for the meeting and you conclude he is not going to be a productive team member. You then decide to ignore him for the rest of the meeting. This approach to drawing conclusions follows the Ladder of Inference. From all the available data that you could focus on regarding Jose, you selected his misuse of statistics. From this selected data, you interpreted that to mean he was unprepared. That led to the conclusion that Jose would be a poor team member, which led you to take action and to ignore him during the rest of the discussion.

What influences your perception of what data is important or how to draw inferences? The Ladder of Inference suggests that the context, assumptions, and values influence what data you select and how you draw inferences and make conclusions. For example, suppose the meeting you and Jose attended had been scheduled for a long time and that it had been stressed that everyone was to be prepared. This might explain why you focused on the misstatement of statistics. Alternatively, perhaps you have made the assumption that all team members should be prepared for the meeting or have as a key personal value the importance of preparation. This may account for why you focused on that particular data and drew the conclusions you did.

The Ladder of Inference can help you explain position clearly and inquire into the others' positions and perspectives. Using the Ladder of Inference, you can clearly explain your position. Starting with the left-hand side of the ladder, you might say things like this:

I think the situation calls for . . .
One of the assumptions I am making . . .
It is important to me because . . .

These kinds of statements help clarify for other group members the assumptions and values that influence the kind of data you select and how you make interpretations and conclusions. Starting on the right-hand side of the ladder, you might say things like this:

The data I'm using to base my inferences on is . . .
What this data means to me is . . .
This leads me to conclude . . .
Based on my interpretations and conclusions, I think we need to do . . .

The Ladder of Inference provides a way for you to explain your views clearly and in depth.

The Ladder of Inference can also be used to ask questions regarding another's perspective. Consider the following questions:

What assumptions are you making about this situation?
What values are important to you in this situation?
What data are you using to base your interpretations?
Why are you focusing on this data and not other data?
How does it make sense for you to interpret the data in the way that you have?
How do your interpretations influence what conclusions you are making?
Why are you taking the actions you are given your conclusions?

By asking these kinds of questions, it is possible to gain a more detailed understanding of other group members' perspectives.

Framing

Sometimes group members become stuck in their thinking. The way they have described or framed the issue may be continuing the conflict. For example, a work team may be having conflict over the men's treatment of the women on the work team. The way the group may have framed the conflict is in terms of sexual harassment. Yet each time the group talks about sexual harassment the group gets into major conflict—the men deny they are engaging in sexual harassment and the women maintain they are. No amount of explaining your viewpoint or inquiring into other members' viewpoints is going to help the group get beyond the conflict. The more group members explain their position or the more they inquire into the views of other group members, the more they come into conflict.

One way to refocus the group is to reframe the discussion topic or issue. **Reframing** is restating something in a new constructive way. It helps soften and neutralize hostile comments, encourage progress, clarify, and introduce creative possibilities. In this instant, the group may reframe the topic to one of creating positive working relationships as opposed to sexual harassment. This reframe may allow the group to talk about the issue more productively as it shifts the responsibility for maintaining a good working relationship to all group members. Reframing can be accomplished in a variety of ways (see Table 13.2).

Knowledge Link

How do giving accounts and explanations, framing, and providing social support build quality relationships?

Providing Social Support

Earlier in this chapter, we discussed the importance of constructing a supportive group climate. Supportive group climates are created when people use communication that is empathetic, descriptive, aimed at solving problems, spontaneous, conveys equality, and expresses an openness to different ideas. How can group members convey supportiveness to other group members? Two skills are particularly useful to helping create supportive climates within groups: acknowledging and reflecting.

Acknowledging comments help members indicate that they understand one another, their situation, their process, and their actions. Group leaders and members can acknowledge a variety of issues, feelings, and attitudes during a group meeting. For example, it is possible to acknowledge the following:

- problems and difficulties ("It sounds like one of the problems you perceive is . . .")
- what people want and need ("In order for you to feel we have arrived at a good solution, you need . . .")
- differences and issues ("Where we differ in the group over this issue is . . .")
- hard work and positive contributions ("I appreciate the hard work you have put in on this task.")
- positive, respectful interaction ("It really helps the discussion when we keep personal attacks out of it . . . ")
- recognition of others ("Bob has done a tremendous job on this project . . .")
- progress on the task ("Wow, we've come a long way since we started. Let's summarize what we've done so far . . .")
- shared concerns and common ground ("What we share is . . .")
- areas of consensus ("It sounds like most of us agree that . . .")
- decisions that have been made ("So, what we have decided is . . .")

TABLE 13.2

Reframing Strategies

Reframing allows you to reinterpret what an event or issue means for people. Reframing can get people to think about an event or issue in creative and constructive ways.

REFRAMING STRATEGY	EXAMPLE	PURPOSE
Reframe from past to future	*Member:* I'm tired of people not putting out enough effort. *Leader:* So you want to see more effort in the future, right?	Focusing on the future may open up new ways of viewing the present
Reframe from negative to positive	*Member:* I feel overworked. *Leader:* It sounds as if the group really respects the quality of work you do and gives you a lot of work.	Focusing on the positive can be motivating and encouraging
Reframe from personal attack to problem definition	*Member:* People are just not following through on their assignment. They are just so incompetent and inconsiderate. *Leader:* So part of the difficulty is failing to complete the assignment in a timely fashion.	Focusing on the problem verses the person can diminish feelings of defensiveness
Reframe from a demand to a goal or need	*Member:* If I don't get some help with this work, I quit! *Leader:* It sounds like you need some assistance to get your work done.	Focusing on what needs to be done as opposed to issuing demands opens up the space for creative solutions
Reframe from an individual concern to a group concern	*Member:* I'm just worried that I don't have the skills to do the work I've been assigned. *Leader:* So it would help if the group could work together to make sure you are assigned work that makes sense.	Placing the concern on the whole group takes pressure off the individual
Reframe from a concern to a vision	*Member:* I just don't want to do this project. It's too boring. *Leader:* So you would like to have a project that's exciting and interesting.	By focusing on a vision, people begin identifying what they like and what motivates them

Acknowledgment serves two important functions. First, it allows group members to keep track of where they are in the discussion. By highlighting points of difference and consensus, how much progress has been made, and decisions that have been made, group members know where they are in the discussion. Thus they are better able to participate and control their environment in order to bring about desirable goals. Second, acknowledgment can heighten motivation. When the contributions of group members are recognized, when positive moments during the interaction are praised, and when hard work is acclaimed, group members know what is expected and will be more likely to exert the effort to accomplish the task.

A second skill is **reflecting** and concerns repeating someone's feelings about what they have said. It helps check understanding, helps participants feel confirmed and acknowledged, and helps group members understand the emotional dimension of what others are saying. Here are some possible reflections one could offer during a group meeting:

- Reflect strong expressions of emotion: "You seem very upset."
- Reflect feelings that are especially pertinent to a member's position, interest, values, or perspective: "I see you really feel that all group members need to give the same level of effort to completing the project."
- Reflect feelings that may not be heard by other members of the group: "So Sandra, you feel pretty happy that Bri got her work in on time."
- Reflect feelings that come across more nonverbally than verbally: "This can be kind of stressful, huh?"

Reflecting the feelings of group members recognizes the validity of their feelings and beliefs. Reflecting allows people to feel as if they have been heard, which helps build supportive climates.

CHALLENGES TO COMPETENCE

Group life provides many challenges to managing relationships. When have you been challenged to maintain high-quality relationships in small groups? What caused you to be challenged? Although there are many challenges to maintaining high-quality group relationships, we suspect you may have encountered two major challenges in your group experience: (1) differing goals, expectations, and needs, and (2) people being in differing stages of relationship with the group.

As highlighted in Chapter 11, group members have multiple motivations for entering a group and these multiple motivations also influence how they go about creating relationships with other group members. For example, think of a time when your instructor or professor assigned a "group" project for a class. Many times these group projects are difficult because the group members have different expectations regarding the project. For some, they want to put out great effort to get an "A" because they feel it is important to do good work. For others, they may be satisfied with a "C" because the class is not in their major and not viewed as important. Similarly, part of Rob's difficulty in the chapter-opening vignette may have emerged from the fact that different board members had different expectations of what they wanted Rob to do. Some wanted him to maintain the status quo and others desired change. A key challenge to small groups is how to identify people's expectations, and if they are different, how to work with them.

A second challenge that small groups face is the stability of membership in the group. Although it is possible for a small group to remain intact from its beginning until its end, it is more likely that over time, group members will drop out and new members will join. For example, take a university department. Over time, some instructors and professors will stay and others will leave. When faculty leave, they are typically replaced by new instructors and professors. Why does this pose a challenge? On one hand, it may not. Group turnover can provide an opportunity for renewal and rejuvenation. New instructors and professors may provide fresh ideas, insights, and programs and foster innovation. On the other hand, faculty who have been in the department for a while may be resistant to change.

The impact of fluctuating group membership depends on the stage of development the group is in. If the group is in the orientation phase, shifting new members into that group may not pose a problem because the group is still in the process of developing an understanding of the task and the relationships with one another. Similarly, if the group is in the conflict phase there may be little impact when new members join the group.

Because the group is in the middle of hashing out differences, adding new differences may not pose any difficulty. However, group turnover during the emergence phase may be problematic. By this time the group has established norms about how to act and developed policies and procedures for group behavior. New members at this stage of group development have the possibility of disrupting the group.

Overcoming Challenges to Competence

Managing the complexity of group life can be difficult. Being able to keep the discussion on track, analyze problems and solutions in depth, manage a variety of conflicts, and have the ability to lead change in a group are difficult tasks. These tasks are made even more problematic when we recognize that group members may have different expectations and values and that group turnover can require groups to constantly revisit their norms and operating agreements. We see three major strategies that can be used to address these two challenges: (1) framing the issue in a way that all group members can engage with, (2) exploring the past and the future to develop, and (3) identifying the positions and interests of group members.

ISSUE FRAMING

The foundation for most group work is the group's task or problem that is assigned. For groups to engage in a thoughtful and appropriate selection of alternatives, they must be focused on the key issues confronting the group. Moreover, the issue needs to be framed in a way that allows group members to relate and connect with each other in a productive manner. **Issue framing** is a thoughtful way to define and clarify important questions and choices. Just like a photographer frames a picture highlighting certain features in the photograph and not others, groups frame discussion questions that they will deliberate. If the discussion question is not framed appropriately, the discussion will not address the concerns of the group and may also lead to unwanted conflict.

All group members have positions and interests that influence how they work together in groups. Competent small group communicators are curious about and use communication to identify other members' positions and interests.

NON SEQUITUR © Wiley. Dist. by Universal Press Syndicate. Reprinted.

Issue framing consists of a number of steps aimed at refining the discussion question for the group. Issue framing involves groups beginning with a fuzzy statement of the problem and then developing a more precise wording of the problem. After creating a precise wording of the problem, the group then identifies their choices to solve the problem. Group members and leaders can help the group go through this process by doing the following:

1. Select a concern shared by most of the members of the group. Explore what is important to the group. What matters to them? Do not worry that participants disagree about this question. The hottest issues are often the most important concerns.
2. Word the issue as a neutral question. State the issue as an open question with several possible answers. Do not include a solution in the way the question is worded.
3. Word the question such that more than two options are possible. Avoid "either-or" questions. Leave open several possible choices for answering the question.
4. Find a wording that everyone can live with.

How might Rob have used issue framing to work with the board of directors? First, Rob might have asked what group members thought was their primary concern. They may have agreed it was low audience attendance. Second, Rob might have had the group play with the wording of the question. The group may have discussed the viability of the following three questions:

1. Will a new advertising campaign increase audience attendance?
2. Is a new advertising campaign or dropping ticket prices better?
3. What opportunities do we have for increasing audience attendance?

The first question violates the rule of embedding a solution into the question. The second question not only embeds a solution into the question, it also phrases the question as an "either-or": The group can select one or the other option. The third question is the best because it provides enough focus for the group but does not prescribe for the group what the final solution should be. Moreover, it invites all group members to engage with the issue and to work collaboratively with one another.

EXPLORING COMMON GROUND

Listening for someone's expectations and needs means distinguishing between an individual's position and interest. A **position** is a stated course of action that the person wants to see pursued in the group. An **interest** is the underlying motivation or reason the person wants to pursue a particular position. For example, take the following statements of position:

1. We need a clear time line for completing the project.
2. I just want to make sure this project is doable.
3. I don't want to work on this project. It's a boring idea.

What interests underlie the positions taken in each of these statements? For statement 1, perhaps the group member's interest is to feel safe about being able to complete the project, and one way to achieve this is to have clear-cut time lines. Alternatively, perhaps the person's interest is efficiency—he or she may be involved in balancing a number of other projects. For statement 2, perhaps the group member's interest is self-esteem—the person wants to achieve success and feels this is only possible by taking on projects that are doable. Or the underlying interest might be the amount of effort devoted to the project—a doable project requires less effort than a demanding project. For statement 3, the interest underlying the position could be self-actualization; this group member may not want to work on the project because it will not allow a chance to grow and develop.

Why is listening for someone's interest important? Remember that people in groups may have hidden agendas and by listening for their interest and differentiating it from their position, you may be able to discern their hidden agenda. Listening for people's interests and differentiating them from their position better allows you to identify the multiple motivations of group members and to avoid the bad habit of mistaking a group member's position as his or her motivation.

REVISITING THE GROUP'S COMMISSION

Small groups typically have a specific commission for the task they are performing. A **commission** is a "co-mission" where the group members have an agreed understanding of the purpose of the group, the task it is to perform, and the kinds of actions viewed as appropriate by group members for accomplishing its task. The commission sets the stage for the group's purpose and how group members are to relate and work with each other. A group's commission can become unclear as existing group members leave the group and new members join. One way to ensure that group members retain their understanding of the group's commission is to revisit it periodically. The C-V-A model is an excellent way to help group members revisit their commission (PDC Training Manual, 1999). The **C-V-A model** is a group procedure that structures discussion around three areas: concerns, visions, and actions.

There are three elements in the C-V-A model (see Figure 13.4). Concerns are problems or difficulties that various group members are worried about. For example, what are the problems or difficulties that the AAC board of directors is supposed to tackle and take action on? Visions are ideas about the ideal state, what things should be like. What would the AAC board like to accomplish in the future? By discussing concerns and visions, the parameters of the task the board is to accomplish and their responsibilities become clearer. Actions are about the working agreements that group members have created regarding how they will work together to address the concerns and accomplish the vision. What agreements does the board and the executive director have in place for how they will interact with each other? Do they have a clear understanding of what kinds of actions and roles are expected to be performed by board members and the executive director?

How might Rob use the C-V-A model to help revisit the group's commission? First, he could use it as a checklist to analyze whether the board is in agreement on their commission. Does the group have a similar understanding regarding their concerns, visions, and actions? Second, if Rob feels the board needs to revisit its commission, he could use the C-V-A model to structure the group's discussion. You can start a C-V-A discussion with any of these issues—with concerns, visions, or actions. The important thing is always to move from one point to another. For example, Rob might have had the group discuss each of the following questions in turn:

- What are your concerns? How do they match up with the concerns the board traditionally has had?
- What are your visions for the board? In what ways is the vision similar to or different from visions from previous boards?
- What understandings do we have for how we are to act with one another? Have these understandings changed over time or have they remained the same?

FIGURE 13.4
The C-V-A Model

The C-V-A model is a group procedure tool that can help members understand the purpose of the group, the task it is to perform, and the kinds of actions appropriate for group members to perform. A group discussion can start with any of the three issues; however, effective groups need to cover all three issues.

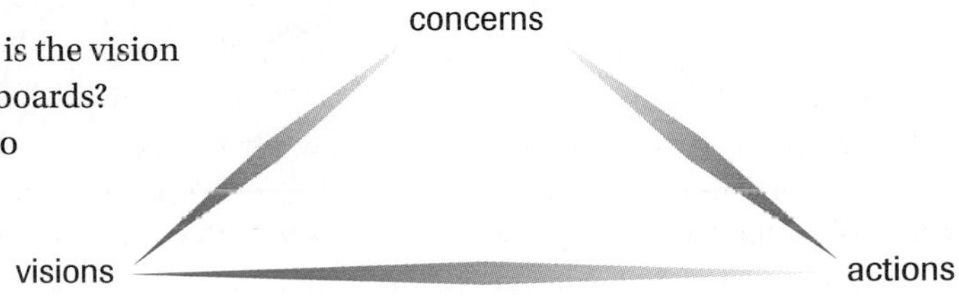

The C-V-A can help the group perform a rigorous analysis on all aspects of defining the commission. By revisiting the group's commission, both old and new group members have a common understanding of what the group needs to accomplish and what their role is in helping the group achieve its task.

Chapter Summary

A key element in developing effective small groups is cultivating high-quality relationships among group members. Developing constructive relationships among group members requires that competent group communicators develop a working knowledge of (1) how to create and sustain group relationships, and (2) how to lead small groups. To understand the nature of relationships within small groups, recognize that groups have a life span characterized by different phases. The phase hypothesis suggests that groups go through the following sequence of phases: orientation, conflict, and emergence. The kinds of relationships required at each phase differ. As group members develop relationships with one another, they are also negotiating their group roles. Group roles may take many forms including task roles, relational roles, and ego-centered roles. The kinds of roles that group members play depends on whether the feedback they receive from other group members confirms or denies the role they are playing.

Creating successful groups necessitates understanding how supportive group environments are created. When small groups create supportive group environments that are characterized by descriptive communication, spontaneity, openness, empathy, and flexibility, they are more likely to work well together. Yet many times over the life of a group, defensive group environments can get created that promote and sustain conflict. Therefore, part of managing relationships within a group is about managing conflict. Group conflicts can occur over interpersonal relationships and the group's emotional climate (affective conflict), the group's task or issues (ideational conflict), and the procedures that should be employed during group discussion (procedural conflict). Managing these various conflicts involves mastering a variety of conflict management styles including accommodating, avoiding, competing, compromising, and collaborating.

One of the key relationships within a small group is between the group leader and other group members. Leadership is a communication process that helps groups organize themselves to achieve desirable goals. Leadership is distinct from being a leader. Leadership is about the give-and-take among leaders and followers, and a leader is an individual who guides the group's activities. Sometimes groups require two leaders—one who focuses on accomplishing the task and the other who concentrates on maintaining productive relationships among group members—in order to manage the equilibrium problem of meeting both task and relational needs.

Leadership involves coordinating the activities of the group. Leaders may use a variety of styles to accomplish their task and may act in democratic or autocratic ways. The style a leader selects may depend on the structure of the task, the maturity of the group, the commitment of the group, and the information that group members require to complete the task. It is particularly important for leaders to be aware of the kinds of leadership behavior that promote change and innovation within groups. When the work the group needs to change is technical work, the leader may adopt a more autocratic style and inform the group members what needs to be accomplished. When the work the group needs to change is adaptive work, the group leader may need to work more collaboratively and democratically with group members to foster innovation.

Understanding how relationships are created and sustained and how leadership can be performed is not enough. The competent small group communicator must also have the necessary skills to manage relationships and lead groups. Three skills are of particular importance. First, constructing accounts and explanations using the Ladder of Inference can help articulate the reasons and motivations of group members that may lead them into conflict or resisting leadership. Second, framing issues in ways that allow group members to work collaboratively helps build supportive group environments and manage conflict. Third, providing social support through the skills of acknowledgment and reflecting facilitates group members so they feel their voices have been heard, which in turn can lead to supportive group environments.

Small group communicators face two significant challenges to their competence: (1) differing goals, expectations, and needs of group members, and (2) the stability of group membership. These challenges can be met by engaging in issue framing—a process that helps the group clarify important questions and choices. These challenges can also be met by having group members explore common ground by articulating their positions and interests and revisiting the group's commission by using the C-V-A model.

Key Terms

group phases
phase hypothesis
group role
supportive group environment
defensive group environment
conflict
affective conflict
ideational conflict
procedural conflict
conflict management styles
accommodating style
avoiding style
competing style
compromising style
collaborating style
leadership
leader
equilibrium problem
democratic leadership
autocratic leadership
technical work
adaptive work
Ladder of Inference
reframing
acknowledging comments
reflecting
issue framing
position
interest
commission
C-V-A model

Building Knowledge

1. What are the three common phases that characterize group life? How important is it for group members to go through each phase in order to have an effective group?
2. What are the three types of group roles that members may create in a group? What influences the likelihood that group members will play particular roles?
3. What are the differences between supportive and defensive group environments? What kinds of communication can help create supportive group environments?
4. What are the defining characteristics of conflict? Under what conditions do you feel group members would engage in affective, ideational, or procedural conflict?
5. Is using a collaborating style the best way to manage group conflict? When might it be desirable to use the conflict management styles of avoiding, accommodating, competing, and compromising?
6. How does the nature of the group task influence the type of leadership that small groups need? What are the different skills associated with technical and adaptive work?
7 What components make up the Ladder of Inference? How might you use the Ladder of Inference to explain your reasoning to other people? To inquire into other people's views?

Building Skills

Individual Exercises

1. Take a group you belong to where you have made arguments or stated conclusions during the discussion. List two or three arguments/conclusions that you made. Using the Ladder of Inference, take each argument/conclusion and answer the following questions:
   a. What assumptions was your conclusion based on?
   b. What data did you select to make your conclusion?

Relational Management Competence Skills Grid

To help you understand how to use this grid, the skills displayed by Rob in the opening vignette of this chapter have been analyzed below. Examine that analysis and then think about a recent relational management situation and what you could have done more competently. First, describe the context of the relational management situation in the spaces provided. Next, analyze your relational management skills based on the skills explained in this chapter for each step in the relational management process. In the first column,

ANALYZING ROB'S RELATIONAL MANAGEMENT SKILLS

Context

CULTURE: Theatre staff and board of directors in North American context

TIME: Weekday evening

RELATIONSHIP: Executive director-board member, staff-board member, executive director-staff

PLACE: In the meeting room of the theater

FUNCTION: Rob must manage the conflicts that are surfacing due to proposed changes

RELATIONAL MANAGEMENT SKILLS	LESS COMPETENT	MORE COMPETENT
GIVING ACCOUNTS AND EXPLANATIONS	Not providing the reasons why the meeting was necessary; not using data to base one's inferences or conclusions; not explaining the reasoning process behind one's conclusion	Stating values or assumptions that inform your position (e.g., "The reason I think this is important is because . . ."); explaining one's reasoning (e.g., "I'm basing my position on . . ."); inquiring into the reasoning other group members use
FRAMING AND REFRAMING	Focusing on the past problem without consideration of the group's dreams; framing issues in ways that privilege one side over another in a group discussion; framing issues in ways that fragment and divide the group	Focusing on the future (e.g., "In the future you'd like to see . . ."); focusing on the positive elements of the situation (e.g., "One of the strengths of this group is . . ."); focusing on the problem not the person (e.g., "The challenge we are facing . . ."); focusing on group versus concern (e.g., "When we as a group focus on . . .")
PROVIDING SOCIAL SUPPORT: • **ACKNOWLEDGING COMMENTS** • **REFLECTING COMMENTS**	Ignoring people's needs; criticizing or diminishing the significance of others' ideas and feelings; recognizing only one side of the issue without giving others' opinions consideration	Acknowledging difficulties or differences among issues (e.g., "It sounds like one of the problems . . ." and ""Where we disagree in the group is . . ."); acknowledging people's needs and wants (e.g., "It sounds that for you to feel good about this, you need . . ."); acknowledging consensus on concerns (e.g., "What we agree on . . ."); reflecting other group members' emotions and feelings (e.g., "You seem really upset.")

briefly describe and give examples of how your skills may have been less than competent. Using these less competent skills as a point of comparison to fill in the second column, describe the skills you think would have been perceived as more competent in the particular context. With practice, you will find you can use this grid to help develop your listening skills for future relational managment situations, as well as to analyze relational management situations you have already experienced.

ANALYZING YOUR RELATIONAL MANAGEMENT SKILLS

Context

CULTURE:

TIME:

RELATIONSHIP:

PLACE:

FUNCTION:

RELATIONAL MANAGEMENT SKILLS	LESS COMPETENT	MORE COMPETENT
GIVING ACCOUNTS AND EXPLANATIONS		
FRAMING AND REFRAMING		
PROVIDING SOCIAL SUPPORT: • **ACKNOWLEDGING COMMENTS** • **REFLECTING COMMENTS**		

c. What inferences did you draw from this data?

d. What kind of future actions did you take based on your conclusion?

Take the arguments/conclusions you have heard in the discussion that didn't make much sense to you. Using the Ladder of Inference, draw up a list of questions you could use to explore the reasoning the person used to draw the conclusion.

2. Draw two columns on a piece of paper. In the left-hand column, list the typical kinds of conflict you have in groups. In the right-hand column, describe the kind of conflict management style you use to solve the conflict. Go back to the left-hand column and classify the conflict as either an affective, ideational, or procedural conflict. Analyze the data in the two columns. Does your conflict management style vary according to the type of conflict?

3. Identify a leader who has recently instituted some change in a group. Interview that group leader and explore what he or she did to create the change. What techniques or strategies did he or she employ to create the change? Did the leader view the change as involving technical or adaptive work?

4 Take a group you belong to and identify an issue or topic that is important to the group. Using the steps involved with issue framing, generate three acceptable discussion questions that could guide the group discussion.

5 Go to the leadership Web site for the Jepson School of Leadership Studies at the University of Richmond at **http://www.richmond.edu/academics/leadership/courses/inex.html**. Examine the course offerings for the school. Given the information on the Web site, prepare a presentation for your class on the important knowledge and skills effective leaders may need to possess.

Group Exercises

1. In a group of 4–5 people, generate a list of common statements that people make which can disrupt a discussion. Using Table 13.2 as a guide, develop three reframes. What kinds of openings do the reframes create to get the discussion back on track?

2. In groups of 4–5 people, select a conflict that might emerge in a small group. Using the five conflict management styles of avoiding, accommodating, competing, compromising, and collaborating, role-play in the group how that conflict would be managed. How does each style sound? What kinds of roles do different group members take when they perform a particular style? Which conflict management style best manages this conflict? Why?

3. In a group of 4–5 people, select an important issue or problem currently being discussed on your campus. Conduct a 30-minute discussion using the C-V-A model starting with the Concerns. Did the C-V-A model keep the discussion on track? Under what conditions would it be more useful to start with Visions or Actions?

4.  Using *InfoTrac College Edition,* look up the article, "Leadership for a new age," Nation's Business, May 1997 v85n5 p18(7) by Sharon Nelton. Read the article. Prepare a presentation for your class that answers these two questions: (1) Why will more democratic leadership styles be more prominent in the future? (2) What allows individuals to become more democratic and participative in their leadership style?

References

Bales, R. F. (1970). *Personality and interpersonal behavior.* New York: Holt, Rinehart & Winston.

Bales, R. F., & Strodtbeck, F. L. (1951). Phases in group problem-solving. *Journal of Abnormal and Social Psychology, 46,* 485–495.

Barge, J. K. (1994). *Leadership: Communication skills for organizations and groups.* New York: St. Martin's Press.

Barge, J. K. (1996). Leadership skills and the dialectics of leadership in group decision making. In R. Y. Hirokawa & M. S. Poole (Eds.), *Communication and group decision making* (2nd ed., pp. 301–344). Thousand Oaks, CA: Sage.

Benne, K. D., & Sheats, P. (1948). Functional roles of group members. *Journal of Social Issues, 4,* 41–49.

Bennis, W. G., & Nanus, B. (1985). *Leaders: The strategies of taking charge.* San Francisco: HarperCollins.

Bolman, L. G., & Deal, T. E. (1997). Reframing organizations: Artistry, choice, and leadership (2nd ed.). San Francisco: Jossey-Bass.

Bormann, E. G. (1975). *Discussion and group methods: Theory and practice.* New York: Harper.

Eagly, A. H., & Johnson, B. T. (1990). Gender and leadership style: A meta-analysis. *Psychological Bulletin, 108,* 233–256.

Eagly, A. H., Karau, S. J., & Makhijani, M. G. (1995). Gender and the effectiveness of leaders: A meta-analysis. *Psychological Bulletin, 111,* 3–23.

Fisher, B. A. (1970). Decision emergence: Phases in group decision making. *Speech Monographs, 37,* 53–66.

Fisher, R., & Ury, W. (1991). *Getting to yes* (2nd ed.). New York: Penguin.

Gibb, J. R. (1961). Defensive communication. *Journal of Communication, 11,* 141–148.

Heifetz, R. A. (1994). *Leadership without easy answers.* Cambridge, MA: Belknap.

Helgesen, S. (1995). *Web of inclusion: A new architecture for building great organizations.* New York: Doubleday.

Kilmann, R. H., & Thomas, K. W. (1977). Developing a forced-choice measure of conflict handling behavior: The "MODE" instrument. *Educational and Psychological Measurement, 37,* 309–325.

Klenke, K. (1996). *Women and leadership: A contextual perspective.* New York: Springer

Kouzes, J. M., & Posner, B. Z. (1995). *The leadership challenge: How to get extraordinary things done in organizations* (2nd ed.). San Francisco: Jossey-Bass.

Lumsden, G., & Lumsden, D. (1993). *Communicating in groups and teams: Sharing leadership.* Belmont, CA: Wadsworth.

Morgan, G. (1997). *Images of organization* (2nd ed.). Thousand Oaks, CA: Sage.

PDC Training Manual. (1999). Albuquerque, NM: Public Dialogue Consortium.

Poole, M. S., Siebold, D. S., & McPhee, R. D. (1996). The structuration of group decisions. In R. Y. Hirokawa & M. S. Poole (Eds.), *Communication and group decision making* (2nd ed., pp. 114–146). Thousand Oaks, CA: Sage.

Putnam, L. L., & Poole, M. S. (1987). Conflict and negotiation. In F. M. Jablin, L. L. Putnam, K. H. Roberts, & L. W. Porter (Eds.), *Handbook of organizational communication* (pp. 549–599). Thousand Oaks, CA: Sage.

Senge, P. M., Kleiner, A., Roberts, C., Ross, R. B., & Smith, B. J. (1994). *The fifth discipline fieldbook.* New York: Currency Doubleday.

Stogdill, R. M. (1948). Personal factors associated with leadership: A survey of the literature. *Journal of Psychology, 25,* 35–71.

Tuckman, B. W., & Jensen, M. (1977). Stages of small-group development revisited. *Group and Organization Studies, 2,* 419–427.

CHAPTER 14

Learning Objectives

After studying this chapter, you should be able to:

1. Explain the foundation of public speaking in rhetoric.
2. Understand how the model of communication competence applies to public speaking.
3. Appreciate the motives for improving your public speaking competence.
4. Define public speaking and describe the types of speeches and delivery.
5. Explain how the competence model applies to public speaking, including motivation, knowledge, and skills.
6. Describe how to adapt a speech to a context by analyzing the listeners and speaking situation.
7. Understand the role of audience competence in public speaking.
8. Discuss the major challenges to motivation and public speaking of communication apprehension and public speaking anxiety.
9. Describe and apply one or more of the strategies for overcoming public speaking anxiety.
10. Characterize the ethical responsibilities of a public speaker.

Introducing Public Speaking

Nicholas felt confident about his communication abilities in most situations. His interpersonal and small group communication skills were well developed. With confidence, he attended parties and joined clubs, eagerly meeting people who frequently became his good friends. For some reason, though, that exuberant self-confidence disappeared when it came to one very important communication event—speaking in public.

As a full-time college student and communication major, Nicholas's required course work included a public speaking class that he had put off until his senior year. Despite his outgoing personality, he had wanted to avoid the experience of presenting a speech to a group of people as long as possible. If a group project required an in-class presentation, Nicholas would volunteer to do most of the research work in order not to be one of the in-class presenters. But secretly he would envy his classmates who appeared confident and in control when they stood up in front of the class to present the results of his work.

Now the time of reckoning had arrived, and Nicholas knew it. He was registered in the public speaking class, not because he wanted to be, but because graduation was only four months away. To his surprise, the course instructor did a great job of coaching the students and they really grew as public speakers. As it turned out, Nicholas did well in the class and even enjoyed it. He improved his research skills immensely using the internet, the campus library, and even an interview to gather highly credible sources of information for his speeches. He learned to present informative and persuasive speeches effectively and was able to do so using an outline to present rather than reading his entire speech. The other students really appreciated his final speech, which described why it is a good idea to improve your public speaking skills—how a person benefits individually and how these skills can be used to benefit society. Nicholas also learned to handle his public speaking anxiety, finishing the course with a B+.

When he went for a job interview after graduating, Nicholas was taken back because the interviewers asked him to present a short impromptu speech summarizing why he wanted the position. When they called back to say that he got the job, what they said was an even bigger surprise. Nicholas's ability to present his thoughts clearly and convincingly in the impromptu speech impressed the interviewers more than anything else he said or did. •••

Nicholas's feelings of anxiety about public speaking are not unique. In fact, researchers agree that public speaking anxiety is one of the greatest fears of most North Americans. In a national survey, respondents were asked to identify their greatest fears. You guessed it—public speaking is the top fear of 45% of adults—feared more than financial problems, heights, deep water, or even dying (Bruskin/Goldring Research; 1993). Table 14.1 presents the survey results.

Despite this initial anxiety, students like you and Nicholas can learn to handle any negative feelings you have about public speaking and, in fact, learn to give speeches quite effectively. Research has proven that this is the case. In one study, students in an introductory public speaking course were tested right before and right after presenting a speech (MacIntyre & MacDonald, 1998). The majority of the students, even those with the highest level of anxiety at the beginning of the speech, showed significant improvement in their perceptions of their own communication competence, and they also perceived the audience as more pleasant and supportive by the end of the speech. In a

Knowledge Link

Is it good to talk about public speaking anxiety at the beginning of a course, or is it better not to discuss it too much?

•••

TABLE 14.1

••• Number One Fear: Public Speaking •••

According to a national survey, public speaking is the top fear of 45% of 1,000 North American adults, followed by financial problems, heights, deep water, and then death. Note that women are more afraid of all of the feared events than men, a result not explained by those who conducted the survey. This gender difference is important, however, as you begin to think about improving your public speaking competence.

FEARED EVENT	TOTAL	WOMEN	MEN
Public speaking	45%	54%	34%
Financial problems	40%	42%	38%
Heights	40%	50%	29%
Deep water	33%	45%	19%
Death	31%	34%	28%
Sickness	28%	34%	21%
Insects and bugs	24%	34%	13%
Loneliness	23%	27%	18%
Flying	22%	30%	15%
Driving/riding in a car	10%	13%	7%
Dogs	10%	11%	8%
Darkness	9%	14%	4%
Elevators	8%	13%	4%
Escalators	8%	13%	4%

SOURCE: Bruskin/Goldring Research (1993).

similar study, students were tested at the beginning and the end of a basic communication course (Rubin, Rubin, & Jordan, 1997). The course had the most favorable effect on students who started out high in communication apprehension and low in communication competence. These students experienced greater changes than anyone else, feeling significantly less afraid and becoming more competent. So it is quite possible to reduce your feelings of apprehension and improve your public speaking competence significantly.

A Model of Public Speaking Competence

Whether you are apprehensive or not, take a look at the model of competence for public speaking in Figure 14.1, which is similar to those presented earlier for interpersonal and group communication but identifies issues specific to public speaking. The three interdependent components of competence—motivation, knowledge, and skills—work together to influence whether the audience perceives a public speaker as competent. If a speaker is motivated and willing to speak publicly, has the essential knowledge and understanding of how to prepare a speech for presentation, and has developed and is able to use all the crucial verbal and nonverbal public speaking skills, then the outcome of perceived competence is likely to occur. As Figure 14.1 also suggests, the speaker adapts the speech to the context using audience analysis, and audience members contribute to competence by being motivated to listen, understanding the listening process, and providing feedback to the speaker.

FIGURE 14.1
A Model of Public Speaking Competence

Competence in public speaking results from the speaker's motivation, knowledge, and skills, and his or her adaptation of the speech to the context. Public speaking competence also includes audience members demonstrating listening competence.

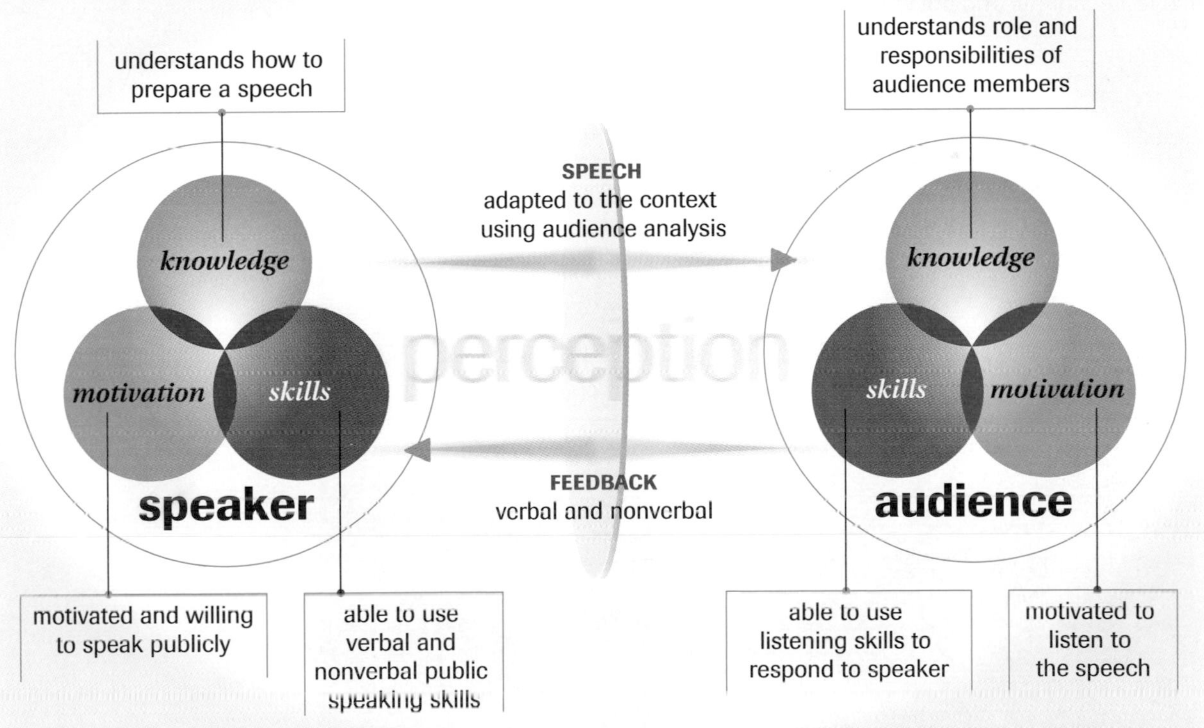

Now that we have briefly seen how this model applies to public speaking, let's explore the historical roots of public speaking in the study of rhetoric and how that tradition provides solid reasons for improving your ability to give a good speech. We examine your assumptions about public speaking and then discuss what public speaking is like today. A more in-depth discussion of the components of public speaking competence, including context and audience analysis, and audience competence, is explored and we finish with practical solutions for dealing with public speaking anxiety.

The Rhetorical Tradition

When Nicholas learned to give a good speech and when you present your next speech, you are both participating in the age-old tradition of rhetoric. Although the term *empty rhetoric* is sometimes used in a negative way to describe the hollow language of contemporary politicians and to suggest that their remarks are hollow or meaningless, the study of rhetoric and public speaking is a noble endeavor with a proud past. **Rhetoric**—the art of influencing an audience through words—dates back many centuries with its roots in the Greek and Roman periods of history.

The Greek Period

Long ago, before 500 B.C.E., a teacher and his student, Corax and Tisias, taught common citizens on the island of Sicily how to argue effectively for themselves in public forums. The work of Corax and Tisias led to the early tradition of rhetoric in ancient Greece. In 481 B.C.E., a group of Greek philosophers called **sophists** began to teach about thinking and speaking persuasively. Other Greek writers later criticized the sophists for focusing too much on technique and not enough on the content of a speech. As a result, like rhetoric,

Public speaking can trace its roots back to the rhetorical traditions of ancient Greece and Rome.

the term *sophistry* is sometimes used today to refer to the empty or meaningless use of language. A sophist named Protagoras, still known today as the father of debate, required his students to first speak in favor of an issue and then argue against it, in order to develop an understanding of the reasoning on both sides of the issue. Isocrates, the father of eloquence, carried on the traditions of the sophists. He had his students learn about a variety of subjects and form political, social, and ethical judgments, so they would become better citizens and more eloquent public speakers.

Plato, one of the most famous Greek philosophers, stressed participation in **dialectic,** a question and answer process used to examine all sides of an issue in search of the truth. Plato's writings frequently took the form of conversations between characters who debated important issues, like the nature of knowledge or the immortality of the soul. Another famous Greek philosopher and writer, Aristotle, saw logic as essential to understanding any subject. He was the first to describe systematically a system of persuasion for Western culture based on logic, emotion, and speaker credibility. That system or set of "appeals" is still used today to help students understand persuasive speaking (see Chapter 18).

THE ROMAN PERIOD

The Romans continued the tradition of public speaking that began with the Greeks. In the 2nd century B.C.E., Cicero combined rhetoric and philosophy in his writings about public speaking. Like the Greeks, he believed good public speakers needed a well-rounded education, but his unique contribution was a structured five-step process for analyzing issues and developing a speech. Cicero's recommendations are covered in Chapter 15 under speech preparation.

In the first century A.D., another Roman, Quintilian, extended the Roman tradition of public speaking by developing a series of questions to encourage creative and critical thinking on issues. He is also credited with a concern for being an ethical as well as effective public speaker. In his writings, he described the ideal speaker as *a good man speaking well.* By that, Quintilian meant that an effective speaker is also ethical and of high character. Of course, Quintilian did not intend to leave women out, but rhetoric, at that time, was an activity only for men.

The basic ideas about rhetoric introduced centuries ago by the Greeks and Romans—thinking critically, becoming a well-informed citizen, and speaking ethically—have endured until the present day. Public speaking continues to be crucial to achieving the ideals of democracy and a capitalist society. The ability of citizens in contemporary society to argue effectively in public, to think and speak persuasively, to debate logically, and to form ethical judgments are essential skills for becoming a better citizen.

Why Public Speaking Is Important?

When you contemplate the challenge of learning to be a better public speaker, it may seem a little daunting. Nonetheless, there are quite a few good reasons for addressing this challenge. The ability to speak well in public yields civic benefits for all of us. If you develop your ability to deliver a good speech, you will possess the skills essential to active participation as a good citizen in your community and in a democratic society. Furthermore, you will present yourself with greater confidence and self-assurance in a variety of communication situations, which will yield benefits in your personal as well as professional life.

A speaker who effectively communicates ideas in public can help bring people together to serve the greater good and create healthy communities.

MOTIVES FOR THE PUBLIC GOOD

Just as in the days of Plato, Aristotle, and Cicero, public speaking continues to have a role in achieving the ideals of democracy in modern society. Public speaking skills significantly contribute to the common good by serving as a powerful tool for effecting change in communities and society. People who can communicate ideas publicly—whether arguing for policy change or championing human rights—are in a better position to contribute in a positive way to the well-being of everyone. By speaking out, they help those who can not be heard coordinate their efforts to create better communities. By being able to speak your mind publicly on behalf of a cause, and with the support of others, you are enabled to mobilize the power and energy of diverse individuals and groups of people so they work together to achieve common goals. In this way, public speaking serves as the primary basis for facilitating the exchange of ideas in a variety of communication situations in the public sphere of democratic society. We can look to great leaders as examples of this: Eleanor Roosevelt, Martin Luther King, Jr., Nelson Mandela, and Cesar Chavez, to name but a few.

On a more personal level, suppose a tuition hike is planned for your campus, one that most students cannot afford. The students keep meeting informally to talk about the problem, but they do not seem to unite with a common voice and do anything about it. By speaking up and offering to be a spokesperson at one of the meetings, you could help the students get their story straight and bring it clearly to the attention of the campus administrators. By presenting their collective ideas effectively, you could see to it that their argument is heard and their concerns and rights respected.

Knowledge Link

Is the pledge of the Greeks and Romans—that citizens should be good public speakers—similar to what you observe today?

PERSONAL MOTIVES

Putting civic motives aside, you will benefit as an individual by improving your public speaking competence. Like Nicholas, if you become a better public speaker, you will feel more confident about yourself and possess an invaluable set of communication skills. You will use your public speaking skills in your personal life giving toasts and eulogies and speaking out and presenting your ideas in groups and at team meetings.

Another personal reason for improving your public speaking skills is that, by doing so, you will become a more critical thinker. **Critical thinking** is the process of evaluating evidence, assumptions, and ideas based on sound reasoning and logic. When you prepare a speech, you collect, evaluate, and organize evidence and ideas logically. These activities involve critical thinking; so while preparing your speech and improving your public speaking skills, you also hone your ability to think critically (Allen, Berkowitz, Hunt, & Louden, 1999). As you learn to prepare speeches for your public speaking class, you will also learn to think critically about many topics from varying perspectives.

Knowledge Link

What are the ways that you could use public speaking in your community to help achieve desirable goals?

PROFESSIONAL MOTIVES

When Nicholas improved his public speaking skills, a surprising benefit came his way. He got the job he wanted because of his improved communication abilities and his effective impromptu speech. You too will use public speaking skills in your work life, presenting reports, briefings, and trainings.

Numerous national surveys and studies identify public speaking skills as crucial to academic and professional success in life (Morreale, Osborn, & Pearson, in press). These surveys have been conducted in many vocations from school to business. In a survey of professors' perceptions of what business students should learn, faculty members replied that they believe students need more instruction in making oral presentations to prepare them for the real world of business (Plutsky, 1996). A report issued by top executives from Fortune 500 companies states that newly hired graduates with impressive academic skills often lack essential communication skills, such as public speaking ("Graduates," 1997). The executives recommend that college graduates be better prepared to communicate publicly.

In another national survey, over a thousand human resource managers were asked two questions: What factors help college graduates get jobs, and what factors influence how well they perform after getting the job (Winsor, Curtis, & Stephens, 1997)? The human resource managers responded that the most important factors in helping college graduates obtain employment are basic oral and written communication skills. The managers added that among the top factors influencing job performance are public speaking and listening skills.

All of these studies indicate how important it is for you professionally to be able to speak competently in public. If you do so with confidence and competence, your ideas will be respected and you will be perceived as a credible individual whose professional presentations are worth paying attention to.

Public speaking skills have been linked to not only getting a job but also how well you succeed in your job.

What Is Public Speaking?

Now that you have seen how becoming a better public speaker brings civic, personal, and professional benefits, it is time to learn more about this valuable way of communicating. What follows is a set of assumptions about public speaking, a definition, and descriptions of various types of speeches and delivery methods.

ASSUMPTIONS ABOUT PUBLIC SPEAKING

Most people, including you, hold general assumptions about public speaking. Although some of these assumptions are true, others are not. Let's clear up these assumptions now. Before you learn any more about public speaking competence, answer the questions in Test Your Assumptions.

Statements 1, 2, 3, and 4 are about the value of public speaking skills. Statement 1 is false, and 2, 3, and 4 are true. As just discussed, speaking with confidence in public is a valuable skill for anyone to acquire. It benefits an individual personally, improves critical thinking abilities, and benefits communities and society as well.

Statements 5 and 6 are false. Although some people appear to have an inborn knack for public speaking, it is a learned skill that can be improved with proper training such as taking a college public speaking course.

Statements 7 and 8 are about fear of public speaking. Statement 7 says that not much can be done to combat public speaking anxiety, which is false. Statement 8 says that some speakers who don't appear nervous actually are. This statement is true. Abraham Lincoln, who appeared calm and in control, actually was very nervous when he spoke publicly. The famous television interviewer Barbara Walters appears unruffled when she is talking to celebrities, but she openly acknowledges her public speaking anxiety.

Having clarified the assumptions, we now consider what public speaking is and how it works. **Public speaking** is communication from one to many. A single person—or sometimes a group of people—present a message to a larger number of people, who usually do not have speaking roles except for asking questions at the end of the presentation. Speeches today can be categorized according to the type of speech—its purpose—and how the speech is delivered.

Test your assumptions

INSTRUCTIONS: Read each of the following statements. Circle the answer that you think best reflects each statement.

TRUE	FALSE	**1.** Public speaking is essential for politicians, community leaders, and teachers, but most people don't need to become better at it.
TRUE	FALSE	**2.** If more people become better public speakers, the quality of collective life in society will improve.
TRUE	FALSE	**3.** Your personal quality of life can be improved if you learn to be a better public speaker.
TRUE	FALSE	**4.** By improving your public speaking skills, you will actually be able to think better.
TRUE	FALSE	**5.** Good public speakers are born that way; it comes to them more naturally than to other people.
TRUE	FALSE	**6.** Training in public speaking will make a person a little better at it, but not a lot better.
TRUE	FALSE	**7.** If a person has public speaking anxiety, not much can be done about it.
TRUE	FALSE	**8.** People who appear self-confident when speaking publicly may still suffer from public speaking anxiety.

Answers: 1: F; 2: T; 3: T; 4: T; 5: F; 6: F; 7: F; 8: T

Types of Speeches

Although in the future you may be asked to give a speech to entertain an audience or commemorate a special event, the two types of speeches covered in most public speaking classes are informative and persuasive. An **informative speech** has the purpose of communicating something new or a new perspective to an audience, and moving listeners to greater understanding or insight. Speakers at training seminars and college professors both have the purpose of sharing new information and achieving new understanding with the audience. A **persuasive speech** has the purpose of influencing an audience's attitudes, beliefs, values, or behaviors. Motivational speakers, religious leaders, and even salespeople all have the purpose of persuading the audience to change in some way. Many political speeches fall into this category. Politicians try to persuade you that their positions on public issues represent what you should think or do.

Knowledge Link

Is the ability to present an informative speech or to present a persuasive speech more valuable for enabling you to contribute to your community?

Types of Delivery

Both types of speeches—informative and persuasive—can be presented using any one of four different methods of delivery: impromptu, extemporaneous, manuscript, or memorized. Each type of delivery involves a different amount of preparation time and is appropriate to use in different public speaking situations.

The **impromptu speech** is delivered with the least amount of preparation, usually with little or no time to plan your remarks. At a social event like a wedding or a surprise party, guests are often invited to provide impromptu remarks about the bride, the groom, or the guest of honor. At a staff meeting at work, you may be called on to present an impromptu description of a project or a plan for solving a company problem. Like Nicholas, when you are told in a job interview, "Tell us about yourself," that is an impromptu speech as well.

Your first speech in a public speaking class also could be an impromptu, perhaps a speech of self-introduction or on another topic assigned by your instructor. If that happens, you can borrow some hints from debaters who are trained to prepare public remarks quickly during fast-paced debates. Debaters' critical thinking skills can be adapted to any impromptu speaking situation, because these speakers have to be good at thinking on their feet and speaking in the moment (Davis & Dickmeyer, 1993). Here's some advice:

- First, keep your composure and try to relax.
- Before you speak, jot down quick notes to focus and organize what you will say.
- Quickly figure out your single most important point and something to illustrate and support it. Keep your remarks organized around that central theme or idea.
- Decide on a simple introduction, middle, and conclusion to organize what you will say.
- When you get to your conclusion, say it and stop speaking. The biggest mistake impromptu speakers make is rambling on and on.

Unlike the impromptu, an **extemporaneous speech** is carefully planned and prepared ahead of time. It is delivered in a conversational tone of voice using note cards or a presentational outline to remember key ideas and information. Although you may have spent a great deal of time researching, organizing, and rehearsing, your delivery of the speech is relaxed and unaffected. Because your note cards or outline contain only key words to remind you of what to say, the wording of the speech varies each time it is presented, creating an illusion of spontaneity.

Extemporaneous speaking is a popular type of delivery in college classrooms, as well as in businesses and organizations. Despite its advantages, with this type of delivery, it can be difficult to keep within your allotted time and say what you intend to say. You can remedy these problems by including less information rather than more, which keeps your speech simpler, and by practicing the speech ahead to be sure you can cover what is on your note cards. Speech instructors agree that students who practice give better speeches and get better grades.

A **manuscript speech** is written out ahead of time and read word for word to the audience. If you were to write out the content of each note card or item from the speech outline for an extemporaneous speech, it would become a manuscript speech. This type of delivery is called for when complete accuracy is necessary, like a speech in a courtroom or a keynote address at an important conference or event.

Although accuracy and formality are advantages, a problem with this type of delivery is making less eye contact and gesturing less as you read the speech. You can handle this problem in these ways. When preparing the manuscript, use more adverbs and adjectives to enliven the speech, and use shorter paragraphs, which are easier to come back to after looking up. Type the manuscript in all capital letters and in a large typeface for ease of reading. And practice with the manuscript, so you memorize some parts and can say them to the audience instead of just reading them.

A **memorized speech** requires the most preparation because it is fully written out and memorized ahead of time, then spoken to the audience word for word. Like a manuscript speech, this type of delivery is used when accuracy is crucial. When the U.S. president presents the state of the union message, often the speech is almost memorized before it is presented. This type of delivery is the most time-consuming method and frequently the least effective because it can appear rehearsed and insincere. Furthermore, if the speech is interrupted for some reason, you may lose your place in the memorized text. These problems can be avoided by practicing the speech so much that you can convey spontaneity and sincerity to the audience when you deliver it.

A Model of Speaker's Competence

Given an understanding of what public speaking is like today, we now examine it more closely through the lens of the model of communication competence. Recall that we introduced you earlier in this chapter to a model of public speaking competence. Let's now discuss the three basic components of public speaking competence outlined in Figure 14.2—motivation, knowledge, and skills—as they relate to the speaker.

Motivation

The importance of the motivation component in improving public speaking competence is underscored by a study of 245 students in a public speaking class (Carrell & Menzel, 1997). The researchers evaluated the impact of students' motivation to learn on their performance in the public speaking course. Those who were more highly motivated significantly outperformed all the other students in the course.

Returning for a moment to Nicholas, why is it he was not motivated to take public speaking before his senior year? Why did he go out of his way to avoid speaking in front of a group of people? Obviously he had a fear of public speaking, and he was probably

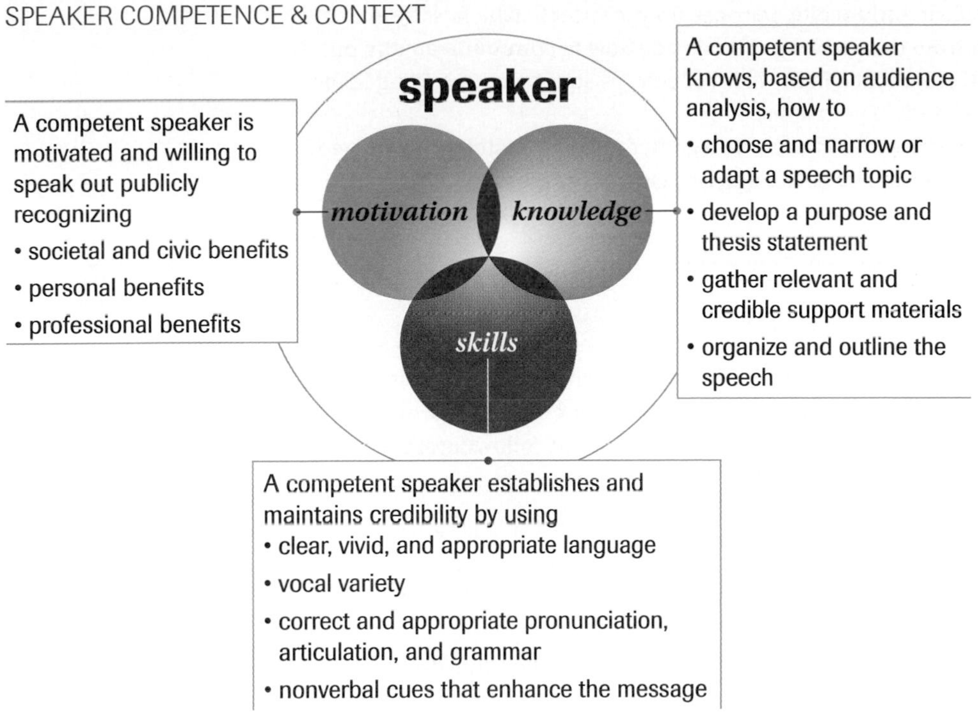

SPEAKER COMPETENCE & CONTEXT

FIGURE 14.2
A Model of Speaker Competence

The basic components of competence—motivation, knowledge, and skills—are essential to preparing and presenting a speech competently. The appropriate and effective use of these components influences the outcome of perceived competence by the audience in any public speaking context.

unaware of the civic, personal, and professional benefits of improving his public speaking skills. Like Nicholas, most people's fears negatively affect their motivation to speak publicly or learn more about public speaking. Interestingly, these fears do not exist for most people when they are younger. Observe small children in kindergarten or the first grade. Most of them are outgoing, if not fearless, when it comes to speaking out among their peers or even adults. So what causes people to change as they grow up, so they lack the motivation to speak in public?

As people grow and mature, they come to see public speaking as a psychological threat to their self-image and self-esteem. Because the members of the audience are watching, listening, and deciding what they think of the speaker, public speaking is perceived as a threat to the self-concept. Our bodies react to this psychological danger with many of the same physical symptoms we experience with physical threats: light-headedness, dry mouth, shaking, shortness of breath, and general bodily tension. As a result, we lack the motivation to speak publicly despite the many good civic, personal, and professional motives for improving public speaking skills.

KNOWLEDGE

In addition to becoming motivated to speak publicly, knowledge of the process and techniques involved in developing a speech is essential to competence. You build this knowledge by following a step-by-step preparation process, as you plan and organize your speech.

1. Based on the results of audience analysis, discussed later in this chapter, you choose and narrow a speech topic that the listeners will find appealing. If a topic has been assigned, you adapt it to the context and audience.

2. Next you determine a clear and specific purpose for the speech, which is the response you hope for from the audience. You decide how to communicate the purpose of the speech to the audience in the form of a thesis statement or central idea that summarizes the content of your speech.
3. Having a purpose in mind for your speech, you gather research materials from credible sources to support your informative claim or persuasive argument.
4. Then you organize those materials into an outline and speaking notes.

Chapter 15 covers each of these steps in more detail.

SKILLS

Along with motivation and knowledge, competent public speaking calls for using a variety of presentation skills that help establish and maintain your **credibility,** which is how believable you are as a speaker when you deliver your speech. The following skills are discussed extensively in Chapter 16:

1. Use language and words that are clear, vivid, and appropriate. Clear language helps listeners understand your message, and vivid language promotes enthusiasm for it. Appropriate language is respectful of all the audience members and does not offend anyone in the audience.
2. How you use your voice is crucial, in that it can heighten and maintain audience attention and interest in your speech. Your message is brought to life using vocal variety, varying your speaking rate and the pitch and intensity of your voice.
3. You also must speak correctly, using pronunciation, articulation, and grammar that is suitable to the particular audience and speaking situation.
4. Finally, you must use all the nonverbal cues described in Chapter 5 to support and enhance your spoken message. Your physical appearance and how you move, gesture, and use eye contact and facial expressions are all important to public speaking competence.

Context & Audience Analysis

As you first learned in Chapter 2, the context in which communication takes place influences and shapes the communication event. Therefore, competence in public speaking calls for adapting what you say and how you say it to the particular context. Like Nicholas, the contexts in which you will present your speeches in college will probably be in a public speaking course or in a class that requires individual or group presentations. Outside of school, you will give presentations at work, at community gatherings, and at various social events. To adapt to these as well as other contexts and prepare and present your speech effectively, you must first engage in audience analysis.

Audience analysis is the process a speaker uses to ascertain relevant facts and information about the listeners and the speaking situation that will shape how the speech is prepared and delivered. The key word here is *relevant.* You do not need to find out everything about the audience and situation, but you do need to be aware of anything that will affect how the listeners perceive and react to you and your speech. In Chapter 3, you learned how variations in perception result in people interpreting communication events and messages quite differently. By engaging in audience analysis, you anticipate these reactions and then prepare and present your speech based on what you've learned about both the listeners and the particular speaking situation. Check out the competence approach to audience analysis in Figure 14.3 and then read about how this is done.

Which component of public competence represents the biggest challenge to most people as they strive to become better public speakers and why?

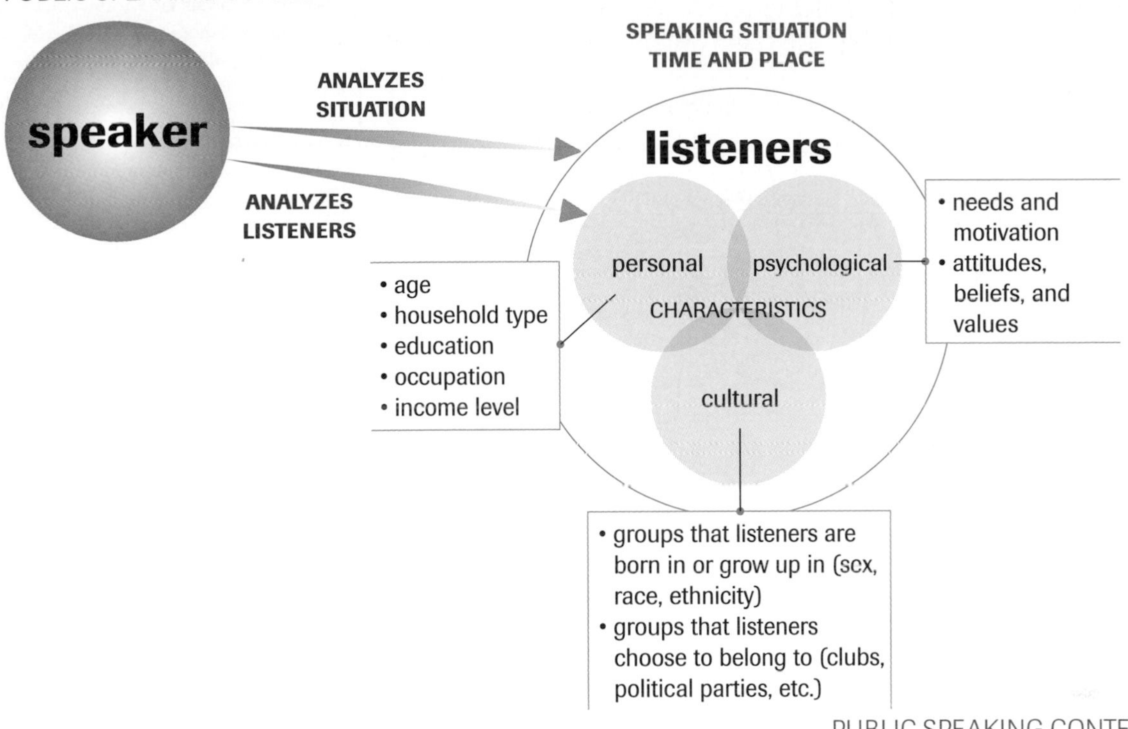

FIGURE 14.3
Competence and Audience Analysis

A competent speaker adapts to any public speaking context by analyzing both the listeners and the speaking situation in order to learn relevant facts and information that are used to prepare and deliver the speech.

Analyzing the Listeners

Experts in public speaking say that the number one reason a speech fails to achieve its goal is because the speaker does not know his or her listeners well enough (St. John, 1995). Three sets of characteristics about the listeners are important to know about: (1) personal characteristics, (2) psychological characteristics, and (3) cultural characteristics (Morreale & Bovee, 1997). As you analyze these characteristics, it is helpful to think about the composition of the audience on a scale ranging from highly homogeneous (the audience members are much like one another) to highly diverse (the audience members are not very much alike). If there is a high level of homogeneity or similarity, it will be easier to choose a topic that will appeal to the majority of your listeners. A higher level of diversity in personal, psychological, or cultural characteristics will represent a greater challenge, but one you must consider as you choose or develop a topic and prepare your speech.

You can learn about the characteristics of the other students in your class by talking to them directly and asking questions about their interests, preferences, and activities. Or with the consent of your course instructor, you could conduct an informal or written survey, asking pertinent questions about their perceptions of your topic.

Personal Characteristics

Personal characteristics include objective demographic information about the audience members. Most relevant are the listeners' ages, household types, education, occupation, and income levels.

- Age is often an indicator of the concerns or interests of listeners. For example, you can assume that most young college students are less interested in the details of a

"Good God! He's giving the white-collar voters' speech to the blue collars."

Audience analysis is essential, whether you're running for public office or giving a speech in class.

© The New Yorker Collection 1984 Joseph Farris from cartoonbank.com. All rights reserved.

retirement plan than a group of adults in their 40s or 50s might be. Age also tells you what major historical events the listeners may or may not be aware of. If your audience is fairly homogeneous in age, be sure your topic is one that appeals to the average age of the listeners. If they are diverse in age, provide background information for any ideas with which they may be unfamiliar.

- Household type, who is actually living together in the household, is another personal characteristic that may affect audience reactions. At one time, households in the United States were characterized by a higher level of homogeneity than they are today. For instance, in 1972, married couples with children were the most common household arrangement (45%); in 1998, only 26% of homes were constituted in this way (National Opinion Research Center, 2000) Today's diverse household types include many people living alone, households with two working parents, single-parent families, stepfamilies, intergenerational families with grandparents and grandchildren living under the same roof, and gay and lesbian households. If you reference any aspect of home life in your speech, allow for the fact that your listeners may live in different household types. Choose a topic and develop your speech so it is equally appealing and respectful of all the listeners.
- Knowing the educational level of your listeners will also help you prepare a speech they will relate to and find engaging. To some extent, education shapes what people are interested in. But keep in mind that education and intelligence are not the same. Many highly intelligent and successful people have not attained high levels of academic achievement, but they do have inquiring and quick minds and are interested in a wide variety of topics. Let the educational background of your listeners guide how you

Knowledge Link

Should audience analysis be approached differently depending on whether the audience is highly homogenous or highly diverse? In what ways?

develop your topic. If the topic is one the audience would only know about through more education, fill them in so they can appreciate it.

- What the audience members do for a living and how much they earn can also provide insights into what they will find interesting. Occupational choices reflect people's preferences and likes and dislikes, and the amount of expendable income they have shapes what they are able to do in life and what they want to hear about in a speech. If there is a high level of occupational homogeneity, choose a topic with appeal to common interests. If there is a high level of economic diversity, be sure your topic will be interesting, regardless of income level.

Psychological Characteristics

The audience's **psychological characteristics** that must be analyzed are their needs and motivation and their attitudes, beliefs, and values. These characteristics represent subjective information that frequently is more difficult to determine than objective, personal characteristics. At a glance, you can estimate the average age and even income of an audience, but ascertaining what they might need or value is more difficult.

Public speaking experts agree that it is essential to assess an audience's needs and keep those needs in mind when developing a speech (Langham, 1994). The reason is that most people are motivated to listen more attentively if the information presented relates to a topic or aspects of a topic they need to know about. As you saw in Chapter 11, human needs can be divided into five categories: physiological, safety and security, love, self-esteem, and self-actualization (Maslow, 1954). If your speech focuses on satisfying one of these needs, such as ensuring public safety in troubling times or achieving a higher level of self-esteem or self-actualization through one's work, the audience is more likely to be motivated to pay attention to what you say.

Along with listeners' needs, their attitudes, beliefs, and values impact their reactions to a speech. As you learned in Chapter 3, these aspects of an individual are integral to each person's self-concept. Figure 14.4 illustrates how these characteristics are imbedded in a person's psychological makeup, with values at the core or center of the person, overlaid by their beliefs, and then by their attitudes. For the purpose of audience analysis, the following descriptions clarify these three psychological aspects of a person and how they are interrelated.

FIGURE 14.4
Attitudes, Beliefs, and Values

Because values are at the very core of a person, surrounded by his or her beliefs and then attitudes, people's values are the hardest to influence or change.

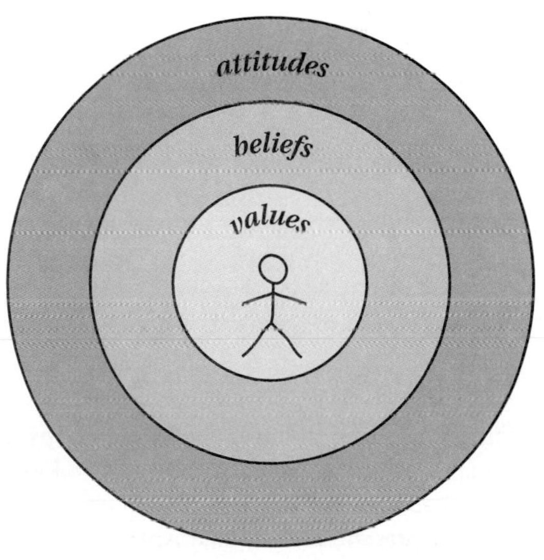

- **Attitudes** are psychological reactions to another person, object, or concept that affect people's behaviors. Our attitudes represent what we like or dislike, our positive or negative inclinations, ranging on a continuum from favorable to neutral to hostile. For instance, if you have a generally positive attitude toward work, most days you will go to your job cheerfully.
- **Beliefs** are people's basic convictions about what is true or false, based on their own knowledge and experience. Beliefs represent what we have learned or come to know, as a result of our exposure to others and to our culture. If you hold the belief that people should work hard to get ahead, you will apply yourself at work and give your all to your job.
- **Values** are deeply rooted clusters of attitudes and beliefs that reflect what a person considers very important or unimportant,

very worthy or unworthy. As such, our values act as the criteria we often use for making choices and judgments in life (Johannesen, 1996). If you highly value professional attainment and achieving status in the workplace, that value will shape your behaviors and choices. When offered a promotion, regardless of peripheral negative consequences, you will accept the offer.

Your speech will be more effective if, in addition to personal characteristics, you carefully analyze the psychological characteristics of your listeners' attitudes, beliefs, and values. They are more likely to listen to and remember information that supports or is at least compatible with their existing attitudes. Because beliefs are based on what people think is true, it will take presenting facts or highly persuasive evidence to influence beliefs. Values are harder to change than attitudes or beliefs. However, a speech related to your audience's values will hold their attention because they really care about it. This does not mean you should misrepresent your own attitudes, beliefs, or values in your speech, which would be unethical as a public speaker.

Knowledge Link

Does the concept of the "post-modern self" affect how a public speaker should analyze the attitudes, beliefs, and values of an audience? How so?

Cultural Characteristics

Some communication scholars say that culture—defined in Chapter 2 as the enduring patterns of thought, value, and behavior that define a group of people—affects and shapes everything listeners perceive, learn, understand, and know (Chesebro, 1996). Therefore, cultural characteristics of audience members influence what they expect from a speech and how they react to it.

Cultural characteristics of importance to public speaking come from two kinds of groups to which listeners belong: those they are born into or grow up in—such as their biological sex, race, and ethnicity—and groups they may choose to belong to—such as their religion, clubs, political parties, or other sorts of organizations. By becoming aware of the groups your listeners belong to, you can prepare a more effective speech that appeals to and respects their culturally diverse experiences and perspectives. If, for example, they are active in political organizations, a speech on presidential electioneering would be appealing.

Using audience analysis, you can identify cultural commonalties of interest based on group membership while respecting the ways in which listeners may be culturally different. This is particularly important in contemporary society, because today's audiences represent a culturally diverse and rich mix of backgrounds and interests (Nolan, 1999). Listeners may be diverse in matters such as religious affiliation, political preference, and racial and ethnic background. In fact, statisticians tell us that the United States is becoming increasingly multicultural and multiracial. Table 14.2 presents projections on diversity in the United States to 2050. The CloseUp on Diversity provides more concrete guidelines for analyzing a diverse audience and adapting your speech so it is appropriate to the audience and effective in the context.

ANALYZING THE SITUATION

Besides analyzing the listeners' personal, psychological, and cultural characteristics, a competent speaker also analyzes the **speaking situation,** which includes both time and place. **Timing** involves how much time you have to speak and when the speech is scheduled to be presented. The **place** aspect of the speaking occasion, as described in Chapter 2,

TABLE 14.2

••• Diversity in the United States by 2050 •••

By the year 2050, the racial and ethnic demographics of United States society will shift significantly. A competent and ethical public speaker prepares and presents with sensitivity to the diversity of contemporary audiences.

RACE/ETHNIC	JULY 1, 2005	JULY 1, 2015	JULY 1, 2025	JULY 1, 2050
White	199,802	205,019	209,117	207,901
Minorities	86,179	105,115	125,933	186,029
Hispanic	36,057	46,705	58,930	96,508
Black	35,485	39,512	43,511	53,555
American Indian	2,183	2,461	2,744	3,534
Asian	12,454	16,437	20,748	32,432

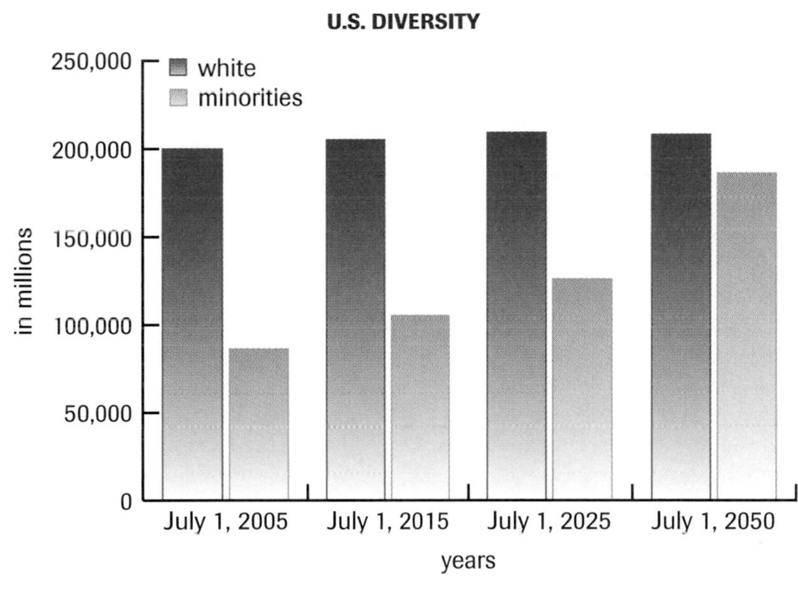

SOURCE: U.S. Bureau of the Census (2000), Population Projections.

relates to the context in which the speech is presented, the environment, and the physical surroundings.

Time

When you consider how much time you have to present, remember that one of the worst things you can do as a public speaker is run overtime. If your speech runs too long and you seem to be rambling on and on, you will lose your audience's attention and appear disorganized. But if your speech runs too short and you fail to fill up the time allotted, your audience may think you do not have much to say and you did not gather sufficient information for the speech. The best way to stay within the time constraints is to prepare carefully and practice your speech out loud ahead of time to see how long it takes to

CloseUp ON DIVERSITY

Analyzing a Diverse Audience

MOST STATISTICIANS AGREE that the United States is becoming increasingly diverse. What's more, they predict that one of the most important social trends that will directly affect most people in the future will be changes in the racial and ethnic makeup of the nation. The prediction is that the overall proportions of the white and nonwhite populations in the United States will shift significantly by the middle of the new millennium (see Table 14.2). Whites are currently a significant majority, but by or before 2050, they will account for just over half the total population, and the other half will be made up of a mix of other racial and ethnic groups—African Americans, Hispanic Americans, Asian Americans, and so forth.

Given how diverse society is becoming, competent public speakers are ethically bound to prepare and present their speeches with sensitivity to diverse audiences. One way to accomplish that is through culturally sensitive audience analysis. When speakers analyze an audience, they tend to think about the audience members in collective groups with common or similar characteristics. This type of analysis helps create a speech that appeals to the listeners' commonalties and similarities. Although it may be useful to prepare a speech that appeals to the audience as a collective group of listeners, this approach to audience analysis could fail to honor the ways in which the audience is diverse. Balancing the need to prepare a speech that appeals to listeners' similarities with the need to honor the ways in which they are dissimilar is a challenge in today's world. The following suggestions can guide public speaking in a more diverse society:

- *Avoid stereotyping.* Despite the need to consider similarities in the personal and psychological characteristics of the listeners, don't assume any characteristic is always true of all of your listeners simply because they belong to a certain group. Remember, no matter what group they belong to, people are individuals, and they prefer to be treated that way.
- *Avoid ethnocentrism.* Ethnocentrism is the tendency to use your own culture or group as the standard against which others are measured and evaluated. To avoid ethnocentrism as a public speaker, do not assume that your culture and subculture's attitudes, opinions, or behaviors are right or better than those of your listeners. Do not suggest there is one right or normal way to do things that is reflected by your group but not by a group to which your listeners belong.
- *Avoid racial and ethnic bias, as well as gender bias.* Don't make judgments about listeners' preferences, interests, abilities, or knowledge of certain topics based on their race, ethnicity, or gender. In any society, including a highly diverse one, individuality transcends culturally based characteristics.
- *Show an interest in other cultures.* Your listeners will appreciate it if you invite the contribution of diverse opinions or observations from members of other cultures in your audience. Become well informed about the cultural background of the listeners and communicate your interest in them without appearing condescending or insincere.
- *Respect differences in how other cultures communicate.* Adapt your communication style to the audience, but do so without offending your listeners. If you know the audience prefers a certain communication style, perhaps more relaxed or more formal, use that approach when giving your speech.
- *Respect how different cultures organize and present information.* Some cultures prefer organizing ideas linearly, coming directly to the point, presenting the speech purpose, and moving quickly from one point to the next. Other cultures prefer a less direct approach and consider directness impolite and even aggressive. Respect such cultural differences, whether preparing and presenting a speech or listening to someone from another culture give a speech.

SOURCE: Nolan (1999).

present. If it runs overtime, you obviously need to cut something out. If it runs short, you need to enhance the content to lengthen the speech.

A frequently overlooked aspect of timing is the time of day when you will speak. Listeners are more alert around midmorning but tend to become fatigued by midafternoon, so a complex topic may be poorly received later on in the day. If you are required to present complex information in the afternoon, enliven it for your listeners with the inclusion of some information that is easy to pay attention to, like stories or examples or, if appropriate, with effective visual aids.

The timing of a speech also includes how it fits into the sequence of scheduled events. Are you the first, last, or middle speaker? Are you scheduled before, after, or during lunch or dinner? If you are one of the last speakers of the day, you will want to keep your speech as brief as possible. If you allow your speech to interfere with a meal or cause a class to run over, you will lose your audience's attention and goodwill. If you are one of the first speakers on the schedule, be sure you stick to your allotted time out of consideration for those who follow you.

Place

Place, the environment and physical surroundings, includes the arrangement of furnishings and seating for the listeners, audiovisual equipment being used, and any other incidental physical factor that could impact your speech. Experienced public speakers often visit the place where they will speak ahead of time to reduce the possibility of last minute surprises. They check out the location of the speaker's podium, where the listeners are seated, and where they will be seated before and after the speech. Most important, they examine the audio or visual equipment to be sure it will work well during the actual presentation. They examine the lighting in the room to be sure the listeners will be able to see their visual aids while taking notes. When you familiarize yourself with your speaking place, consider doing a practice session in the real environment. As a result, you will encounter fewer problems later, but also feel and appear more confident when the time comes to present the speech.

As you can now see, context and audience analysis, as depicted in Figure 14.3, are essential to public speaking competence. A competent speaker takes the time to adapt to the particular context by analyzing both the listeners and the speaking situation.

Knowledge Link

How can the suggestions described here for analyzing the time and place of a speech be applied to communicating in interpersonal and group contexts?

Audience Competence

A last but significant aspect of public speaking competence is **audience competence,** which involves what you do as a listener whether attending a speech at school, at work, or at a special event. Because the responsibility for competent communication lies with all the participants, not just the speaker, listeners also must take responsibility for the success of the speech-making process.

Take another look at the competence model introduced earlier in Figure 14.1. You will notice that audience members actively participate in the process of public speaking by applying the three basic components of competence. They must be motivated to listen attentively and to receive and tune in to the entire message presented in the speech. They must understand the role and responsibilities of audience members and demonstrate knowledge by constructing meaning out of the entire message and withholding judgment of the speech until the speaker is done. And they must demonstrate listening skills by responding to the speaker and providing verbal and nonverbal feedback.

Audience competence not only enhances the public speaking experience for the speaker but also benefits each audience member. You have an opportunity to learn to be a better speaker yourself by observing what other speakers do well and learning ways to improve your own speeches. By using responding skills effectively, you can seek answers

"Senator, the American people, whom you often mention in your speeches, would like a word with you."

Audience competence involves actively participating in the public speaking process. Some people may think that means visiting the speaker later on in his or her office.

© The New Yorker Collection 1998 J. B. Handelman from cartoonbank.com. All rights reserved.

to questions about the speech topic for your own benefit and for the benefit of other listeners. Furthermore, by providing constructive feedback to the speaker, you can help a classmate improve his or her public speaking competence.

Challenges to Public Speaking Competence

Just as Nicholas did successfully in the opening vignette, you can overcome any fears you may have about public speaking, if you are motivated to do so. But your motivation to prepare and present effective speeches competently can be challenged by communication apprehension and public speaking anxiety. Let's now discuss these two challenges and, most importantly, how you can manage their negative effects.

Communication Apprehension

Communication apprehension is the fear or anxiety an individual experiences as a result of either real or anticipated communication with another person or persons (Richmond & McCroskey, 1995). When it happens to you, like Nicholas, you may experience your hands shaking, sweaty palms, or just a squeamish feeling in the pit of your stomach. The result is a tendency to either avoid communication or suffer from feelings of yet more anxiety when forced to communicate.

Context apprehension refers to whether, as a general rule, you are anxious about communicating in a particular context like interpersonal, small group, or public speaking. For example, many of us are fine talking one on one but experience more anxiety about public speaking. Some researchers believe this apprehension occurs because the communication behaviors of human beings have biological origins, in addition to being learned

(McCroskey & Beatty, 2000). The CloseUp in Chapter 5 explained this communibiological perspective on communication behaviors. According to these researchers, a person is born with a propensity or tendency to be apprehensive and there are significant implications for communication instruction and learning.

There is not sufficient testing as yet to know just how much, if any, of a person's apprehension is biological and how much is learned. However, one research study found that whether it is inborn or not, even people with high levels of apprehension can learn to manage and control it (Ellis, 1995). One of the most problematic forms of context apprehension is public speaking anxiety.

PUBLIC SPEAKING ANXIETY

The most common kind of context-related communication apprehension is public speaking anxiety, popularly referred to as stage fright. **Public speaking anxiety** refers to a person's fear or anxiety associated with a real or anticipated public speaking event. Researchers have studied students' patterns of anxiety about giving speeches and learned the following (Behnke & Sawyer, 1999; Sawyer & Behnke, 1999).

Students, and most people for that matter, demonstrate the highest levels of *physiological* anxiety right at the beginning of a speech. Suddenly, hands shake, legs quiver, and voices quake. Speakers are frequently surprised by these physiological reactions, particularly if they aren't aware of feeling very anxious before the speech. The highest level of *psychological* or mental anxiety occurs during what is called the preperformance period, any time the speaker thinks ahead to giving the speech.

In addition to being aware of when it might occur, it is helpful to know why people have public speaking anxiety in the first place. One cause of anxiety is the psychological threat to your self-esteem, which becomes important when you remember previous negative experiences that happened to you when you spoke in public (Sawyer & Behnke, 1997). Perhaps when you spoke out, someone laughed or failed to take you and your comments seriously. It may have been an incident as inconsequential as making a remark at the dinner table or answering a question incorrectly in an elementary school class. Or it may have been more significant, like presenting a public speech to a large group of influential people and forgetting the most important points you wanted to make. In either case, the lesson was learned: *When I speak publicly, I feel foolish or stupid.*

A second cause of anxiety is identifying with the wrong public speakers as your role models. You watched people speak in public who appeared nervous and made mistakes.

Knowledge Link

Are the symptoms of public speaking anxiety similar to those that people experience in social situations and in interpersonal conversations?

Despite research that says public speaking anxiety is the number one fear of many people, approaching the gallows may be more frightening.

© Tribune Media Services, Inc. All rights reserved. Reprinted with permission.

It may have been someone on television or a speaker presenting a talk at a meeting. You identified personally with those nervous and inept speakers, rather than with someone who speaks with confidence and competence. You said to yourself, "Now that's the kind of speaker I am." The lesson was learned: *When I speak in public, I make mistakes, embarrass myself, and appear inept.*

A third cause of public speaking anxiety is the tendency to hold unrealistic attitudes and expectations about public speaking as a process and about of yourself as a speaker. You may expect some disaster or catastrophic failure to occur when you speak, like blanking out and forgetting everything you want to say. Or you may have an unrealistic desire to be accepted by everyone and to please everybody and have all of the listeners like you. You may think your speech has to be absolutely perfect and flawless in content and delivery. Finally, you may want to feel totally confident and completely calm and in control when you present your speech. All these attitudes and expectations are unrealistic and the lesson you learn is this: I *cannot possibly be a good public speaker and present an effective speech with confidence.*

Table 14.3 summarizes the three causes of public speaking anxiety and suggests some solutions for each cause. See which of the causes you relate to the most, and make note of the suggestions for handling those causes.

TABLE 14.3

••• Public Speaking Anxiety: Causes, Reactions, & Solutions •••

Which of the three causes and reactions to public speaking anxiety is problematic for you? Take a close look at the solutions for handling your negative reactions.

CAUSE & REACTION	POSSIBLE SOLUTIONS
Cause: Previous negative experiences with public speaking. *Your Reaction:* Avoid public speaking so you won't look foolish and stupid.	Try to forget the past and don't allow it to shape the present.
Cause: Identification with the wrong role models. *Your Reaction:* Avoid public speaking because you'll make mistakes and embarrass yourself.	Make a conscious effort to identify with speakers who appear confident and in control. Watch those people and think about yourself as a public speaker who is just like them.
Cause: Four unrealistic attitudes and expectations about public speaking. *Your Reaction:* Avoid public speaking because you can't possibly do it well. 1. Premonition of disaster or catastrophic failure. 2. Desire for total acceptance. 3. Desire for absolute perfection. 4. Desire for total confidence.	Become aware of which unrealistic attitudes affect you as a public speaker. 1. Realize that it is unlikely anything catastrophic will occur. If something does go wrong, it isn't the end of the world. 2. Realize it's impossible for you to please everyone all the time, just as it's impossible for everyone to please you all the time. Be yourself and do the best job you can. 3. Don't expect perfection. Realize that no speech is perfect; then accept your imperfections and learn from mistakes. Don't dwell on what goes wrong. 4. Expect anxiety. Realize that fear is natural and everyone has it. Accept your insecurities, knowing the audience members can't see your fears and are probably more supportive of you than you realize.

Overcoming Challenges to Public Speaking Competence

Now that you understand the challenges of communication apprehension and public speaking anxiety, we can discuss ways to overcome any anxiety you may have. Before you will be able to prepare and present a speech competently, these two challenges must be addressed. Communication researchers and classroom instructors have tested and experimented with different kinds of treatments and discovered that stage fright can be reduced successfully in a variety of ways (Robinson, 1997).

Reducing Public Speaking Anxiety

Public speaking students who engaged in small group activities to address anxiety every week throughout an entire semester decreased their level of communication apprehension significantly (Crump & Dudley, 1996). Regular participation in workshops on reducing anxiety made a difference for another group of students (Hopf, 1995). Viewing videotapes designed to reduce public speaking anxiety helped still other students. Students who viewed videotapes of themselves giving speeches reported a decrease in apprehension and an increase in perceptions of their own communication competence, in work and social settings, but with the largest improvements for the classroom setting (Ayres, Ayres, Baker, & Colby, 1993; Hinton & Kramer, 1998).

As you think about the challenge of reducing any public speaking anxiety you may have, you can choose among three competency-based approaches: systematic desensitization, cognitive modification, and goal setting (Watson, 1990).You may find that you prefer one of these methods over another, or you may benefit from using more than one technique at the same time.

Systematic Desensitization

Systematic desensitization is a process that desensitizes a person's feelings and emotional reactions to public speaking by using positive visualization and encouraging the person to relax when contemplating a particular speaking event. With this approach, the anxious speaker learns to relax while visualizing each step leading up to giving a speech. Here is how systematic desensitization works.

An instructor or a trainer teaches you general methods of relaxation, and then asks you to envision a series of situations that lead up to a feared public speaking event. First, you think about a comfortable, nonthreatening situation such as the day you registered for the public speaking class along with several other courses. Then you visualize increasingly more threatening and anxiety-producing situations. You get the course syllabus, you read about the speaking assignments, you choose a topic for your first speech. As you learn to relax in each situation, the trainer helps you use more advanced visualization techniques, like recalling the situation and trying to see, hear, and feel what it actually would be like. Eventually, you should be able to relax, without feeling an overwhelming amount of anxiety, while thinking about the fear-producing event of presenting a speech.

Systematic desensitization works because you cannot be relaxed and fearful at the same time. By repeatedly visualizing a feared communication event, but relaxing at the same time, you gain control of the fear.

Cognitive Modification

Cognitive modification is a process that changes or modifies unrealistic beliefs about public speaking. This approach is similar to what was referred to as belief restructuring in Chapter 8 for interpersonal communication. In much the same way, cognitive modification enables a public speaker to confront his or her beliefs and fears and question their validity and value. It works as follows.

Start by identifying any unrealistic beliefs and expectations you hold about yourself as a public speaker. Write down any unrealistic or negative thoughts and expectations that come to mind when you think about an upcoming public speaking event, such as "I'm certain something terrible will happen while I'm giving my speech, and there's nothing I can do about it." Then rewrite each thought in a more reasonable and positive way, for example, "It's unlikely anything will go wrong, and by planning and practice I can help avert any problems." Throughout the preperformance period, jot down any negative thoughts and rewrite them positively. Periodically, review the positive thoughts. Some speakers even post their new statements by their computers or the work area where they prepare their speeches. It is important to note that the unrealistic statements are extreme, misleading, and produce high anxiety. In contrast, the revised statements are less extreme, more realistic, and result in a more moderate emotional reaction.

Cognitive modification works because it provides you with a different way of looking at yourself. It derails your negative thinking and replaces it with positive statements about yourself as a public speaker.

Knowledge Link

How is belief restructuring for managing social anxiety similar to or different from cognitive modification for alleviating public speaking anxiety?

Goal Setting

Goal setting is a process for alleviating anxiety that makes use of a structured plan for changing a person's public speaking behaviors. Using this approach, the speaker formulates personal goal statements about public speaking, identifies desirable behaviors and criteria for accomplishing each goal successfully, and then follows the steps necessary to accomplish the goals. Goal setting works like this.

You begin by identifying a general area of improvement for your goals, such as reducing your overall level of communication apprehension. For that general area, you formulate specific goal statements in behavioral terms, such as contribute more frequently and confidently to class discussions, contribute more frequently to small group discussions, and discuss ideas (for speeches) more comfortably with your professor. Next, you write

Virtual reality is now being used for treating a variety of phobias, including public speaking anxiety.

down behaviors and criteria for success for each statement, so you have benchmarks for accomplishing each goal. The success criteria might be make a minimum of one contribution per day to class discussions, offer two comments in each group discussion in which you participate, and discuss your ideas with your professor once a week.

Goal setting works because it provides a tangible framework for accomplishing behavioral change. If you follow the steps to accomplish your goals, change is inevitable; and when you start behaving confidently, you begin to feel more confident.

In addition to these three basic approaches to reducing anxiety, another new technique holds great promise. Virtual reality is now being used to treat public speaking anxiety. The CloseUp on Technology describes this unique approach.

Ethics & Public Speaking

In addition to overcoming challenges, a final crucial aspect of public speaking competence is your ethical responsibilities as a speaker. No one can specifically prescribe these responsibilities for you because ethics are based on each person's individual values. Therefore, no absolute sense of ethics can clearly specify ethical and unethical public speaking behaviors for everyone.

Furthermore, the competing ethics of different cultures can be challenging to you as a public speaker. What you consider ethical may be quite different from what some of your listeners think. You may value openness and candor above all else, whereas audience members think concealing information that may upset others is more ethical. As you use your own values—honesty, integrity, and respect, for example—to make decisions about what to say, you must consider the impact of your decisions on all the members of your audience.

Suppose, for example, you find yourself about to present a speech you think has a very worthy goal, such as giving money to a charitable cause to which you are strongly committed. You learn some information through your research that would hinder accomplishing that goal. Perhaps a large percentage of the contributed funds go to support administrative costs and not to help the needy. Would it be ethical to suppress the information or misrepresent it in your speech? If you value honesty above all else, you would disclose what you know to your audience. If, however, you believe the end sometimes justifies the means, you might think it acceptable to suppress or misrepresent the information. In order to make decisions such as this one, the standards for ethical communication introduced in Chapter 2 can be applied to public speaking. Those standards suggest the following definition for what it means to communicate ethically in the public speaking context: An **ethical public speaker** knows and respects the guidelines for speaking appropriately in the given situation and uses public speaking skills to accomplish his or her goals effectively while considering the effects of the speech on everyone involved.

Based on this definition, and keeping in mind the key variable of culturally influenced values, here are some guidelines ethical public speaking:

- Research your speech carefully and present all relevant information and points of view. Does the information you present portray your topic accurately and truthfully to the audience? Suppressing information or using misleading data or evidence in your speech is unethical.
- Document your sources carefully and give credit where credit is due—recommendations for doing this are covered in Chapter 15. Have you properly acknowledged the sources of information in your speech? It would be unethical to plagiarize the work of anyone else and present it as your own.

CloseUp ON TECHNOLOGY

Virtual Reality & Public Speaking Anxiety

A NEW AND INNOVATIVE APPROACH is available for overcoming phobias—which are persistent, illogical fears of a specific thing or situation. Using technology and computers, virtual reality treats phobias by placing the phobic person in a controlled environment that replicates his or her anxiety-causing situation. This treatment has been used successfully to help people overcome a fear of heights, flying, spiders, driving, and even a problem called agoraphobia, which is a fear of open places that results in being afraid to leave one's house. Now virtual reality assisted therapy is also being used to treat the fear of public speaking.

Researchers at Clark Atlanta University pioneered the treatment of fear of public speaking with visual reality therapy. Undergraduate students were placed in front of a virtual auditorium that gradually filled with virtual people. Simulation of crowd noises included laughter, commentary, and applause. The students' treatment schedule during eight weekly sessions consisted of presenting speeches that were 10 to 15 minutes in length. During the sessions, the students exhibited physical symptoms that matched those that most speakers experience during real public speeches—increased heart rate, lump in the throat, dry mouth, sweaty palms, loss of balance, and weakness in the knees. At the end of the treatment period, most students experienced a significant reduction in all of their anxiety symptoms, and sometime later they reported they were able to speak comfortably in front of large groups of people—real people.

Although virtual reality-assisted therapy is administered through computers, it also employs standard therapeutic techniques. Being immersed in a fear-producing setting has long been considered valuable as a form of exposure therapy, because it helps the phobic person develop a tolerance to the fear. With traditional exposure therapy, the person is either forced to confront the actual frightening physical situation or he or she tries to imagine being in the situation. As a third form of exposure therapy, virtual reality exposure occurs in a virtual setting that is safer, less embarrassing, less costly in some cases than reproducing the real-world situation, and more realistic than merely imagining the danger. An additional advantage of a computer-controlled fear experience is that the person can regulate the level of anxiety and reduce or increase the amount of fear experienced according to his or her personal tolerance level.

Despite these promising results, critics of visual reality therapy say its developers still need to answer some important questions. How well do the positive benefits transfer to the real world, and how long will these benefits last? How much of the real situation needs to be simulated in order for the technique to work—is it necessary to hear, see, and feel the fear-producing event? For example, in the case of spiders, feeling seems to be as important as seeing. And how long does a person have to be exposed to a fear-producing situation in order to become less afraid? Is one 50-minute exposure as beneficial as five 10-minute sessions?

Notwithstanding these questions about its application and use, visual reality therapy holds out hope for a new and effective way to treat an age-old phobia, the fear of public speaking. For those so afflicted, it offers a treatment method that is much like systematic desensitization as discussed in this chapter, but perhaps the virtual approach is even better. Cicero, the Roman orator who suffered from public speaking anxiety, would have been impressed with what computers are now capable of doing for those who are afraid.

SOURCES: Hodges (May-June 1995); Strickland, Hodges, North, & Weghorst. (1997).

- Be honest about who you are, your opinions, and your attitudes. This will help you establish both your credibility and your competence with your listeners. Are you presenting yourself and what you think accurately and truthfully? Misrepresenting your credentials, qualifications, or opinions—or not standing for what you believe—are not ethical behaviors.
- Avoid coercion and manipulating people's emotions and reactions by what you say. Have you presented overly emotional evidence simply to accomplish the goal of your speech? It would be unethical to upset or offend anyone in the audience unnecessarily just to accomplish your goal.

- Most important, consider the consequences and potential impact of your speech. Do your goals infringe on the rights and interests of anyone else? If you encourage your listeners to follow advice that is not in their best interest, that is unethical.

This chapter has introduced you to public speaking as a way of communicating that is valuable to you as a member of a community and society, and to you as an individual. You are now ready to acquire the knowledge essential to preparing and presenting an effective speech. Chapters 15 and 16 cover speech preparation and presentation.

Chapter Summary

Like the other ways of communicating, public speaking is best approached using the model of communication competence. Public speaking is part of the historical tradition of rhetoric, dating back to the early Greeks and Romans who emphasized critical thinking and speaking persuasively and considered public speaking a vital tool for improving society. Public speaking competence continues to serve the public good in society today and yields personal as well as professional benefits for individuals. Public speaking involves a single person or group of people presenting a message to a larger number of people. Two main types of speeches are informative, which communicates something new or a new perspective, and persuasive, which attempts to influence beliefs, attitudes, values, or behaviors. Speeches can be delivered in any one of four ways: impromptu, extemporaneous, manuscript, and memorized. Each type of delivery involves a different amount of preparation time and is appropriate for different speaking situations.

Revisiting the model of competence, the interdependent components of motivation, knowledge, and skills work together to influence whether a speaker is perceived as competent. Public speaking competence also requires speakers to adapt to the context by engaging in audience analysis and audience members to demonstrate listening competence.

Two challenges to motivation are communication apprehension and public speaking anxiety. The four types of apprehension are context, situational, audience, and trait. Public speaking anxiety is the most common kind of context apprehension. People have public speaking anxiety as a result of previous negative experiences, identifying with negative role models, or holding unrealistic attitudes and expectations of themselves as public speakers. This anxiety can be reduced using systematic desensitization, cognitive modification, or goal setting. In addition to overcoming anxiety and learning how to prepare and present a speech, a competent speaker must also assume ethical responsibilities when speaking in public.

Key Terms

rhetoric
sophists
dialectic
critical thinking
public speaking
informative speech
persuasive speech
impromptu speech
extemporaneous speech
manuscript speech
memorized speech
credibility
audience analysis
personal characteristics
psychological characteristics
attitudes
beliefs
values
cultural characteristics
speaking situation
timing
place
audience competence
communication apprehension
context apprehension
public speaking anxiety
systematic desensitization
cognitive modification
goal setting
ethical public speaker

Building Motivation

See Self-Assessment on page 413.

Building Knowledge

1. How can we continue to preserve the values of rhetoric and public speaking originally discussed by the Greeks and Romans in the best interest of our communities and democratic society?
2. Some scholars believe the ability to speak well enhances the ability to think critically. Do you agree or not? Explain and support your answer with examples from your own experience.
3. Does every citizen in a free and democratic society have the responsibility to develop public speaking competence in order to participate actively and contribute to community life? Explain your answer.
4. Of the four methods of delivery—impromptu, extemporaneous, manuscript, or memorized—which will be most useful to you and why?
5. Of the three sets of factors involved in audience analysis (personal, psychological, and cultural), which plays the biggest part in how an audience reacts to a speech? Explain your answer.
6. According to some researchers, communication apprehension is a trait some people are born with. Do you agree? Support your choice.
7. Discuss the three basic approaches to reducing public speaking anxiety. Which would work best for you, and why?
8. What does being an ethical public speaker mean to you personally? Discuss the most important attributes of ethics in public speaking. Provide examples of an ethical and an unethical public speaker, drawn from your own experience or what you have observed in the media and press.

Building Skills

Individual Exercises

1. To develop your ability to think critically, try questioning your own beliefs by expressing those beliefs out loud. Express some strong belief you hold, explain it with as much supporting data as possible, and then evaluate it. Keep sharpening your ideas by sharpening your ability to express them.
2. Practice audience analysis using this role-playing technique. Assume the role of another person (the course instructor, your employer, or another student). Write down several observations about and reactions to your possible speech topic, as if you were looking at it through the other person's eyes.
3. To better understand values and audience analysis, take the *Values and Lifestyles* questionnaire on the internet at **http://future.sri.com/vals/valsindex.html**.
4. Using the *InfoTrac College Edition,* develop a better understanding of how professionals reduce public speaking anxiety by reading a 1997 article by Fritz Kreisler in *Behavioral Health Treatment, 2* (4), entitled "Use peer power in treatment for public-speaking phobia."
5. Try employing systematic desensitization to change how you feel about giving a speech. Put yourself in a relaxing environment, perhaps at home listening to soothing music. Lie down or sit in a comfortable chair and close your eyes. Envision yourself in a series of situations that coincide with the steps you will take to prepare your next speech. Completely relax while thinking about each step in the speech preparation process. First relax your toes, then your feet, then ankles, and move up through your body to the top of your head. Relax as you envision each step, and then see if you can envision yourself feeling relaxed when presenting a speech.
6. Try using cognitive modification to change your unrealistic beliefs about public speaking. Think ahead to your next assigned speech and write down any beliefs and expectations you can think of about either the speaking event or yourself as a public speaker. Number each belief and then rewrite each as a more positive and reasonable expectation. Type up the new beliefs and print them out using a fairly large font on your computer. Make several copies and post them in conspicuous places for several days to help change your

thinking. Crumple up and throw away the piece of paper with your old thoughts after you have revised them into new beliefs.

7. Use goal setting to handle your anxiety by developing your skills. Choose an aspect of public speaking that is problematic for you and write it at the top of a pad of paper. For that general area, list several specific behavioral goal statements, which, if achieved, would change how you behave relative to the problem area. Next to each goal statement, write behaviors and criteria for success for that goal.

Group Exercises

1. With a group of several other students, attend a formal speech on or off campus. Answer the following questions about the speech: What benefits accrued as a result of the speech and to whom? What was the speaker's purpose in speaking? What type of delivery was used and was it effective for that speech?
2. At the conclusion of a lecture in your public speaking class, divide into small groups. Discuss how competent you were as audience members and strategies for becoming better at audience competence.
3. Form groups of 5–6 students. Engage in audience analysis of your public speaking class. Analyze your classmates as listeners and the classroom as a public speaking situation.
4. Form groups of 3–4 students. Have each student in the group select a preferred anxiety-reducing approach from the three described in this chapter and write out a personal action plan for remedying his or public speaking anxiety. Share and critique each student's action plan.

References

Allen, M., Berkowitz, S., Hunt, S., & Louden, A. (1999). A meta-analysis of the impact of forensics and communication education on critical thinking. *Communication Education, 48,* 18–30.

Ayres, J., Ayres, F., Baker, A., & Colby, N. (1993). Two empirical tests of a videotape designed to reduce public speaking anxiety. *Journal of Applied Communication Research, 21,* 132–147.

Behnke, R. R., & Sawyer, C. R. (1999). Milestones of anticipatory public speaking anxiety. *Communication Education, 48,* 165–172.

Bruskin/Goldring Research. (1993, February). *America's number 1 fear: Public speaking* (p. 4).

Carrell, L. J., & Menzel, K. E. (1997). The impact of preparation and motivation on learning performance. *Communication Education, 46,* 262–272.

Chesebro, J. (1996). Communication vistas: Futures from a 1996 perspective. *Spectra, 32* (9), 2.

Crump, C. A., & Dudley, J. A. (1996). Methods for dealing with communication apprehension in higher education: Speech instruction via use of small group modalities. (ERIC Document Reproductive Service No. ED 390 100.)

Davis, M. J., & Dickmeyer, S. G. (1993, November). Critical thinking pedagogy: Opportunities to take limited preparation beyond the realm of competition. Paper presented at the 79th annual meeting of the National Communication Association, Miami, FL.

Ellis, K. (1995). Apprehension, self-perceived competency, and teacher immediacy in the laboratory-supported public speaking course: Trends and relationships. *Communication Education, 44,* 64–78.

Graduates are not prepared to work in business. (1997, June). *Association Trends,* p. 4.

Hinton, J. S., & Kramer, M. W. (1998). The impact of self-directed videotape feedback on students' self-reported levels of communication competence and apprehension. *Communication Education, 47,* 151–161.

Hodges, M. (1995, May-June). Facing real fears in virtual worlds. *Technology Review, 98,* 16–18.

Hopf, T. (1995). Does self-help material work? Testing a manual designed to help trainers construct public speaking apprehension reduction workshops. *Communication Research Reports, 21,* 34–38.

Johannesen, R. L. (1996). *Ethics in human communication* (4th ed.). Prospect Heights, IL: Waveland.

Langham, B. (1994). Speaking with style. *Successful Meetings, 43* (7), 94–96.

MacIntyre, P .S., & MacDonald, J. R. (1998). Public speaking anxiety: Perceived competence and audience congeniality. *Communication Education, 47,* 359–365.

Maslow, A. H. (1954). A theory of human motivation. *Psychological Review, 50,* 381.

McCroskey, J. C., & Beatty, M. J. (2000). The communibiological perspective: Implications for communication in instruction. *Communication Education, 49* (1), 1–6.

Morreale, S., & Bovee, C. (1997). *Excellence in public speaking.* Fort Worth, TX: Harcourt, Brace, Jovanovich.

Morreale, S., Osborn, M., & Pearson, J. (in press). *Why communication is important: An annotated bibliography.* Journal of the Association for Communication Administration. Annandale, VA: Association of Communication Administration.

National Opinion Research Center. (2000). General social survey 1972–1998. Retrieved February 5, 2000 from the World Wide Web: http://www.norc.uchicago.edu/online/emerge.pdf.

Nolan, R. W. (1999). *Communication and adapting across cultures: Living and working in the global village.* Westport, CT: Bergin & Garvey.

Plutsky, S. (1996). Faculty perceptions of students' business communication needs. *Communication Quarterly, 59,* 69–74.

Richmond, V. P., & McCroskey, J. C. (1995). *Communication: Apprehension, avoidance, and effectiveness* (4th ed). Scottsdale, AZ: Gorsuch Scarisbrick.

Robinson, T. E. (1997). Communication apprehension and the basic public speaking course: A national survey of in-class treatment techniques. *Communication Education, 46,* 188–197.

Rubin, R. B., Rubin, A. M., & Jordan, F. F. (1997). Effects of instruction on communication apprehension and communication competence. *Communication Education, 46,* 104–114.

Sawyer, C. R., & Behnke, R. R. (1997). Communication apprehension and implicit memories of public speaking state anxiety. *Communication Education, 45,* 211–222.

Sawyer, C. R., & Behnke, R. R. (1999). State anxiety patterns for public speaking and the behavior inhibition system. *Communication Reports, 12* (1), 33–41.

St. John, S. (1995). Get your act together. *Presentations, 9*(8), 26–33.

Strickland, D., Hodges, L., North, M., & Weghorst, S. (1997). Overcoming phobias by virtual exposure. *Communications of the ACM, 40,* 34–40.

U.S. Bureau of the Census (2000). Population projections. Retrieved January 3, 2000 from the World Wide Web: http://www.census.gov/population/www/projections/natproj.html.

Watson, A. K. (1990). Helping developmental students overcome communication apprehension. *Journal of Developmental Education, 14,* 10–17.

Winsor, J. L., Curtis, D. B., & Stephens, R. D. (1997). National preferences in business and communication education. *Journal of the Association for Communication Administration, 3,* 170–179.

Building Motivation

Self-Assessment: Rate each of the following public speaking situations, indicating the typical level of competence you feel you can or do achieve. Use the scale of 1–4 provided, with 1 minimal competence and 4 high competence. Rate one component (motivation) through all the situations, and then rate the next component (knowledge), and then the third (skills).

Motivation	Knowledge	Skills
1 = Distracted, disinterested, or no motivation to be competent	**1** = Completely inexperienced and ignorant about how to behave	**1** = Completely incapable of behaving competently in the situation
2 = Somewhat nervous, but some motivation to be competent	**2** = Minimal experience and knowledge about how to behave	**2** = Barely capable of behaving minimally competently
3 = Somewhat confident and motivated to be competent	**3** = Somewhat experienced and knowledgeable about how to behave	**3** = Fairly capable of behaving competently
4 = Highly confident and motivated to be competent	**4** = Highly knowledgeable about all aspects of how to behave	**4** = Highly capable of behaving competently

Public Speaking Situation:	Motivation	Knowledge	Skills
1. Presenting a speech to a group of people from cultures very different from your own			
2. Talking to a group of senior citizens to convince them to support your favorite cause			
3. Presenting the toast to the bride and groom at a wedding			
4. Presenting a group project to your class at school and serving as the main speaker for the group			
5. Presenting a project summary at your new job to all of upper management			
6. Presenting the student speech at your college graduation			
7. Giving an impromptu speech at a political meeting to gather support for a cause you really believe in			
8. Interviewing for a job and presenting a speech about your background and why you are right for the job			
TOTAL SCORES			

Interpreting Your Scores: For each context level, total your ratings for each column (motivation, knowledge, skills). You should end up with three scores. The possible range of scores per column is 8–32. A score of 8–14 indicates you are minimizing your competence and have significant room for improvement in this area of competence. A score of 15–28 means you think you are average at speaking in public. A score of 29–32 indicates a perceived high level of competence.

CHAPTER 15

Learning Objectives

After studying this chapter, you should be able to:

1. Understand the nature and importance of speech preparation competence
2. Choose, narrow, and adapt your speech topic.
3. Develop a speech purpose and write a thesis statement.
4. Gather relevant and credible support materials to accomplish your speech purpose.
5. Choose an organizational pattern for your support materials.
6. Understand the basics of outlining and prepare a working, formal, and presentational outline.
7. Develop an introduction, body, transitions, and conclusion for your speech.
8. Use various types of visual aids, including computerized presentation tools.
9. Understand the major challenges to speech preparation and be able to overcome them.

Understanding Speech Preparation

Althea approached speech preparation the way many students do, facing a blank computer screen the night before her speech. She had chosen a topic and done her research for a speech presentation for her marketing class Tuesday morning. But when she got home from school at 8 o'clock Monday night, she hadn't yet organized her support materials or prepared an outline for her speech. She found herself with a mountain of information that lacked organization and focus. By midnight, she had sifted through her research material and achieved some semblance of a speech outline but had no energy left to practice the presentation. So she went to bed, planning to arrive early enough at school to practice with her friend, Richard, who was probably well prepared for his presentation.

Richard was ready to present his speech. When the assignments were given out, he took the time to get acquainted with other students in the class before choosing his speech topic. He was surprised to learn that most of his classmates were interested in giving their in-class speeches on marketing topics, but they were not well informed about the need for on-the-job public speaking skills. Based on that bit of information, Richard chose public speaking in a business setting as his speech topic. The purpose of his speech was to motivate other business majors like himself to think about the benefits of continuing to improve their public speaking skills beyond graduation. He observed how people at his current job presented various reports and briefings, and he interviewed his manager in person and the developer of a Web site about public speaking in the work setting using email. He located several good sources of information on the internet and in the campus library. He had prepared an outline for presenting the speech and developed and practiced a computerized presentation as a visual aid.

You can probably guess what happened in the marketing class on Tuesday morning. Not only did Richard get a better grade than Althea, his speech was better received and he felt more confident presenting it. He presented his speech effectively, because he understood the importance of speech preparation for competent public speaking. ●●●

Researchers have provided evidence of how important it is to prepare carefully before you speak in public. One research study, involving 119 public speaking students, investigated the relationship between preparation and public speaking performance (Menzel & Carrell, 1994). The quality of the students' speech performances, as indicated by their grades, was directly proportional to total preparation time, including the amount of time spent conducting research, time spent preparing a visual aid, the number of times the speech was rehearsed before an audience, and the amount of time spent rehearsing silently and out loud. Students who spent more time on all these preparation activities got better grades on their speeches than students who spent less time. The lesson is clear: Speech preparation is a crucial part of public speaking competence.

Preparing With Competence

Competent speech preparation involves a series of steps similar to those recommended by Cicero, the great Roman orator. Cicero outlined five canons for public speaking: invention, arrangement, style, memory, and delivery. Invention and arrangement are the classical equivalent to the speech preparation steps described in this chapter. Invention calls for discovering or creatively *inventing* what you will say—the content of your speech. Arrangement focuses on how you organize or arrange what you will say. Cicero's canons of style, memory, and delivery are the classical equivalent to speech presentation (see Chapter 16).

A Competence Model for Preparing a Speech

A contemporary application of Cicero's notions of invention and arrangement is presented in the model in Figure 15.1, which outlines the essential steps to preparing a speech with competence. This model visually highlights the knowledge component and speech preparation steps necessary to public speaking competence, as introduced in Chapter 14.

Knowledge Link

Are all speech preparation steps equally essential to competence? Are any not quite as essential?

●●●

1. Based on audience analysis, choose and narrow a topic for your speech or adapt an assigned topic to the particular audience.

2. Develop a clear and specific purpose for your topic and determine the best way to present that purpose to the audience in the form of a thesis statement, the central idea of the speech.

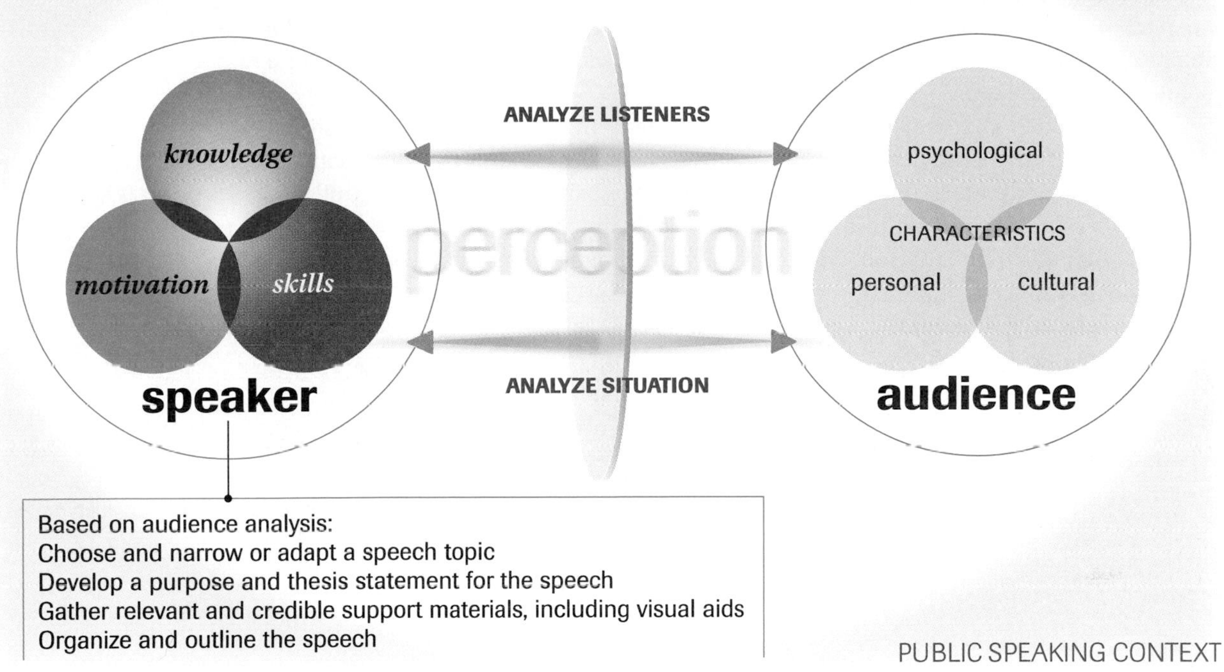

FIGURE 15.1
A Competence Model for Speech Preparation

Competence in preparing a speech results from the speaker choosing and narrowing or adapting a topic for the speech based on careful audience analysis of the listeners and the situation; determining a purpose for the speech and a thesis statement that summarizes that purpose; gathering highly credible support materials and evidence to accomplish the speech purpose, including effective visual aids; and organizing the information gathered in outline form.

3. Gather relevant support materials from credible sources of information to accomplish the speech purpose and link those support materials reasonably and clearly to your central idea.
4. Organize the information in an outline to focus your development and writing of the speech and to use when you present the speech extemporaneously to the audience.
5. If appropriate in the particular context, develop visual aids to enhance your verbal presentation.

Choosing & Narrowing a Topic

The first preparation step, essential to public speaking competence, is choosing and narrowing a speech topic. If your instructor has assigned you a topic, your job is to adapt and narrow it for the particular audience. Reflect on everything you have learned about your listeners through audience analysis—all of their personal, psychological, and cultural characteristics. The following guidelines will help you accomplish this step competently.

FINDING A GOOD TOPIC

It is important to understand the difference between a general subject area and a speech topic. A **subject area** is a general area of knowledge such as the American civil war, college life, communication, contact sports, or organic chemistry. A **topic** is a specific facet or aspect of a subject area. For example, the subject area of Richard's speech was public speaking. Based on analyzing his audience's needs, he chose presenting speeches in a business setting as a topic.

The best place to start is with a subject area you find interesting or know something about. Unfortunately, many students in public speaking classes struggle with choosing topics because they don't think their own experiences and interests are significant enough to talk about to a public audience, which is definitely not the case (Monaghan, 1986). A good topic is one that appeals to you; if you're interested in it, you'll prepare and present a better speech.

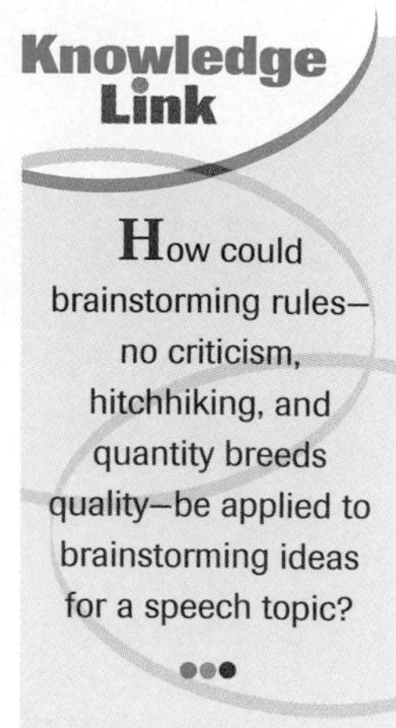

Explore your own experiences and interests for a possible topic by using an approach that marketing experts call *thinking outside the box* or personal brainstorming (Rubel, 1995). Think imaginatively about your own interests and write down everything that comes to mind. Then examine your list for a subject area of interest and a topic within it. You could also use the techniques presented in Chapter 12 and meet with a group of your classmates to brainstorm possible topics.

Besides searching your own mind and experiences for a topic, browse through newspapers, magazines, and books at the local bookstore or library for ideas. Or try using the internet to find a topic. Go to one of the several Web sites on the internet that includes an *idea generator* (**http://www.lib.odu.edu/research/idea/ideagenerator.shtml**). You use an idea generator to search main categories or subject areas such as arts & humanities, business & public administration, sports, recreation & leisure (see Figure 15.2). For each category, the idea generator provides an extensive list of possible speech topics.

Here's another way to come up with a topic: Think about what you have already learned about the audience's attitudes, beliefs, and values. The student speech at the end of this chapter, "Very Fake Badges—Very Real Guns," provides an example of a speaker using this approach (Benton, 1995). The award-winning student speech is about the use of private police officers in today's society, and how these officers are neither sufficiently trained nor subjected to the same rigorous scrutiny as public police officers. The speaker alerts his listeners to the seriousness of this problem by appealing to their personal values of safety and security and their common need for a reliable police force.

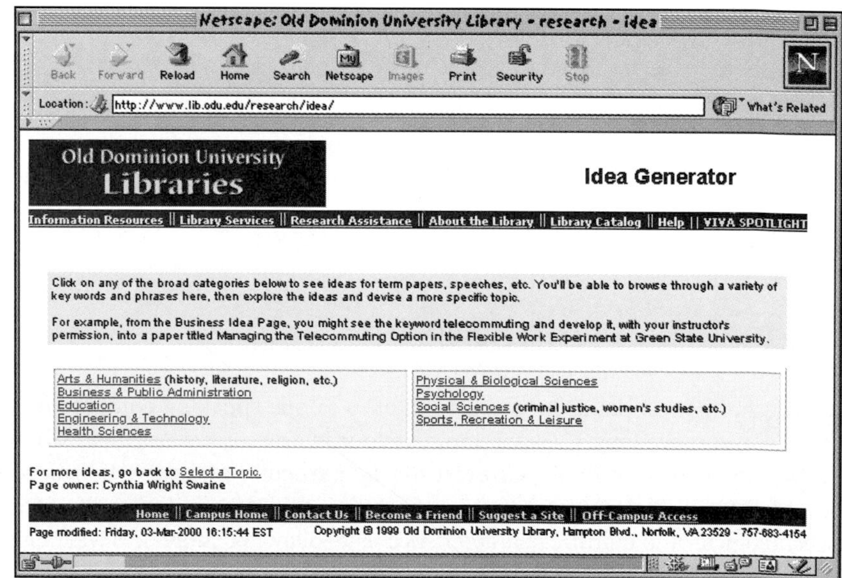

FIGURE 15.2
Finding a Subject and Topic Using the Internet

A Web site such as this one with an idea generator will help you find a subject area and then a speech topic.

ADAPTING & NARROWING THE TOPIC

Remember that whatever topic you choose, it must be adapted and narrowed so it's appropriate for the audience and speaking situation. First, decide on an approach to the topic that will appeal to the particular audience. Then narrow and limit what you'll cover in the speech. A common mistake is preparing a speech that contains too much information. If your speech is focused and narrow, your listeners will find it easier to understand and follow. And narrowing the topic simplifies the preparation process. A speech topic that is too broad is difficult and unmanageable to research.

Narrow a topic by getting more and more specific about what you will cover until it reaches a manageable level. Think about what the audience really needs or wants to know about it. Also consider the level of explanation and background description that will be necessary for them to understand it. Benton's speech illustrates this narrowing process. He may have started with the subject area of crime, narrowed his focus to public safety, then to police protection in society, and finally to the topic of the dangers of using private police.

Developing Purpose & Thesis

Once you're satisfied with your speech topic, step 2 is to clarify what you hope to accomplish by speaking. All successful speeches are built around a purpose and contain a thesis statement. Without them your listeners will not be able to follow what you say (Leeds, 1995).

General Purpose

Speeches can have any one of several **general purposes** or goals as discussed in Chapter 14: to inform the listeners and extend their understanding of something; to persuade them to change an attitude, belief, value, or behavior; or to entertain or commemorate a special event. The two main types we explore, based on their general purpose, are speeches to inform (covered in detail in Chapter 17) and speeches to persuade (covered in Chapter 18). Bond Benton's speech about private police has the general purpose to persuade.

Specific Purpose

Every speech also has its own **specific purpose** or goal, a statement of the response the speaker would like from the audience. The specific purpose, written as a single infinitive statement, summarizes what you want the audience to know, do, or feel as a result of your speech. Benton's speech provides this example:

> To persuade the audience that the use of private police is dangerous and offer solutions to relieve the problem.

As this example illustrates, a good specific purpose is clear, realistic, and audience focused. Because it's clear, it can guide your work throughout the entire preparation process, letting you know exactly what to research and what to include in your speech. By being realistic, it limits the goal of your speech to what can be accomplished in the amount of time allowed. By being audience focused, it describes the response you would like from the audience.

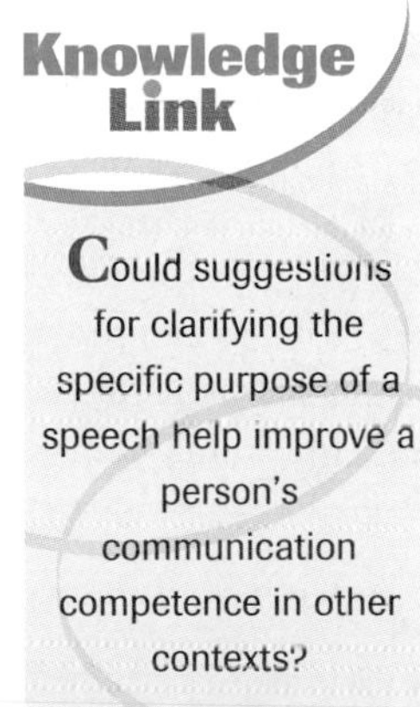

Thesis Statement

Building on the specific purpose, the next step to competence is to formulate a thesis statement, which is said out loud to the audience when you actually deliver the speech. The **thesis statement** in a sentence or two outlines the specific elements that support your speech goal. A good thesis tells the audience exactly what you want them to know,

TABLE 15.1

Understanding Subject, Topic, Purpose, & Thesis Statement

In the opening vignette, Richard used this process to narrow and focus what he would cover in his speech.

SPEECH DETAIL	EXPLANATION
Subject area	Public speaking
Narrowed topic	Public speaking in business settings
General purpose	To persuade
Specific purpose	To motivate the audience to continue to develop and improve their public speaking skills beyond graduation
Thesis statement	Today, through reinforcing the value of public speaking in the business setting and providing specific resources for additional development, I hope to persuade you to continue to improve your public speaking skills beyond this class.

understand, and remember when your speech is done. Write it as a simple, declarative sentence or two that restates the speech purpose and states the main points which support that purpose. Although you may formulate a thesis statement early in the speech development process, you'll likely revise and reword it as you research your topic.

Richard's speech, described in the chapter-opening vignette, offers the following thesis statement :

> Today, through reinforcing the value if public speaking in the business setting and providing specific resources for additional development, I hope to persuade you to continue to improve your public speaking skills beyond this class.

See Table 15.1 for an example of subject area, topic, general purpose, specific purpose, and thesis statement from Richard's speech.

Gathering Support Materials

After you choose a topic and develop a purpose and thesis statement, step 3 of the competence model involves finding information to support and accomplish the speech purpose. To help you with this essential step to competence, we now discuss various sources of information, including personal observations and experiences, informational interviews, the internet, and the library.

PERSONAL OBSERVATIONS & EXPERIENCES

Information gathered by observing others and descriptions of your own experiences lend support and credence to factual information and help you relate better to your listeners. In the opening vignette, Richard observed people at his job giving briefings and reports and he shared those observations in his speech. To come up with a story or personal experience for your speech, think about your topic and whether you have done something, known someone, or witnessed something that relates to it. Tell the audience that story and because it's personal to you, you'll tell it well.

If you decide to use observations or personal experiences, the competence model calls for doing so in an ethical manner. That means presenting this form of support material truthfully. Any story represents your viewpoint and *only* your viewpoint, so acknowledge that fact to your listeners and do not draw generalizations from your individual experiences. Presenting a biased description could damage your credibility. It is also unethical to distort the telling of an event to serve your own purpose or to tell someone else's story without giving him or her credit for it.

INFORMATIONAL INTERVIEWS

Interviewing is another effective way to gather information for your speech from an expert or from someone whose life experience relates to your topic. An informational interview can help you gather testimony and convincing evidence. For example, Richard interviewed his manager to get her viewpoints on the importance of public speaking in a work setting.

An interview with an expert or a person with experience relative to your topic can yield great information for your speech.

Before you decide to use an interview to gather information, determine whether this method will provide the kind of evidence you need. Do you have sufficient factual information but need the opinion of an expert or the testimony of someone experienced in your topic? If so, can you arrange an interview with a person who would be a credible source? After you've identified someone to interview, contact that interviewee and offer a choice of several ways for the interview to occur—in person, by phone, or by email—and then choose a mutually satisfactory time. Definitely consider the possibility of an electronic interview. You could locate an expert on your speech topic using the internet and submit your interview questions to him or her by email, which Richard did with the developer of a Web site on public speaking in business (Jones & Polak, 1993).

Preparation is the key to a successful interview, so plan carefully what you'll ask and how you'll ask it (Stewart, 1991; Yaskin, 1990). Develop interview questions ahead of time, rank-ordering them from the information you need the most to that which you need the least. Include open-ended questions that the interviewee cannot answer with a simple yes or no, and prepare several follow-up questions for each open-ended question. For instance, Richard might have asked his manager to describe ways she had seen other workers use public speaking skills effectively at work. A follow-up question could be: "Tell me how that speaker used various verbal and nonverbal skills to present so effectively."

Since most interviews involve interpersonal communication, what skills outlined in Chapter 10 would enhance your ability to create meaning in the interviewing context?

During the interview itself, be prepared to skip questions if the discussion moves in an unexpected direction. Above all, be flexible, polite, and respectful of the interviewee's time. Only tape-record the interview if you have permission to do so. Review your notes immediately after the interview looking for themes or major ideas that support your thesis. Is there a meaningful quotation that will enliven your speech? If so, be sure to contact the interviewee and ask for permission to use it.

In the following passage from Benton's speech, he quotes from a phone interview with a regular police officer who works in a city that employs private police to patrol a college campus. This quote from the phone interview is used to explain why big cities are hiring private police:

> The reason actions like this have been necessitated is simple: Cities right now are experiencing a dramatic rise in crime, while in turn they are receiving less money to run their police forces. And although private police represent a big risk, they are very cheap.

USING THE INTERNET

In addition to personal experiences and interviewing, the internet can be either a great resource for researching a speech or a frustrating waste of time. Used effectively, the internet provides avenues for researching your speech that include electronic mail (email) and listservs, newsgroups and chat rooms, and the World Wide Web.

Email is useful for communicating directly with people who can help you research your speech. People may go to great lengths to help others who are looking for information. If you locate an email listserv of a group of people interested in the subject area of your speech, you can send an inquiry about your topic to many people at once. By joining an email discussion list, not only can you send messages to everyone on it, you will get any email messages that other participants send. Also you can participate in a newsgroup or an electronic chat room that discusses your subject area or speech topic and ask questions in real time of people who are potential experts on your topic. The addresses of expert individuals, email lists, and chat rooms are often available from associations or organizations interested in a subject area. Two sites on the internet itself, Deja.Com (**http://www.deja.com**) and Reference.com (**http://www.reference.com**), provide search tools to help locate electronic discussion groups. Meta-List (**http://www.meta-list.net/**) is a search engine you can use to search more than 200,000 public email lists and newsletters by keyword or category.

The World Wide Web on the internet provides access to an overwhelming number of Web sites, any of which may contain useful information for your speech. The Web is seen as such a viable tool for preparing speeches that a debate program now incorporates its use in a forensic event entitled "electronic extemporaneous speaking" (Voth, 1997). Students on both sides of a debate topic are given access to the internet for 30 minutes to help construct a 7-minute speech. The event is said to have a positive impact on students' research, organizational, critical thinking, and speaking skills.

When accessing the World Wide Web, there are many search engines to choose from, which are not all alike and won't conduct the same kind of search for you (Berkman, 2000). You can choose among hierarchical indexes, standard search engines, alternative search engines, and meta search engines.

A hierarchical index, such as Yahoo (**http://www.yahoo.com**), is extremely selective. People trained to categorize information examine Web sites and put them in categories and subcategories. When you do a search, it is much more likely that what you find will be relevant to your topic.

Standard search engines, AltaVista (**http:www.altavistacom**), Excite (**http://www.excite.com**), Go Network (**http://infoseek.go.com**), and Hotbot (**http://www.hotboth.com**), use software "spiders" that act as personal mini-search engines that search the entire Web and calculate mathematically how relevant the pages are to your search terms. They return a large rank-ordered list of sites that represent the best match to what you request. For example, the first listing will most likely have a 97% to 100% probability of providing relevant information. As you dig deeper into the list, the percentages decrease. Check the first 25 to 30 Web sites returned. Try to avoid commercial sites (*.com) that often try to sell a particular product instead of just providing information. Sites linked to universities and colleges (*.edu) are good places to look for scholarly research. Nonprofit organizations (*.org) can be an additional source of information because they have access to large volumes of research data in a particular field. Don't use standard engines at all when you have a very broad subject, because of the sheer number of sites the search will yield. Instead, use a hierarchical index to find more relevant, well-catalogued sites.

Alternative search engines take different individual approaches to searching the Web. For example, Northern Light (http://www.northernlight.com) ranks Web sites as a standard engine does, but displays the results in categories and groups rather than as a single listing, which can be quite helpful. With the alternative engine Ask Jeeves (http:www.askjeeves.com), you don't enter keywords. Rather, you type a question in plain English such as "Is there life on Mars?" Jeeves has recorded millions of questions that users ask and supplies you Web sites to answer that particular question.

Search engines that search other engines are called meta engines. The Invisible Web (http://www.invisibleweb.com) offers links to more highly targeted search sources instead of just hundreds or thousands of Web pages. The meta engine Dogpile (http://www.dogpile.com) searches the best known as well as lesser known search engines. SearchEdu is a meta engine that indexes and searches over 20 million Web sites in the educational domain, despite the commercial identifier in its address (http://www.searchedu.com). SearchGov is a meta engine for governmental sites (http://www.searchgov.com).

To maximize results, use any engine's Help icon for tips on conducting your search. If you need general help in using the internet, a Web site called Internet Navigator (http://www.lib.utah.edu/navigator/) provides an introduction to the internet and how to use it most productively.

Richard in the opening vignette used the internet to search for information on his speech topic. He first entered the phrase "public speaking" using the search engine AltaVista, as illustrated in Figure 5.3. The result was 2, 252,898 possible hits or sites that he could visit to research his topic. Obviously, his topic was too broad but he knew how to narrow it while still using AltaVista. He narrowed the search by using the Boolean operand plus (+) and entering "public speaking + career success + business environment" and came up with 738,653 hits. By using the plus sign (+) between the words, Richard had asked the search engine to use the phrases together to create a combined search and thus narrow and focus it. By contrast, when an asterik (*) is used to separate phrases (a wildcard), the search is conducted looking for all pages with any material pertaining to the phrases separately.

Richard didn't have time to research all 738,000 hits returned via his Boolean search. However,

FIGURE 15.3
Using the Internet to Gather Support Materials

Using a search engine like AltaVista, enter the right combination of search terms using a Boolean operand like a plus (+) sign to locate Web sites of relevance to your speech topic. Sometimes, it takes trying different combinations of key terms before you come up with the right combination for your topic.

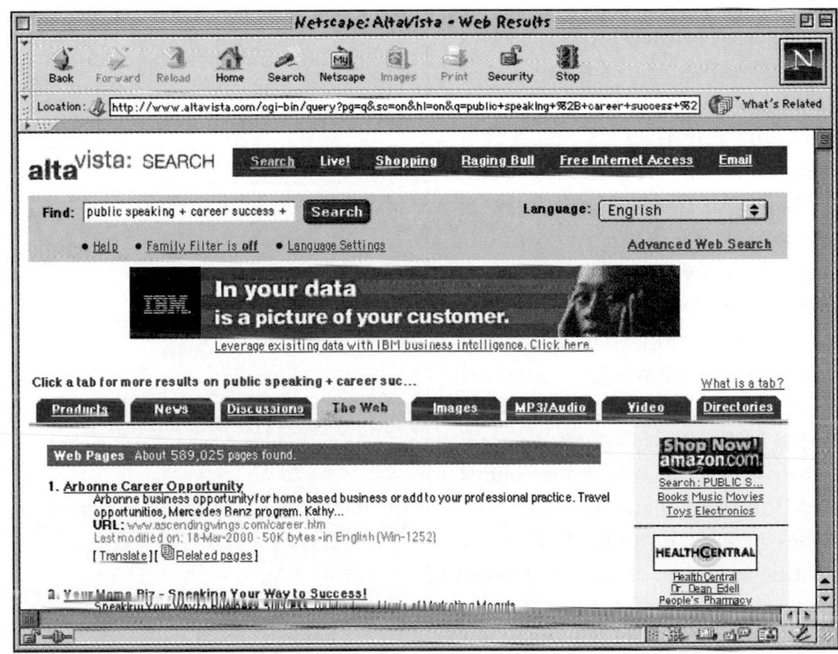

after reviewing 30 potential Web sites, he found several that related to his topic of public speaking in businesses. Let's look at what Richard found:

- He visited the Web site of Kareem Abdul-Jabbar, a famous basketball player, whose excellent public speaking skills helped him emerge as an international spokesperson on the importance of education. Richard could use the story of how Kareem uses public speaking to promote a cause he believes in and encourage his listeners to continue to grow as public speakers (http://www.kareem.com/speaker.htm).
- He went to the Web site of an organization called Leading-Edge Management Trainers that provides public speaking training online for businesspeople. The site had just been updated and the credentials of its developers were impressive. So Richard sent an email message to Peter Martin, one of the developers and owners of the company, and then conducted an online interview with him (http://www.public-speaking-training.co.uk/).
- Richard also found a comprehensive Web site, SeminarMaster.com, that could help students continue to improve their public speaking skills in various business settings after graduation (http://www.selfgrowth.com/public.html).

Richard not only found interesting information on the internet, he also made sure the Web sites were credible sources. Later in this chapter, we talk in some detail about how to evaluate Web sites critically, an essential skill if you choose to use the internet to research your speech.

FIGURE 15.4
Using the Database *InfoTrac College Edition*

InfoTrac College Edition indexes many academic articles and is easy to search using key terms.

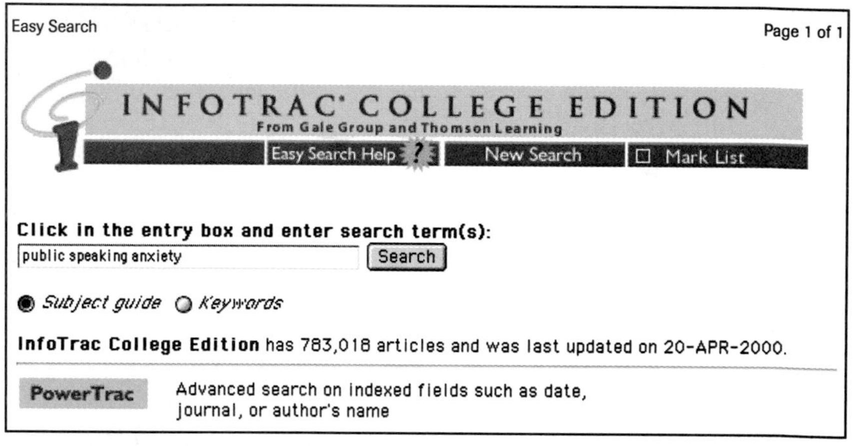

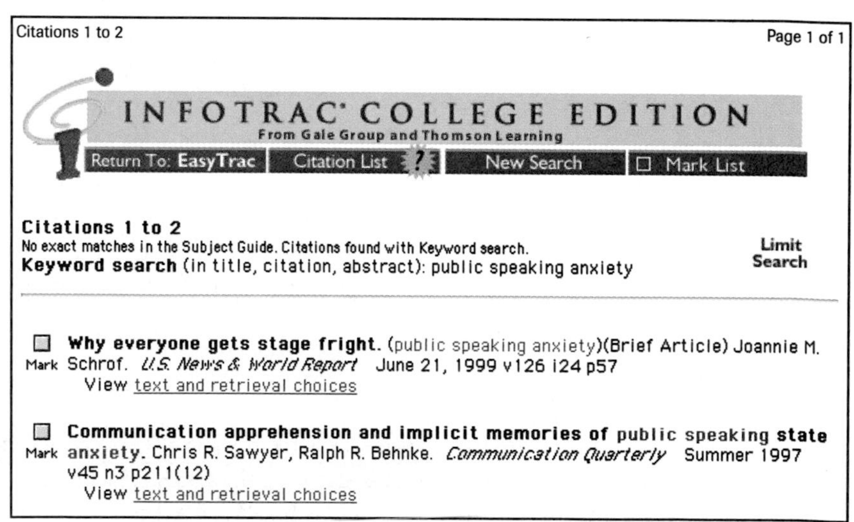

USING THE LIBRARY

In addition to the internet, many other sources of information in the library on your campus can be accessed in printed form as well as in thousands of computerized databases.

A **computerized database** is a collection of information that contains abstracts and full-text versions of documents and publications or indexes to information located elsewhere. Such online databases are housed in the library computer system or accessed using the internet. An example of these is *InfoTrac College Edition,* shown in Figure 15.4, an excellent computerized database that indexes articles in journals in most academic fields. Some databases also are available and can be accessed on CD-ROMs. The National Communication Association, for instance, places CommSearch in most school libraries, which indexes all the major academic journals in the communication field.

Your school or local library has these computerized databases, as well as reference books, newspapers and periodicals, and government documents.

Reference Books

The library houses many diverse reference works such as almanacs, biographies, dictionaries, directories, encyclopedias, statistical reports, and collections of quotations—most of which are available in print, online, and on CD-ROM.

Almanacs are compilations of statistics and other facts about nations, politics, the labor force, natural phenomena, and so on. The *Statistical Abstract of the United States,* an annual publication of the Department of Commerce, contains information about life, work, and government in the United States. Best known almanacs are the *Information Please Almanac,* the *World Almanac and Book of Facts,* and the *Universal Almanac.*

If you want information about a famous person, living or dead, you could check a biographical reference book. *Who's Who in America* and *Who's Who in the World* are available in print and on a CD-ROM called the *Complete Marquis Who's Who Plus.* Two indexes to biographical books, the *Biography Index* and *Current Biography,* will direct you to short biographies or whole books about famous people.

The multitude of different sources of information in the library will supply a wealth of support materials for your speech.

Dictionaries not only help clarify unfamiliar terminology, you can sometimes use the definition of a word in the speech itself. The 20-volume *Oxford English Dictionary* is available in print and on CD-ROM, and specialized dictionaries are available for technical and professional fields.

Directories contain information about various professions, special interest groups, and organizations. Listed organizations supply information for researching your speech and often the name of a person to contact about it. For example, you could use the *Encyclopedia of Associations* to find an organization whose members are experts on your speech topic and then contact that organization for a referral.

Encyclopedias can serve as good starting points for research because they cross-reference subjects and list additional readings and names of experts in a field. Single-volume encyclopedias such as *The Columbia Encyclopedia* and *The Random House Encyclopedia* provide quick but brief introductions to subject areas; useful multiple-volume encyclopedias are *The New Encyclopedia Britannica* and the *Encyclopedia Americana.* Specialized encyclopedias cover particular subject areas like art, philosophy, religion, technology, and ethnic studies. Two of the best known electronic encyclopedias available on CD-ROM are *Microsoft Encarta* and *Compton's Multimedia Encyclopedia.*

Books of quotations, organized by subject, topic, or source, could provide a clever or meaningful quote for your speech. Most popular are *Bartlett's Familiar Quotations* and the *Oxford Dictionary of Quotations.* Retail bookstores carry lesser known collections such as *The 637 Best Things Anybody Ever Said* by Robert Byrne and *The Guinness Book of Poisonous Quotes* by Colin Jarman.

Newspapers & Periodicals

Newspapers and periodicals are good sources of current information about politics, business, media, crime, fashion, weather and the many events that shape and influence society. Past issues of these publications can provide historical perspectives on topics and events. This vast source of information includes daily, weekly, and other newspapers, as well as regularly published periodicals. Periodicals include popular magazines, trade journals, business magazines, and academic journals.

Indexes to newspapers and periodicals can be searched by topic or keyword to find an article on practically any speech topic. The popular *New York Times Index* can be searched in print volumes and online to locate current or historical articles that can then be read in full text on microfilm or online. *The Reader's Guide to Periodical Literature* indexes many popular magazines such as *People* or *Newsweek.* There are also specialized indexes in subject areas like communication, education, or psychology. If you're interested in a historical and academic perspective on your topic, the *Cumulative Contents Index* provides indexing to more than 3,000 academic journals dating back to the 19th century. Most popular indexes are available in printed form, online, or on CD-ROM; or you can go directly to print newspapers and periodicals or their electronic version on the World Wide Web.

Government Documents

Most U.S. government departments and offices regularly collect and publish information and data to keep the public informed. The subjects covered in governmental publications are endless ranging from college enrollment, to the unemployment rate, to census data, population projections, and economic forecasts. Like other large sources of information, indexes and catalogs are available in the library to simplify the process of searching for the right government document.

All of this governmental information is in the public domain, which means it can be easily accessed on the internet by visiting the Web site for the governmental department like the Department of Education, Justice, or Labor. Also, the Government Printing Office publishes the *Monthly Catalog of United States Government Publications,* available online at **http://www.gpo.gov**, or a print version can be ordered from that Web site. At the Web site of the U.S. Senate (**http://www.senate.gov**) and the House of Representatives (**http://www.house.gov**), you'll find information on bills being debated and passed in Congress that may provide valuable information for your speech.

In addition to his internet search, Richard visited the campus library to find support materials for his speech. Heeding the advice of his helpful school librarian, he used the computerized database on the CD-ROM CommSearch to research academic communication journals and found several articles that talked about how important public speaking skills are to professional success. In the *Encyclopedia of Associations* he learned about the National Speakers Association, an organization that provides information about experts in a variety of industries and disciplines who, in addition to their jobs in business, also reach out to audiences in their respective fields as trainers, consultants, and public speakers. He also located a quotation by Lee Iacocca, then president of the Chrysler Corporation, who spoke out often about the value of public speaking in organizations and the importance of communication to managerial success.

Knowledge Link

Which library source is potentially the best for support materials, and which is the best starting point for researching a speech?

Organizing & Outlining

The fourth step in competent preparation is to organize the support materials and develop an outline for your speech, the step the Greek rhetorician Cicero called "arrangement." The importance of this step to public speaking competence was emphasized by the Roman rhetorician Quintilian who said, "In speaking, however abundant the matter may be, it will merely form a confused heap unless arrangement be employed to reduce it to order and to give it connection and a firmness of structure" (Butler, 1950).

To give your speech connection and structure, we next consider various ways to organize your support materials. Then we discuss how you can use outlines to both prepare and present your speech.

ORGANIZATIONAL PATTERNS

A variety of organizational patterns can be used to organize the body of your speech. The most common patterns are topical and chronological, which are very effective for informative speeches. *Topical* speech organization arranges information according to subtopics or subcategories of the speech subject. The subtopics do not have to occur in any particular order. *Chronological* speech organization, in contrast, presents information based on time, and it is important to order the subtopics in the sequence they occurred. Other patterns, such as problem-solution and a technique called the motivated sequence, lend themselves more to persuasive speeches. Table 15.2 provides a preview of the various organizational patterns we discuss in detail in Chapters 17 and 18. For now, we discuss a basic approach to organizing and outlining that will work for any speech.

TABLE 15.2

••• Types of Organizational Patterns •••

An organizational pattern is used to structure the main part or body of your speech. Certain patterns lend themselves more easily to informative speeches and others to persuasion, but this is not an absolute rule. Your job is to choose the right organizational pattern to accomplish the purpose of your speech.

Organizing the Informative Speech

1. *Topic:* Divides information about the topic into subtopics or subcategories
2. *Chronology:* Describes changes or developments in any situation or circumstance, historical or sequential
3. *Space:* Organizes information based on the positioning of objects in physical space or relationships among locations.
4. *Comparison and contrast:* Describes or explains how a subject is similar to or different from something else.
5. *Cause and effect:* Examines why something happens or happened and the results

Organizing the Persuasive Speech

1. *Problem-solution:* Identifies a problem and then proposes a solution to solve it.
2. *Motivated sequence:* Moves through a sequence of five steps designed to motivate and persuade listeners psychologically
3. *Claim-warrant-data:* Moves audience from accepting data that's presented, through a warrant that links the data to the speaker's claim.
4. *Refuting the opponent:* Dismantles the opponent's argument to indicate the superiority of the speaker's argument
5. *Comparing alternatives:* Examines two or more alternatives, and then makes an appeal for the speaker's preferred choice

BASICS OF OUTLINING

Most outlines look much like the basic structure for a speech presented in Figure 15.5. They contain an introduction, a body, and a conclusion. This approach to organizing speeches dates back to when the Greek orators Corax and Tisias taught citizens how to organize arguments in their own defense for presentation in court. That centuries-old model contained a prologue, an argument or proof, and an epilogue, which parallels the introduction, body, and conclusion approach still used today. Remember that the organizational pattern you choose is used to structure the *body* of your speech outline and not the introduction and conclusion.

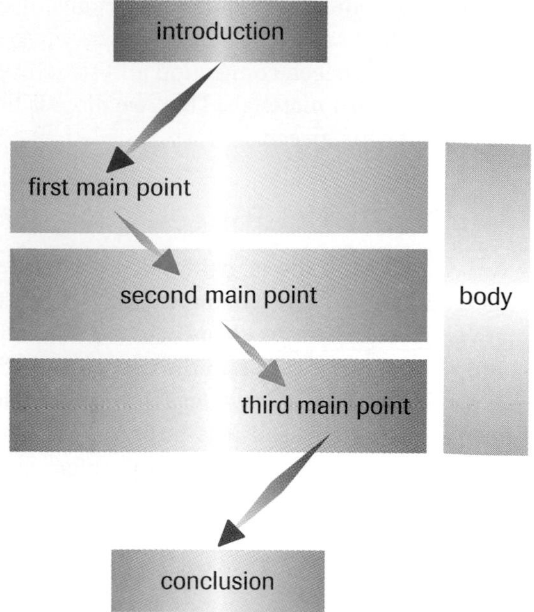

FIGURE 15.5
Basic Structure for a Speech Outline

When you organize a speech, fit your ideas into a structure for a speech outline that contains an introduction, a body, and a conclusion.

Based on the simple structure of introduction, body, and conclusion, the outline itself should resemble the **standard outline format** presented in Figure 15.6. This format makes use of an alphanumeric system with a consistent pattern of numbers and letters to indicate subordination of ideas. Indented headings and subheadings indicate how the points in the outline relate to each other, with main points to the extreme left and subpoints indented in a consistent manner throughout the outline. Here's a simple example of how this alphanumeric system works:

I. First main point (Roman numeral)
  A. First subpoint (capital letter)
    1. Support material (standard number)
      a. Support material (lowercase letter)
      b. Support material (lowercase letter)
    2. Support material (standard number)
  B. Second subpoint (capital letter)
II. Second main point (Roman numeral)
  A. First subpoint (capital letter)
  B. Second subpoint (capital letter)

Here are a few suggestions to help you develop your outline. Always have at least two main points labeled by a Roman numeral in any speech. And for each main point, have at least two subpoints labeled by a capital letter. So if you have "I" you always have "II"; if you have "A," you always have "B," and so on. Also, the main parts of the speech—the introduction, body, and conclusion—are not identified with Roman numerals. Examine the standard outline format in Figure 15.6 for further reinforcement.

TYPES OF OUTLINES

As you develop your speech and get ready to present it, you'll likely make use of three different types of outlines. All three make use of the basic outlining format: a working outline, a formal outline, and a presentational outline.

A **working outline** contains most of the detailed information from your research efforts that you arrange and rearrange as you plan your speech. It acts as a foundation for organizing and reorganizing your support materials and ideas into main points. This outline is, in essence, a rough draft of your speech. You'll change it often as you experiment with different ways of organizing the information you have gathered together, and then it

FIGURE 15.6
Standard Outline Format

All speeches can be organized using a standard outline format such as this one that contains all of the components essential to an effective speech.

Standard Outline Format

Speech Title .... Indicates the speech topic (piques curiosity)
General Purpose .... Type of speech—to inform, to persuade, or to entertain
Specific Purpose .... Statement of the response the speaker would like from the audience

INTRODUCTION

I. Attention-getting or lead-in device .... Motivates histeners to pay attention

II. Establish Credibility

III. Thesis statement .... Restates in a sentence or two the speech purpose and the main points supporting that purpose

IV. Preview of main points ..... Alerts listeners to what to expect

BODY .... Supports central claim by presenting a series of main points and supporting material

I. First main point .... Key idea that proves claim and supports thesis statement

- A. First subpoint
  1. Support material
  2. Support material
- B. Second subpoint
  1. Support material
  2. Support material

(A–B) . . Supports main point

TRANSITION .... Word, phrase, or sentence that demonstrates how the main points relate to each other

II. Second main point .... Key idea that proves claim and supports thesis statement

- A. First subpoint
  1. Support material
  2. Support material
- B. Second subpoint
  1. Support material
  2. Support material

(A–B) . . Supports main point

TRANSITION .... Word, phrase, or sentence that demonstrates how the main points relate to each other

CONCLUSION .... Signals to listeners speech is ending and reminds them of the thesis statement or central idea

I. Review of main points ...... Summarizes speech meaning and purpose through review of content

II. Restatement of thesis ...... Restates the speech purpose and refers back to the introduction

III. Closing device or attention-getter .... Leaves listeners with a memorable idea and message

Introduction

Quote from Kareem Abdul-Jabbar's Web site

- http://www.kareem.com/speaker.htm

Body

Importance of public speaking skills related to business

- Studies on how important public speaking skills are to professional success
  - Association Trends article
  - Journal article
- Opinion of my manager

How to improve skills after graduation

- Advice from email interview with Web site developer, Peter Martin
- The National Speakers Association
- Advice from SeminarMaster.com Web site
  - http://www.selfgrowth.com/public.html
- My opinion based on observing others at work

Conclusion

- Inspiring quotation about public speaking by Lee Iacocca
  - speeches of Lee Iacocca by M. Seeger, p.11

FIGURE 15.7 Richard's Working Outline

Richard's working outline contains the support materials he gathered from the internet, the library, and from his own experience and an interview at work.

will serve as the base on which you create a more formal outline. In Figure 15.7, Richard's working outline for his speech shows how he began the process of organizing his support materials.

A **formal outline** contains all of the information from the final version of your working outline, organized and presented using the alphanumeric system in Figure 15.6 for labeling main points and subpoints. Use this outline to examine your main points visually, to check whether you have enough but not too many subpoints under each main point, and to review the logic of how your ideas are arranged and relate to one another. Orderliness, neatness, and logic are essential, and often professors require this outline to include appropriate citations for the sources of information used in the speech.

Richard's formal outline is presented in Figure 15.8. Make particular note of how Richard quickly captures his audience's attention with a quote from a popular public

FIGURE 15.8
Richard's Formal Outline

This formal outline for Richard's speech on public speaking in business settings evolved from his working outline.

SUCCESS SPEECH

Speech Title: Speaking Your Way to Success in Business
General Purpose: To persuade
Specific Purpose: I want to motivate my audience to continue to develop and improve their public speaking skills beyond graduation.

Introduction

I. *Attention Getter:* Many people know Kareem Abdul-Jabbar as one of the world's greatest basketball players. But did you know Kareem Abdul-Jabbar is also an international spokesperson? Kareem has developed a rewarding second career, by being able, in his own words "to convey knowledge that people may not be aware of" through public presentations.

II. *Establish Credibility:* Kareem is a good example of what I have learned through research; continuing to develop and improve your public speaking skills beyond graduation is important because public speaking skills are crucial to professional success.

III. *Thesis Statement and Preview of Main Points:* Today, through reinforcing the value of public speaking in the business setting and providing specific resources for additional development, I hope to persuade you to continue to improve your public speaking skills beyond this class.

Body

I. Numerous national studies and surveys have identified public speaking skills as crucial to a person's professional success in life.
   A. Report of top executives from Fortune 500 companies
      1. Newly hired graduates lack essential communication skills.
      2. Graduates need communication skills, such as public speaking (Graduates, 1997).
   B. National survey of over 1000 human resource managers
      1. The most important factors in helping college graduates get jobs are basic oral and written communication skills.
      2. Top factors influencing job performance are public speaking and listening skills (Winsor, Curtis, & Stephens, 1997).
   C. Statement from my manager on the value of public speaking skills on the job (Richard's manager, personal communication, January 23, 2000.

Transition: Now that we have seen how important public speaking is in the business world, I'd like to share some ideas about how to improve your public speaking skills beyond graduation.

II. There are a variety of opportunities for improving your public speaking skills once you leave college and begin or continue gainful employment.
   A. Email interview with Peter Martin
      1. Developer of the Web site, Public Speaking Training for Business Men and Women.
      2. Suggestions for continued growth as a speaker (P. Martin, personal communication, January 21, 2000).

B. The National Speakers Association: Represents individuals in a variety of industries and disciplines who, in addition to their jobs in business, reach out to audiences in their respective fields as trainers, consultants, and public speakers.

C. SeminarMaster.com
   1. A comprehensive Web site.
   2. Provides links to 68 sites about improving public speaking skills in business (http://www.selfgrowth.com/public.html).

D. Personal advice
   1. Observation of colleagues improving speaking skills through practice.
   2. Colleagues who improved public speaking skills were more successful.

Conclusion

I. *Review:* Now we clearly see how beneficial public speaking skills are to professional success in life and how many opportunities are available to continue to grow as a public speaker well beyond the confines of this classroom.

II. *Restatement of Thesis and Reference Back to Introduction:* Continuing to improve your public speaking skills—just as Kareem Abdul-Jabarr did—is to your personal advantage in business and industry.

III. *Closing Device/Attention Getter:* As Lee Iacocca, the legendary president of Chrysler Corporation once said: "Communication has been my most valuable management tool." Iacocca firmly believes that you can have brilliant ideas, but if you can't get them across, your ideas won't get you anywhere.

References

Abdul-Jabbar, K. (February, 2000). Kareem Abdul-Jabbar [5 pages]. Retrieved January 16, 2000 from the World Wide Web: http://www.kareem.com/speaker.htm.

Graduates are not prepared to work in business. (1997, June). *Association Trends,* 4.

Martin, P. (April 10, 1998). Public Speaking Training for Business Men and Women: Leading-edge Management Trainers [5 pages]. Retrieved January 15, 2000 from the World Wide Web: http://www.public-speaking-training.co.uk.

National Speakers Association (1999). In T. E. Sheets (Ed.), *Encyclopedia of associations* (35th ed.) (p.1126). Farmington Hills, MI: The Gale Group.

Seeger, M. (1994). *Speeches of Lee Iacocca.* Detroit: Wayne State University Press.

Wheeler, W. (1999). SeminarMaster.com, Inc. [8 pages]. Retrieved January 15, 2000 from the World Wide Web: http://www.selfgrowth.com/public.html.

Winsor, J. L., Curtis, D. B., & Stephens, R. D. (1997). National preferences in business and communication education. *Journal of the Association of Communication Administration, 3,* 170–179.

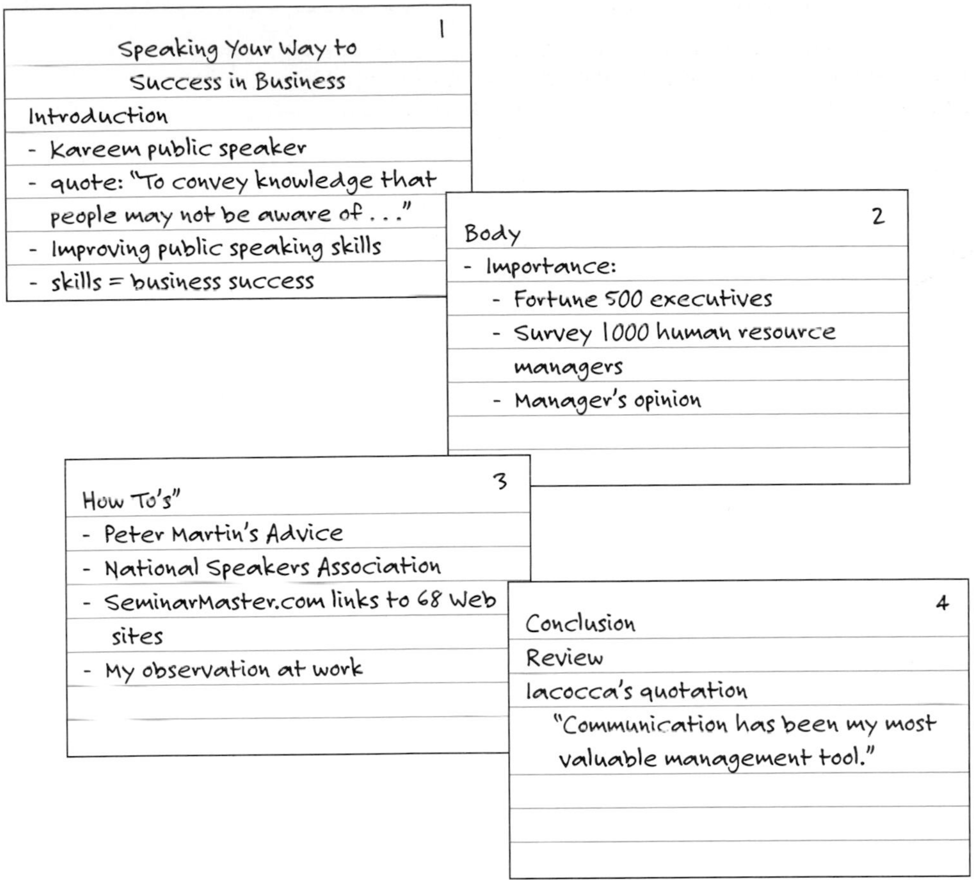

1

Speaking Your Way to
Success in Business

Introduction
- Kareem public speaker
- quote: "To convey knowledge that people may not be aware of . . ."
- Improving public speaking skills
- skills = business success

2

Body
- Importance:
  - Fortune 500 executives
  - Survey 1000 human resource managers
  - Manager's opinion

3

How To's"
- Peter Martin's Advice
- National Speakers Association
- SeminarMaster.com links to 68 Web sites
- My observation at work

4

Conclusion
Review
Iacocca's quotation
"Communication has been my most valuable management tool."

FIGURE 15.9
Richard's Presentational Outline

Richard's outline for giving his speech is written on 3" × 5" cards and contains only the keywords necessary to keep him on track and remember what to say. If this outline contains too much information, you end up referencing it too much and losing the spontaneity essential to extemporaneous speaking.

figure and then establishes his credibility by referencing his own extensive research on his speech topic.

The speaking or **presentational outline** is what you use when you give your speech. It contains only enough information to remind you of what to say at a glance. You prepare it from the formal outline, selecting out just enough details to remind you of what to say. This could take the form of a brief **keyword outline** on a single sheet of paper, or you could put notes on one side of a 3" × 5" card. Either way, including too much information won't allow you to see points at a glance and may cause you to lose your place in the speech. That said, avoid becoming note dependent—meaning that you refer to your notes too often and lose contact with the audience when giving the speech. A presentational outline for Richard's speech is provided in Figure 15.9.

As these three types of outlines confirm, most speeches do have three main parts: an introduction, body, and conclusion—with main points and subpoints supporting each section. We discuss these three main parts of a speech next.

INTRODUCTION

The **introduction** sets the tone for the speech and establishes your credibility as a speaker and your sources of information. The main functions of the introduction are to capture your listeners' attention, establish speaker and source credibility, present your main claim and say why it's important, and preview what the speech will be about.

An attention-getting device for the introduction could be a startling statement, a question, a quotation, a personal experience, a story, or a reference or compliment about the audience or speaking occasion. In Richard's speech he used a quotation from Kareem Abdul-Jabbar as an attention getter. In Benton's speech about private police officers, the speaker starts out with the following short story:

> What's a guy to do? You steal a car, assault two minors, carry an automatic submachine gun, and get arrested on charges of cocaine possession. What can you do for an encore? Well, if you're John Padilla of Long Island, New York, you get hired by the city as a privately employed police officer.

The thesis statement, the central idea of the speech, follows the attention-getting device in the introduction. In addition to stating the single most important idea of the speech, a good thesis makes a statement about why the speech is important to the audience. Benton sums up his thesis by asking a simple question in the introduction: "Should *our* public safety be sold to the lowest bidder?"

After you capture the listeners' attention, establish credibility, and present the thesis, provide a *preview* of the content of the speech. Its purpose is to indicate what your listeners should anticipate and be listening for. Sometimes the preview specifically states the main points of the speech that are to follow; in other speeches this is not a good idea. If your speech is designed to build to a suspenseful conclusion or if you first want to impress a hostile audience with your evidence, you may not want to mention your main points in the preview. Notice how cleverly Benton uses language in his preview:

> . . . we will begin by taking aim at the problem of private policing by looking at the system's inherent harms and how those harms have become so widespread. We'll then try to arrest a few solutions at both the governmental, but most importantly, at the personal level, as well.

Some speakers will try anything to get the audience's attention!

Reprinted by special permission of Cowles Syndicate, Inc.

THE NEIGHBORHOOD

First, get your audience's attention.

BODY OF THE SPEECH

The **body of the speech** supports your central claim through the presentation of a series of main points. The **main points** are key ideas that, when taken together, prove the claim and support the thesis statement. As you develop a working outline for your speech, identify the main points and decide on the best way to organize them to accomplish the purpose of the speech.

An effective speech contains at least two main points but no more than five, because listeners can retain only a limited amount of information at one time. All main points should be worded in a parallel manner and contain approximately the same amount of information and number of subpoints.

Within the body of the speech, the main points are connected using **transitions**—words, phrases, or sentences—that demonstrate how the points relate to each other. Transitions are also used to connect the introduction to the body of the speech and the body to the conclusion.

Transitions let listeners know you're ending one idea and they preview what's coming next. They also can serve as an internal summary telling the audience what you've covered so far. A transition could be something as simple as saying: "Next, I'd like to describe . . ." or "Having examined the problem of . . . , let's consider a solution. . . ." Here are several examples of transitions from Benton's speech:

- *From the introduction to the body of the speech:* "To better understand this dilemma, we will begin by . . ."
- *From main point 1 to main point 2:* "At this point, we have observed some of the harms inherent in private policing. . . . We can now go about looking at some pragmatic solutions to this difficult dilemma."
- *From the body to the conclusion:* "Today we have examined the problem of private policing. . . ."

CONCLUSION

The **conclusion** lets the listeners know your speech is ending and reminds them of your central idea. An effective conclusion brings a sense of finality to your speech and emphasizes the significance of your message. Its main functions are to review the content of the speech and summarize its meaning and purpose, refer back to the introduction and reinforce the thesis, and leave the audience with a final attention getting-message. Just as in the introduction, the closing device can be a question, a short story, a quotation, or an inspirational appeal.

In closing his speech, Richard called on his classmates to visit a Web site to learn more about continuing to improve their public speaking skills and he used a quotation as a closing device. Here is the conclusion from Benton's speech with each section identified by its function:

- *Review of the content of the speech:* Today we have examined the problem of private policing, by first examining how these officers are unequipped for their roles as police and how this problem has become so widespread in society. We then examined some simple and pragmatic solutions to this problem at both the societal and, finally, at the personal level.
- *Reinforcement of thesis:* Thomas Jefferson once stated that one corrupt officer of the law is more deplorable than a thousand thieves.
- *Final message and call to action:* If we as individuals and as a society don't take action against the problems that private policing has created, we stand on the verge of proving this old adage true.

There are pitfalls to avoid while preparing and presenting a conclusion. Try not to start your conclusion with a phrase like "Now, in conclusion . . ." or "To wrap up . . ." Instead, begin your concluding story or comments, and the audience will clearly understand you are ending the speech. Avoid presenting new information in the conclusion because the conclusion should end the speech and not expand it, and don't apologize or make excuses for anything you said. When you've finished the conclusion, just stop talking and avoid comments like "Well, I guess that's all I have to say." Finally, if you plan to take questions, pause after the conclusion and then ask if anybody has questions or comments.

Candidates for public office face challenges just like you as they craft conclusions for their speeches.

DOONESBURY © G. B. Trudeau. Reprinted with permission of UNIVERSAL PRESS SYNDICATE.

Using Visual Aids

After you've organized your support materials in outline form, the final step in competent speech preparation is to develop visual aids. Scholars who study persuasive communication have confirmed the effectiveness of visual images (Messaris, 1997). They have learned that people may forget texts and lists, but they will recall visual images. As we have all seen too many times, when the Federal Aviation Agency wants to illustrate how a plane crash occurred, they know how to make extensive use of visual images with computerized replications of the disaster.

Visual aids assist in illustrating or supporting the content of a speech and add interest and excitement to it. They are useful when you need to clarify a difficult concept, present a complex idea, or demonstrate a process the audience would have difficulty understanding.

Types of Aids

Your choice of a visual aid is only limited by your imagination and creativity, and how much time you are willing to spend preparing it. If you decide to use a visual aid, types to choose from include objects and models, diagrams and drawings, pictures, photographs, maps, charts and graphs, and tables and lists.

Objects & Models

Objects are useful visual aids when you want to show your listeners what something looks like or how it works. A baseball cap could be used in a speech about the record for hitting home runs. A set of gardening tools would be helpful if you're explaining aspects of horticulture. If you use an object of any kind, be sure it's large enough for all audience members to see, but small enough so you can conceal it until the point in your speech when it becomes relevant. To avoid distracting the audience from what you're saying, only show the object when you're actually talking about it and try not to pass it around during the speech.

In cases when the object you would like to use is too large and cumbersome to bring in or too small for the listeners to see clearly, you can show your audience a model rather than the object itself. Architects, for example, provide models of buildings when they present their ideas to clients. If you want to talk about the solar system and how planets relate to one another, a scaled-down model using plastic balls would make a good visual aid.

Knowledge Link

Which types of visual aids could help a group leader define and analyze a problem, identify criteria for solving it, and generate and evaluate solutions.?

Diagrams & Drawings

If you prefer not to create a model, you can use a diagram or a drawing to explain how something looks or operates. These types of aids are particularly useful for explaining steps in a process or for simplifying and clarifying relationships. If you want to explain how a car engine works, a diagram will help the listeners follow your explanation. If a builder wants to show a client the façade of a building, a drawing would work well. Diagrams and drawings help listeners understand ideas that words alone can't adequately describe, but they must be clear and accurate.

Pictures, Photographs, & Maps

If your speech would benefit from a realistic depiction of a person, a place, or an object, a picture or a photograph is helpful. The realism of a picture or photo can bring an idea or a concept to life more effectively than a diagram or drawing. For example, a photograph of the face of a young child would humanize a request to contribute to a charity for children in developing countries. A picture or photograph needs to be large enough to be seen by everyone, and it should be cropped or framed to eliminate any distracting details.

When you want to pinpoint a location or highlight a geographical area, you can use a map as a visual aid. Maps also can help you talk about concentrations of people or industries, weather patterns, landmarks, transportation routes, or phenomena such as voter behaviors or crime patterns. If your speech is about a historical period, a map of what the world or area looked like at that time makes an intriguing visual aid. Benton's speech would have been enhanced by the use of a map of the United States pinpointing the locations where these private officers are used most extensively.

Charts & Graphs

When you're planning to present statistics or a series of numbers to support a point in your speech, you need a visual aid that will help your listeners easily grasp the meaning of the figures. Putting statistics into a chart or a graph clarifies the relationships among the

Would noodles for brains be a good speech aid?

CALVIN AND HOBBES © Watterson. Reprinted with permission of UNIVERSAL PRESS.

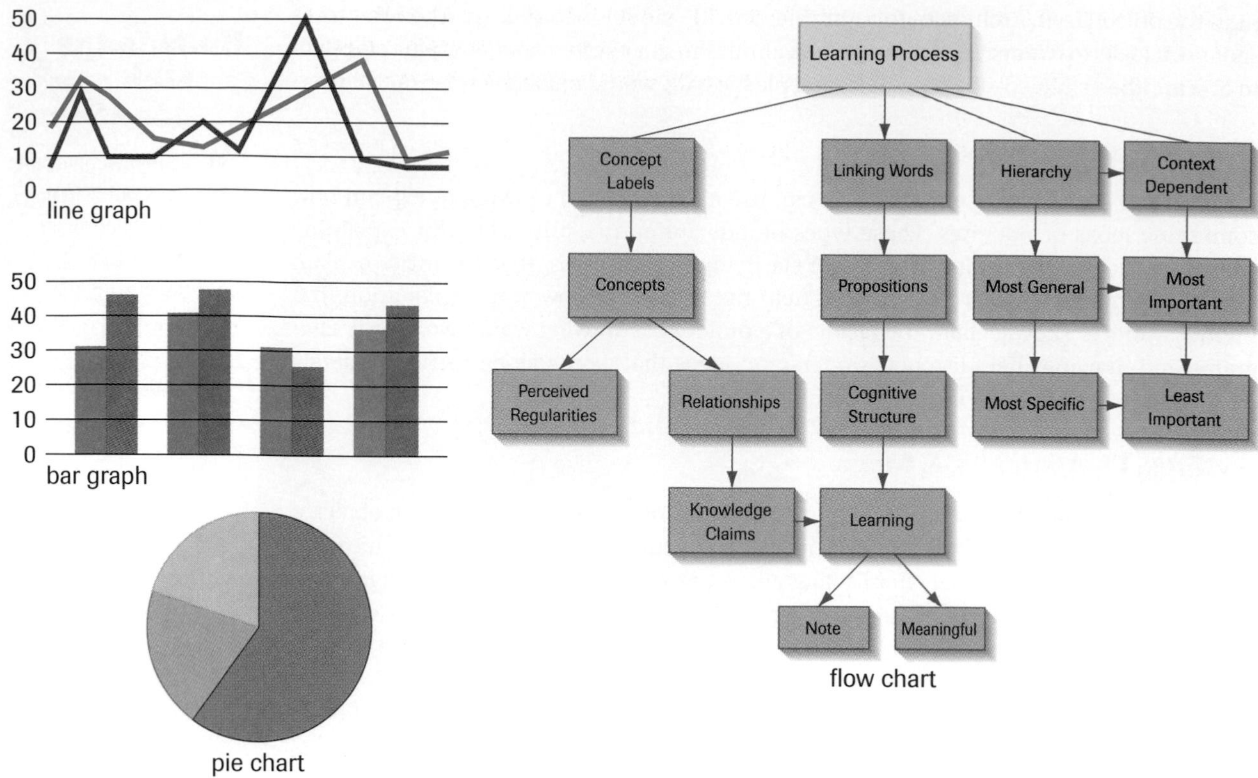

FIGURE 15.10
Types of Charts and Graphs

Using charts and graphs as visual aids helps clarify relationships among numbers and explain trends or patterns that you mention in your speech.

numbers and reveals any trends or patterns. Among the most frequently used charts and graphs are line graphs, bar graphs, pie charts, and flow charts (see Figure 15.10).

A line graph is used to show changes over time or the relationship of two or more sets of numbers. Because line graphs are simple to read, you can show the patterns of change in more than one series of numbers without confusing the audience. A bar graph portrays numbers as rectangular bars, making a series of numbers even easier to read and understand. You can use a bar graph to compare two or three sets of numbers or to show trends over time. When you want to portray numbers as parts of a whole, use a pie chart. Each slice of the pie represents one part of the whole. Most of the time, it's best to put the largest slice of the pie at 12 o'clock and arrange the other slices clockwise in descending order of size. A flow chart is effective for illustrating a sequence of steps. A symbol or a geometric shape represents each step on the chart, so the listeners can trace a path through the sequence.

Tables & Lists

When you want to organize, summarize, and present detailed information, use a table, an all-text visual aid in which numbers or words are arranged in a grid of columns and rows. Articles in academic journals often present the results of research studies in table form.

By using short phrases for headings and minimizing text entries, you can include a lot of data in a small space. In a speech, you can use color in a table to focus your audience's attention on specific information. But avoid confusing the audience with too much color or too much information and detail.

Like tables, lists are all-text visual aids that can communicate a lot of information in a simple way. You can use lists to communicate to the audience at a glance which items are most important, by arranging the items in ascending or descending order. If the items on your list are of equal importance, arrange them in the order that you prefer to talk about them. Lists are most effective if you keep them short and to the point. The types of visual aids just discussed are typical of what could be presented in list form, but you would want to determine the most logical order for them.

METHODS OF PRESENTATION

Once you've chosen the type of visual aid to use, decide on the method you'll use to present it. You can choose between two methods: unprojected and projected aids. **Unprojected aids** don't require the use of electricity to present them. **Projected aids** make use of electricity and include computer-assisted aids.

Unprojected Aids

Unprojected visual aids—the chalkboard, flip charts and poster boards, and handouts—are among the easiest to use. They are inexpensive, unbreakable for the most part, and can be used in lighted rooms for ease of note taking. But they can be cumbersome, hard for large groups to see, and may require you to turn your back on the the audience. For suggestions on using each of the unprojected aids competently, see Table 15.3.

TABLE 15.3

Suggestions for Using Unprojected Visual Aids

Flip Charts and Posters

1. Decide where you'll position and display the flip chart or poster ahead of time.
2. Don't block the audience's view of the chart or poster, and don't face it while you're speaking.
3. Conceal material, then reveal it as you discuss it.

Handouts

1. Use handouts to help the listeners follow or recall your main points, but don't let them take over your presentation.
2. Wait to distribute your handouts until the end of your speech, so audience members don't read them while you're speaking.
3. If the handouts are essential to understanding your speech, distribute them before you start but not during the speech itself, which is time consuming.
4. If you use a computerized presentation and have printed handouts of the computer images, distribute those ahead of time. Then the audience members can listen to you rather than writing everything down off each computer image.

TABLE 15.4

••• Suggestions for Using Projected Visual Aids •••

Slides

1. Put the slides in order and set up the projector ahead of time.
2. Load and test slides and focus the projector before the speech.
3. Practice using the remove control.

Overhead Transparencies

1. Don't cram too much information and detail onto one overhead.
2. Test transparencies for size, focus, and visibility ahead of time.
3. Conceal information on the transparency, until it's time to talk about it.
4. Practice standing next to the projector or the projected image, whichever you prefer.
5. Use a pointer or pen to point to the screen or projector.
6. Shut off the projector when it's not in use.

Audiotape and Videotape

1. Cue up tapes or images to the correct start point ahead of time.
2. Check picture quality and volume ahead of time.
3. Practice using the remote control.

Projected Aids

Projected visual aids—including slides, overhead transparencies, videotapes, audio tapes, and computer-generated images—can be more trouble to prepare but are potentially more impressive than unprojected aids. They are more dramatic and colorful, easier for members of large groups to see, and can create a desired mood or effect for your speech. Their disadvantages are their higher cost and limited availability in some situations, the possibility of breakdowns, the potential to be noisy, and they're not as easily used in a lighted room. Hints for the competent use of projected aids are presented in Table 15.4.

Computerized Presentations

Of all the projected visual aids, computerized presentations are increasing the most in popularity (Ringle & Thompson, 1998). You use a computer to create and display text, photographs, drawings, diagrams, maps, charts, tables and lists, and even video clips. If you have an internet browser and a connection to the internet during your presentation, computerized presentations also allow you move easily from a computerized presentation to the internet.

To put together a computerized presentation, you need a specialized software program like PowerPoint, a computer on which to develop the presentation, and a suitable projector for presenting it. Then with some training and practice, you can create slides on your computer screen and use them to present your speech. If you haven't used a computerized presentation software program before, an easy way to get started is with the tutorial assistant built into most programs. For example, PowerPoint contains a tutorial called AutoWizard. For additional instruction, computer centers on college campuses often provide free training.

Although programs like PowerPoint are increasing in popularity in business and education, the use of computerized visual aids in public speaking also has its detractors (Brandt, 1998; Zuckerman, 1999). According to some critics, such programs cause speakers to prepare presentations that take the life and vitality out of public speaking. To support their claim, they ask us to imagine what Martin Luther King, Jr.'s "I Have a Dream" speech or Ronald Reagan's "Challenger" speech would have been like if either of those great speakers had presented with PowerPoint. Of course, these special occasion speeches were persuasive and commemorative and did not lend themselves well to computerized visual aids. You can see and hear a segment of King's speech at a Web site on compressed video to decide what you think (**http://www.mccsc.edu/~bhsntech/**).

Despite this criticism, computerized presentations have become standard in business settings. Provided you don't allow the visual aid to upstage you as a speaker, being able to use a computer program like PowerPoint is essential to public speaking competence. It is important to prepare relatively simple visual graphics, so you can speak to the audience when presenting rather than reading off the slide. Control the quantity of information and the amount of action used in each slide or graphic display. Table 15.5 contains suggestions for the effective use of computerized visual aids, several of which apply to traditional overheads as well.

Figure 15.11 provides an ineffective example as well as two simple but effective PowerPoint slides for Richard's speech. Slide 1 contains too much text and uses font sizes that are too small. The two columns of text use different font sizes, which is visually distracting. The other two slides are not particularly flashy, but they contain the right amount of information to focus the speaker's remarks. They use simple graphics that come with the PowerPoint software, the font sizes are appropriate and easy to read even at a distance, and each slide focuses on only one concept.

TABLE 15.5

Suggestions for Using Computerized Visual Aids

1. Be sure each slide focuses on only one main concept and information to support that topic.
2. Use a font size for the text that can be read easily by all audience members no matter where they are sitting. Use 36-point type for major headings, 24 points for subheads, and at least 18 points for text.
3. Use a typeface that is visually pleasing but simple, such as Times New Roman, Courier, Arial, or Helvetica.
4. Use uppercase and lowercase type because reading text printed in all capital letters is difficult.
5. Enliven your slides by using the clip art that comes with programs like PowerPoint. Just clip and paste it onto the slide wherever you want it.
6. Use a color scheme that is pleasing to the eye but not so bold it's distracting. PowerPoint allows you to choose among preselected blends of colors for slides.
7. Keep visual transitions between slides fairly simple. If you're using a computer program, use a consistent transitional device or dissolve to move from one visual to the next. Don't have lines of text flying in from all different directions throughout the presentation.
8. Finally, if you make use of anyone else's work as part of your computerized presentation, get permission and give credit when necessary.

INEFFECTIVE

Speaking Your Way to Success in Business

- Importance of Public Speaking Skills in Business
  - Fortune 500 executives state that newly hired graduates lack public speaking skills.
  - 1,000 human resource managers say most important factors influencing job performance are public speaking and listening.
  - My manager's statement about the value of public speaking skills
- Improving Your Public Speaking Skills After Graduation
  - Textbook author Hamilton Gregory provides suggestions for continuing improvement.
  - The National Speakers Association represents trainers, consultants, and public speakers.
  - SeminarMaster.com

EFFECTIVE

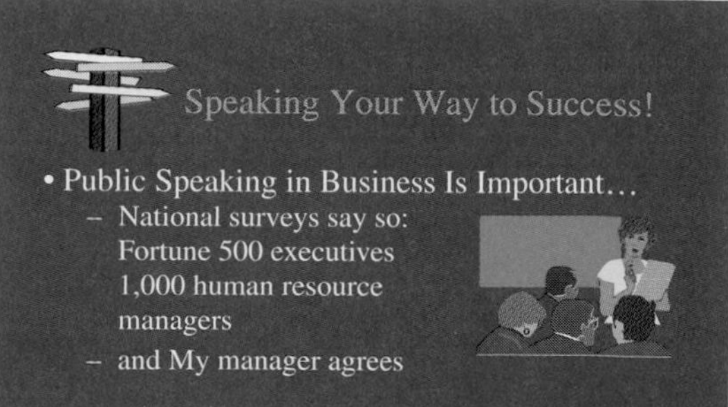

Continue to improve your skills...

- How to keep getting better . . .
  - Hints from an expert public speaking trainer
  - Get advice from SeminarMaster.com
  - Observe successful speakers where you work

FIGURE 15.11
Examples of PowerPoint Slides

Learning to use computerized presentation software is easy, but learning to use it competently is another matter. Here is an example of an effective and ineffective PowerPoint slides. Why are the slides on the right more effective?

If you plan to use any type of visual aid, whether it's a flip chart or computerized presentation, remember this last suggestion to help you prepare it competently. To test the quality of your visual aid, see if it passes this "nice test:"

N = Necessary to the speech and to prove your thesis, not just an add-on.
I = Impacts the audience in the way intended.
C = Clear and simple.
E = Easily seen or heard by all audience members.

Challenges to Preparing With Competence

As you prepare your speech, following the steps to competence just described, be aware of the following challenges to preparation: establishing source credibility, validating sources from the internet, and documenting and citing your sources of information.

ESTABLISHING SOURCE CREDIBILITY

How credible you appear as a speaker relates in part to **source credibility.** The audience makes critical judgments about your intentions as a speaker based on their evaluation of the quality of the information you present, and those judgments impact your credibility significantly.

Communication researchers refer to this critical dimension of credibility as the "goodwill" or intent you have toward the audience (McCroskey, 1999). A speaker of goodwill is one whose intention it is to present information and support materials that the listeners can rely on as truthful, reliable, and relevant to the topic at hand. A challenge when preparing your speech is to gather the kind of information that will enhance your credibility while accomplishing the purpose of your speech.

VALIDATING INTERNET INFORMATION

A second challenge to competent speech preparation relates to how you choose and use information from the internet. Many sites on the World Wide Web lack the controls of traditional publishers such as accuracy checking and getting proper permission for information that is posted. There are literally millions of Web pages where information is presented as factual and it is actually just someone's opinion. Scholarly resources do abound, but they are presented right along with unfounded, inaccurate, and out-of-date claims and information (McBride & Dickstein, 1998). The challenge when searching the internet for support materials is validating these sources of information.

Knowledge Link

Depending on the particular public speaking situation, is one of these challenges to preparation more relevant than the others? In what way?

DOCUMENTING SOURCES OF INFORMATION

A third challenge to preparation is providing appropriate documentation for all the sources of information you use in your speech. Not only must you gather useful information, you also have the responsibility of letting the audience know where you obtained it. That means that during the speech, you state your sources of information to the audience, and you prepare a list of references for their perusal and to accompany your outline, using appropriate forms of citation to document your sources. This list of references, appropriately citing source material in a speech is called a **references.** References for a speech are similar to a **bibliography** for a written work.

Overcoming Challenges to Preparation Competence

Speakers who are aware of these three challenges and take the steps necessary to address them are much more likely to be perceived as competent when presenting their speeches. Here are some specific recommendations for addressing these challenges.

HOW TO ESTABLISH SOURCE CREDIBILITY

As you prepare your speech, you examine a wide array of sources of information—from other people, from the internet, and from the library. You use critical thinking skills to evaluate support materials to determine which ones are most useful for your speech.

As we mentioned in Chapter 14, critical thinking involves evaluating evidence, assumptions, and ideas, which is precisely what you must do as you research your speech and select those support materials that are most credible. In study after study, communication researchers have demonstrated how important these critical thinking skills are (Allen, Berkowitz, Hunt, & Louden, 1999). And if you do this job well, your ability to think critically about your topic will be obvious to the audience when you present the speech, the listeners will judge you as a speaker of goodwill, and that will decidedly

CloseUp ON PUBLIC SPEAKING

Critical Thinking & Credibility

RESEARCHERS HAVE LEARNED that critical thinking and communication are inextricably intertwined (Allen, Bekowitz, Hunt, & Louden, 1999). A summary of research studies found that training in public speaking, discussion, and debate has a significant positive impact on critical thinking abilities. Students learn more, and their critical thinking skills improve.

Critical thinking has several advantages for you as a public speaker. As you prepare a speech, you research support materials, examine the evidence, and then form opinions about it. As a result, you become well informed on the topic. When you present your evidence, the listeners know that you know what you're talking about and that you examined the topic with an open mind. Your well-informed judgments will promote respect from the audience, thus enhancing your credibility. Furthermore, thinking critically while researching your speech enables you to present your ideas with more confidence, because you know you can support your claims and defend your opinions. This confidence also enhances your credibility.

Here are some suggestions for improving your critical thinking skills:

- Be open to new ideas, but research the necessary information to document those ideas.
- Seek to understand new ideas by examining all the information and evidence.
- Consider all ideas, whether your own or someone else's, from different viewpoints.
- Probe and examine assumptions by questioning and challenging them.
- Understand the difference between a fact and an opinion—you can verify a fact but not an opinion.
- Explore contradictions and differences in opposing viewpoints.
- Weigh all the evidence before forming a judgment.
- Draw conclusions only after examining all alternatives and possibilities.

Do not . . .

- Accept unsupported claims or assertions.
- Rush to judgment and form an opinion without examining the evidence.
- Assume all information posted on the internet is authoritative and reliable.

SOURCE: Allen et al. (1999).

enhance your credibility. The CloseUp on Critical Thinking provides suggestions for thinking critically when researching and preparing a speech.

HOW TO EVALUATE INTERNET SOURCES

It is also your responsibility as a competent public speaker to validate the authenticity of any electronic source you include in your speech (Goldsborough, 1999). If you are using a Web site as a source of information, begin with its home page to determine what you can about its authors or developers. Ask yourself the following questions, which are typical of what college librarians ask, as you evaluate an internet source (University of Colorado, 2000):

- What is the goal of the site and is it stated anywhere? Who is the audience?
- How accurate and reliable is the information on the site when compared to similar information from other sources?
- Are sources for the information provided? Is the origin of the content documented and are facts verifiable?

- Is the information on the site current and is there an indication of when it was posted or updated?
- How broad is the coverage of the topic and is it explored in depth?
- Is the information on the site presented objectively or does it appear to be biased? Is the information fact, opinion, or propaganda?
- Finally, who are the developers of the site and what are their credentials? How reputable is the organization or institution with which the site is associated? Is it clear who is responsible for the site and can the author(s) be contacted?

In addition to these questions, other guidelines for evaluating Web sites are available on the internet itself. A governmental site provides a checklist of criteria for evaluating sites (**http://www.ed.gov/databases/ERIC_Digests/ed426440.html**); and a site developed by the librarians at the University of California, Los Angeles, is also helpful (**http://www.library.ucla.edu/libraries/college/instruct/critical.htm**.

HOW TO PROVIDE SOURCE CITATIONS

In addition to choosing credible information and validating your Web sites, it is also crucial to provide appropriate credit for the intellectual property you use in your speech—your sources of information.

When you present your speech and provide information that is not your own opinion or experience, you have an obligation to state the source of it when you speak. That does not mean you read the entire reference verbatim as it appears in your reference list. Rather, you refer to the source as you bring up each piece of support material or evidence, particularly if it's a highly credible source. Benton's speech provides several examples of how the speaker made reference to the relevant sources of information:

1. According to the *New York Times* of July 13, 1993, the average training period of a private police officer is . . .
2. In fact, according to the *Journal of Social Problems*, August 1992, private officers are 20 times more likely . . .
3. Commenting on the city's move away from private police, Ray Collin, a lifelong south side resident, stated . . .

To provide documentation of your sources in a reference list to accompany your outline, there are several approaches that are well respected in most academic environments (American Psychological Association, 1994; Modern Language Association, 1995). These associations produce handbooks of guidelines to assist you in preparing references for various sources of information. By using these guidelines to document your sources of information, you convey to the audience that you are aware of the need for academic honesty, which means carefully documenting what you have chosen to include in your speech and properly attributing the sources. You can develop a list of references for your speech by using the American Psychological Association guidelines illustrated in Table 15.6. More extensive guidelines are available in printed form and on the internet (**http://www.tsufl.edu/library/5/citation.htm**).

The steps to competent speech preparation outlined in this chapter helped Richard prepare a speech that turned out successfully. Preparation is the key to effective presentation. Like Richard, you should now be motivated to prepare a good speech, understand how to prepare a speech effectively, and possess the skills necessary to competent speech preparation. Chapter 16 discusses the motivation, knowledge, and skills essential to presenting a speech with competence.

TABLE 15.6

Suggestions for Preparing a List of References

The American Psychological Association (APA) provides a popular format for a reference list. Here are examples of the types of references students are most likely to use in a speech. A style format book is available from APA that you can consult for more complicated references.

Nonperiodicals (Books, Reports, Brochures, Manuals, Audiovisual Media)

Authors' name(s) and Initial(s). (Date). *Title of book or report.* City, State: Publisher.

> Morreale, S., Spitzberg, B., & Barge, K. (2000). *Human communication: Motivation, knowledge, and skills.* Belmont, CA: Wadsworth.

Periodicals (Journals, Magazines, Newsletters, etc.)

Authors' name(s) and Initial(s). (Date). Title of article. *Title of Periodical, volume #,* page #'s.

> Winsor, J.L., Curtis, D.B., & Stephens, R.D. (1997). National preferences in business and communication education. *Journal of the Association for Communication Administration, 3,* 170–179.

Convention or Conference Paper

Authors' name(s) and Initial(s). (Date Including Month). *Title of paper.* Paper presented at the Name of Convention, City, State, or Country.

> Spitzberg, B.H., & Duran, R.L. (1994, May). *Toward an ideological deconstruction of communication competence.* Paper presented at the International Communication Association Conference, Sydney, Australia.

Web Site

Developers' name(s) and Initial(s). (Date). Name of Web Site [# of pages]. Retrieved month, day, year from the World Wide Web: Web address.

> Ruckelshaus, P.. & Earling, A. (1999). Executive Communications Group [15 pages]. Retrieved January 13, 2000 from the World Wide Web: http://www.ecglink.com/frmain.html.

ERIC Document

Authors' name(s) and Initial(s). (Date). *Title of document.* City and State: Source of Document. (ERIC Document #)

> Stotsky, S. (May, 1992). *The connection between language education and civic education.* Bloomington, IN: ERIC Digest. (ERIC Document Reproduction Service No. ED 348 318)

Personal Communication (Email, Phone Conversations, Interviews, etc.)

Do not include personal communication events in the list of references. Only cite them in the text as follows:

> (K. Abdul-Jabbar, email communication, January 20, 2000)

SOURCE: American Psychological Association (1994).

Chapter Summary

Research studies support the importance of speech preparation to public speaking competence. A competent speaker chooses or adapts a speech topic to the audience and situation. A good topic is found in personal experiences and interests, outside sources, or on the internet. The speaker identifies the general and specific purpose of the speech and writes a thesis statement, which is the central idea or claim of the speech. Support materials are gathered to accomplish the purpose from personal observations and experiences, informational interviews, the internet, and from the library. When gathering sources of information for a speech, critical thinking skills are used to evaluate and choose credible and appropriate support materials and evidence.

The next step in speech preparation is organizing the information and support materials in outline form. Organizational patterns sequence information in the most effective way for the informative and for the persuasive speech. A working outline serves as a foundation for organizing and reorganizing the support materials into main points. A formal outline contains all the information from the final version of the working outline, organized and presented using the alphanumeric system to label main points and subpoints. The presentational outline contains only enough information to remind the speaker of what to say at a glance, when presenting the speech. Most speeches have three main parts: an introduction, body, and conclusion. The introduction establishes the speaker's credibility, orients the listeners to the speech, and engages them in what will be said. The body of the speech supports the central claim through the presentation of a series of main points that, taken together, prove the central claim and support the thesis. Within the body of the speech, transitions indicate how the main points are related to each other. The conclusion lets the listeners know the speech is ending and reminds them of the central idea of the speech. While developing an outline, the speaker plans and develops visual aids to enhance the effectiveness of the presentation. Both unprojected and projected visual aids can be used to illustrate or support the content of a speech.

Finally, competent preparation entails an awareness of and ability to overcome the challenges of establishing source credibility, validating sources from the internet, and providing appropriate documentation of sources of information in citation form.

Key Terms

subject area
topic
general purpose
specific purpose
thesis statement
computerized database
standard outline format
working outline
formal outline
presentational outline
keyword outline
introduction
body of the speech
main points
transitions
conclusion
visual aids
unprojected aids
projected aids
source credibility
references
bibliography

Building Knowledge

1. If a speaker uncovers a source of information that contradicts the claim in his or her thesis statement, what should be done and why? What is the ethical thing to do?
2. Based on how diverse the United States is becoming, what are the ramifications for a speaker when he or she is gathering evidence and support materials and organizing a speech?
3. How apparent should the speaker's organizational pattern be to the listeners? How can a speaker effectively let the audience know how the speech is organized?

4. How might an introduction or conclusion be inappropriate or offensive? What kinds of introductions and conclusions should a speaker avoid?
5. Some speakers prefer to write out their speeches in manuscript form and then develop a speaking outline. Is that a good idea? Explain your answer.
6. Is the increased use of computerized presentations good or bad? Is it debasing public speaking and rhetoric? Explain your answer.

Building Skills

Individual Exercises

1. Develop a list of speech topics by using personal brainstorming. Take three sheets of paper and label the sheets as these subject areas: Work Life/Academics, Leisure Activities, and Social Concerns/Issues. Then write one word or phrase under each subject area. Under Academics, you might write psychology; under Leisure Activities, maybe music; under Social Concerns, perhaps the environment. Next, list five possible speech topics for each subject area and word.
2. Using *InfoTrac College Edition,* enter a keyword or phrase as a "subject search" that represents the topic of your next speech. Locate a minimum of three sources of information for your speech, at least one of which was published in the last two years.
3. Locate a site on the internet that contains support materials which appear useful for your next speech. Evaluate the quality of that site using the Web Page Evaluation Worksheet at **http://www.duke.edu/~de1/evaluate.html**.
4. Locate support materials for your speech topic by searching with a keyword at **http://www.infoplease.com**, which is a Web site that searches nine categories of almanacs and dictionaries, a thesaurus, and an encyclopedia.
5. Take the sources of information gathered from exercises 2, 3, and 4, and organize them using the standard outline format described in this chapter.
6. Sharpen your ability to evaluate Web sites with the online exercise in evaluating electronic information at **http://www.lib.calpoly.edu/infocomp/modules/05_evaluate/**.
7. Locate a source of support materials for your next speech using Meta-List.net, which is a search engine for over 200,000 electronic mailing lists. Find a discussion list or newsletter relevant to your next speech topic and contact that source for information at **http://www.meta-list.net**.

Group Exercises

1. Break into small groups of 3–4 students. Choose a speech topic such as these: Do violent video games cause teen violence? Should we abolish all affirmative action laws? Have each team gather support materials to support or refute the topic. Establish a time limit (one class period or the week between class meetings) for gathering information. Have each team present its findings and vote on whose information is most effective.
2. In small groups, discuss the next speech you'll present in class. Exchange ideas about topic, speech purpose, thesis statement, possible major points, support materials, and organizational patterns.
3. In a group with 3–4 students, develop a set of recommendations for the use of visual aids in Richard's speech from the vignette and for the speech about private police officers.

References

Allen, M., Berkowitz, S., Hunt, S., & Louden, A. (1999). A meta-analysis of the impact of forensics and communication education on critical thinking. *Communication Education, 48,* 18–30.

American Psychological Association (1994). *How to cite information from the internet and World Wide Web.* Retrived January 15, 2000 from the World Wide Web: http://www.apa.org/journals/webref.

American Psychological Association (1994). *Publication manual of the American Psychological Association* (4th ed.). Washington, DC: Author.

Benton, B. (1995). Very fake badges—very real guns. *Winning Orations of the Interstate Oratorical Association* (pp. 31–33). Northfield, MN: Interstate Oratorical Association.

Berkman, R. (2000, January 21). Searching for the right search engine. *Chronicle for Higher Education,* p. B6.

Brandt, D. S. (1998). Digital presentations: Make your delivery effective. *Computers in Libraries, 18*(5), 35–38.

Butler, H. E. (Trans). (1950). *The institutio oratoria of Quintilian, 3*(7), 2–3. Cambridge, MA: Harvard University Press.

Goldsborough, R. (1999, July). Suggestions to help you survive workplace 'infoglut.' *Communication Briefings, 18,* 8a–8b.

Jones, P., & Polak, J. (1993). Computer-based personal interviewing: State-of-the-art and future prospects.

Journal of the Market Research Society, 35 (3), 221–233.

Leeds, D. (1995). People shouldn't wonder, 'what was that about?' *National Underwriter, 99* (14), 12–13.

McBride, K., & Dickstein, R. (1998, March 20). The Web demands critical reading by students. *The Chronicle of Higher Education,* p. B6.

McCroskey, J. C. (1999). Goodwill: A reexamination of the Construct and its measurement. *Communication Monographs, 66,* 90–103.

Menzel, K. E., & Carrell, L. J. (1994). The relationship between preparation and performance in public speaking. *Communication Education, 43, 17–26.*

Messaris, P. (1997). *Visual persuasion: The role of images in advertising.* New Delhi: Sage.

Modern Language Association. (1995). *MLA handbook for writers of research papers* (4th ed.). New York: Author.

Monaghan, T. A. (1986). *Finding speech topics and supporting material.* (ERIC Document Reproduction Service No. ED 270 834)

Ringle, W. J., & Thompson, W. D. (1998). *TechEdge: Using computers to present and persuade.* Needham Heights, MA: Allyn & Bacon.

Rubel, C. (1995). Out of ideas? Try thinking 'out of the dots.' *Marketing News,* 29(23), 19.

Stewart, C. J. (1991). *Teaching interviewing for career preparation.* Bloomington, IN: ERIC Document Reproduction Service No. ED 334 627.

University of Colorado. (2000). *Evaluating web resources.* Colorado Springs: Author.

Voth, B. (1997). Catching a wave in the Internet surf: Electronic extemporaneous speaking. *Argumentation and Advocacy, 33,* 200–206.

Yaskin, S. (1990). Interviews: Are you prepared? *School Press Review, 66*(1), 10–16.

Zuckerman, L. (1999, April 17). Words go right to the brain, but can they stir the heart? *New York Times,* pp. A17–A19.

Exemplary Student Speech

Bond Benton, then of Wichita State University, Kansas, took first place in a National Interstate Oratorical Association contest for college students with this persuasive speech. Benton opens with a gripping attention-getting device and then informatively describes the problem of cities using private police officers to enhance the public force. Having painted a vivid picture of the problem with a variety of support materials, he goes on to his second main point, which is solutions to the problem. Benton concludes with a review of his speech and a memorable quotation from a credible source, Thomas Jefferson. The strengths of this speech are the speaker's extensive use of solid and varied evidence, his logical and easy-to-follow organizational pattern, and his vivid use of language.

Very Fake Badges—Very Real Guns

by Bond Benton

(1) What's a guy to do? You steal a car, assault two minors, carry an automatic submachine gun, and get arrested on charges of cocaine possession. What can you do for an encore? Well, if you're John Padilla of Long Island, New York, you get hired by the city as a privately employed police officer. Still on probation for a narcotics conviction, Mr. Padilla attended the obligatory two-week training session, then took to the street. While on duty, Padilla fired sixteen shots at a car parked in front of a local high school, killing two young men and critically wounding three others. Commenting on the incident, Padilla's mother stated that he may in fact be mentally unstable.

(2) Well, putting Mrs. Padilla's brilliant detective work aside, our society faces a new dilemma. More and more cities are employing private police, who are roughly the equivalent of security guards, to perform functions previously performed by fully accredited state officers. According to the *Los Angeles Times* of September 4, 1994, the current demand for crime prevention, coupled with the era of shrinking budgets, has created a situation in which, by the end of the century, state-employed private police officers will outnumber their traditional counterparts 3:1. Already, these officers do $1.6 billion in damage each year, killing over 300 people.

(1) *Introduction:* This speech starts right out with a powerful story as an attention-getter. Next, the speaker introduces and explains the topic of the speech—the problem of cities using private police. Facts and statistics are used to suggest how serious the problem is.

(2) Vivid language brings the thesis statement to life as the speaker refers to "people who carry very fake badges and very real guns."

(3) Very soon, this nation may become inundated with people who carry very fake badges and very real guns. And in examining all this we must ask ourselves the question: Should our public safety be sold to the lowest bidder? With careful examination of the costly dangers of employing state-sponsored private police, we can indeed see that the answer is no.

(4) To better understand this dilemma, we will begin by taking aim at the problem of private policing by looking at the system's inherent harms and how those harms have become so widespread. We'll then try to arrest a few solutions at both the governmental, but most importantly, at the personal level, as well.

(5) But initially, we will examine some of the dangers associated with private police.

(6) To understand these negative effects, you only need examine the minuscule amount of training the officers receive. According to the *New York Times* of July 13, 1993, the average training period of a private police officer is only fifteen days. Additionally, any background check of an applicant is haphazard at best. While this may be adequate for the crack security force that eyes the customers at a shopping mall, the article notes that such training can't even begin to cover all of the basic knowledge a traditional police officer uses everyday.

Take for example, Michael Huston, a Vietnam veteran whose family claimed he was mentally disabled. Hired as a private police officer in 1992, Huston patrolled the Hollywood area of Los Angeles. After witnessing a burglary at Universal Studios, Huston decided that his best course of action was to burn down the portion of the studios in which the burglary occurred, since he was unable to track down the suspects. After doing $25 million in damage to several of the movie sets, Mr. Huston then reported the incident to a superior, hoping to earn praise. Later at a trial, Huston claimed that another person who lived inside him had caused the damage. And incidents such as this are not isolated.

(7) The *Los Angeles Times* of November 28, 1993, states that private police officers, while numbering fewer than their traditional counterparts, do 74% more property damage each year when figured on the national average. And these numbers shouldn't be that surprising as the article cites a recent survey that indicated that when it comes to using firearms, 40% of all private police officers are self-taught.

(8) But, as if poor training coupled with high liability isn't enough, private security officers would also probably not fit the classification of being exceedingly culturally sensitive. In fact, according to the *Journal of Social Problems,* August 1992, private officers are 20 times more likely to commit an act of police brutality against an African-American suspect than their white counterparts. According to the *Chicago Tribune,* March 28, 1993, racism in the private police that patrolled the predominantly black southside was so pervasive, the community actually celebrated when the department disbanded. Commenting on the city's move away from private police, Ray Collin, a lifelong southside resident stated, "I think we'll have more security, now that we got rid of those damn security guards."

(9) Well, now that we have examined the risks of the state using private police officers, it would seem that only a few misguided, penny-pinching areas would use such an incredibly flawed system on a mass scale.

(10) However, the *Journal of Criminal Justice,* June 1994, states that virtually every community in America utilizes private police officers. In fact, in a telephone interview that I conducted with Frank Jones of the Tempe Police Department, I was told the city we are in right now employs private police officers in a patrolling and investigative capacity, particularly in the area in and around this campus.

(11) And the reason actions like this have been necessitated is simple: Cities right now are experiencing a dramatic rise in crime, while in turn they are receiving less money to run their police forces. And although private police represent a big risk, they are very cheap. According to the *New York Magazine* of March 13, 1995, private police officers earn as little as one tenth the salary of traditional police. As former state trooper and current New York city councilman Luis Lopez stated, "When issues like this come up I usually abstain from voting. I have big doubts about these guys, but there's no way I can vote against them."

(3) Having introduced the topic, the speaker now provides a specific preview of the main points that will be covered in the speech.

(4) *First Main Point:* Here the speaker begins his first main point, which is the dangers of private policing.

(5) The first danger is the poor training that private police officers get. This subpoint is first supported with statistical information from the New York Times and a moving story of a Vietnam veteran who became a private police officer.

(6) The damage caused by private police also illustrates the problem of poor training.

(7) The speaker makes a nice transition from the danger of poor training to the second subpoint under dangers—private police lack cultural sensitivity. Sources of information for this subpoint are articles from an academic journal and a respected newspaper and a quotation.

(8) In this transition, the speaker again uses vivid language to introduce the third danger, the widespread use of private police.

(9) A journal article and the results of a telephone interview with a police officer illustrate the extent of the problem.

(10) Here the speaker explains that the problem is widespread because private police officers are paid very little.

(11) *Second Main Point:* This internal summary and preview leads to the second main point, some solutions to the problem.

Lopez's doubts are echoed in the minds of many politicians, yet as long as America demands a greater police presence on the streets, with continuing apprehension about any tax increases, hiring private officers will remain a politically viable solution to this dilemma.

(12) At this point, we have observed some of the harms inherent in private policing by first looking at the dangerously low quality of service that the officers provide, and secondly, understanding how this problem has become so widespread in our society. With this new understanding, we can now go about looking at some pragmatic solutions to this difficult dilemma.

(12) First, the speaker cleverly acknowledges that there are situations where private police officers should be used.

(13) Now, it would be unwise to imply that all of these officers are corrupt and incompetent, or that there is no role for private police in our society.

(13) The author of a book on the topic and a respected newspaper provide the first solution, which is the need for more official screening of private police.

(14) In fact, Les Johnson in his 1993 book *The Rebirth of Private Policing* states that well-trained private police officers are integral to private industry and that they may play a very helpful role in helping the public in areas such as clerical work and traffic duty. Yet, before this can occur, Johnson contends that steps need to be taken to clean up the process by which the applicants are both screened and trained. Determining little things, like is the potential officer a rapist or murderer, would be a beneficial start in this direction. As the *Los Angeles Times* of January 28, 1995, explains, the current situation dictates that cities can't do the job alone, but at the very least, private police must be checked by a policy that dictates they are part of the solution, rather than part of the problem.

(14) An academic journal is the source of a second solution—community based crime prevention programs like Neighborhood Watch.

(15) The government would also do well to examine other options in the area of crime control before they put all their eggs in the private policing basket. The *Journal of Planning*, June 1994, states that community-based crime prevention programs may actually be preferable to private police in terms of cost, effectiveness, and long-term support. Simple measures, such as setting up neighborhood watch programs, give citizens advocacy in owning their own self-protection. Yet, perhaps the greatest advantage to such programs is that they rely on internal solutions to solving crime, rather than counting on the visibly inefficient help that outside forces attempt to provide.

(15) The speaker now provides a third solution of his own—individual action on the part of the audience members.

(16) Yet all these measures are invalid unless individuals take action on them. And, amazingly enough, you don't even have to write your representative in congress. In hearings on private security held before the U.S. House of Representatives, Dr. John Chavela, professor of law enforcement administration at Western Illinois University, stated that this battle will be decided largely at the local level. Essentially what this means, is that simply educating yourself to actions occurring in your community is a crucial first step. By making a phone call to your mayor regarding these concerns about private policing or even joining your local neighborhood watch program, you can have an immeasurable impact.

Now such measures may be well and good in the long run, but there are basic steps that need to be remembered when dealing with the problems that this issue presents in the meantime. First of all, by law, all privately employed state police officers must wear uniforms and badges designating them as such. If you are ever a victim of a crime and aren't comfortable talking with one of these officers, simply request to see a fully accredited police official. But, most importantly, if you ever witness any suspicious-looking action on the part of a private officer, inform the local authorities immediately. As the *New York Times*, November 4, 1993, states, public scrutiny is the only way the actions of these individuals can be monitored and effectively dealt with.

(16) A final solution is offered—question the credentials and report suspicious actions of private police. An article from the New York Times is used to support this recommendation.

(17) Today we have examined the problem of private policing, by first examining how these officers are unequipped for their roles as police and how this problem has become so widespread in society. We then examined some simple and pragmatic solutions to this problem at both the societal and, finally, at the personal level. Thomas Jefferson once stated that one corrupt officer of the law is more deplorable than a thousand thieves. If we as individuals and as a society don't take action against the problems that private policing has created, we stand on the verge of proving this old adage true.

(17) *Conclusion:* The speaker first reviews the contents of the speech—its main points. Then a quotation by Thomas Jefferson is used as a closing device along with a call for action.

CHAPTER 16

Learning Objectives

After studying this chapter, you should be able to:

1. Understand the nature of presentational competence and the importance of speaker credibility.
2. Explain the role of language and words in public speaking and the importance of clarity, vividness, and appropriateness.
3. Describe how a public speaker uses rate, pitch, and volume to heighten and maintain audience interest in a speech.
4. Define pronunciation, articulation, and grammar and explain their correct and appropriate use by a public speaker.
5. Describe how nonverbal cues are used to support and enhance a speech, including appearance, posture and body movement, gestures, facial expression, and eye contact.
6. Discuss the major challenges to presentational competence speech preparation and be able to overcome them.

Presenting Your Speech

Wen Shu and Sergio were pleased when they received personal invitations from the Office of Academic Advancement to accompany the chancellor of their campus on a speaking tour around the state. They were told that the purpose of the tour was to promote the university and encourage students from rural areas to come to the city to attend their school. The tour party would consist of the chancellor and several teachers and students from around the state and county, as well as international students. At every stop on the tour, each student, including Wen Shu and Sergio, would present a five-minute speech about their positive experiences at the university. After the excitement of the invitation subsided, Wen Shu and Sergio started immediately to prepare what they would say. When their speeches were fully outlined, they practiced together and critiqued each other's performances. Then they revised their outlines based on each other's reactions and presented the revised speeches to their course instructor.

The professor told Sergio that he projected his voice extremely well, but he had a few problems with language and word choice—how he said what he said. He used fancy words and jargon that might be unfamiliar to the students to whom he would be speaking. He had just taken a communication theory class and he included some of what he had learned in his speech to illustrate course content at the college level. As a result, his choice of words obscured his message rather than clarifying it. Furthermore, he mispronounced some words and didn't articulate sounds correctly and tended to use some uhms and uhs without knowing it. The professor told Sergio to rework several parts of the speech and practice it more with Wen Shu before embarking on the tour.

The professor liked Wen Shu's use of language and commended her excellent pronunciation and use of grammar, particularly because English was not her first language. She chose her words carefully and spoke at just the right level for the students in the audience. Despite those strengths, the professor said that Wen Shu communicated nervousness and a lack of confidence nonverbally. She rocked from one foot to the other and, unlike Sergio, she spoke quietly and kept looking down and doodling nervously on her speech outline. In addition, no matter what content she presented, her face was almost expressionless, even when she told an emotional story about being the first in her family to leave China to go to college in the United States. The professor told Wen Shu to videotape her speech and concentrate on improving several of the more problematic nonverbal cues before starting the tour.

Both Wen Shu and Sergio did a great job on the tour. Sergio watched the students' reactions to his speech and when he thought something he said was unclear, he modified his remarks right then and there. Wen Shu succeeded in using nonverbal cues much more effectively. At the end of the tour, the chancellor thanked both students personally for their participation. Their public speaking skills and training had paid off, and both students were pleased with a job well done. •••

Perhaps you have experienced some of the same difficulties as Sergio and Wen Shu when giving a speech. If so, you are not unique—until most people receive training in public speaking, they have no way of knowing how to present a speech effectively. It's like any other skill—skiing, playing tennis, or even using a computer—training and practice are essential to developing effective skills. In fact, researchers have found that formal training in public speaking is the best way for people in the workplace and students to improve their public speaking skills.

In one study, employees from all different kinds of organizations—manufacturing, service, production, and research companies—received presentation skills training (Seibold, Kudsi, & Rude, 1993). A significant number of the trainees reacted positively to the training, reporting that they believed they had improved their public speaking skills a great deal. In addition, their co-workers said the 194 training participants improved significantly in 12 out of 16 presentation skills. Those skills encompassed all the verbal and nonverbal aspects of giving a speech covered in this chapter. In other studies, college students just like you who took a public speaking course exhibited significant gains in overall public speaking competence and in how well they used language, their voices, their ability to speak correctly, and nonverbal cues (Ellis, 1995; Morreale, Hackman, & Neer, 1995).

This research suggests that training in public speaking works and, through training, you can improve your ability to give an effective speech. Moreover, improving your presentation skills will be valuable to you just as those skills were valuable to Wen Shu and Sergio. When you're faced with the challenge of presenting a speech—at school, at work, or in your public life—you'll know how to present it competently.

Presenting With Competence

Competent speech presentation today closely resembles what the Roman orator Cicero described as style, delivery, and memory (May, 1988). By style, Cicero meant the distinctive way a speech is presented that makes it recognizable or memorable to the audience. According to Cicero, style is achieved primarily through the speaker's use of language. Wen Shu's instructor was giving her stylistic advice when encouraging her to use language more effectively. By delivery, Cicero was referring to the actual presentation of the speech to the audience. A skillful delivery involves the effective use of the voice and all the nonverbal cues that Sergio incorporated in his presentation. Memory was an important skill in Cicero's day, but as we explained in Chapter 14, that type of delivery is no longer as popular except for special occasions.

A COMPETENCE MODEL FOR PRESENTING A SPEECH

The presentation skills covered in this chapter are similar to the principles introduced by Cicero centuries ago. The model in Figure 16.1 depicts these presentation skills and the skills component that is essential to public speaking competence, as first introduced in Chapter 14. Motivation, knowledge, and skills work together to influence whether a public speaker is perceived by the audience as competent. As a component of that competence model, the following skills are crucial to being perceived as competent by your listeners:

1. Use language and words that are clear, vivid, and appropriate.
2. Vary the rate, pitch, and volume of your voice.
3. Use correct and appropriate pronunciation, articulation, and grammar.
4. Embody a variety of nonverbal cues in your presentation: appearance, posture, body movement and gestures, facial expression, and eye contact.

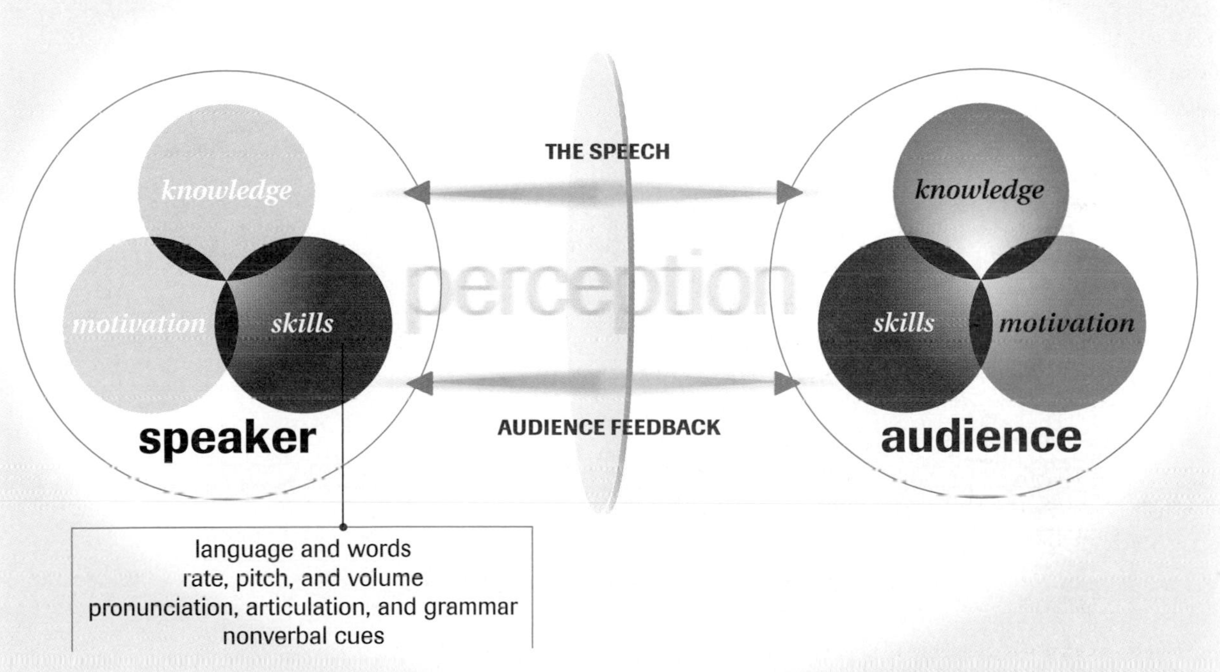

FIGURE 16.1
A Model of Presentational Competence

Competence in presenting a speech results from the speaker using language and words that are clear, vivid, and appropriate; varying the rate, pitch, and volume of the voice; using correct and appropriate pronunciation, articulation, and grammar; and using a variety of nonverbal cues to support and enhance the spoken message.

Before examining each of these four skills closely, we first consider how their use affects your credibility as a speaker. You already have learned about the credibility derived from the sources of information and support materials you include in your speech. Equally important to public speaking competence is speaker credibility.

Knowledge Link

Of the four public speaking skills, does one stand out as more essential to communication competence? If so, which skill and why?

●●●

SPEAKER CREDIBILITY & PRESENTATIONAL COMPETENCE

Perceptions of a speaker's communication competence, as described in Chapter 2, are based on observing the person's communication behaviors in a given context. Your competence as a public speaker results from the audience's impression of you, which is influenced in part by how you use presentation skills in the particular context. Whether you're giving a speech at a pep rally on a college campus or a formal presentation in a boardroom of a major corporation, the appropriate and effective use of presentation skills for the particular context will decidedly affect the impression you make and therefore your credibility as a speaker.

Speaker credibility can be defined as the impressions the listeners form of the public speaker in a given public speaking context, at a given time. Note that these impressions change over time, as Figure 16.2 illustrates.

Your **initial credibility** is based on what the audience knows about you before hearing you speak. If they've heard you are well informed or an expert on your topic, your initial credibility is higher. If they know nothing about you, which could be the case in a public speaking class, your initial credibility is based on their first impression of you. That is why what you say and do in the introduction to your speech is pivotal to your credibility.

Derived credibility develops as your audience listens to you speak. Based on what you say and how you behave, audience members form and change their impressions of you.

"Let's run through this once more—and, remember, you choke up at Paragraph Three and brush away the tear at Paragraph Five."

How would you rate this speaker's credibility?

© The New Yorker Collection 1988 Donald Reilly from cartoonbank.com. All rights reserved.

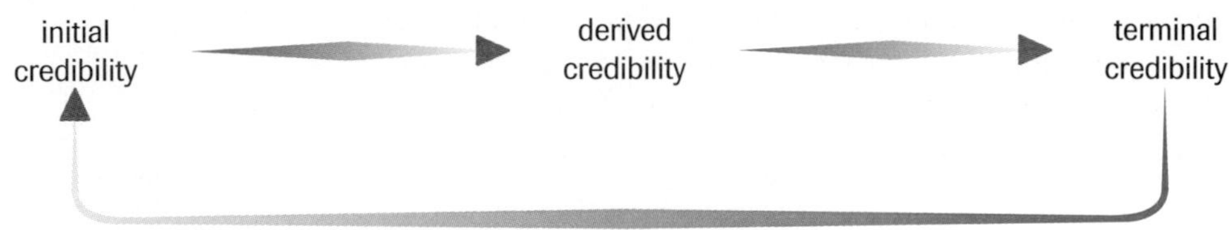

FIGURE 16.2
How Speaker Credibility Develops Over Time

Your initial credibility is what you bring with you to the speaking situation. You develop derived credibility, as you speak, and your terminal credibility is what the audience takes away with them.

As we discussed in Chapter 15, the credibility of your sources of information is important during your speech. But your presentational skills, discussed in this chapter, are equally significant. Do you behave and speak like a person who is an expert and well informed on the topic, whose remarks can be trusted?

Finally, **terminal credibility** is the long-term impression you leave behind—what happens after the listeners go home and think about your speech. As they receive more information and reflect on what you said and how you said it, their impressions of your competence as a speaker will change and solidify.

According to some communication scholars, speaker credibility is an all-important element, whether the goal of communication is persuasion or the generation of understanding (McCroskey & Young, 1981). Moreover, communication experts say that perceptions of a speaker's competence, trustworthiness, dynamism, and credibility are highly influenced by the dynamics of verbal communication such as volume, pitch, rate, and pronunciation, as well as postural movements, gestures, facial expression, and eye behavior (Fatt, 1999). In one experimental study, college teachers used what are called immediacy behaviors in the classroom: smiling frequently, using vocal variety and gestures, and walking relaxedly around the room. As a result these teachers were perceived as significantly more credible by the students (Thweatt & McCroskey, 1998). The message is clear. As you present persuasive and informative speeches, use all of the presentation skills discussed here to enhance your speaker credibility.

Knowledge Link

In order to create the impression of competence and credibility, how can a public speaker discover what is perceived as credible?

The Eloquence of Words

As Sergio's experience in the opening vignette indicated, the competent use of words and language is essential to giving a good speech and establishing and maintaining your credibility with any audience. By changing how he used language to describe the content of a college course, Sergio communicated better with the future college students in his audience. This significance of oral language and the importance of the spoken word is a topic that has been studied extensively by communication scholars (Ong, 1988).

Martin Luther King, Jr.'s celebrated "I Have a Dream" speech is an excellent example of using words competently and eloquently (Logue, 1997). In fact, when *USA Today* identified the top 100 speeches of the century, that speech was in the number one slot. The speech is still remembered by many people today, even though King wrote and delivered it decades ago in 1963 at the March on Washington for Jobs and Freedom. The great impact of that speech is due in part to how King delivered his message of peace and equality for all races before a crowd of 200,000 gathered at the Lincoln Memorial in Washington, D.C. Just reading the following well-known section of King's speech will give you an idea of how competently and eloquently he used language:

The Reverend Dr. Martin Luther King, Jr.'s "I Have a Dream" speech is an example of great public speaking that has withstood the test of time.

> [L]et freedom ring from the prodigious hilltops of New Hampshire. Let freedom ring from the mighty mountains of New York. Let freedom ring from the heightening Alleghenies of Pennsylvania! Let freedom ring from the snowcapped Rockies of Colorado! Let freedom ring from the curvacious peaks of California! But not only that; let freedom ring from Stone Mountain of Georgia! Let freedom ring from Lookout Mountain of Tennessee! Let freedom ring from every hill and molehill of Mississippi. From every mountainside, let freedom ring.

Competent language, such as King demonstrated, enhances the listeners' understanding and enthusiasm for a speech by the use of words that are clear, vivid, and appropriate. Although most people could not deliver the "I Have a Dream" speech anywhere near like King did, clear, vivid, and appropriate language are nonetheless essential skills for all competent speakers.

Knowledge Link

Is it always a good idea to present a speech using language eloquently?

CLARITY

The importance of clarity to communication competence was first introduced in Chapter 2. In the case of public speaking, **clear language** uses words in such a way that the listeners understand and can easily comprehend the meaning of the speaker's message. If your listeners have to try to figure out what you mean, they'll be distracted from listening to your speech. You achieve clarity by being sensitive to how the meanings of words and phrases vary from one person to another, and by using words that are concrete and familiar to your listeners.

Meaning

Chapter 4 stated that language can and should be used to clarify the meaning of a spoken message. Words are symbols that mean different things to different people, and different things in different situations. The ramifications of this are significant for a public speaker. When you present a speech to an audience of 20 people, there are 20 opportunities for what you say to mean something different to the listeners. For example, suppose you use a term in your speech like "partner," a word that was identified in Chapter 4 as an ambiguous word. If you tell the audience that you are sharing your partner's opinion with them, some listeners could think that you mean your business partner, while others might imagine that they are hearing the opinion of your "loved one." One effective way to avoid this sort of ambiguity and achieve clarity is to use more concrete words.

Concreteness

To help your listeners interpret your words as you intend them, use language and words that are more concrete than abstract. As you saw in Chapter 4, the ladder of abstraction categorizes language by placing concrete words lower on the ladder and abstract ones on the higher rungs (Hayakawa, 1964). A concrete word refers to something specific your audience can visualize, such as an object, person, or specific place. In contrast, an abstract word is more general and describes something less able to be visualized, such as a category of objects, a type of person, a kind of place, or an idea. Figure 16.3 provides some simple examples of concrete versus more abstract words.

In the introduction to "I Have a Dream," Martin Luther King, Jr. used abstract words to call attention to racial discrimination as a problem that hadn't gone away: "Fivescore years ago, a great American, in whose symbolic shadow we stand, signed the Emancipation Proclamation. . . . But one hundred years later, we must face the tragic fact that the Negro is still not free." The abstract word in this statement is *free,* and the audience would have no way of knowing what King meant by it. Later in the speech, King did clarify his meaning by providing examples.

Familiarity

In addition to using concrete language to achieve clarity, it is also helpful to use words with which your listeners are familiar. Every field of knowledge has its own jargon, specialized or technical terms, but the use of unfamiliar words clouds rather than clarifies the meaning of a speech. For example, slang or the use of words that are only known in a particular region or by a particular group of people can lead to misunderstandings. If you use regionalisms understood in some regions of the country but not in others, such as surfer slang, cowboy slang, or homeboy slang, the meaning of your message will not be clear to all your listeners. The everyday expressions that some of your listeners understand immediately may have little or no meaning to others. A phrase such as "it's raining cats and dogs" or "the ball is in your court" may be easily understood by many people in the United States, but confusing to people from other countries. The same holds true for people from different cities or even social groups.

By contrast, when you express yourself using clear, concrete, and familiar language, you help the audience understand and relate to your message. It may be tempting to use more elaborate language, but you run the risk of mispronouncing or misusing a fancy word, which would damage your credibility. Furthermore, if you make a point clear the first time, there is no need to repeat it in a variety of ways in order for your listeners to understand, and you can pay more attention to using vivid language that will enliven your speech.

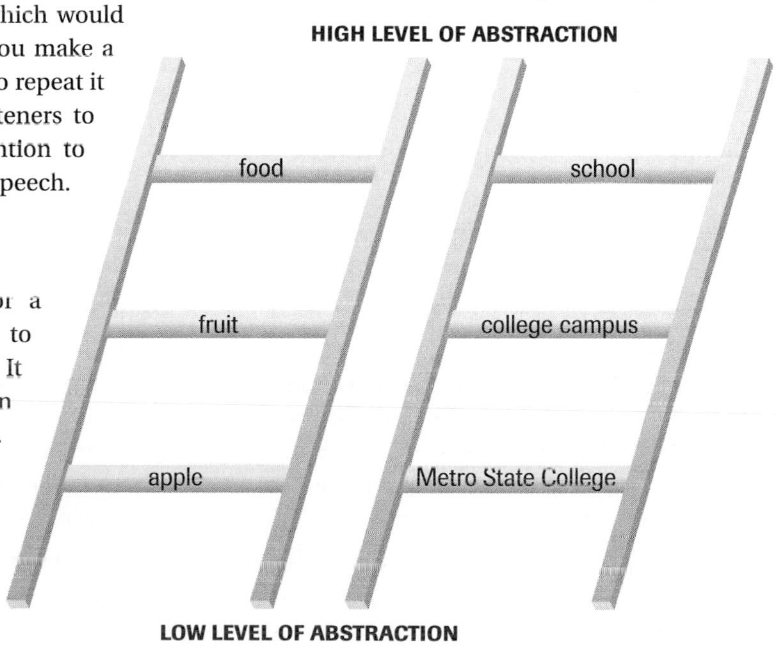

VIVIDNESS

Vivid language promotes enthusiasm for a speech by bringing the speaker's message to life and moving the audience emotionally. It makes a speech memorable and its main points engaging and real for the listeners. Remember that Cicero said real **style** is achieved primarily through the speaker's use of language. The kind of style and vividness Cicero was referring to will add great impact to your speech. In fact, researchers have found that the

FIGURE 16.3
Concrete vs. Abstract Words

The use of concrete words helps your listeners easily visualize what your words mean, thus promoting greater clarity.

powerful use of language affects perceptions of a speaker's dynamism, status, and credibility, as well as the listeners' attitudes toward what the speaker is recommending (Haleta, 1996, Sparks, Areni, & Cox, 1998). Powerful language and the vividness and style recommended by Cicero can be achieved through the use of imagery and figures of speech.

Imagery

Imagery is the creation of visual pictures and other sensory experiences through description. When listeners can almost see, feel, taste, smell, or hear something, they're much more likely to be impressed by it and remember it. For example, when Wen Shu described leaving China to come to college in the United States, she probably drew mental and emotional pictures of the event for her listeners. She may have talked about her feelings on the very first day on a new campus, including details of about how big the campus seemed at first and how she sat in the back of the room on the first day of class. She might have included descriptions of how other students reacted to her and how she reacted to them.

Figures of Speech

In addition to imagery, there are several figures of speech—simile, metaphor, analogy, the rhetorical question, alliteration, and repetition—any and all of which will bring the style Cicero talked about to your speech. These **figures of speech** help the listeners visualize, identify with, or really think about the points you're trying to make. You probably use these techniques in everyday conversation without realizing it, but their intentional use in a speech is quite effective.

A **simile** is an explicit comparison that compares two unlike things using the words *like* or *as.* Wen Shu could have used a simile by saying that stepping on to the new campus on the first day of class was like a Broadway star stepping on to the stage for the first time on opening night. Here are a few more examples of similes:

He's as big as a house.
You eat like a bird.
The winner of the race ran like greased lightning.

A **metaphor** implies a comparison between two dissimilar things, but it does so without using the words *like* or *as* (Ausmus, 1998). Here's an example: "Communication apprehension can either be the anchor that weighs you down or the shoulder you stand on to reach new heights in public speaking."

An **analogy** is an extended simile or metaphor that asks the listeners to accept that things which sound alike in most respects will be alike in the respect being discussed. Here's an example: "Overcoming anxiety is like taking a journey to an unknown place. The first step is always the hardest and perhaps a bit scary. But as you move along and become familiar with the new terrain, your anxiety subsides. And when you reach your destination, you think it wasn't so hard getting there after all."

A **rhetorical question** is asked for effect rather than to elicit a response. When you ask a rhetorical question in your speech, you're inviting your listeners to answer silently to themselves and then continue thinking about the question as you provide an answer to it. This figure of speech is frequently used as the attention-getting device in the introduction to a speech. Here are two different ways Sergio or Wen Shu could have used a rhetorical question to start their speeches:

Have you begun to ask yourself where you want to be 10 years from now?

> As you sit here today, are you satisfied with the plan you now have for achieving your goals after you graduate? Are you ready to hear about another plan?

Alliteration is the repetition of the same consonant sound in a series of words or phrases to draw attention to certain ideas and help listeners remember what is said. When you use alliteration, the sounds add a subtle but memorable dimension to your message. Sergio may have appealed to the students to get started planning for college by saying "The key to prosperity is preparation, planning, and placing yourself in the front row of class this fall."

When the speaker repeats the same word or phrase several times in a section of a speech, it is called **repetition**. This repetition helps emphasize or tie several ideas together so your audience remembers and understands the connections you've made. It also helps to reinforce your point and make it memorable. King's "I Have a Dream" speech is full of repetition. Here is but one example:

> Go back to Mississippi, go back to Alabama, go back to South Carolina, go back to Georgia, go back to the slums and ghettos of our northern cities, knowing that somehow this situation can and will be changed.

By now you may be thinking that vivid language and style are just for public speaking experts, but that's not the case. Anyone can use vivid language in a speech, simply by planning ahead. You can use a simple simile or metaphor to illustrate any point you want to make. Write out a rhetorical question or several sentences ahead of time that use alliteration or repetition. If you choose to use a simile or metaphor, try to personalize it for the audience by using personal pronouns like *you, us, we,* or *let's* (Harris, 1994). For instance, it would be more effective to say "Most of us experience opening-night jitters during our first speeches," rather than "Many students experience anxiety during their first speeches."

Vivid language, imagery, and figures of speech are the best ways to bring your message to life for the listeners.

APPROPRIATENESS

In Chapter 4 we pointed out that language carries with it certain expectations of what we are obligated, permitted, or prohibited from saying—more simply, what is appropriate. In a public speaking situation, **appropriate language** presents information in a way that respects and treats all audience members as equals without being condescending or using biased language and stereotypes.

Condescending Language

To be respectful and treat your audience members as equals, adapt what you say to their knowledge of your topic and avoid the use of condescending language that speaks down to them. If your audience is unfamiliar with the topic, provide details about what they may not understand, but do so without setting yourself up as the only expert on the topic. If information is presented in a condescending manner, you risk the audience members not listening to what you have to say. Casualness with technical jargon and other information also communicates disrespect and negatively impacts your listeners' attitude toward your message and you as a speaker. Rather than enhancing your credibility, condescending use of language will harm it.

But don't go to an extreme to build rapport with the audience by presenting information in any way that isn't comfortable for you. Instead, present your speech in your own

Biased Language

Another way to use language appropriately is to avoid the use of biased words or phrases that derive their meaning from stereotypes, based on gender, race, ethnic group, age, sexual orientation, or disability. Most people know to avoid overt racial slurs but may carry with them certain stereotypes that will influence what they say in a manner that may insult others. A subtle bias in language could unintentionally offend or insult an individual member or some segment of the audience. By contrast, the use of unbiased language makes a positive statement about your credibility and serves to bring audiences together and encourage open discussion of even the most controversial topics.

Gender-biased language can result from something as simple as using male pronouns more often than female ones. Referring to *he* more often than *she* may suggest the speaker respects men more than women. Gender bias also results from using words that designate certain occupations or professions as male and others as female. You can change that by making a few substitutions in the words you use to designate certain jobs, such as saying *flight attendant* rather than *stewardess; firefighter* rather than *fireman; chairperson* rather than *chairman;* and, *humanity* rather than *mankind.* Remember, doctors, politicians, astronauts, and executives can be male or female, so avoid language that assumes a gender bias in any role. Moreover, rather than refer to someone as a woman lawyer or a male nurse, leave off the gender descriptor, unless it's really necessary to understand your point. Table 16.1 provides specific suggestions for using gender-neutral language in your speech.

The guidelines for avoiding gender-biased language apply equally to other types of bias. Stereotypically pairing certain professions or occupations with certain races or ethnic groups or remarking on the race or ethnic background of a person in a certain profession is a form of subtle language bias. For example, to refer to a Jewish lawyer implies that lawyers are expected to be Jewish. At an even more subtle level, to refer to an African American doctor may somehow communicate that an African American doctor is an unusual occurrence. Without intending to do so, this type of language can subtly offend some of the listeners in your audience. Leave off the reference to ethnicity or race when mentioning a person's profession.

Unless your audience needs to know the gender, race, or age of the person you're talking about, omit that information from your speech. Likewise, leave out references to a person's disability unless that information is relevant. Eliminate from your speech any words or phrases that categorize people based on stereotypes or that patronize people in any way.

The CloseUp on Diversity describes a way of using language that is free of bias and honors diversity in contemporary society. A new approach to using language called **multicodality** suggests that competent speakers retain their unique way of using words and language while incorporating some of the unique language patterns of the listeners into what is said—a technique researchers call code switching.

At this point, you may be thinking it is quite a challenge to incorporate clarity, vividness, and appropriateness in what you say. However, by developing a few well-planned and effective phrases or sentences that draw mental pictures and evoke emotions, you can improve your speech immensely. By carefully wording and writing out these parts of your speech ahead of time, you will ensure that you say them just as you intend (see Table 16.2).

TABLE 16.1

••• Avoiding Biased Words & Phrases •••

Simple changes in language will help you become a gender-neutral public speaker.

1. Replace phrases that contain *man* or *woman* with gender-neutral terms.

Instead of	*Substitute*
Policeman	police officer
manpower	labor force
waitress	waitperson
workman	laborer

2. Restructure sentences to eliminate sexist language.

Instead of	*Substitute*
The fabric in the dress is man-made.	The fabric in the dress is synthetic, not natural.
What are the average man-hours it will take to do the job?	How many hours will it take to do the job?
When will a new chairman be assigned?	When will someone be appointed to the chair's position?

3. Use plurals to avoid gender-specific pronouns.

Instead of	*Substitute*
When a staff member arrives, tell him to sit in the front row.	As staff members arrive, tell them to sit in the front row.
A public speaker should plan the handouts he will use ahead of time.	Public speakers should plan the handouts they will use ahead of time.

4. Mention women first as often as men.

Instead of	*Substitute*
Men and women experience public speaking anxiety in the same way.	Women and men experience public speaking anxiety in the same way.
He or she will help us out.	She or he will help us out.

SOURCE: Detz (1992).

TABLE 16.2

••• Using Clear, Vivid, & Appropriate Language •••

Use clear, vivid, and appropriate language to promote understanding and avoid offending your listeners.

1. Clear language promotes understanding and comprehension of meaning.

- Be sensitive to variations in meaning
- Use concrete rather than abstract words
- Use familiar words

2. Vivid language promotes enthusiasm, brings the message to life, and moves the audience emotionally.

- Use imagery to create visual pictures
- Use figures of speech

  Simile compares unlike things using *like* or *as*

  Metaphor compares dissimilar things without using *like* or *as*

  Analogy extends a simile or metaphor

3. Appropriate language respects and treats listeners as equals and avoids biased language and stereotypes.

- Adapt language to listeners' knowledge base but avoid being condescending
- Avoid biased words or phrases based on stereotypes about gender, race, ethnic group, age, or disability

The Sound of Your Voice

The words you say are communicated to the audience by the sound of your voice. A popular communication axiom—a self-evident truth—states that it isn't what you say but how you say it that counts! As a competent speaker, you need to become aware of how you use your voice and strive for variety and contrast, which will introduce dynamism, an essential aspect of credibility, to what you say. When you present a speech, use **vocal variety** to heighten and maintain audience attention and interest in your message by varying the rate (fast vs. slow), pitch (high vs. low), and volume (loud vs. soft) of your voice.

Rate

Rate is the speed at which a speaker delivers a speech. As mentioned in the Chapter 6, most people speak at around 125 words per minute, and people listen at least four times faster. Good public speakers vary their rate, sometimes talking fast and sometimes slower, but always speaking at a pace the audience can understand. Although you don't want to aim for a specific rate of speech, you can adjust your rate to the topic of the speech. A serious subject deserves a slower and more deliberate rate; less serious subject matter can be delivered a bit faster. Experienced speakers also vary their rate based on the mood they want to create, for example, talking faster creates a sense of excitement.

Many beginning public speakers tend to talk too fast because they're nervous, which makes it difficult for their listeners to absorb what is said. By contrast, a speaker who talks too slowly bores listeners and gives them time to shift their focus away from the speech. When a speaker delivers a speech at the same rate throughout, it sounds monotonous and the listeners may tune out the entire speech.

The key to avoiding these problems is variety in rate. To vary your rate, change the length of the silent pauses that fall naturally between words, phrases, or sentences. Even while speaking fairly quickly, a silent pause can be used to emphasize a point and allow your listeners a moment to think about it (Clair, 1998). Pauses also act as silent transitions from one thought to the next, letting the listeners know that you've completed one idea and you're moving on to another.

One benefit of pausing silently is that it helps you reduce your use of **vocalized pauses,** which are the meaningless sounds or words a speaker utters during moments of silence, such as *like, uh, you know,* and *OK.* These filled pauses, which usually result from nervousness, interrupt the flow of a speech and can be distracting to the listeners. The easiest way to substitute a silent pause for a vocalized pause is to record yourself giving a speech. Once you become aware of the vocalized pauses you tend to use, you can train yourself to take a quick breath instead.

Pitch

Pitch is the highness or lowness of the speaking voice. All speakers have a natural pitch at which they usually speak, but competent speakers try to achieve a more effective pitch by varying and adjusting it to a slightly lower or higher timbre (Wolff, 1998). A change in pitch, called an *inflection,* reveals the emotional content of the message and tells the listeners whether a speaker is asking a question or making a statement. Raising your pitch at the end of a sentence, for example, indicates a question is being asked. Sometimes

CloseUp ON DIVERSITY

Language & Multicodality

INTERCULTURAL COMMUNICATION experts agree that communicating with people of different cultural backgrounds than your own can be challenging for a variety of reasons (Martin, Hecht, & Larkey, 1994). Difficulties may arise from differences in verbal and nonverbal communication patterns or from communication preferences. Given these realities, a competent public speaker needs to look for ways to bridge the differences among people and build rapport and understanding with culturally different and diverse audiences.

An approach to using language called *multicodality* can help. Multicodality is similar to being multilingual in that speakers retain their own unique way of using words and language, while learning to use some of the language codes and patterns of their listeners. Widely studied by scholars in linguistics, communication, and sociology, researchers refer to this as *code switching,* which means you switch from your own way of encoding a message and encode it the way other person or persons would.

These researchers noticed how bicultural and bilingual people use code switching as a solution to culturally based communication differences (Auer, 1998). The speakers switch back and forth from one language to another within one conversation. This phenomenon has been documented in young children in homes where two or more languages are spoken. It also occurs among multilingual adults, who bounce back and forth from one language to another—like Spanish/English speakers, Russian/English, Chinese/English, or French/English.

Sometimes code switchers only switch a word or two to clarify meaning. For instance, in Canada, French/English bilinguals use the English word *fun* because the French language lacks a good counterpart. Other times, speakers use a word that is more readily understood in the dominant or popular culture. English speakers in French-speaking countries often use the word *dépanneur* to mean convenience store. When two people of different cultures first meet, they often code-switch to learn what language will be most comfortable for talking with one another.

Besides switching from one language to another, code switchers also switch from one dialect to another within the same language. One researcher, on a trip to Italy, overheard an Italian friend switch from standard Italian into a regional dialect—Genovese. She questioned the friend about such strategic use of the Genovese dialect in common conversation, and the friend explained why he code switches. By peppering his language with the regional dialect, he can quickly establish rapport with a stranger and, as a result, more easily establish a sense of informality and community with another person.

There is a lesson for the public speaker to be derived from observing what people who share multiple cultures are doing naturally. If code switching helps these multicultural people build rapport and understanding, it can help a public speaker do the same thing. A public speaker who is multicodal would first become familiar with any distinctive verbal or nonverbal cultural codes or language patterns of the listeners in the audience. Then those codes or patterns could be used in the speech to build rapport and to communicate an awareness and value of the listeners' culture.

If you're speaking to a group of people from a highly expressive culture, such as Italian Americans, you could use language that is more expressive and exuberant. With an audience of black businesspeople, you might quote black authors and leaders. If you're speaking to an audience of high school students, you could incorporate adjectives and descriptors that might be popular at the time with that audience. That said, it's important to note that public speakers should not forsake their own way of communicating to embrace the code of the listeners, nor should they use the other code in an insincere or condescending manner. Rather, aspects of the listeners' codes should be incorporated within the speaker's message to communicate interest and respect.

SOURCES: Auer (1998); Martin, Hecht, & Larkey (1994).

inexperienced speakers do this at the end of their speeches, even when they don't intend to ask a question.

When a person speaks publicly, anxiety may cause the vocal pitch to rise to a squeak, giving away the fact that the speaker is nervous. It's hard to listen to a speaker with a continuously high-pitched voice, but equally distracting is a speaker who uses a monotone pitch and stays in a narrow, unchanging pitch range for an entire speech. The speaker's voice has a droning sound to it that most listeners find boring. By varying your pitch, you keep your listener's attention and emphasize important points in your speech. Experienced speakers determine an optimal pitch for their voices and vary it with control when speaking publicly.

VOLUME

Volume is the intensity, the loudness or softness, of the speaker's voice. Competent public speakers vary their volume based on the size of the audience, the size of the room, and the amount of background noise they may be speaking against. Being heard is so important that experienced speakers often arrive early for speaking engagements to test out audio equipment and acoustics to be sure all audience members will able to hear without straining. They speak loud enough so everyone can hear them, but they are also careful not to overpower the listeners with a booming or loud voice. When a speaker's volume is too loud, the listeners may feel their space is being invaded, making the speech an unpleasant experience.

In the opening vignette, Wen Shu had a problem with volume that many beginning speakers have. People who are new to public speaking either don't talk loud enough or they let their voices quietly fade out at the end of a thought. A lack of confidence in oneself and in one's own voice accounts for this lack of sufficient volume. As a public speaker, you can use volume and vocal variety most effectively by developing the use of your public voice (see Figure 16.4).

PUBLIC VOICE & PRIVATE VOICE

A **public voice** makes use of increased variety in rate and pitch and increased volume, so your words are easily heard and understood by the entire audience. Your private voice is the one you use in interpersonal conversations, or even in self-reflection or when thinking out loud. Although your private voice seems quite natural, you need to become accustomed to a louder public voice for giving speeches, even though it may sound strange at first.

To achieve a public voice, experiment with giving your speech using the full range of rate, pitch, and volume your voice is capable of. As you do that, use your voice to call attention to important parts of your speech. The faster and louder you say something, the

FIGURE 16.4
Public Voice vs. Private Voice

Public voice makes full use of variety in rate, pitch, and volume and is more appropriate for public speaking situations than your private voice.

TABLE 16.3

Varying Rate, Pitch, & Volume of the Voice

By varying the rate, pitch, and volume of your voice, you can maintain the listeners' attention and interest in what you're saying.

1. Vary rate.
- Vary rate by talking fast and then talking more slowly (but be sure you can be understood).
- Talk more slowly and more deliberately for a serious subject.
- Talk faster for less serious subject matter.
- Use silent pauses.
- Avoid vocalized pauses.

2. Vary pitch.
- Adjust pitch to a slightly lower or a slightly higher timbre.
- Use inflections to reveal emotional content.
- Don't raise pitch at the end of a sentence, except to ask a question.

3. Vary volume.
- Vary volume but speak loudly enough to be heard.
- Don't overpower listeners with a loud voice.
- Develop a public voice for presenting speeches.

more emotion and excitement you assign to it. By slowing down, dropping your pitch, or decreasing your volume, you can call attention to an idea in a more subtle way. The three aspects of vocal variety are briefly summarized in Table 16.3 to help you remember how to do it.

The Value of Correctness

In addition to paying attention to language and vocal variety, competence results from speaking correctly and appropriately for the given context in which the speech is presented. The failure to do so can have several negative results for you as a public speaker. First, your listeners may not understand what you're saying, for example, if you mispronounce a word. Second, an error calls attention to itself and distracts the listeners from your message. Third, errors in speech damage your credibility as a speaker. Consequently, a competent speaker pronounces words correctly, articulates speech sounds clearly, and uses correct grammar.

Pronunciation means stressing and accenting the right syllables in a word. **Articulation** is forming individual speech sounds correctly with your mouth, so they combine to produce an understandable word. **Grammar** is the rules and structure for putting words together in sentences.

Pronunciation & Articulation

Most speakers try to pronounce words correctly and appropriately for the given audience. But people grow up pronouncing words like others around them; plus, regional and ethnic dialects affect pronunciation patterns. As a result, without knowing it, many familiar words are frequently mispronounced. *Library* may be said out loud as *lyberry. Government* is *guvermint. Ask* is *ax. Just* is *jist. Get* is *git.* If you have any doubt about how to pronounce a word, look it up in the dictionary and see which syllables should be accented in order to pronounce the word correctly.

Besides pronunciation problems, speakers frequently fail to articulate speech sounds correctly. Most people know that *awtuh* should be *ought to.* They know the right way to pronounce it, but they may not bother to articulate it correctly. Clear and correct articulation depends on how the speaker's mouth actually forms sounds, which could be affected by factors such as chewing gum while speaking or even wearing braces. More often, poor articulation results from simply not paying attention to how you form sounds when you speak. Common articulation problems are errors of omission, substitution, addition, and slurring.

- **Omission** means leaving out and not saying part of a word. The most common omissions are word endings, such as when the *ing* at the end of a word becomes *in. Working* becomes *workin* and *speaking* becomes *speakin.* Sometimes parts are omitted from the middle of a word as well as the end of it. *Listening* becomes *lis-nin.* Another form of omission occurs when a speaker doesn't pronounce the consonants at the end of words, like d's and t's. *Grand* becomes *gran* and an *appointment* becomes an *appointmin.*
- **Substitutions** occur when the speaker replaces part of a word with an incorrect sound. At the beginning of a word, the "d" sound may be substituted for the "t" sound. The result is that people say *dese, dem,* and *dose* instead of *these, them,* and *those.* Sometimes the ending of *th* is substituted by just *t,* and the word *with* becomes *wit.*
- **Additions** occur when a speaker adds extra parts to a word. An *athlete* becomes an *athalete; regardless* becomes *irregardless,* which isn't actually a word.
- **Slurring,** running sounds and words together, is another common articulation problem public speakers must overcome. It's caused by the speaker saying two or more words at once, or overlapping the end of one word with the beginning of the next. Pairs of words that end with the word *of* or the word *to* are often slurred together: *sort of* becomes *sorta; want to* becomes *wanna.* To avoid such slurring in a public speech, alternative phrasing can be used. Instead of saying *alotta* something, it's more effective to refer to *many, quite a few,* or *an array of.*

GRAMMAR

Finally, correct language calls for avoiding grammatical errors. If listeners are distracted by a mistake in grammar, their attention turns from what you are saying to the error itself. Moreover, if you commit an error in grammar, it calls into question your authority as a speaker and thereby damages your credibility. The listeners will think, perhaps wrongly so, that you don't know enough about the topic to be talking about it.

Most people pay close attention to the grammatical structure of sentences when they are writing, but they are less careful about grammar when they speak in public. The typical kinds of errors most people make are simple ones such as the erroneous use of the verb *to be:* "All of them was there" or "Sergio and Wen Shu was late for class" are incorrect uses of the verb to be. *All* is a plural noun, so should take the plural form of the verb. "All of them were there" and "Sergio and Wen Shu were late for class" are grammatically correct.

Less flagrant but equally erroneous is the incorrect use of pronouns such as *self, me,* and *I* . *Self* is a reflexive pronoun used to reflect on a noun or another pronoun to add emphasis. "I myself accept the invitation to speak" is correct. "Wen Shu and myself accept the invitation" is wrong; it should be "Wen Shu and I accept the invitation."

I and *me* can be the subject or object of the sentence. When used as the subject in a sentence, *I* is correct; when used as the object in a sentence *me* is correct. "Thanks for inviting

Knowledge Link

How could guidelines for vocal variety help improve communication in interpersonal situations and in small groups?

TABLE 16.4

••• Using Correct Pronunciation, Articulation, & Grammar •••

By speaking correctly, you ensure that the listeners understand what you say. Errors distract from your message and reflect negatively on your credibility.

1. **Pronounce words correctly.**
   - Avoid regionalisms and dialect.
   - Look up words that you can't pronounce ahead of time.
2. **Articulate speech sounds correctly**
   - Avoid the errors of omission, substitution, and addition.
   - Avoid slurring.
3. **Use correct grammar**
   - Avoid the incorrect use of the verb *to be*.
   - Use the pronouns *self, me,* and *I* correctly.
   - Use the correct subject/verb agreement for problem words such as *data* and *media.*

Wen Shu and I" is wrong; "Thanks for inviting Wen Shu and me" is correct. "Wen Shu and me accept the invitation" is wrong; "Wen Shu and I accept the invitation" is correct.

Subject/verb agreement errors often happen when a word is confusing in regard to its plural and singular forms. *Data* and *media* are good examples. *Datum* and *medium* are the singular form of these nouns; *data* and *media* are the plural forms. So the correct subject/verb agreement would be "The data from the study are interesting; the media were expected to wait until the speaker arrived." Incorrect use would be "The data is interesting and the media was expected." A summary of these recommendations for the use of pronunciation, articulation, and grammar is presented in Table 16.4.

The Importance of Nonverbal Cues

In addition to all the aspects of verbal communication just discussed, understanding and using nonverbal cues to support and enhance the spoken message is crucial to public speaking competence and therefore to your credibility as a speaker. In Chapter 5 you learned that nonverbal cues have a large impact on how people react to messages. That is true, but when people speak in public, they sometimes forget about the messages they are sending nonverbally. That is what happened to Wen Shu until her instructor called her ineffective nonverbal cues to her attention and she watched herself on videotape. The nonverbal cues important to public speaking are appearance, posture and body movement, gestures, facial expression, and eye contact.

APPEARANCE

Think about the initial impression you'll make on your listeners when you stand up and walk to the podium or lectern. Recall the discussion of first impressions in Chapter 5 and modify your **appearance** accordingly—your clothing, shoes, jewelry, hairstyle, and even hair adornments. All these nonverbal cues influence what the audience thinks of you even before you begin to speak, and consequently, they affect your initial credibility.

You want to present yourself in the best possible light, without manipulating your appearance in any way that would seem artificial to the audience or make you uncomfortable. In general, avoid trying out a new hairstyle or outfit when you give your speech. A new hairstyle can go wrong or take too much preparation time, and you may not feel comfortable in new clothes. Feeling relaxed but attractive is the best appearance to put forward to any audience.

When thinking about your appearance and the impression you want to make, consider the results of a study of fashion in the classroom (Morris, Gorham, Cohen, & Huffman, 1996). The study investigated the effects of clothing on students' perceptions of their instructors. Three styles of attire were compared: formal professional (business suits, dress shoes, etc.), casual professional (pants suit, casual dress), and casual (faded jeans, T-shirt, flannel shirt). The more formal the attire, the greater the increase in ratings of instructor competence. If that holds true for instructors in the classroom, the same approach can work for you. If you want to be perceived as competent and credible, dress somewhat more formally.

Posture & Body Movement

You're dressed to impress and there you sit, waiting to present your first speech. When it's your turn, stand up straight, hold your head up, and walk with confidence to the front of the room. A confident walk conveys a sense of self-assuredness that will move the audience to respect you. Further, by acting self-assured, you will actually begin to feel more confident.

After arriving at the lectern, stand relaxed but maintain an alert body posture, with your shoulders held up and in line with your hips and knees. This posture will communicate that you're in control and ready to speak. **Posture** is defined as a position or attitude of the bodily parts, and that is just what it communicates, your attitude. For instance, if you slouch and lean on the podium or lectern, your posture communicates a lack of confidence and enthusiasm.

During your speech, move about voluntarily and purposefully within the speaking area. By moving with purpose, you can emphasize a transition or focus the audience's attention on an important point you want to make. If you're about to tell a story, move closer to the audience while telling the tale to draw them in, and then back to your notes as you conclude it and move on. By moving toward the audience or from one side of the lectern to the other, you decrease the distance between you and the listeners, which communicates that sense of immediacy and involvement that positively impacts perceptions of credibility (Thweatt & McCroskey, 1998).

Although it's effective to move purposefully to make a point, moving about aimlessly can signal nervousness. Pacing, or letting your body rock unconsciously from one foot to the other, distracts listeners from what you're saying and communicates public speaking anxiety. So only use body movement intentionally, and try to become aware of any unconscious movements that may distract your listeners from your message.

Gestures

Whether standing or moving, competent speakers keep their hands and arms free and relaxed, so they are ready to incorporate natural movements or gestures into their presentations. Gestures are used to reinforce what is said, emphasize important points, and make presentations more interesting to watch. Because most people gesture naturally when speaking one on one, gesturing when presenting a speech will make the presentation seem more natural and relaxed.

Gestures also communicate openness to the audience and a sense of involvement. A small gesture communicates less involvement, and a larger gesture communicates greater involvement. Most speakers gesture with their arms somewhere between their waist and shoulders, but the most important thing is to gesture in a way that's natural for you and matches the content of what you're saying. Here are a few hints for gesturing naturally:

- Vary your gestures from one hand to the other and sometimes gesture with both hands at the same time. Many speakers use their dominant hand more, leaving the other arm hanging like a limp dishrag.
- When you aren't gesturing, let both arms relax and drop your arms to your sides naturally.
- If you feel unsure about what to do with your hands, rest them lightly on the lectern at any time during your speech. This will help you appear much more in control of what you're saying.
- Try to hold your gestures longer when speaking publicly than you do in normal conversation, avoiding quick or jerky movements.
- Don't clasp your hands for too long in front or in back of you; this will keep you from gesturing.
- Avoid gesturing in a way that appears artificial to the audience. If you feel your gestures are contrived, they will certainly appear that way to the audience.

Two more nonverbal cues you can use to your advantage as a public speaker are facial expression and eye contact. In one study of U.S. college students, their use of these two forms of nonverbal communication had a positive impact on their credibility. A relaxed facial expression compared with a nervous facial expression, and direct eye contact rather than indirect, resulted in higher credibility ratings of the students as speakers (Aguinis, Simonsen, & Pierce, 1998).

FACIAL EXPRESSION

Facial expression is the vehicle you use to communicate how you feel about what you're saying to the audience. Your facial expression reflects the mood or tone of your speech, but may reveal mixed feelings. If you don't believe in your claim, your facial expression will reveal your doubt. If you're nervous, your facial expression may be too strained and you won't appear enthusiastic about the topic. Instead, try for a facial expression to match and reflect the content of your speech. If it's on a lighthearted topic, your facial expression should reflect this. If your topic is serious, look serious. Moreover, try to avoid either a deadpan expression—no feeling at all—or a smile pasted on your face.

As we mentioned in Chapter 5, research indicates that men and women use facial expressions differently when speaking (Borisoff & Merrill, 1992). Women express more emotion on their faces and smile more, even if they're unhappy or the message is not worth smiling about. If a woman is presenting a speech on a serious topic and smiles too much, it is confusing to the audience. Another problem results when a woman speaker emotes too much or displays too much emotion on the face, which can be distracting to the listeners. By contrast, men tend to limit the amount of emotion they display on their faces, so listeners in an audience might not be able to tell how they feel about what they're presenting. The way to get around these gender differences is simply to match your facial expression to the content of your speech. Whether you are a man or a woman, use facial expressions that are appropriate to your topic and communicate your true feelings about it.

Eye Contact

Eye contact is a tool you can use to promote a sense of involvement with audience members. In North America, eye contact communicates honesty, openness, and respect for others—all crucial aspects of credibility for a public speaker. If you avoid making eye contact with listeners in an audience of North Americans, they may perceive you as nervous at best or deceitful at worst.

To get better at using eye contact as a public speaker, mentally divide your audience into four quadrants, like a window with four panes. Look directly at and speak to at least one person in each quadrant at some point during the speech. Don't just gaze in their direction, but actually stop and make eye contact with a specific member of the audience seated in each quadrant. Not only will this communicate interest and involvement to the entire audience, you also will learn how your listeners are reacting to your speech. If they're losing interest, you can speed up or talk a little louder to regain their attention. If it's appropriate to do so, you can invite audience participation by asking questions about their opinion of what you're saying. Table 16.5 provides a summary of all the nonverbal cues that help to present a speech most competently.

TABLE 16.5

••• Nonverbal Communication & Public Speaking •••

Make use of a variety of nonverbal cues to support and enhance your verbal message.

1. Appearance

- Modify your appearance to make a good first impression.
- Don't modify your appearance in a way that looks artificial or makes you uncomfortable.

2. Posture and body movement

- Walk confidently.
- At the lectern, relax but maintain an alert body posture.
- Move about in the speaking area voluntarily and purposefully.
- Avoid pacing, body rocking, or fiddling with objects.

3. Gestures

- Make use of both hands and gesture naturally.
- Relax and drop arms to your sides when not gesturing.
- Rest hands lightly on the lectern.
- Hold gestures longer.
- Don't clasp hands in front or in back of you.

4. Facial expressions

- Use your face to communicate how you feel about your speech.
- Let your facial expression reflect the mood and tone of the speech.
- Avoid a deadpan expression.
- Match your facial expression to what you're saying.

5. Eye contact

- Use eye contact to communicate interest and involvement to the audience.
- Use eye contact to gauge how the listeners are reacting to your speech.

Challenges to Presenting With Competence

Like Wen Shu and Sergio, you are now aware of all the presentation skills that will help you present your speech more competently and credibly. As you ready yourself to present your next speech, you also need to be aware of several challenges that could impact your presentational competence: maximizing a competent delivery, managing audience reactions to what you say, and presenting most effectively with visual aids.

Knowledge Link

How can a public speaker figure out what verbal/nonverbal behavior is appropriate and thus achieve a truly competent delivery?

MAXIMIZING A COMPETENT DELIVERY

By now you may need some kind of guideline for making decisions about using all the presentation skills just described in this chapter. The Frank and Ernest cartoon provides one suggestion—"just wag your tail now and then." On a more serious note, deciding what you should do or not do when presenting your next speech is a challenge for any speaker. Given the options of all the verbal and nonverbal skills just discussed, figuring how to present your speech most competently can be a challenge.

MANAGING AUDIENCE REACTIONS

Depending on the type of speech you're presenting, you may find you need to manage audience feedback and answer questions at the conclusion of your speech. Distractions of various types also may occur during your speech, such as a cell phone ringing or even a heckler expressing his or her opinion in a distracting manner. A challenge to presentational competence is knowing what to do and being able to handle these situations.

PRESENTING WITH VISUAL AIDS

In Chapter 15, you learned how to prepare effective visual aids, but preparation is only half the job. When you incorporate a visual aid of any kind in your speech, doing so with competence can be challenging. Poorly used, a visual aid distracts from your speech rather than enhancing it.

Nonverbal cues made easy . . . just wag your tail now and then!

Frank & Ernest reprinted by permission of Newspaper Enterprises Association, Inc.

Overcoming Challenges to Presentational Competence

A speaker who is aware of these three challenges, and who is able to handle them when presenting a speech, will be perceived as competent and will leave a lasting impression as a credible speaker. Here are some recommendations for addressing these challenges.

HOW TO MAXIMIZE DELIVERY COMPETENCE

First of all, as you think about making the best possible impression with your use of presentation skills, remember that impressions of competence are influenced by the context in which the communication takes place. What is appropriate and effective in one public speaking context may be inappropriate and ineffective in some other context. Given that caution, Frank Dance, an expert on public speaking, offers a useful recommendation for deciding how to use the presentation skills outlined in this chapter most competently (Dance, 1999). Dance coined the phrase **transparent delivery,** which means presenting a speech in such a way that the audience doesn't focus on the elements of the delivery but instead pays full attention to the message—thus the delivery itself is transparent.

To achieve a transparent delivery, watch yourself present a speech on videotape. Examine how you use all the various presentation skills and think about how they will impact the audience's reactions to your speech. If the use of certain words helps clarify and create interest in your speech, then use those words. If increasing the volume of your voice encourages the listeners to pay attention to you, increase your volume. If slurred speech might cause audience members to wonder what you're saying, work on your articulation. If a certain gesture calls attention to itself and not to a point you want to make, don't gesture in that way. In sum, do what enhances your speech and avoid anything that interferes with its delivery. Then once you have decided on your strengths as a presenter and what skills you should make most use of, practice your speech several times on videotape, just as Sergio and Wen Shu did as they prepared for the statewide tour promoting their campus. Like those students, several rehearsals of an extemporaneous speech are pivotal to a competent presentation of it.

HOW TO HANDLE FEEDBACK, QUESTIONS, & DISTRACTIONS

As you learned in Chapter 14, audience members have the responsibility to provide feedback to the speaker, which often occurs during a question and answer session at the conclusion of the speech. Your goals during such a session are to answer any questions that are raised, easy or difficult ones; demonstrate your appreciation of the audience's participation; and benefit personally from the listeners' feedback by learning about their reactions to your speech. Here are some how-to's for managing a Q&A session competently:

- Do your homework ahead of time. Compile a list of questions you may be asked and prepare answers for all of them.
- Take responsibility for being the time manager during the Q&A session. Try to get to as many questions as possible by answering each question pointedly and moving quickly to the next question.
- If a listener's question actually contains several questions, divide the question up and answer its parts separately.

- If a question is particularly complex, repeat and clarify it before answering it.
- If a listener asks for clarification of something specific you said in the speech, return to the overhead or poster containing that information while you answer the question.
- If you don't know the answer to a question, admit you don't know but tell the questioner you'll get back to him or her later with an answer.

A competent speaker plans ahead for the questions that could be asked in a tough Q&A session.

Sometimes during a Q&A session, audience members raise challenging questions or offer dissenting opinions. By inviting the audience to ask questions, you open the door to a dialogue that may or may not always be amicable. As a result, you may find yourself engaged in a debate in front of a room full of people with an audience member who strongly disagrees with your point of view—sometimes to the extent that the listener is actually heckling you. You can turn this situation to your advantage by viewing it as an opportunity to receive constructive feedback and clarify your point of view. By anticipating opposing or negative comments, you can be well prepared to address them (Rafe, 1994). Here are a few hints for handling a tough Q&A session:

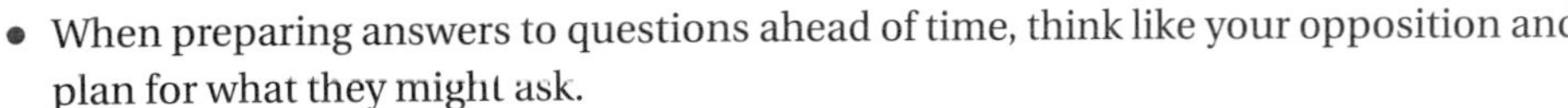

- When preparing answers to questions ahead of time, think like your opposition and plan for what they might ask.
- If asked a difficult question you can't answer, maintain your composure and either tell the person you'll get back to him or her or ask other audience members for their input. You can't be expected to know everything, so handling the situation respectfully will boost your credibility, not harm it.
- If faced with a biased or threatening question, rephrase the question more objectively, then answer it without reacting emotionally or being drawn into a one-on-one debate. Try to give the best answer you can without appearing evasive.
- Above all, remain calm, and admit when you may be mistaken or don't have an immediate answer to every question. Invite and encourage open dialogue and you'll be respected for doing so.

Another situation that a competent speaker must know how to handle is the unexpected distraction. Despite all good preparation, a visual aid fails to work as it should—a poster board falls over or an overhead projector fails to work. Or something happens to an audience member; he or she starts to cough or, of course, a cell phone goes off during your speech. The best approach to handling any of these situations is simply to pause briefly, then continue. Clearly, everyone realizes what has happened, so acknowledge the distraction and then continue with your speech. That may mean picking up the poster board, doing without your overheads, or asking the owner of the cell phone to take the call in the hallway. Another recommendation of speech teachers who were asked the cell phone question is this: At the beginning of your speech, ask your listeners to turn off their phone and pagers, unless they are needed for emergency reasons.

HOW TO PRESENT WITH VISUAL AIDS

Visual aids competently incorporated into your presentation make it more appealing and easier to follow. If you decide to use a visual aid as part of your speech, include it in at least one practice session before you actually present with it. By doing this, you will answer several crucial questions you don't want to be asking yourself on the actual day of your presentation.

You need to decide ahead of time where you'll set up and display the aid and where you'll stand relative to it. If you're using a projected image of some kind, experiment with standing next to the projector or next to the projected image. Both of these locations are equally effective, but you need to choose which feels most comfortable to you. Also experiment with pointing to each item on the aid as you talk about it, or just letting the listeners read for themselves what is displayed. Practice with a pointer if you're going to use one, and plan what you'll do with it when it's not in use. Here's a summary of suggestions for competently presenting with a visual aid effectively:

- Speak to the audience, not to the visual aid. If you face the aid, the audience won't hear what you're saying.
- Use a pointer, a pencil, or a laser pointer, if you want to focus audience attention on the part of the aid you're talking about.
- If possible, cover up the sections of the aid you have yet to discuss. Reveal each section just as you begin to talk about it.
- Don't read the entire text of the aid to the audience, unless you want to emphasize a definition or description of something contained in it.
- Don't shuffle through handouts or transparencies while you're presenting. Instead, have them in the right order ahead of time and plan for how you'll pick them up and where you'll put them after presenting with them.

Wen Shu and Sergio improved their presentation skills and were able to contribute effectively to the work of the traveling campus team. In the same way, by examining your own presentation skills and thinking about your strengths and your weaknesses as a presenter, you can identify specific skills that may need improvement. When you give your next speech, concentrate on several of the skills covered in this chapter and try to improve in those areas. With practice, you'll get better and better and become a highly competent public speaker.

Chapter Summary

Research studies show that training in public speaking is the best way to improve public speaking skills. The competent use of language and words, vocal variety, pronunciation, articulation, and grammar, and nonverbal cues influences the audience's impressions of a speaker's credibility.

Competent language enhances the listeners' understanding and enthusiasm for a speech by the use of words that are clear, vivid, and appropriate. Vividness and style are achieved through the use of imagery and the following figures of speech: simile, metaphor, analogy, the rhetorical question, alliteration, and repetition. In addition

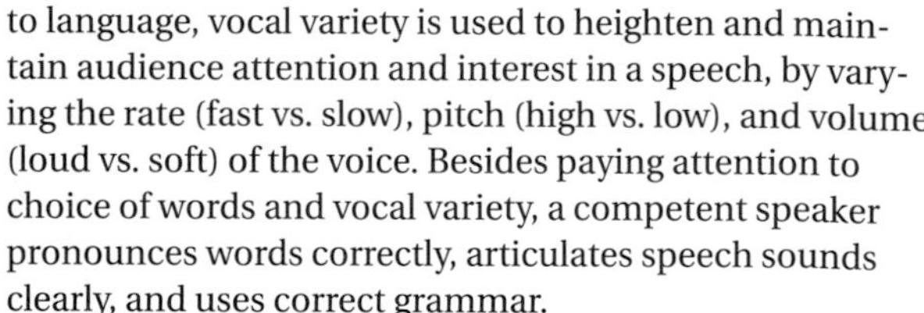

to language, vocal variety is used to heighten and maintain audience attention and interest in a speech, by varying the rate (fast vs. slow), pitch (high vs. low), and volume (loud vs. soft) of the voice. Besides paying attention to choice of words and vocal variety, a competent speaker pronounces words correctly, articulates speech sounds clearly, and uses correct grammar.

Beyond words and how they are spoken, a competent speaker understands and uses the following nonverbal cues to support and enhance the spoken message: appearance, posture and body movement, gestures, facial expression, and eye contact. To make best use all of these presentation skills, public speaking competence calls for addressing the challenges of maximizing the quality of the delivery and practicing the speech, managing audience feedback, questions, and distractions, and presenting effectively with visual aids.

Key Terms

speaker credibility
initial credibility
derived credibility
terminal credibility
competent language
clear language
vivid language
style
imagery
figures of speech
simile
metaphor
analogy
rhetorical question
alliteration
repetition
appropriate language
multicodality
vocal variety
rate
vocalized pauses
pitch
volume
public voice
pronunciation
articulation
grammar
omission
substitutions
additions
slurring
appearance
posture
facial expression
eye contact
transparent delivery

Building Knowledge

1. How can a speaker who lacks initial credibility enhance the first impression he or she makes on the audience?
2. Competent language calls for using words that are clear, vivid, and appropriate. However, words that are clear may not be very vivid, and words that are vivid may not be appropriate for the particular audience or speaking situation. How can a speaker balance the use of all three types of words?
3. As speakers strive for variety in rate, pitch, and volume, how can they retain the authenticity of their own voice? How can speakers develop a public voice different from their private voice?
4. Is it always appropriate for a speaker to use correct pronunciation, articulation, and grammar? How can a speaker strike a balance between speaking correctly and speaking in a way that suits a particular situation and audience for whom correctness may not be particularly effective?
5. Of all the nonverbal cues a speaker can use, which do you think is the most important and why—appearance, posture, body movement, gestures, facial expression, or eye contact?
6. If during a Q&A session, an audience member asks a question but isn't satisfied with your answer, what can and should a competent speaker do?

Building Skills

Individual Exercises

1. Make a videotape of your next speech during one of your practice sessions. Watch yourself and evaluate your presentation skills, based on the content of this chapter. Identify your strengths and weaknesses and make a list of what you will try to improve when you actually present the speech to an audience.
2. Attend a live lecture or speech. Evaluate the speaker's presentation skills using the content of this chapter.
3. If you are using *InfoTrac College Edition,* enter public speaking as a subject search, which will result in at least 30 articles. Select several articles that appear to offer helpful hints on presenting a speech, such as "How to be a successful speaker," by Michael Hypes and others, *The Journal of Physical Education, Recreation & Dance,* January 1999 (70), 50–54; "Keeping up public appearances: Master the fine art of public-speaking and give a great presentation every time," by Audrey Arthur, *Black Enterprise,* July 1997 (27), 54; "Speak easy: A few hints for anyone who hates to give speeches," by Phyllis Gates, *Working Woman,* February 1997 (22), 60–62. Read the articles and synthesize a list of hints that you could use as the topic of an in-class speech.
4. Go the Web site of the Public Address Division of the National Communication Association, which links to many other sites that contain speeches. The linked sites include, among others: Democratic Leadership Speeches in the U.S. House of Representatives, Gifts of Speech: Women's Speeches From Around the World, National Press Club Transcripts of Speeches, Presidential Speeches from the National Archives, and Speeches on Human Rights. Find a speech that appeals to you and, using its text, examine the speaker's use of language. Is it clear, vivid, and appropriate? Does the speaker use correct grammar and figures of speech effectively? (**http://www.vanderbilt.edu/Ans/Comm/Courses/pad/padlinks.html**)

Public Speaking Presentation Competence Skills Grid

To help you understand how to use this grid, the skills displayed by Sergio and Wen Shu in the opening vignette of this chapter have been anlayzed below. Examine that analysis and then think about a recent speech and what you could have done more competently. On the next page, first describe the context of the speech in the spaces provided. Next, analyze your presentation skills based on the four presentational skills explained in this chapter. In the first column, briefly describe and give examples of how your skills were less than competent.

ANALYZING WEN SHU AND SERGIO'S PRESENTATION SKILLS

Context

CULTURE: A Chinese and a Mexican American student on a statewide speaking tour

TIME: Daytime and evening

RELATIONSHIP: Older students–younger students; student–faculty

PLACE: Rural high schools

FUNCTION: To promote the university and encourage students to attend it

PRESENTATION SKILLS	LESS COMPETENT	MORE COMPETENT
WORDS & LANGUAGE	Sergio used fancy words, jargon, and unfamiliar terms.	Sergio needs to speak clearly, vividly, and appropriately for the particular audience. Wen Shu chose her words carefully and spoke at the right level.
VOCAL VARIETY	Wen Shu spoke too quietly.	Wen Shu needs to vary her vocal variety and increase her volume. Sergio projected his voice effectively.
PRONUNCIATION, ARTICULATION, & GRAMMAR	Sergio committed errors in pronunciation and articulation and used filled pauses.	Sergio needs to pronounce words and articulate sounds correctly and pause silently. Wen Shu pronounced clearly and used grammar correctly.
NONVERBAL CLUES	Wen Shu rocked from one foot to the other, kept looking down, doodled nervously, and had an expressionless face.	Wen Shu needs to use posture, gestures, body movement, facial expressions, and eye contact to enhance her verbal message.

Using these less competent skills as a point of comparison to fill in the second column, describe the skills you think would have been perceived as more competent in the particular context. With practice, you will find you can use this grid to help you plan how to present future speeches more competently and avoid behaviors that could be perceived as less competent.

ANALYZING YOUR PRESENTATION SKILLS

Context

CULTURE:

TIME:

RELATIONSHIP:

PLACE:

FUNCTION:

PRESENTATION SKILLS	LESS COMPETENT	MORE COMPETENT
WORDS & LANGUAGE		
VOCAL VARIETY		
PRONUNCIATION, ARTICULATION, & GRAMMAR		
NONVERBAL CLUES		

Building Skills (Cont'd)

5. A Web site devoted to Martin Luther King, Jr. has a segment of the "I Have a Dream" speech on compressed video and translated into several languages (**http://www.mccsc.edu/~bhsntech/**). Evaluate King's use of language, particularly the figures of speech described in this chapter.
6. On the internet, access a site that provides the texts of State of the Union speeches, such as **http://www.whitehouse.gov**. Select a speech that interests you and present an analysis of its content in a speech to your class.
7. Visit the Web site of the G. Robert Vincent Voice Library at **http://www.lib.msu.edu/vincent/**, where you can hear excerpts from the speeches of over a dozen U.S. presidents. Choose a president and evaluate the speaker's use of vocal variety.

Group Exercises

1. With one other student, visit the Web site Wired Style: Principles of English Usage in the Digital Age, which provides definitions for new terms, buzzwords, and acronyms. Try to find some words or terms that each of you could use to enliven your language in your next speech.
2. Get another student to be your rehearsal and practice partner. Ask your partner to watch carefully how you present your speech. Then have that person critique your posture, body movement, gestures, facial expression, and eye contact. Reverse roles, watch, and then critique your partner's nonverbal cues.
3. Ask your practice partner to provide you feedback during your in-class presentation on two factors: volume and speaking rate. Your partner should sit toward the rear of the room and communicate with you using four hand signals. A flat hand, facing up and lifted toward the ceiling means "Increase your volume, you're talking too softly." A single finger pointed up and held at the mouth means "Softer, you're too loud." A circular motion with the hand means "Speed it up, you're too slow." A stretching motion with both hands means "Slow it down, you're talking too fast."
4. In small groups, practice your ability to walk to, stand in, and move around in the speaking area. Have each student take a turn walking to the speaking platform, standing at the lectern, and moving deliberately away from the lectern to another part of the speaking area. Group members should provide feedback to each student.
5. In small groups, practice presenting your speech using your visual aid. Again, the group should provide feedback to each student.
6. If there are bilingual or trilingual students in the class, get in groups and discuss those students' personal experiences with code switching.

References

Aguinis, H., Simonsen, M., & Pierce, C. (1998). Effects of nonverbal behavior on perceptions of power bases. *Journal of Social Psychology, 138*(4) 455–470.

Auer, P. (Ed.). (1998). *Code-switching in conversation: Language, interaction, and identify.* London: Routledge.

Ausmus, W. A. (1998). Pragmatic uses of metaphor: Models and metaphor in the nuclear winter scenario. *Communication Monographs, 65,* 67–82.

Borisoff, D., & Merrill, L. (1992). *The power to communicate: Gender differences as barriers* (2nd ed.). Prospect Heights, IL: Waveland Press.

Clair, R. P. (1998). *Organizing silence: A world of possibilities.* Albany: SUNY Press.

Dance, F. E. X. (1999, July). Successful presenters master the art of being transparent. *Presentations,* p. 80.

Detz, J. (1992). *How to write and give a speech.* (pp. 60–61). New York: St. Martin's Press.

Ellis, K. (1995). Apprehension, self-perceived competency, and teacher immediacy in the laboratory-supported public speaking course: Trends and relationships. *Communication Education, 44,* 64–78.

Fatt, P. T. (1999, June-July). It's not the way you say, it's how you say it. *Communication World, 16*(6), 37–41.

Haleta, L. L. (1996). Student perceptions of teachers' use of language: The effects of powerful and powerless language on impression formation and uncertainty. *Communication Education, 45,* 16–28.

Harris, R. M. (1994). Practically perfect presentations. *Training & Development, 48*(7), 55–58.

Hayakawa, S. I. (1964). *Language in thought and action.* New York: Harcourt Brace.

Logue, C. M. (1997). *Representative American speeches 1937–1997.* New York: Wilson.

Martin, J. N., Hecht, M. L., & Larkey, L. K. (1994). Conversational improvement strategies for interethnic communication: African American and European American perspectives. *Communication Monographs, 61,* 236–255.

May, J. M. (1988). *Trials of character: The eloquence of Ciceronian ethos.* Chapel Hill: University of North Carolina Press.

McCroskey, J. C., & Young, T. J. (1981). Ethos and credibility: The construct and its measurement after three decades. *Central States Speech Journal, 32,* 24–34.

Morreale, S. P., Hackman, M. Z., & Neer, M. (1995). Predictors of behavioral competence and self-esteem: A study assessing impact in a basic public speaking course. *Basic Communication Course Annual, 7,* 125–141.

Morris, T., Gorham, J., Cohen, S., & Huffman, D. (1996). Fashion in the classroom: Effects of attire on student perceptions of instructors in college classes. *Communication Education, 45,* 135–148.

Ong, W. (1988). *Orality to literacy: The technologizing of the word.* London: Routledge.

Rafe, S. C. (1994). Talking "green" with hostile publics. *Public Relations Journal, 50,*(4), 38–39.

Seibold, D., Kudsi, S., & Rude, M. (1993). Does communication training make a difference? Evidence for the effectiveness of a presentation skills program. *Journal of Applied Communication Research, 21,* 111–131.

Sparks, J. R., Areni, C. S., & Cox, K. C. (1998). An investigation of the effects of language style and communication modality on persuasion. *Communication Education, 65,* 108–125.

Thweatt, K. S., & McCroskey, J. C. (1998). The impact of teacher immediacy and misbehaviors on teacher credibility. *Communication Education, 47,* 348–358.

Wolff, M. (1998). Perfect pitch. *Success, 45*(8), 18.

CHAPTER 17

Learning Objectives

After studying this chapter, you should be able to:

1. Describe what informative speaking is and why it's important.
2. Outline the three types of informative speeches based on their objective.
3. Distinguish among the five ways to organize an informative speech and understand how to outline each organizational pattern.
4. Understand how to use definitions, descriptions, examples, stories, testimonies and quotations, and facts and statistics to support an informative speech.
5. Discuss the role of ethics in informative speaking.
6. Identify three challenges to competent informative speaking and explain how to overcome them.

Speaking to Inform

By the time Patricia started to prepare her informative speech, she had already learned a lot about speaking with competence. Now it was time to apply her newly learned preparation and presenting skills and go for an "A" on the informative assignment in her public speaking class. She chose a topic she knew something about—the popularity of coffeehouses and increase in coffee drinking in American society. Because of her job at the bookstore café near campus, she had observed how much business had grown over the last few years. Plus, she thought the topic would appeal to her classmates, most of whom visit the café frequently. Patricia located some impressive statistics in the library demonstrating a year-by-year increase in coffee consumption, so she decided to describe how much patterns in coffee drinking had increased in the United States during the past decade and why that happened. To support her speech, she interviewed students who visited the café, who explained why they liked coming there and drinking coffee with their friends.

When she presented her speech in class, "The Joy of Java," Patricia expected the other students to be fascinated with her speech, but that wasn't what happened. Some of them even appeared a little bored as Patricia told them about the increase in coffee drinking, as opposed to other forms of libation like alcoholic beverages. Her grade improved over her last speech as she had hoped, but she wondered why her classmates weren't more attentive. After class, she was anxious to review the professor's feedback form to find out what she did well and what she could have done better. She was sure her topic was a good one for the audience. But had she provided too much or too little information—and was it the right information? Was the speech organized in a way that was easy to follow? Why weren't her classmates motivated to learn more about the dramatic increase in coffee drinking?

The instructor said that her presentation style was fine, and she definitely had chosen a topic the other students could relate to. She had organized the speech well and it was easy to follow, as she proceeded from talking about how much coffee consumption had increased to why that had happened. But to get the attention of the other students, the instructor said Patricia needed to be more inventive and creative in her use of examples and stories to liven up her facts and statistics. Her testimonies were effective, but she should have used a few direct quotations from the students about why they enjoy coffee drinking. She could have opened her speech with a story to illustrate how students make new friends in the bookstore café. Patricia had done a good job, but she still had something to learn about giving an informative speech. •••

This chapter covers key ideas about speaking to inform that will help you prepare and present an informative speech most competently. As with any other communication context, taking a competence approach to informative speaking is essential. Figure 17.1 visually depicts how each of the components of competence—motivation, knowledge, and skills—influences the outcome of perceived competence in any informative speaking situation. The content of this chapter tells you how to achieve that competence.

We begin by clarifying what an informative speech is and why it's an important form of public speaking competence. Then we describe three types of informative speeches followed by suggestions for organizing and outlining these speeches and using support materials effectively. The chapter concludes with the challenges to informative speaking that a competent public speaker must consider and overcome.

SPEAKING TO INFORM

A competent speaker
- appreciates the importance of informative speaking in the information age
- realizes that promoting understanding and encouraging retention of information is difficult
- respects the importance of ethics when speaking to inform

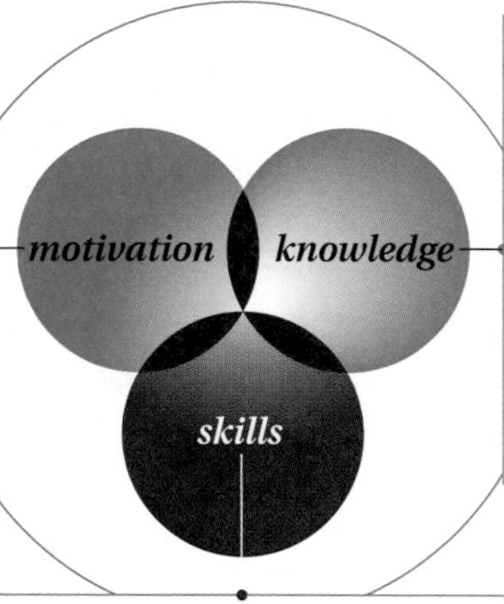

A competent speaker understands
- what informative speaking is
- the three types of informative speeches and how to use them competently
- the challenges to speaking to inform

A competent speaker is able to
- use the five organizational patterns to speak informatively
- develop an outline for an informative speech
- gather and use support materials to inform
- overcome the challenges to informative speaking

FIGURE 17.1
A Competence Approach to Informative Speaking

As in all communication contexts, motivation, knowledge, and skills are essential to speaking to inform. The use of these components influences whether a speaker presents an informative speech competently or incompetently.

Understanding the Informative Speech

An informative speech may range from a description of the intangible, like understanding the law of gravity, to a set of tangible instructions, like how to change a flat tire or prepare for final exams. Whether the speech is intended to describe or explain something or instruct the audience about how something works, it's considered informative.

WHAT IS AN INFORMATIVE SPEECH?

As we stated in Chapter 14, the purpose of an informative speech is to communicate new information or a new perspective on a topic to an audience and bring the listeners to greater understanding or insight. Given that purpose, an informative speech could be about an object, process, event, person, issue, or concept.

An informative speech about an object could be about a national or local memorial. The newest memorial to United States President Franklin D. Roosevelt has garnered national attention for its unique design.

If you choose to present a speech about an object, it is usually about something tangible that can be seen, touched, or otherwise experienced through the physical senses, such as a car, a computer, a place, or even a monument of some kind, like the Vietnam Memorial or the newer Franklin D. Roosevelt Memorial, both of which are in Washington, D.C. If you decide to describe a system or sequence of steps that lead to a result or change taking place, such as the steps involved in applying for a loan or shopping for a new car or computer, that is an informative speech about a process. An event speech describes something that has occurred, such as a historical event—the dawning of the new millennium—or a noteworthy event that has happened in your community—like the results of an election or reactions to a local catastrophe. A speech about a person describes an individual in much the same way that an object speech describes an object. An issue speech examines a debatable topic from various points of view, such as abortion, environmental concerns, or the banning of certain music and books. If you choose to present a concept speech, it would be about abstract ideas—theories, principles, or values—such as the theory of relativity, or ideas about democracy, ethical communication, freedom of the press, or human rights.

WHY INFORMATIVE SPEAKING IS IMPORTANT

Regardless of the topic, developing the ability to present an informative speech may be one of the most important public speaking competencies you'll learn, because you'll use these skills frequently. In the information age in which we live, the majority of us earn our living by handling information in some way and conveying it to one another. Therefore, informative speaking is a crucial aspect of most people's community and professional lives.

A professor's lecture obviously is an informative speech, but businesspeople too are often called on to present information. In the corporate and professional world, informative speaking can take the form of a briefing that summarizes large amounts of information, a report of progress on projects and activities, or a training that provides instructions about how to carry out a task or assignment.

Knowledge Link

How can informative speaking play a valuable role in creating communities, as described in Chapter 1?

In giving any of these informative speeches, the goal is to promote understanding of the information presented, as well as to encourage the audience to retain a significant amount of the message. According to one listening expert, after as little as 10 minutes of a lecture or informative speech, some listeners' experience "micro-sleep," during which they only partially attend to what is said (Roberts, 1998). As a result, one day after hearing an informative speech, they recall only about half of it. Two weeks later, they're fortunate if they recall even 25% of what was presented. Given these realities, improving your informative speaking competence is a must, and that begins with an understanding of the three different types of informative speeches.

Types of Informative Speeches

Informative speeches can be categorized based on their objective. Three possible objectives for an informative speech are speaking to describe, explain, or instruct. These are general objectives, similar to the general purpose for a speech discussed in Chapter 15, but they are tailored to informative speaking. They emphasize audience understanding or their abilities—what the audience should know or be able to do by the end of the speech.

Knowledge Link

Would speaking to describe, explain, or instruct be most helpful in coordinating relationships within a group?

SPEAKING TO DESCRIBE

Descriptions are used when the listeners are unfamiliar with the topic of the speech and need new information in order to understand it. If you want the audience to become aware of and remember something new, your objective is to describe or provide a verbal picture of it. If your speech is about a vacation to an exotic or unfamiliar place, you will need to describe what it's like there, perhaps by contrast to more familiar places. If you want to introduce a new product line to your sales force, it's necessary to describe the new items and their advantages over older products. This informative objective could be stated as follows. Take note in this example of how concrete the speaker's expectation of the audience is.

> The sales force members will understand and be able to describe four advantages of the new product line, by comparison to last year's products.

SPEAKING TO EXPLAIN

Explanations are necessary to clarify something that is already known but not well understood, or to explain how something works. If you want the listeners to understand why something exists or has occurred, or how it operates, your objective is to explain it. If your speech is about public speaking anxiety, the other students are probably familiar with what it is, but they would appreciate an explanation of why they have it and what can be done about it. If your speech is about an increase in violent crime or drug usage, you could explain why the problem exists and what measures are being taken to address the situation. To clarify the distinction between an informative and persuasive speech, if you were to move beyond explaining the problem and take a position on how to combat crime or drug use, your speech would become persuasive. An informative objective for this speech would be this:

> The audience will be able to explain the underlying causes of the increase in violent crimes, as well as three strategies now in use to combat this problem.

SPEAKING TO INSTRUCT

Instructions are useful when the objective is to teach the audience something or tell them know how to use it. If you want the listeners to be able to apply what is presented, you provide instructions. For example, if you want the other students to be able to use a particular method for reducing public speaking anxiety, you need to provide instructions for applying that method. If a new product available through your company needs to be demonstrated by a salesperson, instructions in its use should be provided in an instructional speech. Here's an informative objective statement for that speech:

> Each salesperson will understand how to use the new product and be able to perform the six steps essential to its use.

To appreciate the importance of clarifying the objective of an informative speech, think about Patricia's speech at the beginning of this chapter. After choosing the topic of coffee consumption, Patricia decided, perhaps unintentionally, that her speech was to be both descriptive and explanatory. Her objectives were to describe the surprising changes in coffee drinking patterns in the United States, and to explain why those changes had occurred. Given that she had two objectives, Patricia needed to provide sufficient information to accomplish both effectively. She provided statistics to support her claim of an increase in coffee drinking, but she had testimonial evidence only from students in the coffee shop explaining why the increase had occurred. That oversight may have accounted in part for her speech not being quite as effective as she would have liked. If she decided to stay with both objectives, she should have researched the second objective more, perhaps contacting marketing experts at coffee companies for additional explanations of the increase in coffee consumption.

A sample student speech at the end of this chapter further illustrates the importance of understanding the relationship between the objective of a speech and what is included as its content. The speech is about the wonders of the technology of virtual reality. Like Patricia's speech, it has two objectives—to describe and to explain—but the speaker provides substantial information to accomplish both of these:

1. To describe what virtual reality is, its capabilities and its limitations.
2. To explain how virtual reality works.

Organizing & Outlining an Informative Speech

The principles of speech organization and outlining we discussed in Chapter 15, although important for all speeches, are especially helpful for a competent speaker who wants to achieve the objective of his or her informative speech. Because the goal is often to communicate an abundance of new information, good organization is essential for the audience to understand what is presented and not be overwhelmed by it. Furthermore, informative speeches are frequently about complex or complicated topics that can be hard to understand.

A communication researcher reported on why it's difficult to organize and present complex topics in informative speeches, stating that listeners may not understand new and complex ideas for three reasons (Rowan, 1995). The information in the speech may be confusing because it involves difficult concepts or language, structures or processes that are hard to envision, or ideas that are difficult to understand because they are hard to believe. In all of these cases, Rowan suggests first analyzing the informative topic to discover what aspects of it will be most difficult for your listeners to understand and then organizing and outlining your speech accordingly. Developing a working outline for your speech (see Chapter 15) will help you with this task. You will be able to determine what complex information must be included, the best position for it in you speech, and what form of support is essential to understanding it.

The five possible ways to organize an informative speech are by topic, chronology, space, comparison and contrast, and cause and effect. These five organizational patterns are most often used for informative speaking, but several of them clearly could be used for a persuasive speech. Cause and effect, for example, is frequently recommended for both informative and persuasive speeches.

As you learn about these five organizational patterns, understand that an informative speech outline has the same basic parts discussed in Chapter 15—an introduction, body, and conclusion. However, the main points of the body of an informative speech are organized using one of these five patterns, as shown in Figure 17.2. As each is discussed, an example is provided to show you how to use it to organize the body of your speech.

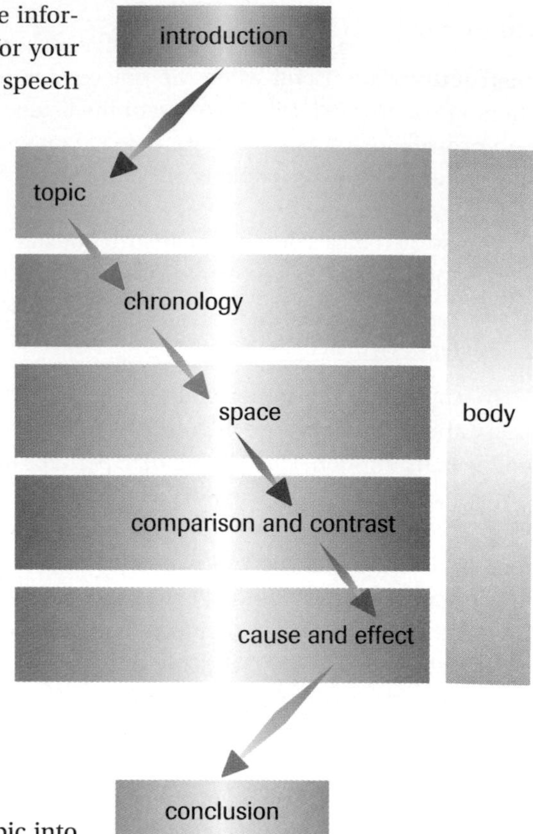

FIGURE 17.2
Organizing the Informative Speech

The body of an informative speech is structured using any one of five different organizational patterns. The introduction and conclusion remain the same as we discussed in Chapter 15.

TOPIC

Topical organization divides information about a subject and topic into subcategories that will constitute the main points of the body of the speech. This structure is advantageous when your topic naturally clusters into subcategories or lists of items you want the listeners to understand or know how to use. Various aspects of an object or a person, steps in a process, or dimensions of a concept are subtopics of a topic that can be effectively organized by topic. The body of the visual reality speech at the end of this chapter is organized by topic and covers four main points. Figure 17.3 contains an outline for that speech to illustrate how the four subtopics make up the main points for the body of the speech.

One problem with topical organization is that the main points may sound unrelated, if you fail to provide clear transitions as you move from one point to the next. Also, you risk boring the audience and sounding like you're droning on and on, from one topic of discussion to another. To avoid this problem, structure an introduction that builds a strong case for the importance of your topic and use a visual aid to help your listeners stay with you as you move through the main points.

The following main points contained in a commencement address at Elmira College in Elmira, New York, were organized categorically and could have been presented effectively using a visual aid (Houghton, 1997). The speaker could have displayed these "Six Values to Cherish" on a small graduation scroll, as a handout to all the students:

1. The unknown . . . so you are curious about the world.
2. Uncertainty . . . so you learn to deal with change.
3. Bad judgment . . . so you use it as a tool and a lesson.
4. Pain . . . so you understand it as part of growth.
5. Disappointment . . . so you learn to value humor and laughter as its remedy.
6. Vulnerability . . .so you will listen and be sensitive to others and their vulnerabilities.

FIGURE 17.3
Outline for the Virtual Reality Informative Speech

This informative speech is organized topically with four main points making up the body of the speech.

Virtual Reality Outline

INTRODUCTION

I. Narrative about Rifstorc Nurthmuson (attention getter)
II. VR will revolutionize computer industry (statement of significance)
III. We will examine what VR is, its capabilities, and future applications (preview)

BODY

I. Description of intricacies, concepts, components of VR
 A. Definition
 B. How people control computers
 C. Eyephones and how they work
 D. Dataglove and how it works
II. Capabilities of VR
 A. Uses by engineers, architects, and surgeons
 B. Uses by consumers (e.g., toy company, instant vacations)
III. Limitations of VR
 A. Need for software containing essential information
 B. Inability to perfectly simulate reality (e.g., can see but not feel)
 C. Crude picture and jerky movement
 D. High cost
IV. Future applications of the technology
 A. Clean up nuclear disaster
 B. Repair spacecraft
 C. Long distance and internal surgery
 D. Pilot training
 E. VR teleconferencing

CONCLUSION

I. VR is extraordinary (restatement of significance)
II. How VR works and its capabilities (review)
III. Rifstorc Nurthmuson may become more than a scenario character (closing device)

CHRONOLOGY

Chronological organization is used to describe changes or developments in any situation or circumstance. It can be historical—linked to actual dates—or sequential—related to a sequence of steps that occur or are performed over time.

A historical structure would work well if you're describing an event such as a war, the founding and development of your college, or the development and decline of the labor movement in the United States. In a speech about the labor movement, a historical structure could be used to structure the main points of the body of the speech in this way:

I. 1792–1929: Labor unions grew to be powerful economic force in United States.
II. 1930–1950: Union membership grew in the 1930s and 1940s and began to decline in the 1950s.
III. 1960–present: Membership has continued to decline; labor unions are searching for a foothold in the information age economy.

Two problems can occur if you organize a speech historically. First, the audience may not think something that happened so long ago is relevant to them. If that's the case, demonstrate the relevance of the speech topic to their lives early in the speech. Second, you'll bore the audience if your speech is little more than a recounting of dates and times. To avoid that problem, include precise dates only to provide a context for appreciating the significance of the event, and make the particular time in history memorable using lively and colorful examples of life back then.

Because a sequential time structure is effective in describing the series of steps in a process, you could use this pattern to describe how the stock market ebbs and flows, or how weather systems form and move around the globe. A topic such as the steps a student takes to choose the best college could be presented using the following sequential pattern:

- **I.** Gather information on schools that offer the desired major.
- **II.** Investigate scholarships and financial aid available.
- **III.** Apply to top three choices and await acceptance notification.
- **IV.** Visit the campuses where accepted, meet with faculty and advisers, and make a decision.

SPACE

Spatial organization presents information based on the positioning of objects in physical space, or relationships between locations. This structure works well when you want the listeners to visualize the arrangement of objects, locations, or distances. For example, if you're describing what your home is like, or the architectural design of a building or a mall, you would structure your speech spatially around the layout of the building. Space organization would also work well to describe the shifting battle lines held by the North and South during the Civil War; the best places to visit in a major city like London or New York; or even the various regions of the human brain and their functions, which could be organized like this:

- **I.** Cerebellum
- **II.** Cerebral cortex
- **III.** Pituitary
- **IV.** Thalamus
- **V.** Spinal cord

The main problem with space organization is making certain that the listeners follow along and can visualize the spaces you are describing. Providing a map, layout, or diagram of the spaces, like the one in Figure 17.4, will solve that problem.

FIGURE 17.4
Visual Aid for Organizing by Space

A speech about the functions of the different areas of the brain could use a diagram of the various areas.

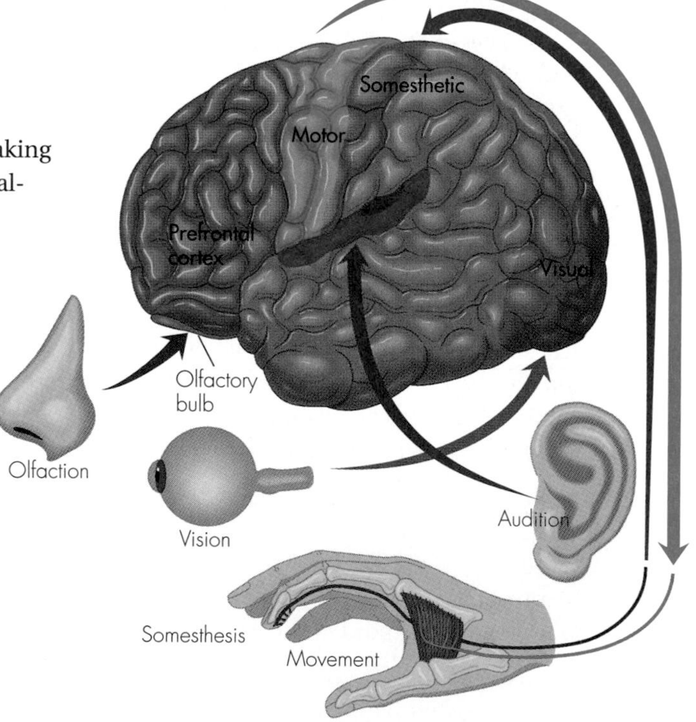

COMPARISON & CONTRAST

Organization by **comparison and contrast** is used to describe or explain how a subject is similar to, or different from, something else. Comparison means pointing out the similarities; contrast means pointing out the differences. This structure works well if the subject of the speech can be easily related to something the audience already knows about. It's also useful when significant similarities or differences between the subject of discussion and something else will help the audience understand and appreciate the subject better.

For example, comparison and contrast would be useful for describing a visit to another country. You could first describe how the country is similar to one the listeners are familiar with, and then talk about how the country and its customs are dissimilar. A speech on health care reform could compare and contrast programs in the United States to those in other countries by using these two main points as the body of the speech:

I. How the U.S. health care program is like (compares to) that in Canada and England.
II. How the U.S. health care program is unlike (contrasts to) programs in other countries.

One problem when using comparison and contrast is structuring the speech so the listeners know whether you're talking about a similarity or a difference. You could present all the comparisons first, followed by all the contrasts; then your speech would be like the health care speech and have two major points, one on similarities and one on differences. Another approach would be to select important aspects of the subject and talk about the similarities or the differences of each aspect of the subject. Then the body of the speech would have as many main points as aspects that you choose to talk about. Here's the health care example again, organized based on aspects of the issue:

I. Historical background to the two health care systems
II. Benefits and costs of both systems for patients
III. Advantages and disadvantages for health care providers
IV. Advantages and disadvantages for health care facilities

CAUSE & EFFECT

Organization by **cause and effect** examines why something happens (the causes) and what happens as a result (the effects). This structure is good for understanding an event or an action of an individual, an organization, or an institution. It is also useful for describing a controversial issue, because it can illustrate connections between the issue and its consequences. A cause-and-effect speech could be used to describe significant historical events, such as women winning the right to vote or the development of nuclear power as an energy source. The emergence of social problems like teenage violence in schools or an increase in smoking by young people would work well by using cause-and-effect organization.

Be aware that you may want to reverse the order and describe the effects or results first and then their cause. This reverse approach is recommended when the audience is already interested in the topic and knows something about it. By first calling attention to the significant impact of the effects, you heighten interest in the causes before you discuss them. That's what Patricia did in her speech about coffee drinking. She first described the effects—how much coffee consumption had increased in the United States—and then the cause—why people are drinking more coffee. In a speech about smoking, you could first describe the effects—the devastation of lung cancer—before you proceed to the cause—marketing cigarettes to young people. Here's how the body of that speech could be structured:

I. Statistics on the increase in lung cancer and early deaths (effect)
II. Story about a young person who died of lung cancer (effect)
III. Number of dollars tobacco companies spend annually to reach a young market (cause)
IV. Ads designed to appeal to young smokers (cause)

Two cautions are in order when using cause-and-effect organization. First, be sure you are clear about whether you are speaking to inform or to persuade, because this organizational pattern lends itself to both types of speeches. For instance, the informative speech about smoking would become persuasive if you urged the audience to take some action about the situation. Second, be certain you have a true cause-and-effect relationship and the situation or cause you're describing is really what is causing the effects or results. To be both competent and ethical, you must be sure it's a causal relationship and not just a series of coincidences.

To decide which of the five organizational patterns will work best for organizing and outlining the body of your informative speech, think about the actual content of the speech—what it is about. Depending on whether the speech is about an object, process, event, person, issue, or concept, one or more of the organizational patterns just described will be most effective. Table 17.1 summarizes suggestions for organizing the body of your informative speech based on what the speech is about.

Knowledge Link

Which of the five organizational patterns just described for informative speeches is most likely to be useful for persuasive speeches as well?

TABLE 17.1

Organizing Informative Speeches

Depending on the content of the informative speech, certain organizational patterns will work better than others.

IF THE SPEECH IS ABOUT . . .	THEN ORGANIZE IT THIS WAY :
An object	*By topic:* Use if aspects of the object you're describing naturally cluster into categories. *By chronology:* Use if aspects of the object can easily be visualized in a spatial relationship to one another.
A process	*By chronology:* Use if the process you're describing occurs sequentially over time or as a sequence of steps. *By space:* Use if the steps in the process can be easily visualized as connected to each other.
An event	*By chronology:* Use when an event or a series of events can be described as they occurred over time. *By cause and effect:* Use when the event can be understood by describing why it happened and what resulted.
A person	*By topic:* Use when you want to describe various aspects, characteristics, achievements, or actions of a person. *By comparison and contrast:* Use to understand a person based on how she or he is either like or unlike someone else. *By cause and effect:* Use to understand the cause and effects of the person's actions or decisions.
An issue	*By cause and effect:* Use to promote understanding of an issue by presenting why the issue exists and what is happening as a result. *By comparison and contrast:* Use to provide insights into an issue, based on how it is like or unlike another issue. *By topic:* Use to describe the main ideas that comprise the issue.
A concept	*By topic:* Use to describe main ideas that comprise the concept. *By comparison and contrast:* Use to provide insights into an unfamiliar concept by describing how it is like or unlike something else.

Using Support Materials to Inform

Deciding how to organize your informative speech is a crucial step to preparing an informative speech competently. But to make your speech as effective as possible, you also need to be inventive and creative in how you use support materials. In Chapter 15 you learned about the sources of information from which to gather support materials, such as your own experiences and those of other people, from the internet, and from the library. From these sources of information, the support materials you will have at your disposal are definitions and descriptions, examples, stories, testimonies and quotations, and facts and statistics. These forms of support are essential to informative speaking, and they are equally effective for use in persuasive speeches—the topic of Chapter 18.

DEFINITIONS & DESCRIPTIONS

Clarity and precision in an informative speech are achieved in part by providing definitions and descriptions. In Chapter 2, you learned that clarity is essential to communicating competently, whether with one other person or with a large audience. To achieve clarity, first realize that uncommon terms which are new or unfamiliar to the listeners must be explained. You can accomplish this by defining the new word or term and providing a description of it early in your speech. Second, members of the audience may interpret common and familiar words that you use in different ways. So if a familiar word or phrase is serving as a key term in your speech, provide a simple and concise definition of it to let your listeners know exactly how you're using it. Words like *abortion, affirmative action,* or *welfare* need to be defined. Use a dictionary to determine the most acceptable definition for the key term.

Knowledge Link

Would definitions and descriptions be most valuable in a speech to describe, a speech to explain, or a speech to instruct?

Kelly Smith (1998), a student at Ball State University, provided both a definition and a description of the topic of her speech—toxoplasmosis . She defined toxoplasmosis as "a disease that results from an airborne parasite that attacks the nervous system of its host."

When she realized the new term needed yet more clarification, Kelly provided the following description of it:

> Toxoplasmosis is a disease that can result in fatigue, blindness, and even death. It is mainly spread by something we see in neighborhoods every single day—cats. What happens is a cat

DOONESBURY By Garry Trudeau

Don't follow this advice for using strategies and support materials in your speech!

Doonesbury © G. B. Trudeau. Reprinted with permission of UNIVERSAL PRESS SYNDICATE.

eats an animal, who [that] has been infected with the disease such as a rat. The disease grows in the cat's small intestines, until it is discarded in the cat's stool. The stool releases tiny spores called oocysts, which infect the air around it. Therefore, when someone breathes in these oocysts they become infected with the disease toxoplasmosis.

Examples

Another simple but effective form of support is the example. An **example** is a specific item, person, or event that helps explain or illustrate an idea, clarify a difficult concept, or make anything you say more interesting or real to the audience. You can choose between using real examples or hypothetical ones. A **hypothetical example** is something that hasn't actually happened but could happen, which can be just as effective as a real example. In using a hypothetical example, you ask your listeners to imagine a situation related to the speech topic. It is important that a hypothetical example be plausible. For instance, in Patricia's speech about drinking coffee at the café, she could have said, "Imagine how nice it would be to relax after a tough exam with a few friends sipping cups of cappuccino together!"

A competent speaker carefully plans the use of powerful examples, realizing that one strong example is more effective than several inadequate ones. In a speech about the problem of pharmacists and insurance companies switching prescription drugs on patients, Mike Wagner (1998) at University of Nebraska, Lincoln, used this example:

> Take Marie Williams, a school bus driver in Richmond, Virginia. Last January, her pharmacist told her that in order to stay covered, Marie would have to begin taking Prinivil instead of Zestril. Because she couldn't afford the $208 uninsured bottle of Zestril, Marie went with the cheaper Prinivil. Three days later, she blacked out as she pulled out of her school bus parking lot due to an adverse drug reaction with the inappropriate substitute. Motivated by a fear of cost, patients like Marie Williams are forced to accept substitutions.

Lauren McGarity (1998), a student at Rice University, used a somewhat shorter but equally effective example to illustrate the financial loss common citizens sustain as a result of publicly funded stadiums and privately owned sports franchises in big cities:

> The November 16, 1997, *Buffalo News* provides the example of Oriole Park or Camden Yard which costs Baltimore residents more than $14 million a year. The net economic gain in employment and tax revenues is only $3 million a year. But because we believe these team's tall tales, we start to fear the economic impact of losing a team.

Knowledge Link

Would examples and stories be most valuable in a speech to describe, a speech to explain, or a speech to instruct?

Even though examples such as these are effective, it would not be competent or ethical to use an example to prove a point, if you know it's only an isolated incident that is not true on a larger scale. For instance, if the majority of sports stadiums are profitable for the cities where they are located, and the Oriole stadium is one of the few that are losing money, it would be unethical to use Camden Yards as an example.

Stories

When you tell a story, which is actually just a long example, it serves the same purpose—to illustrate an idea, clarify a concept, or make a point more interesting or real. The ability to tell a good story is one of the most valuable skills a public speaker can have—it fuels a speech with energy and engages the audience in its action (Weber, 1995). It is also an ideal tool for eliciting an emotional response from the audience and setting the tone or mood for a speech as part of the introduction (Wylie, 1998). If you recall, Patricia's professor at the beginning of this chapter said her speech would have been more engaging if she had started out with a personal story of how two classmates met and became good friends while drinking coffee at the bookstore café.

Here's a great story that was used to illustrate the importance of telling the truth. It was the attention-getting device in the introduction to a speech presented by the chairman of the Federal Communications Commission to a telecommunications group in Washington, D.C. (Kennard, 1998):

> I'll never forget the time two of my buddies decided to drive all the way to Los Angeles for a long weekend. They had an exam on Monday morning and they fully intended to get back in time. But they had a little too much fun in LA and didn't get back until Monday afternoon, too late for the exam. So they slinked into the professor's office and one of them told a little fib. He said they had been on their way to class to take the exam but had gotten a flat tire and that's why they were late. They begged the professor for a chance to take the exam. To their surprise, the professor seemed rather accommodating: A flat tire, eh? OK, you can take the test. My friends were amazed that the professor had fallen for the flat tire story. And so after putting the students in separate classrooms, the professor gave them an exam that consisted of a very simple question: Which tire?

A person who can tell a good story is sometimes referred to as a *raconteur.* Here's a raconteur telling a tale that is entrancing the listeners.

A story like this one certainly would grab the audience's attention. However, a story that is either poorly told or not relevant to the content of your speech can have a negative impact on your credibility. To avoid this situation, choose your story carefully, be sure it's relevant to your topic, and don't include it just to fill up time or amuse the audience. Keep the story short and concise, and, if possible, describe real people and events. Create a mental picture of the action that takes place in the story by describing what actually happened or what someone actually did.

TESTIMONIES & QUOTATIONS

Two more valuable forms of support make use of someone else's words to support the ideas in your speech. **Testimony** utilizes the opinion of an expert or the account of an event by a witness to it. A **quotation** makes use of a person's exact words. Either or both of these techniques can be used to provide authoritative evidence for your speech, when your own credibility with the listeners isn't as impressive as you would like. In Patricia's speech about drinking coffee, she provided testimony from visitors to the bookstore café, but her professor said she should have also used some direct quotations from coffee manufacturers.

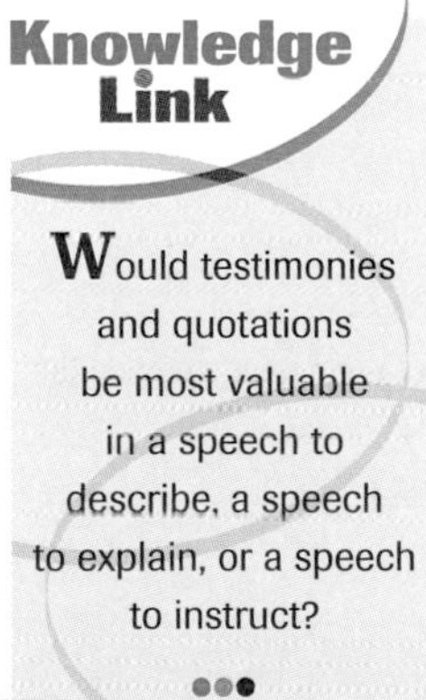

For a testimony or quotation to be effective, choosing the right source is imperative. Find experts or people who hold respected positions in the subject area you are speaking about, preferably someone your listeners know about. You can use a person who is not highly expert, if he or she has experience relevant to your speech topic. You can use a person who is not well known, if you tell the audience why the individual's opinion is important. In a speech about noise-induced hearing loss, Jodi Becker (1998) of the University of Wisconsin, Eau Claire, made effective use of testimony and a very emphatic quotation:

> For an average person, hearing loss can begin at a mere 80 decibels, states Dr. Robert Ghent of the Musician's Hearing Institute in a personal interview conducted on October 14, 1998. The three hazard zones where every day we all come in contact with this deafening level of noise are near our stereos, in our workplace, and our home environment. When asked if loud music causes hearing damage, Dr. Ghent replied, "Absolutely!"

Here's another example of the use of testimony and a quotation by Dave Naze (1998) of Rock Valley College in a speech that argued for refocusing on reading as the best answer to educational problems in the United States:

> We as a nation must follow the words of John G. Ramsay, professor of education studies at Carleton College. Ramsay argues in *Vital Speeches of the Day,* of September 1, 1997, that America needs to implement a first "R" school philosophy; that first "R" being "reading." Ramsay believes that in the world of political, technological and cultural changes, "reading will remain the most powerful, efficient, in-depth, and balanced way of gathering, sorting, and understanding information."

Facts & Statistics

A final way to provide support for an informative speech, as we already highlighted in Chapter 15, is to present facts and statistics. A **fact** is an individual piece of information that listeners could verify for themselves if they wanted to. To be effective, a fact should be highly relevant to the speech topic, and it should contain enough evidence that it can stand on its own as a solid piece of information. Tammy Frisby (1998) a student at Concordia College, used the following facts to call attention to the dangers of gum disease:

1. In medical terminology, gum disease is a low-grade infection, but gum disease or periodontal disease or gingivitis still has the ability to put you at risk for life-threatening medial problems.
2. The American Dental Association is now convinced that America's most common infection is also a risk factor for America's number one killer of adults, heart disease, and America's number one killer of infants, prematurity.

Knowledge Link

Would facts and statistics be most valuable in a speech to describe, a speech to explain, or a speech to instruct?

FIGURE 17.5
Visual Aids to Clarify and Simplify an Informative Speech

As recommended in Chapter 15, a visual aid can be used in an informative speech to dramatize a descriptive statistic, such as the small percentage of people who receive bone marrow transplants versus how many need them.

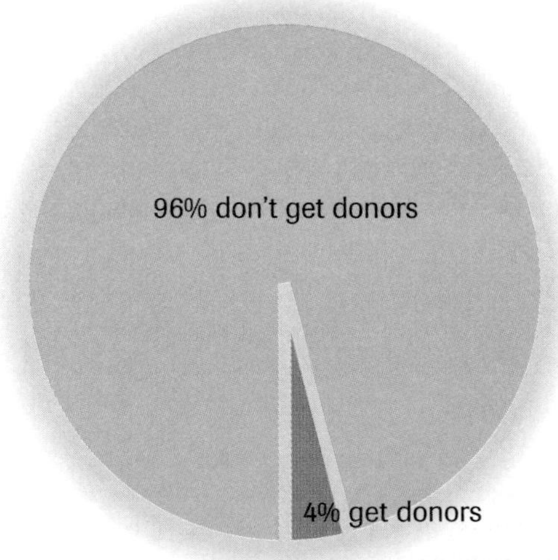

Statistics are numerical summaries of facts, figures, and research findings that provide pictures of data about people, ideas, or patterns of behavior. In the "Floss or Die" speech about gum disease, Frisby used statistics, as well as facts, to provide evidence for her claims:

1. The Veterans Administration Normative Aging Study followed 1,231 participants beginning in the 1960s. The participants who started out with bad gums have had twice the death rate from heart disease.
2. A study begun in the 1990s by the Harvard School of Public Health found that participants with gum disease had two-thirds greater risk of heart disease.
3. A 1997 research report from the University of Carolina concluded that pregnant women with gum disease were more than 7 times as likely to deliver prematurely, making gum disease responsible for 45,500 of all the premature babies born in the United States each year at a price tag of $1 billion in neonatal care costs.

A type of statistic you can use as support in your speech is descriptive. **Descriptive statistics** describe or present pictures of what whole groups of people do, think, or are like. They summarize the behaviors or the attitudes of everyone in the group. The Veterans Administration Normative Aging Study mentioned in Tammy Frisby's speech is a good example of this type of statistic. It presents information describing what happened to an entire group of 1,231 people as they grew older. In a speech about the need for bone marrow donors, David Slater (1998) of Wayne State University also uses a descriptive statistic to reveal what is happening to an entire group of people who need bone marrow transplants (see Figure 17.5).

> The *Las Vegas Review* of September 17, 1997, reports that, in this country alone, 30,000 people per year are diagnosed with any one of the life-threatening diseases for which marrow donation is a viable cure, but sadly less than 4% receive the marrow they need—not because of a lack of potential donors but because of a lack of registered donors.

If you use statistics, select your figures carefully and don't overwhelm the audience with numbers. More is not necessarily better—in fact, it can be confusing. If you need to present a lot of numbers, provide a simple interpretation of the statistics, perhaps in the form of a visual aid. Chapter 15 discussed the use of charts and graphs to present statistics more clearly. Also consider simplifying and strengthening your statistical evidence by combining it with a strong example. The example makes a situation or event real and personal, and statistics indicate that the example is widespread.

Knowledge Link

How can the concept of appropriate communication (introduced in Chapter 2) help you make decisions about ethical informative speaking?

Ethics & Informative Speaking

Just as ethics is important to speech preparation in general, it plays a crucial role when preparing an informative speech. As you plan your speech and choose support materials and evidence, you will face similar ethical challenges and have to make similar ethical decisions. Should you use statistics or other support materials that would accomplish your informative objective but perhaps misrepresent the truth or lead your listeners to faulty conclusions? If you discover some evidence that could be manipulated ever so slightly to make your informative speech more interesting, is this use of inaccurate or misleading information really unethical? The CloseUp on ethics and informative speaking discusses the ethics involved in deciding what support materials to use and how to present your informative speech most ethically.

CloseUp on Ethics

Ethics & Informative Speaking

AN IMPORTANT PART of public speaking competence is being able to make ethical decisions as an informative speaker. In public as well as corporate life, examples of ethically questionable informative speaking abound. When Bill Clinton's personal conduct was under scrutiny in early 1999 because of his relationship with a White House intern, then President Clinton gave a televised informative speech to the American public. His remarks were considered unethical by some critics who said Clinton used language ambiguously to misrepresent the nature of his relationship with the intern, Monica Lewinsky.

In corporate America, there have been numerous cases of CEOs and managers presenting information unethically to employees. They bring in management consultants to interview employees about their job assignments, supposedly with the goal of redesigning and streamlining the corporation's structure. After giving speeches about corporate plans to streamline and maximize profits for everyone's benefit, jobs are later eliminated and massive layoffs ensue. Incidents such as these raise serious questions about what it means to present information in an ethical manner.

To the extent that you are able to achieve your own objectives for an informative speech while respecting the prevailing rules of conduct, that speech is more likely to be ethical. That means you present information and support materials to accomplish your objective, but you do so with respect for prevailing cultural rules. If you recall from Chapter 2, members of the National Communication Association developed a *Credo for Ethical Communication* that provides insight into the cultural rules for communicating ethically in U.S. society (1999).The prologue to the credo states that "Ethical communication enhances human worth and dignity by fostering truthfulness, accuracy, honesty, and reason are essential to integrity in communication."

Using this cultural rule, ethical informative speaking can be defined as "Communication that provides sufficient information to the listeners such that they can make informed choices about matters of strategic importance to themselves."

In the final analysis, it is up to you to prepare and present your informative speech as ethically as possible. Strive for an optimal balance of appropriateness and effectiveness, knowing that it's acceptable to attempt to achieve the objective of your speech (effectiveness), but not at the price of violating any prevailing cultural rules for ethical communication (appropriateness), such as distorting the truth or presenting information inaccurately. Furthermore, share any information with your listeners that they need to know, in order to make informed choices about any matter of importance to them mentioned in your speech.

SOURCE: NCA (1999).

Challenges to Informative Speaking

When a speaker fails to present an informative speech competently, it is usually because of one or more of the following three reasons. The speaker chose an inappropriate subject or topic, faulty information was used to support the topic, or the speech was poorly organized. Novice speakers are most likely to have problems with these challenges, whereas more experienced speakers have learned through trial and error how crucial these are to giving informative speeches competently.

INAPPROPRIATE SUBJECT OR TOPIC

The process of topic selection was thoroughly discussed in Chapter 15. Choosing from the wrong subject area or selecting an inappropriate topic because of poor audience analysis is a serious mistake that will result in a speech with little appeal for your audi-

TABLE 17.2

Choosing a Topic for a College Classroom Speech

Topic selection for an informative speech should take into account the knowledge base of the listeners, realizing how rapidly people's cultural frames of reference change. Students born in the 1980s who are entering college at the beginning of the new century may not be familiar with some or all of the cultural reference points described here.

CULTURAL FRAMES OF REFERENCE OF COLLEGE STUDENTS

- They were born and grew up with Microsoft, IBM, PCs, in-line skates, NutraSweet, fax machines, film on disks, and unregulated quantities of commercial interruptions on television.
- There has always been a woman judge on the Supreme Court, and women have always been traveling into space.
- They have never needed a prescription to buy ibuprofen.
- They never heard anyone say "Book 'em Danno," "Good night, John-boy," or "Kiss my grits" in prime time.
- Strikes by highly paid athletes have always been part of professional athletics.
- The moonwalk is a Michael Jackson dance step, not a Neil Armstrong giant step.
- They have no meaningful recollection of the Reagan era and may not know he had ever been shot.
- They have never feared a nuclear war.
- Their lifetime has always included AIDS.
- They have always had an answering machine and might wonder why people say "dial" a telephone.
- They cannot fathom not having a remote control.
- The expression "You sound like a broken record" means nothing to them.
- Popcorn has always been cooked in a microwave.
- There has always been MTV.

SOURCE: *The Chronicle of Higher Education* (1997, September 3).

ence. This challenge to informative speaking can be well illustrated by thinking about what an audience of today's entry-level college freshmen is probably like. If you fail to consider these students' life experiences and their cultural knowledge base, you won't choose a topic they will find engaging. For a list of cultural references that would have little to no meaning for today's college students, see Table 17.2.

FAULTY INFORMATION

In addition to topic selection, another challenge to informative speaking is the use of faulty information. Three problems can occur with this challenge—too much, too little, or the wrong information.

Information overload is a common problem. The speaker includes more information than is necessary to accomplish the informative objective of the speech, more than can be covered in the time allotted, or too much high-level information. Chapter 7 talked about why this overload happens in contemporary society—because people have access to so much information through technology. Thus the temptation is great to overload the speech with information that the audience can't possibly absorb in the time allowed.

Including too little information in an informative speech can also be a problem, however. This problem stems from assuming you already know enough about the subject or topic so you don't need to research it. You don't discover support materials that would help achieve the informative objective and then you present information your audience already knows about and may find totally dull.

Figuring out how much or how little information to include is important, but the quality of that information is also of concern. Each minute of an informative speech is precious, so only present information that the audience can relate to and that helps accomplish the informative objective. Using the wrong information can cause any informative speech to fail.

Knowledge Link

Of the three challenges to competence in informative speaking just described, which is the biggest problem for speakers and why?

•••

POOR ORGANIZATION

A third challenge to giving an informative speech competently is failing to organize the speech so the listeners easily understand it. A common mistake new speakers make is not realizing how hard it is for listeners to follow and absorb a large amount of new information. Because you become familiar with the content of your informative speech, you may not realize how overwhelming it may sound when your listeners hear it for the first time. If they have to spend their time trying to figure out the maze of new information that you present, your informative speech just won't be effective.

Overcoming Challenges to Competence

Competent informative speaking calls for choosing the right topic, supporting the informative objective with the right information, organizing the information simply and logically, and finally, motivating each audience member to want to listen to the speech.

CHOOSE THE RIGHT TOPIC & INFORMATION

When you decide on a topic for your informative speech, even if it evolves from your own knowledge and experience, examine it in light of its appeal to the listeners. Does it represent information they will care about and want to know more about? Or will you have to work too hard to motivate them to care? As a competent informative speaker, either choose a topic to which your listeners will easily relate or take responsibility for providing background information to help them appreciate and understand it.

Table 17.3 contains a list of possible topics for informative speeches. Use the list to identify a topic of interest to your audience by applying a strategy the rhetoricians of classical Greece called **common places,** or *koinoi topoi* (Wallace, 1972). According to the Greeks, these were standardized ways of finding something to say based on common knowledge or awareness of a subject. The Greek word for place (*topos*) refers to the places

TABLE 17.3

••• Topics for Informative Speeches •••

Here's a list of possible topics for your speech based on the nature of its content. You may find a topic for your informative speech by examining these suggestions.

CONTENT OF SPEECH	POSSIBLE TOPICS FOR EACH TYPE OF SPEECH
An object speech	Things you collect—books, stamps, antiques; an extraordinary place you've visited or know about—a town, city, state, or country; a new gadget—a palm computer, CD recorder, or household item.
A process speech	Things you do or know how to do—snowshoeing, skiing, hiking, traveling, refinishing furniture, cooking, saving money, spending, getting along with others, living in another country, planning your life.
An event speech	A local or national current event, a noteworthy event from history, an event that marked a turning point in history, an event that occurred in the life of a noteworthy person, a special event that occurred in your life.
A people speech	A contemporary or historical person of significance to the audience, someone you know or have known of particular interest.
An issue speech	Nuclear disarmament, affirmative action, recycling, conservation laws and practices, violence in the media, grading systems, substance abuse and regulation, health care and policies, political and governmental policies or programs, abortion laws and practices, unions and strike policies, lifestyles.
A concept speech	Nuclear power, multiculturalism/diversity, the world ecosystem, media literacy, the information age, ethical communication, theory of evolution, principles of communication, democracy, friendship, love.

in your mind where an approach to a speech topic can be found. Today, the plural term *topoi* is used to refer to categories or subject areas for speeches. For instance, you could begin with a common topoi on the list in Table 17.3, such as things you collect; then you could approach that topic with your audience in mind by explaining how to get started collecting items that may increase in value. You could start with the topoi of the world ecosystem, then describe the impact on people in your community of the U.S. government's ecological policies.

Once you're satisfied with your topic, locate information to support it that is right for the audience. As you choose support materials, be sure they represent information that will be perceived as meaningful and relevant by the particular listeners. Provide definitions and descriptions of any terms and concepts they wouldn't otherwise understand. Be sure your examples and stories are ones they will relate to and your facts and statistics will impress them as significant. Finally, be sure you use an appropriate amount of information, not too much and not too little. Practice your speech ahead of time to know if you can comfortably present the amount of information it contains in the time allowed.

"I'll tell you what this election is about. It's about homework, and pitiful allowances, and having to clean your room. It's also about candy, and ice cream, and staying up late."

Choosing the right topic for the audience is important regardless of the age of the listeners!

© The New Yorker Collection 1996 Robert Weber from cartoonbank.com. All rights reserved.

ORGANIZE SIMPLY & LOGICALLY

Regardless of which organizational pattern you use for your informative speech, err on the side of using it with simplicity. Although the temptation may be great to impress the audience with lots of information presented in a complex way, instead present a clear and uncomplicated informative message that is easily understood. Realize that what sounds simple to you may sound complex to the listeners, when they first hear it. So pare it down to the essentials, to what is simple, basic, and necessary for accomplishing your informative objective.

In addition to presenting your information simply, present it logically, so the listeners can easily follow your line of reasoning. Use any one of the organizational patterns described earlier to arrange the main parts of the body of your speech logically. Because an informative speech does contain a lot of new information, be sure to use clear transitions, words, and phrases, to help the audience stay with you. "Now that you understand the causes, it's important to examine the situation we are all facing today." "Let's carefully trace how this situation has evolved over time, by beginning with what took place in the early 1980s."

MOTIVATE LISTENERS TO LEARN

No matter how carefully you choose information and organize your informative speech, it may not be as effective as you would like if your listeners aren't motivated to listen to it. Remember that Patricia's informative speech about coffee drinking was effective in many ways, but she didn't involve or motivate her listeners to care about what she had to say.

One way to motivate listeners to learn is to involve them in caring about the topic early in the speech. Figure out an aspect of the topic that would be intriguing to the audience, and incorporate it into your introduction. Come up with an attention-getting device, a story, or a startling statistic related to that aspect of your topic. The following introduction to the speech on virtual reality is an excellent example of making an informative speech topic appealing to the audience:

> Rifstorc Nurthmuson's Macintosh computer alerts him to a hazardous waste emergency. He quickly pulls on his Datasuit and Dataglove and slips his Eyephones over his eyes in order to enter virtual reality. Rifstorc teleoperates a robot located at the site of the accident through his Datasuit and glove. These devices calculate every motion he makes, right down to each finger and knuckle. These motions are transmitted to the robot, who performs exactly the same movements as Rifstorc. He sees what the robot sees through his Eyephones, giving him the illusion that he is actually cleaning up the toxic mess. As Rifstorc "experiences" the accident site and begins the cleanup, the robot follows his actions and actually does the work.
>
> Virtual reality promises to revolutionize the computer industry. As *Forbes* magazine of February 5, 1990, states, "according to the visionaries and futurists who abound in Silicon Valley, virtual reality is where the computer user of the 21st century will telecommunicate, design, and do research."

Once you've motivated the audience to want to learn more, assure them that you will provide good and reliable information on the topic. Even if they decide they're interested in what you're going to say, that interest will fade if you appear not to know what you're talking about. A solid preview will assure them that you have gathered good information and organized it effectively for them. Here's the virtual reality preview, which clearly states what will be covered in the informative speech:

> In order to appreciate how this technology will affect our lives, today we will examine what virtual reality is, what its capabilities are, and what future applications it may hold.

Finally, as you proceed through your informative speech, keep your listeners actively involved in what you are saying. Educators and teachers are well aware that listeners learn more if they become active participants in their own learning process (Ebert-May, Brewer, & Allred, 1997; Rubin & Hebert, 1998). As a competent speaker, of course you use polished delivery skills and nonverbal cues to encourage audience involvement—eye contact, moving toward the audience, gesturing as you speak. But there are other creative ways to address the challenge of motivating listeners to learn.

You can encourage your listeners to get involved and relate to your speech topic by asking them questions. Patricia could have involved her audience members by asking, "How many of you really like a good cup of coffee to start the day? Raise your hands." If your speech is about public speaking anxiety, you could ask, "Have you ever used an anxiety-reducing technique that really worked for you?" Questions such as these could be developed for practically any informative speech. Or if time allows and you're talking about a topic that lends itself to an informal mini-quiz, you could hand out a questionnaire with a few questions related to your topic.

Another way to promote involvement in an informative speech is to make use of volunteers from the audience. Even if you only use one or two volunteers, other members of the audience will feel more involved in your speech as a result. You could have volunteers demonstrate a dance step, an exercise, or even point to areas on a map as you talk about them. Finally, and if time allows, a simple way to encourage audience involvement is to conclude with a short question and answer period.

The steps to giving an informative speech outlined in this chapter would have helped Patricia present her "Joy of Java" speech with greater competence. They will help you as well as you determine the type of informative speech to present, how to organize it, and how to use support materials most beneficially. The next and final chapter on public speaking will introduce you to similar concepts, but as they apply to persuasive speaking.

Chapter Summary

The purpose of speaking to inform is to communicate new information or a new perspective to an audience about an object, process, event, person, issue, or concept. These public speaking skills are important to people's community lives and their work life in today's information age. Informative speeches can be categorized based on their objective, including speeches to describe, explain, or instruct. Descriptions are used when the listeners are unfamiliar with the topic of the speech and need new information in order to understand it. Explanations are used to clarify something that is already known but not well understood, or to explain how something works. Instructions are useful when the objective is to teach the audience something or tell them how to use it.

Organizing an informative speech effectively is crucial to achieving its objective. The five ways to organize the body of an informative speech are by topic, chronology, space, comparison and contrast, and cause and effect. Organization by topic divides information about a subject and topic into subtopics or subcategories. Organization by time is used to describe changes or developments in any situation or circumstance, which can be historical or sequential. Organization by space organizes information based on the positioning of objects in physical space, or relationships between locations. Organization by comparison and contrast is used to describe or explain how a subject is similar to or different from something else. Organization by cause and effect examines why something happens (the causes) and what happens as a result (the effects).

To present an informative speech most effectively, a competent speaker is inventive and creative in the use of these support materials: definitions and descriptions, examples, stories, testimonies and quotations, and facts and statistics.

Three challenges to informative speaking are a subject or topic that is inappropriate; the use of faulty information, either too much, too little, or the wrong information; and poor organization, which results in the speech not being easily understood by the listeners. To overcome these challenges, a competent speaker chooses a subject and topic the listeners can easily relate to, provides the right support materials to help the listeners appreciate and understand the topic, organizes the speech simply and logically, and finally, motivates the listeners to learn, by encouraging a sense of involvement in the speech.

Key Terms

descriptions
explanations
instructions
topical organization
chronological organization
spatial organization
comparison and contrast organization
cause-and-effect organization
example
hypothetical example
testimony
quotation
fact
statistics
descriptive statistics
common places

Building Knowledge

1. Is informative speaking one of the most important communication skills a person can acquire? Whether your answer is yes or no, explain your reasoning.
2. Could one informative speech have all three objectives: to describe, explain, and instruct? If yes, provide an example. If no, explain why not.
3. Of the five ways to organize an informative speech—by topic, chronology, space, comparison and contrast, and cause and effect—is any one of them easier or harder to use? Explain your answer.
4. In your opinion, which of the various types of support materials are most essential for giving an effective informative speech? Explain your reasoning.
5. If your personal code of ethics about informative speaking is different from members of your audience, what should you do about making ethical choices as a public speaker?
6. Of the three challenges to informative speaking presented in this chapter, which causes the most problems for you as a public speaker? In addition to the suggestions offered, what else can you do about that challenge?
7. Analyze the speech about virtual reality based on what you have learned about informative speaking in this chapter. Is there anything the speaker could have said or done that would have made this speech even more effective?

Building Skills

Individual Exercises

1. Make three columns on a piece of paper. Label your columns Types of Informative Speeches, Speech Topic, and Organizational Pattern, from left to right. In column 1, list the three types of informative speeches, based on objective. In column 2, come up with one speech topic that appeals to you for each type of speech. In column 3, decide which organizational pattern would work best for each topic you listed.
2. Analyze the speech about virtual reality at the end of this chapter to determine how well you think it achieves its informative objective. What did the speaker do most effectively to achieve his objective?
3. Attend an informative public speech or lecture. Identify the type of speech presented and how it's organized. Analyze the speech based on the challenges to informative speaking presented in this chapter—choice of subject and topic, use of information, and organization.
4. If you are using *InfoTrac College Edition,* choose a topic for an informative speech and enter that topic as a keyword search. Locate 3–4 pieces of information that could be used as support material (definition, example, testimony, fact, statistic) for that topic.
5. Visit The Quotations Home Page at http://www.geocities.com/~spanoudi/quote.html. This site contains links to 30 collections and over 21,000 quotes. Find a quotation that could be used for the topic you chose for Exercise 4.

Group Exercises

1. Form a small group of 4–5 students and choose any one of the topics presented in Table 17.3. Each student in the group should write the topic on a piece of paper and decide on an objective and organizational pattern for that topic. Compare and discuss each student's ideas.
2. Attend an informative speech in a small group with several other students (a lecture will do). Each student should analyze the speech based on the speaker's use of support materials and the challenges to informative speaking—choice of subject and topic, use of information, and organization. After you leave the presentation, compare your evaluations.
3. Form groups of four students and choose one of the topics listed in Table 17.3 under issue speeches. Form pairs and assign to the first pair the development of an informative objective and an outline using the comparison and contrast organizational method. The second pair should use cause-and-effect organization to develop an objective and outline for the topic. Compare the two outlines to see which organizational pattern worked best and discuss why. Then stay in the group of four students and discuss what types of support materials would help achieve the objective of each outline.
4. In a small group of 4–5 students, practice telling a personal story to the group. Have each group member think about one of these topics: your most memorable communication experience; an event that influenced the course of your life; another person who contributed something memorable to your life. Give each person 5 to 10 minutes to outline and organize his or her thoughts. Then have each person tell his or her story and the rest of the group provides feedback to the storytellers.

References

Becker, J. (1998). Noise induced hearing loss: Unheard of hazard zones. In LoSchnoon (Ed.) *Winning Orations* (pp. 146–149). Mankato, MN: Interstate Oratorical Association.

Ebert-May, D., Brewer, C., & Allred, S. (1997). Innovation in large lectures-teaching for active learning. *BioScience, 147*(9), 601–608.

Frisby, T. (1998). Floss or die. In L. Schnoon (Ed.), *Winning Orations* (pp. 67–70). Mankato, MN: Interstate Oratorical Association.

Harris, S. (1992). Virtual reality: Immersion in an artificial world. In R. L. Johannesen, R. R. Allen, and W. A. Lunkugel (Eds.), *Contemporary American Speeches.* Dubuque, IA: Kendall Hunt.

Houghton, J. R. (1997, April/May). Six values to cherish. *Executive Speeches, 11*(5) 65–69.

Kennard, W .E. (1998, April). Remarks to Educom Networking. Educom Conference, Washington, DC.

McGarity, L. (1998). The great stadium swindle. In L. Schnoon (Ed.), *Winning Orations* (pp. 122–125). Mankato, MN: Interstate Oratorical Association.

National Communication Association (1999). Summer Conference on Ethical Communication. Annandale, VA: National Communication Association.

Naze, D. (1998). The computer delusion. In L. Schnoon (Ed.), *Winning Orations* (pp. 28–31). Mankato, MN: Interstate Oratorical Association.

Roberts, C. (1998, March). *Developing willing listeners: A host of problems and a plethora of solutions.* Paper presented at the annual meeting of the International Listening Association, Kansas City, KS.

Rowan, K. E. (1995). A new pedagogy for explanatory public speaking: Why arrangement should not substitute for invention. *Communication Education, 44,* 236–250.

Rubin, L., & Hebert, C. (1998). Model for active learning: Collaborative peer teaching. *College Teaching, 46*(1), 26–31.

Short subjects: What you should know about this year's freshmen. (1997, September 3). *The Chronicle of Education,* p. A12.

Slater, D. (1998). Sharing life. In L. Schnoon (Ed.), *Winning Orations* (pp. 63–66). Mankato, MN: Interstate Oratorical Association.

Smith, K. (1998). Toxoplasmosis. In L. Schnoon (Ed.), *Winning Orations* (pp. 34–37). Mankato, MN: Interstate Oratorical Association.

Wagner, M. (1998). The American drug cartel. In L. Schnoon (Ed.), *Winning Orations* (pp. 79–81). Mankato, MN: Interstate Oratorical Association.

Wallace, K. (1972). Topoi and the problem of invention. *Quarterly Journal of Speech, 58,* 387–395.

Weber, D. E. (1995). *Applied storytelling: Narrative skills for communicators.* Short course presented at the 81st Annual Meeting of the Speech Communication Association, San Antonio, TX.

Wylie, A. (1998, February-March). Story telling: A powerful form of communication. *Communication World, 15*(3), 30–33.

Exemplary Informative Speech

Steve Harris at the National Forensic Association Tournament held at Marshall University in Huntington, West Virginia, in April 1991 presented the following informative speech. At the time, Harris was a junior majoring in economics and international relations at the University of Wisconsin, Madison. The speech has two objectives—to describe and to explain the technology of virtual reality (VR). It would be categorized as a combination of an object and process speech; it describes the intangible object of virtual reality and its capabilities and limitations, but it also explains the process of how virtual reality works. Despite the fact that the speech was presented in 1991, its description of VR is highly informative and, in fact, forecasts some of the contemporary uses of VR mentioned in Chapter 14, such as using it to reduce public speaking anxiety.

Virtual Reality: Immersion in an Artificial World

By Steve Harris

(1) Rifstorc Nurthmuson's Macintosh computer alerts him to a hazardous waste emergency. He quickly pulls on his Datasuit and Dataglove and slips his Eyephones over his eyes in order to enter virtual reality. Rifstorc teleoperates a robot located at the site of the accident through his Datasuit and glove. These devices calculate every motion he makes, right down to each finger and knuckle. These motions are transmitted to the robot, who performs exactly the same movements as Rifstorc. He sees what the robot sees through his Eyephones, giving him the illusion that he is actually cleaning up the toxic mess. As Rifstorc "experiences" the accident site and begins the cleanup, the robot follows his actions and actually does the work.

(1) *Introduction:* At the very beginning of the introduction, the speaker immediately intrigues the audience with a hypothetical example of virtual reality (VR).

(2) Virtual reality promises to revolutionize the computer industry. As *Forbes* magazine of February 5, 1990, states, "according to the visionaries and futurists who abound in Silicon Valley, virtual reality is where the computer user of the 21st century will telecommunicate, design, and do research."

(2) In this statement of significance, the speaker emphasizes the importance of VR, supporting the claim with several dramatic quotations. He thus establishes the credibility of several of his sources of information. However, note that the speaker does not establish his own credibility by indicating that he has become well-informed about VR and can be considered a reliable source of information on the topic.

(3) In order to appreciate how this technology will affect our lives, today we will examine what virtual reality is, what its capabilities are, and what future applications it may hold.

(3) Now that the speaker has told the listeners that the topic is important, this preview tells them what three aspects of VR will be covered. The speech will be organized into three categories: what VR is, its capabilities, and its future applications.

(4) Author Stewart Brand notes in *Compute* magazine of October 1989, that yesterday's virtual reality was the moving theater—the creation of an artificial world. He writes about today's technology, "Virtual reality is as much of an immersion in an artificial world as you can get without piping it into your nervous system." We'll now look at the intricacies of virtual reality, or VR, look at its concepts, and examine its technical components. *Computer* magazine of the same month defines virtual reality as the creation of artificial worlds of experience. It continues, "Virtual reality devices place you inside a controlled hallucination—the ultimate simulation." In fact, many people have found the experience so compelling, they compare VR to drugs. This coupling was further advanced by a *Wall Street Journal* article entitled "A Kind of Electronic LSD?"

(4) *Body of the Speech:* The speaker begins the first main point—what VR is and how it works—with a description and a definition.

(5) Virtual reality's basic technology stems from a revolution in how we control computers. According to *Business Week* of February 20, 1989, most computers are manipulated through a keyboard and several cumbersome command keys. Virtual reality surpasses the mouse in ease of operation by allowing you to control computer functions through your own movements and gestures. Virtual reality allows you to control computers more naturally. "If you let people manipulate spatial things, you're taking advantage of something they already knew before they knew the word *computer,*" says Paul McAvinney, chairperson of Sensor Frame Corporation, a VR research company.

(5) To better understand VR, the speaker compares how people control computers normally and how they control them using VR.

(6) Another company developing this technology is VPL Research located in Silicon Valley, California. They are actively involved in producing hardware equipment used in controlling virtual reality software. The VR system already developed by VPL utilizes two pieces of high-tech equipment. First is a pair of goggles, called Eyephones, that resemble a scuba mask. But you can't see through Eyephones, because a miniature television screen is positioned over each eye. These screens bombard the user with a 3-dimensional image. A plastic cube on top of the Eyephones headpiece transmits data to a computer, via a cable running out the back, about the wearer's position in space. The cable runs from the headpiece to an ordinary personal computer.

The second piece of equipment is called a Dataglove. *Rolling Stone* magazine of June 14, 1990, describes it as an average spandex rubber glove with several fiber cables wired to it. These cables are connected to the same computer as are the Eyephones to communicate where your hand is in space.

(6) Next, the hardware used in VR is described, starting with Eyephones and then the Dataglove, including a description of how each piece of equipment works.

(7) *Forbes* magazine of February 5, 1990, explains that as the hand is flexed, the light flow along each finger changes enough to be ready by a sensor, which in turn transmits these data to the computer. As you make a motion with your hand, the computer shows

(7) A reliable source of information, *Forbes* magazine, is used to provide a detailed description of how the VR equipment functions.

you what you're doing in the computer environment through your Eyephones. What you see is a disembodied hand on the tiny television screens inside your Eyephones. In essence, you see your motions take the form of a computer-generated hand that can manipulate computer-generated objects. Not only confined to grabbing objects, the Dataglove also signals the computer to move in the computer-generated environment. If you point to the left, the computer pans that direction, as seen on the Eyephones. Point up and you can fly.

(8) David Churbuck, writing for *Forbes* in the February 5, 1990, edition, claims to have first grabbed a fish and then pulled it over his head. He states, "I'm inside a hollow fish with two eyes at the far end." Virtual reality has simplified computer use beyond imagination. Although its technology is unique and revolutionary, it is still simple. Work is being done to perfect a full Datasuit that will measure every motion of every part of the body. Then this technology will become truly amazing.

(8) A direct quotation enlivens the description of how VR equipment works and what it feels like when you're using it.

(9) Turning now to VR's capabilities and limitations, we find that the implications of this technology are staggering. People now have the power to create quickly and easily.

(9) A clear transition alerts the listeners of the move to the next main points, VR's capabilities and limitations.

(10) Molecular engineers can "pick up" and view a single molecule from all directions. They can reach in and sculpt or mold objects directly on a screen, without typing in commands one at a time as was needed previously. As mentioned in the *Futurist* of May/June 1990, architects can tour a building with a client in virtual reality, moving walls and doorways with ease before plans are committed to paper. A surgeon can practice surgical techniques with such a system. The computer would simply read the doctor's hand motions and display the effect on the body organ being resected.

(10) First, the uses of VR by engineers, architects, and surgeons are described.

(11) But virtual reality will certainly not leave the average consumer behind. In fact, *Business Week* of February 20, 1989, claims that Mattel, Inc. has contracted with VPL Research to provide a $75 version of the Dataglove for use with its Nintendo Videogame system. But virtual reality's uses extend much further than toys. People will soon be able to take instant vacations anywhere in the world with the help of fiber optics. The *Wall Street Journal* of July 10, 1990, states that fiber will provide remarkably crisp audio and video in order to transport you to another time or place. Not only limited to a Caribbean beach, the president of VPL, Jaron Lanier, claims that programs can be developed to allow us to experience life in ancient Egypt or over the rainbow in the land of Oz.

(11) Then, uses by average consumers are provided with examples to involve audience members more personally in the discussion.

(12) All of these features, however, are not yet possible. In order for a person to virtually travel to another place, computer software must first be created containing information such as the location of buildings and the appearance of landscape. Another cosmetic problem mentioned in the *Utne Reader* of March/April 1990 is that it cannot yet perfectly simulate reality.

(12) Again, a clear transition lets the listeners know the speaker is moving on to a discussion of the present limitations of VR, starting with the need for new software to be created and the inability of VR to simulate reality perfectly.

(13) When you pick up a virtual baseball, you can see on your Eyephones that you are grasping it, but you cannot actually feel the baseball in your hand. As reported in *Forbes* of February 5, 1990, researchers are developing a method to provide tactile feedback, so the user can touch and feel computer-generated objects. In addition, 3-dimensional sound and eye tracking are features being developed. Eye tracking will enable wearers to pan and zoom in response to eye movement instead of head movement.

(13) Using the simple example of picking up a baseball makes the limitation of seeing but not feeling with VR very real.

(14) But VR's limitations extend beyond nonperfect simulations. The picture provided by the program software is described in *Maclean's* magazine of June 4, 1990, as "crude, Saturday morning cartoon quality." Also, the computer is not powerful enough to keep with your movements. As a result, you see a jerky movement in virtual reality. Although a more advanced, powerful computer would solve the previous problem, the research companies have rejected it based on cost. Currently, according to *Maclean's* of the same date, the Eyephones cost over $11,000, the Dataglove $10,500, and the entire package about $267,000. So although virtual reality's capabilities are amazing, its limitations are significant and being diligently overcome at the VR development labs of VPL Research, Sendor Frame, and Autodesk, Inc.

(14) A third limitation, VR's crude picture quality and jerky movement, is explained using quotations that also indicate how costly VR still is.

(15) The possible future applications for virtual reality have the potential to alter almost all aspects of life. The *Utne Reader* of March/April 1990 mentions a few applications. Wearers could perform ultraprecision work with the aid of robots, such as cleaning up after a nuclear disaster without endangering human life. NASA intends to develop a VR system to enable a technician to repair spacecraft and satellites from earth. Medicine will also be transformed by virtual reality. A doctor in one country could perform surgery in another by donning virtual reality hardware connected to a robot. *The Futurist* of May/June 1990 states that VR could be used for "internal surgery." A micro-robot would be guided by a human surgeon seeing the inside of the patient through virtual reality.

(16) If plans for a full Datasuit become realized, Wimbledon could take place in Virtual reality. *Forbes* magazine of February 5, 1990, claims that if Boris Becker and Ivan Lendl were placed in Datasuits and Eyephones, Wimbledon could take place in both Sweden and Germany.

(17) But let's get back to reality. Plans are already underway by General Electric, NASA, and the army to develop a helicopter training simulator. The system uses fiber optics to create amazing video displays. Its lifelike images of simulated crashes can make promising pilots physically ill. Another realistic application down the line may make business more efficient. The *Wall Street Journal* of July 10, 1990, states that costly business travel could be reduced if companies used virtual reality for teleconferencing. If fact, large meetings may one day be possible with every member in a different part of the country. Using fiber optics, you could see a lifelike image of everyone and hear them with crystal clarity. *Rolling Stone* of June 14, 1990, quotes an Autodesk Corporation document as saying, "It is quite likely that the technology will supplant commuting." Although these futuristic applications may seem far-fetched, most researchers predict that many of the statements here will be fully realized with the next decade.

(18) Virtual reality is an extraordinary new technology that may very well change our lives. While its more amazing applications may be realized only in future years, for now VR devices such as the Dataglove and Eyephones allow us to manipulate computers more naturally. Virtual reality's capabilities affect science, art, medicine, and space exploration. One day, systems based on today's technology may alter our lives completely. Eventually, Rifstorc Nurthmuson, in addition to getting a better name, may become more than just a scenario character and begin saving real lives using virtual reality.

(15) At this point, the speaker moves to the final main point, possible future applications of VR.

(16) Vivid, almost extraordinary, examples are used to illustrate future uses of VR.

(17) Here the speaker describes more realistic applications, using testimony and quotations from respected publications.

(18) *Conclusion*: The speaker begins the conclusion by restating the significance of VR as a new technology. Then the speaker reviews the content of the speech: how VR works, its hardware, and its multiple capabilities. The speech concludes by using a reference back to the hypothetical character from the introduction as a closing device.

SOURCE: Harris (1992).

CHAPTER 18

Learning Objectives

After studying this chapter, you should be able to:

1. Describe persuasive speaking and explain its importance and ethical dimensions.
2. Identify the three types of persuasive speeches and guidelines for using each type.
3. Understand how to use logical, emotional, and credibility appeals to persuade.
4. Describe the five ways to organize a persuasive speech.
5. Identify challenges to effective persuasive speaking and explain how to overcome them.

Speaking to Persuade

Spencer was about to finish his first semester at Southeast University. He had taken a public speaking class because he knew it would help him give better speeches in other classes and at work. The final assignment in the class involved preparing and presenting a persuasive speech. The instructor recommended that students choose a significant topic or issue they felt strongly about, but also one that would appeal to the student audience. Spencer reviewed the list of suggested topics but didn't see anything on the list that spoke to him. Although many of his classmates were politically active and environmentally aware, Spencer didn't really feel passionate about either of those subject areas.

Then two weeks before the assignment was due, Spencer ran into Carol, a classmate who was quite involved in campus politics. As she had done before, Carol tried to persuade Spencer to help her fight the good fight on behalf of the interests and concerns of students on campus. She described a few of the current problems she was working on with a student activist organization, such as insufficient parking and the latest tuition increase. She said that if Spencer and other students didn't organize to fight for their rights, campus administrators would assume they didn't care what was happening on campus and they would continue to raise the tuition whenever they felt like it.

Carol's argument impressed Spencer so much that he attended a meeting of the student activist group with her that afternoon. Later that evening, Spencer thought about how Carol had been able to persuade him, a relatively nonpolitical type of person, to get involved in campus life. He felt his eyes had been opened to the administration's shifting priorities and their indifference to students' needs. He had even signed a petition to protest tuition hikes and to protect other important student rights. But how had Carol motivated him to overcome his ambivalence and finally act by attending the student meeting?

Carol had effectively persuaded Spencer by changing what he believed to be true and thereby moving him to action. She had presented a logical argument, reminding Spencer that the last tuition increase was only a year ago and the size of this year's increase would be greater than the inflation rate. She told him how much the campus was spending to recruit new students and that money was coming directly out of his pocket and those of other students. She appealed to him emotionally by explaining how hard it can be for many students at Southeast to absorb the repeated tuition hikes. Many hold part-time and even full-time jobs to pay their own school expense. Another tuition increase would mean working more hours and taking fewer courses. A committed and credible role model herself, Carol appeared to care genuinely about the welfare of others. She stressed the impact and the importance of every contribution to that one united voice for all students. It wouldn't take much of Spencer's time to participate and add to that collective voice.

Not only was Spencer pleased to be working with Carol and the other students, he realized there was another immediate benefit—he had found a topic for his persuasive speech. He would try to persuade his classmates in the public speaking class to sign the petition and join him in protesting the tuition hike. And that was a topic Spencer could get excited about and make relevant to his audience. ●●●

This chapter covers the key elements and techniques of competent persuasion, similar to what Carol used to influence Spencer to become more of a student activist. As with informative speaking, taking a competence approach to persuasive speaking is essential. Figure 18.1 shows how the three components of competence—motivation,

SPEAKING TO PERSUADE

A competent speaker
- appreciates the importance of persuasive speaking in a free society
- realizes how difficult it is to persuade people to change
- respects the importance of ethics when speaking to persuade

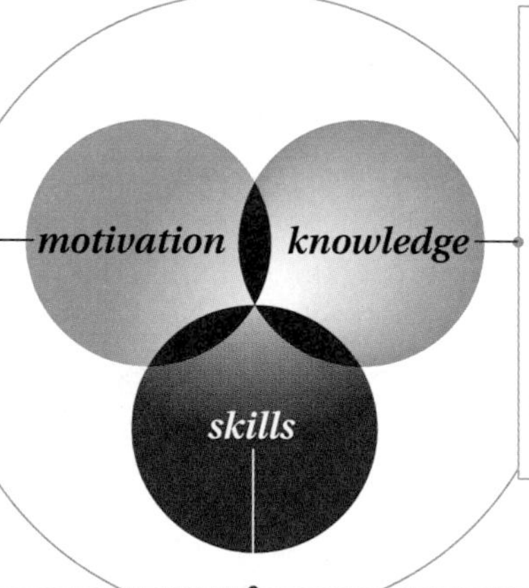

A competent speaker understands
- what persuasive speaking is
- the four types of persuasive speeches and how to use them competently
- the challenges to speaking to persuade

A competent speaker is able to
- use the five organizational patterns to speak persuasively
- use three types of appeals to persuade effectively
- develop an outline for a persuasive speech
- overcome the challenges to persuasive speaking

FIGURE 18.1
A Competence Approach to Persuasive Speaking

As in all communication contexts, motivation, knowledge, and skills are essential to persuasive speaking. The use of these components influences whether a speaker presents a persuasive speech competently or incompetently.

knowledge, and skills—influence the outcome of perceived competence when presenting any persuasive speech. The content of this chapter explains just how you can achieve that competence.

We begin by building an understanding of persuasive speaking, including its importance and its ethical dimensions. Then we describe three types of persuasive speeches, followed by strategies for making an argument persuasive and methods for organizing these speeches. The chapter concludes with a look at the major challenges to competent persuasive speaking and ways to overcome those challenges.

Understanding the Persuasive Speech

We defined *persuasion* in Chapter 1 as the use of communication to reinforce, modify, or change attitudes, beliefs, values, or actions. Hence the persuasive speech, as stated in Chapter 14, is intended to influence these characteristics of the audience (Stiff, 1994, p.4). In the case of Spencer's attitude toward student activism, Carol's purpose in talking to him was to change his past negative attitude and encourage him to adopt different future behaviors, which she did successfully.

WHAT IS PERSUASIVE SPEAKING?

Some public speaking experts say that all speeches are inherently persuasive. According to this perspective, whenever you present information, you're attempting to persuade the audience that the information is true. Therefore, all public speaking—including speeches to inform—is partly persuasive. To understand this viewpoint better, let's compare persuasive speaking to informative speaking.

As you saw in Chapter 17, an informative speaker uses information purely to promote understanding. By contrast, as you will see in this chapter, a persuasive speaker uses information to influence listeners. As a result, persuasive speeches are organized differently from informative ones. Furthermore, although both types of speakers are concerned with the audience's attitudes toward the information presented, the listeners' specific position on the topic is vital to persuasive speaking, because the ultimate goal is to influence that position.

The persuasive speech differs in several ways from the informative speech, but it shares some qualities as well. Both types of speeches start out with a specific purpose, first try to gain the audience's attention, and then present suitable information to accomplish the speech purpose. Good organization is also crucial to both types of speeches. Moreover, both types of speakers must be aware of the importance to the audience of what they present.

Knowledge Link

Does viewing communication as persuasion (as suggested in Chapter 1) reinforce that all public speeches are persuasive?

WHY PERSUASIVE SPEAKING IS IMPORTANT

Persuasive speaking has been considered an important aspect of social life for centuries. In *The Rhetoric,* his famous book on persuasion, the Greek philosopher Aristotle wrote about how crucial it is for people to discover the available means of persuasion in any situation (Roberts, 1954). Aristotle identified four social values for rhetoric and persuasion.

First, it prevents the triumph of fraud and injustice. It is not enough just to know what is right; people must be able to argue for what is right. Second, rhetoric and persuasion are an effective method of instruction for the public. It is not sufficient just to understand an argument; a speaker must also be able to instruct the audience in a persuasive manner. Third, persuasive rhetoric helps people see and understand both sides of an argument. Public debates on policies and legislative issues are examples of this. They allow citizens to determine what they believe to be true by listening to the persuasive arguments of political leaders. Fourth, rhetoric and persuasion are a viable means of defense. According to Aristotle, just as people need to be able to defend themselves physically, they should also be able to fend off verbal attacks persuasively.

As we discussed in Chapter 14, the effective use of persuasive speaking skills continues to be the foundation of a free and open society. People use persuasion in contemporary society to examine various sides of important issues and then make informed decisions. Whether at the local or national level—in legislatures, schools, businesses, or public meetings—people use persuasive speaking to debate and then set organizational and public agendas for their communities. At town meetings in small New England villages, in cities at meetings of community groups such as tenants' rights associations and food cooperatives, at local schools and zoning boards, speaking to persuade plays an important role in creating communities, as Chapter 1 emphatically pointed out.

In fact, the ability of citizens to express their positions persuasively is so crucial to a free society, teachers in public schools are encouraging even young students to learn to express their ideas clearly and speak persuasively (Lindquist, 1995). In one study of students in an eighth grade class, the ability to speak persuasively was identified as essential to the mastery of other lifelong learning skills (Moebius, 1991). Students who learned to develop and deliver persuasive speeches also learned to understand and respect different points of view, to support their beliefs with evidence, and to present their opinions more effectively.

THE ETHICS OF PERSUASIVE SPEAKING

Given the importance of persuasive speaking skills to society, it is critical to understand ethical persuasion. Persuasive speaking could be misunderstood and confused with coercion or manipulation, which are not ethical ways of influencing others. **Coercion** is a negative form of influence that occurs when a speaker persuades others to act in a particular way out of fear of reprisal, or by using force, or giving the listeners no choice but to cooperate. In Nazi Germany, some people were coerced by Hitler's speeches to betray their friends and family members who were providing safe havens for Jews. They were afraid that if they didn't cooperate, they themselves would be accused of disloyalty to the Nazi party.

Manipulation is also a negative and unethical form of influence used to control people's actions or reactions in a devious or deceitful way. Political campaign speeches sometimes border on manipulation when they misrepresent an opponent's programs or positions on an issue. For example, a candidate for elected office might suggest that his or her opponent wants to end medical coverage or take away social security benefits from the elderly, when that may not be the case.

By contrast to these unethical approaches, ethical persuasion leaves the decision about what to think or do up to the person or the audience members. The speaker presents information, without coercing or manipulating the listeners, and allows them to make up their own minds. As a result, the listeners are more likely to continue to hold the new opinions or engage in the desired behaviors in the future. When a person or audience member is coerced or manipulated into changing, there is less commitment to the new opinion or desire to continue the activity later on.

In contemporary society, professionals such as public relations practitioners and lawyers could be tempted to manipulate the truth because of their need to present a positive image of their products or clients (Barney & Black, 1994). This challenge is further

Knowledge Link

What ethical responsibilities do persuasive speakers have when aiding others in creating communities?

confounded by the fact that what is considered ethical and unethical communication varies from one person to the next, depending on the cultural background of the communicators. Building on the information about ethics introduced in Chapter 1, the CloseUp on ethics and persuasive speaking highlights the ethical challenges these professionals and public speakers often face.

Types of Persuasive Speeches

As with informative speeches, persuasive speeches can be categorized based on the speaker's objective. The three types of persuasive speeches attempt to *reinforce* the listeners' attitudes, beliefs, and values; *change* their attitudes, beliefs, and values; or *move the listeners to action.*

As you'll recall, three of these audience characteristics—attitudes, beliefs, and values—were discussed in Chapter 15 as crucial to audience analysis. Now you can use what you know about analyzing these characteristics to develop an effective persuasive speech. This entails figuring out your audience's probable reaction to and position on your persuasive topic and developing your speech based on that information. Table 18.1 provides examples of how to analyze potential audience reactions to some typical persuasive topics.

That said, this categorization system for persuasive speeches is misleading in that it suggests the three types are discrete and unrelated to one another. In reality, the types of

Knowledge Link

How can nonverbal cues be used most competently when presenting each of these types of persuasive speeches?

•••

TABLE 18.1

••• Attitudes, Beliefs, Values, & Behaviors •••

When preparing a persuasive speech topic, you must determine the audience's attitudes, beliefs, values, and possible behaviors. That information will help you develop a speech that's more likely to achieve your persuasive objective.

TOPIC/ISSUE	ATTITUDE	BELIEF	VALUE	BEHAVIOR
Prayer in Public Schools	Favorable toward nondenominational prayer	It's the responsibility of the public school system to encourage moral values	Morality and religious values	Petition the school board to rule in favor of prayer in schools
Capital Punishment	Favorable toward life sentences for those committing murder or other violent crimes	It's wrong to take another person's life	Sacredness of all human life	Vote against putting people to death by use of the electric chair or lethal injection
First Amendment Rights	Favorable toward no control or interference by the government on the internet	People have a right to express their opinions in any way they prefer	Individual liberty	Vote for a hands-off policy relative to Web pages and pornography on the internet
Euthanasia	Favorable toward assisted suicide	People have a right to control their own destiny	Freedom of choice	Encourage the use of living wills that allow people to die as they choose

CloseUp ON ETHICS

Ethics & Speaking to Persuade

PUBLIC SPEAKERS FACE particularly challenging ethical dilemmas when they are speaking to persuade. An objectivity ethic says public speakers should share only the truth with their audience. But a persuasion ethic suggests persuaders may want to present their argument in its most favorable light. Advocates such as lawyers believe the persuasion ethic is defensible and laudable in a participatory democracy. In a free and democratic society, when all sides of an issue are argued openly, ultimately the truth is revealed. Furthermore, the presentation of varying perceptions of the truth is justified by the democratic ideal that everyone has a right to express the truth as he or she sees it. Given this ethical dilemma, here are guidelines for making decisions about ethical persuasive speaking:

- *Don't allow the end to justify the means.* Your end in a persuasive speech is to accomplish your persuasive goal. But if you withhold information in order to accomplish that goal, you're assuming the audience isn't capable of weighing all the evidence and making a good decision. If you suppress or distort information or deliberately lie in order to adapt your speech to the audience, that is unethical. As a public speaker, you are ethically responsible to present all viewpoints—openly and fairly—so your listeners will be in a position to form their own opinions.
- *Don't use numbers or statistics to mislead the audience.* Most people think statistical studies are precise and reliable, so they're easily persuaded by the use of statistics to support an argument. However, researchers who generate statistics, and public speakers who make use of them, can interpret and slant what numbers mean. Using the persuasive ability of statistics to misrepresent what is true is not ethical. If you discover statistics that contradict your position, you have an ethical responsibility to report that evidence to your listeners.
- *Don't misrepresent your position on the topic to the listeners.* If the listeners strongly disagree with your position, it may be tempting to distort or misrepresent your claim or position. To say what you do not mean, to fabricate enthusiasm for a topic, or to endorse a policy with which you disagree is unethical.
- *Don't use emotion to distract the listeners from the truth.* Emotional evidence can sometimes be more effective than a logical argument. Therefore, you may be tempted to use an extremely emotional story or example to persuade the audience of the rightness or importance of your claim. That is acceptable only if you have carefully considered the impact of that evidence on the audience. Moreover, to use emotion as a substitute for sound reasoning is unethical.

speeches sometimes overlap. You may find yourself presenting a speech that has more than one objective, for example, to change both the attitudes and the behaviors of your listeners. In the opening vignette, Carol's objective was to change Spencer's attitudes and his actions and behaviors. We now examine the three types of persuasive speeches more closely.

SPEECHES TO REINFORCE ATTITUDES, BELIEFS, & VALUES

If the audience members are already favorably disposed toward your topic and position, your objective is to reinforce that favorable response and encourage them to an even greater degree of commitment. A **speech to reinforce** is intended to influence listeners by strengthening their convictions and taking advantage of their tendency to seek out and attend to messages with which they already agree. Most listeners are more likely to pay attention to and remember information that supports or resembles their own attitudes and opinions (Furnham & Procter, 1989–1990). So by reinforcing your listeners' attitudes, beliefs, or values, you'll increase the likelihood that they'll pay attention and remember what you say.

This type of speech works well if there is a need to raise your listeners' consciousness about an issue or concern. They may already agree with your position but have no sense of urgency about the topic. In this case, you want to encourage them to care more about it. For example, if your audience believes governmental aid to education is (or is not) a good idea, your job would be to reinforce their current beliefs and influence them to pay more attention to the current messages of political candidates who agree with your position.

To reinforce listeners' attitudes and beliefs, provide them with additional information that supports their existing attitudes and what they already believe to be true. Reinforce their values by indicating your respect for what they hold to be right or important (Johannesen, 1997). You needn't say you agree with them, if you do not. But merely by respecting their values, you build rapport and goodwill, which enhances your credibility as a persuasive speaker and helps accomplish the objective of speaking to reinforce.

SPEECHES TO CHANGE ATTITUDES, BELIEFS, & VALUES

If the audience's present attitudes, beliefs, and values are not to your liking—if they contradict or prevent you from achieving your own goals—then your objective is to change the listeners' present response to a more desirable one. A **speech to change** is intended to convince the audience to change what they like or dislike, what they hold to be true or untrue, or what they consider important or unimportant.

In order to change listeners' attitudes—what they like or dislike—you have to first provide them with information that motivates them to listen to you and then try to modify or change their attitudes. You could accomplish this by reinforcing an attitude they already hold to get their attention and establish mutual understanding, and then make your own point. For example, if you're presenting a speech against government regulation of the internet to listeners who are politically conservative, you would want to reinforce their existing attitudes that are probably favorable toward minimizing government regulations. If the audience is more liberal, you would reinforce their concerns about the loss of freedom of speech that might occur through governmental regulation. Then you would provide your argument against regulation.

The best way to change listeners' beliefs—what they hold to be true or untrue—is to present them with solid facts and evidence from highly credible sources. Because beliefs are based on what people know, if you want to change beliefs, you need compelling evidence to counteract their previous experiences and knowledge. Information from credible sources, as well as your own credibility as a speaker, are essential to convince the audience that their current beliefs are not necessarily true and they should change them.

To change your listeners' values—what they consider important or unimportant—is to make a fundamental change in something very basic to each individual (Johannesen, 1997). Because values are imbedded in a person's self-concept, they are much harder to change than attitudes or beliefs. Therefore, success in changing listeners' values is rare, but appealing to values is an effective technique for influencing attitudes and beliefs.

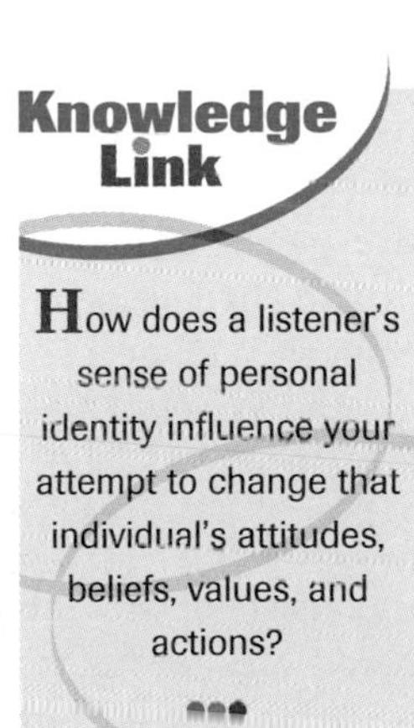

SPEECHES TO MOVE LISTENERS TO ACTION

If the audience's behaviors are not what you would like them to be, then your objective is to influence or change what the listeners do—their actions. A **speech to move to action** is intended to influence listeners to either engage in a new and desirable behavior or discontinue an undesirable behavior. If you give a speech and ask your listeners to vote for your candidate, buy a product, or start recycling their trash, you are asking them to adopt a new behavior. If your speech asks them to stop smoking or littering, the action you're recommending is one of discontinuance.

To change people's behaviors, it is important to realize that attitudes, beliefs, and values shape and direct behaviors. For example, you may hold a favorable attitude toward climbing the corporate ladder, believe that education is the best way to get a good job, and value professional success. As a result of these attitudes, beliefs, and values, you'll engage in behaviors such as trying hard to succeed at work, going directly from high school to college, or returning to college after several years in the work force.

Consequently, if you want to change people's behaviors—which is hard to do—you must demonstrate that their current behaviors aren't consistent with their attitudes, beliefs, or values. Most people prefer to think that they act according to what they believe and value. If you can demonstrate to your listeners that another set of behaviors is more consistent with their attitudes, beliefs and values, your speech is more likely to result in at least some behavioral change.

To understand fully the three types of persuasive speeches just discussed, take a look at the student speech at the end of this chapter, "The Forgotten Four-Letter Word," which took first place at the Interstate Oratorical Association's Winning Orations Competition in 1999 (Meinen, 1999). The speech is about the public's current lack of compassion and concern about AIDS and how people have been lulled into complacency about the disease. The speaker disagrees with the listeners' present convictions about AIDS and so does not attempt to reinforce those attitudes and beliefs. Rather, the objective is to change existing attitudes and beliefs and thus move the audience to action. Here's an excerpt from the introduction to the speech that summarizes the speaker's objective:

> Our well of compassion has run dry, and we're all too eager to relegate AIDS to a growing list of historical atrocities. Closing our eyes won't make a monster of this magnitude go away. Instead, we must revive our compassion and interest by first, discovering why we've become immune to this vicious virus, next detailing the effects of our plague of indifference, and finally, curing ourselves of AIDS compassion fatigue.

Making Your Argument Persuasive

As you now know, each of the three types of persuasive speeches calls for a particular strategy for making it most persuasive. But whether you're trying to influence attitudes, beliefs, values, or actions, you can make your argument much more persuasive by using one or more of three types of persuasive appeals. An **appeal** is the subtle technique speakers use to get the audience to accept their persuasive argument.

Current thinking on this topic is derived from the classical tradition of rhetoric, when in the 4th century B.C.E., Greek rhetoricians recommended that persuasive speakers make use of **logos**—a form of logical appeals, **pathos**—emotional appeals, and **ethos**—or credibility appeals. Although there is some debate about which of these appeals is most effective—logic, emotion, or credibility—persuasion experts agree that all three techniques can be effective depending on the particular situation, the audience, and the persuasive goal (Stiff, 1994).

Logical Appeals

A **logical appeal** is based on knowledge and reasoning, which involves how people think. It consists of presenting evidence and encouraging the listeners to draw a conclusion based on that information. Logical arguments are particularly effective for audiences made up of people from Western or North American cultures, who prefer to make deci-

"Edwardson, this address brings the art of obfuscation to a new high."

Despite what this speaker thinks, obfuscating (blurring) the message is *not* the best way to present a logical appeal. Rather, present a plausible argument that is perceived as convincing and reasonable by your listeners.

© 2000 Bernard Schoenbaum from cartoonbank.com. All rights reserved.

sions based on examining evidence and information. At the beginning of this chapter, Carol persuaded Spencer to become a student activist partly by using a logical argument. She provided solid evidence of how and why unfair tuition increases were taking place on their campus.

Logical arguments can be made in two ways—using deductive or inductive reasoning. **Deduction** is a process of reasoning in which a specific conclusion follows necessarily from a general principle that is often made up of a major and a minor premise. If the audience accepts the two premises as true, then they must also accept that the specific conclusion is true. Here's a classic example that teachers of rhetoric often use to illustrate deductive reasoning:

Major premise: *All of humanity are mortal.*
Minor premise: *Socrates is a human.*
General conclusion: *Socrates is mortal.*

Here's how a college professor might use deductive reasoning to arrive at a conclusion:

Major premise: *College students will avoid public speaking whenever they can.*
Minor premise: *The students in my class are typical college students.*
Specific conclusion: *I must require all students to present a portion of the group presentation project, in order to ensure that each student takes a speaking part.*

Induction is a process of reasoning in which a general conclusion follows from the examination of a series of specific instances or examples. If the listeners accept the specific instances and examples as true, then they must also accept the general conclusion as true. The more credible the specific examples and illustrations, the more logical the conclusion will seem to the listeners. Using the topic of students presenting a group project, the professor could use an inductive argument to come to a general conclusion in this manner:

Instance: *John did not take a speaking role in his group's presentation this semester.*

Knowledge Link

What are the ramifications of the use of schema to organize information (as noted in Chapter 2) for developing a persuasive speech using logical appeals?

Instance: *Arisa declined a speaking role last semester.*

Instance: *Two other professors told me students in their classes have chosen not to speak during group presentations.*

General conclusion: *All college students will avoid speaking during group presentations, if they possibly can.*

In the student speech about AIDS, a logical argument is used to change what the listeners think. The speaker first summarizes why compassion fatigue about AIDS exists by stating that "AIDS has slowly faded from our national consciousness chiefly due to hype surrounding an AIDS cure and grossly misleading statistics." Then the following evidence is presented inductively to encourage the listeners to draw the desired conclusion:

- Newspapers are saying that AIDS ended (Urvashi Vaid, *Advocate,* December 24, 1997)
- Hype-filled headlines about a cure are fueling compassion fatigue and offering a false sense of security (*Scientist,* January 1998; *Advocate,* February 17 1998)
- Misleading and low AIDS statistics are reinforcing compassion fatigue, for example, the Center for Disease Control now counts only full-blown AIDS, not HIV infection (*Harpers,* July 1998)
- The death rate is down because of improved care, but HIV infection rates are up (*Journal of American Medical Association,* August 19 1998)
- Slightly lower numbers do exist in the United States, but the disease has reached pandemic proportions, not just epidemic, in developing countries (*Lancet,* July 11, 1998)

EMOTIONAL APPEALS

An **emotional appeal** is based on psychology and passion, which involves how people feel. Despite what most people would like to think, they are not always logical. If your argument appeals to your listeners' emotions, it will get their attention and hold it. By reaching them emotionally and convincing them that they should care about your topic, you will more likely achieve your persuasive goal.

Direct mail requests or phone calls asking you to help the less fortunate—the homeless, the hungry, or helpless animals—frequently use emotional appeals in the form of dramatic photographs or heart-wrenching stories. By making a contribution, they tell you you'll feel you have made a difference in the lives of those who need your support and your money.

To use emotional appeals effectively, you can appeal to any of a variety of your listeners' emotions, such as love, hate, sympathy, guilt, or even fear. A **fear appeal** is based on changing listeners' attitudes or behaviors through the use of an anxiety-arousing message. This type of appeal is useful in situations where you need to motivate the audience to pay attention and get more involved in your topic (Roser & Thompson, 1995). A fear appeal is not inherently an ethical or unethical approach to persuasion. For example, campaigns promoting antismoking or breast self-exams often use fear appeals appropriately to convince people of the danger of the given health issue.

In order for a fear appeal to be effective, it must include information that poses a real threat or danger to the listeners, and it must prescribe an effective action for handling the threat (Stiff, 1994; Witte, 1994). Moreover, the listeners must believe the threat is real and could actually happen, and the speaker and his or her information must be perceived as highly credible. In a study of the use of fear appeals, parents were effectively persuaded to immunize their preschool children against disease after they were given highly credible

Some speakers' credibility precedes them; others have a harder time appearing expert and trustworthy.

© 2000 Charles Barsotti from Cartoonbank.com. All rights reserved.

information stating that getting immunizations is realistic, available, affordable, safe, and effective (Smith, 1997). That said, fear appeals should be used cautiously. Realize that too strong a fear appeal will backfire, particularly if the listeners are not provided information for dealing with the fear-inducing situation or problem.

Emotional and logical appeals can be used effectively together to accomplish the objective of a persuasive speech. Listeners typically respond to the emotional content of a speech first and then examine the logical evidence. So combining emotion and logic, in that order, can be particularly effective. In a speech about the increasing danger of using cell phones while driving, Kevin Sackreiter (1998) of South Dakota State University used emotion effectively in an attention-getting story, followed by logic in the form of statistics:

Knowledge Link

How could a persuasive speaker ethically combine emotional and logical appeals to promote competent decision making in groups?

- In June 1996, a woman and her three children were driving back from a dentist appointment on Highway 14 near Janesville, Wisconsin. Traveling in the other direction was a construction worker in his pickup truck. The construction worker was talking to a landscaper on his cellular phone. While looking down at the phone, the builder lost control of his vehicle, crossed the center line, and hit the family's minivan head on. Both the 35-year-old mother and her 3-month-old son were killed in the crash. Her daughters survived, although one was seriously injured. The builder, who was treated and released from the hospital, walked away with only a minor traffic citation. This incident is just one example of the increasing problem that cellular phones cause on our national highways.
- The National Police Agency reported that in one American city during the month of June 1996 there were 128 accidents involving injury and one involving death that could be related to cellular phone use.
- In 1995, the number of Americans who signed up for new cell-phone service exceeded the national birthrate . . .
- According to the *Company Press Release* of April 13, 1998, there are currently 54 million cellular telephone subscribers in the United States with 10 million new users added each year.
- These numbers are especially significant, when we look at how many of these cellular phones are used while their owner is driving. According to the *Automotive Wire* of April 13, 1998, cellular phone industry studies indicate that 80 percent of cellular usage

occurs behind the wheel of an automobile. The use of cellular phones while driving is a very substantial problem throughout the United States.

CREDIBILITY APPEALS

A **credibility appeal** is related to how listeners perceive the reputation, prestige, and authority of the speaker. In Chapter 15, you learned about source credibility and in Chapter 16 about speaker credibility. As discussed in those chapters, if you establish the credibility of your sources of information and of yourself as a speaker, you are more likely to be believable and therefore persuasive. By contrast, if the audience disrespects or distrusts you, you'll have a harder time persuading them, regardless of any logical or emotional appeals you use. Furthermore, if you lack credibility, they may not even have an interest in what you have to say (Taylor, 1996).

Because their reputations precede them, some speakers are automatically perceived to be highly credible. But how can a novice speaker establish credibility with an audience? Three factors influence whether you will impress your audience as credible: expertise, trustworthiness, and charisma.

- *Expertise:* You need to be perceived by the listeners as someone who is competent and in command of the subject of your speech. This kind of competence involves knowing the topic well, being prepared to talk about it, and bringing your own experience to the discussion. If you prepared your speech according to the guidelines in Chapter 15 and can establish source credibility, the audience will respect you as more expert. Or if you have experience of relevance to the topic, for example, if you hold a degree in economics, your listeners will accept your explanation of the laws of supply and demand. Similarly, if they know that you successfully stopped smoking, they'll more likely listen to your advice.
- *Trustworthiness:* You need to be perceived as a person of high character, so listeners feel they can believe what you say. This aspect of credibility was referred to in Chapter 15 as a speaker of goodwill. Character involves honesty and objectivity. Without a doubt, being an honest person who tells the truth will enhance your credibility, because sincerity and openness can quickly build the trust that is crucial to audience respect. In addition, you can demonstrate character by speaking objectively about your speech topic. Mentioning opposing viewpoints and quoting sources which challenge your position suggest to the audience that you are a person of integrity.
- *Charisma:* Finally, you need to be perceived as a speaker with charisma, which means the audience finds you engaging, likable, and enthusiastic. All of the nonverbal cues for competent public speaking outlined in Chapter 16 will help you become more charismatic and therefore a more credible speaker. Such a speaker is dynamic, energetic, and enthusiastic and therefore able to gain and hold the audience's attention. There have been many charismatic speakers in the world of politics—Bill Clinton, Mikhail Gorbachev, Barbara Mikulski, Ronald Reagan, and even dictators such as Saddam Hussein arguably have charisma. Whether you agree with the politics of these leaders or not, their ability to impress audiences was due in part to their personal charisma.

Despite being perceived by many voters as charismatic and expert on some topics, Bill Clinton's credibility was called into question because of his honesty and trustworthiness.

Organizing & Outlining the Persuasive Speech

The general principles of speech organization discussed in Chapter 15 apply to the persuasive speech as well. An effective persuasive speech is carefully organized and structured to accomplish its objective. There are five ways to organize a persuasive speech that will help accomplish the objective of influencing the audience. The problem-solution pattern and the motivated sequence are the best known and most popular. Claim-warrant-data is an effective technique taken from writings about argumentation and logical reasoning. Refuting the opponent or comparing alternatives are useful when it's necessary to take opposing arguments into account.

Knowledge Link

Of the five organizational patterns, which would prove most valuable to a speaker who is attempting to facilitate coordination among community members?

PROBLEM-SOLUTION

Problem-solution organization first identifies a problem and then proposes a workable solution to solve it. This organizational pattern can be used to plan the body of the speech, using the basic structure introduced in Chapter 15. Draft an introduction, body, and conclusion, but cover only two main points in the body of the speech. Your first main point describes the problem and persuades the audience that the problem must be overcome. The second main point proposes a solution to overcome the problem. For an outline of problem-solution organization, see Figure 18.2.

Carol attempted to get Spencer involved in campus life by using problem-solution organization. She described what she saw as a crucial problem on campus and offered a constructive solution to it.

- *Problem:* Campus administrators make decisions with too little concern for the students' welfare.
- *Solution:* Get involved in campus life and contribute to policy-making decisions.

FIGURE 18.2
The Problem-Solution Pattern

This organizational pattern for a persuasive speech is structured similarly to the standard outline format described in Chapter 15. The body of the speech is organized as a problem and a solution.

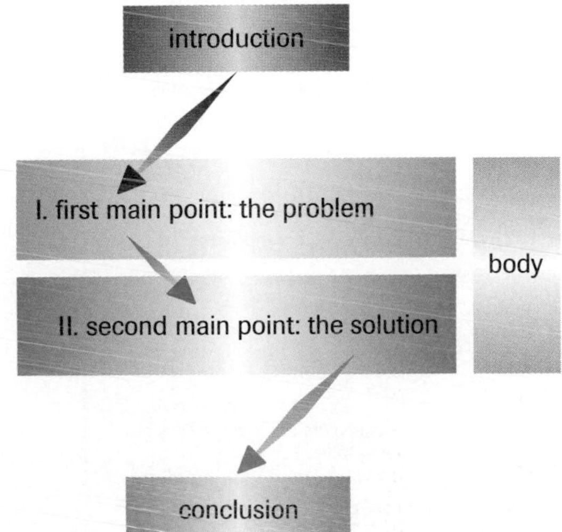

Motivated Sequence

An enhanced version of problem-solution organization has dominated the persuasion literature for years since it was first introduced in 1935 by Alan Monroe, a professor at Purdue University. The **motivated sequence** organizational pattern is a persuasive structure that moves through a sequence of five steps, designed to motivate and persuade listeners psychologically (Monroe, 1935). This pattern is effective because it makes use of a natural sequential pattern of human thought: gaining the listeners' attention, convincing them of a need or problem, offering a solution to satisfy the need or solve the problem, and then helping them visualize the solution and take action relative to it.

Returning to the basic speech structure you learned from Chapter 15, you present the attention step in your introduction, the need and satisfaction steps in the body of the speech, and the visualization and action steps in your conclusion. These five steps are outlined in Figure 18.3 and described here. Excerpts and a discussion of the speech about AIDS and compassion fatigue are used to help you understand how to use each step. The speaker's outline of the AIDS speech is presented in Figure 18.4.

Step 1: *Get the audience's attention.* In this first step, create interest in the topic of your speech and a desire on the part of your listeners to hear what you have to say. Also provide a statement of the purpose of your speech and forecast the importance of the need or problem that will be the general theme of your speech.

Here's how the speaker began the AIDS speech and drew the audience's attention to the problem (see I. in the speech outline):

> In 1981, two strange diseases first grabbed the attention of the American public. The first, a mental malaise born of our overabundance of seemingly insurmountable societal ills. We

Motivation Sequence Organizational Pattern

Speech Title	Indicate the issue of persuasion (pique curiosity).
General Purpose	Type of speech—to persuade.
Specific Purpose	State whether the speech has the objective to influence the audience's beliefs, attitudes, values, or behaviors about a need or problem.
Five Sequential Steps	
INTRODUCTION	
I. ATTENTION (STEP 1)	Grab the audience's attention and forecast the theme of the speech.
BODY	
II. NEED/PROBLEM (STEP 2)	Describe the problem or need, provide evidence of its importance, and relate it to the audience's desires and/or needs.
III. SATISFACTION/ SOLUTION (STEP 3)	Present a plan of action to address the problem or need.
CONCLUSION	
IV. VISUALIZATION (STEP 4)	Describe the results of the proposed plan or consequences of the audience's failure to change or to act
V. ACTION (STEP 5)	Summarize main ideas and call for the audience to change their beliefs or to act or react in the desired manner.

FIGURE 18.3
Outline of Motivated Sequence Organizational Pattern

As with any speech, your outline for this organizational pattern should state the title and general and specific purpose of the speech. Then the motivated sequence goes on to include the five sequential steps: attention, need, satisfaction, visualization, and action.

called it compassion fatigue, best described by the July-August 1981 *Utne Reader,* as the inability to care any more about social issues like refugees, homelessness, famine, natural disasters, the environment, or the Holocaust. The second was a new disease initially brought to our attention by its savage spread through the homosexual community. We called it AIDS and watched in horror as it polarized society and stopped discriminating on the basis of sexual preference, victimizing every demographic group and defying modern medical advances.

The July 1998 *Scientific American* reports that AIDS has recently been renamed a pandemic, having left mere epidemic status behind. And compassion fatigue? It's just added HIV to its list, somewhere between homelessness and the Holocaust, as something we just can't find the heart to care about anymore.

Step 2: *Establish that a need or problem exists.* In this step, describe and develop the need or problem by providing evidence of its existence and importance. Use examples, testimony, statistics, and other forms of support to emphasize the seriousness of the situation. Explain why the problem exists and relate it to the listeners by pointing out how it affects them. Motivate them to feel that a decision needs to be made or some action taken.

The AIDS speech carefully follows this recommendation, as the outline in Figure 18.4 shows. First, the problem (II. A in the outline) is described and its importance emphasized:

- 16,000 people contract AIDS daily
- 1.3 million died of AIDS last year
- 650,000 people are now HIV positive

Next, the speaker explains why the problem of compassion fatigue exists (II.B):

> Despite our exposure to death and destruction, facts and figures, names and quilt squares, AIDS has slowly faded from our national consciousness chiefly due to hype surrounding an AIDS cure and grossly misleading statistics.

The negative results of the problem (II.C) are then described as the following attitudinal and behavioral effects:

- Americans no longer taking AIDS seriously
- Unwillingness to let go of AIDS stereotypes and prejudices
- Lack of AIDS activists and increase in risky behavior
- Perceptions by youth of invulnerability to AIDS

Step 3: *Propose a satisfying solution.* This step is used to present a plan of action to meet the need or solve the problem you established in the previous step. Explain to the listeners how your plan addresses the need or problem better than any other solution. To do this, you may have to demonstrate how your solution is superior to others.

The speaker in our speech example presented two action steps that are necessary to solve the problem of AIDS compassion fatigue (III. in the outline):

- National focus must shift to include research on AIDS prevention as well as on a cure for AIDS
- Citizens must change their attitudes and revive AIDS activism

Step 4: *Help the audience visualize the solution.* This step helps the audience to imagine the benefits of the solution you propose or the negative consequences of not adopting your solution. You ask your listeners to picture the proposed plan being implemented, or what the world will look like if they fail to act. Here's the brief but effective negative visualization step from the AIDS speech:

> By the year 2000, one out of every three of us will know someone infected with the HIV virus. We may be immune to the stories and statistics, but none of us is safe from the reality of AIDS.

AIDS Speech Outline

Speech Title: The Forgotten Four-Letter Word
General Purpose: To persuade
Specific Purpose: To change the listeners' attitudes and behaviors regarding AIDS as a pandemic

INTRODUCTION

I. ATTENTION (Step 1)
   A. In 1981, two strange diseases—compassion fatigue (*Utne Reader,* July-August 1981) and AIDS
   B. AIDS as a pandemic (*Scientific American,* July 1998)

Transition: Our well of compassion has run dry, and we're all too eager to relegate AIDS to growing list of historical atrocities.

BODY

II. NEED/PROBLEM (Step 2)
   A. Description of problem
      1. 16,000 contract AIDS daily, 1.3 million died last year, 650,000 HIV positive (*Business Week,* February 16, 1998)
      2. Revive compassion by discovering why we're immune, the effects, and the cure of AIDS compassion fatigue
   B. Why problem exists
      1. Hype surrounding AIDS cure
         a. Newspapers say AIDS ended (Urvashi Vaid, *Advocate,* December 24, 1997)
         b. Hype-filled headlines fuel compassion fatigue (January 1998, *Scientist;* February 17, 1998, *Advocate*)
      2. Misleading statistics
         a. Centers for Disease Control counts only full-blown AIDS, not HIV infection (July 1998, *Harper's*)
         b. Quotes of death rate down, but HIV infection rates are up (August 19, 1998, *Journal of American Medical Association*)
         c. Slightly lower numbers in U.S. but a pandemic in developing countries (July 11, 1998, *Lancet*)
   C. Results of the problem
      1. Attitudinal effects
         a. Americans no longer take AIDS seriously (October 1997, Gallup Poll)
         b. Unwilling to let go of AIDS stereotypes and prejudices (Spring 1998, *Albany Law Review*)
      2. Behavioral effects
         a. Lack of AIDS activists and increase in risky behavior (July 13,1998, *MacLean's;* April 7, 1997, *U.S. News and World Report*)
         b. Perceptions by youth of invulnerability to AIDS (January 5, 1998, *AIDS Weekly Plus;* April 8, 1998, *Journal of American Medical Association*)

Transition: With this haunting question in mind, we must develop a practical and realistic prescription for our compassion fatigue on both a national and personal level.

III. SATISFACTION/SOLUTION
   A. National focus of research, time, and money must shift to include AIDS prevention as well as AIDS (January 5, 1998, *AIDS Weekly Plus;* May 1998, *American Bar Association Journal*)
   B. Citizens must change their attitudes and revive AIDS activism (July 1998, *Scientific American*)

FIGURE 18.4
Working Outline Using the Motivated Sequence in the AIDS Speech

The speech about AIDS and compassion fatigue illustrates the effective use of this approach. Each step in the motivated sequence is identified with a Roman numeral, and the alphanumeric system for outlining is used to indicate subordination of points and subpoints. When you prepare a formal outline using this approach, be sure to apply the tenets for formal outlining presented in Chapter 15.

AIDS Speech Outline (Cont'd)

CONCLUSION

IV. VISUALIZATION
- A. In 2000, 1 of 3 of us will know someone with HIV
- B. None of us is safe from AIDS

V. ACTION
- A. Most effective wake-up call is from high-risk communities and individualized grassroots efforts that start small, make biggest steps
- B. Solution is in our hands
- C. Forensics community should take risk and speak out, not succumb to compassion fatigue

Step 5: *Motivate the audience to take action.* Finally, ask the audience to act on the solution that you proposed to solve the problem. First summarize your main ideas as you would in any conclusion. Then clearly identify the specific action that is called for. If your objective is to change attitudes or beliefs, try to motivate the audience to reconsider their past positions and believe what you propose instead. If you want the listeners to change their behaviors, urge them to take the specific actions you recommend to solve the problem.

In the following action step, the AIDS speaker first points out that individualized efforts can make a difference, and then asks the audience members to take action about the problem:

- The most effective wake-up call is from high-risk communities; individualized grassroots efforts that start small, make biggest steps
- Solution is in our hands
- Members of the forensics community (the audience members) should take risk and speak out

CLAIM-DATA-WARRANT

Claim-data-warrant, often referred to as the *Toulmin model,* is a persuasive structure that historically was used to analyze arguments in the practice of debate and argumentation (Brockriede & Ehninger, 1960; Toulmin, 1958). Using this organizational pattern, the goal is to move the audience from accepting data that are presented through a warrant that links the data to the claim itself. The speaker draws on the types of logical appeals described earlier in this chapter and engages in practical reasoning offering the listeners a sensible argument for changing what they think or do. As Figure 18.5 indicates, with this structure, the body of your speech consists of three parts:

1. The claim or thesis of the speech: This is the statement you want your listeners to accept as true—a final proposition or conclusion to your argument. The claim answers this question: *What should the listeners accept as so?*
2. The data or evidence you provide to support the claim: These are the support materials and information that prove the truth of the claim. Your data answer this question: *What have you got to go on? Why should the listeners accept what you say as so?*
3. The warrant or reasoning that links the data to the claim. The warrant answers these questions: *How do you get there? What is the link between the data and the claim?*

DATA (therefore) **CLAIM**

nuclear power plants are more efficient → the government should build more nuclear power plants

(since) **WARRANT**
more cost-efficient forms of energy are needed

FIGURE 18.5
Claim-Data-Warrant Organizational Pattern

This structure could be used to provide an argument for the federal government constructing more nuclear power plants.

The key to using claim-data-warrant effectively is to provide sufficient data to support the claim and to link the data to the claim through careful reasoning. Krista Kim (1998), a student at Santa Rosa Junior College, used a modified version of claim-data-warrant in the following excerpts from her speech about crimes against the developmentally disabled:

Claim: Today we will take a look at crime striking the developmentally disabled, to understand that this is a real problem, which requires our immediate attention.

Data:

1. According to a recent report by the *San Francisco Chronicle* on October 20, 1997, developmentally disabled citizens are more likely to be victims of robbery than any other citizens.
2. Besides being targets of robbery, developmentally disabled citizens are also targets for sexual abuse.
3. Another crime that the developmentally disabled are subject to is poor quality care.

Warrant: Because of society's ignorance concerning their treatment . . . today the developmentally disabled are being harmed because of both ignorance and institutional problems.

REFUTING THE OPPONENT

Refuting the opponent organization dismantles your opponent's argument in order to persuade the audience that your argument is superior. In using this type of organizational pattern, your goal is to convince the audience that the opposition's ideas are false, misinformed, or in some way harmful.

There are two basic approaches for refuting the opponent, either of which can be used as the main points to structure the body of your speech. The first is to convince the audience that the other argument is flawed—that something is wrong with your opponent's line of reasoning. You examine his or her argument for any inconsistencies or errors in how evidence is presented or interpreted. The second approach is to convince the listeners that the actions recommended by your opponent will lead to undesirable results or consequences. You refute your opponent's argument by stressing its negative ramifications for your audience.

If you decide to use refuting the opponent, avoid engaging in personal attacks and stay strictly with the issues involved. Use solid evidence to criticize only your opponent's argument; attacking a person can backfire and damage your own credibility. Moreover, mudslinging and personal attacks are unethical approaches to persuasion and therefore not competent.

Knowledge Link

Can a public speaker use refuting the opponent as an organizational pattern and still persuade ethically?

Refuting your opponent by using personal attack can backfire and reflect negatively on your credibility as speaker.

Comparing Alternatives

Comparing alternatives organization first asks listeners to examine two or more alternatives, and then it makes a strong appeal for the preferred choice. This organizational pattern is designed to convince the audience that among all the possible ways to solve a problem, there is but one choice that has significant advantages over the others.

To use this organizational pattern, you present a series of alternatives and provide reasons to reject each alternative, except the one you're persuading the audience to favor or adopt. You present all the other alternatives, and then the alternative you prefer last. Just as with refuting the opponent, you can use comparing alternatives to structure the body of your speech. You would then have several main points, each containing a different alternative, and ending with the presentation of your preferred choice.

Comparing alternatives is useful if the listeners will later be exposed to counterarguments from other speakers. Candidates running for political office or people presenting policy speeches can make good use of comparing alternatives. When a politician or policymaker presents a new program, there are usually other opinions or alternative ways to handle the issue. As a result, the speaker often reviews the other alternatives, refuting each and leaving only his or her proposal as the logical choice.

Challenges to Persuasive Speaking

Persuasive speeches can represent a great challenge to a public speaker. You are attempting to actually influence your listeners and most people are highly resistant to being influenced. So your speech may fail for the same reason most persuasion fails—it's difficult to get people to change the attitudes, beliefs, values, and behaviors they have spent years developing. This failure may result from speakers failing to consider the hostility level of the audience or using faulty reasoning.

Hostile Audience

When presented with a persuasive argument, listeners often unconsciously engage in a form of inner speech or **counterargument** that argues against the persuasive message being presented and for the listener's entrenched position or point of view. This silent counterargument encourages listeners to build a case against your persuasive message rather than listening to the arguments you're presenting. Therefore, thinking about the audience's reactions ahead of time is crucial to giving a successful persuasive speech.

It is particularly important to consider your audience's position on your topic when the majority of the audience members strongly disagree with your position or have an unfavorable attitude toward, you, your topic, or the particular situation. If you're facing such a hostile audience, that is a great challenge to effective persuasion. To deal with this challenge, you must anticipate all possible audience reactions to your speech and present your topic in a way that deals with, if not overcomes, audience hostility.

FAULTY REASONING

In addition to the audience's hostile attitudes, another challenge to persuasion arises from speakers committing **logical fallacies,** which are errors in reasoning and logic that lead the listeners to false conclusions. These speakers are so intent on achieving their persuasive goals that they present evidence or information that is in error, unreasonable, or misrepresents the truth in some way. Whether intentional or unintentional, if fallacies in reasoning are detected, they reflect negatively on your credibility as a speaker and call into question your integrity and ethical standards.

Overcoming Challenges to Competence

Given these challenges to persuasive speaking, it may be tempting to not even try to influence listeners or convince them to change. However, a competent speaker can anticipate the audience's reactions, avoid errors in reasoning, and motivate listeners to change.

ANTICIPATE AUDIENCE REACTION

Because the hostility level of the audience represents a challenge to persuasion, you want to prevent counterargument from even getting started. One way to accomplish this is to present information in your speech so it builds toward a positive response. If the audience's attitude toward your topic is negative, don't state a straightforward claim or thesis in your introduction, which will precipitate counterargument. If you state a claim or viewpoint with which the listeners disagree, that could prejudice them against your message before they even hear your argument. Instead, use the thesis to forecast the general theme of your speech. Present neutral but valid information first, and state your claim after the audience has heard your evidence.

If your goal is to persuade a hostile audience to change, it is essential to determine ahead of time just where they stand on your topic. You need to know the audience's attitude toward, information level about, and ego involvement in your topic. Consider the following three questions about your listeners as you prepare your persuasive speech.

1. *Attitude:* Are they friendly or hostile toward your position on the topic? If your listeners are hostile, use a balanced appeal. Reinforce the merit of their position on the topic, letting them know you respect their point of view (Allen, 1991). Tell them you'll be discussing several perspectives on the topic and that you plan to discuss the merits of each perspective. Present your speech using provisional and conditional language, and don't directly attack or criticize their point of view. Also, don't misrepresent your own position, which would be dishonest and unethical.

2. *Information level:* How much does the audience know about the subject area or topic? Are they well informed, somewhat informed, or misinformed? If your listeners are well informed, don't bore them or waste their time by telling them what they already know. Instead, establish your credibility on the topic and give them new information before trying to persuade them to your way of thinking. If they're uninformed, link the new material to information they already know. And if they're misinformed, rather than criticizing or correcting them directly, present alternative ways of looking at the issue.

3. *Ego involvement:* How much do they care about the topic? To what degree are their egos tied up in it? Ego-involved listeners are particularly hard to persuade because as soon as they realize your position is different from theirs, they stop listening and start creating counterarguments. So if your listeners have a high degree of ego involvement in your topic, and if their position on it is quite different from yours, avoid overstating your case or explicitly stating your persuasive goal (O'Keefe, 1997).

Knowledge Link

Does a persuasive speaker use attribution theory (as described in Chapter 3) when anticipating audience reactions and future behaviors?

Several preparation techniques can help you deal with the audience reaction factor ahead of time and minimize negative reactions. First, pretend you're preparing a speech for the opposite side of the argument. For instance, if you're planning a speech that advocates euthanasia, do some library research examining the arguments of those who oppose it. This will alert you to the attitudes, beliefs, and values of an audience that is hostile to this topic. Second, have a friend or colleague listen to your speech and play devil's advocate. Ask this person to poke holes in your argument and tell you why he or she disagrees with your position. With this feedback, revise your speech to build a stronger case to persuade a hostile, well-informed, and ego-involved audience.

Reason with Integrity

In addition to anticipating the audience's reactions and attitudes, you can enhance your credibility by paying close attention to how you reason and present evidence. Carefully examine all your support materials and organize them logically. By making a conscious effort to avoid errors in reasoning and logical fallacies, you let your audience know that you are a public speaker of integrity who subscribes to the highest standards of ethical conduct. Logicians have identified literally hundreds of logical fallacies to avoid, but the following examples show some of the dangers inherent in failing to reason with integrity.

- ***Ad hominem*** This fallacy occurs when a speaker attacks another person as opposed to the argument the person is making. *Ad hominem* is Latin for "to the man." Candidates in political campaigns commit this error in reasoning by attacking their opponents and failing to stick to the issues, sometimes in subtle ways. For example, attacking the opponent and labeling him or her a left-wing liberal or a right-wing conservative would focus the audience's attention on the other person and not on her or his argument. Unfortunately, some candidates for public office have discovered that this approach to negative campaigning has a benefit. It works.
- ***Non sequitor*** When a claim does not directly follow from the presented support material a *non sequitor* occurs. While the claim may be correct and true, it does not necessarily follow from the evidence presented. A *non sequitor,* literally, means that a statement does not follow from anything previously said. For example, a speaker who is discussing health care could discuss the benefits of nationalized health insurance, but would commit a *non sequitor* by concluding with a claim about the benefits to defense industry.
- ***Red Herring*** This fallacy diverts the audience's attention from the real issue by presenting irrelevant arguments or issues. The expression "red herring" derives its meaning

Knowledge Link

How can a public speaker avoid some of the fallacies in reasoning by using knowledge of the rules that help sort out what certain words and phrases mean?

from the practice of dragging a smelly fish across a trail to divert the attention of hunting dogs. For instance, this technique might be used in a budget debate on a college campus about financial aid policies. A speaker could divert attention from financial aid issues by bringing up the red herring of insufficient funds for additional parking lots.

- ***Slippery Slope*** When a speaker suggests one event automatically leads to a series of other undesirable events, it is called *slippery slope* reasoning. The speaker implies that if the listeners take one action, they are setting themselves up to slide down a slope from which there is no return. This implication that a situation results from a single cause, when in fact it had multiple causes, is another way of misleading an audience. If you know there are additional causes, you have an obligation to describe them to the audience. For example, to suggest that teenage pregnancy is only the result of coming from a broken home is erroneous. There are many other contributing factors such as poor school attendance, lack of parental support, and peer influence.
- ***Straw Man Argument*** With this type of logical fallacy, the speaker attacks an entire argument by selecting a weak example or aspect of it, discrediting that example, and thus defaming the entire argument. The speaker sets up a "straw man" that is easy to challenge and knock over. In a business or corporation, the personnel manager could say that the company should not be subject to affirmative action policies because women are already sufficiently represented in the work force. The issue of affirmative action is more complex than simply female representation, so this would be the use of a "straw woman" argument.
- ***Sweeping or hasty generalization*** A sweeping generalization that clusters ideas, people, or objects into one indiscriminate group and implies that all of the items in the group are the same obscures vital and relevant differences. For example, a sweeping generalization would be to say "athletes are bad students," or "AIDS is the penalty people pay for having casual sex," or "all Americans eat too much." A hasty generalization results from moving to a conclusion based on too few specific cases or examples. If a speaker describes one basketball or soccer player who is a notoriously bad student and generalizes to all players, he or she is making a hasty generalization.

MOTIVATE LISTENERS TO CHANGE

Given that you have anticipated your audience's reactions and constructed your persuasive argument with integrity, you still need to do everything you can to motivate your listeners to change. In Chapter 8, you learned about positive and negative communication motives, that people communicate for both positive and negative reasons. Similarly, when giving a persuasive speech, you can offer your listeners either a positive or a negative reason for changing.

Positive motivation calls for indicating the good results the audience can expect if they choose to change. Negative motivation involves pointing out the bad results that will occur if the audience chooses not to change. You can combine the two types of motivators effectively in one speech. When Carol was persuading Spencer to become a student activist, she told him how much the campus would benefit from his contributions—a positive motive. Similarly, she described the results of letting administrators run the campus and make decisions without input from the students—a negative motive.

The advice provided in this chapter helped Spencer present an effective speech on student activism. No doubt most of the students in the class signed his petition opposing the ominous tuition hike. Like Spencer, if you follow the guidelines provided here for preparing and presenting persuasive speeches competently, you too will influence listeners and reinforce, modify, and change their attitudes, beliefs, values, and behaviors.

Chapter Summary

A persuasive speech attempts to influence the audience's attitudes, beliefs, values, or actions. Because of its goal to influence, a persuasive speech is organized differently from an informative speech and is more concerned with the listeners' specific position on the speech topic. However, both types of speeches start with a clear purpose and objective and use effective support materials, and both types of speakers are concerned about the effect of their speech on the audience. Aristotle emphasized the importance of persuasive speaking skills in society, which continue to be crucial today. In using these skills, an ethical speaker avoids coercion or manipulation to influence an audience.

The three types of persuasive speeches, based on the speaker's objective, attempt to (1) reinforce the listeners' attitudes, beliefs, and values; (2) change attitudes, beliefs, and values; or (3) move the listeners to action. Whether the speech is intended to influence attitudes, beliefs, values, or actions, a competent speaker uses one or more of three types of appeals. A logical appeal is based on knowledge and reasoning, what people know, and makes use of deductive or inductive reasoning to influence listeners. An emotional appeal is based on psychology and passion, how people feel, and calls on emotions such as love, hate, sympathy, guilt, or even fear in order to influence the audience. A third type of appeal, credibility, is based on the listeners' perceptions of the reputation, prestige, and authority of the speaker. The speaker's perceived expertise, trustworthiness, and charisma affect perceptions of credibility.

A persuasive speech can be organized in any one of five ways. Problem-solution organization first identifies a problem and then proposes a solution. The motivated sequence consists of five steps: attention, need, satisfaction, visualization, and action. Claim-data-warrant organization moves listeners from data that are presented through a warrant that links the data to the speaker's claim. Refuting the opponent organization dismantles the opposing argument. Comparing alternatives examines two or more alternatives and makes an appeal for the preferred choice.

Challenges to persuasive speaking include speakers failing to consider the hostility level of the audience and using faulty reasoning. To overcome these challenges, a competent speaker anticipates the audience's reactions, reasons with integrity, and motivates listeners to change.

Key Terms

coercion
manipulation
speech to reinforce
speech to change
speech to move to action
appeal
logos
pathos
ethos
logical appeal
deduction
induction
emotional appeal
fear appeal
credibility appeal
problem-solution
motivated sequence
claim-data-warrant
refuting the opponent
comparing alternatives
counterargument
logical fallacies
ad hominem
non sequitor
red herring
slippery slope
straw man argument
sweeping or hasty generalization

Building Knowledge

1. If there is a fine line between persuasion and manipulation, what might you as a persuasive speaker say or do to avoid becoming coercive?
2. Of the three types of persuasive speeches—to reinforce, change, or move to action—which poses the greatest ethical challenge for a public speaker and why?

3. If effective persuasion sometimes requires adapting and modifying your position on a topic for a hostile audience, when would that adaptation or modification become unethical? Explain your answer.
4. When considering the use of appeals in a persuasive speech—logical, emotional, or credibility appeals—what aspects of the speech will help you decide what appeals to include?
5. Is any one of the persuasive organizational patterns better to use or more effective than the others? Explain your answer.
6. Which of the challenges to persuasive speaking do you find personally challenging and why? What can you do about that challenge?
7. Analyze the speech about AIDS and compassion fatigue based on what you have learned about persuasion in this chapter. Is there anything the speaker could have said that would have made this prize-winning speech even more effective?

Building Skills

Individual Exercises

1. Identify several topics for a persuasive speech. Label five columns on a piece of paper as follows: topics, attitudes, beliefs, values, and actions. List your speech topics in the left-hand column and then answer these questions for each topic in the remaining four columns. What would the other students in the class believe about the topic? What attitude would they hold toward it? What values might be related to the topic? What actions or behaviors might they demonstrate regarding the topic?
2. On the internet, visit a site that contains links to historical or contemporary speeches, such as The National Gallery of the Spoken Word at http:www.ngsw.org/. Go to one of those links and find a persuasive speech that interests you. Read the speech and identify what type of persuasive speech it is, what types of appeals are used, and its organizational pattern. Based on your analysis, decide how effective you think the speech is.
3. If you are using *InfoTrac College Edition,* go to Joseph Nolan's article, How to campaign: Advice from the Greek and Roman orators in *Vital Speeches,* April 1, 1996, V62, n12, p 369–374. Nolan provides advice about how contemporary politicians could make use of the recommendations of classical teachers of rhetoric. Examine and evaluate Nolan's suggestions.
4. Make a list of the occasions you can remember during the last year or so, when you changed your mind or your behavior in some way. What happened that persuaded you to change? Make a list of the occasions you can remember when someone or something (like an advertisement) tried to influence or persuade you but failed. Why did that persuasive act fail, and what could have improved its effectiveness?

Group Exercises

1. Form groups of four students and choose a topic for a persuasive speech that appeals to all of you—something you know or care about and the other students in your class would find interesting. As a group, decide on a position on the topic and state that position as a specific purpose statement for a persuasive speech. Decide what type of persuasive speech to develop for the topic and what type(s) of appeals will work best. Choose the best way to organize the speech.
2. Form dyads and develop a case for your credibility as public speakers. Each person should choose a topic for a persuasive speech and determine how to build his or her credibility when presenting that speech. Compare how each student would build a case for his or her expertise, trustworthiness, and charisma.
3. Attend and evaluate the effectiveness of a persuasive speech either on or off campus with a small group of students, based on the contents of this chapter. After you leave the presentation, compare your analyses.

References

Allen, M. (1991). Meta-analysis comparing the research of one-sided and two-sided messages. *Western Journal of Speech Communication, 55,* 390–404.

Barney, R., & Black, J. (1994). Ethics and professional persuasive communications. *Public Relations Review, 20,* 233–248.

Brockriede W., & Ehninger, D. (1960). Toulmin on argument: An interpretation and application. *The Quarterly Journal of Speech, 46* (1), 44–53.

Furnham, A., & Procter, E. (1989–1990). Memory for information about nuclear power: A test of the selective recall hypothesis. *Current Psychology Research and Reviews, 8,* 287-297.

Johannesen, R. L. (1997). *Ethics in human communication* (4th ed.). Prospect Heights, IL: Waveland Press.

Kim, K. (1998). The invisible crimes. In L. Schnoor (Ed.) *Winning Orations* (pp. 6–9). Mankato, MN: Interstate Oratorical Association.

Lindquist, T. (1995). Talking the talk: How to teach kids the gentle art of persuasion. *Instructor, 105* (4), 26–28.

Meinen, S. (1999). The forgotten four-letter word. In L. Schnoor (Ed.) *Winning Orations* (pp. 26–29). Mankato, MN: Interstate Oratorical Association.

Moebius, M. (1991). What do you believe? Persuasive speeches in eighth grade. *English Journal, 80,* 38–42.

Monroe, A. H. (1935). *Principles and types of speech.* Glenview, IL: Scott, Foresman.

O'Keefe, D. J. (1997). Standpoint explicitness and persuasive effect: A meta-analytic review of the effects of varying conclusion articulation in persuasive message. *Argumentation and Advocacy, 34,* 1–13.

Roberts, W. R. (Trans.). (1954). *The rhetoric,* by Aristotle. New York: Modern Library.

Roser, C., & Thompson, M. (1995). Fear appeals and the formation of active publics. *Journal of Communication, 45,* 103–121.

Sackreiter, K. (1998). Phone calls that kill. *Winning Orations* (pp. 116–119). Mankato, MN: Interstate Oratorical Association.

Smith, S. L. (1997). The effective use of fear appeals in persuasive immunization: An analysis of national immunization intervention messages. *Journal of Applied Communication Research, 25,* 264–292.

Stiff, J. B. (1994). *Persuasive communication.* New York: Guilford.

Taylor, L. (1996). How did "a great deal of interest" for my talk dwindle to "unexpected lack of demand"? *New Statesman, 128,* 63–64.

Toulmin, S. (1958). *The uses of argument.* Cambridge, England: Cambridge University Press.

Witte, K. (1994). Fear control and danger control: A test of the extended parallel process model. *Communication Monographs, 61,* 113–134.

Exemplary Persuasive Speech

The following persuasive speech about the public's lack of compassion and concern about the pandemic of AIDS was presented by Sarah Meinen of Bradley University at the 127th Annual Contest of the Interstate Oratorical Association in April 1999 and took first place in the competition. The objective of the speech is to change the listeners' attitudes, beliefs, and behaviors relative to AIDS. The speech carefully follows the five steps of the motivated sequence organizational pattern and makes effective use of logical appeals and the inclusion of credible sources of information.

The Forgotten Four-Letter Word

By Sarah Meinen

(1) In 1981, two strange diseases first grabbed the attention of the American public. The first, a mental malaise born of our overabundance of seemingly insurmountable societal ills. We called it compassion fatigue, best described by the July-August, 1981 *Utne Reader* as the inability to care any more about social issues like refugees, homelessness, famine, natural disasters, the environment, or the Holocaust. The second was a new disease initially brought to our attention by its savage spread through the homosexual community. We called it AIDS and watched in horror as it polarized society and stopped discriminating on the basis of sexual preference, victimizing every demographic group and defying modern medical advances.

(1) *ATTENTION STEP:* The speaker first calls the audience's attention to a two-part problem, the public's compassion fatigue about social issues and the disease of AIDS.

(2) The July 1998 *Scientific American* reports that AIDS has recently been renamed a pandemic, having left mere epidemic status behind. And compassion fatigue? It's just added HIV to its list, somewhere between homelessness and the Holocaust, as something we just can't find the heart to care about anymore.

(2) A respected publication is used to tell the listeners that the problem of AIDS is still so serious it has reached pandemic proportions.

(3) This speech is not about a freshly discovered rare disease. It's not about a faulty new technology or an obscure but deadly industrial chemical. Rather, AIDS is familiar and this familiarity is the problem. Our well of compassion has run dry, and we're all too eager to relegate AIDS to a growing list of historical atrocities.

(3) In this preview and thesis statement, the speaker uses language effectively to forecast the content of the speech.

(4) As the February 16, 1998, *Business Week* claims, we don't want to hear that 16,000 people contract HIV everyday, that 2.3 million died of AIDS last year alone, that 650,000 Americans are now HIV positive. However, closing our eyes won't make a monster of this magnitude go away. Instead, we must revive our compassion and interest by first, discovering why we've become immune to this vicious virus; next, detailing the effects of our plague of indifference; and finally, curing ourselves of AIDS compassion fatigue.

(4) *PROBLEM STEP:* The speaker makes effective use of logical appeals to substantiate the problem. This first subpoint of the problem step is a description of the magnitude of the problem that is supported with three hard-hitting statistics.

True, 1997 was a banner year for AIDS research. True, the number of AIDS deaths reached a record low last year. True, scientists scrambled to assemble the sketchy outlines of an AIDS vaccine. But 1997 was also the year we stopped carrying a banner for AIDS, the year new cases of HIV infection continued to shatter already ominous records, the year we found our own AIDS vaccine: apathy, disinterest, indifference.

(5) Despite our exposure to death and destruction, facts and figures, names and quilt squares, AIDS has slowly faded from our national consciousness chiefly due to hype surrounding an AIDS cure and grossly misleading statistics.

(5) The second subpoint is previewed by outlining why the problem exists—because of misinformation about a cure for AIDS and misleading statistics.

"The other day," says columnist Urvashi Vaid in the December 24, 1997, *Advocate*, "someone called to tell me that AIDS has ended. I mean, he'd read it in the *New York Times*, so it had to be true. I wondered if anyone from the *Times* had called to break the news to Neil who died just three months ago," Vaid says as he recalls reading similar headlines in *Time, Newsweek,* and *U.S. News.*

(6) The January 1998 *Scientist* argues that these hype-filled headlines fuel our compassion fatigue, offering us a false sense of security. It's easy to forget about AIDS if we don't consider it a threat anymore. For example, says the February 17, 1998, *Advocate*, media coverage abounds about the development of an AIDS vaccine, which promises to eradicate HIV. Lost in the fine print, however, are the vaccine's innumerable problems; it won't be testable for at least five years, will only protect against the most basic, least drug-resistant strains of the quick-to-mutate HIV virus, and will only benefit a fraction of 1 percent of AIDS patients, those who have recently been tested and remain unexposed to any HIV drugs.

(6) Credible evidence that explains the hype about a cure is provided here.

(7) Misleading AIDS statistics are also fatiguing our AIDS compassion, says the July 1998 *Harper's*. For example, the Centers for Disease Control and Prevention has changed the way it reports AIDS statistics, but it hasn't changed the way it labels them. The CDC used to count cases of HIV infection and full-blown AIDS. Now it only counts full-blown AIDS cases.

(7) Examples of statistics that mislead the public about the gravity of AIDS are carefully explained.

The August 19, 1998, *JAMA* points out that even though AIDS death rates look lower, HIV infection rates are more important and prove that AIDS continues to claim new victims. "Drugs keep victims alive longer," says Jack Killen, head of the National Institute of Allergy and Infectious Disease Division of AIDS, "but these people can't live on AZT cocktails and protease inhibitors forever."

The July 11, 1998, *Lancet*, reminds us that despite slightly lower U.S. numbers, the AIDS pandemic has grown out of control in developing countries. In Botswana and Rwanda, HIV lurks in 25% of the population and threatens to increase infant morality by 75% in the next 10 years. "These are the statistics we don't hear," says Dr. Anthony Fauci, head of the U.S. Institute of Allergies and Infectious Disease. "But these are the same statistics which prove AIDS is still the greatest threat facing humanity."

(8) AIDS has been too grim, too overwhelming, and it's been around too long. We may be over AIDS, but AIDS is not over, and we must focus on both the attitudinal and behavioral effects of compassion fatigue.

(8) The third subpoint is now previewed—the results of the problem—its negative attitudinal and behavioral effects on the public.

(9) A Gallup Poll taken in October 1997 reveals that today, only 29% of us consider AIDS a serious problem. Ten years ago, 66% of us did. Only 30% of us are concerned about contracting the disease, compared to 42% of Americans a decade ago. AIDS simply is old news, yesterday's worry, blasé, passé, overdone, a has-been disease.

(9) Americans are no longer taking AIDS seriously.

(10) Additionally, the Spring 1998 *Albany Law Review* claims that we are unwilling to let go of old AIDS stereotypes and prejudices. Our "it can't happen to us" mentality is surpris-

(10) Stereotypes are continuing about who is getting AIDS and who is not.

ingly resilient in the face of statistics that tell us heterosexual sex is the number one way to contract AIDS in 1998.

(11) Behaviorally, says the July 13, 1998, *MacLean's*, our compassion fatigue has produced both a lack of AIDS champions and an increase in risky behavior. The April 7, 1997, *U.S. News and World Report* argues that lately AIDS activism is strictly backstage activity for many of Hollywood's elite, who have abandoned red ribbons because, as Gerry Ansel, spokesman for AIDS Project Los Angeles, says, "they have become a cliché." It's no longer chic for movie stars to support AIDS awareness, and sadly where trendy Hollywood goes, the American public follows. AIDS bracelets have been cast aside, and red ribbons are unpinned as we search for a fresh, new cause champion.

(11) Because of the lack of concern, there are now fewer AIDS activists championing the cause.

(12) But the most alarming result of our compassion fatigue, says the January 5, 1998, *AIDS Weekly Plus*, is the cavalier way we treat the disease. A Yale University School of Medicine study reports that 9 out of 10 adolescents believe they are invulnerable to AIDS even though 20% of those same kids have seen a friend or relative die of the disease, and half of them regularly engage in sex without condoms. "This study is important," says Dr. Michael Merson, director of public health at Yale, " because it tells us that despite the wealth of information that's out there, young people have still not internalized the dangers of AIDS." Have not internalized or just don't care, asks the April 8, 1998, *JAMA*.

(12) Adolescents and young people are engaging in risky sexual behavior as a result of thinking they are invulnerable to AIDS.

(13) With this haunting question in mind, we must develop a practical and realistic prescription for our compassion fatigue on both a national and personal level. First, the January 5, 1998, *AIDS Weekly Plus*, says that the focus must shift from an AIDS cure to AIDS prevention. "While we don't want AIDS vaccine and drug research to stop," says Michael Shriver of the National Association of Peoples with AIDS, "we believe that more time, research and money needs to go into feasible prevention programs." These programs, he says, need to begin with awareness and concern. The May 1998 *American Bar Association Journal* agrees, arguing that if we don't shift our focus soon, by the time we find a cure, there'll be no one left to save.

(13) *SOLUTION STEP:* The speaker now recommends a twofold solution to the problem. It is time to shift national attention to include research on prevention as well as an AIDS cure.

(14) Devising utopian research and prevention plans is useless, claims the July 1998 *Scientific American*, unless we as citizens change our attitudes and revive AIDS activism. We need to be critical consumers who refuse to be pacified with optimistic statistics and miracle cures. We need to evaluate AIDS information carefully, analyzing numbers, questioning source validity, and separating hope from hype. Most importantly, we need to find a way to care about AIDS again. Wear a red ribbon. Walk in the John Keats March for AIDS. View the AIDS quilt. Volunteer at a local hospice. Do whatever you have to do to be shocked, to be scared, to be involved, to be compassionate, and to keep this pandemic from being ignored, dismissed, or forgotten.

(14) Additionally, individual citizens must change their attitudes and help revive activism about the problem.

(15) By the year 2000, one out of every three of us will know someone infected with the HIV virus. We may be immune to the stories and statistics, but none of us is safe from the reality of AIDS.

(15) *VISUALIZATON STEP:* Here the speaker briefly envisions what life will be like if nothing is done about the problem that has been described. This is a form of negative visualization, a gentle fear appeal.

(16) The July 1998 *Scientific American* claims that the most effective AIDS wake-up calls are made by vocal people in high-risk communities; individualized grassroots efforts that start small, make the biggest steps. Is that a loud enough call to action? This time, the solution really is in our hands. This community has the ability to speak passionately, the platform to affect an enormous audience, and the clout to command attention. The forensics community has a choice. We can take a risk and speak out, knowing our voices may be lost but hoping someone hears. Or we can stand idly by, succumb to our compassion fatigue, and watch AIDS claim our best and our brightest.

(16) *ACTION STEP:* The speaker first points out that individualized action can be effective. Then the listeners are called on to take risks, speak out, and not succumb to compassion fatigue about AIDS.

Appendix: Competence in Interviewing Contexts

Marie had done very well in school, graduating cum laude in communication, and looked forward to getting a job in human resources in a local firm. She had heard the campus job center had a good library for researching the job market, so she spent several days looking up contact information for local companies and hours poring over the want ads in the local papers. She sent out dozens of letters with résumés and was disappointed when after two months, she had only received one call for an interview.

To prepare for the interview, Marie used what she knew from her communication courses, such as dressing professionally, practicing her response to some of the questions she assumed would be asked, and asking people what they knew about the company. On the day of the interview, she arrived early just to have some time to relax, and just before entering the personnel office, she took several deep breaths, stretched, and focused on her introductory demeanor. She felt good and ready.

She soon found herself sitting in a cold office staring at a secretary, who informed Marie that the interviewer was backed up and the interview wouldn't begin for another 30 minutes. After about 20 minutes of sitting in an uncomfortable chair, a person exited the interviewer's office looking visibly shaken and distressed. After another few minutes, a stern-looking man in his early 50s, who looked a lot like the sophomore accounting professor Marie was so terrified of, introduced himself as Arthur to Marie and escorted her into his office.

Arthur explained that the job was demanding, would involve a fair amount of overtime, and travel at least 20 weeks a year to the various locations of the company, such as Cincinnati, Detroit, Lincoln, Houston, and Phoenix. In addition, the job required skill at Powerpoint presentation software and PeopleSoft human resources accounting software. Marie recognized almost immediately that she probably couldn't compete for the job. After a few standard questions about her background and interests, Marie was completely surprised by the following request: "In this job, you constantly get surprised by employee questions during your presentations. Let's see how you handle yourself on your feet. Stand up, and tell me an interesting story that has a moral you would apply to an issue of sexual harassment in the workplace." ●●●

Few of us would be composed and creative enough to handle such a situation without a fair degree of awkwardness and potentially incompetent actions. Despite using what communication knowledge and skills she learned in school, Marie rapidly realized that she was not prepared for what she was encountering. She became nervous because of all the factors she simply had not anticipated, such as the coldness of the waiting room, the resemblance of the interviewer to a person she disliked, the recognition that she probably did not have the skills required in the job, and the shock of a request she simply had never anticipated. She realized that she had not done sufficient homework on the nature of the job or its requirements. Finally, she found her own skills limited by the extent to which the interviewer controlled the encounter and directed her comments. In short, Marie found competence rather elusive in this interview. It was not as she expected, and she began reevaluating the value of her education in the job market and the career she had assumed for so long that she would pursue.

Interviews As a Context for Competence

Our perplexed would-be employee realizes something very important about the interview context. Every single action has the potential for communicating something about the candidate's competence. Behavior in interviews is constantly being evaluated in terms of its appropriateness. Every interview almost by definition makes the effectiveness of one's performance a highly valued objective of the context.

Most of the interviewing process can be viewed from the perspective of interpersonal communication competence. Although public or group presentations may be involved in some interview contexts, most interviews are still conducted interpersonally. The model of interpersonal communication competence elaborated in Chapters 8 through 10 provides an appropriate approach to understanding competence in interviewing. Motivation in interviewing can be examined in terms of recognizing the goals and values of interviewing. That is, why do people engage in interviews, and how valuable can success in interviewing be? Knowledge is examined in terms of understanding the types of interviews, and what information is relevant to success in the interview context. Skills are examined in terms of those identified as essential for interpersonal communication competence; attentiveness such as listening, composure such as anxiety management, coordination such as handling questions, and expressiveness such as verbal and nonverbal behavior. Thus, this chapter examines the model of communication competence in a particular context that virtually everyone faces eventually: the interview. We describe the whats, whys, and hows of interviews as well as the challenges and ways of overcoming these challenges. An **interview** can be defined as an encounter oriented toward the possibility of mutual gain through the exchange of information, a process consisting largely of question-and-answer sequences. Several features of this definition need further consideration.

The possibility of *mutual gain* is always implicit in interviews. The interviewee is seeking something, whether it's help with a personal problem, recognition for expertise in a given topic area, or a job. The interviewer is seeking to help, to complete an assignment, or fulfill his or her duties for an organization. It is the possibility of mutual gain that leads people to engage in interviews even when many do not lead to the outcomes the participants hoped to achieve.

Interviews involve *information exchange.* Many people assume that the interviewer receives information and the interviewee gives information. This stereotype of interviews is incorrect on at least two counts. First, as we have explained, communication is transactional, which means that information is being indirectly exchanged whenever people are communicating. You are interpreting the other person's nonverbal messages and attributing meaning to his or her comments and questions, even when the person is doing little more than asking questions.

Second, interviews almost always involve the direct exchange of information. That is, both parties ask questions, provide answers, and attempt to reach conclusions about each other. For example, if you are a journalist, interviewing a student for a story for the school newspaper, the student interviewee is likely to ask questions such as what the story is for or about, when it will run, and who else is likely to be interviewed. If you are interviewing for a job, you are likely to ask about the organization's benefits, who you will report to, and so forth. For example, in college campus screening interviews, interviewers spend much more time providing information about their organization than they do asking questions (DeBell, Montgomery, McCarthy, & Lanthier, 1998). If you are being interviewed by a counselor because you've been experiencing too much anxiety and stress over school, you may well inquire about the counselor's experience, where he or she trained, and whether he or she has much experience with this kind of problem. In short, even when a person is being interviewed, the person is also interviewing to some extent.

Interviews consist of much more than questions and answers. But questions and answers are one of the most identifiable features of almost any interview (Ramsay, Gallois, & Callan, 1997). Compared to everyday conversation, for example, interviews tend to be much more question and answer oriented. Most conversations involve considerable exchange of information, but most of it moves along topical lines, in which each participant follows up the prior statement with a statement of personal experience that is similar or related in its ideas to what was just said. In interviews, however, it is generally the question that determines the relevance of the next utterance. Consider the following two examples:

Typical Conversation

JOSH: So, I kind of hung out after class a second and waited for her to grab her books and stuff, and start walking out the door. Just then I smiled at her and asked her where she was going, like would she want to go study or something. She said 'Yes, sure,' and so we got some coffee and compared notes. I got her number later.

SARA: A guy did something like that with me just a couple of weeks ago in astronomy. I had always thought he was kind of cute, but I never figured he'd be interested in me.

JOSH: I see your major was communication. Did you have a minor?
SARA: I minored in political science. I thought I might be able to use it in political consulting someday.

JOSH: So you're interested in consulting? Presentation, development, or both?
SARA: I think I'd be stronger as a trainer and presenter, but I hope I would also be good at designing consulting curriculum and programs.

In the typical conversation, each person seems to want to further discussion about himself or herself, realizing that discussion of the other person's ideas is part of the process of talking about one's own interests. There may or may not be a particular agenda or outcome being sought. In contrast, the interview is designed to optimize the flow of information needed to reach certain decisions. Does this person get the job? Is this the place I want to work? Can this person help me? Is this person at risk? Does this person have the information I need for my report? Is my opinion important enough to be quoted? Outcomes such as these are sought in various types of interviews, and certain information needs to be exchanged if the best interview outcomes are to be achieved.

Before examining the types of interviews and the role of knowledge in interviews, it is reasonable to ask why. Why do we need interviews at all, and why do we go through them when so many people seem to dislike them? As in all aspects of communication, people engage in interviews for important reasons, and understanding these reasons can enhance your motivation in interview contexts.

Why? Motivation in the Interview

Why are you studying this textbook? Why are you taking this course in communication? Presumably, you hope you will learn things that can help you in life, whether this simply means getting a degree or achieving particular career goals. The short-term tasks of studying for exams and preparing assignments are short-term goals designed to fulfill the longer term goals of making the life of your choosing in the future. So it is with interviews. Interviews are short-term goals that serve as a bridge to long-term goals.

INTERVIEW CONTEXTS

Three interview contexts—organizational, investigative, and therapeutic—help illustrate the potential importance of interviews. The **organizational interview** is a transaction between institutional representative(s) and a prospective employee for the purpose of ascertaining the appropriateness and terms of contracting the services of the interviewee. It is most often associated with decisions of job, career, and hiring, and generally implies salary or remuneration, but may also include such situations as varied as interviewing to be a volunteer for a nonprofit campaign or pet adoption. The importance of the interview can be immense. Proportional to other forms and contexts of communication, at the individual level there may be few situations in which so much depends on so little communication as that in the selection interview. For example, job salary is often negotiated based on the impression you make on an interviewer during a 10- to 30-minute organizational interview as well as on your salary history. Even within an industry, potential salaries can vary substantially for a given type of job. Building a résumé depends greatly on your initial experience and the credibility of your early job experiences. Although people are increasingly changing careers several times during their lives, the early salaries often dictate the base from which future salaries are negotiated. It is difficult to go to a second job asking for $150,000 if your prior job paid $27,000. However, $5,000 less in your starting year's base salary, prorated out to retirement over 40 to 45 years, can mean the difference of hundreds of thousands of dollars. Thus if a positive impression during an organizational interview means the difference of a higher or lower base salary, you can see its fiscal importance.

Success in the organizational interview is about more than money. Consider if you get passed by on the one job you really desire and end up having to take a position with a job description you don't want, in an industry you dislike. Again, all this may depend on one, or a few, job interviews, collectively lasting less than a few hours. By the same token, the organization is investing a lot in the interview as well. The estimated average cost of attracting a high-quality manager or professional is $2,000 (DeBell et al., 1998). Given that the candidate bases his or her decision to accept a job in part based on the interviewer's or recruiter's communication skills (Turban, Forret, & Hendrickson, 1998), all parties involved in the interview have a significant interest in the competence of the interview process (Kikoski, 1998).

If the prospect of the employment selection interview seems intimidating, consider the importance of the investigative interview, also called the informational interview. The **investigative interview** is a transaction between parties in which the interviewer is seeking information from the interviewee for the purpose of enhancing decision making and understanding of a specified issue or situation. It typically is associated with journalistic interviews, but may include situations as varied as a police interrogation or sexual harassment investigation. Heads of state and company presidents have kept or lost their jobs because of an ill-placed phrase or a poorly chosen word when speaking to a journalist. Sportscasters have been drummed out of the business for making racist remarks, and sports players have been kept out of the hall of fame for admitting gambling problems in interviews. At the more mundane, but equally important, level virtually everything we know through the media is generated, illustrated, or reinforced through the interview process. Imagine a news story with no expert testimony or statements, or a biography of a celebrity with no questions asked of the star or the star's acquaintances. The investigative interview is a powerful force for knowledge, discovery, and the pursuit of truth. Indeed, the interview may become even more important in a world of instant access to information and information overload. People need experts more than ever to help discern between valid and invalid information. The investigative interview will continue to be a tool through which such opinion formation is determined.

The therapeutic interview is another interchange of great importance (Evans, Coman, & Gloss, 1996). The **therapeutic interview** is a transaction between parties in which the parties are seeking information from a service provider or provider representative relevant to enhancing the interviewee's mental or physical health. Generally, people think of the therapeutic interview as the "doctor-patient" exchange in which a patient tells a physician about symptoms, but it includes other situations such as psychological and marital counseling. When you go to a doctor because you are ill or distressed, the encounter in which you explain your problems is an interview (Evans, Coman, & Gross, 1996; Farnill, Hayes, & Todisco, 1997). The health professional needs to gather exact information about your underlying problems. An incorrect diagnosis, whether physical, mental, or emotional, can lead to incorrect therapies (pharmaceutical or psychological) that can do more harm than good. Thus it is vital in the therapeutic interview that the health professional obtain valid and relevant information.

INTERVIEW GOALS

The importance of interviews seems obvious. But how does recognizing the importance of interview goals lead to greater motivation, and thus competence? Analyzing your goals in an interview can help motivate your interview performance. As you will recall, goals are those outcomes you are seeking from a communication process. You may want a paycheck (i.e., a job) or a life's project (i.e., a career). You may want reassurance that your ailment is nothing serious, or you may want to alter your entire range of health habits.

As we indicated earlier, interacting competently in interviews is typically a short-term goal in the service of a longer term goal. Understanding the longer term goals can help focus the short-term goals, and lead to more competent interview experiences. Do you want a job or a career? A job is something that pays you a salary. A career is making a living from something you want or need to do, or for which you feel your talents are particularly well suited.

Do you want to treat your symptoms, or do you want to be cured? If you tell a counselor that you are severely stressed or depressed because of exams, you may receive a month's prescription of medication or an appointment for a counseling session. If you explain you grew up in a family environment in which failure was severely punished and approval was almost never forthcoming for outstanding accomplishments, the cure may involve much more therapy than merely a month's medication or one counseling session.

Do you want to meet a deadline or write an award-winning story? If you merely want to complete a story for a deadline, a brief boilerplate interview by phone may be enough. But if you want to write award-winning stories, you may need to engage in extensive preinterview research and secure a block of time to pursue an in-depth interview. In summary, assessing your goals plays a significant role in guiding your actions in the interview itself. Furthermore, as illustrated through these examples, goals also determine your motivation to a large extent as well. The more important the goal, the more preparation, the more openness, the more honesty, and the more your performance are likely to matter to the outcome.

What? Knowledge in the Interview

Assuming you have analyzed the goals of an interview, and concluded it is important, you must obtain the knowledge you need to perform competently when the interview actually happens. You may have learned much about communication through this course and other courses, and you interact with people every day of your life, so you may feel prepared for job interviews. This is most likely an illusion, and a risky one at that. Interviews are different, and often quite different, from most everyday encounters. They have rules and importance that few everyday encounters have. Understanding the types of interviews, and the rules and roles you play in these types, is vital to developing knowledge of competent interview performance.

IDENTIFYING TYPES OF INTERVIEWS

When someone mentions that he or she just participated in an interview, you are likely to picture a situation like Marie experienced. However, there are many different types of interviews. Consider, for example, the list of interview types in Table A.1. This list is not exhaustive, but it does illustrate the extent to which interviews are reflected throughout the landscape of modern society. Interviews may be different from everyday interaction, but you are likely to encounter some form of interview almost every day.

TABLE A.1

Typical Types of Interviews

Type	Purpose
Organizational Interviews	
Institutional Interviews	
Selection	To determine who is chosen for employment
Appraisal	To assess a person's performance adequacy in a position
Grievance	To investigate the merits of an employee's complaint or accusation of an infraction
Disciplinary	To investigate an infraction or inform an employee of organizational decisions regarding the infraction
Feedback	To obtain information relevant to organizational functioning (e.g., exit interviews of departing employees, product/customer satisfaction surveys, etc.)
Information Seeking	To understand more about a given person or organization, with the intent to make better future decisions
Negotiation/persuasion Interviews	To ascertain information relevant to the prospects for a mutually beneficial exchange or contract among parties (e.g., interviewing parties to a conflict, a salesperson interviewing a potential client, etc.)
Investigative Interviews	
Media Interviews	
Journalistic	To obtain information and commentary relevant to an investigative report intended for publication or display
Conference	To obtain remarks and elaboration of remarks of a person for broadcast (e.g., press conference, scientific conference, etc.)
Research Interviews	
Survey	To obtain information for a particular study project or set of questions, with preprepared questions, via telephone, computer, or face-to-face
Focus Group	To obtain rich, open-ended information to discover reactions and/or opinions of people who have an experience in common (e.g., interviewing people who have just seen an advertisement or movie, etc.)
Ethnographic	To obtain rich, open-ended information to discover individuals' perceptions of a given culture of experience (e.g., interviewing homeless people or illegal aliens about their experiences, etc.)
Relational Interviews	To obtain information relevant to relationship maintenance or resolution of relational problem (e.g., inquiring how a spouse's day went, a first date interchange of information to determine if a second date is likely, etc.)
Interrogation Interviews	To seek information relevant to a mystery, crime, or potentially problematic event (e.g., police interrogation of prisoner or witness, FBI interview with prospective employee regarding potential security risks, etc.)
Therapeutic Interviews	
Physical	To obtain information relevant to treating physical illness or enhancing physical wellness (e.g., a doctor or chiropractor diagnosing illness, or a physical therapist preparing you for a massage, etc.)
Mental/Emotional	To obtain information relevant to enhancing emotional well-being (e.g., a rabbi counseling a couple about to be married, a psychiatrist counseling a student witness after a shooting at school, etc.)

Each type of interview is likely to have its own rules, roles, and expectations. Some are bilateral, whereas others are more unilateral. **Bilateral interviews** are those in which both parties, the interviewer and the interviewee, have relatively equal power and roles in the interview. A relational interview is likely to be characterized by extensive reciprocity and interchange of roles. Both relational partners are likely to inquire about the other's day or the other's feelings. In contrast, **unilateral interviews** are typified by considerable division of power and roles. For example, in an interrogation, typically the interviewer has almost total control over the asking of questions, the environment, the procedure, and so forth (Sear & Stephenson, 1997).

During your lifetime, you may be a part of many, if not most, of these interviews. However, some of these types of interviews are both more typical and more problematic than other types. We have chosen to focus primarily on organizational or selection interviews, investigative or journalistic interviews and therapeutic or helping interviews.

IDENTIFYING YOU

Now that you have an idea of the types of interviews, it is important to understand which you may face, and how you should present yourself in those interviews. Recall from Chapter 9 that many social situations are guided by rules and scripts. Interviews are guided more than most situations. The interviewers probably will have conducted dozens, perhaps hundreds, of the type of interview you are encountering. This familiarity with the type of communication and the specific topic means the interviewer is likely to have a fairly set agenda to pursue. Each person and each specific ailment may be unique, but a doctor will have interviewed thousands of patients and experienced many similar types of ailments. Over time, the doctor will get a sense of what information is needed when in order to diagnose that type of illness. Similarly, a personnel interviewer may have interviewed hundreds of prospective employees for a certain type of position. A journalist often will have conducted hundreds of journalistic interviews. Each story may be unique, but there are still crime beats and sports stories that are highly similar.

If interview situations are often scripted, it follows that interviewers often have a set of expectations for what is likely to happen in the interview and a set of expectations for what needs to happen when and what the interviewee is apt to be like. As we have discussed several times throughout this text, the extent to which you fulfill or violate expectations has significant implications for your competence. Therefore, you must be able to examine how you will appear in an interview situation, and the extent to which the other person will see you as you need to be seen. In short, are you who you want to be in the interview?

You probably behave at least somewhat differently around your best friend than you do around your parents or grandparents. Yet you are also "yourself" in both situations. People adapt their behavior to the situation to be appropriate and effective. Interviews are no different. You adapt your behavior to fit the interview situation, and yet you generally want the other person to see the "real" (or at least, the "best") you in the interview. To be competent, therefore, know who you are and how you want to be seen in the interview.

"Know thyself" is a far more difficult prescription than it seems. Many careers today did not even exist a decade ago. Some illnesses can be diagnosed today that could not be diagnosed a decade ago. Some stories won't get uncovered if you don't appear sincere and objective, even if at some level you are suspicious and biased. In short, it is important to analyze any potential interview encounter and determine what is expected of you, and to what extent you can balance your true self with what is expected. Recall from Chapter 2 that competence carries with it ethical implications. Sometimes you can be effective in the short term through deception, but such deception tends to be more threatening to long-term effectiveness because if it is found out, it is likely to be viewed as inappropriate by others. Those others may subsequently distrust you, or even shun you. A journalist who lies to interviewees about keeping sources secret is not likely to get many other interviews with sensitive sources if it gets out that confidential information was leaked by the journalist. Similarly, employees who severely exaggerate their abilities (e.g., software capabilities) in selection interviews may find themselves unable to meet the demands of the job and to perform.

To know yourself and how you want to appear, engage in **self-analysis,** the systematic examination of your own values (e.g., how important are material possessions, lifestyle, etc.), career objectives, and likes and dislikes regarding work and service. Part of this analysis will have already taken place if you have examined your goals for the interview. But your goals also depend on how well you know yourself. Numerous career, aptitude and vocational surveys, and books are available to assist you in determining your core values and interests. When you have a better sense of self, it will be easier for you to determine how to construct the desired impression in an interview.

For example, if you are intending to look for a job, and through self-analysis you confirm that you like working with people and in particular, with disadvantaged people, you are unlikely to need to dress up in a formal business suit for the types of interviews you will be pursuing. In contrast, if you determine that you really like the role of training executives in their communication skills, you probably need to dress very formally and professionally for job interviews. If you want to be in front of groups of people presenting complex information, it will be wise to be prepared to demonstrate Powerpoint or similar presentational software mastery.

IDENTIFYING THE ORGANIZATION

Marie miscalculated her interview in several ways, but one of the most correctable was in the background research she did on the organization. There are various ways an organization, a doctor, a rabbi or minister, journalist, or interviewee can be researched. Virtually every campus, library, and employment agency has a collection of resources for investigating the nature of companies and organizations, from their charters to their size to their public or private status to their benefits. Many organizations host a Web site. If you locate a particular organization's Web site, look for the words "About Us" or "Company Profile" to learn more about that particular group. People can be investigated through newspaper indexes, through regulating professional associations, and by interviewing the organization to which they belong.

IDENTIFYING THE FIT BETWEEN YOU & THE ORGANIZATION

The word *interview* begins with the prefix "inter," which means "between," and implies something is going on between two or more persons. Interviews are not supposed to be simple one-way flows of information. At the same time someone may be interviewing you, you should be obtaining information that will help you determine your course of action as well. In a selection interview, as the interviewee you need to obtain information that will allow you to decide if you want to accept the job should it be offered. If interviewed by a physician or nurse, you would need to determine if that person is sufficiently caring and skilled to get at the problem. Even in HMOs, you can exercise some choice over who treats you by choosing your primary physician. If interviewed by a journalist, also determine if you trust the journalist to do justice to your comments. In short, a competent interview requires that both (or all) parties to the encounter fulfill their roles and obtain the information relevant to their respective decisions. Regardless of the role you play in an interview, as interviewer or interviewee, you need to analyze your goals, who you are, and then obtain the information necessary to determine whether these provide a good fit for you.

How? Skills in Interviews

The world of interviewing has changed extensively in recent years. Interviews are now often multistage events, in which preliminary interviews occur via computer screening of electronically submitted résumés. Subsequent interviews may occur in a group context in which a panel of interviewers ask the interviewee questions from various locations in a teleconference or videoconference. Sometimes interviews involve following an employee during his or her typical day. Negotiations for higher level positions often involve discussion of benefits from health insurance and child care to housing allowances and stock options. In this brave new world of interviewing, remember that at its core, the interview is still a communication event in which the interviewee has only a limited amount of opportunity in which to impress the interviewer. Likewise, the interviewer only has a limited opportunity in which to make the right decisions regarding the interviewee. Thus communication competence is essential to success in the interview context, whichever role you play. Furthermore, the same skills that tend to lead to success in interpersonal encounters are those that tend to lead to competence in interviewing contexts: attentiveness, composure, coordination, and expressiveness.

ATTENTIVENESS

Attentiveness in the interview context consists primarily of listening and empathy skills. The most obvious type of interview in which attentiveness is illustrated is in therapeutic interviews. Research shows that patients evaluate the competence of physicians in large part based on the physician's attentiveness to their concerns (Cegala, McNeilis, McGee, & Jonas, 1995; Tamburrino, Lynch, Nagel, & Mangen, 1993). Personnel interviewers list eye contact, listening, and feedback response as among the most deficient skills among interviewees (Peterson, 1997). The ability to pay attention, appear focused on the other person, orient body posture toward the other person, reveal involvement in the other person's statements and concerns, and demonstrate understanding of the other person's agenda and statements all reveal attentiveness. The interview can be a very distracting encounter, and the extent to which you let your thoughts become self-focused detracts from your ability to pay attention to the other person in the encounter.

COMPOSURE

Composure, appearing relaxed and confident, is a vital skill in the interview context. Interviews differ from most other interpersonal encounters in their relative formality. Interviews make people nervous because they tend to have more well-defined roles, and because they explicitly involve high stakes (i.e., important goals) and interpersonal evaluation. In other words, many of the same reasons that make public speaking so frightening, such as being judged by others, are what make people anxious about interviews.

One of the characteristics being evaluated in many interview situations is the interviewee's ability to maintain self-control and composure in a stressful situation. How people handle stress and pressure is certainly of interest to a potential employer. Many personnel interviewers, for example, mention the importance of "self-confidence," "fluency control," "pressure situations," and "preparation" as important skills interviewees need to display (Peterson, 1997). Indeed, appearing self-confident, using positive language, and demonstrating preparation are among the most important rules to follow in job interviews (Ramsay et al., 1997). Displaying composure in an interview, whether interviewee or interviewer, consists of vocal confidence and assertiveness, control of posture and movement, and avoiding nervous tapping, fidgeting, and verbal slips or incoherent rambling. Composed persons appear to know what they are doing, and are confident in doing it.

COORDINATION

Coordination is the ability to manage turn taking, transitions, topic flow, and beginnings and endings of interaction. In the interview context, much of the direction and movement of the episode is determined by the interviewer, but both participants play a significant role in how smoothly and competently such action takes place. For example, one of the most obvious aspects of coordination in interviews is how well questions are answered. Part of answering a question competently involves the topical relevance of the answer to the question, the rapidity with which the answer is provided, the extent to which the answer seems to address all the implications of the question, and the extent to which the answer avoids unnecessary digression or inefficiency of response. Indeed, in a survey of personnel interviewers, "topic relevance," "response organization," and "response clarity" were among the most commonly mentioned skill inadequacies noted among interviewees (Peterson, 1997). Displaying verbal fluency and providing focused answers are among the most important rules to follow in a job interview (Ramsay et al., 1997).

Part of the coordination on the interview's part is asking questions that get at the information relevant to the goal of the interview. Several types of questions are useful for pursuing relevant information during interviews. The first step any interviewer needs to take is to decide what primary and secondary questions will facilitate collecting the information they require. **Primary questions** introduce a particular topic during the interview. **Secondary questions** are follow up or probing questions that elaborate on the material that surface through primary questions. Sometimes asking a primary question will elicit the needed relevant information; however, many times a primary question only scratches the surface of the information that the interviewer requires. Therefore, it is useful for interviewers to determine before the interview what information they need to collect during the interview and to select primary and secondary questions that meet their purpose. For example, during an employment interview, an interviewer may want to know more about a job applicant's work history. The interview may then use the following primary and secondary questions to inquire into this area:

- Primary question: What jobs have you held previously?
- Secondary question: What has been your favorite job? Least favorite? Why?
- Secondary question: What skills have you learned as a result of your work experience?
- Secondary question: What was the biggest challenge you faced on the job?

As you can see, the primary question introduces the notion of work history and the secondary questions probe likes and dislikes about their work experience, skills, and challenges.

Once an interviewer has determined the general topics for the interview by selecting their primary and secondary questions, interviewers need to go back over these questions and work with their phrasing in order to elicit the desired information. Three types of questions are particularly useful.

First, interviewers need to determine whether open or closed questions are most helpful in collecting relevant information. **Open-ended questions** permit any range of response as potentially appropriate. Questions such as "Why did you decide to live here?" and "What motivated you to become a communication major?" illustrate open-ended questions. **Close-ended questions** are useful for some types of information, but not others. Close-ended questions typically prefigure simple answers as sufficient. That is, the question implies what answers could be appropriate as responses, and these answers tend to be relatively simple. Questions such as, "So you grew up in Texas?" imply a "yes" or "no" answer, with the possibility of brief elaboration (e.g., "Yes, well, mostly, but my parents were in the military, so we moved around a lot.").

Second, interviewers may want to select hypothetical or behavioral questions. **Hypothetical questions** ask the interviewee to respond to what-if situations. For example, in a job interview, an interviewer may ask the applicant the following kinds of questions, dealing with specific topics:

- Difficult employees: "What would you do if a co-worker continually came to work late and you needed to motivate that co-worker to come to work on time?"
- Conflict: "Imagine that a co-worker has just made an incredibly inappropriate remark to you. What would you do?"
- Leadership: "Suppose you were promoted to supervisor. What kind of leadership style would you use?"

Hypothetical questions are particularly useful if you want to assess skills and abilities that an individual may not yet have had an opportunity to develop as well as assessing how this individual may act in future situations.

Several interviewers, however, prefer behavioral questions to hypothetical questions. **Behavioral questions** solicit detailed and specific responses from interviewees that are grounded in their past behavioral experience. Interviewers may prefer these types of questions to hypothetical questions because they may believe that past experience best predicts future experience. (Cunningham, 2000). Examples of behavioral questions include:

- Difficult Employees: "Think of a time when you had to work with a difficult co-worker. How did you manage that situation?"
- Conflict: "Tell me about a situation where you had to manage a conflict between yourself and another co-worker."
- Leadership: "Describe an instance where you acted as a leader. What did you do?"

When using behavioral questions interviewers typically thoroughly explain the situation, specifically describe the action they performed, and describe the results of the action.

Finally, interviewers need to determine whether they should ask objective or interpretive questions. **Objective questions** are fact-based questions that ask the interviewer for impartial descriptions of events and situations. For example, during a therapeutic interview, a client may ask a series of objective questions in order to acquire the client's personal history (e.g., "You became married when?" "How many children do you have?"). While objective questions may be useful for obtaining relatively straightforward information that is not open to dispute, such as how many people belong to a family, one's marital status, and so on, interviewers may want to ask questions that provide glimpses into the way people think, their attitudes, and their beliefs. In such instances, interviewers may be better served by asking interpretive questions. **Interpretive questions** solicit a person's subjective opinions and perspectives. For example, during a therapeutic interview, a therapist may ask interpretive questions such as "How do you make sense of the situation?" or "What do you think would happen if . . .?" in order to gain an understanding of the client's opinions and perspectives on the situation.

Competence in interviewing involves not only the skillful use of these kinds of questions by the interviewer, but the skillful recognition of them by the interviewee. Therefore, it may be useful for interviewees to brainstorm possible questions that may be asked in an interview and to anticipate how to respond to such questions. For example, in organizational interviews such as job interviews it may be useful to anticipate and plan responses to typical questions. A number of books and articles list typical interview questions asked during employment interviews (see Stewart & Cash, 2000).

EXPRESSIVENESS

Expressiveness is the ability to appear animated, involved, and energized in communication. Messages have both verbal and nonverbal aspects, and both are important to making a memorable and vivid impression on another person. In the interview context, expressiveness consists of facial and vocalic expressiveness, gesturing, and articulateness of pronunciation and opinion expression. Interviewers, for example, note that many applicants are deficient in "vocabulary," "descriptive language," "gesturing," "voice projection," "volume control" and "facial expressiveness" (Peterson, 1997). The vast majority of job interviewers point to the articulateness of an employee as an element of the interviewee's desirability as a prospective employee (Wright & Multon, 1995), and "ability to express ideas" has been shown to be a significant determinant of interviewer impressions of candidates (Wade & Kinicki, 1997). Expressiveness can distinguish a merely capable interviewee from a memorable interviewee (Bobevski, Holgate, & McLennara, 1997). For example, in a study of interviewees with physical disabilities, those with good nonverbal communication skills were rated as significantly more employable than those with poor nonverbal communication skills (Wright & Multon, 1995). That is, regardless of a person's technical competence for a job, his or her communication competence, in particular expressiveness, can significantly determine whether or not this person will be hired (Bretz, Rynes, & Gerhart, 1993).

Challenges to Competence in the Interview

Given the importance of communication skills to everyday organizational activity (McPherson, 1998), it is no surprise that demonstrating communication competence in the interview is widely taken to be an important indicator of an interviewee's ability to function in the organization (Argyle, Furnham, & Graham, 1981; Ramsay et al, 1997). In addition, the competence of the interviewer is often taken to be an indicator of the competence of the interviewer's organization itself (Turban et al., 1998).

A recent survey was sent to 500 personnel interviewers in a midwestern city (Peterson, 1997). Almost 70% of the interviewers strongly agreed with this statement: "Oral and nonverbal communication skills significantly impact hiring decisions." Almost exactly as many strongly agreed that "higher level positions require more effective communication skills." In all, half of the respondents strongly agreed that jobs in the 21st century require "increased communication skills." However, only about 5% strongly agreed, "Job applicants display adequate communication skills." Clearly there seems to be significant room for improvement of communication competence in the interview context. Why are interviews so difficult to manage competently? Next we consider two important and interrelated challenges to competence in interview contexts: anxiety and impression management.

ANXIETY MANAGEMENT

Many aspects of situations can make people nervous. Most interview contexts seem to combine a host of these aspects. In the employment interview context, a job or possibly even a career is at stake. The situation is generally formal, unfamiliar, and constrained in terms of time and opportunity for you to get to know one another. In medical or therapeutic interviews, illness or wellness may be at stake. The prospect of disclosing very private, perhaps very negative, information about one's self looms in almost all such interviews. Again, the situation may be formal, unfamiliar, or perhaps even cold and intimidating. In journalistic interviews, the interviewee must consider that every word may reflect on his or her competence, and each word may show up in print or be broadcast on television or the internet. The interviewer in a journalistic interview is aware that most interviewees are doing a favor to give the interview, and may easily become uncooperative if the interview is not handled competently. In summary, interview contexts often involve high stakes, unfamiliar situations, high levels of formality and constraint, limited amounts of time, and considerable focus of attention on what limited amounts of communication can be displayed. It is not surprising that people are anxious in such encounters.

IMPRESSION MANAGEMENT

Anxiety is a common problem in interview contexts because of the potential for evaluation. But to some extent, we are always being evaluated in communication. So what makes interview situations so different? One key difference is that the competence of a person's impression is itself explicitly at stake in interviews. Not only is a job, one's health, one's expertise, or one's honesty at stake, but a person's *worth* (at least in the eyes of the interviewer) is at stake as well. Is a patient's illness "worth" the physician's valuable time? Is the expert's expertise worth quoting in the story? Is the candidate worth hiring? These are either real stakes or we often believe they are the stakes of interviews.

We are accustomed to managing our impression, our face, in everyday communication. But interviews are concentrated episodes of interaction. They provide a limited amount of time in which to make a distinct impression. And the impression we are trying to make is expressly one of competence. Unlike some situations in which you may or may not be motivated to be competent (e.g., trying to end a conversation with someone who just doesn't seem to understand), in interviews it is taken for granted that you want to appear competent.

Finally, impression management is more of an issue in interviews because the rules of job interviews are so much more defined than in most other situations (Ramsay et al., 1997). In many situations you can afford to take risks with rules, or work your way out of rule violations assuming the rule is either not very important or not very well defined. But what rules in a job interview could be said to be unimportant or unclear? Interview contexts are part of our cultural consciousness. People who have never been in a formal job interview, for example, have nevertheless probably seen or heard dozens or hundreds of depictions of such situations. A good example of the rule-bound nature of job interviews is reflected in the area of illegal questions. The Equal Employment Opportunity Commission (EEOC) and the federal government have created several guidelines regarding the kinds of questions that can be asked during job interviews. The intent of this regulation to prohibit job discrimination in hiring decisions. These laws and regulations change, which makes it important for competent interviewers to know the current law. Even so, there are several questions that interviewers should never ask during employment interviews.

1. Don't ask applicants whether they currently have children or are planning to have children. This has the potential to lead to gender discrimination.
2. Don't ask for an applicant's age. Questions about age have the possibility of leading to age discrimination.
3. Refrain from asking questions that probe whether the applicant has physical or mental disabilities that may interfere with their job performance. Disabilities can be

explored once a job offer has been made, conditional on completion of physical, medical, or job-skills tests.

4. Don't' ask questions that try to identify physical characteristics such as height or weight. Obesity can be considered a disability.
5. Don't ask female candidates from their maiden name. Such questions establish marital status and candidates cannot be discriminated on the basis of marital status.
6. Don't ask about citizenship because you may be setting yourself up for a national-origin lawsuit. You may ask for documentation that indicates that the employee has a legal right to work in the U.S.
7. Don't ask questions about arrest records; such records are not proof of anything. Employers *are* entitled to inquire into convictions of crimes. (adapted from Pouliot, 1992).

Job interviewers cannot take risks violating these rules; it can lead to significant legal action against the company. At the same time, what is a job applicant to do if asked illegal question. On the one hand, a job applicant could stand by his or her ground and refuse to answer the question. However, the likelihood that a job will be offered decreases because you are directly confronting and potentially embarrassing the interviewer. On the other hand, a job applicant could answer the question and create a favorable impression, but might feel as if he or she has personal standards.

With so many rules, a person is constantly struggling with being himself or herself, and at the same time, communicating within the relatively strict rules of the interview context. If you merely conform to the rules, you may appear like every other candidate, patient, or expert. So you must distinguish yourself. But how do you do this given that your behavior must conform to a well-defined set of rules? The struggle between self-expression and rule conformity represents one of the most significant challenges of interview situations.

Overcoming Challenges in the Interview

One of the most frustrating experiences of newly graduated college students is the discovery that much of the job market expects its candidates to have job experience. But how are you supposed to get experience unless they hire you? And how were you supposed to get experience in a real career when you were going to college full or part time? There is no easy answer to these questions, but they do illustrate the importance of experience. It is both important to getting a job and to competence in the interview situation itself.

THE VALUE OF EXPERIENCE

Remember the things that make people anxious in interview situations: high stakes, unfamiliarity, formality and constraint, and a high degree of focus on your communication. Most of these can be managed through increasing your experience and familiarity with interviews. One of the best approaches to developing experience and familiarity with the interview context is through information-seeking interviews (Charles, Fleetwood-Walker, & Luck, 1985).

In **information-seeking interviews,** a person seeks to understand more about a given person or organization, with the intent to make better future decisions. People sometimes engage in information-seeking interviews with prospective physicians, therapists, or health-care organizations to decide which one ultimately to select. In the most common type of information-seeking interview, candidates interview various organizations primarily to find out more about a given job market, employer, or set of career options.

Information-seeking interviews often are relatively straightforward. A person calls the personnel or human resources department of an organization and asks for an information-seeking interview. If the organization engages in such interviews, a time is set up and the person goes in with a set of questions to ask the organizational representative about various career opportunities in the field that the organization represents. A competent information seeker will have done what homework is possible in researching the organization and have a prepared set of questions to ask. A competent information seeker will also be prepared, should the interview take such a turn, to talk about himself or herself as a prospective employee, and what he or she aspires to in a career.

Such interviews are in part about helping the interviewer make better decisions in knowing what to expect, and what to seek, in the job market. But they serve other important functions as well. Sometimes, the organizational representative likes the information seeker, and either takes his or her résumé for future consideration, or suggests other organizations at which the seeker may find opportunities. So information-seeking interviews sometimes lead directly to contacts and to jobs. Most importantly, however, is that even if they don't lead directly to jobs, they are a relatively low-risk way of improving your familiarity with the process of interviewing, the differing environments of organizational interviewing, the rules of information exchange in interviews, and with selling yourself.

THE VALUE OF KNOWLEDGE

If experience and familiarity help develop skills, they also help develop knowledge. Knowledge is especially important in contexts in which there are right and wrong ways of doing things. As we indicated previously, interviews tend to be very rule-bound contexts (Ramsay et al., 1997). For example, at home when you are working at your desk, you might put your feet up on the desk. Your professor may even do this. But it would almost certainly be a rule violation for you to put your feet up on an interviewer's desk during an interview. Some rule violations would not be very disruptive (e.g., wearing dirty clothes to an interview), but others would tend to be very disruptive (e.g., speaking while being spoken to, telling lies), and would tend to lower the interviewer's evaluation of your competence (Argyle et al., 1981).

The rules of each interview type listed in Table A.1 are likely to be somewhat unique. For example, a doctor's examination of a patient obviously involves a very different set of topics, and generally would be expected to follow a somewhat different set of stages, than a job interview. In a diagnosis interview, the doctor might start with some small talk (e.g., How have you been? How did that last prescription work?), ask about the specific problem, and then ask questions relevant to diagnosing the particular ailment. The patient would be expected to be informative early, and perhaps later be inquisitive, for example, after the physician has suggested a diagnosis and treatment. The job interview, in contrast, tends to have an opening of small talk, some review of how the interview will proceed, an exchange of information and review of items on a candidate's résumé, a review of the interview and any follow-up processes to expect, and postinterview small talk (DeBell et al., 1998). So each type of interview is likely to have its own topics and its own sequence of information exchange. But certain rules are likely to generalize across interview contexts as well.

Interview contexts generally follow rules similar to everyday conversation, but perhaps with greater expectation of these rules being followed. Many of these rules were summarized by Grice (1975) in terms of **conversational maxims.** The **maxim of quantity** says a response should be informative, but provide only the information required by the previous statement or question. The **maxim of quality** requires that responses be honest. The **maxim of relevance** suggests that responses should be topically related to the prior statements. Finally, the **maxim of manner** indicates that responses should be orderly and clear. Many other rules could be identified in any given context, but these maxims represent a reasonably solid foundation for competence in an interview situation, as they do in most everyday conversation.

Appendix Summary

The interviewing context is both unique and yet similar to other communication contexts. It is unique in the significance of the goals at stake, the relative formality of the rules, and the relative difference in status and roles of the participants. Despite these differences, interviewing is similar to other communication contexts, especially interpersonal contexts, in that the competence model of motivation, knowledge, and skills applies equally to both contexts. Competent interviewing involves being motivated to be competent, knowledgeable in the types and expectations of interviews, and skilled in interviewing. Skills, like interpersonal communication in general, involve attentiveness, composure, coordination, and expressiveness.

The challenges to competent interviewing include the level of anxiety candidates tend to experience, brought on largely by the formality and significance of the context. The other major challenge is the intensity with which a person's face, a person's impression, is onstage in an interview context. Competent management of these challenges involves achieving experience and familiarity through information-seeking interviews and understanding the rule-based nature of interview contexts.

Key Terms

- interview
- organizational interview
- investigative interview
- therapeutic interview
- bilateral interview
- unilateral interview
- self-analysis
- attentiveness
- composure
- coordination
- primary questions
- secondary questions
- open-ended questions
- closed-ended questions
- hypothetical questions
- behavioral questions
- objective questions
- interpretive questions
- expressiveness
- information-seeking interviews
- conversational maxims
- maxim of quantity
- maxim of quality
- maxim of relevance
- maxim of manner

Building Skills

Individual Exercises

1. Develop a draft of a résumé. Develop a heading that summarizes your career objectives and values. Then show your résumé to a family member, a professional, and a fellow student to receive feedback. Be sure you ask for feedback not only on formatting but also on content. What did you learn about yourself during this process? How well can you summarize who you are in the form of a résumé?

2. Engage in three information-seeking interviews. If you are interested in conducting organizational interviews, select professionals in an industry that represents your current career objective. If you are interested in journalism, select three professional journalists or managers of journalistic enterprises. If you are interested in one of the helping professions, select administrators or helping professionals. Take careful notes at each interview, and at the end, summarize what you learned from the interviews in terms of what changes you would, or intend to, make to your education. How were the interviews different from what you expected?

3. Videotape or audiotape five minutes of an interview of an expert (e.g., *Larry King Live*, *Charlie Rose*, etc.), and

transcribe the entire interview. Then critique the interview. What would you have done differently, asked differently, followed up on differently? Where, if anywhere, did the interviewer not manage the interview well? What is the one question that should have been asked that wasn't?

Group Exercises

1. Choose a fellow student in your class and exchange the résumés you developed for individual activity 1. Given a week with each other's résumé, (1) do some research of classified ads and write a job description that would be relevant to the other person's résumé, (2) develop a set of 20 questions you would want to ask the other person if you were an interviewer for an organization that would advertise such a job, and (3) engage in an actual 15-minute interview in which you are interviewing the other student, and then reverse roles and engage in a 15-minute interview in which the other person is interviewing you for your job. How competent were you as an interviewee? As an interviewer? Complete a conversational skills rating form on your own behavior as an interviewee and as the other person as an interviewee. Give each other your ratings of the other person as an interviewee, and compare to your own self-evaluations. How do they compare?
2. After the activity has been completed, exchange lists of questions with each other. Provide written feedback to each other by rewriting questions and developing at least one closed-ended question and one open-ended question for each topic area covered. Furthermore, add questions not asked that you wish had been.

References

Anderson, R., & Killenberg, G. M. (1998). *Interviewing: Speaking, listening, and learning for professional life.* Mountain View, CA: Mayfield.

Argyle, M., Furnham, A., & Graham, J. A. (1981). *Social situations.* Cambridge: Cambridge University Press.

Bobevski, I., Holgate, A. M., & McLennan, J. (1997). Characteristics of effective telephone counselling skills. *British Journal of Guidance and Counselling, 25,* 239–249.

Bretz, R. D., Rynes, S. L., & Gerhart, B. (1993). Recruiter perceptions of applicant fit: Implications for individual career preparation and job search behavior. *Journal of Vocational Behavior, 43,* 310–327.

Cegala, D. J., McNeilis, K. S., McGee, D. S., & Jonas, A. P. (1995). A study of doctors' and patients' perceptions of information processing and communication competence during the medical interview. *Health Communication, 7,* 179–203.

Charles, D., Fleetwood-Walker, P., & Luck, M. (1985). Communication skills: Information-seeking interviews. *Journal of the Operational Research Society, 36,* 883-890.

Cunningham, J. (2000). Behavioral interviewing. Unpublished manuscript. Baylor University, Waco, TX.

DeBell, C. S., Montgomery, M. J., McCarthy, P. R., & Lanthier, R. P. (1998). The critical contact: A study of recruiter verbal behavior during campus interviews. *Journal of Business Communication, 35,* 202–223.

Evans, B. J., Coman, G. J., & Goss, B. (1996). Consulting skills training and medical students' interviewing efficiency. *Medical Education, 30,* 121–128.

Farnill, D., Hayes, S. C., & Todisco, J. (1997). Interviewing skills: Self-evaluation by medical students. *Medical Education, 31,* 122–127.

Grice, H. P. (1975). Logic and conversation. In P. Cole & J. L. Morgan (Eds.), *Syntax and semantics* (Vol. 3, pp. 41–58). New York: Academic Press.

Kikoski, J. F. (1998). Effective communication in the performance appraisal interview: Face-to-face communication for public managers in the culturally diverse workplace. *Public Personnel Management, 27,* 491–513.

McPherson, B. (1998). Student perceptions about business communication in their careers. *Business Communication Quarterly, 61,* 68–79.

Peterson, M. S. (1997). Personnel interviewers' perceptions of the importance and adequacy of applicants' communication skills. *Communication Education, 46,* 287–291.

Pouliot, J.S. (1992, July). *Topics to avoid with applicants. Nations Business,* XX, 57-58. Pulakos, E. D., Schmitt, N., Whitney, D., & Smith, M. (1996). Individual differences in interviewer ratings: The impact of standardization, consensus discussion, and sampling error on the validity of a structured interview. *Personnel Psychology, 49,* 85–102.

Ralph, A., & Thorne, E. (1993). Defining and enhancing competent interview behaviour using the verbal interaction analysis system. *Scandinavian Journal of Behaviour Therapy, 22,* 65–87.

Ramsay, S., Gallois, C., & Callan, V. J. (1997). Social rules and attributions in the personnel selection interview. *Journal of Occupational and Organizational Psychology, 70,* 189–203.

Scar, L., & Stephenson, G. M. (1997). Interviewing skills and individual characteristics of police interrogators. *Issues in Criminological and Legal Psychology, 29,* 27–34.

Schmidt, W. V., & Conaway, R. N. (1999). *Results-oriented interviewing: Principles, practices, and procedures.* Boston: Allyn & Bacon.

Shepherd, E. (1993). Ethical interviewing. *Issues in Criminological and Legal Psychology, 18,* 46–56.

Spitzberg, B. H. (1995). *Instructional assessment of interpersonal competence: The Conversational Skills Rating Scale.* Annandale, VA: Speech Communication Association.

Spitzberg, B. H., & Hurt, H. T. (1987). The measurement of interpersonal skills in instructional contexts. *Communication Education, 36,* 28-45.

Stewart, C. J., & Cash, W. B. (1999). *Interviewing: Principles and practices* (9 ed.). NY: McGraw-Hill.Tamburrino, M. B., Lynch, D. J., Nagel, R., & Mangen, M. (1993). Evaluating empathy in interviewing: Comparing self-report with actual behavior. *Teaching and Learning in Medicine, 5,* 217–220.

Turban, D. B., Forret, M. L., & Hendrickson, C. L. (1998). Applicant attraction to firms: Influences of organization reputation, job and organizational attributes, and recruiter behaviors. *Journal of Vocational Behavior, 52,* 24–44.

Wade, K. J., & Kinicki, A. J. (1997). Subjective applicant qualifications and interpersonal attraction as mediators within a process model of interview selection decisions. *Journal of Vocational Behavior, 50,* 23–40.

Wright, G. E., & Multon, K. D. (1995). Employer's perceptions of nonverbal communication in job interviews for persons with physical disabilities. *Journal of Vocational Behavior, 47,* 214–227.

Glossary

a

ability potential to perform some set of behavior consistently
abstraction dimension of skills that skills exist at many different levels
access extent that different types of media and options in these media are available
accommodating style conflict management style low in assertiveness and high in collaboration
acknowledging comments communication that helps members indicate that they understand one another
acquaintance stage point of first contact between people
action assembly mental process of putting behaviors together in the pursuit of goals
actions behaviors performed by a person
ad hominem verbal attack on another person rather than the argument the person is making
adaptability ability to alter skills appropriately as contexts and conversations evolve
adaptive work group problems and solutions that are not clearly defined and place the responsibility for change on group members
addition adding extra parts to a word
affect blend blending of two or more affect displays into one facial expression
affect displays facial expressions
affective conflict conflict involving the interpersonal relationships formed among group members and the group's emotional climate
affective/cognitive dimension of motives degree to which interpersonal communication is motivated by emotions, or by thoughts and intentions
affiliation emotional and evaluative dimension of relating
aggressive communication expression of your rights or views in a way that violates other's rights or views
agreement when two people have similar values or beliefs about something
alliteration repetition of the same consonant sound in a series of words or phrases to draw attention to certain ideas
allness tendency to conclude that what is believed to be true of one part is true of the whole
analogy extended simile or metaphor that suggests that things which seem alike in some respects will be alike in the respect being discussed
appeal technique speakers use to persuade an audience to accept their argument
appearance presentation of one's physical self
appropriate language language that is respectful, noncondescending, unbiased and fitting to the context
appropriateness communication that fits a given context
articulation shaping individual speech sounds correctly to produce an understandable word
artifacts objects in an environment that make nonverbal statements about the identity and personality of their owner
assertiveness expression of your rights or views in a way that does not violates other's rights or views
attentiveness employing good listening and empathy skills
attentiveness skill of showing interest, concern, and attention in an interaction
attitudes psychological reactions to another person, object, or concept that affect people's behaviors
attribution theory framework for determining the motives underlying another's behavior
audience analysis ascertaining relevant information about listeners and a speaking situation that will shape how a speech is prepared and delivered
audience competence audience ability to listen attentively, receive the entire message presented in the speech, and respond appropriately
autocratic leadership leaders having more power than followers and using one-way communication to direct and guide the actions of followers
autonomy-connection dialectic tension between the desire to be unconstrained and independent in actions and thoughts, and the desire to be intimate and connected with another person
avoiding style conflict management style low in both assertiveness and collaboration

b

behavioral interdependence when an individual's messages affect and are affected by other people's messages
behavioral questions solicit detailed and specific responses grounded in past behavior
belief restructuring cognitive modification—process of systematically using thought to overcome beliefs about your self-concept that impair your competence
beliefs people's basic convictions about what is true or false, based on their own knowledge and experience
bibliography list of source references or related material
bilateral interview both the interviewer and the interviewee have relatively equal power and roles in the interview
blind self aspects of the self known to others but not to the self
body of the speech the middle part of a speech that supports the central claim through the presentation of a series of main points
bottom-up process starting at the level of specific behaviors and working up to a general evaluation of competence
brainstorming group process of generating many uncriticized ideas to improve the chances that high-quality, creative ideas will emerge
brainwriting written method for brainstorming
breadth number of topics we may choose to disclose about ourselves; the number of different communication media to which a person has access

c

carification questions questions that invite another person to elaborate on his or her meaning
cause-and-effect organization information organized by why something happens (the causes) and what happens as a result (the effects)
channel medium through which a message is sent
chronemics intentional and unintentional use of time to communicate
chronological organization presentation of information in a time sequence
claim-data-warrant persuasive structure that has been used to analyze arguments in the practice of debate and argument (*See* Toulmin)
clarity precision of the message
clear language word use that is easy to understand and comprehend
closed-ended questions questions that give the respondent limited options in answering
closedness-openness dialectic contradiction between the desire to preserve your privacy and wanting to share yourself with another person

coercion negative form of influence that occurs when a speaker persuades others to act in a particular way out of fear of reprisal, or by using force, or giving the listeners no choice but to cooperate
cognitive modification process that changes or modifies a person's unrealistic beliefs
collaborating style conflict management style high in both assertiveness and collaboration
collaboration capability ability of group members to work interdependently in the future
collective behavior joint action that links people together
collectivist orientation giving group goals priority over individual goals
commission understanding among group members of the purpose of the group, the task it is to perform, and appropriate actions for accomplishing its task
commitment decision to maintain a relationship over a period of time
common places categories or subject areas for speeches
communication process of managing messages for the purpose of creating meaning
communication apprehension fear or anxiety of either real or anticipated communication with another person or persons
communication competence use of verbal and/or nonverbal behavior to accomplish preferred outcomes in a way that is appropriate to the context communicator
community group of people who come together in the same physical, mental, or virtual space to interact and/or pursue a common goal
comparing alternatives organizing pattern that examines two or more alternatives and makes an appeal for the preferred choice
comparison and contrast organization presentation of information organized based on similarities and differences to something else
comparison questions questions that invite examination of similarities and differences
compensation responding with behavior functionally opposite of what you are seeing in the other
competence model for listening the listener applies motivation, knowledge, and skills to the listening process
competence principle plans are selected on the basis of their efficiency in competently achieving a plan's goals
competent language use of words that are clear, vivid, and appropriate
competent listener someone who is motivated, knowledgeable and skillful at listening effectively in a variety of situations
competing style "win-lose" approach to conflict that is high in assertiveness and low in cooperation
completeness extent that the medium represents the nonverbal and emotional content of messages
composure ability to maintain self-control and composure in a stressful situation
composure skill of displaying control and confidence
compromising style "lose-lose" approach to conflict with each party agreeing to make concessions to the others to find a middle course
computerized database collection of information accessed and organized by computer
computer-mediated communication(CMC) any human symbolic interaction through digitally based technologies
conclusion final part of a speech whose main functions are to review and summarize the content, and to reinforce the thesis
concurrence seeking trying to achieve a consensus regarding a decision
conflict interaction among interdependent people who perceive others as opposing their goals, aims, or values and having the potential to frustrate them in achieving these goals, aims, or values
conflict management styles distinguishable patterns of behavior that represent different forms of managing disputes
consistency maintaining similar ways of behaving across contexts and conversations
constitutive rules rules to help sort out the meaning of words or phrases
constructing meaning how listeners attribute and assign meaning to a speaker's message, and mentally clarify their understanding of it
constructing meaning competence motivated, knowledgeable, and skilled assignment of meaning to a speaker's message
constructs continuum of dimensions or traits that make up personalities
content dimension of messages ideas and meanings of words or behaviors
content knowledge knowing what topics, words, meanings, and such are required in a situation
context frame within which action occurs
context apprehension fear or anxiety about communicating in a particular context such as interpersonal, small group, or public speaking
context interdependence when a group's environment affects and is affected by a group's actions
context levels number of communicators in a communication and the extent the direction of the communication among them is determined by the nature of the episode.
contextual alteration changing something about a situation to see how a person reacts
contextual types routine ways we think about and respond to a communication episode
convergent thinking evaluating and narrowing a wide range of alternatives to select the one most appropriate to the task at hand
conversational maxims generally understood rules and expectations of conversation competence; include maxims of quantity, quality, and manner
conversational narcissism appearance in your communication of caring only about yourself
coordination ability to manage turn taking, transitions, topic flow, and beginnings and endings of interaction
coordination skill of managing the flow of an interaction
cosmopolitan communicators communicators who acknowledge the existence of a number of different, valid meanings for words
counterargument form of inner speech that argues against the persuasive message being presented and for the listener's entrenched point of view
credibility appeal persuasion related to how listeners perceive the reputation, prestige, and authority of the speaker
critical thinking process of evaluating evidence, assumptions, and ideas based on sound reasoning and logic
cultural characteristics audience characteristics relevant to public speaking that come from the groups they are born into, grow up in, or may choose to belong to
culture enduring patterns of thought, value, and behavior that define a group of people
C-V-A model group procedure that structures discussion around concerns, visions, and actions

d

decision selection among alternative explanations or proposals
decision acceptability degree a decision meets standards of quality, quantity, and timeliness set by the people who will use or be affected by the decision
decision making process of selecting among competing alternatives
decline stage relationship stage in which communication reveals increasing tensions or struggles in maintaining the desired relationship definition
decoding assigning meaning to a message
deduction process of reasoning in which a specific conclusion follows necessarily from a general principle
deep interruptions interruptions that take over a speaker's turn in the middle of a speaker's statement
defensive group environment environment characterized by a lack of trust and cooperation among group members

deficit language language that focuses attention on people's deficiencies and problems
democratic leadership two-way communication among people with equal power who jointly make decisions
depth the importance and relevance of information to our core sense of self; the various options available within a medium
derived credibility impressions your listeners form as they listen to you speak
description informative speech that gives new information when the listeners are unfamiliar with the topic
descriptive statistics describe or present pictures of what whole groups of people do, think, or are like
development stage relationship stage in which people pursue a mutual definition of the relationship
devil's advocate procedure process of challenging a group's thinking by introducing contrasting viewpoints and ideas with the assumption that the more minority opinions are included in the final decision, the higher quality the decision
dialectic process of questions and answers used to examine all sides of an issue in search of the truth
dialogue communication process that explores differing perspectives and ideas on problems, issues, or topics; a way of communicating that allows people to stand their own ground while being open to other perspectives
dissolution stage relationship stage where communication negotiates an end to the relationship
divergent thinking generating multiple ideas and alternatives about issues, problems, and solutions
drivers causes of a particular problem
dystopia vision of a world in which everything has gone wrong

e

effectiveness extent communication accomplishes valued outcomes
efficiency amount of resources such as people, time, and money relative to benefits
emblem nonverbal cue that has meaning for a certain cultural group, substitutes for a word and translates almost directly into a word phrase
emoticons whimsical icons that communicate the emotion underlying a verbal statement
emotional appeal persuasion based on psychology and passion
empathic assertion attempt to recognize and grant legitimacy to others in a situation while simultaneously expressing your own rights or views
empathy ability to experience the feelings similar or related to those of another person
enclave culture group of people who find a way to maintain their religious or ideological beliefs and still live in a secular society
encoding putting a thought into words and transmitting it through a channel or a medium to a receiver
episode sequence of messages that has a clear beginning, end and set of constitutive and regulative rules
equilibrium problem challenge to maintain a constructive tension between getting a group task done and maintaining a positive group environment
equivocal communication communication that speaks with many voices or messages
ethical public speaker a speaker who appropriately and effectively speaks to accomplish goals, while also considering the effects of the speech on everyone involved
ethnocentric communicators communicators who recognize only their own meanings for words as valid and reject alternative meanings as wrong
ethnocentrism characterized by or based on the attitude that one's own group is superior
ethos credibility appeals
example specific item, person, or event that helps explain or illustrate an idea, clarify a difficult concept, or make anything you say more interesting or real to the audience
expectancy fulfillment evaluating communication outcomes relative to anticipated outcomes
explanation informative speech that clarifies something that is already known but not well understood
expressiveness ability to appear animated, involved, and energized in communication
expressiveness skill of animating verbal and nonverbal communication
extemporaneous speech speech carefully planned ahead of time but delivered in a conversational tone using notes for key ideas
eye contact looking directly at a person

f

facial expression nonverbal cues from the face showing emotion and mood
fact individual piece of information that can be verified
fear appeal persuasion based on changing listeners' attitudes or behaviors through the use of an anxiety-arousing message
feedback communication to the speaker that conveys the listener's understanding of and reaction to a message
feng shui Chinese approach to spatial arrangement suggesting that artifacts have unique powers when arranged in a certain way
figures of speech expressions that give color and drama to speech
first impression bias schema formed during the initial meeting of a person that influences how later information about this person is processed
fishbone diagram visual mapping tool to help group members identify and discuss important factors affecting a desired outcome
force field analysis process for analyzing the reasons for a problem and obstacles to its elimination
formal outline final version of a working outline, organized and presented using the standard outline format
full-thin dimension of voice vocal range from deep and forceful resonance to more rapid and shallow resonance
function what the communication behavior attempts to, or actually, accomplishes
functionalist approach assumption that particular decision-making functions leading to high-quality decision making can be identified
fundamental attribution error common bias of assuming that other people's behavior derives from internal characteristics, while viewing one's own behavior due more to a context or situation

g

gender role socialization process in which girls and boys receive explicit and implicit messages that convey how they should behave in a given culture
general purpose speaker's goal to inform or persuade
generalized others entire social group or community to which one belongs
gestures large and small movements of the hands and arms that communicate meaning within a society or culture
goal outcomes, objectives, or purpose sought by communication
goal interdependence when group members share goals
goal setting process for alleviating anxiety that makes use of a structured plan for changing a person's behaviors
grammar rules and structure for putting words together
group context interactions among a number of people, typically three to twelve, and usually take place in a more formal, task-oriented context
group culture values, norms, and beliefs that guide a group
group discussion most importnant type of conversation in small groups when focusing on decision making
group environment climate in which group members communicate
group phases stages in the group's life span where there are clearly defined purposes and themes for the group activities
group procedure process for performing a function that is central to the group

group role set of prescribed behaviors that individuals are expected to perform
groupthink norm that makes consensus the highest priority and diminishes the vigilant appraisal of possible alternatives to a final decision

h

haptics touch; tactile contact among people
hasty generalization conclusion based on too few specific cases or examples
hate speech speech attacks on other people on the basis of race, ethnicity, gender, religion, or sexual orientation
hearing automatic process that involves the physiological reception of sounds
hidden agenda motivation that is kept secret and may include a publicly offered false motivation
hidden self parts of the self known to the self but not to others
hypothetical example something that hasn't actually happened but could happen
hypothetical questions solicit responses to what-if situations

i

ideational conflict conflict centering on the arguments and issues concerning decision alternatives
illustrator nonverbal cue that complements and accents a verbal message
imagery creation of visual pictures and other sensory experiences through description
i-message statement that labels the speaker's own behavior
implicit personality theory uses one or a few personality traits to draw broad inferences about others
impromptu speech speech delivered with the least amount of preparation
indexing using language that places an issue, event, or person in a specific time or context
individualistic orientation giving individual goals priority over group goals
induction process of reasoning in which a general conclusion follows from the examination of a series of specific instances or examples
information overload feeling of being overwhelmed because of having more media content and access to and from people than can be processed meaningfully
information transfer model linear view of communication in which a message is sent by a source through a channel to a receiver
information-seeking interviews interviews that seek to understand more about a given person or organization, with the intent to make better future decisions
informative speech communication that offers something new to an audience, and attempts to move listeners to greater understanding or insight
ingratiating communication behavior in interactions that appears to be only interested in seeking favor from the other person
initial credibility impressions listeners have formed of you before hearing you speak
instructions informative speech that teaches something or shows how to use something
interaction barriers obstacles to listening resulting from verbal battles, inflammatory language, or cultural differences
interactional context context in which there are opportunities for all participants to engage
interactive model model that emphasizes two-way communication, viewing communication as a circular process in which both communicators are senders and receivers of messages
interactivity extent that the parties interacting through a medium can communicate simultaneously
interdependence when two elements are related to and mutually affect one another
interest underlying motivation or reason a person wants to pursue a particular position
interpersonal communication process of exchanging signs or symbols that create meaning in an interactive context of few people
interpersonal context informal interaction among people involved in social and/or personal relationships
interpretive questions solicit a person's subjective opinions and perspectives
interview encounter-oriented toward the possibility of mutual gain through the exchange of information, a process consisting largely of question-and-answer sequences
intimacy warmth, closeness, caring, and feeling connected
introduction beginning part of speech whose purpose is to capture attention, present the main claim, and preview the speech
investigative interview transaction between parties in which the interviewer is seeking information from the interviewee for the purpose of enhancing decision making and understanding of a specified issue or situation.
invitational rhetoric away of speaking that treats the speaker and the audience as equals and invites the audience to enter the speaker's world and to see it as the speaker does
issue framing thoughtful way to define and clarify important questions and choices

j

johari window theory of relational openness based on the dimensions of self and other

k

keyword outline brief organization of keywords used to remind a speaker of what to say
kinesics body communication that focuses on how people communicate through movement and posture, gestures, and the face and eyes
knowledge in communication, consists of the content of what we say and do, and the procedures by which this content can be performed
knowledge-gaining strategies behaviors a communicator uses to obtain information about others

l

ladder of abstraction S. I. Hayakawa's description of language on a continuum from very concrete to the abstract
Ladder of Inference tool to help group members explore the reasoning behind their conclusion by evaluating their assumptions, values, and beliefs, data and procedures
language rule-guided system of symbols that allows us to take messages and utterances in the form of words and translate them into meaning
language community group of people who has developed a common set of constitutive and regulative rules which guide the meaning of words and appropriate reactions to them
leader individuals within a group who guide and direct the group's activities
leadership communication process that helps groups organize themselves to achieve desirable goals
linguistic tyranny use of a set of words having a certain value or connotation to describe and control the outcome of a situation
listening learned psychological process in which you receive the message, assign meaning to it, and send feedback to the speaker
listening to empathize and understand focusing on the speaker's feelings and attitudes while gaining information
listening to evaluate and critique critically analyzing the meaning and merits of a speaker's message
listening to learn and comprehend listening that involves a search for facts and ideas
logical appeal persuasion based on knowledge and reasoning
logical fallacies errors in reasoning and logic that lead the listeners to false conclusions

logos logical appeals
looking-glass self self as formed by relationships with other people
love positive emotional state regarding another person, consisting of three basic dimensions: intimacy, passion, and commitment

m

main points key ideas that prove the claim and support the thesis statement of a speech
manipulation negative and unethical form of influence used to control people's actions or reactions in a devious or deceitful way
manuscript speech speech that is written out ahead of time and read word for word to the audience
mastery extent that a user understands how to use the media
maxim of manner responses should be orderly and clear
maxim of quality requires that responses be honest
maxim of quantity a response should be informative, but provide only the information required by the previous statement or question
maxim of relevance responses should be topically related to the prior statements
maximizing communication inappropriately assertive or aggressive, but effective, communication
meaning interpretation people assign to a message
media access extent that CMC technologies are available to the intended audience
media richness extent that a medium recreates or represents all of the information available in the original message
media sensitivity awareness that different media possess different characteristics that systematically affect their appropriateness and effectiveness in different contexts
memorized speech speech that is fully written out and memorized ahead of time, then spoken to the audience word for word
message ambiguity extent that a message has either unknown or multiple meanings
message complexity amount of detail, density, and integration of information in a message
message emotionality extent that a message attempts to communicate the sender's feelings
message overload distracting quantity of messages
messages words, sounds, actions, and gestures that people express to one another when they interact
metalogue a set of shared understandings and assumptions
metaphor implied comparison between two dissimilar things without using the words *like* or *as*
micro-momentary facial flash expression that flashes across the face so quickly it is imperceptible
mindfulness paying close attention to the task at hand
mindlessness engaging in activities without consciously monitoring their operations or processes
minimizing communication inappropriate and ineffective communication that fails to achieve a desired outcomes, and may alienate other
minority reports perspectives generated by a subgroup to reflect thinking and ideas that provide an alternative perspective to the majority opinion.
mixed message nonverbal cue that contradicts a verbal message
modern self notion that the self is comprised of an "I" and a "Me"
molar skills skills that are broad and general in nature
molecular skills skills that are very specific and objective
motivated sequence organizational pattern that uses five steps—attention, need, satisfaction, visualization, and action—designed to motivate and persuade listeners
motivation extent a communicator is drawn toward or pushed away from communicating competently in any context
multicodality keeping one's own unique way of using words and language while incorporating some of the unique language patterns of the listener(s)
multiple self concept that we create many different versions of "self" across contexts

n

natural media face-to-face media such as spoken words, gestures, posture, and all the other verbal, nonverbal, and listening processes using solely body and mind
need for affection need for receiving and giving warmth and positive regard to others
need for control amount of power an individual needs in a relationship
need for inclusion need to maintain satisfactory relationships and associations with others
need fulfillment when an individual joins and participates in a group based on personal and social need
negative motivation factors that result in fear, anxiety, or avoidance
nested decision making prioritizing questions to ask early in a process that serve as the foundation for subsequent questions and lead to the answer of the major question
noise interference coming from the environment that distracts from the communication
nominal group technique (NGT) generating ideas individually and evaluating them as a group
non sequitor statement that does not follow from anything previously said
nonfluencies frequent use of distracters and interrupters that slip out when you speak
nonverbal communication all behaviors, attributes, and objects of humans—other than words—that communicate messages and have shared social meaning
nonverbal cue any human behavior that communicates a nonverbal message if assigned meaning by a sender, receiver, or social group
norm pattern of behavior that recurs over time

o

objective questions fact-based questions asking interviewee for impartial descriptions of events and situations
oculesics using eye contact to communicate
omission leaving out, not saying, part of a word
open self what is known to the self and to others
open-ended questions encourage a wide range of possible responses
openness extent that the messages sent through the medium are public
optimizing communication communication that achieves preferred outcomes in a way that preserves the relationship
organizational interview transaction between institutional representative(s) and a prospective employee for the purpose of ascertaining the appropriateness and terms of contracting the services of the interviewee

p

paralanguage all the nonverbal elements involved in using the voice
paraphrasing summarizing and restating the meaning of a speaker's message in one's own words
passion arousal, sexual and otherwise, associated with interpersonal attraction
passive communication avoidance of self-expression or the accommodation to others' concerns before your own
pathos emotional appeals
people factors attraction to the people who are members of the group
perception active process of making sense of external environment and internal experience
personal characteristics objective demographic information about the audience
personal development decision processes that enhance the personal well-being of group members and facilitate their growth and development
personal space how people distance themselves from one another
personality traits cognitive and social qualities in a person that affect the level that he or she joins and participates in groups

perspective taking seeing the world as the other person sees it
persuasion use of communication to reinforce, change, or modify an audience's attitudes, values, beliefs, or actions
persuasive speech speech intended to influence an audience's attitudes, beliefs, values, or behaviors
phase hypothesis small groups must go through phases in a prescribed order to be effective and make high-quality decisions
physical barriers interferences from the physical environment and distracting characteristics or behaviors of the speaker or the listener
pitch highness or lowness of the speaking voice
place environment or physical surroundings where the communication takes place, including lighting, temperature, available space for movement, objects in the space, and media
plan intentional description of the actions involved in achieving a goal
plan adjustment use of feedback to change elements of a plan
politically correct (PC) language words and phrases that attempt to remove or compensate for any traces of sexism, racism, ageism, heterocentrism or potentially offensive, derogatory meanings
position stated course of action that a person wants to see pursued
positive motivation result of efforts and desires that drive performance toward excellence
positive/negative dimension of motives impact of interpersonal communication on others
Postmodern self self as actually made up of many different selves, not just one stable self
posture position or attitude of the bodily parts
power ability to influence and control another person's thoughts, feelings, or actions
predictability-novelty dialectic tension between seeking stability and pattern in relationships while thriving on a degree of unpredictability and surprise
presentational outline key ideas taken from a formal outline with just enough details to remind a speaker what to say
primary questions introduce a particular topic during an interview
principle of consistency we make attributions about people based on the similarity of their characteristics or actions across time and space
principle of controllability we try to determine if the cause of a particular action as internal or external, and the extent to which a person is able to alter or change the outcome
principle of distinctiveness we make attributions about people based on whether particular characteristics and actions are associated with specific outcomes unique to the situation
principle of locus we attampt to determine the extent to which a cause of some outcome is internal or external to a person
prior success principle plans are based on previous plans when previous plans seem effective and appropriate
problem gap between an ideal state and the current state of events
problem solving process in which members assess problems and formulate solutions
problem-solution organizational pattern that first identifies a problem and then proposes a workable solution
procedural conflict differences of opinion on what procedures to use during group discussion
procedural knowledge how to assemble, plan, and perform content knowledge in a particular situation
projected aids visual aids that use electricity, including computer-assisted aids
pronunciation accenting of syllables in a word
prototypes best example of a particular concept
proxemics study of how people move around in and use space to communicate
psychological barriers mental and emotional distractions to listening
psychological characteristics the audience's needs, motivation, attitudes, beliefs, and values
public speaking communication from one to many
public speaking anxiety fear or anxiety associated with a real or anticipated public speaking event
public speaking context involves one or a small group of people whose task is to speak to a larger number of people, with the general assumption that the audience will have little or no "speaking" role
public voice delivery modified by variety in rate, pitch and volume, to be easily heard and understood by an entire audience

q

questioning explicit or implicit use of verbal or nonverbal behavior to request information from another person
questions of conjecture questions that ask what might happen in the future
questions of fact questions focusing on the accuracy of a particular claim
questions of policy questions that focus on actions that should be taken to solve a problem
questions of value questions that explore issues of intrinsic importance, worth, utility, and desirability of objects, attitudes, and beliefs
quotation a person's exact words

r

rate speed at which a speaker delivers a speech
receiver the ultimate audience for a message
receiving consciously paying attention to verbal and nonverbal aspects of an entire message
receiving competence motivated, knowledgeable, and skilled attention to a speaker's message
reciprocation responding with behavior similar to what you are seeing in the other communicator
reciprocity degree the communicators match each other's levels of disclosure
red herring speech that diverts the audience's attention from the real issue by presenting irrelevant arguments or issues
reflecting repeating someone's feelings about what he or she said
reflective thinking model formulation by John Dewey of the series of steps decision makers follow to make high-quality decisions
refocusing question question that focuses attention toward developing creative responses that meet contradictory needs
reframing stating something in a new and constructive way
refuting the opponent persuasive speech organization that dismantles the opposing argument
regulative rules rules that guide a response
regulator nonverbal cue that helps regulate and coordinate communication among people
relational dialectics captures the tensions that exist among competing and yet interdependent aspects of communication
relational interview obtain information relevant to relationship maintenance or resultion of relational problem
relational knowledge knowing how to manage social relationships among group members, build positive group environments, and manage potential conflict
relational maintenance use of communication to sustain preferred relational definitions or states
relational skills ability to send messages that promote and maintain appropriate and effective working relationships among group members
relationship ongoing, interdependent process of interaction between two or more people
relationship dimension of messages way communicators define their relationship to one another
relevance how closely related the information disclosed is to the topic being discussed
repertoire set of all roles a person is capable of playing or enacting and the set of behaviors or actions that comprise the role
repetition use of the same word or phrase several times to emphasize or tie several ideas together

responding process the listener uses to let the speaker know the message has been received and to clarify understanding of it
responding competence motivated, knowledgeable, and skilled communicating to the speaker that the message has been received and understood
restraining forces factors that prevent groups from addressing and solving a problem
rhetorical eloquence public speaking that follows the rules for effective public speaking within a given culture or community
rhetorical exhaustion when a party decides that it has exhausted all avenues for talk as a means to settle disputes
rhetorical question question asked for effect rather than to elicit a response
role patterns and style of lines and behaviors a person is able to perform across contexts
role taking imagining the meaning that others attribute to one's own behavior
rules followable prescriptions for behavior in a given context

S

sanction behavior communicating a negative evaluation
Sapir-Whorf hypothesis theory that language determines what we see in the world and how we think
schema concept that organizes information into a coherent and meaningful pattern
script story that needs to occur in a given sequence; expected sequence of events that is coherent to the individual
secondary questions follow up or probing questions that elaborate on the material that surfaces through primary questions
self-analysis systematic examination of your own values, career objectives, and likes and dislikes regarding work and service
self-centered communicators communicators who think primarily of their own goals, needs, and actions, and of others only as it fits their needs
self-disclosure process by which we reveal ourselves to others
self-fulfilling prophecy behavior or interactions based on unproven assumptions as if those assumptions were true
self-monitoring attending to one's own situation for information to form the most competent responses to a situation
self-oriented/other-oriented dimension of motives concerns whether an interpersonal message was generated to meet the self's needs or to meet someone else's needs
self-serving bias the tendency to attribute positive outcomes to our selves and negative outcomes to others.
showing questions questions that invite the respondent to focus on specific actions or activities
shyness tendency to withdraw from social activities
signal monitoring looking for signs that an interaction is not going well because too little or too much of a skill is being performed
significant others important people who shape one's life
significant symbols verbal or nonverbal messages that have shared meaning
signified object or phenomena that is represented by a word or symbol
signifier word, or symbol that we associate with an object or phenomena
simile explicit comparison of two unlike things using the words *like* or *as*
simplicity principle communicators are likely to simplify their plans, or make only slight alterations to rather than complicate them
skill repeatable, goal-directed behaviors
skillful listener someone who possesses a set of listening skills, and is able to choose among and use those skills
slippery slope the suggestion that one event automatically leads to a series of other undesirable events
slurring running sounds and words together
small group three or more people who perceive themselves to be a group, are interdependent, and communicate with one another
social anxiety real or imagined fear of interacting in an interpersonal encounter
social commitment the values and political positions we hold
social constructionism theory that language creates our perceptions of reality and the mode of our relational interactions
social facilitation small group's potential for stimulating higher levels of performance among its members
social loafing giving insufficient effort to complete a task with the expectation that other group members will pick up the slack
social location place we occupy according to race, ethnicity, class, gender, sexual orientation, and categorizations
social penetration process by which relationships unfold
social self self as emerging from and determined through relationships with other people
sophists group of Greek philosophers who taught about thinking and speaking persuasively
source original producer of a message
spatial arrangement the way spaces are laid out and relate to one another
spatial organization presentation of information based on the positioning of objects in physical space, or relationships between locations
speaker credibility impressions the listeners form of the public speaker in a given public speaking context, at a given time
speaking situation time and place for a speech
specific purpose statement of the desired audience response
speech to change speech intended to convince the audience to change what they like or dislike, hold to be true or untrue, or consider important or unimportant
speech to move to action speech intended to influence listeners to either engage in a new and desirable behavior or discontinue an undesirable behavior
speech to reinforce speech intended to influence listeners by strengthening their convictions and taking advantage of their tendency to seek out and attend to messages with which they already agree
speed lag between the production and sending of the message, and the receipt of that message
stakeholder analysis identification of individuals who will be affected by a decision and analysis of how each would view the group's decision
standard outline format outline that makes use of an alphanumeric system with a consistent pattern of numbers and letters used to indicate subordination of ideas
statistics numerical summaries of facts, figures, and research findings that provide pictures of data about people, ideas, or patterns of behavior
status level of respect and power a person, or a person's position, is given by those who interact with that person
status ratio difference between the sender's status and the receiver's status
stereotypes characteristics we believe to be true of a category ascribed to a given person or situation
straw man argument an attack on an entire argument by selecting a weak example or aspect of it, discrediting that example, and thus defaming the entire argument
style quality of expression
subject area general area of knowledge
subplans steps that need to be taken to achieve a given stage of a larger plan
substitution replacing part of a word with an incorrect sound
sufficing communication appropriate, but ineffective communication
supportive group environment environment that fosters collaboration and shared achievement of group goals
sweeping generalization clustering ideas, people, or objects into one indiscriminate group and implying that all of the items in the group are the same, obscuring vital and relevant differences

symbol word, sound, action, or gesture that arbitrarily refers to a person, idea, or object
symbol system set of relationships among signifiers or among signifiers and the objects they represent
systematic desensitization process of reducing the intensity of a person's feelings and emotional reactions to a specific situation

t

table text arranged in a grid of columns and rows
talkovers instances in which a person says something during someone else's turn to talk
task activity way to differentiate among groups according to the program or function the group serves
task factors an attraction to the specific task, activity, or goal a group performs or hopes to accomplish
task knowledge knowledge about performing a particular group activity and making decisions appropriate to it
task skills messages a person performs that help the group make a decision
technical work group problems that have clear definitions, solutions, and means of implementation
technological media devices that translate, amplify, or otherwise alter the information from natural media
technophobia fear of incompetence in computer mediated communication
tense-lax dimension of voice vocal range from the harshness of a piercing voice to a continuous more muffled and relaxed voice
terminal credibility long-term impression you leave behind after a speech
territoriality how people stake out space for themselves
testimony opinion of an expert or the account of an event by a witness to it
therapeutic interview transaction between parties in which the parties are seeking information relevant to enhancing the interviewee's mental or physical health from a service provider or provider representative
thesis statement central idea of a speech
time collective and individual perception of the sequence and progression of events
time management skill of balancing the relative proportion of time each communicator gets to speak during a conversation
timing consideration of a speaking situation's time allotment and scheduling
tinkering learning approach that involves experimenting and trial and error
top-down process starting with a general evaluation of competence and working down to the specific behaviors that comprise the evaluation
topic specific facet or aspect of a subject area
topic development conversational management of a subject under discussion
topic initiation introducing a topic for discussion
topical organization presentation of information about a subject and topic divided into subtopics or subcategories
Toulmin model persuasive structure that moves an audience from accepting data that are presented, through a warrant that links the data to the claim itself (*see* claim-data-warrant)
transactional model people are senders and receivers of messages simultaneously and communicators bring their own personal fields of meaning to all communication situations
Transcendent eloquence quality of communication that embraces differences among people and uses these differences as a basis for constructive change
transitions words, phrases, or sentences that demonstrate how main points relate to each other
transparent delivery presenting a speech in such a way that the audience focuses on the message rather than the delivery
trigger words words or phrases that cause emotional reactions, intensify conflicts, and discourage competent listening

u

understanding extent someone comprehends the intended meaning of a message.
unilateral interview typified by considerable division and inequality of power and roles
universal moral respect people of differing viewpoints should be allowed access to participate in interpersonal, group, and societal conversations over significant issues
unknown self parts of self unknown to both the self and others
unprojected aids visual aids that don't use of electricity

v

valence extent that a message has good or bad implications for the sender
values deeply rooted clusters of attitudes and beliefs that reflect what a person considers very important or unimportant, very worthy or unworthy
vigilant interaction commitment to rigorous problem assessment, goal development, and alternatives generation and evaluation
virtual community computer-mediated community where people with common interests can participate in conversation via email, list serv, and "chat" technology
visual aids visual images used to illustrate, support, or enliven the content of a speech
vivid language word use that promotes enthusiasm for a speech by bringing the speaker's message to life and moving the audience emotionally
vocal variety varying vocal rate, pitch, and volume to add interest
vocalized pauses meaningless sounds or words a speaker utters during moments of silence
volume intensity, the loudness or softness, of the speaker's voice

w

we-message statement that labels and describes the joint behaviors of two or more people
wide-narrow dimension of voice vocal range from lower frequency tones produced by a relaxed vocal tract to higher frequency tones produced by tense vocal tracts
working outline foundation for organizing materials and ideas into main points during the drafting of a speech

y

you-message statement that labels another person and involves some evaluation of that person's behavior

Photo Credits

Chapter 1 Page xxii, David Harry Stewart/Tony Stone Images; page 4, Bob Daemmrich/The Image Works; page 12, Sidney/Monkmeyer Press; page 15, Steven Rubin/The Image Works, page 23, David Harry Stewart/Tony Stone Images.

Chapter 2 Page 26, Bob Daemmrich/The Image Works; page 31, Merrim/Monkmeyer Press; page 48, Bob Daemmrich/The Image Works.

Chapter 3 Page 54, Clark/Monkmeyer Press; page 57, Michael Newman/PhotoEdit; page 67, Terry Eiler/Stock Boston; page 81, Bob Mahoney/The Image Works; page 82, Clark/Monkmeyer Press.

Chapter 4 Page 88, Marshall/The Image Works; page 97, A. Ramey/PhotoEdit; page 100, AFP/Corbis; page 110, Michelle Bridwell/PhotoEdit; page 113, Marshall/The Image Works.

Chapter 5 Page 116, Mark Romine/Tony Stone Images; page 126, Dr. Paul Ekman/Human Interaction Laboratory; page 128, Brian Haimer/PhotoEdit; page 130, Rudi Von Briel/PhotoEdit; page 139, Mark Romine/Tony Stone Images.

Chapter 6 Page 144, Richard Lord/PhotoEdit; page 154, Bob Daemmrich/The ImageWorks; page 158, Kerbs/Monkmeyer Press; page 165, Michael Newman/PhotoEdit; page 166, Richard Lord/PhotoEdit.

Chapter 7 Page 172, ©1994 Fox Broadcasting/Photofest; page 184, Brian Haimer/PhotoEdit; page 190, Michael Newman/PhotoEdit; page 194, Michael Newman/PhotoEdit; page 196, ©1994 Fox Broadcasting/Photofest.

Chapter 8 Page 204, Marc Dolphin/Tony Stone Images; page 226, Michael Newman/PhotoEdit; page 231, Marc Dolphin/Tony Stone Images.

Chapter 9 Page. 236, Bachmann/PhotoEdit; page 239, Patrick Ward/Stock Boston; page 253, David K.Crow/PhotoEdit; page 258, Bachmann/PhotoEdit.

Chapter 10 Page 264, Bonnie Kamin/PhotoEdit; page 284, Bonnie Kamin/PhotoEdit.

Chapter 11 Page 292, Richard Hutchings/PhotoEdit; page 295, Archives/The Image Works; page 318, Richard Hutchings/PhotoEdit.

Chapter 12 Page 322, David Young-Wolff/PhotoEdit; page 349, David Young-Wolff/PhotoEdit.

Chapter 13 Page 354, Bonnie Kamin/PhotoEdit; page 366, Hulton Getty/Liaison Agency; page 380, Bonnie Kamin/PhotoEdit.

Chapter 14 Page 382, Jon Feingersh/Stock Boston; page 390, (l) Hulton Getty/Liaison Agency; (r) Tom Pantages; page 392, Bob Daemmrich/Stock Boston; page 393, Michael Newman/PhotoEdit; page 410, Bob Mahoney/The Image Works; page 413, Jon Feingersh/Stock Boston.

Chapter 15 Page 418, Tom Rosenthal/SuperStock, Inc.; page 422, Old Dominion University; page 425, Michael Newman/PhotoEdit; page 427, AltaVista; page 429, Tom Rosenthal/SuperStock, Inc.; page 451, Tom Rosenthal/SuperStock, Inc.

Chapter 16 Page 452, Tony Freeman/PhotoEdit; page 458, Hulton Getty/Liaison Agency; page 476, Tony Freeman/PhotoEdit.

Chapter 17 Page 486, David Young-Wolff/PhotoEdit; page 489, Patricia Canova Tipton/Index Stock; page 508, David Young-Wolff/PhotoEdit;

Chapter 18 page 514, David Young-Wolff/PhotoEdit; page 533, Pool/Luke Frazza/Liaison Agency; page 537, David Young-Wolff/PhotoEdit.

Index

d

e

j

k

l

m

q

r